中国民政统计年鉴

（中国社会服务统计资料）

CHINA CIVIL AFFAIRS' STATISTICAL YEARBOOK

(Statistics of China Social Services)

2014

中华人民共和国民政部　编

Compiled By Ministry of Civil Affairs of the People's Republic of China

中国统计出版社
China Statistics Press

图书在版编目（CIP）数据

中国民政统计年鉴 ：中国社会服务统计资料. 2014 ：汉英对照 / 中华人民共和国民政部编.
-- 北京 ：中国统计出版社, 2014.7
ISBN 978-7-5037-7130-9

I.①中… II.①中… III.①民政事务－统计资料－中国－2014－年鉴－汉、英 IV.①D632-66

中国版本图书馆CIP数据核字（2014）第151028号

中国民政统计年鉴－2014（中国社会服务统计资料）

作　　者／ 中华人民共和国民政部
责任编辑／ 郭　栋　　李　冲
封面设计／ 郭　威
出版发行／ 中国统计出版社
通信地址／ 北京市丰台区西三环南路甲6号　　邮政编码／100073
电　　话／ 邮购 (010)63376909　　书店 (010)68783171
网　　址／ http://csp.stats.gov.cn
印　　刷／ 河北天普润印刷厂
经　　销／ 新华书店
开　　本／ 880×1230mm　　1/16
字　　数／ 1320千字
印　　张／ 43
版　　别／ 2014年8月第1版
版　　次／ 2014年8月第1次印刷
定　　价／ 280.00元

本书附同版本CD-ROM一张，光盘内容以书面文字为准。
如有印装错误，本社发行部负责调换。

《中国民政统计年鉴－2014》

（中国社会服务统计资料）

编委会和编辑出版人员

编者说明

《中国民政统计年鉴－2014》(中国社会服务统计资料)是一部全面反映2013年中国社会服务发展的资料性年刊。2013年度社会服务统计资料是根据各省、自治区、直辖市以及计划单列市民政厅（局）报送的社会服务业统计年报及有关部门的报表编制而成。本书内容由六个部分组成：第一部分是专文，2013年社会服务发展统计公报；第二部分是社会服务主要数据图表；第三部分是社会服务综合统计资料；第四部分是社会服务历年统计资料；第五部分是社会服务当年分省统计资料；第六部分是附录，《中国民政统计年鉴－2013》勘误。本书对各级政府有关部门、从事社会服务研究和教学的人员，以及社会各界了解和研究社会服务发展状况、提高政府管理和决策水平，具有重要的参考价值。

书中涉及到的全国性统计数据均不包括香港特别行政区、澳门特别行政区和台湾省；表格中“--”符号表示数据不足本表最小计量单位；“空格”符号表示该项统计数据为零；“#”表示其中主要项。

本书凝聚了全国民政系统广大规划财务部门统计工作者和有关部门统计人员的辛勤汗水和工作成果。本书的编辑出版得到了各级领导和统计战线同仁们的热情支持和帮助。在此，向所有关心和支持该书出版发行的领导和同志表示衷心的谢意。

目　录

第一部分：专文

第二部分：社会服务主要数据图表

综合

社会工作

成员组织和其他社会服务

第三部分：社会服务综合统计资料

综合

社会工作

成员组织和其他社会服务

第四部分：社会服务历年统计资料

综合

社会工作

成员组织和其他社会服务

第五部分：社会服务当年分省统计资料

综合

行政区划和行政机关

社会服务业态总体情况

社会工作

提供住宿的社会服务活动

为老年人与残疾人提供住宿服务的机构

为智障与精神疾病人提供住宿服务的机构

为儿童提供住宿的社会服务机构

CONTENTS

Part One: Feature Articles

Part Two: Key Data Figures of Social Services

Synthesis

Social Services

Member Organizations and Other Social Services

Part Three: Comprehensive Statistics in Social Service

Synthesis

Social Services

Member Organizations and Other Social Services

Part Four: Statistical Data in Social Service

Synthesis

Social Services

Member Organizations and Other Social Services

Part Five: Social Service Statistics in Provinces in 2013

Synthesis

Administrative divisions and administrative organs

General formation of social service industry

Social Services

Social service institutions with accommodation

Institutions with accommodation for aged and disabled

Institutions with accommodation for mental retardation and psychopath

Institutions with accommodation for children

Other institutions with accommodation

Social service institutions without accommodation

Services for aged

Services for disabled

Member Organizations and Other Social Services

Member organizations

NGOs

Self-governing organizations

Other social services

Service for marriage

Funeral and interment service

Other

Part Six: Appendix

专 文

01

中华人民共和国
2013年社会服务发展统计公报

中华人民共和国民政部

2014年6月16日

2013年，全国民政系统认真贯彻党中央、国务院决策部署，积极履行保障基本民生、创新社会管理、促进国防建设、强化社会服务等方面的职能，扎实推进各项重点工作，民政事业实现了新突破新发展，服务了党和国家工作大局，促进了社会生产力发展，增强了社会活力，增进了发展成果更多更公平惠及全体人民。

一、综合

截至2013年底，全国共有省级行政区划单位34个（其中直辖市4个、省23个、自治区5个、特别行政区2个），地级行政区划单位333个（其中地级市286个、地区14个，自治州30个、盟3个），县级行政区划单位2853个（其中市辖区872个、县级市368个、县1442个、自治县117个、旗49个、自治旗3个、特区1个、林区1个），乡级行政区划单位40497个（其中区公所2个、镇20117个、乡11626个、苏木151个、民族乡1034个、民族苏木1个、街道7566个）。

2013年，共联合检查省界14条，完成了总长度约为11982公里的联检省界任务。

图1 乡镇、街道变化情况

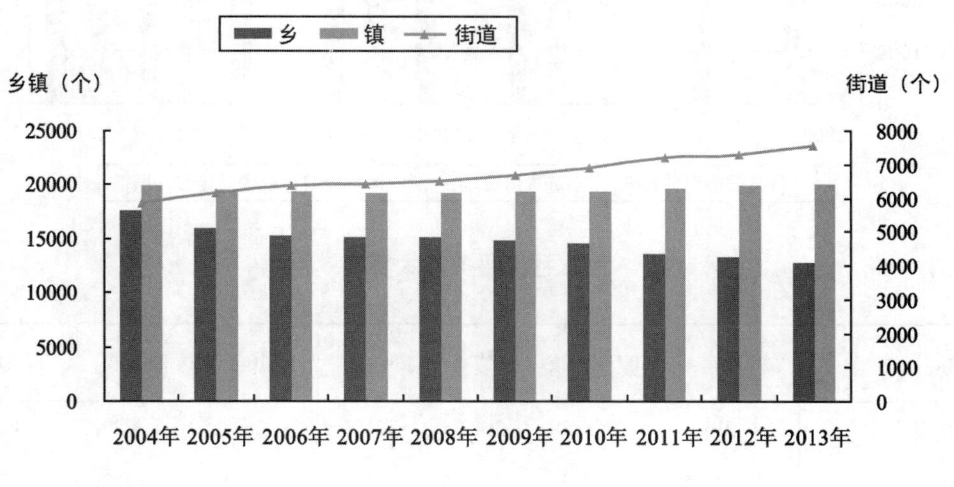

表 1 乡镇、街道变化情况

单位：个

指标	2006年	2007年	2008年	2009年	2010年	2011年	2012年	2013年
乡	15306	15120	15067	14848	14571	13587	13281	12812
镇	19369	19249	19234	19322	19410	19683	19881	20117
街道	6355	6434	6524	6686	6923	7194	7282	7566

截至2013年底，全国共有社会服务机构156.2万个，比上年增长6.8%，职工总数1197.6万人（全国持证社会工作者共计123084人，其中：社会工作师31183人，助理工作师91901人），固定资产总值为6810.2亿元，比上年增长2.0%，增加值为2251.9亿元，比上年增长5.6%，占第三产业的比重为0.9%。

截至2013年底，全国社会服务事业费支出4276.5亿元，比上年增长16.1%，占国家财政支出比重为3.1%，比上年增长0.1个百分点。中央财政共向各地转移支付社会服务事业费为2149.7亿元，比上年增长19.8%，占社会服务事业费比重为50.3%，比上年增加1.6个百分点。社会服务事业基本建设施工项目19116个，全年完成投资总额292.8亿元，比上年增长24.7%。

图2 社会服务基本情况

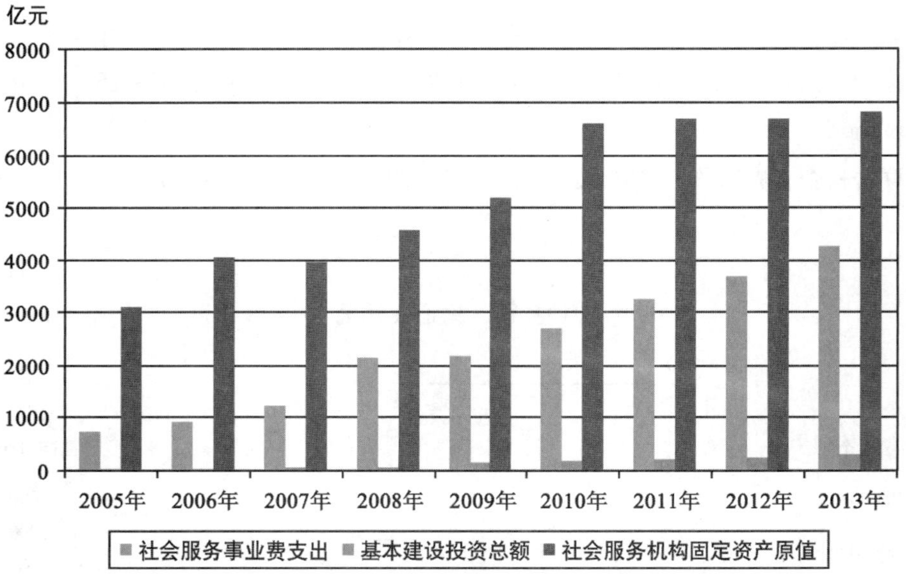

表2 社会服务基本情况

单位：亿元

指标	2006年	2007年	2008年	2009年	2010年	2011年	2012年	2013年
社会服务事业费支出	915.4	1215.5	2146.5	2181.9	2697.5	3229.1	3683.7	4276.5
基本建设投资总额	33.5	47.7	66.6	157.0	183.0	218.5	235.0	292.8
社会服务机构固定资产原值	4066.7	3973.0	4592.8	5198.0	6589.3	6676.7	6675.4	6810.2

二、社会工作

（一）提供住宿的社会服务

截至2013年底，全国各类提供住宿的社会服务机构4.6万个（其中登记注册为事业单位机构1.3万个）；床位526.7万张，比上年增长17.2%；每千人口平均拥有社会服务机构床位3.9张，比上年增长17.3%；收养322.5万人，比上年增长4.2%。

图3 社会服务机构床位

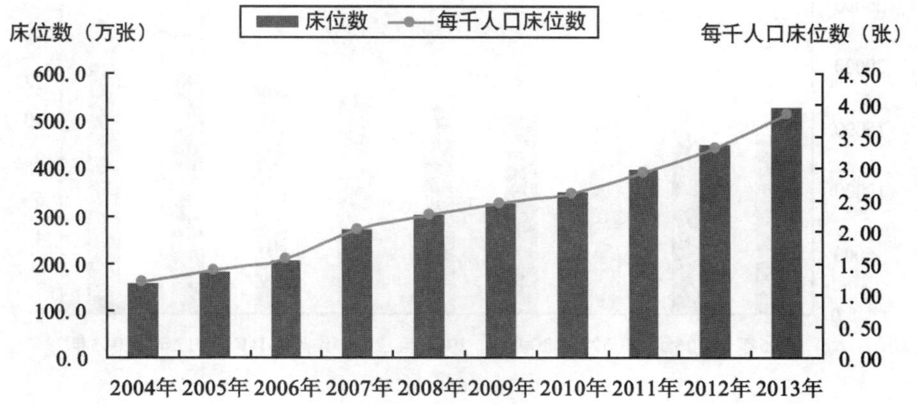

表3 社会服务机构床位

单位：万张、张

指标	2006年	2007年	2008年	2009年	2010年	2011年	2012年	2013年
床位数	204.5	269.6	300.3	326.5	349.6	396.4	449.3	526.7
每千人口床位数	1.56	2.04	2.26	2.45	2.61	2.94	3.32	3.87

1.提供住宿的养老服务。全国各类养老服务机构42475个，拥有床位493.7万张，比上年增长18.9%（每千名老年人拥有养老床位24.4张，比上年增长13.9%）。其中社区留宿和日间照料床位64.1万张。年末收留抚养老年人307.4万人，比上年增长5.5%。

2.提供住宿的智障与精神病服务。全国民政部门管理的智障与精神疾病服务机构共有261个，拥有床位7.4万张，比上年增长10.4%。其中社会福利医院（精神病院）155个，床位数4.5万张，比上年增长9.7%，年末收养各类人员3.7万人；复退军人精神病院106个，床位数2.9万张，比上年增长11.5%，年末收养各类人员2.3万人。

3.提供住宿的儿童福利和儿童救助服务。全国共有儿童收养救助服务机构803个，拥有床位9.8万张，年末收养各类人员5.6万人。其中儿童福利机构529个，比上年增加66个，床位8.7万张，比上年增长12.7%；未成年人救助保护中心274个，床位1.1万张，全年救助生活无着流浪乞讨未成年人18.4万人次。

4.其他提供住宿的社会服务。全国共有其他提供住宿的社会服务机构2438个，床位15.7万张。其中救助管理站1891个，床位9.7万张，全年救助城市生活无着的流浪乞讨人员348.5万人次，其中在站救助296.2万人次，不在站救助52.3万人次；安置农场26个；军供站325个，床位3.7万张；其他收养机构196个，床位2.3万张，年末收养各类人员1.3万人。

（二）不提供住宿的社会服务

1.老龄服务。截至2013年底，全国60岁及以上老年人口20243万人，占总人口的14.9%，其中65岁及以上人口13161万人，占总人口的9.7%。截至2013年底，全国共有老龄事业单位2571个，老年法律援助中心2.1万个，老年维权协调组织7.8万个，老年学校5.4万个、在校学习人员692.0万人，各类老年活动室36.0万个。

图4 60岁及以上老年人口占全国总人口比重

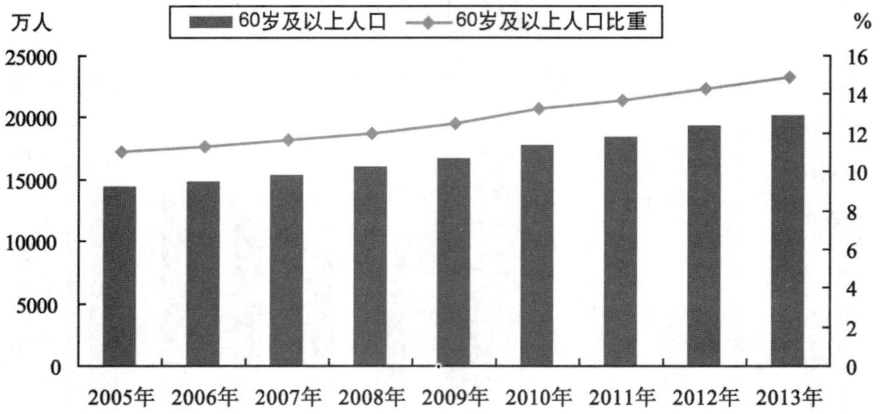

表4 60岁及以上老年人口占全国总人口比重

单位：万人、%

指标	2006年	2007年	2008年	2009年	2010年	2011年	2012年	2013年
60岁及以上人口	14901	15340	15989	16714	17765	18499	19390	20243
60岁及以上人口比重	11.3	11.6	12.0	12.5	13.3	13.7	14.3	14.9

2.儿童福利。截至2013年底，全国共有孤儿54.9万人，其中集中供养孤儿9.4万人，社会散居孤儿45.5万人。2013年全国办理家庭收养登记24460件，其中：内地居民收养登记21033件，港澳台华侨收养197件，外国人收养登记3230件。

图5 家庭儿童收养

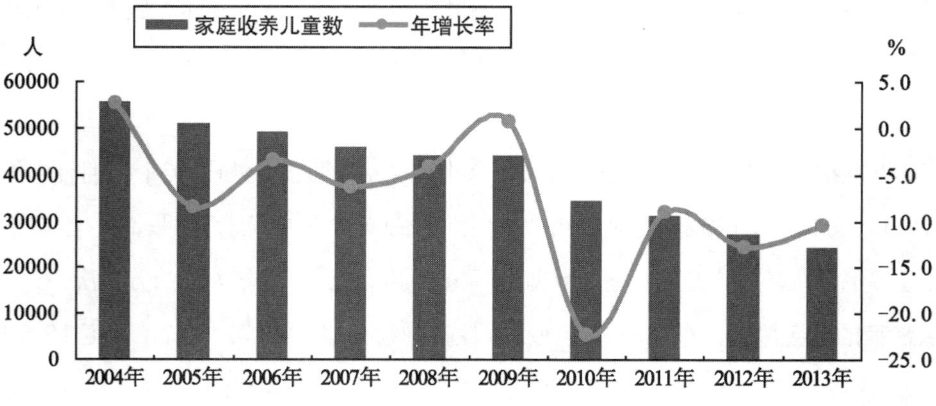

表5 家庭儿童收养

单位：人、%

指标	2006年	2007年	2008年	2009年	2010年	2011年	2012年	2013年
家庭收养儿童数	49148	46047	44115	44359	34473	31329	27310	24460
年增长率	−3.5	−6.3	−4.2	0.6	−22.3	−9.1	−12.8	−10.4

3.**为残疾人提供服务的机构**。截至2013年底，全国共有为残疾人提供服务的机构18227个；增加值为701.5亿元，占第三产业的比重0.27%；吸纳残疾职工53.9万人就业；实现利润106.9亿元；年末固定资产1760.1亿元。

图6 福利企业中的残疾职工

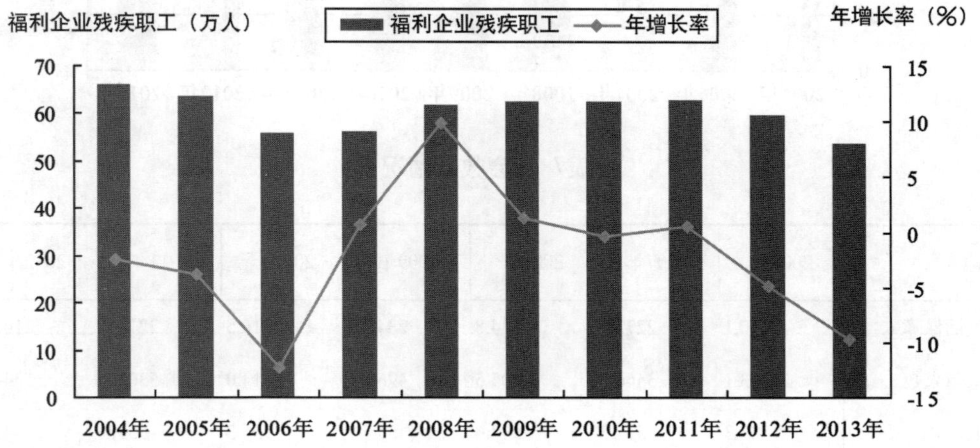

表6 福利企业中的残疾职工

单位：万人、%

指标	2006年	2007年	2008年	2009年	2010年	2011年	2012年	2013年
福利企业残疾职工	55.9	56.3	61.9	62.7	62.5	62.8	59.7	53.9
年增长率	−12.2	0.7	9.9	1.3	−0.3	0.5	−4.9	−9.7

4.社会救助

城市低保。截至2013年底，全国共有城市低保对象1097.2万户、2064.2万人。全年各级财政共支出城市低保资金756.7亿元，比上年增长12.2%，其中中央财政补助资金545.6亿元，占总支出的72.1%。2013年全国城市低保平均标准373元/人、月，比上年增长13%；全国城市低保月人均补助水平264元。

城市"三无"救济。2013年救济城市"三无"8.6万人。

农村低保。截至2013年底，全国有农村低保对象2931.1万户、5388.0万人，比上年同期增加43.5万人，增长了0.8%。全年各级财政共支出农村低保资金866.9亿元，比上年增长20.7%，其中中央补助资金612.3亿元，占总支出的70.6%。2013年全国农村低保平均标准2434元/人、年，比上年提高366元，增长17.7%；全国农村低保月人均补助水平116元，比上年增长11.7%。

农村五保。截至2013年底，全国有农村五保供养537.2万人，比上年下降1.5%。全年各级财政共支出农村五保供养资金172.3亿元，比上年增长18.9%。其中：农村五保集中供养183.5万人，集中供养年平均标准为

4685元/人，比上年增长15.4%；农村五保分散供养353.8万人，分散供养年平均标准为3499元/人，比上年增长16.3%。

图7 社会救助情况

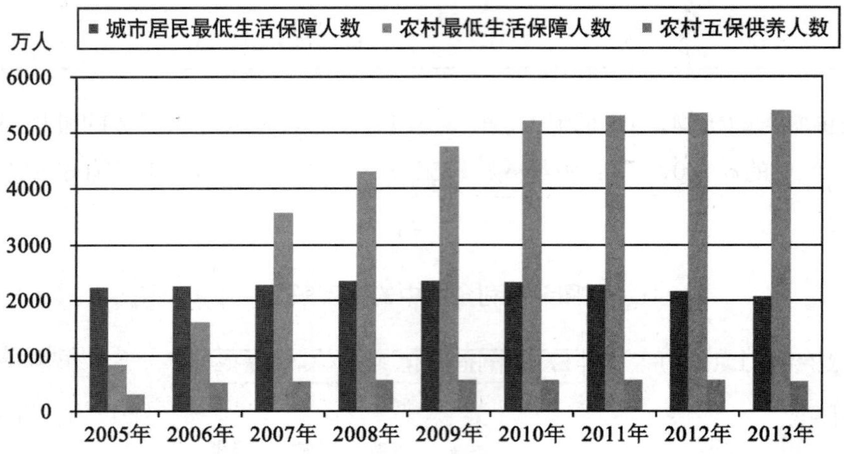

表7 社会救助情况

单位：万人

指标	2006年	2007年	2008年	2009年	2010年	2011年	2012年	2013年
城市居民最低生活保障人数	2240.1	2272.1	2334.8	2345.6	2310.5	2276.8	2143.5	2064.2
农村最低生活保障人数	1593.1	3566.3	4305.5	4760.0	5214.0	5305.7	5344.5	5388.0
农村五保供养人数	503.3	531.3	548.6	553.4	556.3	551.0	545.6	537.2

农村传统救济。2013年农村传统救济73.0万人。

医疗救助。2013年民政部门资助参加城镇居民基本医疗保险1490.1万人，人均资助参保水平96.7元，各级财政共支出资助参保资金14.4亿元；民政部门资助参加新型农村合作医疗4868.7万人，人均资助参合水平61.7元，各级财政共支出资助参合资金30.0亿元；直接医疗救助2126.4万人次，各级财政共支出直接医疗救助资金180.5亿元。

2013年全年累计医疗补助优抚对象454.1万人次，人均补助水平715.8元，各级财政共支出优抚医疗补助资金32.5亿元。

临时救助。2013年临时救助698.1万户次，其中，按户籍性质分类城市家庭323.0万户次，农村家庭375.1万户次；按属地分类当地常驻户口681.0万户次，非当地常驻户口17.2万户次；按救助类型分类支出型临时救助620.5万户次，应急型临时救助77.6万户次。

5.防灾减灾。2013年全国各类自然灾害共造成3.9亿人次不同程度受灾，因灾死亡失踪2284人，紧急转移安置1215.0万人次；农作物受灾面积3135.0万公顷，其中绝收面积384.4万公顷；倒塌房屋87.5万间，严重损坏226.9万间，一般损坏543.4万间；因灾直接经济损失5808.4亿元。国家减灾委、民政部共启动10次预警响应和39次应急响应，协调派出35个救灾应急工作组赶赴灾区，财政部、民政部下拨中央救灾资金102.7亿元，民政部调拨帐篷19.6万顶、棉衣被62.8万件（床）、折叠床8.9万张等救灾物资，累计救助受灾群众8000万人次。受灾群众基本生活得到妥善保障。

图8 因灾死亡（含失踪）人口

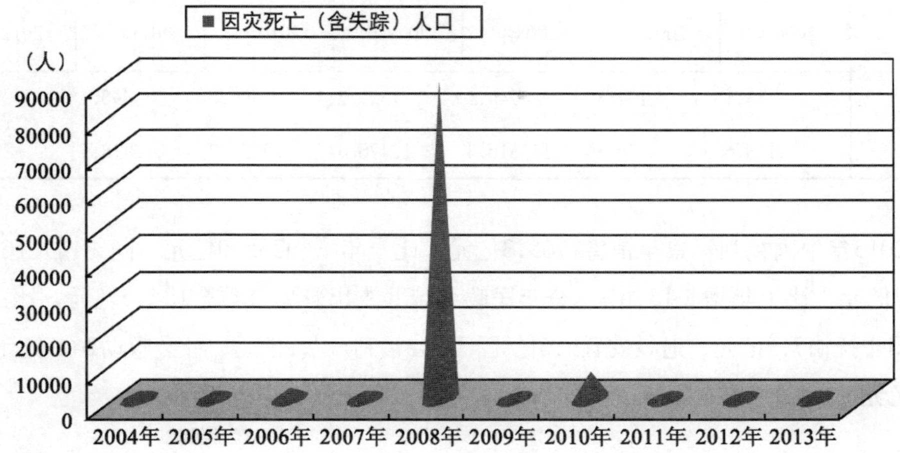

表8 因灾死亡（含失踪）人口

单位：人

指标	2006年	2007年	2008年	2009年	2010年	2011年	2012年	2013年
因灾死亡（含失踪）人口	3186	2325	88928	1528	7844	1126	1530	2284

6.慈善事业。

慈善捐赠。截至2013年底，全国共建立经常性社会捐助工作站、点和慈善超市3.1万个（其中：慈善超市9492个）。全年各地共接收社会捐赠款物566.4亿元，其中：民政部门直接接收社会各界捐款107.6亿元，各类社会组织接收捐款458.8亿元。全年各地接收捐赠衣被10405.0万件，捐赠物资价值折合人民币8.7亿元。间接接收其他部门转入的社会捐款5.0亿元，衣被739.1万件，捐赠物资折款35081.4万元。全年有1246.0万人次困难群众受益。全年有1368.8万人次在社会服务领域提供了3579.7万小时的志愿服务。

图9 接收社会捐款和衣被

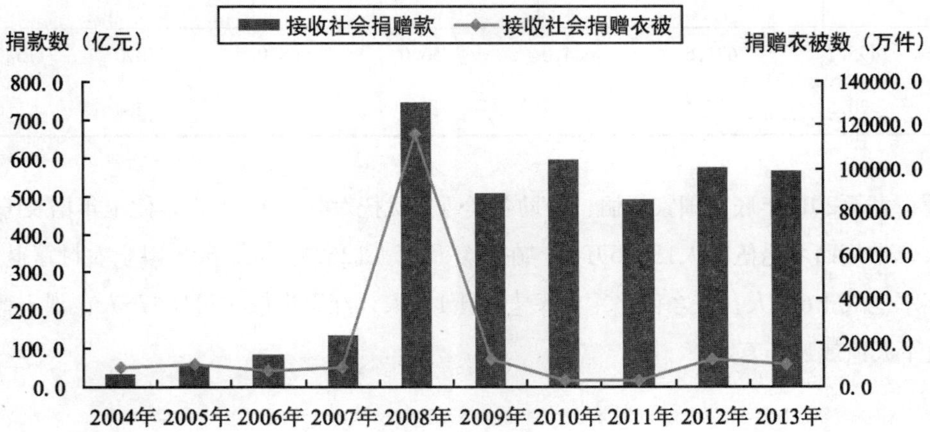

表9 接收社会捐款和衣被

单位：亿元、万件

指标	2006年	2007年	2008年	2009年	2010年	2011年	2012年	2013年
接收社会捐赠款	83.1	132.8	744.5	507.2	596.8	490.1	572.5	566.4
接收社会捐赠衣被	7123.6	8756.8	115816.3	12476.6	2750.2	2918.5	12538.2	10405.0

福利彩票。2013年中国福利彩票年销售1765.3亿元，比上年增加255.0亿元，同比增长16.9%。全年筹集福彩公益金510.7亿元，比上年增长13.6%。全年民政系统共支出彩票公益金195.5亿元，比上年增加36.5亿元；其中：资助用于抚恤7.5亿元，退役安置0.6亿元，社会福利117.1亿元，社会救助26.1亿元，自然灾害2.6亿元，其他41.6亿元。

图10 福利彩票

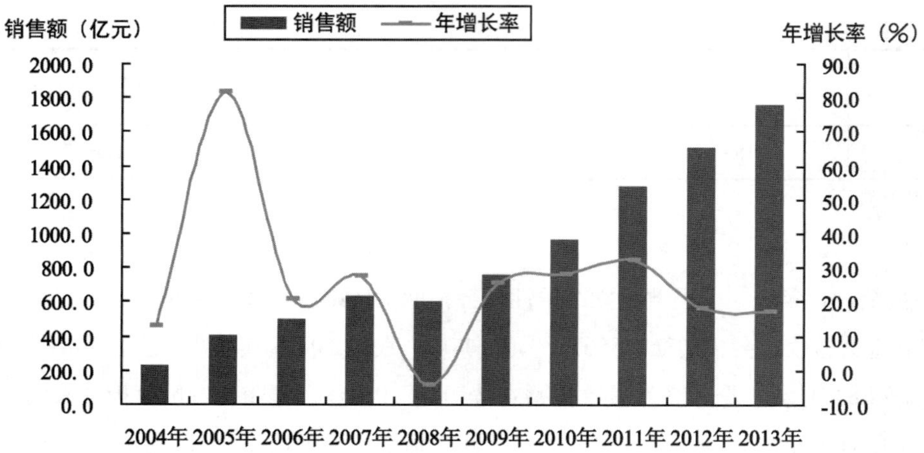

表10 福利彩票

单位：亿元、%

指标	2006年	2007年	2008年	2009年	2010年	2011年	2012年	2013年
销售额	495.7	631.6	604.0	756.0	968.0	1278.0	1510.3	1765.3
年增长率	20.5	27.4	−4.4	25.2	28.0	32.0	18.2	16.9

7.**优抚安置。**截至2013年底，国家抚恤、补助各类重点优抚对象950.5万人，比上年增长0.6%。其中：伤残人员81.2万人，带病回乡退伍军人130.6万人，在乡复员军人126.1万人，60岁以上农村籍退伍军人356.7万人，在乡退伍红军老战士647人，在乡西路军红军老战士117人，红军失散人员18976人；烈士遗属24.0万人，因公牺牲、病故军人遗属12.6万人。

图11 国家抚恤、补助优抚对象

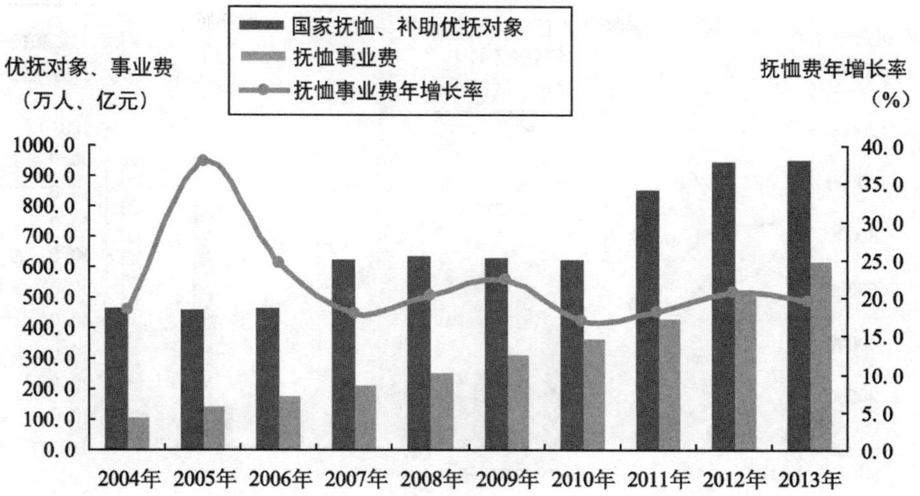

表11 国家抚恤、补助优抚对象

单位：万人、亿元、%

指标	2006年	2007年	2008年	2009年	2010年	2011年	2012年	2013年
国家抚恤、补助优抚对象	462.6	622.4	633.2	630.7	625.0	852.5	944.4	950.5
抚恤事业费	178.8	210.8	253.6	310.3	362.7	428.3	517.0	618.4
抚恤事业费年增长率	24.5	17.9	20.3	22.4	16.9	18.1	20.7	19.6

2013年实际发放烈士褒扬金200人。截至2013年底，全国共有烈士纪念设施管理机构1463个，占地面积4585公顷，机构内烈士纪念设施13602处；零散烈士纪念设施13601处。

2013年共接收军队离退休干部（含退休士官）、无军籍退休退职职工、复员干部3.9万人。军队离退休人员管理中心145个，年末职工0.2万人；军队离退休人员活动中心28个，年末职工0.1万人。

8.**社区服务**。截至2013年底，全国共有各类社区服务机构25.2万个，社区服务机构覆盖率36.9%；其中：社区服务指导中心890个，社区服务中心19014个，比上年增加3517个，社区服务站108377个，比上年增加20446个，养老等其他社区服务机构12.4万个，比上年增加2.8万个。城镇便民、利民服务网点35.9万个。社区志愿服务组织12.8万个。

图12 社区服务机构

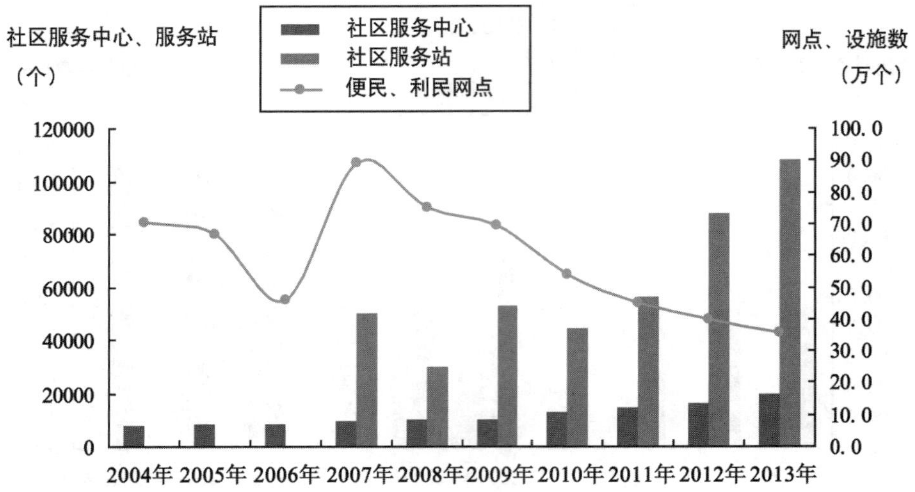

表12 社区服务机构

单位：万个、个

指标	2006年	2007年	2008年	2009年	2010年	2011年	2012年	2013年
社区服务机构	12.5	12.9	14.6	14.6	15.3	16.0	20.0	25.2
社区服务中心	8565	9319	9873	10003	12720	14391	16306	19904
社区服务站		50116	30021	53170	44237	56156	87931	108377
便民、利民网点	45.8	89.3	74.9	69.3	53.9	45.3	39.7	35.9

三、成员组织和其他社会服务

（一）成员组织

1.社会组织。截至2013年底，全国共有社会组织54.7万个，比上年增长9.6%；吸纳社会各类人员就业636.6万人，比上年增加3.8%；形成固定资产1496.6亿元；社会组织增加值为571.1亿元，比上年增长8.7%，占第三产业增加值比重为0.22%；接收各类社会捐赠458.8亿元；全年共查处社会组织违法违规案件3117起，其中取缔非法社会组织46起，行政处罚3071起。

全国共有社会团体28.9万个，比上年增长6.6%。其中：工商服务业类31031个，科技研究类17399个，教育类11753个，卫生类9953个，社会服务类41777个，文化类27115个，体育类17869个，生态环境类6636个，法律类3264个，宗教类4801个，农业及农村发展类58825个，职业及从业组织类19743个，国际及其他涉外组织类481个，其他38379个。全年共查处社会团体违法违规案件2173起，其中取缔非法社会团体21起，行政处罚2152起。

全国共有基金会3549个，比上年增加520个，增长17.2%，其中：公募基金会1378个，非公募基金会2137个，涉外基金会8个，境外基金会代表机构26个。民政部登记的基金会216个。公募基金会和非公募基金会共接收社会各界捐赠302.9亿元。全年对基金会作出行政处罚4起。

全国共有民办非企业单位25.5万个，比上年增长13.1%。其中：科技服务类13729个，生态环境类377个，教育类145210个，卫生类21234个，社会服务类36698个，文化类11694个，体育类10353个，商务服务类5625个，宗教类94个，国际及其他涉外组织类4个，其他9652个。全年共查处民办非企业单位违法违纪案件940起，其中取缔非法民办非企业单位25起，行政处罚915起。

图13 社会组织

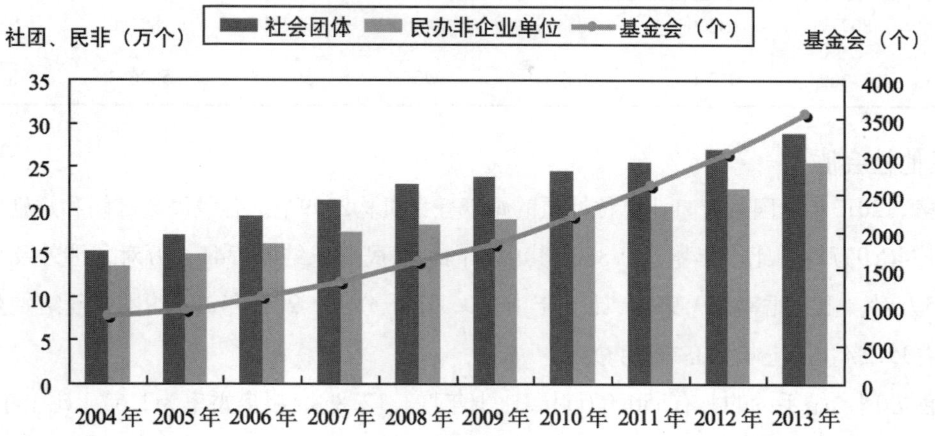

表13 社会组织

单位：万个、个

指标	2006年	2007年	2008年	2009年	2010年	2011年	2012年	2013年
社会团体	19.2	21.2	23.0	23.9	24.5	25.5	27.1	28.9
基金会	1144	1340	1597	1843	2200	2614	3029	3549
民办非企业单位	16.1	17.4	18.2	19.0	19.8	20.4	22.5	25.5

2. 自治组织

截至2013年底，基层群众自治组织共计68.3万个，其中：村委会58.9万个，村民小组466.4万个，村委会成员232.3万人；居委会94620个，比上年增长3.8%，居民小组135.7万个，比上年增加2.2万个，居委会成员48.4万人，比上年增长3.2%。全年共有15.0万个村（居）委会完成选举，参与选举的村（居）民登记数为2.2亿人，参与投票人数为1.7亿人。

图14 自治组织

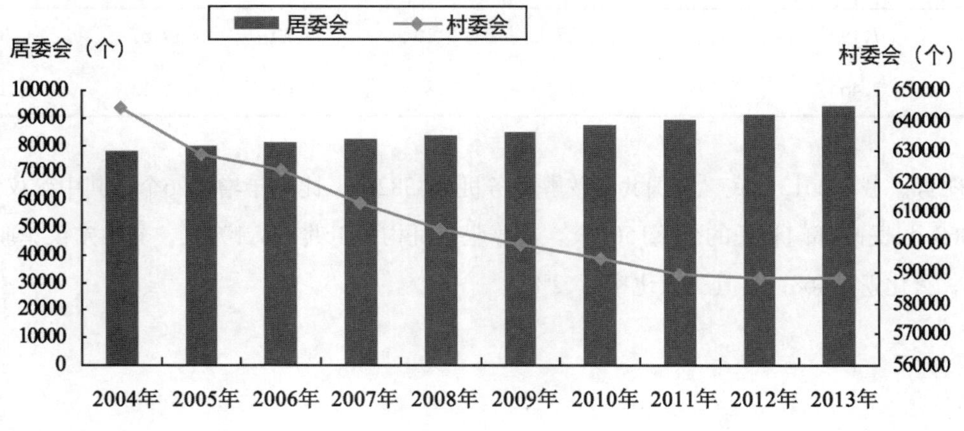

表14 自治组织

单位：个

指标	2006年	2007年	2008年	2009年	2010年	2011年	2012年	2013年
居委会	80717	82006	83413	84689	87057	89480	91153	94620
村委会	623669	612709	604285	599078	594658	589653	588475	588547

（二）其他社会服务

1.**婚姻服务**。2013年全国共有事业单位性质的婚姻登记机构2059个。各级民政部门和婚姻登记机构共依法办理结婚登记1346.9万对，比上年增长1.8%。其中：内地居民登记结婚1341.4万对，涉外及华侨、港澳台居民登记结婚5.5万对。粗结婚率为9.9‰，比上年上升0.1个千分点。2013年25–29岁办理结婚登记占结婚总人口比重最多，占35.2%，比上年提高1个百分点。

2013年依法办理离婚手续的共有350.0万对，比上年增长12.8%，粗离婚率为2.6‰，比上年增加0.3个千分点。其中：民政部门登记离婚281.5万对，法院办理离婚68.5万对。

图15 粗结婚率和粗离婚率

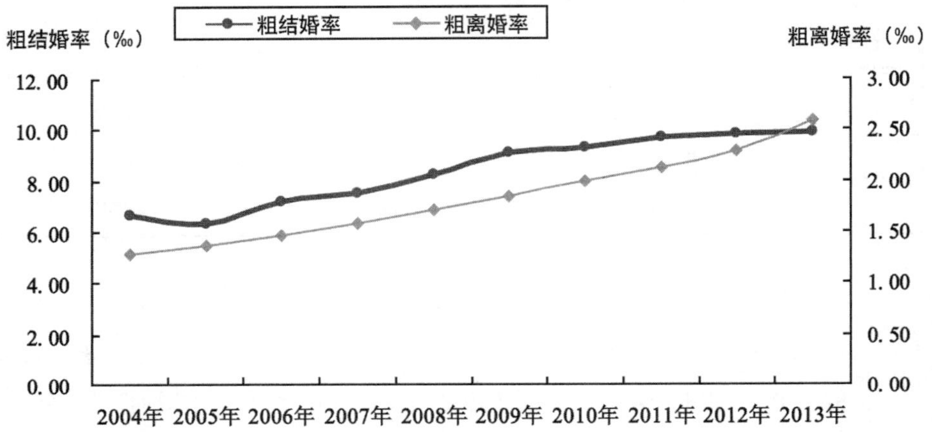

表15 粗结婚率和粗离婚率

单位：‰

指标	2006年	2007年	2008年	2009年	2010年	2011年	2012年	2013年
粗结婚率	7.19	7.50	8.27	9.10	9.30	9.67	9.80	9.92
粗离婚率	1.46	1.59	1.71	1.85	2.00	2.13	2.29	2.58

2. **殡葬服务**。截至2013年底，全国共有殡葬服务机构4382个，比上年增加26个，其中殡仪馆1784个，殡葬管理机构1063个，民政部门管理的公墓1506个。殡葬服务机构职工共有8.1万人，其中殡仪馆职工4.6万人。火化炉5743台，火化遗体468.9万具。火化率48.2%。

图16 火化遗体情况

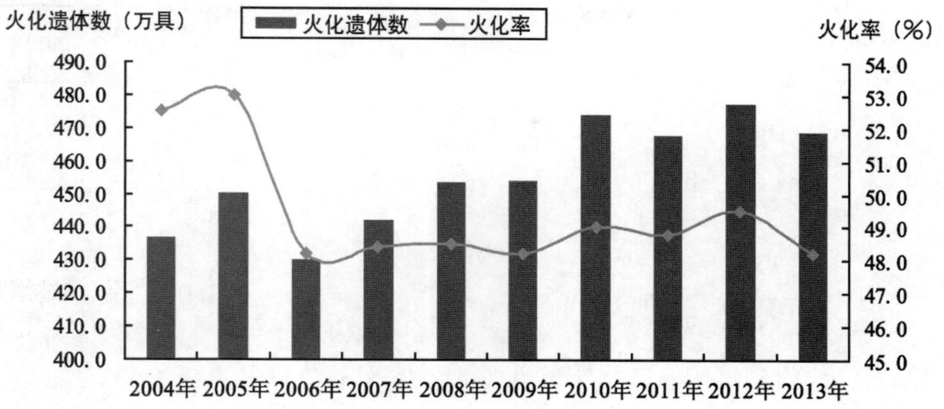

表16 火化遗体情况

单位：万具、%

指标	2006年	2007年	2008年	2009年	2010年	2011年	2012年	2013年
火化遗体数	430.2	442.1	453.4	454.2	474.1	468.1	477.7	468.9
火化率	48.2	48.4	48.5	48.2	49.0	48.8	49.5	48.2

注释：

1.图1和表1中“乡”包含“民族乡、苏木和民族苏木”。

2.财政部、民政部下拨中央救灾资金不包含中央级救灾物资采购经费和中央拨付新疆生产建设兵团救灾资金。

3.2013年社区服务中心里含社区服务指导中心。

4.离婚登记服务中法院判决、调解离婚数据来源于最高人民法院。

5.本资料中的民政对象人数和机构数均为当年实际发生数和法定机构数，与当年批准数、计划数和预算数不可比。

6.本资料部分数据因四舍五入原因，存在分项数据与合计数据不等情况，由此产生的误差，均未作机械调整。

7.各项统计数据均未包括香港特别行政区、澳门特别行政区和台湾省。

Statistical Report of the People's Republic of China on the Development of Social Services in 2013

Ministry of Civil Affairs of
the People's Republic of China
June 16th, 2014

In 2013, the system of national civil affairs earnestly implemented decisions and arrangements of the Party Central Committee and the State Council, actively safeguarded basic livelihood of people,innovated social management, improved national defense construction, and intensified social services.The performance of these functions improved the implementation of key points, made new development of civil affairs, served the overall work of the Party and the country, promoted the development of social productivity, increased social vibrancy and made more development results benefit all people more fairly.

I. Synthesis

By the end of 2013, there were altogether 34 administrative areas at the province level in China (4 municipalities directly under the central government, 23 provinces, 5 autonomous regions and 2 special administrative regions), 333 administrative areas at the prefecture level (286 cities at the prefecture level, 14 prefectures, 30 autonomous prefectures and 3 leagues), 2,853 administrative areas at the county level (872 districts under the jurisdiction of cities, 368 cities at the county level , 1442 counties, 117 autonomous counties, 49 banners, 3 autonomous banners, 1 special zone and 1 forestry district), 40,497 administrative areas at the township level (2 district communities, 20,117 towns, 11,626 townships, 151 sumus, 1,034 ethnic townships, 1 ethnic sumu, 7,566 street communities).

In 2013, the joint inspections covered 14 provincial boundaries (11,982 kilometers).

Figure 1: Changes in Townships, Towns and Street Communities

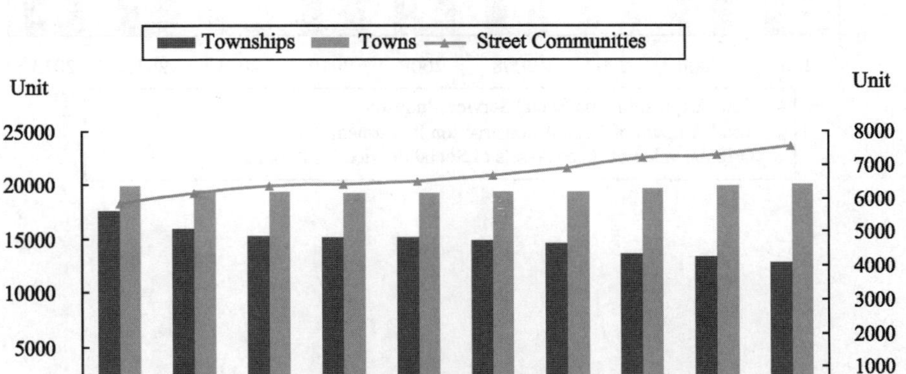

Table 1: Changes in Townships, Towns and Street Communities

Indicators	2006	2007	2008	2009	2010	2011	2012	2013
Townships(Unit)	15306	15120	15067	14848	14571	13587	13281	12812
Towns(Unit)	19369	19249	19234	19322	19410	19683	19881	20117
Street Communities(Unit)	6355	6434	6524	6686	6923	7194	7282	7566

By the end of 2013, there were 1.562 million various registered units on social services, rose by 6.8 percent over the previous year. The total number of staff was 11.976 million, 31,183 of them were social workers and 91,901 of them were assistant social workers. The total fixed assets stood at 681.02 billion yuan, which rose 2.0% over the previous year. The added value reached 225.19 billion yuan, which rose 5.6% over the previous year. It occupied 0.9 % of the proportion of tertiary industry.

By the end of 2013, the total expenditure on social services industry reached 427.65 billion yuan, rose by 16.1% over the previous year. The proportion of total expenditure on social services industry in the share of national financial expenditure was 3.1%, which increased 0.1% over the previous year. The transferred payment of the central government to social services industry amounted to 214.97 billion yuan, which increased 19.8% over the previous year; It took up 50.3 percent of the total social services expenditure, which rose 1.6 percent over the previous year. There were 19,116 construction projects for social services. The total investment reached 29.28 billion yuan, rose by 24.7 percent over the previous year.

Figure 2: Basic Situation of Social Services Industry

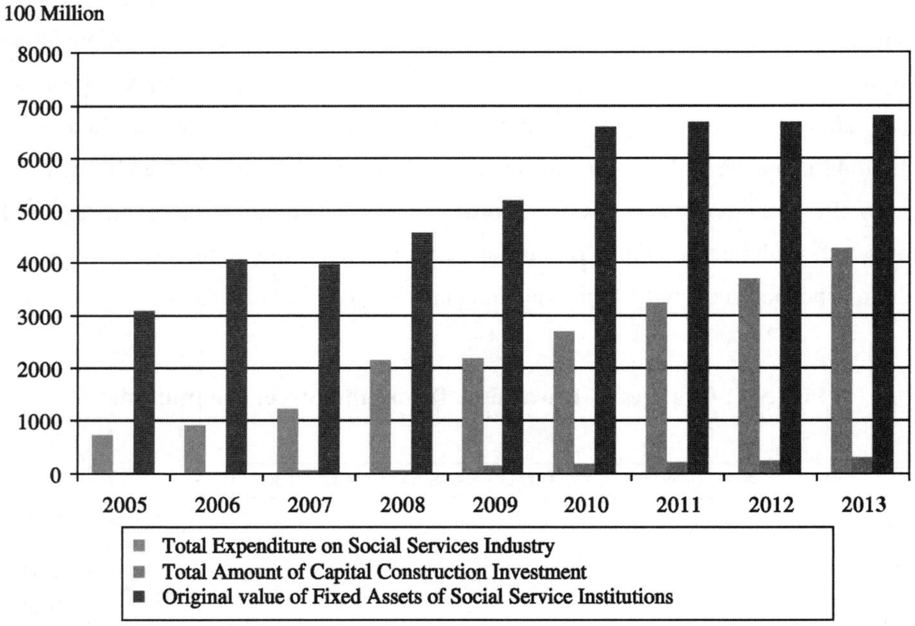

Table 2: Basic Situation of Social Services Industry

Indicators	2006	2007	2008	2009	2010	2011	2012	2013
Total Expenditure on Social Services Industry(100 Million)	915.4	1215.5	2146.5	2181.9	2697.5	3229.1	3683.7	4276.5
Total Amount of Capital Construction Investment(100 Million)	33.5	47.7	66.6	157.0	183.0	218.5	235.0	292.8
Original value of Fixed Assets of Social Service Institutions(100 Million)	4066.7	3973.0	4592.8	5198.0	6589.3	6676.7	6675.4	6810.2

II. Social Services

A. Social Services with Accommodation

By the end of 2013, there were 46 thousand social services institutions with accommodation (13 thousand of them were registered as public institutions). They offered 5.267 million beds, rose by 17.2 percent over that of the previous year. The average number of beds in social services institutions was 3.9 per thousand people, rose by 17.3 percent over the previous year. The number of adoptees in these institutions reached 3.225 million, rose by 4.2 percent over the previous year.

Figure 3: Beds in Social Services Institutions

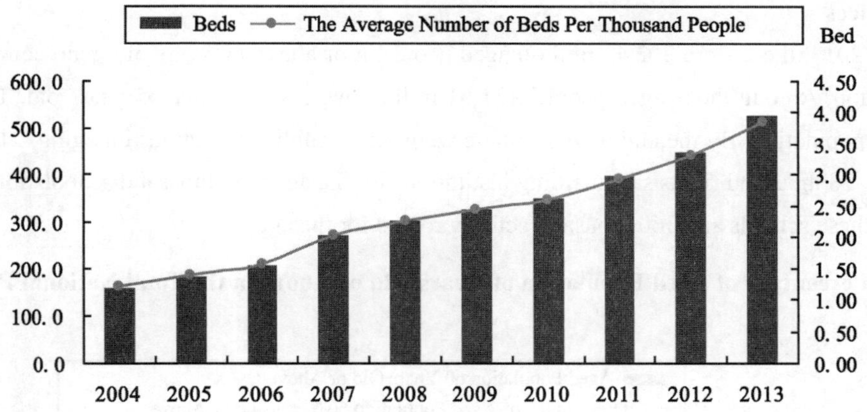

Table 3: Beds in Social Services institutions

Indicators	2006	2007	2008	2009	2010	2011	2012	2013
Beds(10,000 Beds)	204.5	269.6	300.3	326.5	349.6	396.4	449.3	526.7
The Average Number of Beds Per Thousand People(Bed)	1.56	2.04	2.26	2.45	2.61	2.94	3.32	3.87

1. Social Services with Accommodation for the Aged

By the end of 2013, there were 42,475 welfare institutions with 4.937 million beds for the aged in China, which rose by 18.9 percent over the previous year (the average number of beds per thousand seniors was 24.4, rose by 13.9 percent in comparison with last year) . Thereinto, 641 thousand were used for community accommodation and daytime care. At the end of 2013, 3.074 million aged people were adopted, rose by 5.5 percent over the previous year.

2. Service Agencies with Accommodation for Mental Retardations and Psychiatric Disorders

By the end of 2013, there were 261 service agencies for mental retardations and psychiatric disorders under the management of the civil affairs departments with 74 thousand beds, increased 10.4% over the previous year. Thereinto, there were 155 social welfare homes (mental hospitals) with 45 thousand beds, increased 9.7% over the previous year. By the end of year, 37 thousand people were adopted. There were 106 mental hospitals with 29 thousand beds for ex-serviceman, rose by 11.5 percent over the previous year, and 23 thousand people were adopted by the end of the year, rose by 11.5 percent over the previous year.

3. Welfare Homes and Salvation Institutions with Accommodation and for the Children

By the end of 2013, there were 803 adoption and salvation institutions with 98 thousand beds for children, and 56 thousand people were adopted. There were 529 welfare homes for children, rose by 66 in comparison with last year. They offered 87 thousand beds, which rose by 12.7 percent in comparison with last year. There were 274 children relief and management units with 11 thousand beds for the minor vagabonds. They received 184 thousand minor vagabonds in the year.

4. Other Social Service Institutions with Accommodation Services

There were 2,438 other social service institutions with 157 thousand beds. There were 1,891 relief and management shelters with 97 thousand beds. In 2013, they received 3.485 million urban street people who had no means of support. 2.962 million of those got in-shelter reliefs and 523 thousand got out-shelter reliefs. There were 26 arrangement farms. There were 325 military depots for military supplies, which had 37 thousand beds. There were 196 adopt institutions of other kinds, and they offered 23 thousand beds, adopted 13 thousand people by the end of 2013.

B. Social Services without Accommodation

1. Aging Services

By the end of 2013, there were 202.43 million aged people at or above 60 years old, who comprised 14.9 percent of the total population. Among those aged people, 131.61 million were at or above 65 years old. They comprised 9.7 percent of the total population. By the end of 2013, there were 2,571 public institutions on aging, 21 thousand legal aid centers for the aged, 78 thousand rights safeguarding institutions for the aged, 54 thousand schools for the aged with 6.92 million students in these schools and 360 thousand activity rooms for the aged.

Figure 4: Percentage of Aged Population 60 Years Old or Above in the Total National Population

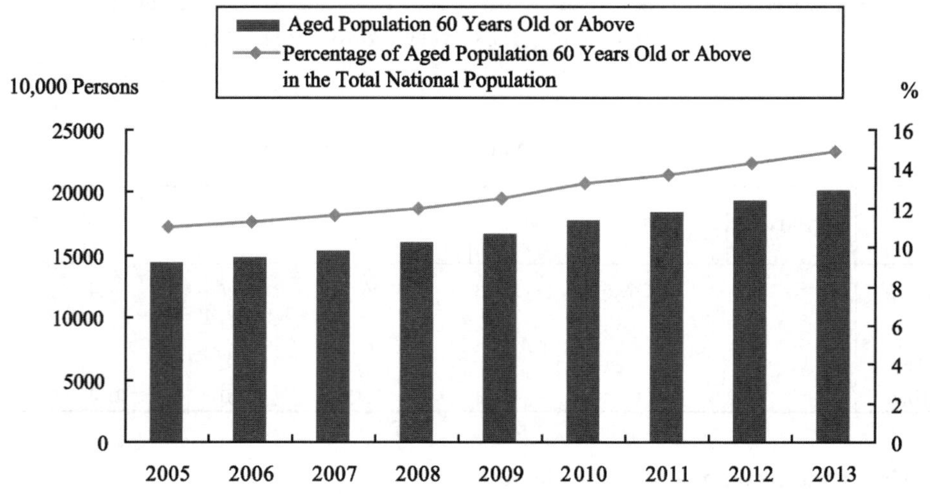

Table 4: Percentage of Aged Population 60 Years Old or Above in the Total National Population

Indicators	2006	2007	2008	2009	2010	2011	2012	2013
Aged Population 60 Years Old or Above (10,000 Persons)	14901	15340	15989	16714	17765	18499	19390	20243
Percentage of Aged Population 60 Years Old or Above in the Total National Population(%)	11.3	11.6	12.0	12.5	13.3	13.7	14.3	14.9

2. Children Welfare

By the end of 2013, there were 549 thousand orphans in China, of which 94 thousand orphans were collectively adopted, 455 thousand orphans scattered. In 2013, registered family adoptions totaled 24,460 cases. Thereinto, 21,033 cases were completed by mainland citizens, 197 cases were completed by overseas Chinese and residents in Hong Kong, Macao and Taiwan, 3,230 cases were completed by foreigners.

Figure 5: Children Adopted by Families

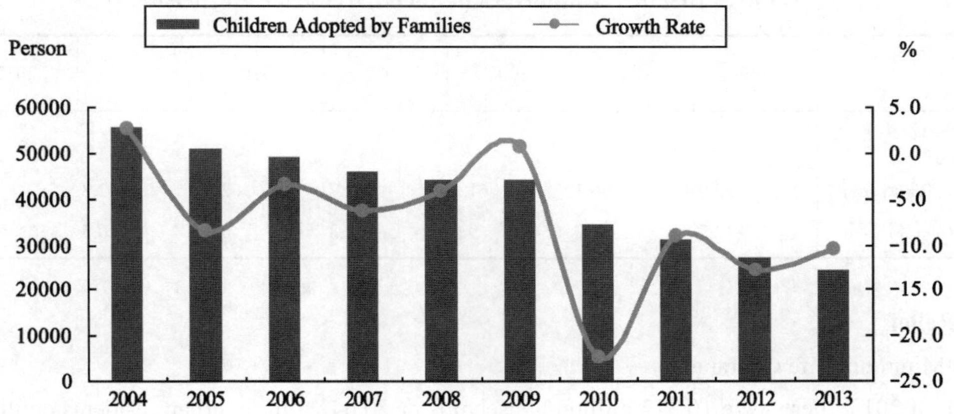

Table 5: Children Adopted by Families

Indicators	2006	2007	2008	2009	2010	2011	2012	2013
Children Adopted by Families(Person)	49148	46047	44115	44359	34473	31329	27310	24460
Growth Rate(%)	-3.5	-6.3	-4.2	0.6	-22.3	-9.1	-12.8	-10.4

3. Agencies Providing Service for Disabled

By the end of 2013, there were 18,227 social welfare agencies providing services for disabled across the country. The added value of social welfare agencies was 70.15 billion yuan, which accounted for 0.27 percent of the tertiary industry. These agencies employed 539 thousand disabled people. The profits reached 10.69 billion yuan. By the end of 2013, the fixed assets valued 176.01 billion yuan.

Figure 6: Disabled Employees in Social Welfare Enterprises

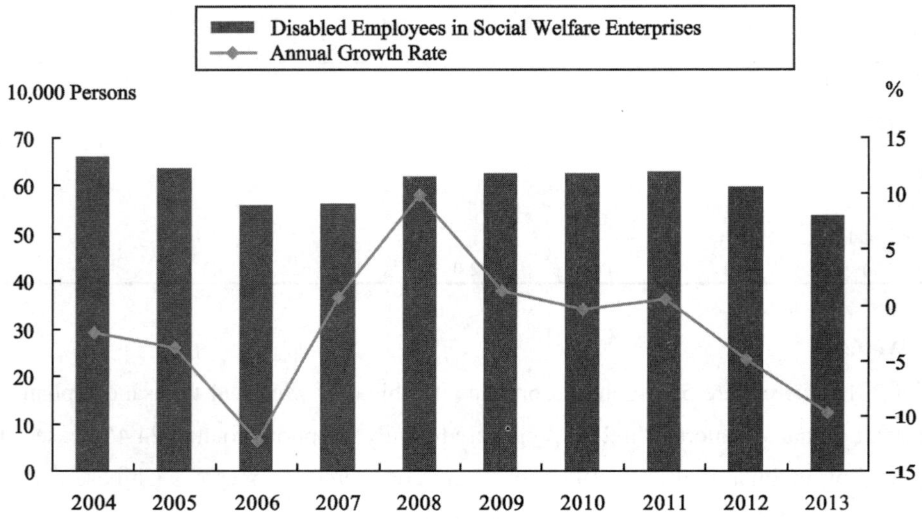

Table 6: Disabled Employees in Social Welfare Enterprises

Indicators	2006	2007	2008	2009	2010	2011	2012	2013
Disabled Employees in Social Welfare Enterprises(10,000 Persons)	55.9	56.3	61.9	62.7	62.5	62.8	59.7	53.9
Annual Growth Rate(%)	-12.2	0.7	9.9	1.3	-0.3	0.5	-4.9	-9.7

4. Social Relief

- Urban Minimum Life Guarantee

By the end of 2013, there were 10.972 million households or 20.642 million urban residents entitled to minimum living allowances. In 2013, the total fiscal expenditure on the urban minimum life guarantee reached 75.67 billion yuan, rose by 12.2 percent over the previous year. There were 54.56 billion yuan came from the central financial subsidy funds, accounted for 72.1 percent of the total expenditure. In 2013, the average expenditure standard of urban minimum life guarantee was 373 yuan per person every month, rose by 13 percent over the previous year. The per capita urban minimum life guarantee was 264 yuan every month.

- Relief of the Urban Three-Without People

In 2013, 86 thousand urban Three-Without people had been relieved.

- Rural Minimum Life Guarantee

By the end of 2013, there were 29.311 million households, 53.88 million people who were covered by the rural minimum life guarantee system, which was an increase of 435 thousand people, rose by 0.8 percent. A total of 86.69 billion yuan was distributed by governments at all levels in the whole year, which was an increase of 20.7 percent in comparison with last year. It contained the central government subsidy of 61.23 billion yuan, accounting for 70.6 percent of the total expenditure. In 2013, the average expenditure standard of rural minimum life guarantee of the country was 2434 yuan per person per year, which was an increase of 366 yuan over that of the previous year, rose by 17.7 percent. The per capita rural minimum life guarantee was 116 yuan every month, rose by 11.7 percent over the previous year.

- Five Guarantees in Rural Areas

By the end of 2013, there were 5.372 million people who had received relief allowances from the five guarantees system in rural areas across the country, decreased 1.5 percent over the previous year. A total of 17.23 billion yuan for rural five guarantees was distributed by government at all levels in the whole year. It was an increase of 18.9 percent over the previous year. There were 1.835 million five guarantees people who were cared collectively in welfare institutions, with an average expenditure standard of 4,685 yuan per person per year, rose by 15.4 percent in comparison with last year. There were 3.538 million people who were cared separately in communities, with an average expenditure standard of 3,499 yuan per person every year, rose by 16.3 percent in comparison with last year.

Figure 7: Situation of Social Relief

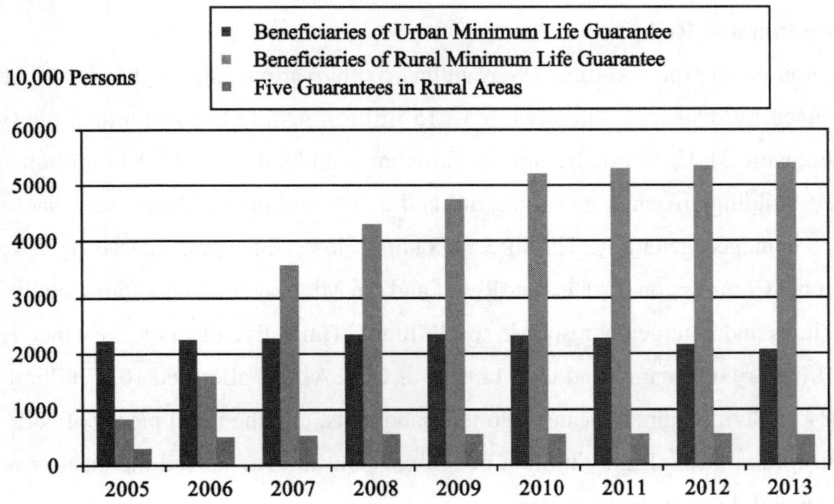

Table 7: Situation of Social Relief

Indicators	2006	2007	2008	2009	2010	2011	2012	2013
Beneficiaries of Urban Minimum Life Guarantee (10,000 Persons)	2240.1	2272.1	2334.8	2345.6	2310.5	2276.8	2143.5	2064.2
Beneficiaries of Rural Minimum Life Guarantee (10,000 Persons)	1593.1	3566.3	4305.5	4760.0	5214.0	5305.7	5344.5	5388.0
Five Guarantees in Rural Areas (10,000 Persons)	503.3	531.3	548.6	553.4	556.3	551.0	545.6	537.2

- Traditional Rural Relief

In 2013, there were 730 thousand residents who received the traditional rural relief.

- Medical Aid

In 2013, civil affairs departments financed 14.901 million urban residents to participate basic medical insurance, with per capita expense of 96.7 yuan. In 2013, the total expenditure on urban medical insurance distributed by the financial system at all levels was 1.44 billion yuan.Civil affairs departments financed 48.687 million people the New Rural Cooperative Medical Care, with per capita fund standing at 61.7 yuan. Governments at all levels financed 3 billion yuan on the medical insurance. There were 21.264 million people (person-times) who received direct aid. The total expenditure on direct medical care distributed by the financial system at all levels reached 18.05 billion yuan.

In 2013, the number of people who were covered by state pension and preferential treatment program and who received medical subsidy reached 4.541 million. The average expenditure was 715.8 yuan per person. The financial expenditure on medical subsidy at all levels totaled 3.25 billion yuan.

- The Provisional Relief

In 2013, there were 6.981 million households that received provisional relief. According to the types of the household registrations, there were 3.23 million that belonged to urban households and 3.751 million that belonged to rural households. According to the classification of the households, there were 6.81 million households that belonged to local permanent residence and 172 thousand households that belonged to non-local permanent residence. According to the types of the provisional relief, there were 6.205 million households that received the provisional relief of expense pattern and there were 0.776 million households that received the provisional relief of emergency pattern.

5. Disaster Prevention and Relief

In 2013, 390 million people (person-times) were influenced by various natural disasters. There were 2,284 deaths and abscondences caused by disasters. There were 12.15 million people (persontimes) who were transferred and resettled urgently. There were 31.35 million hectares of farm crops hit by disasters, 3.844 million hectares of crops were demolished. Collapsed buildings reached 875 thousand and 2.269 million buildings were badly damaged and 5.434 million buildings were damaged generally. The direct economic loss which was caused by disasters stood at 580.84 billion yuan. The National Commission for Disaster Relief and the Ministry of Civil Affairs totally started mechanism of early warning for 10 times and emergency response for 39 times. Thirty five disaster assistance response teams rushed to disaster areas. The Ministry of Finance and the Ministry of Civil Affairs allocated 10.27 billion yuan as central relief funds, and the Ministry of Civil Affairs allocated 196 thousand tents, 628 thousand pieces of cotton-padded clothes and quilts and 89 thousand folding beds. Eighty million people (person-times) received the disaster relief. The basic needs of people afflicted by natural disasters were guaranteed.

Figure 8 : Deaths (Abscondences) Caused by Disasters

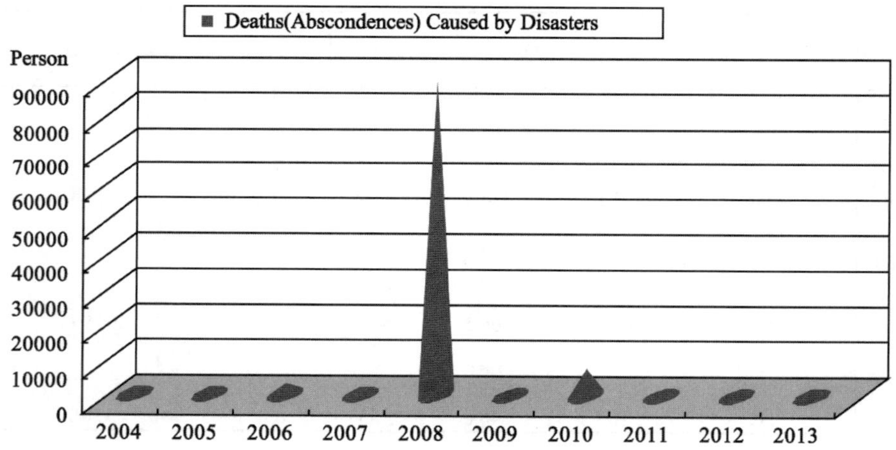

Table 8 : Deaths(Abscondences) Caused by Disasters

Indicators	2006	2007	2008	2009	2010	2011	2012	2013
Deaths (Abscondences) Caused by Disasters (Person)	3186	2325	88928	1528	7844	1126	1530	2284

6. Social Charity

- Charitable Donations

By the end of 2013, there were 31 thousand regular workstations of social donations and charity supermarkets (9,492 of which were charity supermarkets). The total social donations reached 56.64 billion yuan. Of this total, the civil affairs departments received direct donations of 10.76 billion yuan; social organizations received donations of 45.88

billion yuan. In 2013, the donated quilts and clothes reached 104.05 million pieces, valuing at 870 million yuan. The indirect social donations which were transferred from other departments were 0.5 billion yuan, and there were also 7.391 million pieces of indirect-donated quilts and clothes. The donated materials were worth at 350.814 million yuan. Over 12.46 million people (person-times) in difficulties benefited from the charitable donations. There were 13.688 million volunteers (person-times) who provided 35.797 million hours of social services in 2013.

Figure 9: Social Donations and Donated Quilts and Clothes

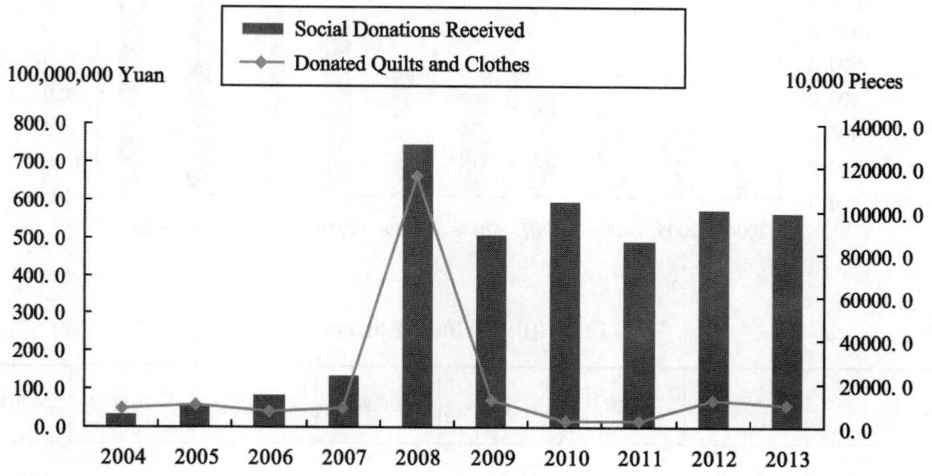

Table 9: Social Donations and Donated Quilts and Clothes

Indicators	2006	2007	2008	2009	2010	2011	2012	2013
Social Donations (100,000,000 Yuan)	83.1	132.8	744.5	507.2	596.8	490.1	572.5	566.4
Social Donated Quilts and Clothes (10,000 Pieces)	7123.6	8756.8	115816.3	12476.6	2750.2	2918.5	12538.2	10405.0

- Welfare Lottery

In 2013, the sales of welfare lottery reached 176.53 billion yuan, an increase of 25.5 billion yuan over the previous year, rose by 16.9 percent over the previous year. The public lottery funds reached 51.07 billion yuan, rose by 13.6 percent in comparison with last year. The expenditure of public lottery funds by the civil affairs departments totaled 19.55 billion yuan, which increased 3.65 billion yuan over the previous year. It included 750 million yuan on state pension, 60 million yuan on the placement of retired serviceman, 11.71 billion yuan on social welfare, 2.61 billion yuan on social relief, 260 million yuan on disaster relief and 4.16 billion yuan on other expenses.

Figure 10: Welfare Lottery

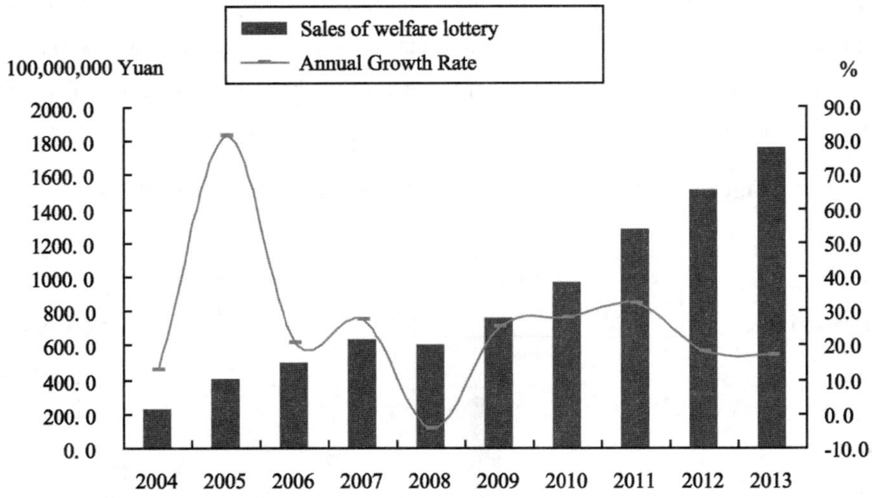

Table 10: Welfare Lottery

Indicators	2006	2007	2008	2009	2010	2011	2012	2013
Sales of Welfare Lottery (100,000,000 Yuan)	495.7	631.6	604.0	756.0	968.0	1278.0	1510.3	1765.3
Annual Growth Rate(%)	20.5	27.4	-4.4	25.2	28.0	32.0	18.2	16.9

7. Preferential Treatment and Placement

By the end of 2013, there were 9.505 million people who were covered by state pension and preferential treatment program, rose by 0.6 percent over the previous year. Of this total, there were 812 thousand wounded servicemen, 1.306 million ailing ex-servicemen, 1.261 million rural retired servicemen, 3.567 million ex-servicemen above 60 years old with rural registration households, 647 veterans of the Red Army in rural areas, 117 veterans of the west-Road Army in the rural areas, 18,976 veterans who lost touch with the Red Army, 240 thousand family members of martyrs, 126 thousand family members of servicemen who died on duty or of illness.

Figure 11: Beneficiaries of State Pension and Preferential Treatment

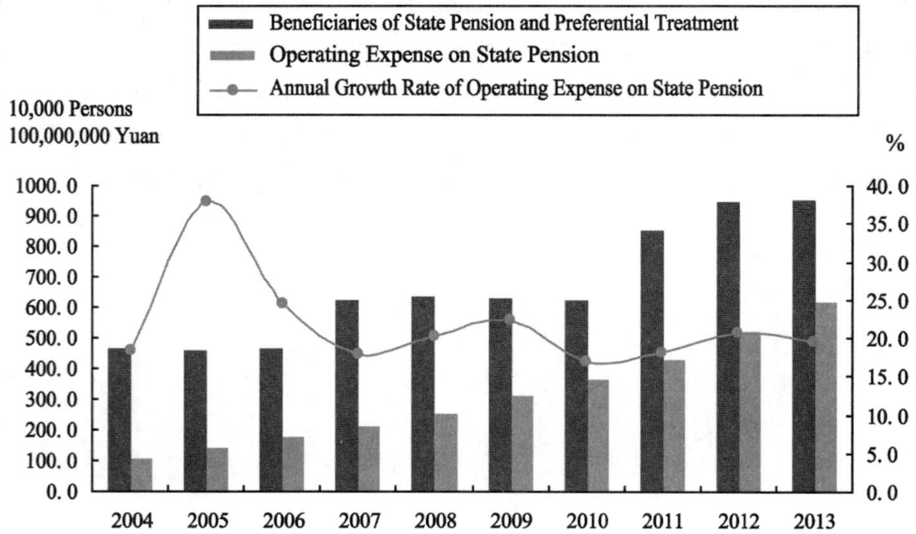

Table 11: Beneficiaries of State Pension and Preferential Treatment

Indicators	2006	2007	2008	2009	2010	2011	2012	2013
Beneficiaries of State Pension and Preferential Treatment (10,000 Persons)	462.6	622.4	633.2	630.7	625.0	852.5	944.4	950.5
Operating Expense on State Pension (100,000,000 Yuan)	178.8	210.8	253.6	310.3	362.7	428.3	517.0	618.4
Annual Growth Rate of Operating Expense on State Pension (%)	24.5	17.9	20.3	22.4	16.9	18.1	20.7	19.6

In 2013, government allocated prizes to 200 martyrs. By the end of 2013, there were 1,463 management units of martyrs' monuments, taking up the space of 4,585 hectares. There were 13,602 martyrs' monuments which were within management units and there were 13,601 scattered monuments.

In 2013, there were 39,000 retired military cadres (includes demobilized sergeants), retirees military employees who had no military registrations and demobilized officer. There were 145 management centers for the emeritus and retired personnels who were from troops and 2,000 employees worked in these management centers. There were 28 activity centers which were granted for the emeritus and retired personnels who were from troops and one thousand employees worked in these places.

8. Community Services

By the end of 2013, there were 252 thousand community service institutions, and the coverage of community service institutions was 36.9 percent. Among these institutions, 890 were community service instruction centers and 19,014 were community service centers, increased by 3,517 over the previous year; There were 108,377 community service stations which increased by 20,446 over the previous year. Other community service institutions (such as institutions for the aged) were 124 thousand, which increased by 28 thousand over the previous year. There were 359 thousand convenience stations and 128 thousand community organizations of volunteers in urban areas.

Figure 12: Community Service Institutions

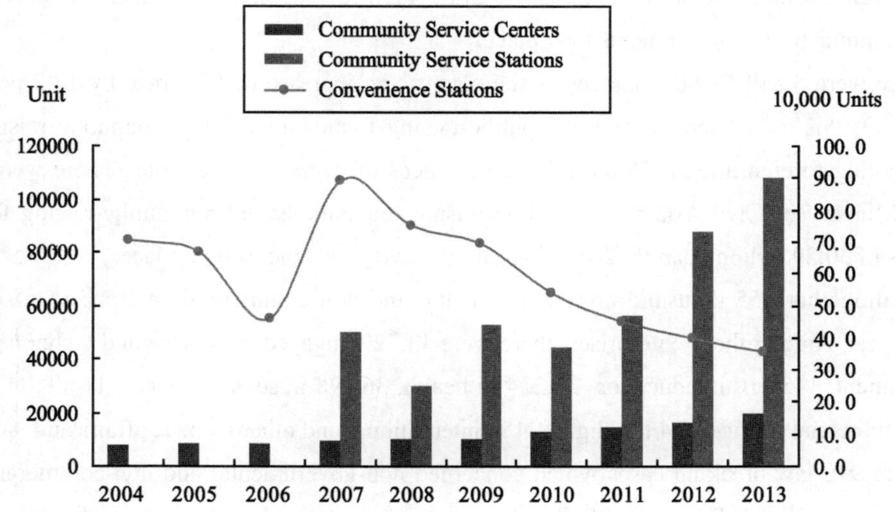

Table 12: Community Service Institutions

Indicators	2006	2007	2008	2009	2010	2011	2012	2013
Community Service Institutions (10,000 Units)	12.5	12.9	14.6	14.6	15.3	16.0	20.0	25.2
Community Service Centers (Unit)	8565	9319	9873	10003	12720	14391	16306	19904
Community Service Stations (Unit)		50116	30021	53170	44237	56156	87931	108377
Convenience Stations (10,000 Units)	45.8	89.3	74.9	69.3	53.9	45.3	39.7	35.9

III. Member Organizations and Other Social Services

A. Member Organizations

1. Non-Government Organizations (NGOs)

By the end of 2013, there were altogether 547 thousand NGOs, rose by 9.6 percent over that of the previous year. There were 6.366 million employees, increased by 3.8 percent over the previous year. The total value of fixed assets was 149.66 billion yuan. The added value of NGOs was 57.11 billion yuan, increased by 8.7 percent over the previous year and it accounted for 0.22 percent in the added value of tertiary industry. The NGOs received donations of 45.88 billion yuan. There were 3,117 law-breaking cases which concerned NGOs and were investigated and penalized. As a result, 46 illegal NGOs were banned and 3,071 administrative punishments took place.

There were 289 thousand social organizations, a growth of 6.6 percent over the previous year. Among these social organizations, 31,031 were engaged in industry and commercial service, 17,399 in science and technology, 11,753 in education, 9,953 in health, 41,777 in social services, 27,115 in culture, 17,869 in sports, 6,636 in eco-environment, 3,264 in legal service, 4,801 in religion, 58,825 in agricultural and rural development, 19,743 in profession, 481 in international and other overseas affairs and 38,379 in other fields. In 2013, there were 2173 law-breaking cases which concerned social organizations and were investigated and penalized. Thereinto, 21 illegal social organizations were banned and 2,152 administrative punishments took place.

In 2013, there were 3,549 foundations across the country, an increase of 520, rose by 17.2 percent over that of the previous year. Of this total, there were 1,378 public-raising foundations, 2,137 nonpublic raising foundations, 8 foundations concerning foreign affairs, 26 representative offices of oversea foundations. There were 216 foundations registered in the Ministry of Civil Affairs. The public-raising foundations and non-public-raising foundations totally received donations of 30.29 billion yuan. In 2013, 4 administrative punishments took place.

There were altogether 255 thousand non-governmental and non-commercial enterprises, rose by 13.1 percent over the previous year. Among these enterprises, there were 13,729 engaged in science and technology service; 377 in ecological environment, 145,210 in education, 21,234 in health, 36,698 in social services, 11,694 in culture, 10,353 in sports, 5,625 in commercial services, 94 in religion, 4 in international and other oversea affairs and 9,652 in other fields. In 2013, there were 940 law-breaking cases which concerned non-governmental and non-commercial enterprises and were investigated and penalized. Thereinto, 25 illegal non-governmental and non-commercial enterprises were banned, and 915 administrative punishments took place.

Figure 13: Non-Governmental Organizations

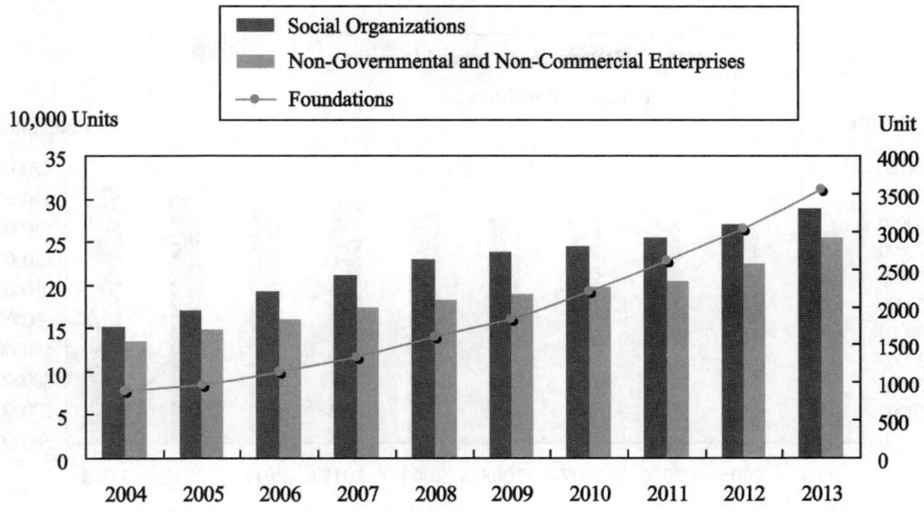

Table 13: Non-Governmental Organizations

Indicators	2006	2007	2008	2009	2010	2011	2012	2013
Social Organizations (10,000 Units)	19.2	21.2	23.0	23.9	24.5	25.5	27.1	28.9
Foundations (Unit)	1144	1340	1597	1843	2200	2614	3029	3549
Non-Governmental and Non-Commercial Enterprises (10,000 Units)	16.1	17.4	18.2	19.0	19.8	20.4	22.5	25.5

2. Self-Governing Organizations

By the end of 2013, self-governing organizations at the grass-roots totaled 683 thousand. Of this total, there were 589 thousand village committees. The number of village groups was 4.664 million. There were 2.323 million members of village committees. There were 94,620 community neighborhood committees, which rose by 3.8 percent over that of the previous year. There were 1.357 million neighborhood groups, which was an increase of 22 thousand over the previous year. There were 484 thousand members of neighborhood committees, rose by 3.2 percent over that in the previous year. In 2013, elections in 150 thousand neighborhood committees and village committees were completed. The registered number of residents and villagers who participated in the elections was 220 million. The number of voters was 170 million.

Table14: Self-Governing Organizations

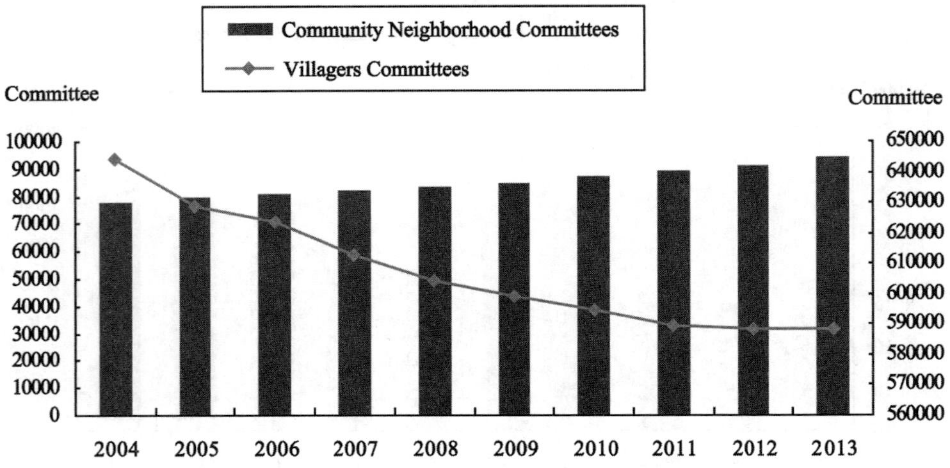

Table 14: Self-Governing Organizations

Indicators	2006	2007	2008	2009	2010	2011	2012	2013
Community Neighborhood Committees (committee)	80717	82006	83413	84689	87057	89480	91153	94620
Villagers Committees (committee)	623669	612709	604285	599078	594658	589653	588475	588547

B. Other Social Services

1. Marriage Service

There were 2,059 service institutions of marriage registration (qualified as public institutions) in China in 2013. The number of people that registered their marriage through civil affairs departments or marriage registration institutions reached 13.469 million couples, rose by 1.8 percent over that of the previous year. Of this total, 13.414 million couples were mainland Chinese residents. There were 55 thousand couples concerning foreigners, overseas Chinese, and residents of Hong Kong, Macau and Taiwan.The crude nuptiality was 9.9 per thousand, rose by 0.1 per thousand over that of the previous year. The proportion of people ranged from 25 to 29 years old accounted for 35.2 percent of all registered for marriage, taking the lead among other age groups and it increased by 1 percent over that of the previous year.

In 2013, there were 3.5 million couples handling divorce, which was an increase of 12.8 percent over the previous year. The crude divorce rate was 2.6 per thousand, which was an increase of 0.3 per thousand over that in 2012. Of this total, 2.815 million couples were registered by the civil affairs departments and those who divorced through courts were 685 thousand couples.

Figure 15: Crude Nuptiality and Divorce Rate

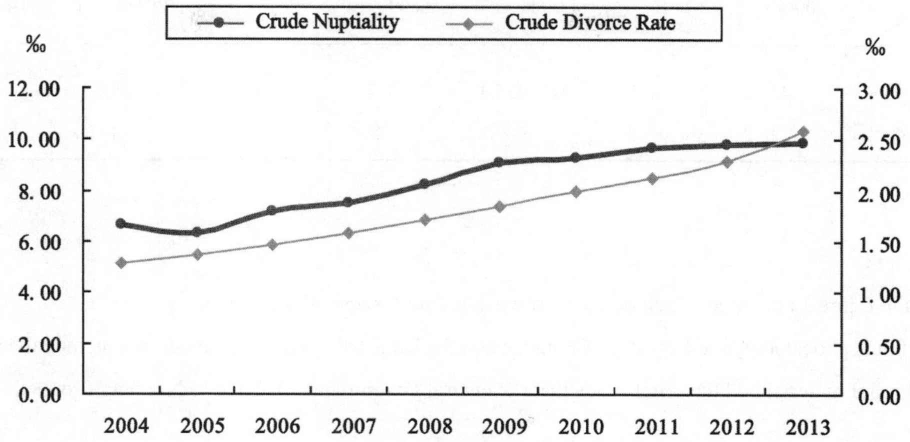

Table 15: Crude Nuptiality and Divorce Rate

Indicators	2006	2007	2008	2009	2010	2011	2012	2013
Crude Nuptiality (‰)	7.19	7.50	8.27	9.10	9.30	9.67	9.80	9.92
Crude Divorce Rate (‰)	1.46	1.59	1.71	1.85	2.00	2.13	2.29	2.58

2. Funeral and Interment

By the end of 2013, there were 4,382 funeral and interment service institutions, with a growth of 26 compared with that of 2012. Of this total, there were 1,784 funeral parlors, 1,063 funeral management units. There were 1,506 public cemeteries under the management of the civil affairs departments. There were 81 thousand staff and workers in the funeral and interment service institutions. Among these institutions, 46 thousand people worked for funeral parlors. There were 5,743 cremators, which cremated 4.689 million remains. The cremation rate standing at 48.2 percent.

Figure 16 : Cremation of Funeral Service

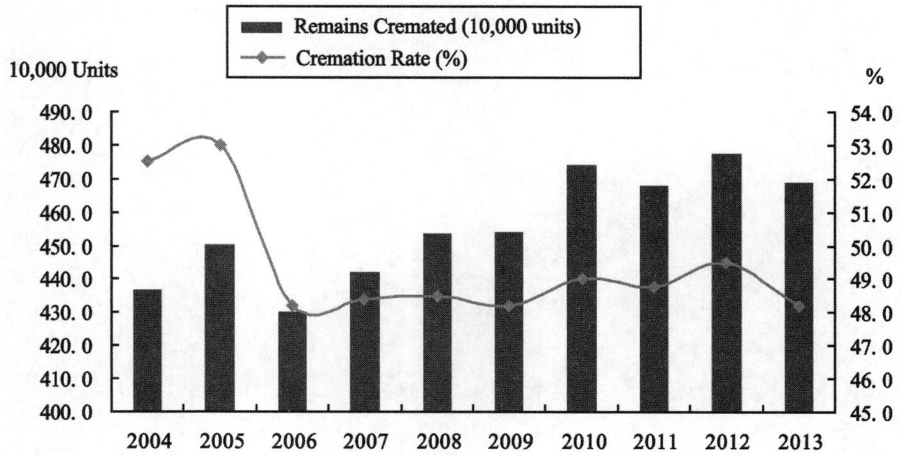

Table 16 :Cremation of Funeral Service

Indicators	2006	2007	2008	2009	2010	2011	2012	2013
Remains Cremated (10,000 Units)	430.2	442.1	453.4	454.2	474.1	468.1	477.7	468.9
Cremation Rate (%)	48.2	48.4	48.5	48.2	49.0	48.8	49.5	48.2

Notes:

[1] Townships in figure 1 and table 1 include ethnic townships, sumus and ethnic sumus.

[2] The relief funds allocated by the Ministry of Finance and the Ministry of Civil Affairs do not include the purchasing funds of central relief material and the relief funds that the central government allocated to Xinjiang Production and Construction Corps.

[3] The community service centers in 2013 contain community service instruction centers.

[4] The statistics of judicial decisions and mediate divorces recorded in the divorce registration service comes from the supreme peoples' court.

[5] In this report, the numbers of people were actual and the numbers of institutions were the numbers of authorized ones. These numbers should not be compared with approved numbers and predicted numbers.

[6] The numbers of items and the numbers of total may not match, this is because some of the statistics in the report were rounded off and no mechanical adjustments have been made for mending the error.

[7] Statistics of Hong Kong, Macau and Taiwan province were not included into the report.

社会服务
主要数据图表

02

图1-1　市、区、县

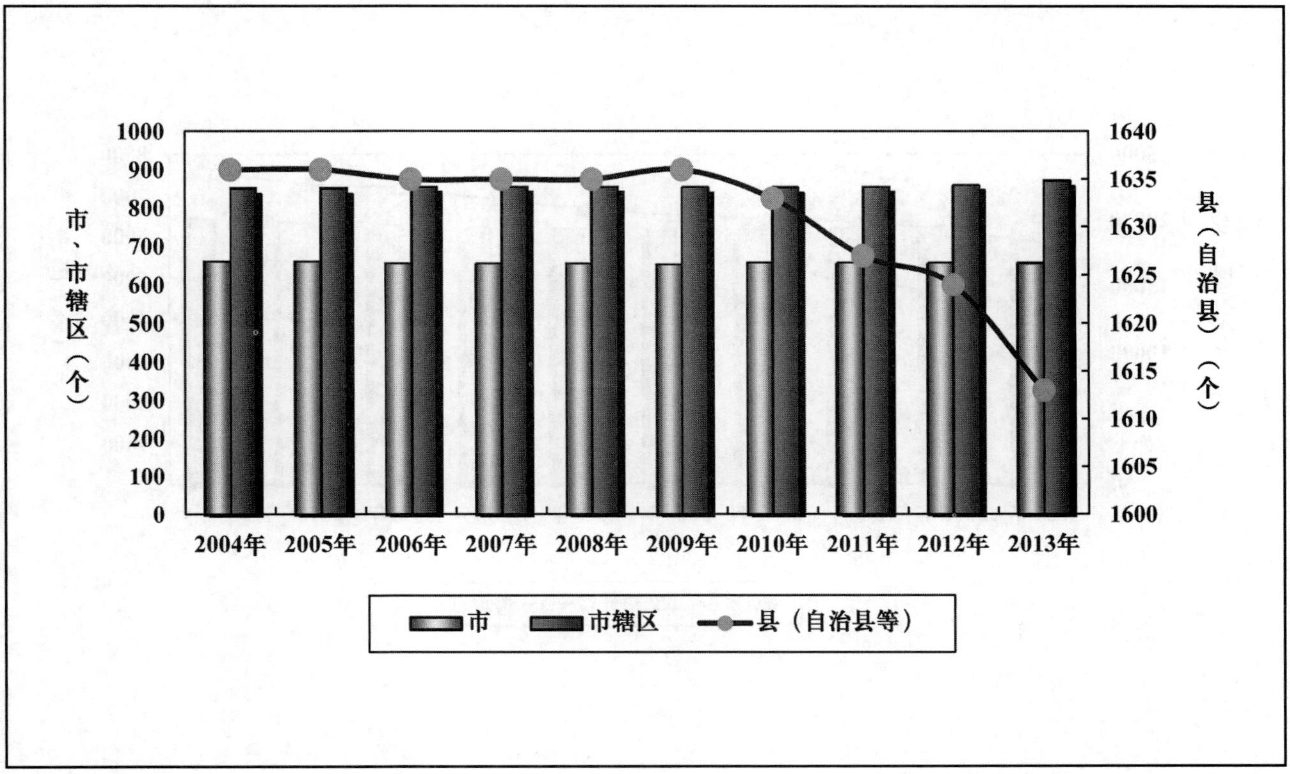

单位：个

指　标	2004年	2005年	2006年	2007年	2008年	2009年	2010年	2011年	2012年	2013年
市	661	661	656	655	655	654	657	657	657	658
市辖区	852	852	856	856	856	855	853	857	860	872
县（自治县等）	1636	1636	1635	1635	1635	1636	1633	1627	1624	1613

注释：市含直辖市、地级市及县级市。

图1-2　乡镇与街道

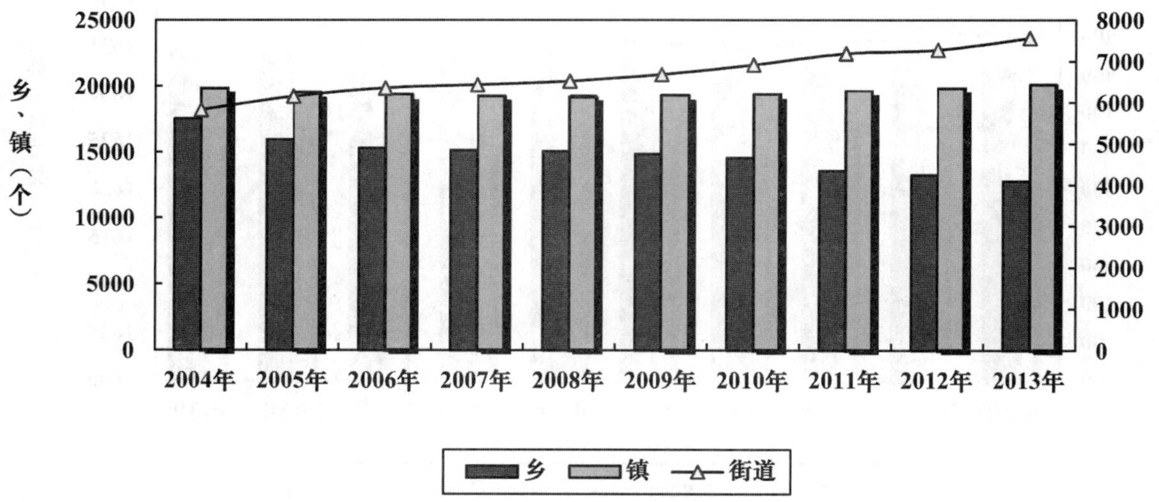

单位：个

指　标	2004年	2005年	2006年	2007年	2008年	2009年	2010年	2011年	2012年	2013年
乡	17534	15951	15306	15120	15067	14848	14571	13587	13281	12812
镇	19892	19522	19369	19249	19234	19322	19410	19683	19881	20117
街道	5829	6152	6355	6434	6524	6686	6923	7194	7282	7566

图1-3　60岁及以上老年人口占全国总人口比重

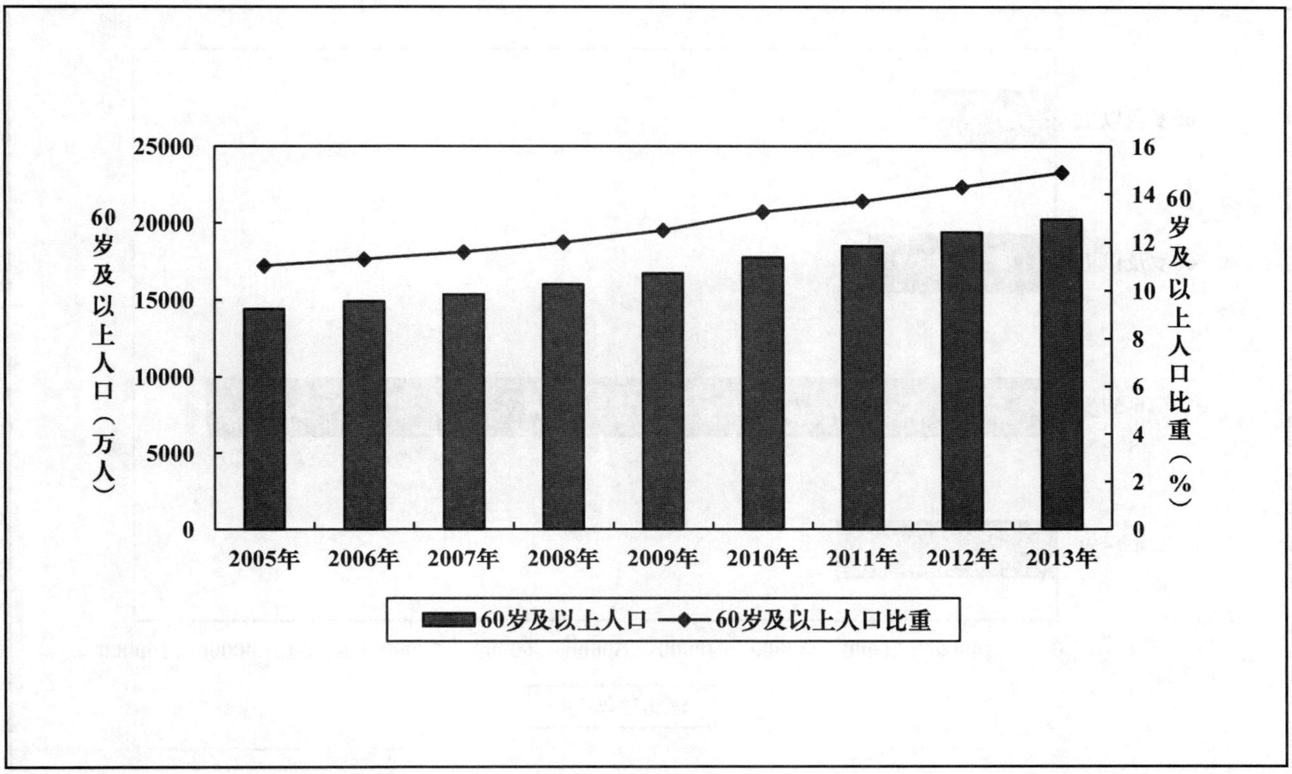

单位：万人、%

指　标	2005年	2006年	2007年	2008年	2009年	2010年	2011年	2012年	2013年
60岁及以上人口	14408	14901	15340	15989	16714	17765	18499	19390	20243
60岁及以上人口比重	11.03	11.3	11.6	12	12.5	13.26	13.7	14.3	14.9

注：本表数据来源于国家统计局。

图1-4　人口年龄结构

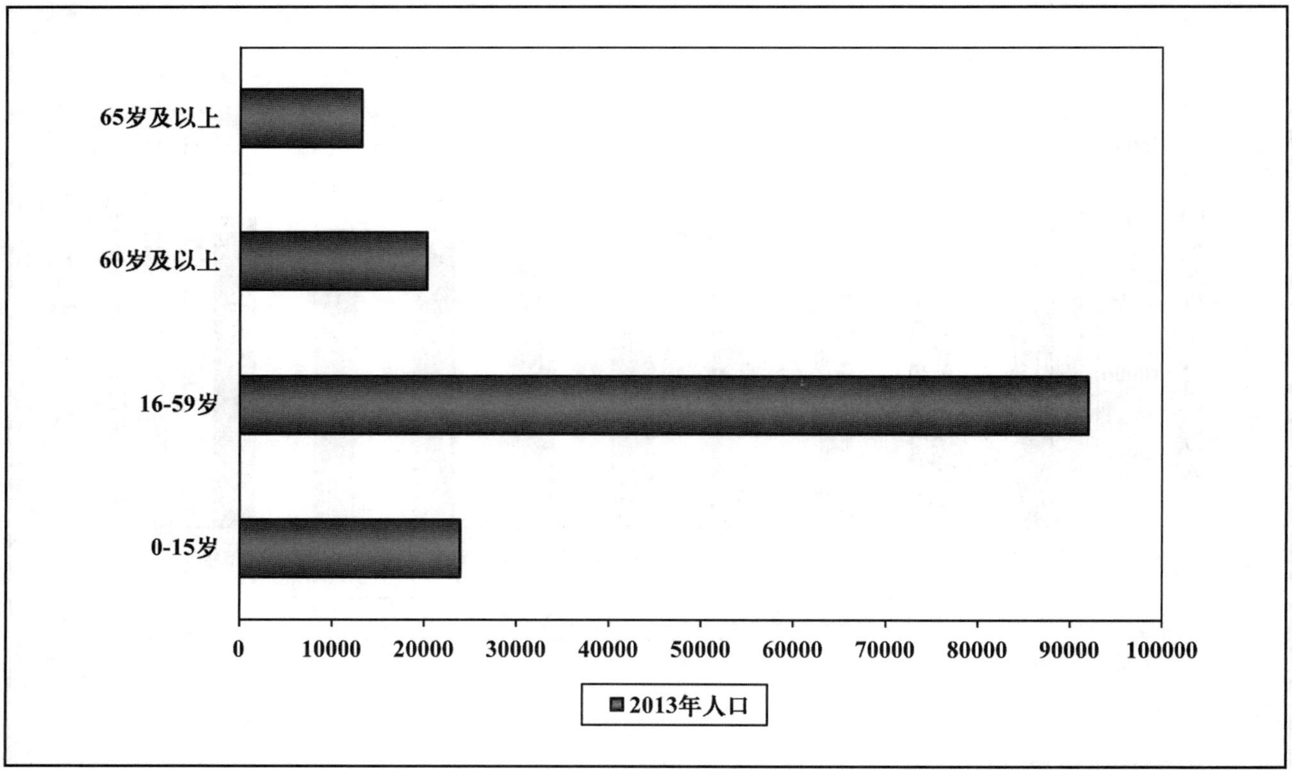

单位：万人、%

指　标	0–15岁	16–59岁	60岁及以上	65岁及以上
2013年人口	23875	91954	20243	13161
不同年龄段人口比重	17.5	67.6	14.9	9.7
比2012年增减百分点			0.6	0.3

图1-5 社会服务机构和职工

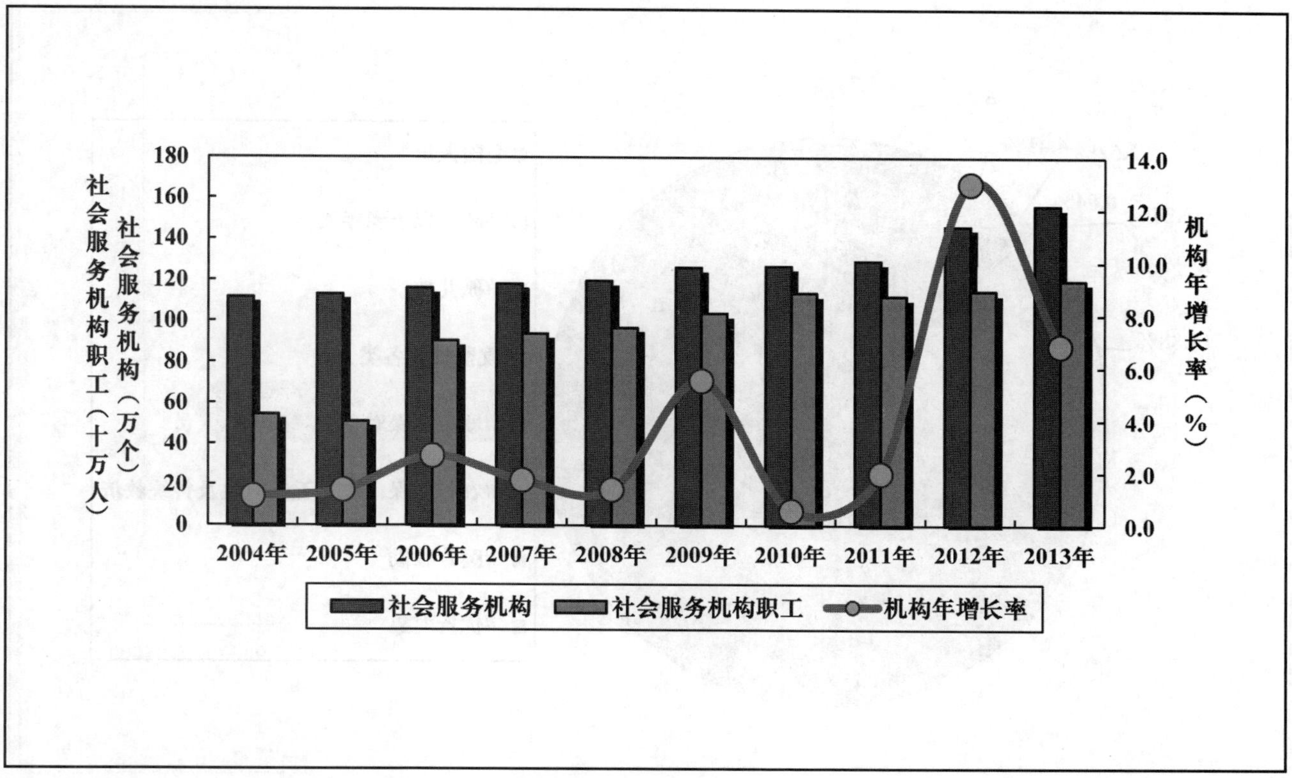

单位：万个、%、十万人

指　标	2004年	2005年	2006年	2007年	2008年	2009年	2010年	2011年	2012年	2013年
社会服务机构	111.5	113.0	116.0	118.0	119.6	126.2	126.9	129.4	146.2	156.2
社会服务机构职工	54.4	50.9	90.4	93.8	96.7	103.8	113.8	112.1	114.7	119.8
机构年增长率	1.1	1.3	2.7	1.7	1.4	5.5	0.6	2.0	13.0	6.8

图1-6　主要社会服务对象占全国总人口比重

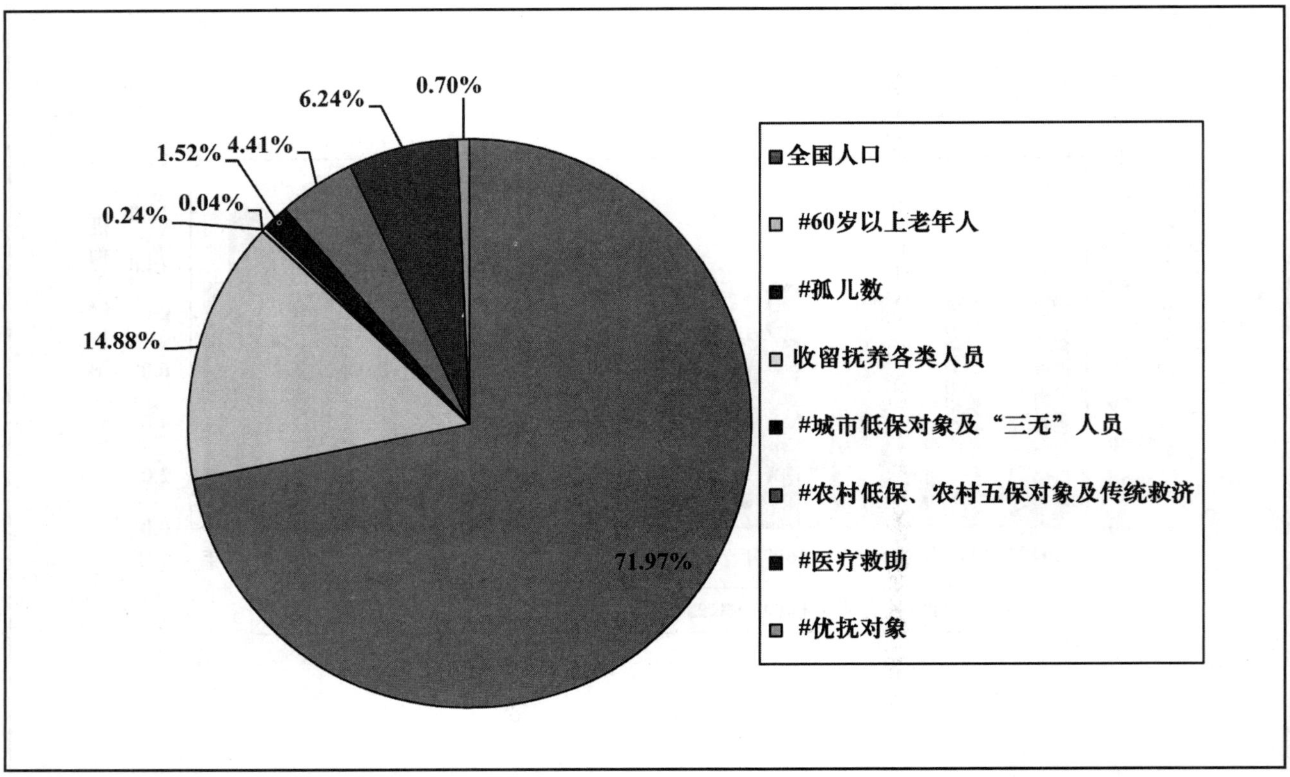

单位：万人、%

指　标	2013年	比　重
全国总人口	136072	100.0
社会服务对象	38127.1	28.02
# 60岁以上老年人	20243	14.88
孤儿数	54.9	0.04
收留抚养各类人员	322.5	0.24
# 城市低保对象及“三无”人员	2072.8	1.52
农村低保、农村五保对象及传统救济	5998.2	4.41
医疗救助	8485.2	6.24
优抚对象	950.5	0.70

图1-7　社会服务机构增加值占服务业增加值比重

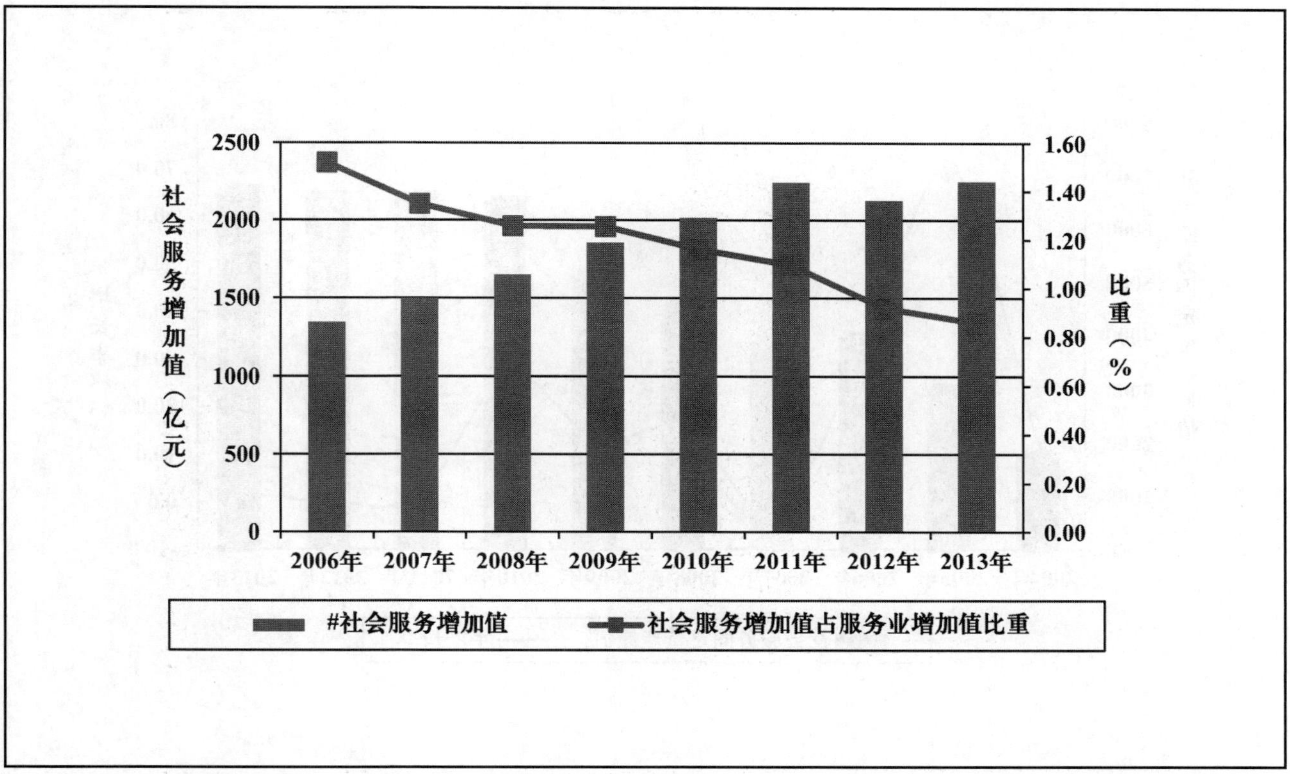

单位：亿元、%

指　标	2006年	2007年	2008年	2009年	2010年	2011年	2012年	2013年
服务业增加值	88554.9	111351.9	131340.0	148038.0	173596.0	204982.5	231626.0	262204.0
# 社会服务增加值	1344.8	1501.2	1650.1	1856.2	2014.5	2246.9	2128.9	2251.9
社会服务增加值占服务业增加值比重	1.52	1.35	1.26	1.25	1.16	1.10	0.92	0.86

图1-8 社会服务固定资产原值

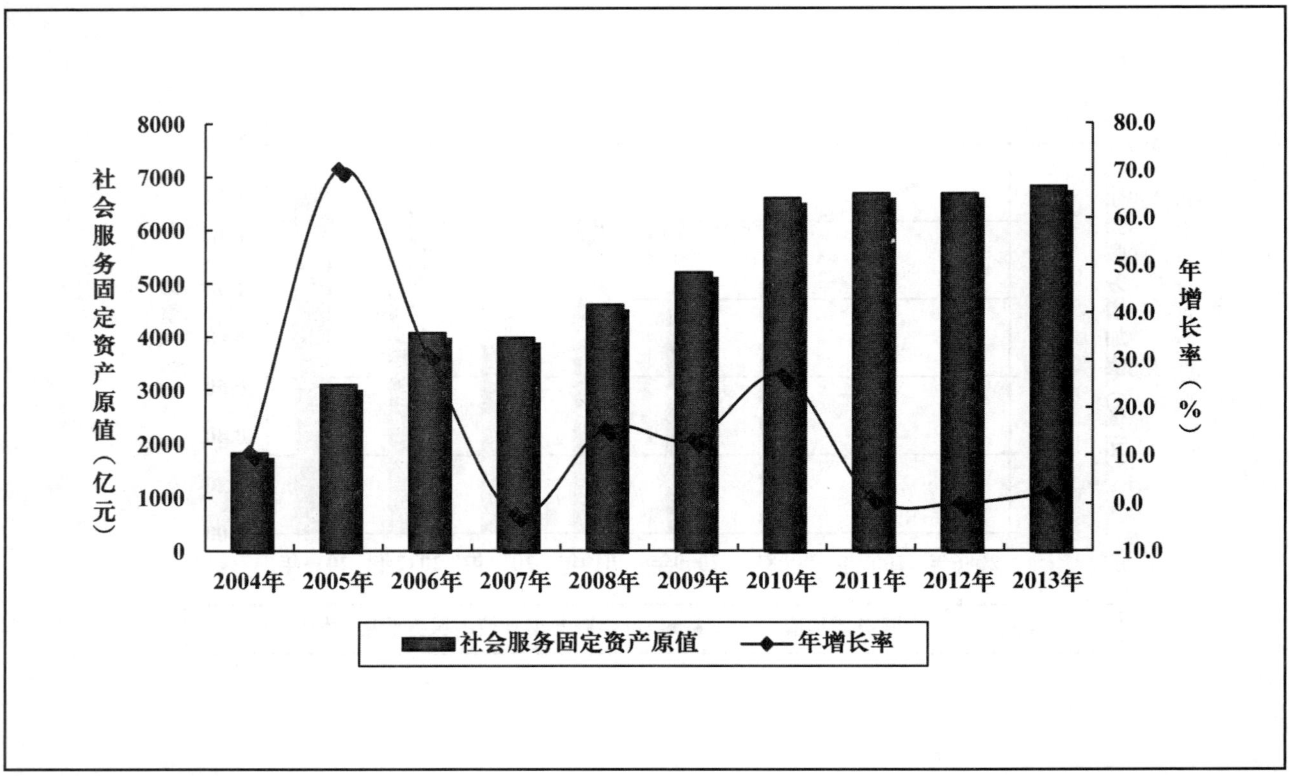

单位：亿元、%

指　标	2004年	2005年	2006年	2007年	2008年	2009年	2010年	2011年	2012年	2013年
社会服务固定资产原值	1818.4	3097.8	4066.7	3973.0	4592.8	5198	6589.3	6676.7	6675.4	6810.2
年增长率	10.6	70.4	31.3	-2.3	15.6	13.2	26.8	1.3		2.0

图1-9　社会服务领域基本建设投资

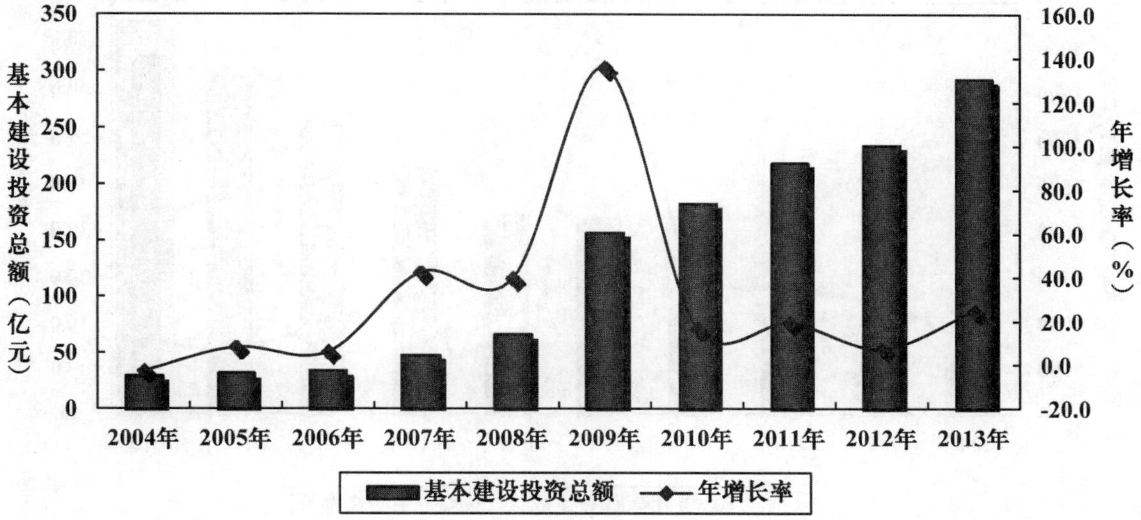

单位：亿元、%

指　标	2004年	2005年	2006年	2007年	2008年	2009年	2010年	2011年	2012年	2013年
基本建设投资总额	29.2	31.6	33.5	47.7	66.6	157.0	183.0	218.5	234.7	292.8
年增长率	-2.7	8.2	6.0	42.4	39.6	135.7	16.6	19.4	7.4	24.8

图1-10　社会服务经费支出

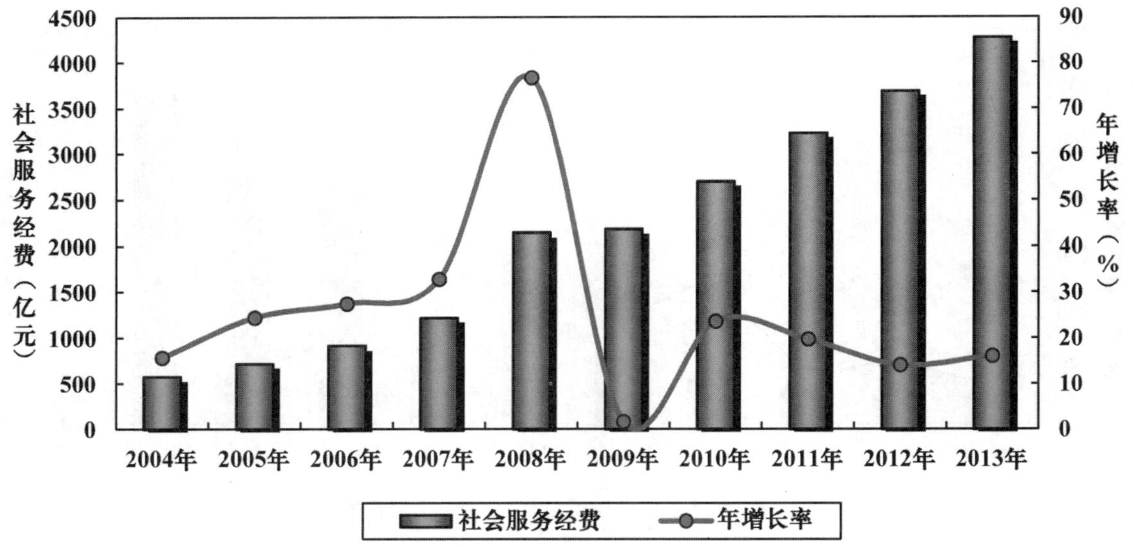

单位：亿元、%

指　标	2004年	2005年	2006年	2007年	2008年	2009年	2010年	2011年	2012年	2013年
社会服务经费	577.4	718.4	915.4	1215.5	2146.5	2181.9	2697.5	3229.1	3683.7	4276.5
年增长率	15.7	24.4	27.4	32.8	76.6	1.6	23.6	19.7	14.1	16.1

图1-11　社会服务经费支出占国家财政支出的比重

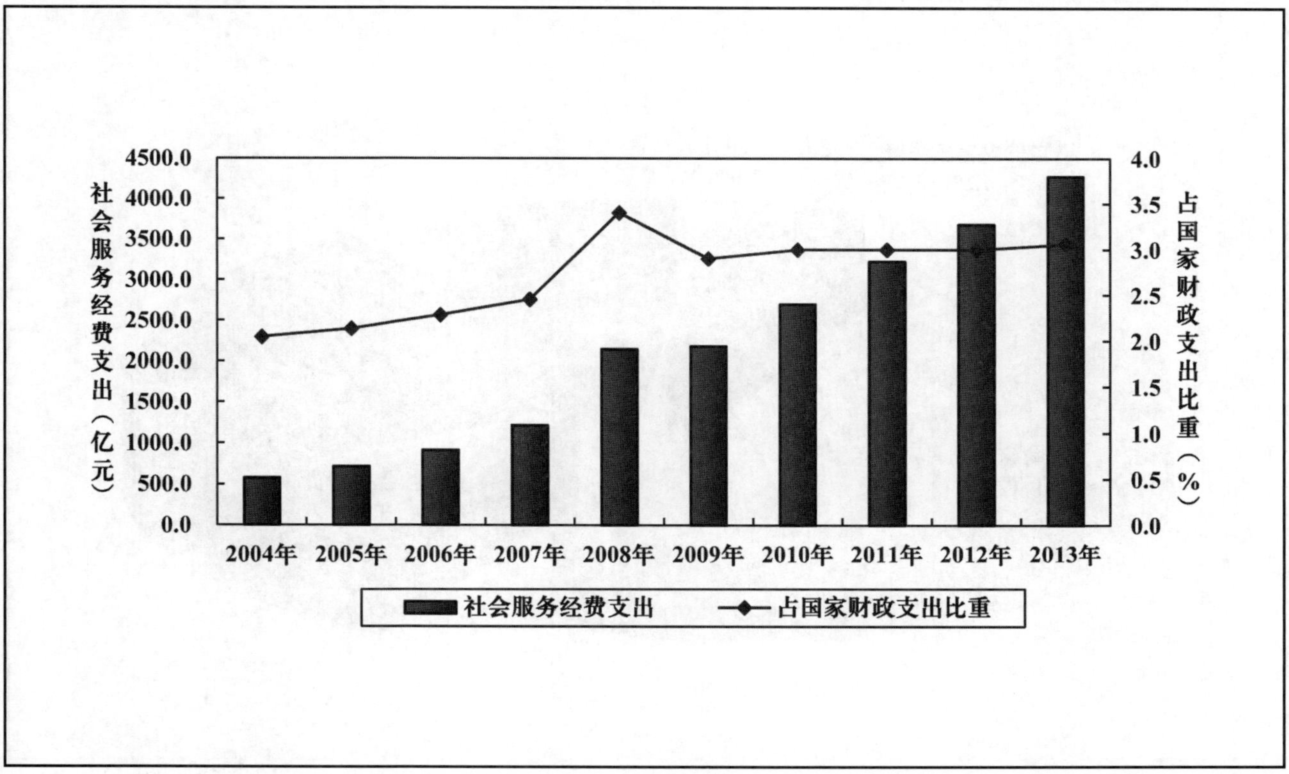

单位：亿元、%

指　标	2004年	2005年	2006年	2007年	2008年	2009年	2010年	2011年	2012年	2013年
社会服务经费支出	577.4	718.4	915.4	1215.5	2146.5	2181.9	2697.5	3229.1	3683.7	4276.5
占国家财政支出比重	2.0	2.1	2.3	2.5	3.4	2.9	3.0	3.0	3.0	3.1

图1-12　社会服务经费按用项支出比重

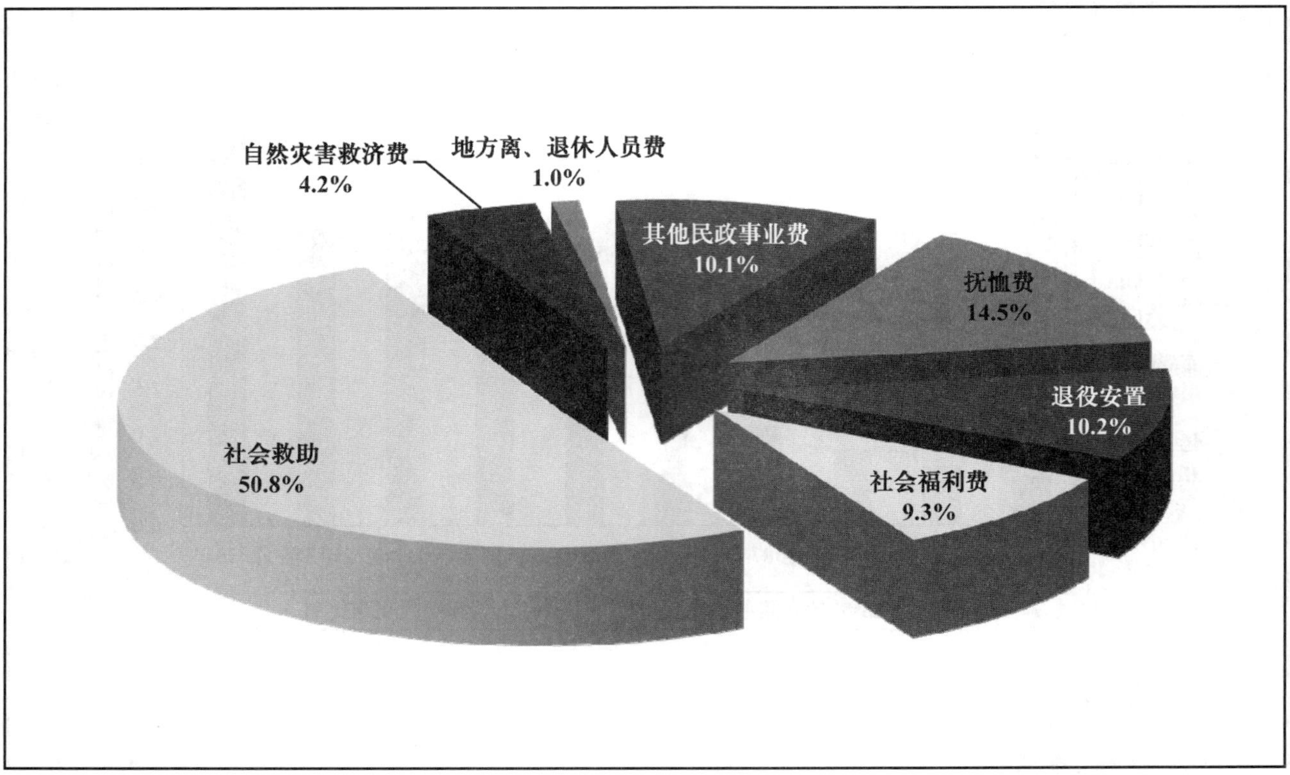

单位：亿元、%

指　标	社会服务经费总支出	抚恤费	退役安置	社会福利费	社会救助	自然灾害救济费	地方离、退休人员费	其他民政事业费
金　额	4276.5	618.4	435.3	397.6	2172.4	178.7	43.6	430.6
比　重	100.0	14.5	10.2	9.3	50.8	4.2	1.0	10.1

图1-13 中央转移支付社会服务经费

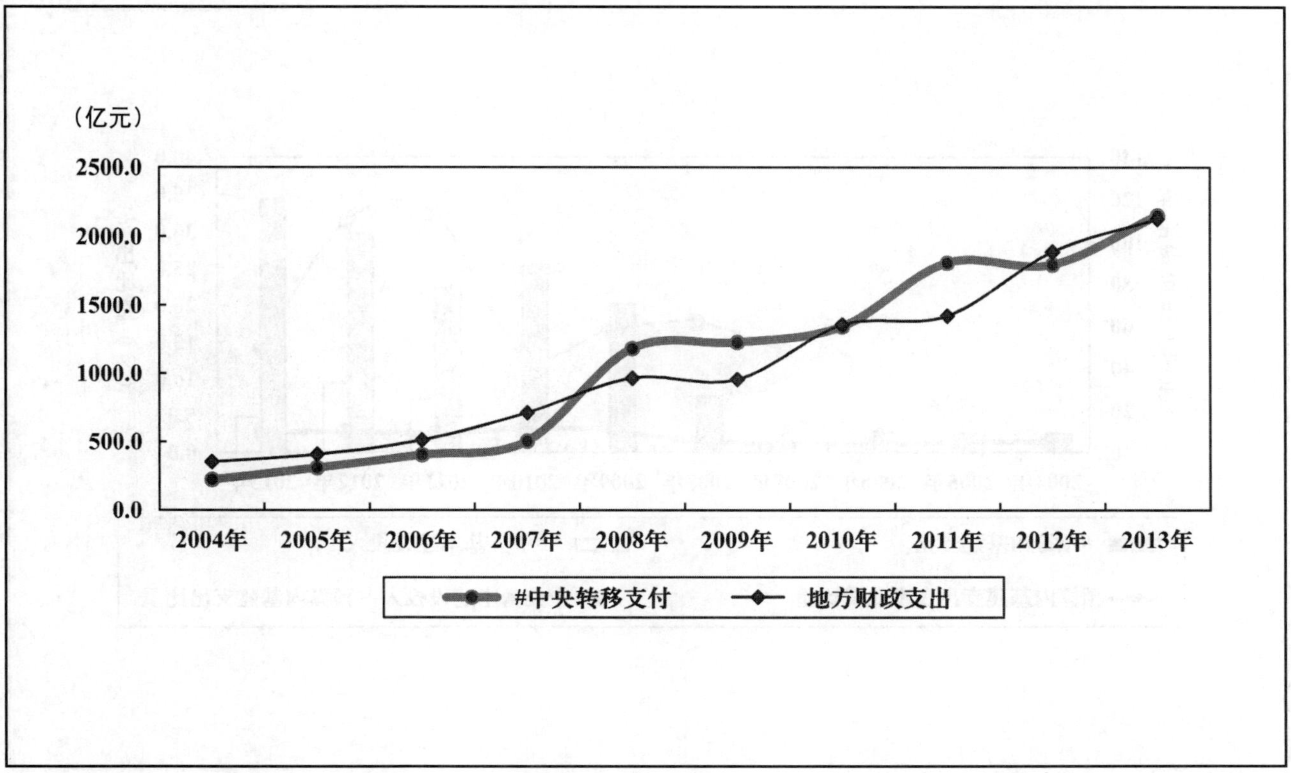

单位：亿元、%

指 标	2004年	2005年	2006年	2007年	2008年	2009年	2010年	2011年	2012年	2013年
社会服务经费支出	577.4	718.4	915.4	1215.5	2146.5	2181.9	2697.5	3229.1	3683.7	4276.5
# 中央转移支付	223.8	310.3	404.0	504.4	1181.1	1227.0	1342.4	1808.0	1794.6	2149.7
地方财政支出	353.6	408.1	511.4	711.1	965.4	954.9	1355.1	1421.1	1889.1	2126.8
中央支付占社会服务经费支出比重	38.8	43.2	44.1	42.6	55.0	56.2	49.8	56.0	48.7	50.3

图1-14 中央投入的基本建设经费占全国预算内基本建设经费比重

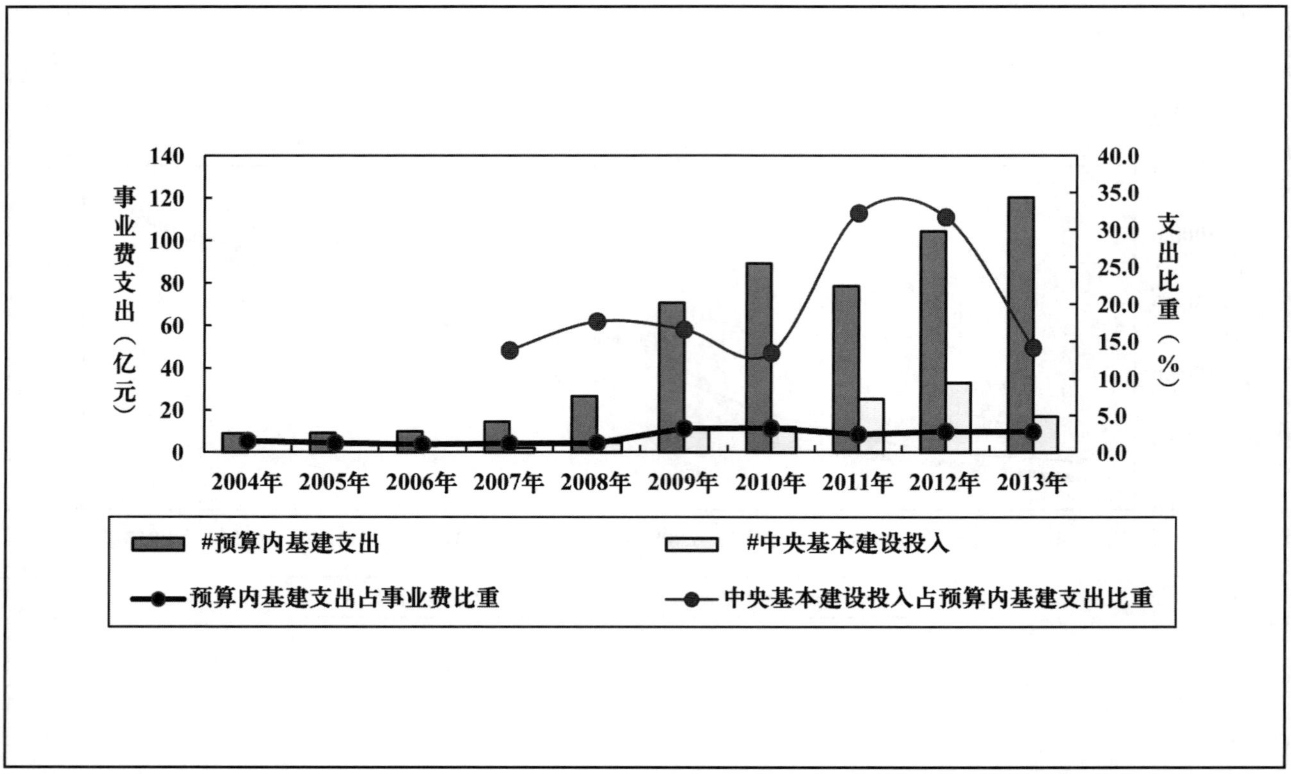

单位：亿元、%

指 标	2004年	2005年	2006年	2007年	2008年	2009年	2010年	2011年	2012年	2013年
社会服务经费支出	577.4	718.4	915.4	1215.5	2146.5	2181.9	2697.5	3229.1	3683.7	4276.5
#预算内基建支出	8.9	9.1	9.9	14.5	26.6	70.6	89.1	78.5	104.2	120.1
#中央基本建设投入				2.0	4.7	11.7	12.0	25.3	33.0	17.0
预算内基建支出占事业费比重	1.5	1.3	1.1	1.2	1.2	3.2	3.3	2.4	2.8	2.8
中央基本建设投入占预算内基建支出比重				13.8	17.7	16.6	13.4	32.2	31.7	14.2

图2-1 社会服务机构床位数

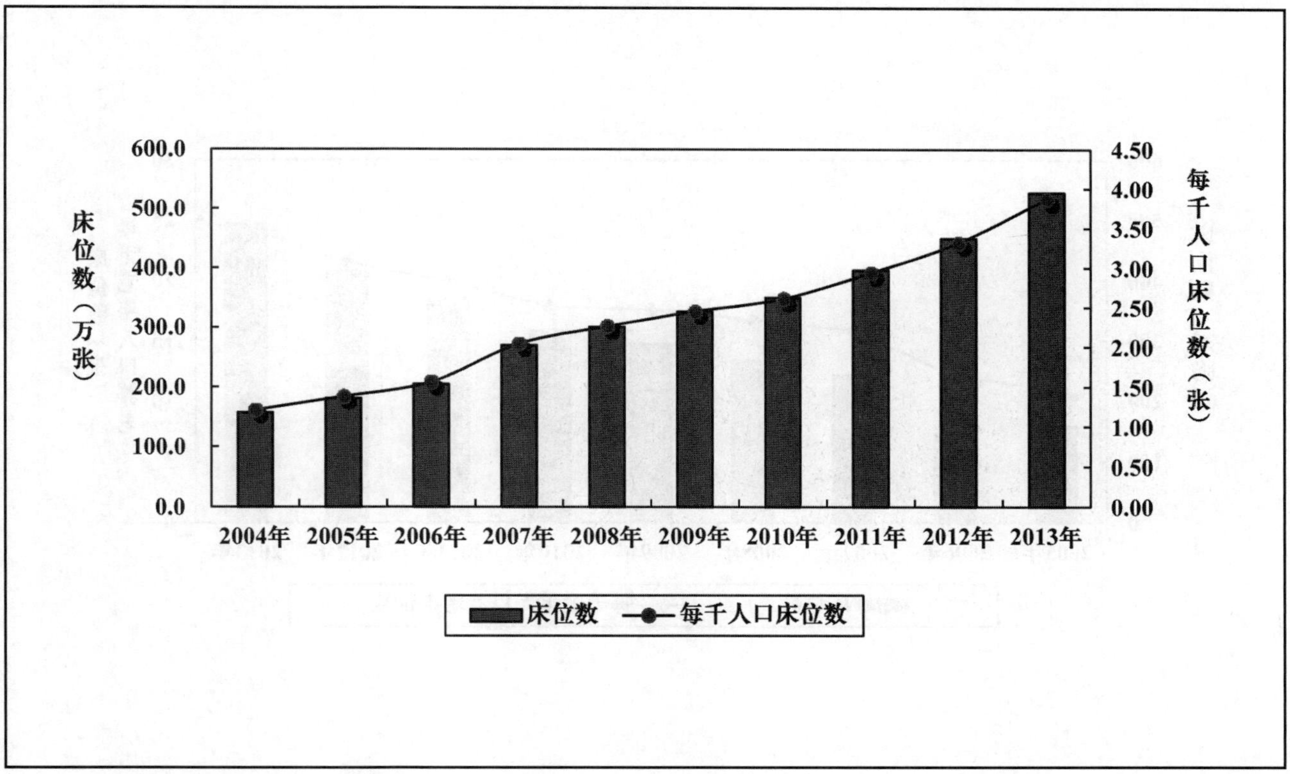

单位：万张、张

指　标	2004年	2005年	2006年	2007年	2008年	2009年	2010年	2011年	20112年	2013年
床位数	157.2	180.7	204.5	269.6	300.3	326.5	349.6	396.4	449.3	526.7
每千人口床位数	1.21	1.38	1.56	2.04	2.26	2.45	2.61	2.94	3.32	3.87

图2-2　养老服务机构床位数

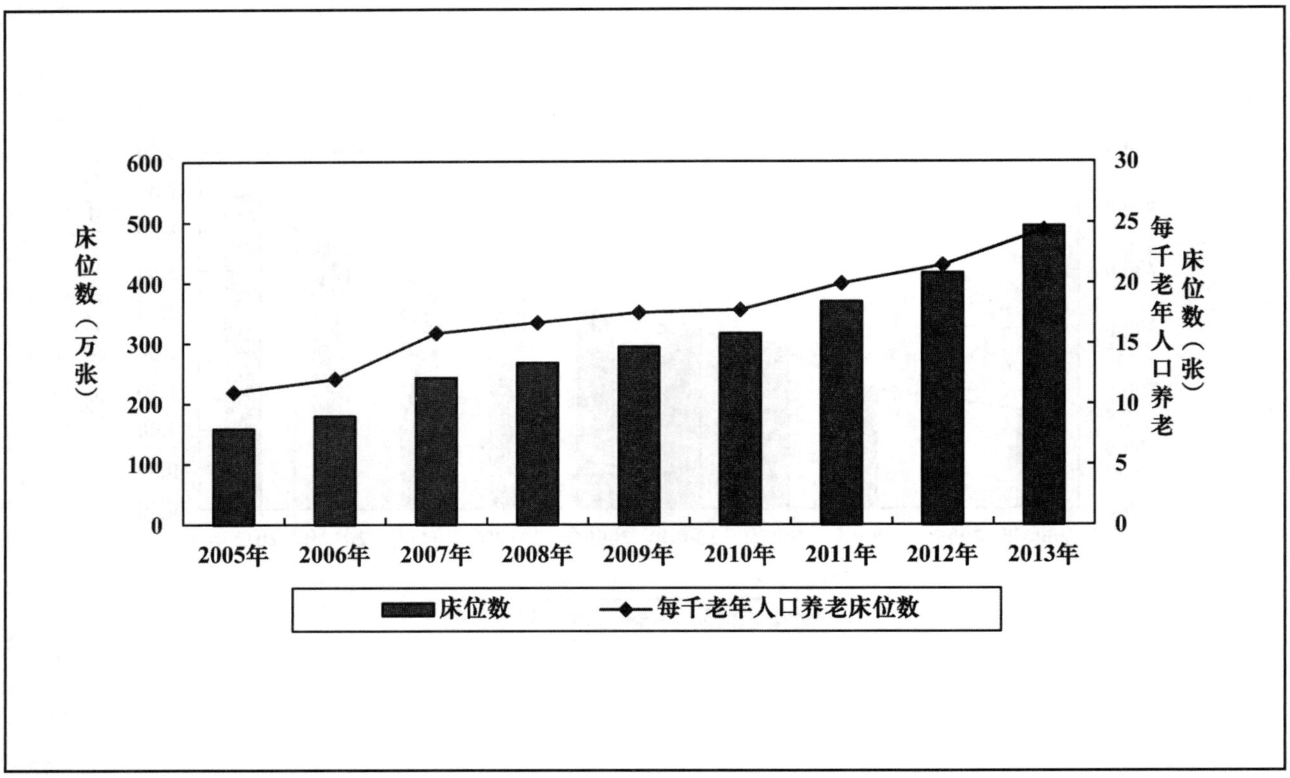

单位：万张、%、张

指　标	2005年	2006年	2007年	2008年	2009年	2010年	2011年	2012年	2013年
床位数	158.1	179.6	242.9	267.4	293.5	316.1	369.2	416.5	493.7
增长率	13.5	13.6	35.2	10.1	9.8	7.7	16.8	12.8	18.5
每千老年人口养老床位数	10.97	12.05	15.83	16.72	17.56	17.79	19.96	21.48	24.39

图2-3 农村养老服务机构

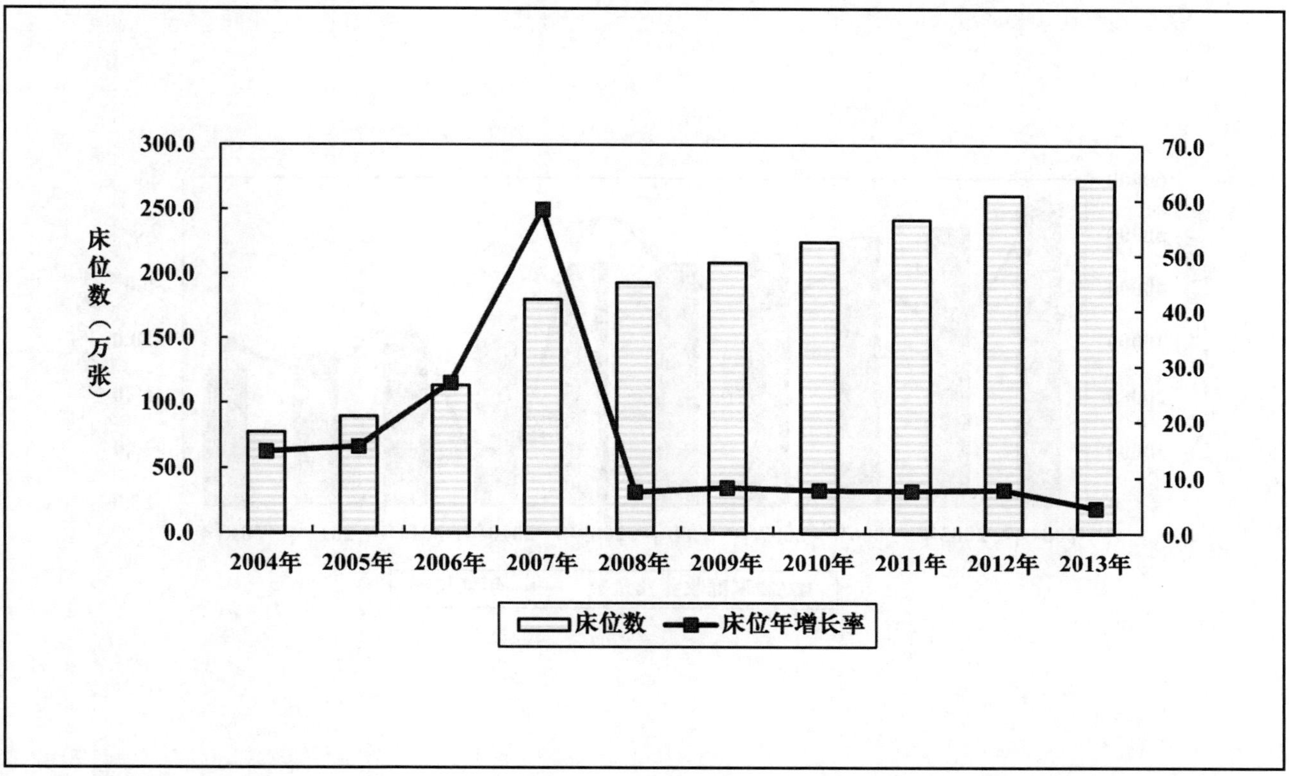

单位：万个、万张、%

指 标	2004年	2005年	2006年	2007年	2008年	2009年	2010年	2011年	2012年	2013年
单位数	2.6	3.0	3.1	3.5	3.0	3.1	3.1	3.2	3.3	3.0
床位数	77.5	89.5	113.6	179.8	193.1	208.8	224.9	242.1	261.0	272.8
床位年增长率	14.6	15.5	26.9	58.3	7.4	8.2	7.7	7.6	7.8	4.5

图2-4 家庭儿童收养

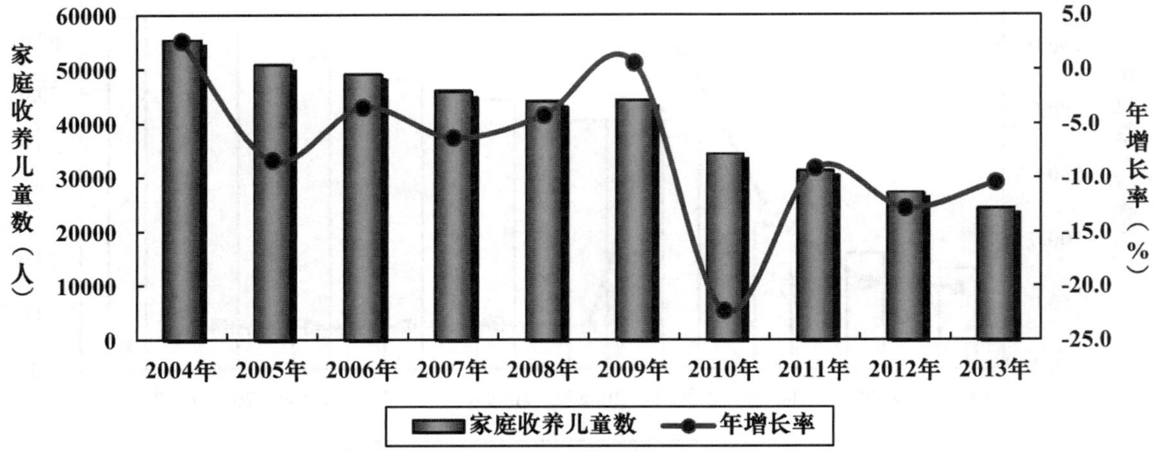

单位：人、%

指 标	2004年	2005年	2006年	2007年	2008年	2009年	2010年	2011年	2012年	2013年
家庭收养儿童数	55572	50921	49148	46047	44115	44359	34473	31329	27310	24460
年增长率	2.6	-8.4	-3.5	-6.3	-4.2	0.6	-22.3	-9.1	-12.8	-10.4

图2–5 为残疾人提供服务机构中的残疾职工

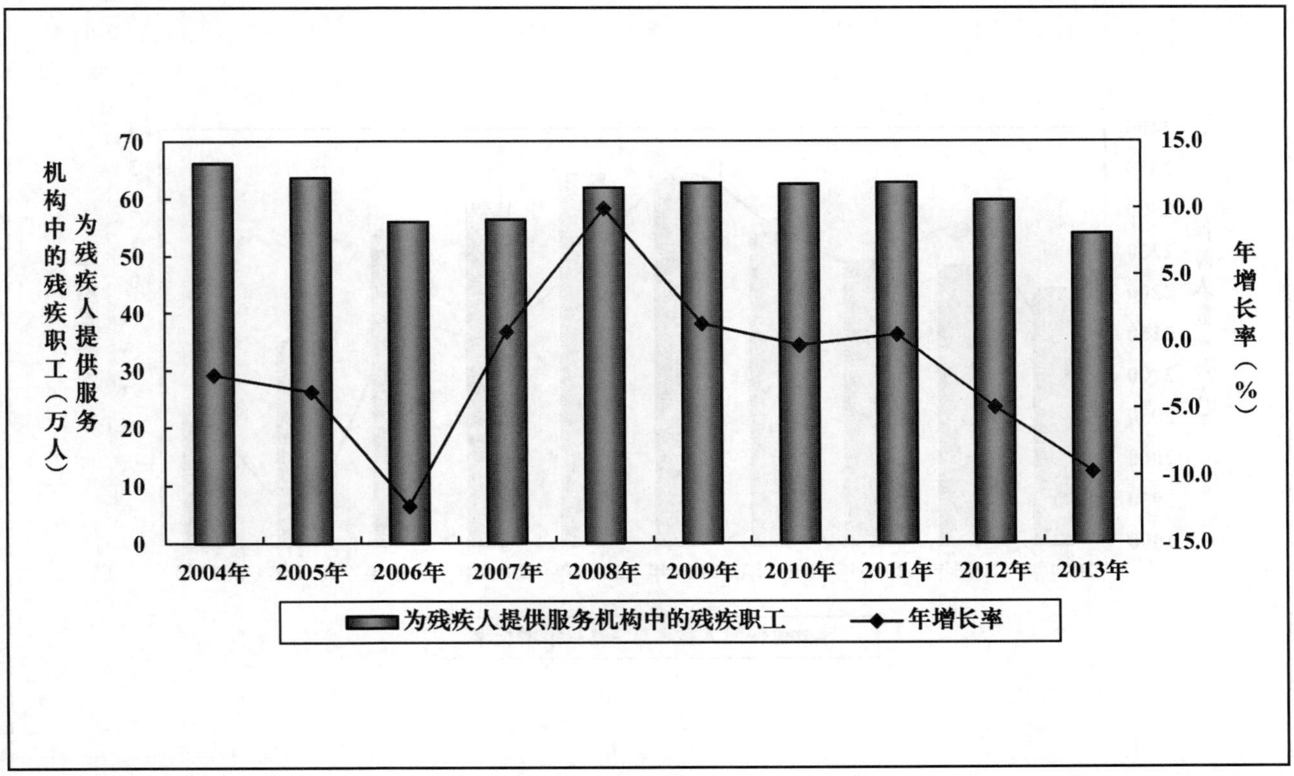

单位：万人、%

指　标	2004年	2005年	2006年	2007年	2008年	2009年	2010年	2011年	2012年	2013年
为残疾人提供服务机构中的残疾职工	66.2	63.7	55.9	56.3	61.9	62.7	62.5	62.8	59.7	53.9
年增长率	-2.5	-3.8	-12.2	0.7	9.9	1.3	-0.3	0.5	-4.9	-9.7

图2-6　城市居民最低生活保障

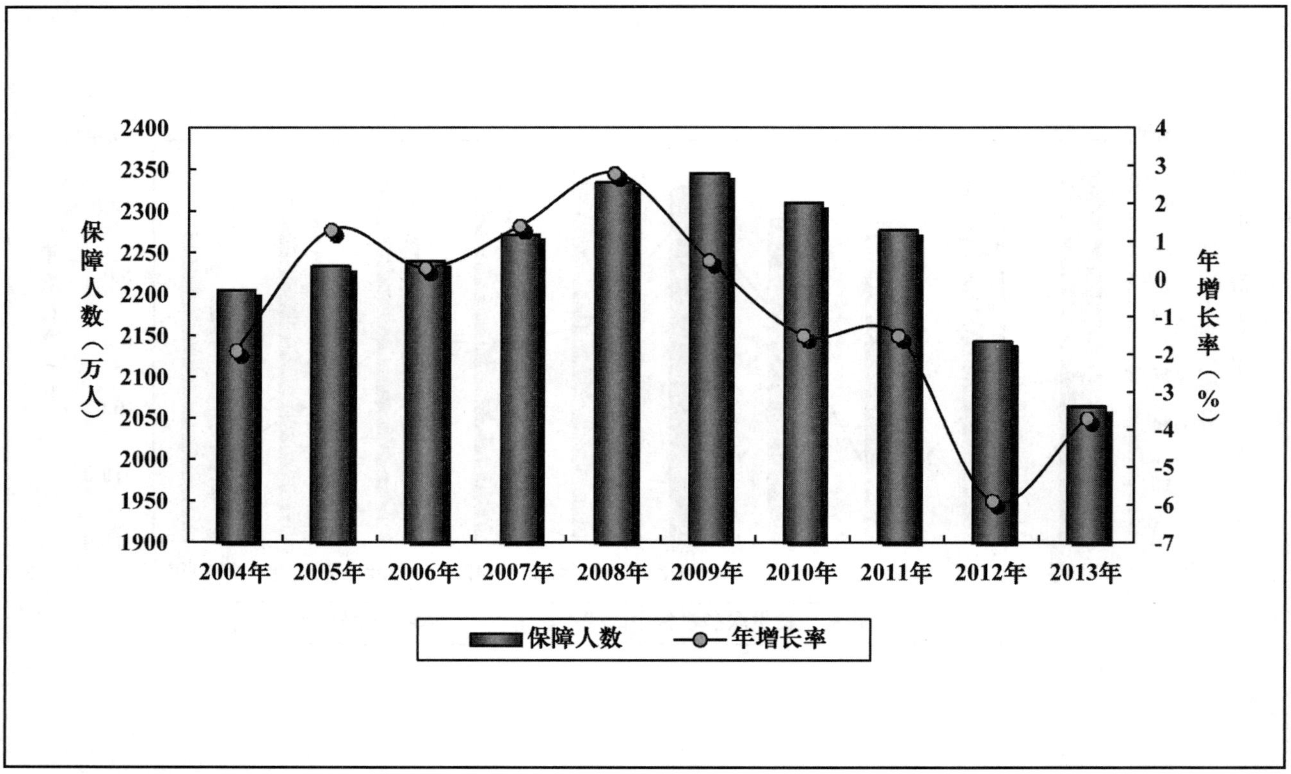

单位：万人、%

指　标	2004年	2005年	2006年	2007年	2008年	2009年	2010年	2011年	2012年	2013年
保障人数	2205.0	2234.2	2240.1	2272.1	2334.8	2345.6	2310.5	2276.8	2143.5	2064.2
年增长率	-1.9	1.3	0.3	1.4	2.8	0.5	-1.5	-1.5	-5.9	-3.7

图2-7　城市居民最低生活保障平均标准与平均支出水平

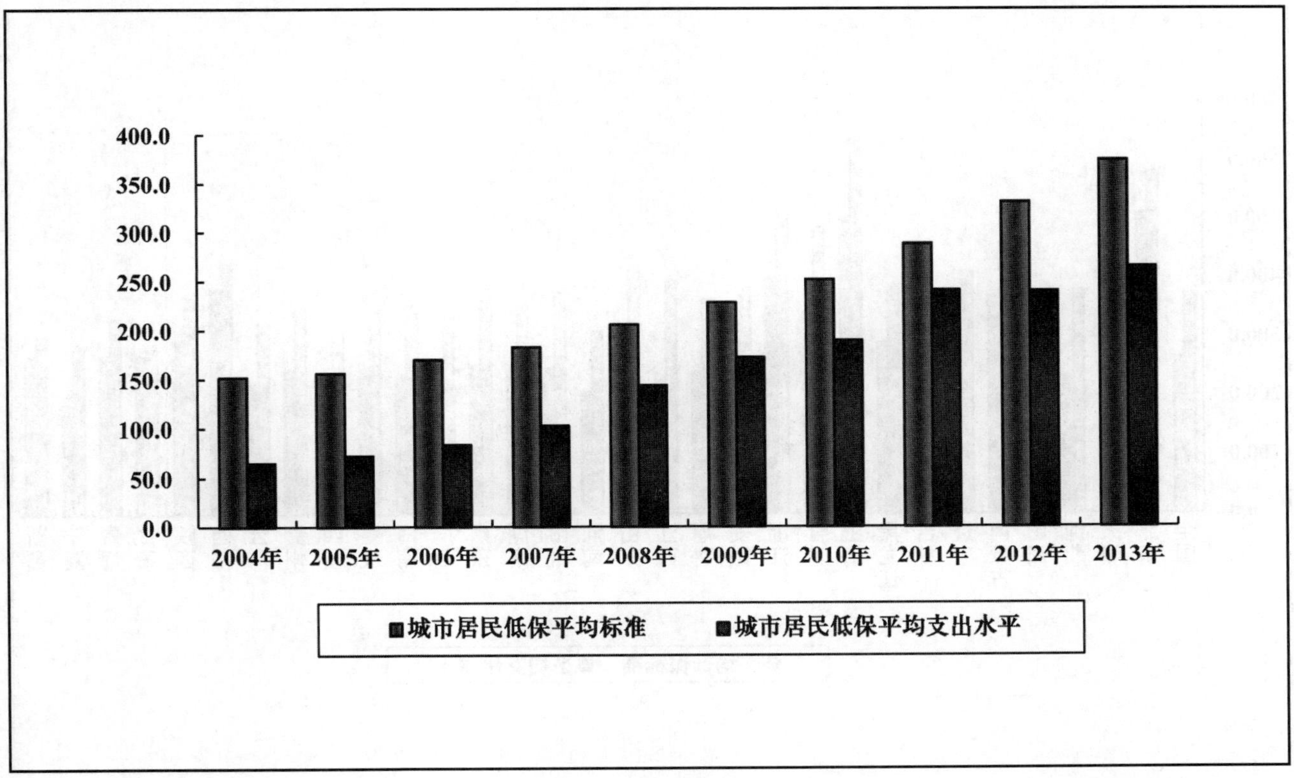

单位：元/人、月

指　标	2004年	2005年	2006年	2007年	2008年	2009年	2010年	2011年	2012年	2013年
城市居民低保平均标准	152.0	156.0	169.6	182.4	205.3	227.8	251.2	287.6	330.1	373.3
城市居民低保平均支出水平	65.0	72.3	83.6	102.7	143.7	172.0	189.0	240.3	239.1	264.2

图2-8　各省城市居民最低生活保障平均标准与支出水平

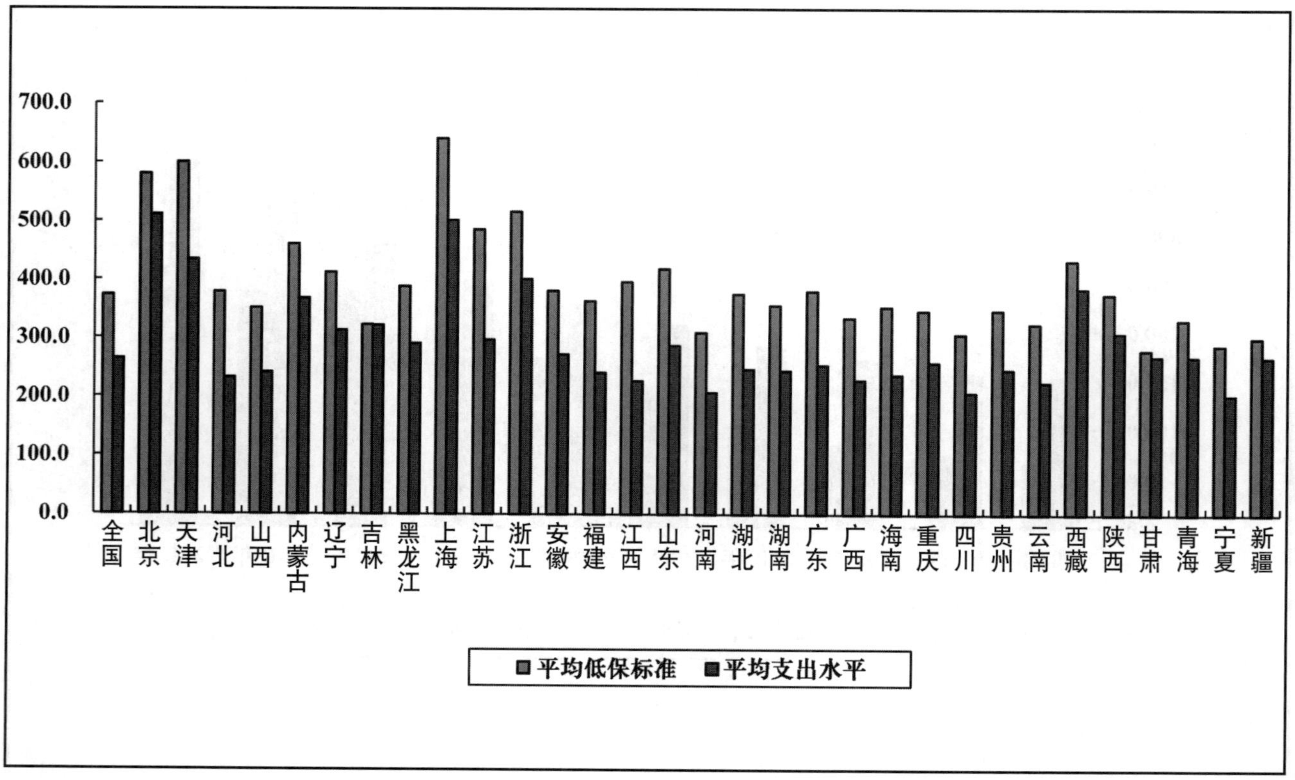

单位：元/人、月

地　区	平均低保标准	平均支出水平	地　区	平均低保标准	平均支出水平	地　区	平均低保标准	平均支出水平	地　区	平均低保标准	平均支出水平
全　国	**373.3**	**264.2**	黑龙江	387.7	290.3	河　南	309.2	207.2	贵　州	347.6	245.9
北　京	580.0	510.9	上　海	640.0	500.9	湖　北	375.1	246.6	云　南	323.9	224.2
天　津	600.0	433.4	江　苏	485.1	296.5	湖　南	356.1	244.4	西　藏	432.4	384.4
河　北	378.5	231.9	浙　江	515.5	400.4	广　东	380.4	253.6	陕　西	374.7	308.3
山　西	351.1	240.7	安　徽	380.5	271.5	广　西	334.7	228.3	甘　肃	279.0	268.9
内蒙古	460.3	367.5	福　建	363.3	240.4	海　南	353.3	237.1	青　海	330.8	267.9
辽　宁	411.5	312.7	江　西	395.7	226.5	重　庆	346.8	257.9	宁　夏	287.6	202.5
吉　林	322.5	321.7	山　东	417.7	286.4	四　川	306.4	206.9	新　疆	300.4	266.7

图2-9 农村最低生活保障

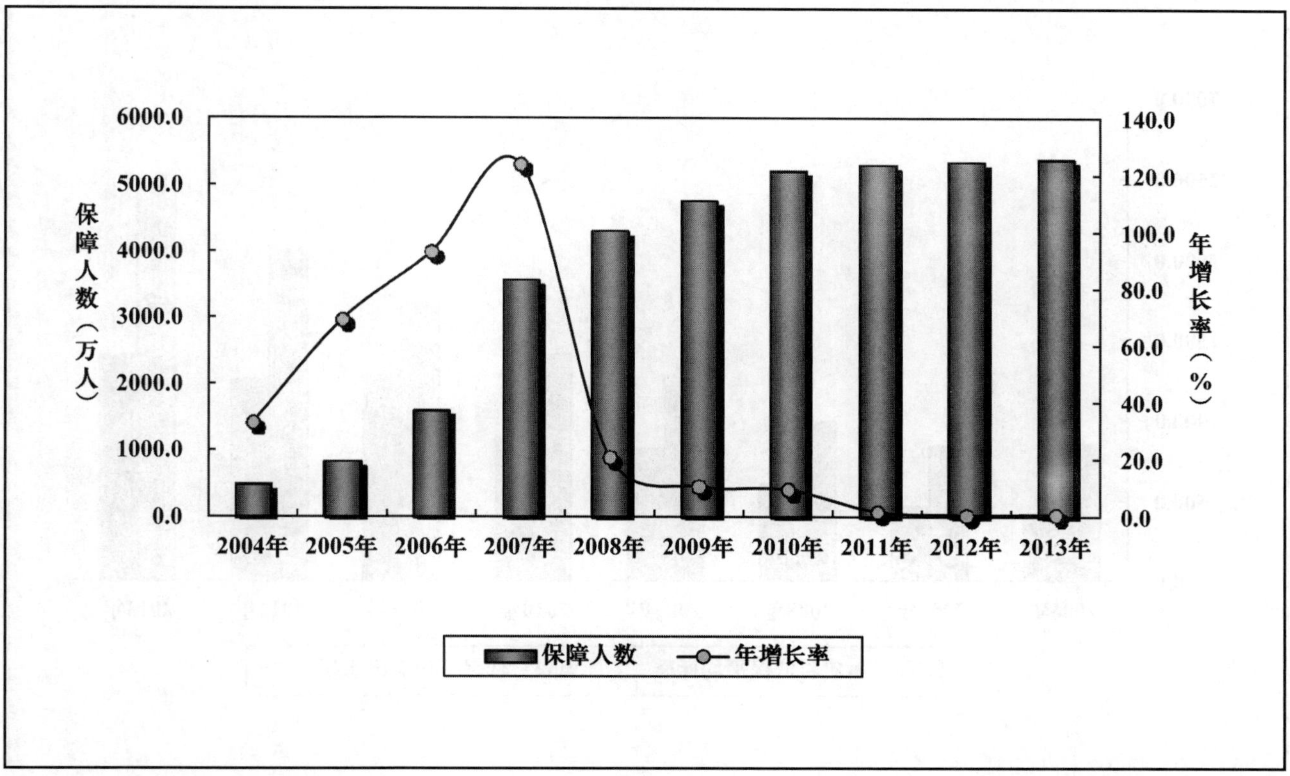

单位：万人、%

指　标	2004年	2005年	2006年	2007年	2008年	2009年	2010年	2011年	2012年	2013年
保障人数	488.0	825.0	1593.1	3566.3	4305.5	4760.0	5214.0	5305.7	5344.5	5388.0
年增长率	32.9	69.1	93.1	123.9	20.7	10.6	9.5	1.8	0.7	0.8

图2-10　农村最低生活保障平均标准与平均支出水平

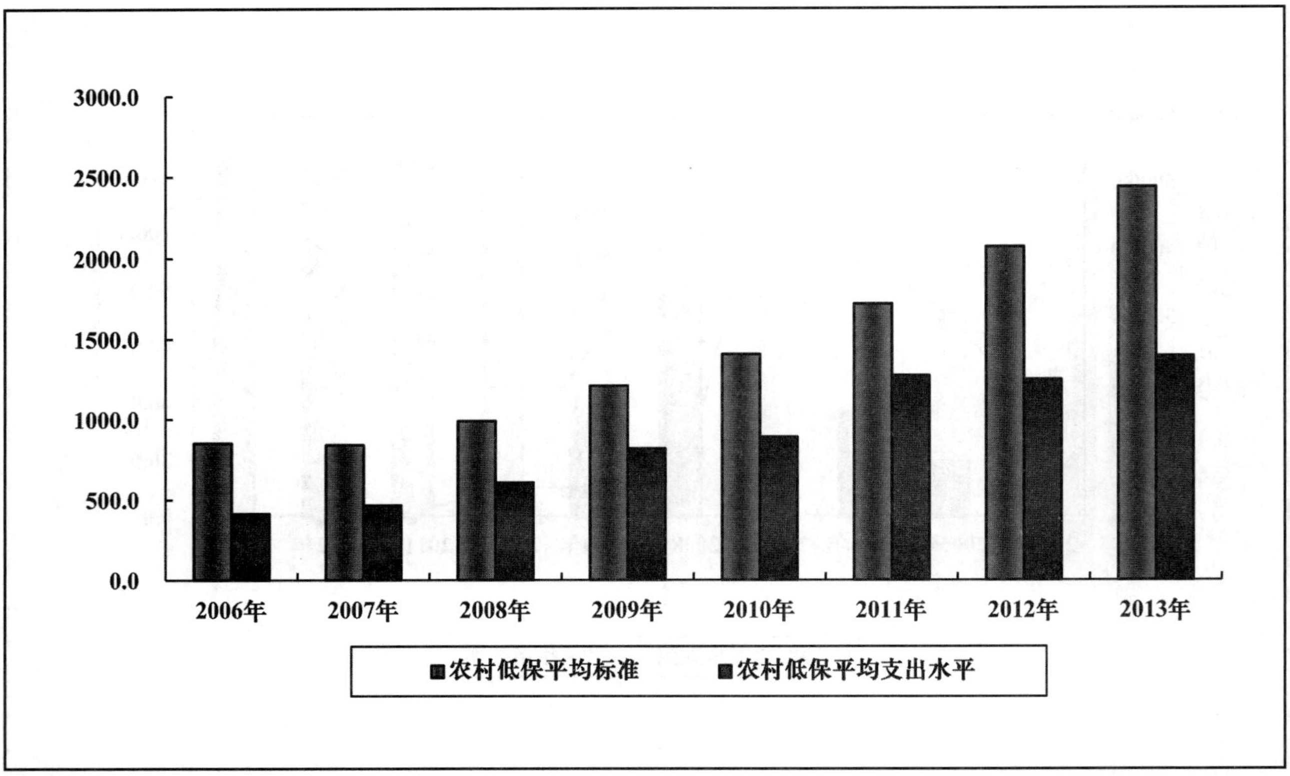

单位：元/人、年

指　标	2006年	2007年	2008年	2009年	2010年	2011年	2012年	2013年
农村低保平均标准	850.8	840.0	987.6	1209.6	1404.0	1718.4	2067.8	2433.9
农村低保平均支出水平	414.0	465.6	604.8	816.0	888.0	1273.2	1247.9	1393.5

图2-11 各省农村最低生活保障平均标准与支出水平

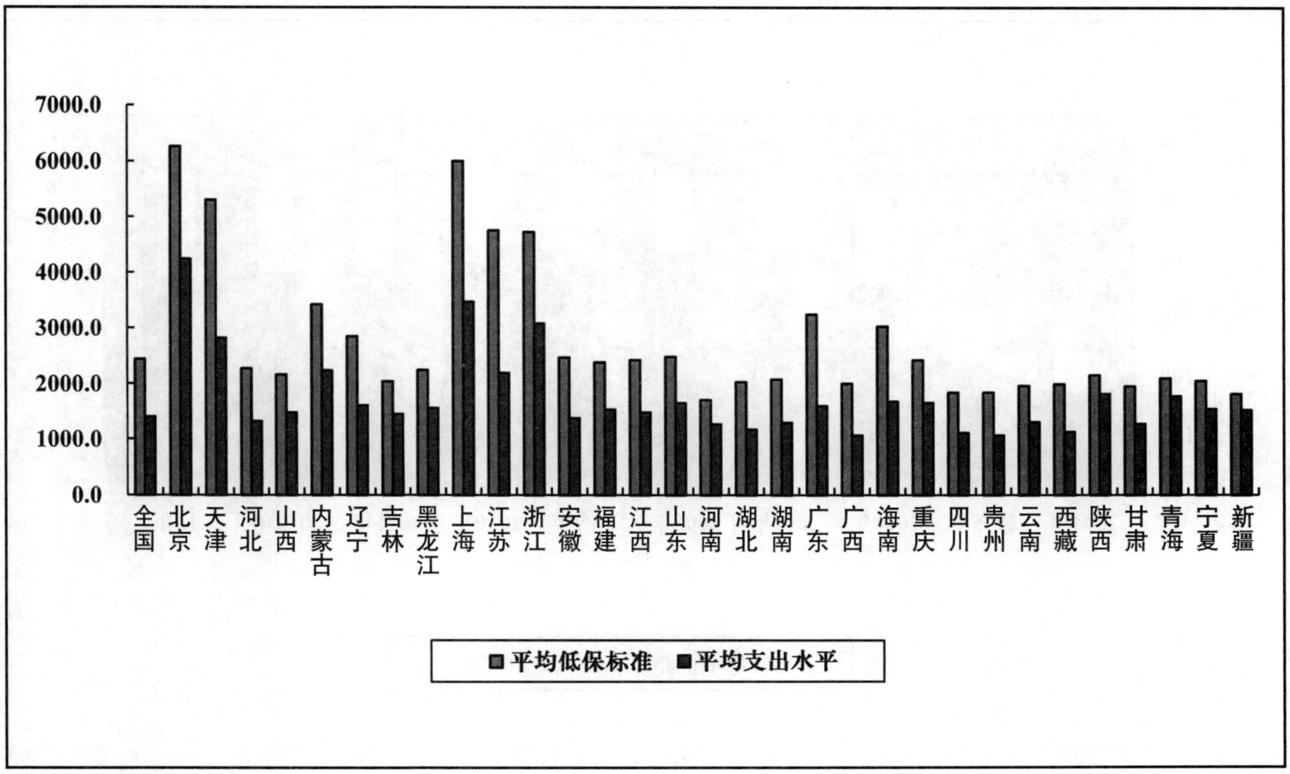

单位：元/人、年

地　区	平均低保标准	平均支出水平	地　区	平均低保标准	平均支出水平	地　区	平均低保标准	平均支出水平	地　区	平均低保标准	平均支出水平
全　国	**2433.9**	**1393.5**	黑龙江	2236.9	1550.9	河　南	1696.8	1255.9	贵　州	1833.0	1059.1
北　京	6258.5	4239.3	上　海	6000.0	3465.0	湖　北	2024.9	1166.7	云　南	1953.5	1299.1
天　津	5304.0	2811.0	江　苏	4752.3	2187.6	湖　南	2068.1	1287.3	西　藏	1980.8	1125.1
河　北	2269.1	1315.3	浙　江	4721.0	3070.8	广　东	3233.3	1588.5	陕　西	2143.4	1800.0
山　西	2157.6	1474.2	安　徽	2463.4	1365.4	广　西	1993.1	1060.5	甘　肃	1939.1	1264.7
内蒙古	3415.0	2231.3	福　建	2375.0	1523.6	海　南	3022.9	1668.4	青　海	2089.0	1759.7
辽　宁	2839.0	1601.7	江　西	2417.0	1470.5	重　庆	2417.4	1643.7	宁　夏	2037.8	1529.2
吉　林	2034.1	1443.5	山　东	2473.1	1639.6	四　川	1832.2	1104.6	新　疆	1804.1	1510.2

图2-12 农村五保供养

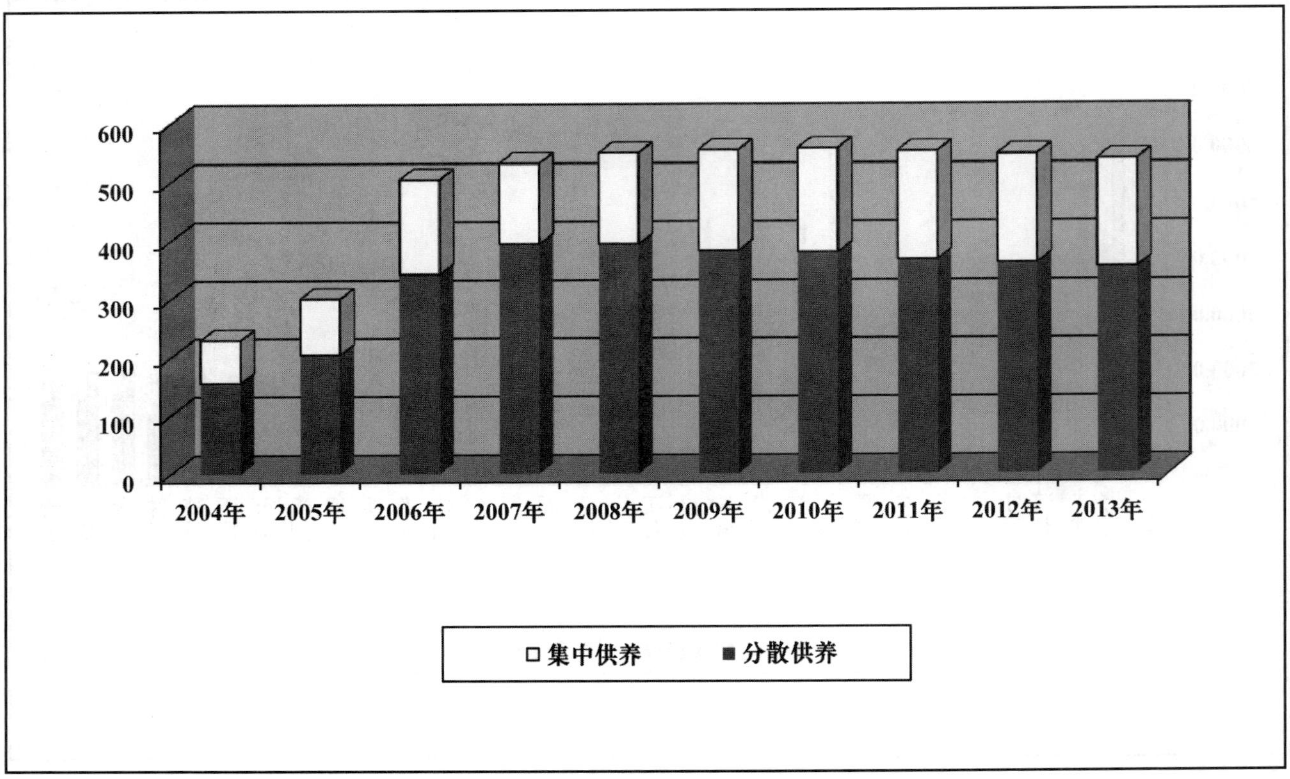

单位：万人

指　标	2004年	2005年	2006年	2007年	2008年	2009年	2010年	2011年	2012年	2013年
供养合计	228.7	300	503.3	531.3	548.6	553.4	556.3	551.0	545.6	537.3
分散供养	155.5	204.0	342.2	393.3	393.0	381.6	378.9	366.5	360.3	353.8
集中供养	73.2	96.0	161.1	138.0	155.6	171.8	177.4	184.5	185.3	183.5

图2-13　各省农村五保集中供养平均标准与支出水平

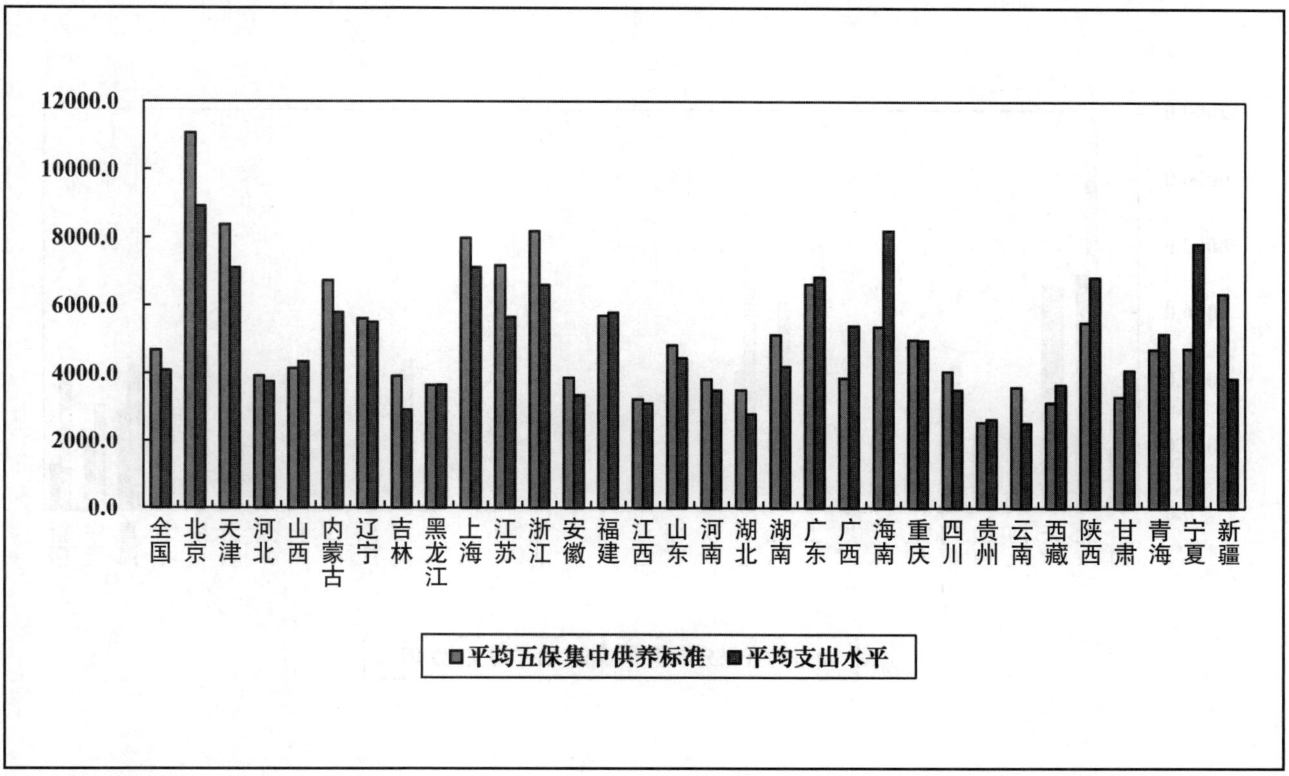

单位：元/人、年

地　区	平均五保集中供养标准	平均支出水平	地　区	平均五保集中供养标准	平均支出水平	地　区	平均五保集中供养标准	平均支出水平	地　区	平均五保集中供养标准	平均支出水平
全　国	**4685.0**	**4078.3**	黑龙江	3647.6	3647.9	河　南	3826.1	3489.4	贵　州	2543.1	2633.5
北　京	11071.1	8921.6	上　海	7980.0	7124.0	湖　北	3497.4	2782.6	云　南	3582.6	2517.4
天　津	8376.7	7109.1	江　苏	7177.7	5648.0	湖　南	5134.3	4192.7	西　藏	3127.0	3664.3
河　北	3921.3	3746.8	浙　江	8178.8	6609.7	广　东	6631.6	6840.0	陕　西	5503.9	6843.2
山　西	4139.9	4338.3	安　徽	3859.8	3347.6	广　西	3855.1	5401.4	甘　肃	3302.8	4090.2
内蒙古	6737.7	5791.1	福　建	5693.5	5784.0	海　南	5371.4	8197.2	青　海	4709.0	5170.8
辽　宁	5607.3	5508.9	江　西	3220.8	3099.0	重　庆	4993.3	4966.7	宁　夏	4741.2	7835.9
吉　林	3915.0	2909.9	山　东	4827.4	4443.2	四　川	4049.7	3508.1	新　疆	6361.3	3857.7

图2-14　各省农村五保分散供养平均标准与支出水平

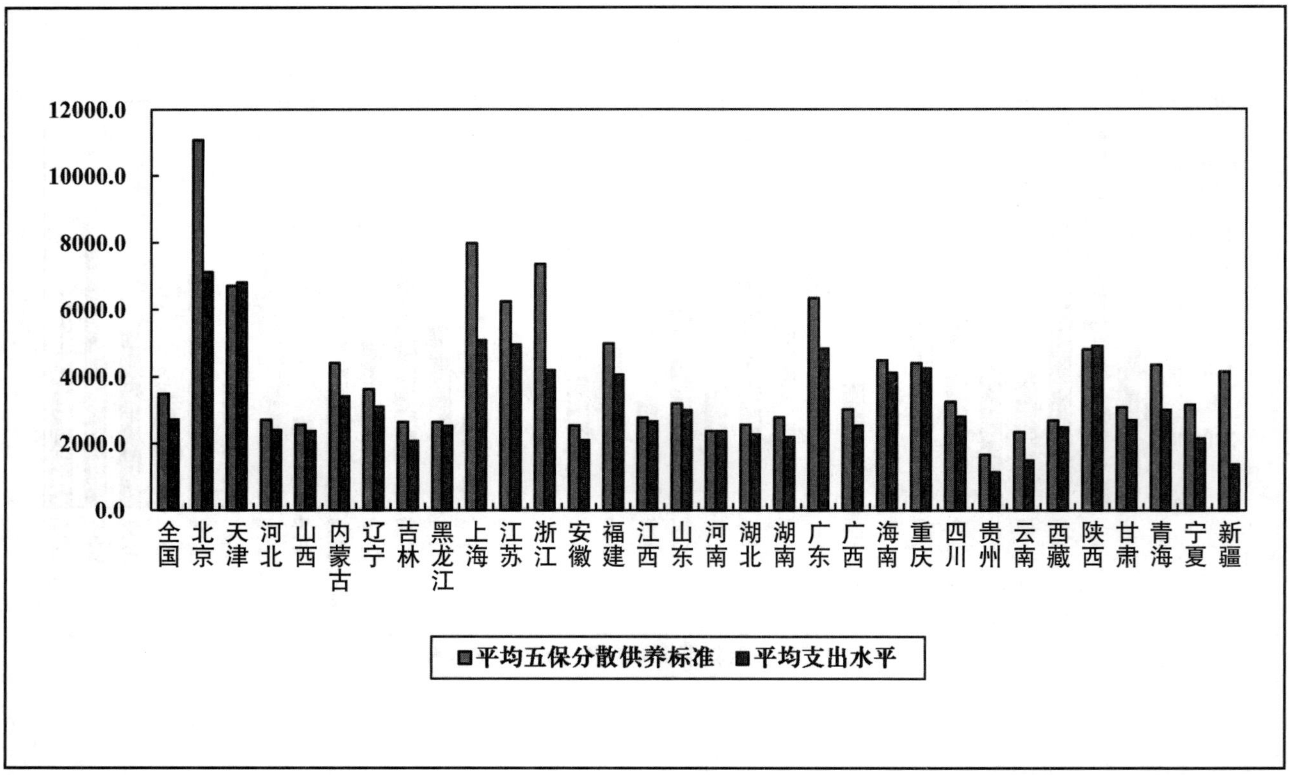

单位：元/人、年

地　区	平均五保分散供养标准	平均支出水平	地　区	平均五保分散供养标准	平均支出水平	地　区	平均五保分散供养标准	平均支出水平	地　区	平均五保分散供养标准	平均支出水平
全　国	**3498.5**	**2724.3**	黑龙江	2643.8	2522.8	河　南	2374.4	2369.4	贵　州	1667.5	1142.6
北　京	11071.1	7110.2	上　海	7980.0	5075.0	湖　北	2569.9	2279.5	云　南	2342.9	1495.9
天　津	6695.6	6797.4	江　苏	6234.4	4948.1	湖　南	2791.4	2196.9	西　藏	2691.1	2487.8
河　北	2709.4	2398.5	浙　江	7346.7	4178.9	广　东	6327.2	4832.0	陕　西	4798.1	4903.8
山　西	2558.2	2371.3	安　徽	2535.1	2099.0	广　西	3033.0	2539.2	甘　肃	3086.5	2704.0
内蒙古	4410.0	3417.1	福　建	4976.4	4054.3	海　南	4485.7	4112.5	青　海	4351.8	3010.3
辽　宁	3634.7	3101.6	江　西	2778.2	2660.9	重　庆	4399.6	4242.4	宁　夏	3170.1	2148.9
吉　林	2643.8	2073.6	山　东	3193.0	2999.1	四　川	3251.5	2807.3	新　疆	4139.8	1372.7

图2-15 社会捐赠

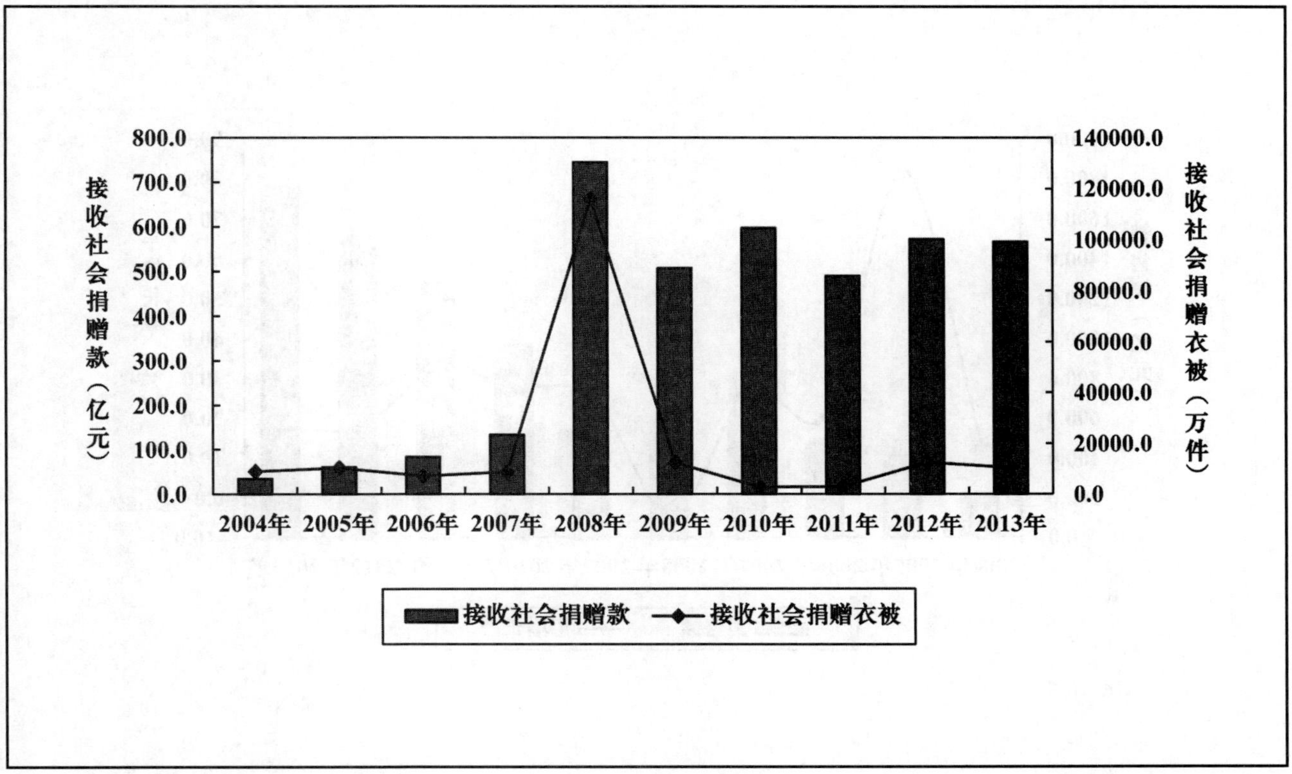

单位：亿元、万件

指 标	2004年	2005年	2006年	2007年	2008年	2009年	2010年	2011年	2012年	2013年
接收社会捐赠款	34.0	60.3	83.1	132.8	744.5	507.2	596.8	490.1	572.5	566.4
接收社会捐赠衣被	8957.2	10355.0	7123.6	8756.8	115816.3	12476.6	2750.2	2918.5	12538.2	10405.0

图2-16　福利彩票

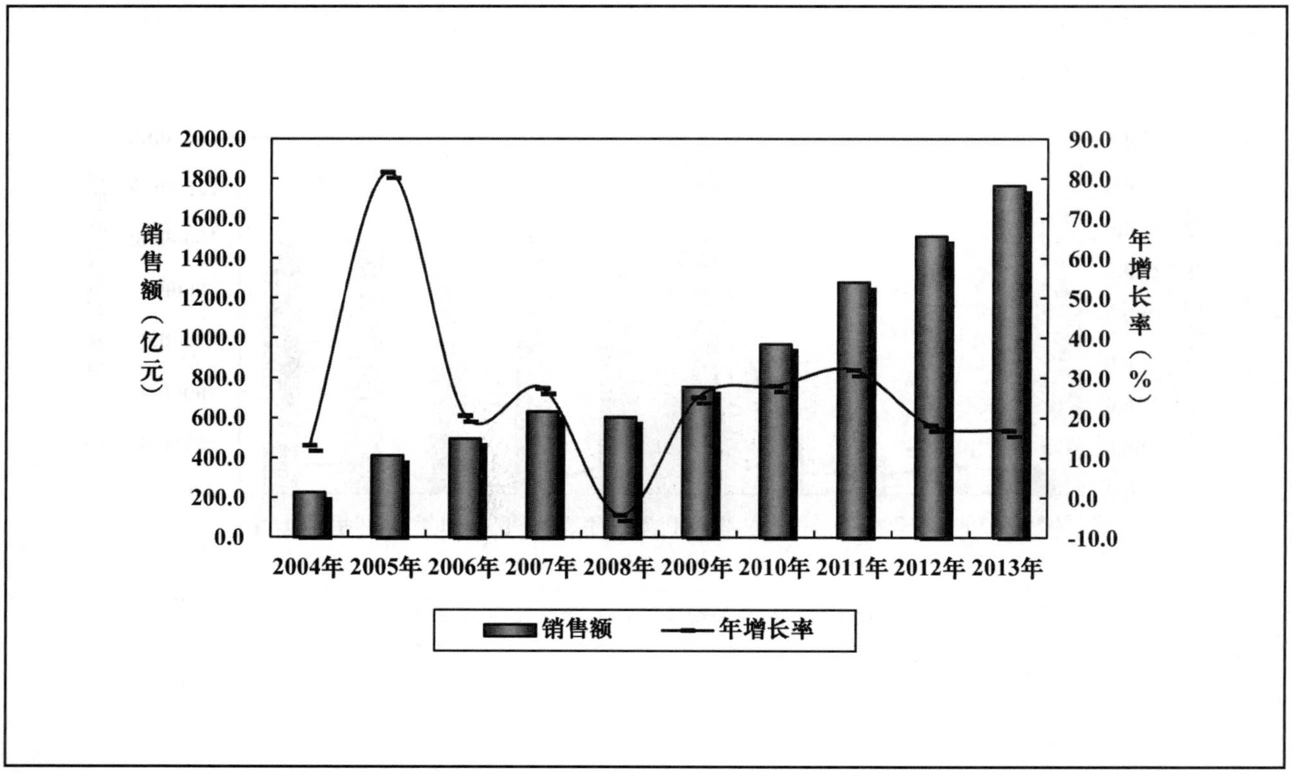

单位：亿元、%

指　标	2004年	2005年	2006年	2007年	2008年	2009年	2010年	2011年	2012年	2013年
销售额	226.4	411.2	495.7	631.6	604.0	756.0	968.0	1278.0	1510.3	1765.3
年增长率	13.1	81.6	20.5	27.4	−4.4	25.2	28.0	32.0	18.2	16.9

图2-17 国家抚恤、补助优抚对象

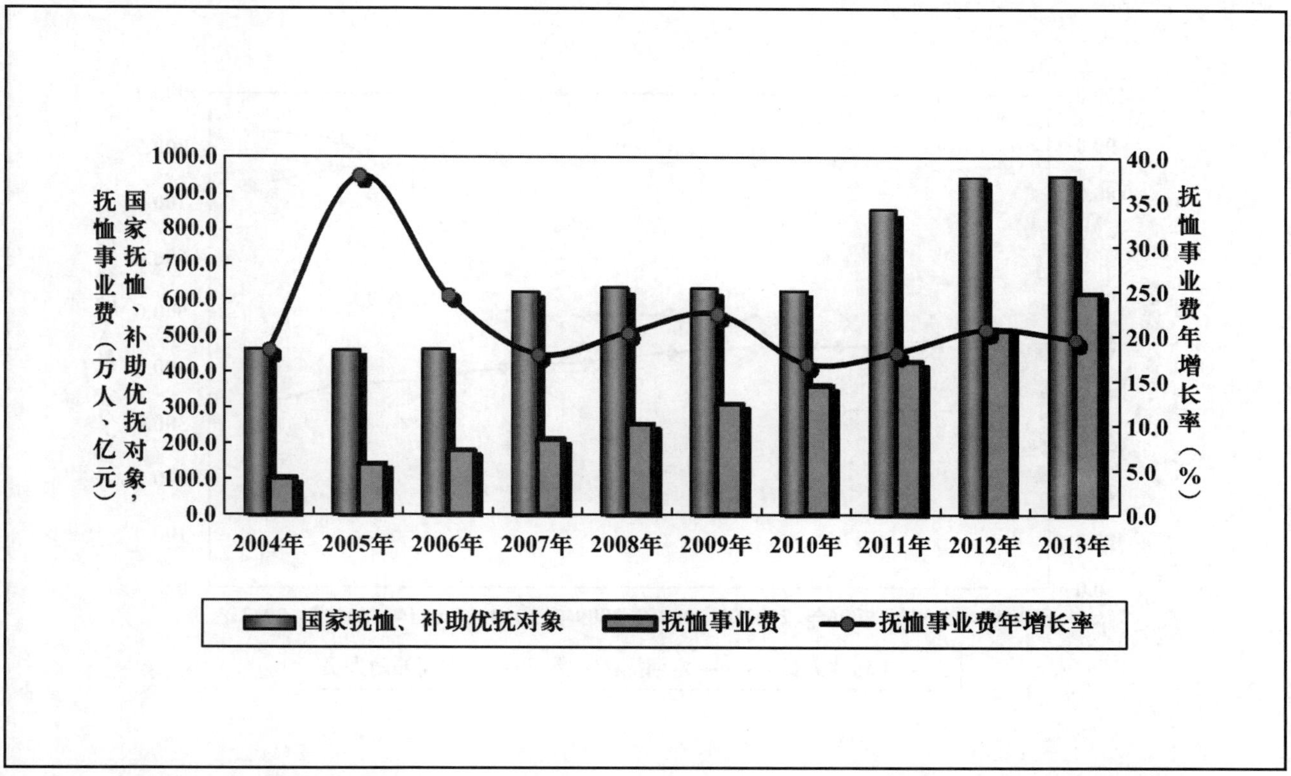

单位：万人、亿元、%

指　标	2004年	2005年	2006年	2007年	2008年	2009年	2010年	2011年	2012年	2013年
国家抚恤、补助优抚对象	462.0	460.3	462.6	622.4	633.2	630.7	625	852.5	944.4	950.5
抚恤事业费	104.1	143.6	178.8	210.8	253.6	310.3	362.7	428.3	517	618.4
抚恤事业费年增长率	18.4	37.9	24.5	17.9	20.3	22.4	16.9	18.1	20.7	19.6

图2-18 优抚对象分类

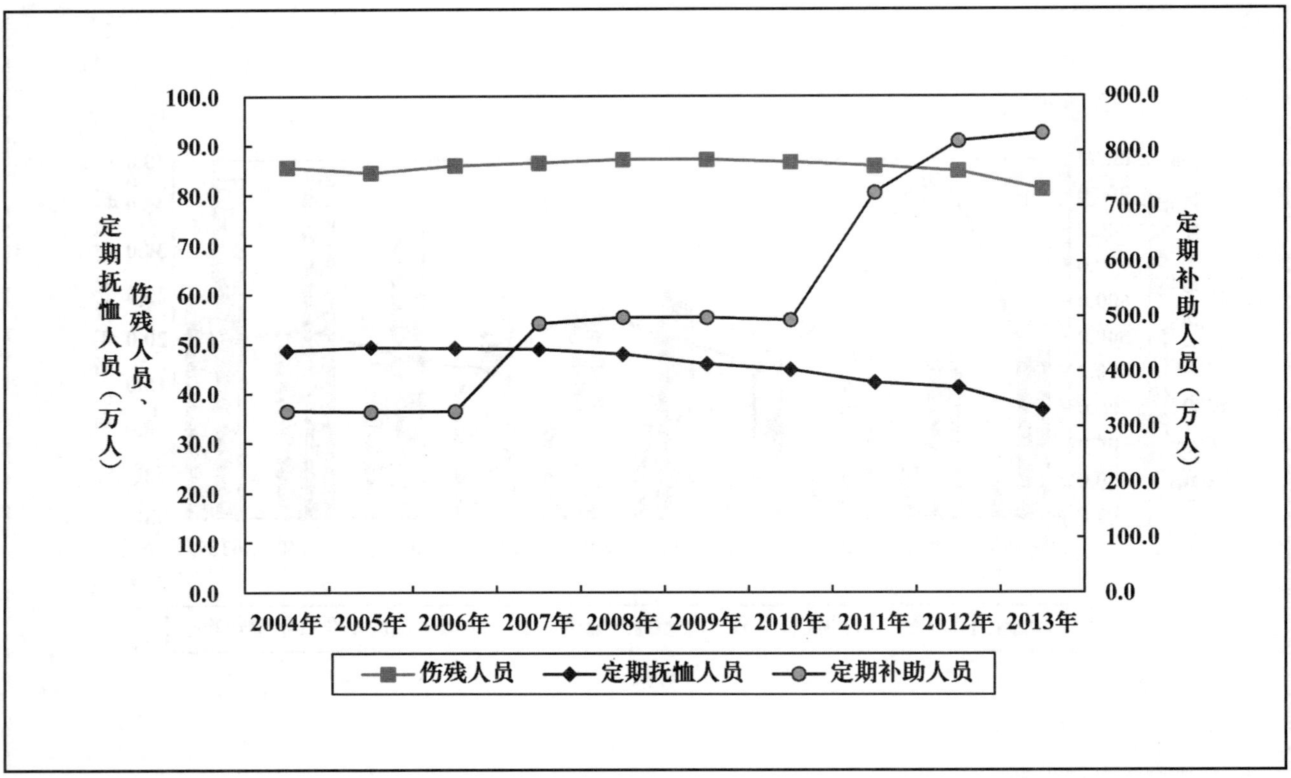

单位：万人

指 标	2004年	2005年	2006年	2007年	2008年	2009年	2010年	2011年	2012年	2013年
伤残人员	85.6	84.5	86.0	86.5	87.2	87.2	86.7	85.9	84.9	81.2
定期抚恤人员	48.6	49.3	49.1	48.9	47.9	45.9	44.8	42.2	41.2	36.6
定期补助人员	327.8	326.6	327.4	487.1	498.2	497.7	493.5	724.4	818.4	832.6

图2-19 接收安置军休干部、军休职工

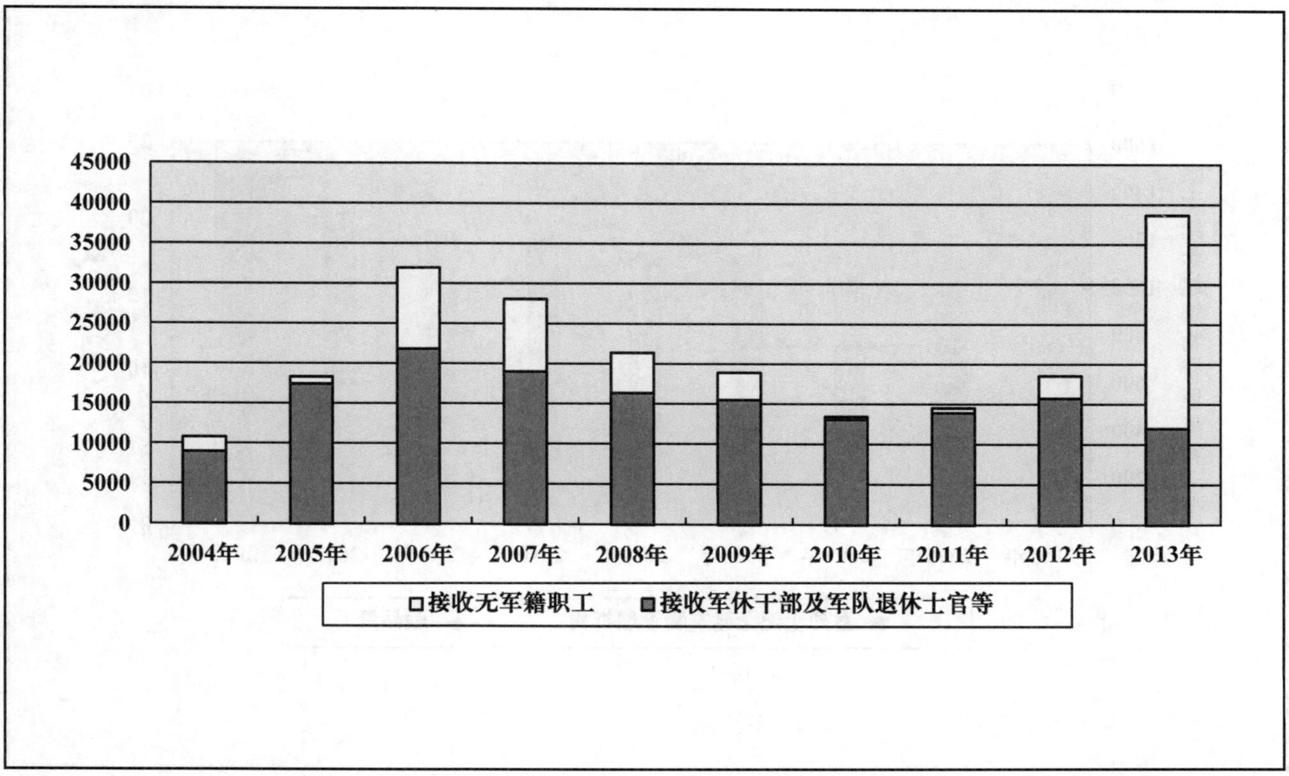

单位：人

指　标	2004年	2005年	2006年	2007年	2008年	2009年	2010年	2011年	2012年	2013年
接收军休干部及军队退休士官等	8974	17416	21832	18997	16331	15492	13070	13901	15723	11997
接收无军籍职工	1820	904	10136	9061	5047	3412	381	629	2847	26709

图2-20 烈士纪念建筑物管理机构和藏品量

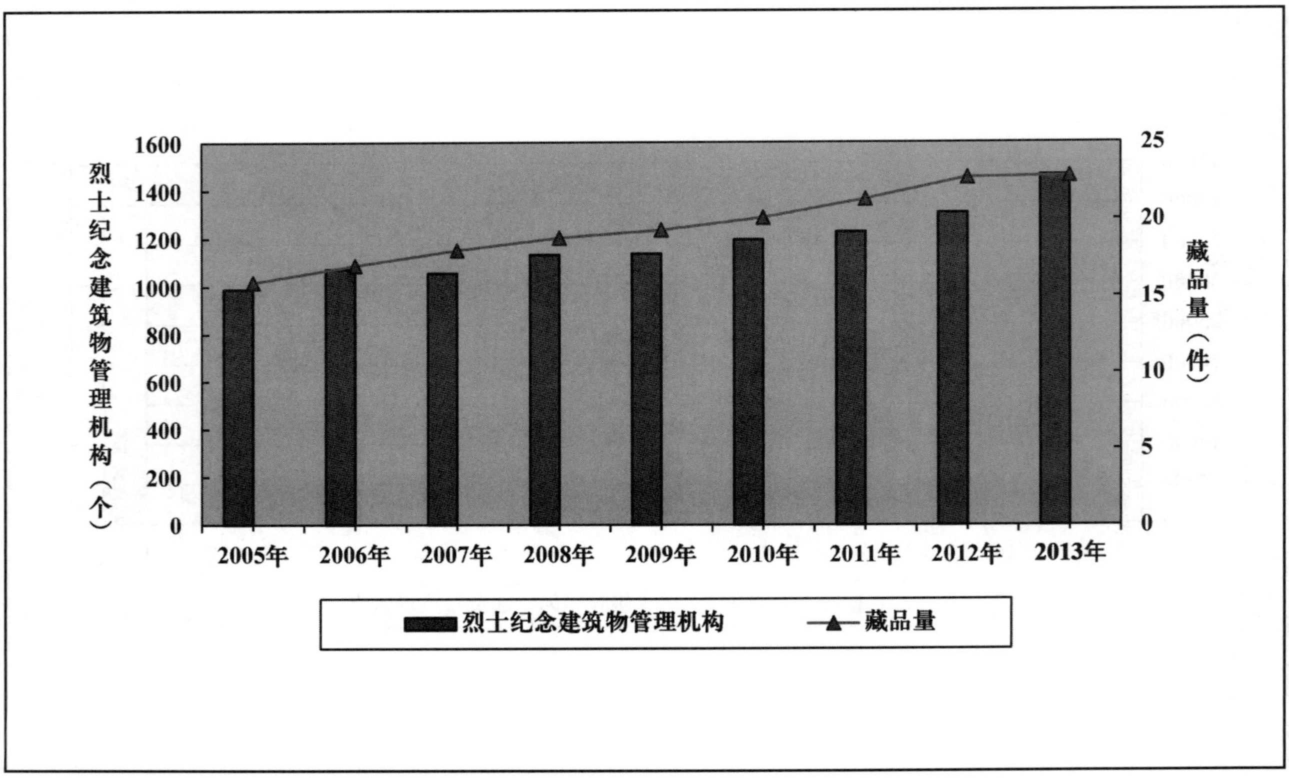

单位：个、万件

指　标	2005年	2006年	2007年	2008年	2009年	2010年	2011年	2012年	2013年
烈士纪念建筑物管理机构	989	1072	1056	1133	1137	1195	1227	1306	1463
藏品量	15.9	17	18	18.8	19.3	20.1	21.3	22.7	22.8

图2-21　烈士褒扬和零散烈士纪念设施

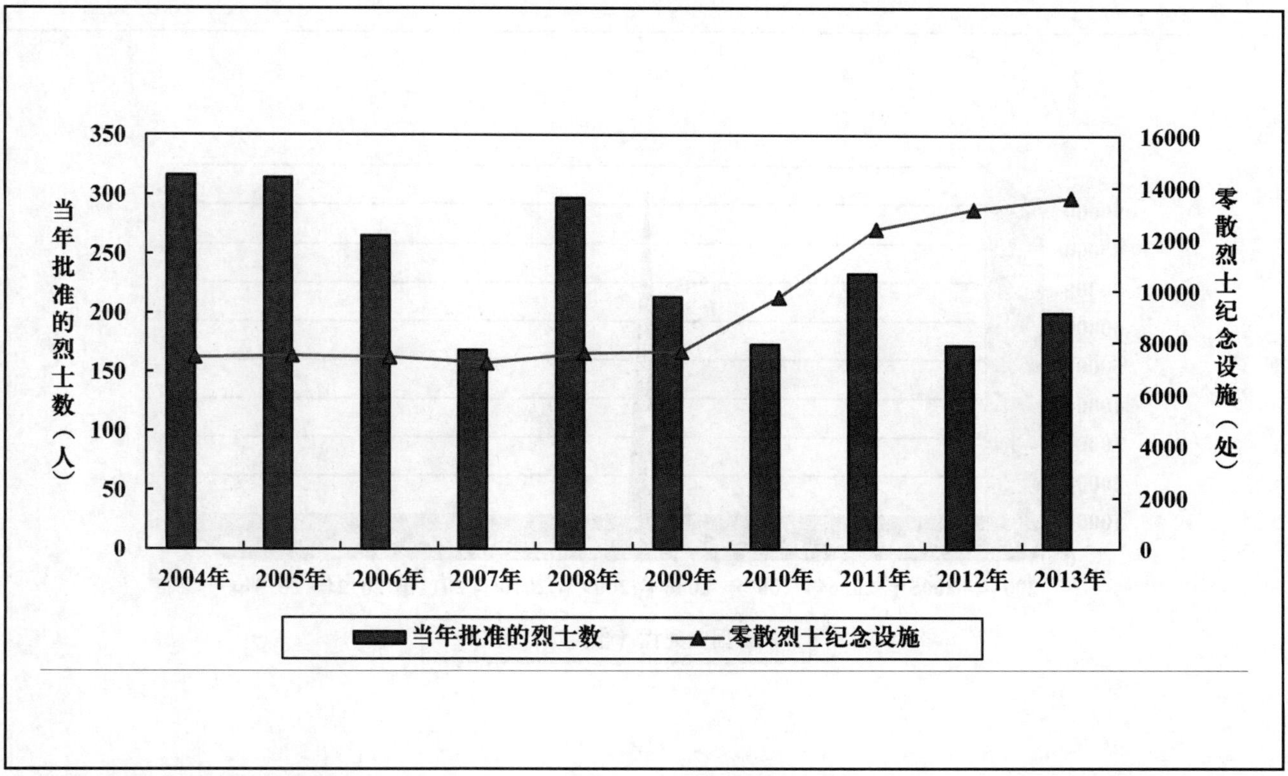

单位：人、处

指　标	2004年	2005年	2006年	2007年	2008年	2009年	2010年	2011年	2012年	2013年
当年批准的烈士数	316	314	265	168	297	213	173	233	172	200
零散烈士纪念设施	7425	7483	7414	7186	7569	7622	9729	12378	13151	13601

图2-22　因灾死亡人口

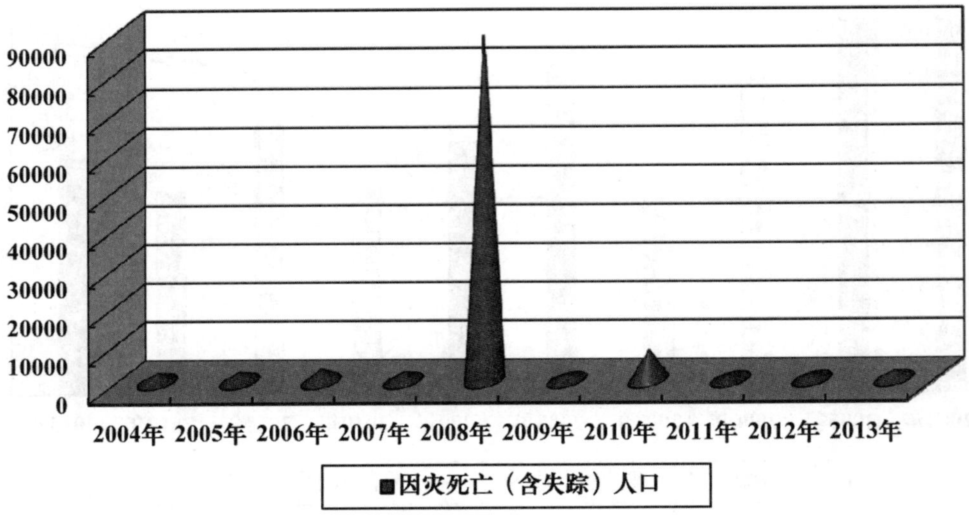

单位：人

指　标	2004年	2005年	2006年	2007年	2008年	2009年	2010年	2011年	2012年	2013年
因灾死亡(含失踪)人口	2250	2475	3186	2325	88928	1528	7844	1126	1530	2284

图2-23 受灾人口

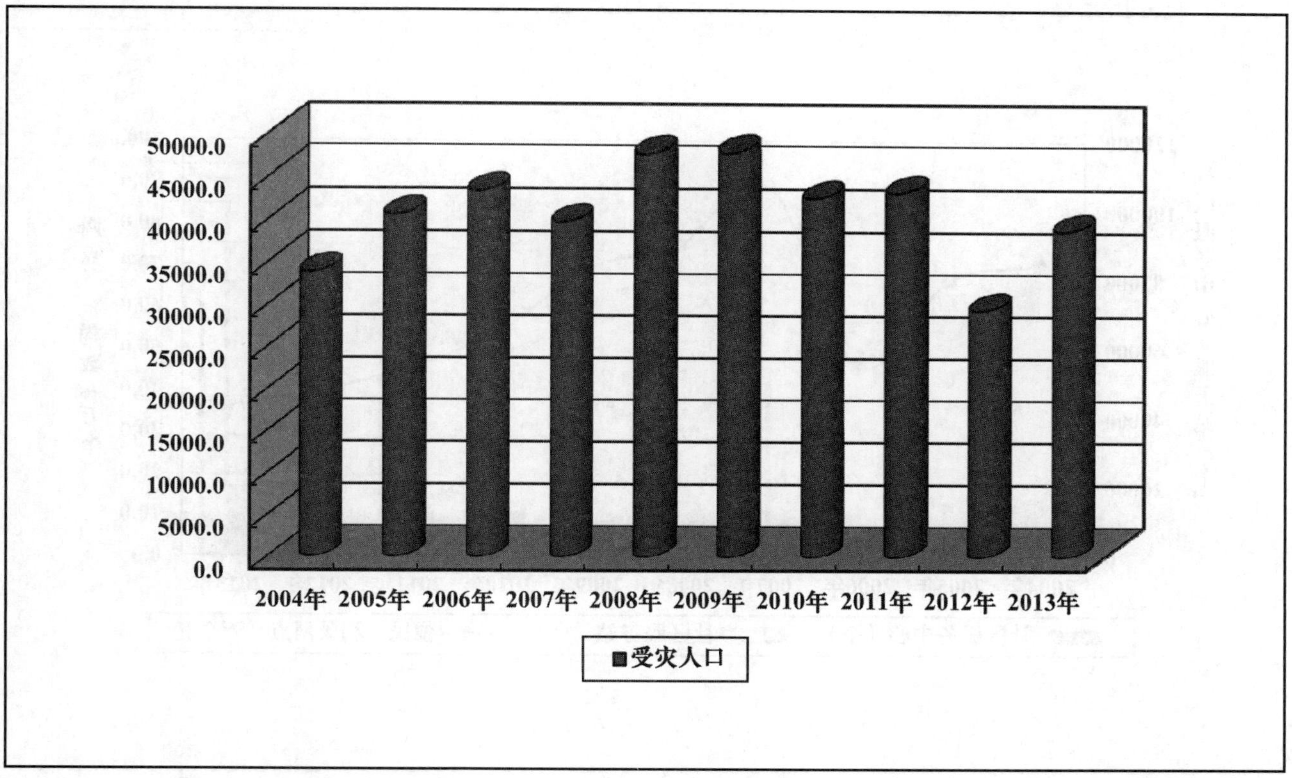

单位：万人次

指　标	2004年	2005年	2006年	2007年	2008年	2009年	2010年	2011年	2012年	2013年
受灾人口	33920.6	40653.7	43453.3	39777.9	47795.0	47933.5	42610.2	43290.0	29421.7	38818.7

图2-24　社区服务机构

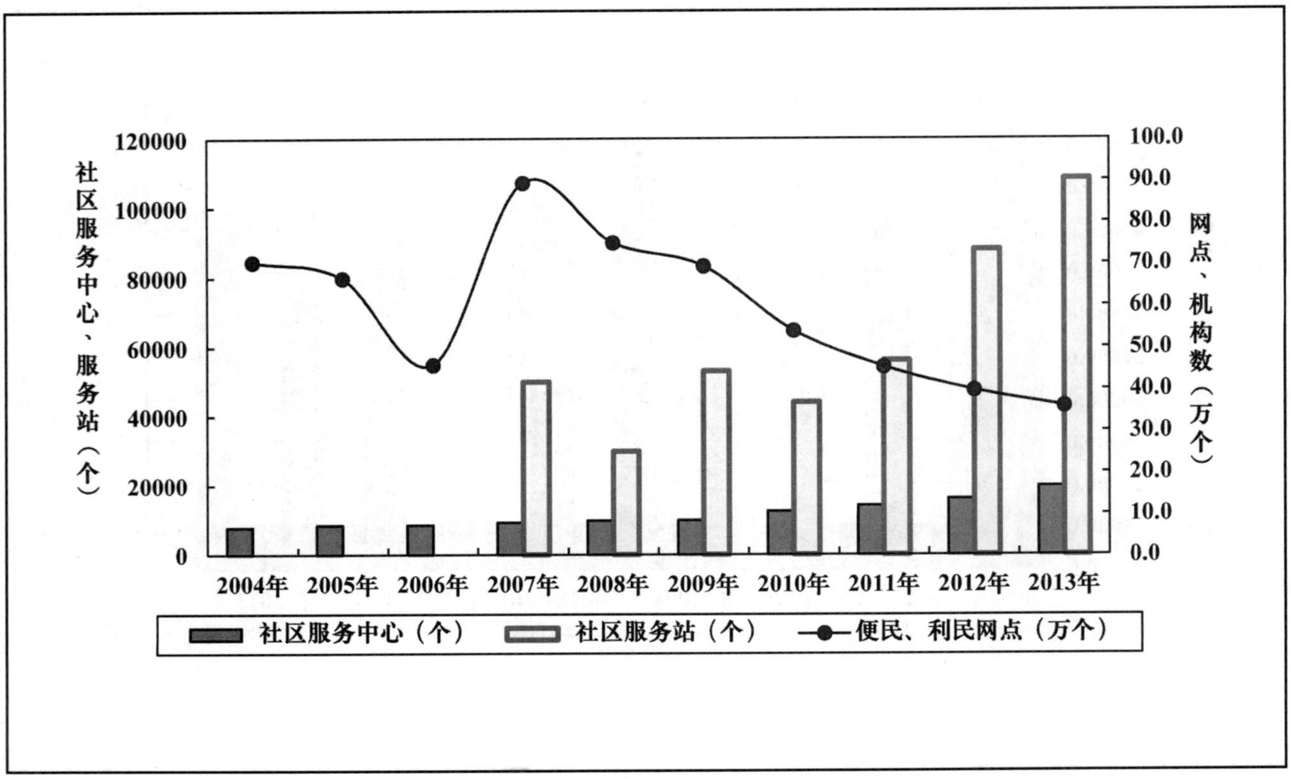

指　标	2004年	2005年	2006年	2007年	2008年	2009年	2010年	2011年	2012年	2013年
社区服务机构(万个)	20.6	20.3	12.5	12.9	14.6	14.6	15.3	16.0	20.0	25.2
社区服务中心(个)	7804	8479	8565	9319	9873	10003	12720	14391	16306	19904
社区服务站(个)				50116	30021	53170	44237	56156	87931	108377
便民、利民网点(万个)	70.4	66.5	45.8	89.3	74.9	69.3	53.9	45.3	39.7	35.9

注释：2013年社区服务中心里含社区服务指导中心。

图2-25 社区服务机构覆盖率

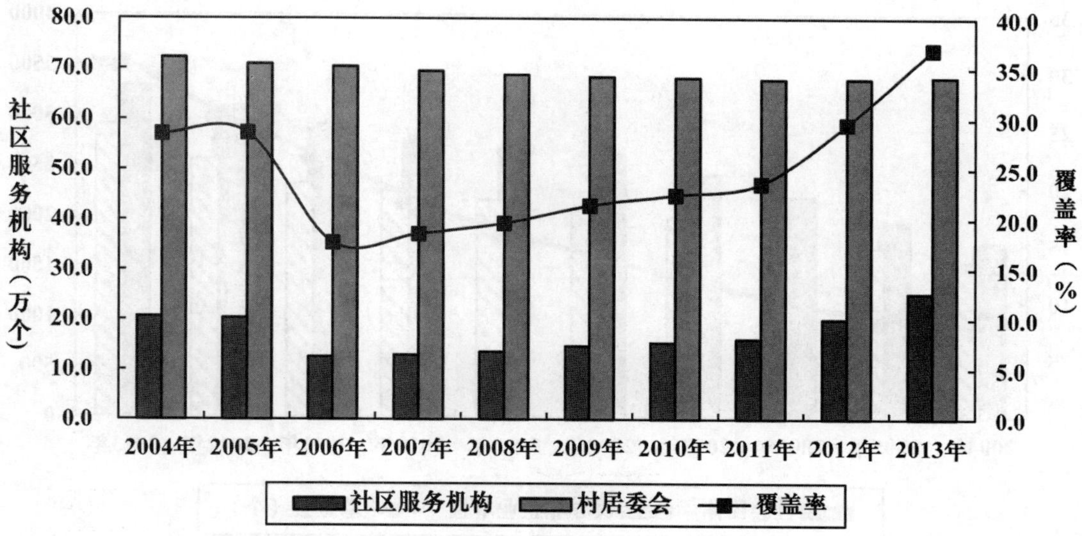

单位：万个、%

指 标	2004年	2005年	2006年	2007年	2008年	2009年	2010年	2011年	2012年	2013年
社区服务机构	20.6	20.3	12.5	12.9	13.5	14.7	15.3	16.0	20.0	25.2
村居委会	72.2	70.9	70.4	69.5	68.8	68.4	68.2	67.9	68.0	68.3
覆盖率	28.5	28.6	17.7	18.6	19.6	21.4	22.4	23.6	29.5	36.9

图3-1　社会组织

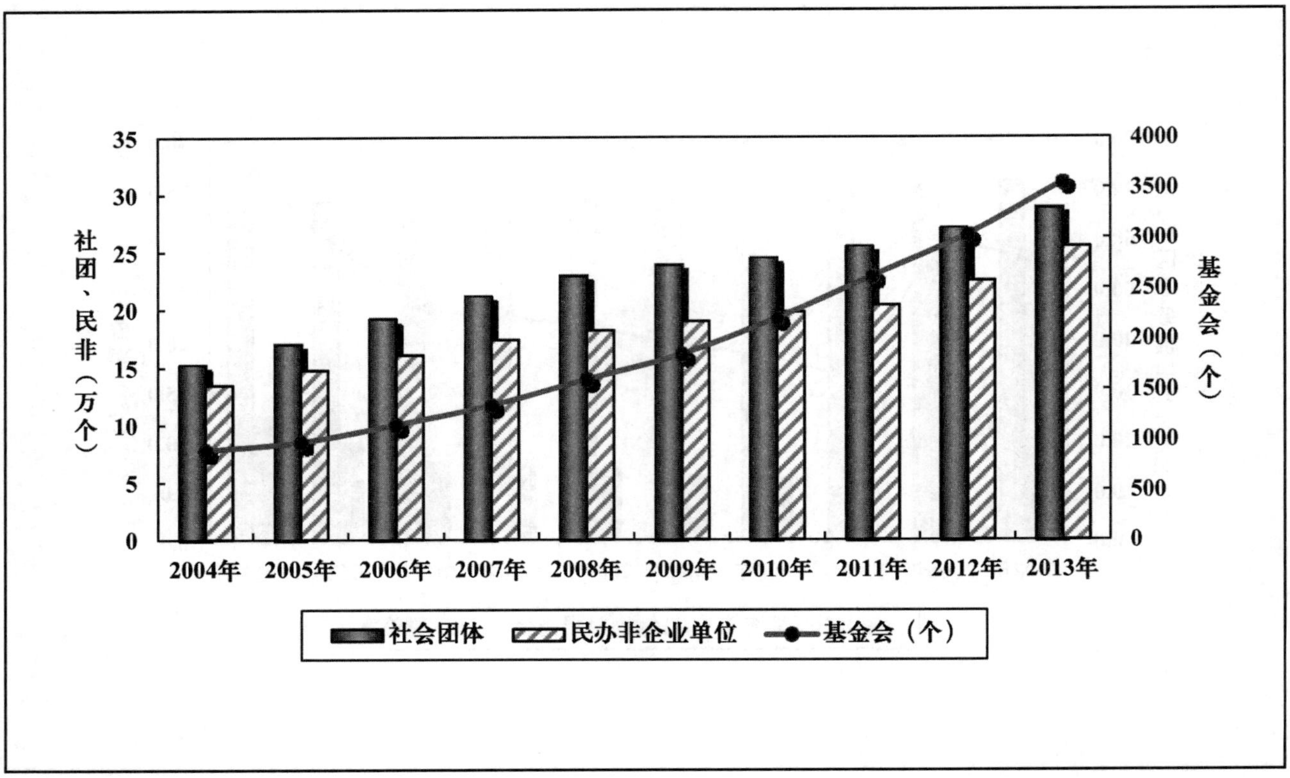

单位：万个、个

指　标	2004年	2005年	2006年	2007年	2008年	2009年	2010年	2011年	2012年	2013年
社会团体	15.3	17.1	19.2	21.2	23.0	23.9	24.5	25.5	27.1	28.9
基金会(个)	892	975	1144	1340	1597	1843	2200	2614	3029	3549
民办非企业单位	13.5	14.8	16.1	17.4	18.2	19.0	19.8	20.4	22.5	25.5

图3-2 自治组织

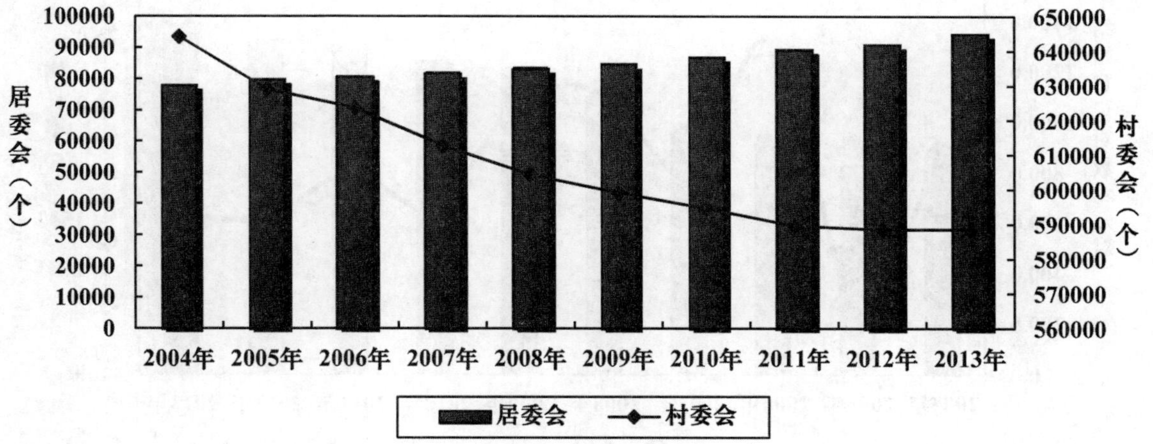

单位：个

指　标	2004年	2005年	2006年	2007年	2008年	2009年	2010年	2011年	2012年	2013年
居委会	77884	79947	80717	82006	83413	84689	87057	89480	91153	94620
村委会	644166	629079	623669	612709	604285	599078	594658	589653	588475	588547

图3-3 结婚登记情况

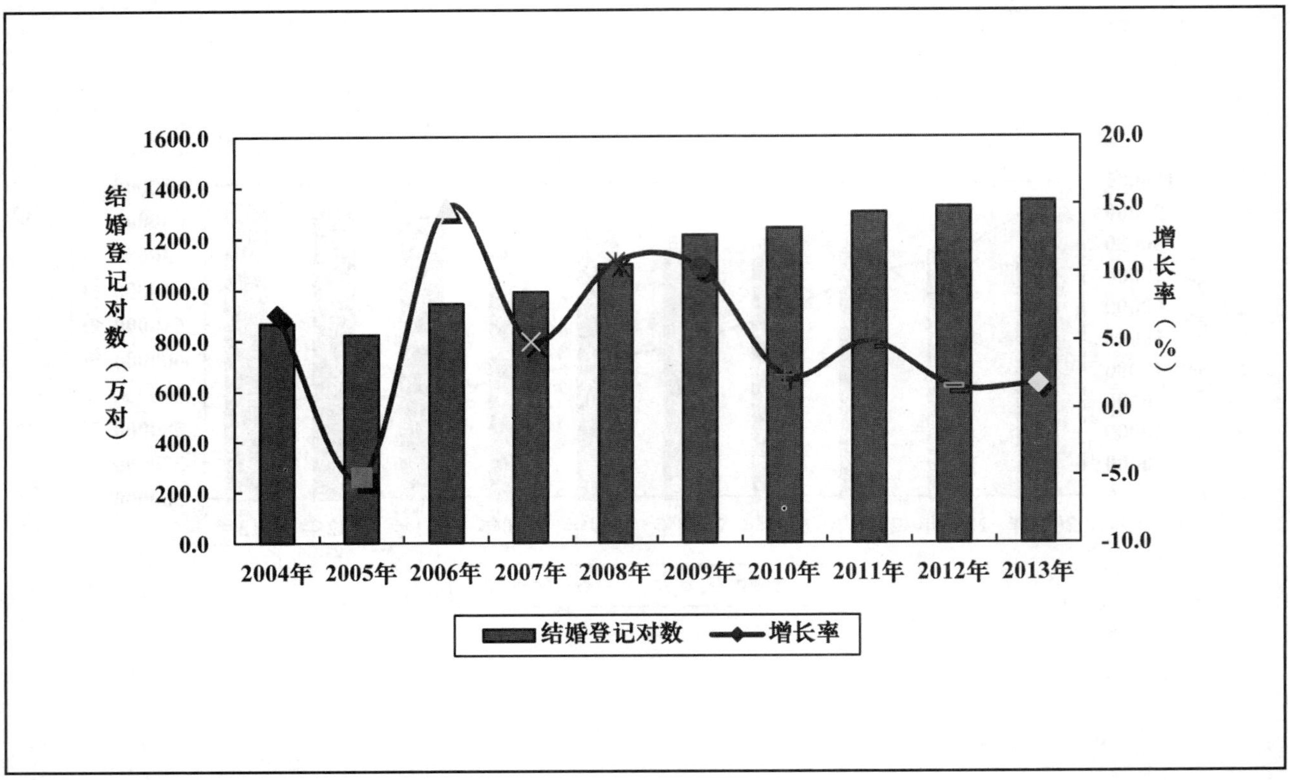

单位：万对、%

指　标	2004年	2005年	2006年	2007年	2008年	2009年	2010年	2011年	2012年	2013年
结婚登记对数	867.2	823.1	945.0	991.4	1098.3	1212.2	1241.0	1302.4	1323.6	1346.9
增长率	6.9	-5.1	14.8	4.9	10.8	10.4	2.4	4.9	1.6	1.8

图3-4　分年龄组结婚登记情况

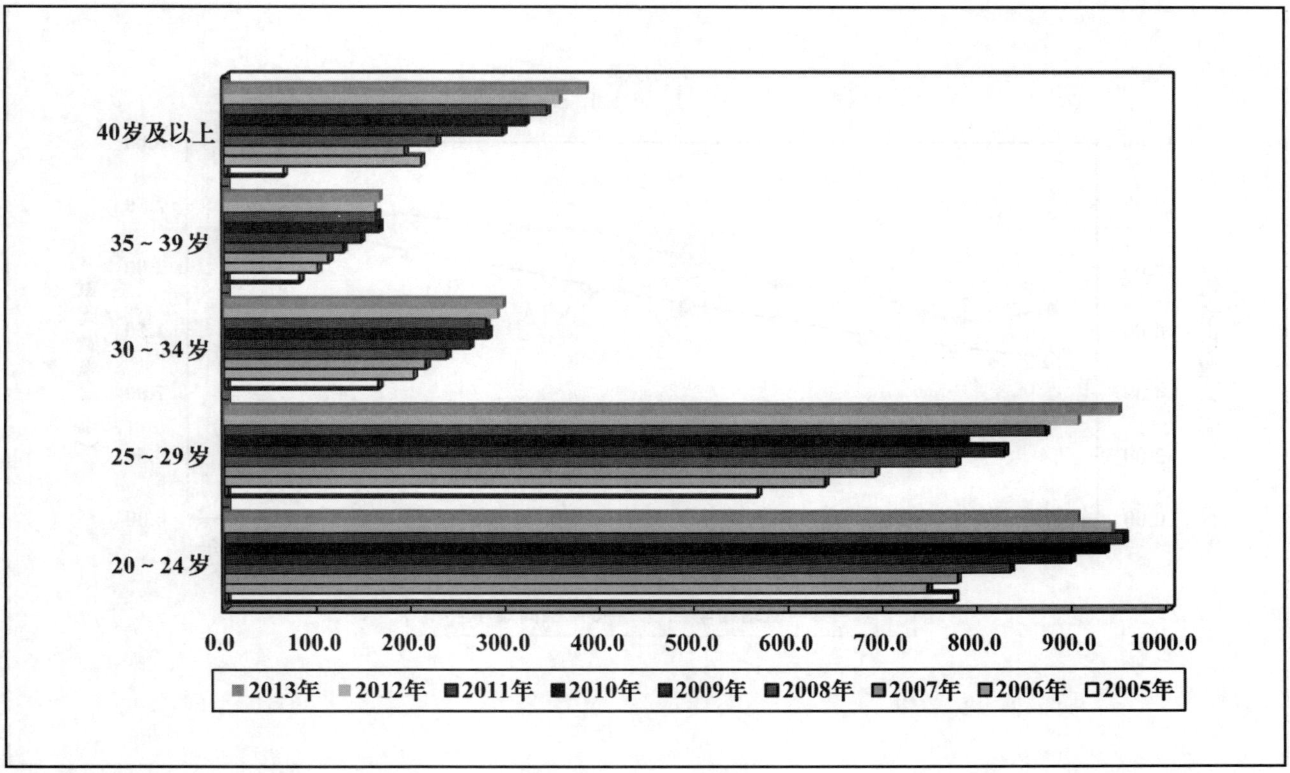

单位：万人

年　份	20～24岁	25～29岁	30～34岁	35～39岁	40岁及以上
2005	773.2	565.0	163.4	80.6	63.8
2006	744.8	636.3	200.8	99.0	209.1
2007	776.7	689.5	214.0	110.9	191.6
2008	832.3	775.7	236.1	126.5	226.2
2009	896.7	826.4	260.3	145.4	295.5
2010	933.4	784.6	279.9	164.5	319.6
2011	953.0	870.2	277.6	161.5	342.4
2012	939.6	904.1	289.0	158.9	355.6
2013	903.4	947.5	295.1	164.3	383.5

图3-5　结婚率和离婚率

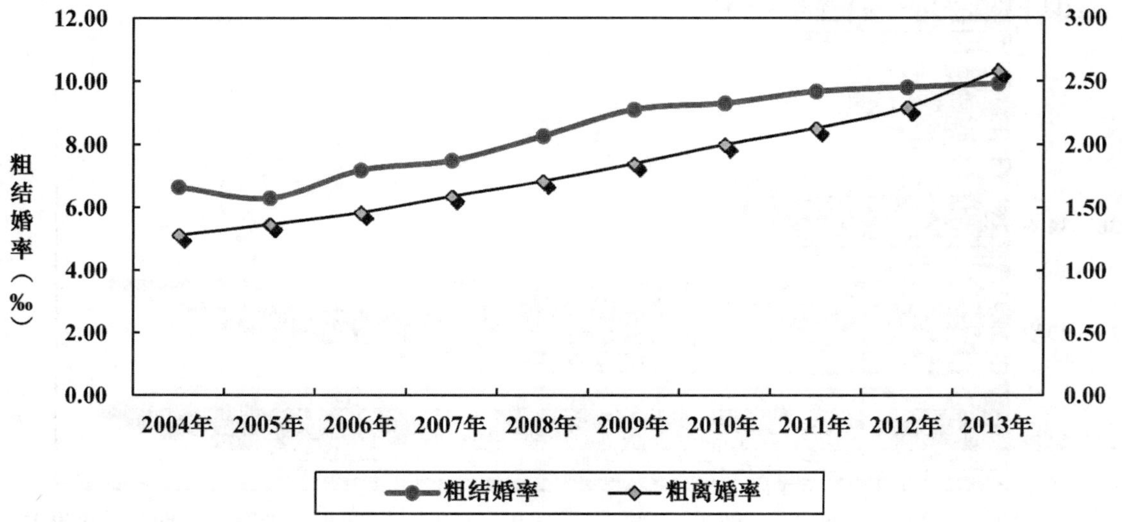

单位：‰

指　标	2004年	2005年	2006年	2007年	2008年	2009年	2010年	2011年	2012年	2013年
粗结婚率	6.65	6.30	7.19	7.50	8.27	9.10	9.30	9.67	9.80	9.92
粗离婚率	1.28	1.37	1.46	1.59	1.71	1.85	2.00	2.13	2.29	2.58

注释：粗结（离）婚率计算方法：结婚对数除以当期人口平均数。

图3-6　民政部门和法院办理离婚情况

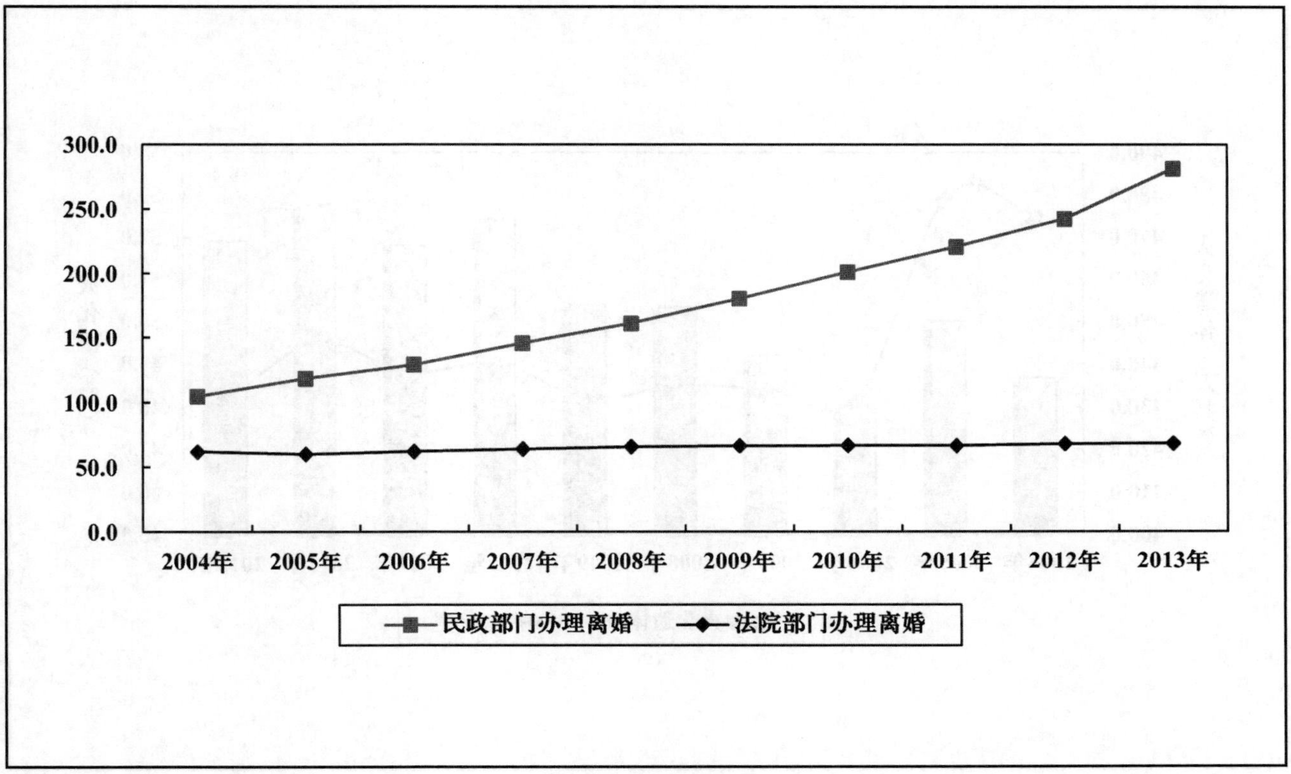

单位：万对

指　标	2004年	2005年	2006年	2007年	2008年	2009年	2010年	2011年	2012年	2013年
民政部门办理离婚	104.6	118.4	129.1	145.7	161.0	180.2	201.0	220.7	242.3	281.5
法院部门办理离婚	61.9	60.1	62.2	64.1	65.9	66.6	66.8	66.7	68.1	68.5

图3-7　火化遗体情况

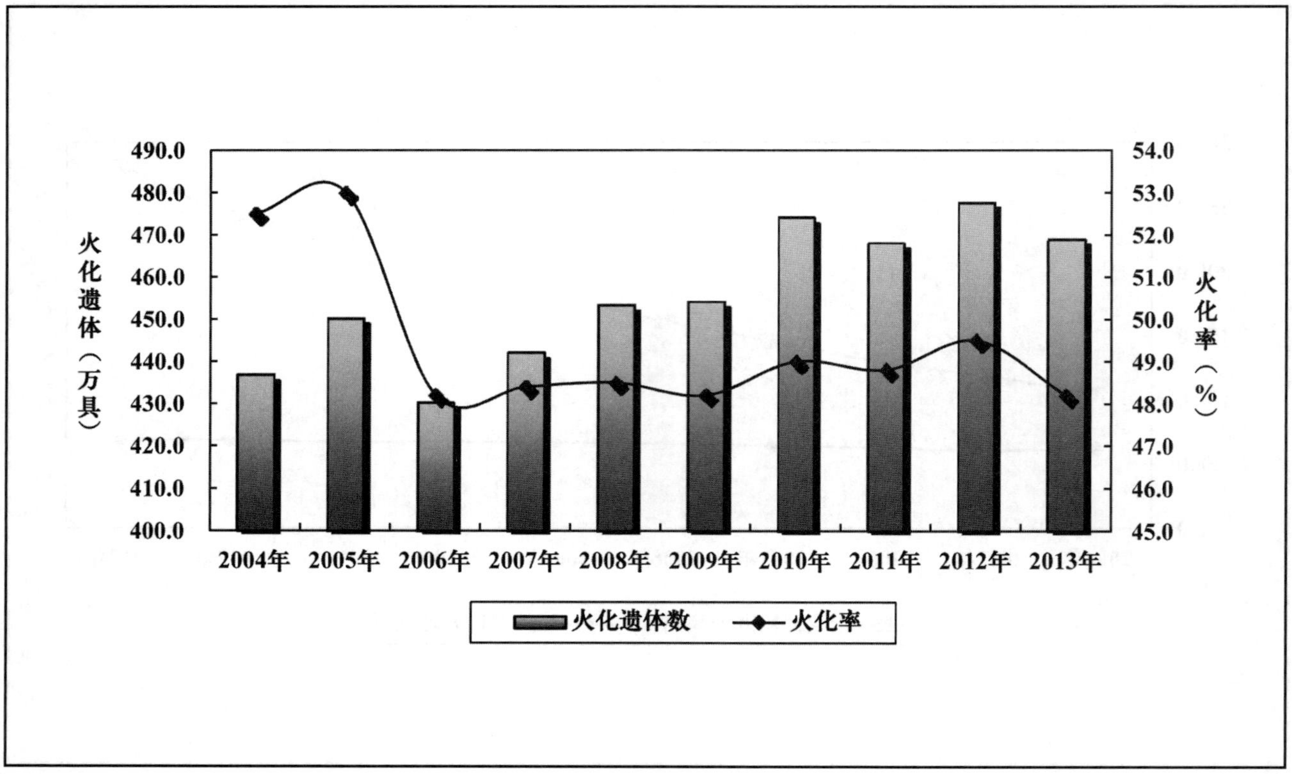

单位：万具、%

指　标	2004年	2005年	2006年	2007年	2008年	2009年	2010年	2011年	2012年	2013年
火化遗体数	436.9	450.2	430.2	442.1	453.4	454.2	474.1	468.1	477.7	468.9
火化率	52.5	53.0	48.2	48.4	48.5	48.2	49.0	48.8	49.5	48.2

社会服务
综合统计资料

03

A-1-1 “七五”—“十二五”时期社会服务发展速度

单位：%

指　标	“七五”时期平均增长速度	“八五”时期平均增长速度	“九五”时期平均增长速度	“十五”时期平均每年增长速度	“十一五”时期平均增长速度	“十二五”时期前3年平均增长速度
一、综合						
行政区划						
镇	5.7	7.7	3.0	-0.8	-0.1	1.2
乡	-11.6	-7.8	-4.7	-7.2	-1.8	-4.2
60岁及以上老年人口					4.3	4.4
事业费支出	11.9	14.8	17.3	25.6	30.3	16.6
固定资产	20.8	22.5	53.1	9.9	16.3	1.1
二、社会工作						
社会服务床位	9.7	4.6	3.0	7.7	13.8	14.6
# 养老床位				5.0	15.3	16.0
智障和精神疾病床位				10.0	8.8	6.7
儿童床位				11.7	11.5	21.2
家庭儿童收养				-2.0	-7.5	-11.8
安置残疾人的福利企业	23.0	7.6	-7.6	-5.2	-6.6	-6.5
为弱势群体筹集资金的福利彩票		54.5	14.6	29.4	18.7	22.2
享受最低生活保障城市居民				40.9	0.7	-3.7
抚恤补助优抚对象	8.5	1.1	-0.3	0.8	6.3	15.0
伤残人员抚恤水平			27.1	18.2	18.5	13.6
烈属和牺牲病故军人家属抚恤水平			6.7	13.5	14.9	19.2
社区服务中心			8.0	5.6	8.2	16.1
三、成员组织和其他社会服务						
社会组织		75.5	-3.2	15.8	6.9	7.0
社会团体				5.6	7.5	5.7
基金会					17.7	17.3
民办非企业单位				45.5	6.1	8.8
自治组织						
村民委员会	1.1	-6.9	-4.7	-3.0	-1.1	-0.3
社区居委会	4.1	2.5	-0.6	-5.9	1.7	3.0
婚姻						
办理结婚登记	2.7	-0.4	-0.2	-0.6	8.6	2.8
办理离婚登记	11.7	5.7	2.8	8.0	8.5	9.3
殡葬						
处理遗体数	5.3	5.5	7.3	3.8	1	-0.4

A-1-2 社会服务发展主要指标预期值

指　标	单　位	2014年 预期值	2015年 预期值	2020年 预期值	2030年 预期值
一、综合					
行政区划					
镇	万个	2.0	2.1	2.2	2.5
乡	万个	1.2	1.2	0.9	0.6
人口	万人	136738.8	137408.9	140808.9	147863.4
60岁及以上老年人口	万人	21143.6	22084.2	27453.5	42425.8
事业费支出	亿元	4986.5	5814.4	12532.9	58229.3
固定资产	亿元	6885.5	6961.6	7354.9	8209.4
二、社会工作					
社会服务床位	万张	581.7	642.4	1055.5	2849.0
# 养老床位	万张	544.8	601.2	984.0	2635.4
智障和精神疾病床位	万张	8.0	8.5	12.2	25.1
儿童床位	万张	10.8	11.8	18.9	48.5
家庭儿童收养	万件	2.1	1.9	1.0	0.3
安置残疾人的福利企业	万个	1.7	1.6	1.1	0.6
为弱势群体筹集资金的福利彩票	亿元	2156.7	2635.0	7172.8	53149.2
享受最低生活保障城市居民	万人	1988.1	1914.8	1586.8	1089.8
抚恤补助优抚对象	万人	993.0	1037.3	1290.7	1998.1
伤残人员抚恤水平	元/人、年	14995.9	17033.2	32204.0	115116.8
烈属和牺牲病故军人家属抚恤水平	元/人、年	11487.3	13692.4	32943.8	190706.6
社区服务中心	万个	2.3	2.7	5.7	25.2
三、成员组织和其他社会服务					
社会组织	万个	58.6	62.7	88.1	173.9
社会团体	万个	30.5	32.3	42.5	73.7
基金会	万个	0.4	0.5	1.1	5.3
民办非企业单位	万个	27.7	30.2	46.0	106.9
自治组织					
村民委员会	万个	58.7	58.5	57.5	55.6
社区居委会	万个	9.8	10.1	11.7	15.6
婚姻					
办理结婚登记	万对	1384.2	1422.5	1630.5	2142.2
办理离婚办理	万对	382.7	418.4	653.6	1595.4
殡葬					
处理遗体数	万具	487.8	507.5	618.4	918.4

注：发展速度为“十二五”时期平均增长速度，其中床位数、抚恤补助优抚对象和处理遗体数用的是1978年至2012年的平均速度。

A-1-3 2009-2013年社会服务业发展主要指标数据

指 标	单 位	2009年	2010年	2011年	2012年	2013年
一、综合						
社会服务基本情况						
机构	万个	126.2	126.9	129.4	136.7	156.2
服务人员	万人	1038.1	1138.4	1120.8	1144.7	1197.6
固定资产	亿元	5198.0	6589.3	6676.7	6675.4	6810.2
增加值	亿元	1849.4	2014.5	2246.9	2128.9	2251.9
事业费	亿元	2181.9	2697.5	3229.1	3683.7	4276.5
# 抚恤	亿元	310.3	362.7	428.3	517.0	618.4
退役安置	亿元	225.7	269.0	302.3	372.1	435.3
社会福利	亿元	124.1	109.9	232.2	319.5	397.6
社会救助	亿元	1098.1	1302.0	1766.3	1866.1	2172.4
自然灾害生活救助	亿元	199.2	237.2	128.7	163.4	178.7
离退休人员经费	亿元	30.0	30.4	35.3	39.0	43.6
其他	亿元	194.5	386.3	336.0	406.7	430.6
# 公益金支出	亿元	113.4	121.2	127.9	159.0	195.5
* 中央转移支付的事业费占全国总事业费比重	%	56.2	49.8	56.0	48.7	50.3
全国总事业费占财政支出的比重	%	2.9	3.0	3.0	3.0	3.1
基本建设投资	亿元	157.0	183.0	218.5	234.7	292.8
# 预算内投资	亿元	70.6	89.1	78.5	104.2	120.1
公益金投资	亿元	26.6	32.3	53.4	51.1	64.7
预算内基本建设投资占事业费比重	%	3.2	3.3	2.4	2.8	2.8
公益金基本建设投资占公益金支出的比重	%	23.5	26.7	41.8	32.1	33.1
乡镇级行政区划						
镇	个	19322	19410	19683	19881	20117
乡	个	14848	14571	13587	13281	12812
# 民族乡	个	1099	1096	1086	1064	1035
街道办事处	个	6686	6923	7194	7282	7566
区公所	个	2	2	2	2	2
老龄人口						
60岁及以上老年人口	万人	16714	17765	18499	19390	20243
占全国总人口	%	12.5	13.3	13.7	14.3	14.9
二、社会工作						
提供住宿的社会服务机构						
单位数	万个	4.4	4.4	4.6	4.8	4.6
床位数	万张	326.5	349.6	396.4	449.4	526.7
# 养老床位	万张	293.5	316.1	369.2	416.6	493.7
智障和精神疾病床位	万张	5.9	6.1	6.5	6.7	7.4
儿童床位	万张	4.8	5.5	6.8	8.7	9.8
其他床位	万张	22.3	21.9	13.9	17.4	15.7
收养人数	万人	256.0	278.2	293.4	309.5	322.5
每千人口社会服务床位数	张	2.5	2.6	2.9	3.3	3.9
每千老年人口养老床位数	张	17.6	17.8	20.0	21.5	24.4

A-1-3续表1

指 标	单 位	2009年	2010年	2011年	2012年	2013年
不提供住宿的社会服务机构						
机构数	万个	9.4	8.8	10.0	13.3	27.7
儿童						
孤儿数	万人	12.8	25.2	49.1	57.0	54.9
家庭收养儿童	万人	4.4	3.5	3.1	2.7	2.4
流浪儿童救助	万人次	16.7	14.6	17.9	15.2	18.1
残疾人						
为残疾人提供服务的机构数	万个	2.3	2.2	2.2	2.0	1.8
残疾职工数	万人	62.7	62.5	62.8	59.7	53.9
社会救助						
最低生活保障						
城市居民最低生活保障人数	万人	2345.6	2310.5	2276.8	2143.5	2064.2
城市居民最低生活保障户数	万户	1141.1	1145.0	1145.7	1114.9	1097.2
城市居民最低生活保障平均标准	元/人、月	227.8	251.2	287.6	330.1	373.3
*城市居民最低生活保障平均支出水平	元/人、月	172.0	189.0	240.3	239.1	264.2
农村最低生活保障人数	万人	4760.0	5214.0	5305.7	5344.5	5388.0
农村最低生活保障户数	万户	2291.8	2528.7	2672.8	2814.9	2931.1
农村最低生活保障平均标准	元/人、年	1210.1	1404.0	1718.4	2067.8	2433.9
*农村最低生活保障平均支出水平	元/人、年	816.0	888.0	1273.2	1247.9	1393.5
五保供养						
农村五保集中供养人数	万人	171.8	177.4	184.5	185.3	183.5
农村五保集中供养平均标准	元/人、年	2587.5	2951.4	3399.7	4060.9	4685.0
农村五保集中供养平均支出水平	元/人、年	2316.0	2460.0	3081.9	3496.6	4078.3
农村五保分散供养人数	万人	381.6	378.9	366.5	360.3	353.8
农村五保分散供养平均标准	元/人、年	1842.7	2102.1	2470.5	3008.0	3498.5
农村五保分散供养平均支出水平	元/人、年	1284.0	1416.0	1774.9	2237.3	2724.3
医疗救助						
民政部门直接救助人次数	万人次	1140.4	1479.3	2144.0	2173.7	2126.4
民政部门资助参加医疗保险人数	万人	1095.9	1461.2	1549.8	1387.1	1490.1
民政部门资助参加合作医疗人数	万人	4059.1	4615.4	4825.3	4490.4	4868.7
生活无着人员救助						
生活无着人员救助	万人次	168.1	171.9	241.0	276.6	348.5
为弱势群体筹集资金的活动						
民政部门接收社会捐赠						
社会捐赠款数	亿元	66.5	179.8	96.6	101.7	107.6
捐赠衣被总数	亿件	1.2	0.3	0.3	1.3	1.0
捐赠其他物资价值	亿元	2.2	4.9	4.8	6.3	8.7
受益人次数	万人次	1522.3	2514.7	1459.7	1325.0	1246.0
社会捐赠接收站、点数	万个	3.3	3.2	3.4	3.1	3.1
销售福利彩票	亿元	756.0	968.0	1278.0	1510.3	1765.3
筹集社会公益金	亿元	243.4	298.8	382.0	449.4	510.7

A-1-3续表2

指　标	单　位	2009年	2010年	2011年	2012年	2013年
优抚安置						
国家抚恤、补助各类优抚对象	万人	630.7	625.0	852.5	944.4	950.5
接收军队离退休人员人数	万人	1.9	1.3	1.5	1.9	3.9
社区服务						
社区服务机构	万个	14.6	15.3	16.0	20.0	25.2
# 社区服务中心	个	10003	12720	14391	16306	19904
社区服务站	个	53170	44237	56156	87931	108377
社区服务机构覆盖率	%	25.6	22.4	23.6	29.5	36.9
便民、利民网点	万个	69.3	53.9	45.3	39.7	35.9
自然灾害情况						
受灾人口	万人次	47933.5	42610.2	43290.0	29421.7	38818.7
因灾死亡（含失踪）人口	人	1528	7844	1126	1530	2284
直接经济损失	亿元	2523.7	5339.9	3096.4	4185.5	5808.4
三、成员组织和其他社会服务						
社会组织	万个	43.1	44.6	46.2	49.9	54.7
社会团体	万个	23.9	24.5	25.5	27.1	28.9
基金会	个	1843	2200	2614	3029	3548
民办非企业单位	万个	19.0	19.8	20.4	22.5	25.5
自治组织	万个	68.4	68.2	67.9	67.9	68.4
村委会	万个	59.9	59.5	59.0	58.8	58.9
社区居委会	万个	8.5	8.7	8.9	9.1	9.5
婚姻服务						
结婚登记	万对	1212.2	1241.0	1302.4	1323.6	1346.9
# 涉外及华侨、港澳台	万对	4.9	4.9	4.9	5.3	5.5
每千居民之结婚宗数	‰	9.1	9.3	9.7	9.8	9.9
离婚办理	万对	246.8	267.8	287.4	310.4	350.0
每千居民之离婚宗数	‰	1.9	2.0	2.1	2.3	2.6
殡葬服务						
火化遗体数	万具	454.2	474.1	468.1	477.7	468.9
火化率	%	48.2	49.0	48.8	49.5	48.2

A-1-4 社会服务发展主要数据与上年比较

指 标	单 位	2013年	2012年	比上年增长(%)
一、综合				
行政区划				
镇	个	20117	19881	1.2
乡	个	12812	13281	-3.5
# 民族乡	个	1035	1064	-2.7
街道办事处	个	7566	7282	3.9
区公所	个	2	2	
老龄人口				
60岁及以上老年人口	万人	20243	19390	4.4
占全国总人口	%	14.9	14.3	0.6(百分点)
65岁及以上老年人口	万人	13161	12714	3.5
占全国总人口	%	9.7	9.4	0.3(百分点)
资产				
民政事业费总支出	亿元	4276.5	3683.7	16.1
# 抚恤	亿元	618.4	517.0	19.6
退役安置	亿元	435.3	372.1	17.0
社会福利	亿元	397.6	319.5	24.4
社会救助	亿元	2172.4	1866.1	16.4
自然灾害生活救助	亿元	178.7	163.4	9.4
离退休人员经费	亿元	43.6	39.0	11.8
其他	亿元	430.6	406.7	5.9
基本建设支出	亿元	292.8	234.7	24.8
固定资产	亿元	6810.2	6675.4	2.0
二、社会工作				
提供住宿的社会服务机构				
单位数	万个	4.6	4.8	-4.2
床位数	万张	526.7	449.4	17.2
收养人数	万人	322.5	309.5	4.2
每千人口社会服务床位数	张	3.9	3.3	18.2

A-1-4续表1

指　标	单　位	2013年	2012年	比上年增长(%)
社会救助				
城市				
城市居民最低生活保障人数	万人	2064.2	2143.5	-3.7
城市居民最低生活保障户数	万户	1097.2	1114.9	-1.6
城市居民最低生活保障平均标准	元/人、月	373.3	330.1	13.1
城市居民最低生活保障平均支出水平	元/人、月	264.2	239.1	10.5
农村				
农村最低生活保障人数	万人	5388.0	5344.5	0.8
农村最低生活保障户数	万户	2931.1	2814.9	4.1
农村最低生活保障平均标准	元/人、年	2433.9	2067.8	17.7
农村最低生活保障平均支出水平	元/人、年	1393.5	1247.9	11.7
农村五保集中供养人数	万人	183.5	185.3	-1.0
农村五保集中供养平均标准	元/人、年	4685.0	4060.9	15.4
农村五保集中供养平均支出水平	元/人、年	4078.3	3496.6	16.6
农村五保分散供养人数	万人	353.8	360.3	-1.8
农村五保分散供养平均标准	元/人、年	3498.5	3008.0	16.3
农村五保分散供养平均支出水平	元/人、年	2724.3	2237.3	21.8
医疗救助				
民政部门直接救助人次数	万人次	2126.4	2173.7	-2.2
民政部门资助参加医疗保险人数	万人	1490.1	1387.1	7.4
农村资助参加合作医疗人数	万人	4868.7	4490.4	8.4
儿童收养				
家庭收养儿童	万人	2.4	2.7	-11.1
为残疾人提供服务的机构				
为残疾人提供服务的机构数	万个	1.8	2.0	-10.0
残疾职工人数	万人	53.9	59.7	-9.7
福利彩票				
销售福利彩票	亿元	1765.3	1510.3	16.9
筹集社会公益金	亿元	510.7	449.4	13.6
优抚安置				
国家抚恤、补助各类优抚对象	万人	950.5	944.4	0.6
安置义务兵、士官人数	万人	44.0	39.3	12.0
接收军队离退休人员人数	万人	3.9	1.9	109.7

A-1-4续表2

指　标	单　位	2013年	2012年	比上年增长(%)
社会捐赠				
社会捐赠款数	亿元	107.6	101.7	5.8
捐赠衣被总数	亿件	1.0	1.3	-20.0
捐赠其他物资价值	亿元	8.7	6.3	38.1
受益人次数	万人次	1246.0	1325.0	-6.0
社会捐赠接收站、点数	万个	3.1	3.1	0.0
社区服务机构				
社区服务指导中心	个	890	809	10.0
社区服务中心	个	19014	15497	22.7
社区服务站	个	108377	87931	23.3
养老等其他社区服务机构	个	123658	95763	29.1
社区服务机构覆盖率	%	36.9	29.5	5.9(百分点)
便民利民网点	个	35.9	39.7	-9.6
三、成员组织和其他社会服务				
社会组织				
社会组织总数	万个	54.7	49.9	9.6
社会团体	万个	28.9	27.1	6.6
基金会	个	3549	3029	17.2
民办非企业	万个	25.5	22.5	10.1
自治组织				
村委会	万个	58.9	58.8	0.2
居委会	万个	9.5	9.1	4.4
婚姻				
结婚登记	万对	1346.9	1323.6	1.8
# 涉外及华侨、港澳台	万对	5.5	5.3	3.8
每千居民之结婚宗数	‰	9.9	9.8	0.1(千分点)
离婚办理	万对	350.0	310.4	12.8
每千居民之离婚宗数	‰	2.6	2.3	0.3(千分点)
殡葬				
火化遗体数	万具	468.9	477.7	-1.8
火化率	%	48.2	49.5	-1.3(百分点)

A-1-5 行政区划与上年比较

单位：个

指　标	2013年	2012年	比上年增减(%)
地级行政区划合计	**333**	**333**	
# 地级市	286	285	0.4
地区	14	15	-6.7
自治州	30	30	
盟	3	3	
县级行政区划合计	**2853**	**2852**	**0.0**
# 市辖区	872	860	1.4
县级市	368	368	
县	1442	1453	-0.8
自治县	117	117	
旗	49	49	
自治旗	3	3	
特区	1	1	
林区	1	1	
乡镇、街道级行政区划合计	**40497**	**40446**	**0.1**
# 镇	20117	19881	1.2
乡	11626	12066	-3.6
苏木	151	151	
民族乡	1034	1063	-2.7
民族苏木	1	1	
街道办事处	7566	7282	3.9
区公所	2	2	

A-1-6 社会服务机构与上年比较

单位：个

指　标	2013年	2012年	比上年增减(%)
社会服务	**1562298**	**1366650**	**14.3**
一、社会工作	**323061**	**179045**	**80.4**
提供住宿的社会服务机构	**45977**	**48105**	**-4.4**
老年人与残疾人服务机构	**42475**	**44304**	**-4.1**
城市养老服务机构	7077	6464	9.5
农村养老服务机构	30247	32787	-7.7
社会福利院	1825	1719	6.2
光荣院	1425	1399	1.9
荣誉军人康复医院	42	43	-2.3
复员军人疗养院	38	41	-7.3
军休所	1821	1851	-1.6
智障与精神疾病服务机构	**261**	**257**	**1.6**
社会福利医院	155	156	-0.6
复退军人精神病院	106	101	5.0
儿童收养救助服务机构	**803**	**724**	**10.9**
儿童福利机构	529	463	14.3
未成年人救助保护中心	274	261	5.0
其他提供住宿的服务机构	**2438**	**2820**	**-13.5**
生活无着人员救助管理站	1891	1770	6.8
安置农场	26	27	-3.7
军供站	325	695	-53.2
其他提供住宿的机构	196	328	-40.2

A-1-6续表

单位：个

指　标	2013年	2012年	比上年增减(%)
不提供住宿的社会服务机构	**277084**	**130940**	**111.6**
老龄机构	2571	2583	-0.5
为残疾人提供服务的机构	18227	20205	-9.8
救助低保服务机构	987	843	17.1
救灾储备单位	784	665	17.9
福利彩票发行机构	940	955	-1.6
军队离退休人员管理中心	145	121	19.8
军队离退休人员活动中心	28	25	12.0
烈士纪念建筑物管理机构	1463	1306	12.0
社区服务机构	251939	104237	141.7
二、成员组织和其他社会服务机构	**1236853**	**1185179**	**4.4**
成员组织	**1230412**	**1178896**	**4.4**
社会组织	**547245**	**499268**	**9.6**
社会团体	289026	271131	6.6
基金会	3549	3029	17.2
民办非企业	254670	225108	13.1
自治组织	**683167**	**679628**	**0.5**
居委会	94620	91153	3.8
村委会	588547	588475	
其他社会服务	**6441**	**6283**	**2.5**
婚姻服务机构	**2059**	**1926**	**6.9**
殡葬服务机构	**4382**	**4357**	**0.6**
殡仪馆	1784	1782	0.1
公墓	1506	1597	-5.7
骨灰堂	29		
殡葬管理单位	1063	978	8.7
三、其他事业单位	**2384**	**2426**	**-1.7**
行政机关	**3492**	**3493**	

A-1-7 社会服务机构职工与上年比较

单位：万人

指　标	2013年	2012年	比上年增减（%）
社会服务	**1197.8**	**1144.7**	**4.6**
一、社会工作	**269.3**	**241.4**	**11.6**
提供住宿的社会服务机构	**42.4**	**39.8**	**6.5**
老年人与残疾人服务机构	**35.6**	**33.1**	**7.6**
城市养老服务机构	11.0	9.3	18.3
农村养老服务机构	16.4	15.9	3.1
社会福利院	4.5	4.2	7.1
光荣院	1.2	1.2	
荣誉军人康复医院	0.5	0.5	
复员军人疗养院	0.3	0.3	
军休所	1.7	1.7	
智障与精神疾病服务机构	**2.5**	**2.3**	**8.7**
社会福利医院	1.4	1.3	7.7
复退军人精神病院	1.1	1.0	10.0
儿童收养救助服务机构	**1.4**	**1.3**	**7.7**
儿童福利机构	1.2	1.1	9.1
未成年人救助保护中心	0.2	0.2	
其他提供住宿的服务机构	**2.9**	**3.1**	**-6.5**
生活无着人员救助管理站	1.8	1.7	5.9
安置农场	0.1	0.1	
军供站	0.6	0.7	-14.3
其他提供住宿的机构	0.4	0.6	-33.3

A-1-7续表

单位：万人

指　标	2013年	2012年	比上年增减（%）
不提供住宿的社会服务机构	**226.9**	**201.6**	**12.5**
老龄机构	1.0	1.1	-9.1
为残疾人提供服务的机构	137.3	149.9	-8.4
救助低保服务机构	0.7	0.6	16.7
救灾储备单位	0.2	0.2	
福利彩票发行机构	1.1	0.9	22.2
军队离退休人员管理中心	0.2	0.2	
军队离退休人员活动中心	0.1	0.1	
烈士纪念建筑物管理机构	1.0	1.0	
社区服务机构	85.3	47.6	79.2
二、成员组织和其他社会服务机构	**926.5**	**901.1**	**2.8**
成员组织	**917.4**	**892.5**	**2.8**
社会组织	**636.7**	**613.3**	**3.8**
社会团体	353.2	346.9	1.8
基金会	1.9	1.9	
民办非企业	281.6	264.5	6.5
自治组织	**280.7**	**279.2**	**0.5**
居委会	48.4	46.9	3.2
村委会	232.3	232.3	
其他社会服务	**9.1**	**8.6**	**5.8**
婚姻服务机构	**1.0**	**0.9**	**11.1**
殡葬服务机构	**8.1**	**7.7**	**5.2**
殡仪馆	4.6	4.5	2.2
公墓	2.5	2.3	8.7
骨灰堂	0.1		
殡葬管理单位	0.9	0.9	
三、其他事业单位	**2.0**	**2.2**	**-9.1**
行政机关	**9.4**	**9.3**	**1.1**

A-1-8 社会服务机构中社会工作师人员情况

单位：人

指 标	社会工作师			助理社会工作师		
	2013年	2012年	比上年增减(%)	2013年	2012年	比上年增减(%)
社会服务	**21917**	**17101**	**28.2**	**43301**	**36436**	**18.8**
一、社会工作	**8014**	**6602**	**21.4**	**15736**	**12278**	**28.2**
提供住宿的社会服务机构	**3256**	**2672**	**21.9**	**3510**	**3233**	**8.6**
老年人与残疾人服务机构	**2250**	**1878**	**19.8**	**2491**	**2335**	**6.7**
城市养老服务机构	603	500	20.6	712	670	6.3
农村养老服务机构	383	388	-1.3	429	444	-3.4
社会福利院	694	507	36.9	864	711	21.5
光荣院	115	115		120	138	-13.0
荣誉军人康复医院	62	66	-6.1	44	54	-18.5
复员军人疗养院	28	26	7.7	19	29	-34.5
军休所	365	276	32.2	303	289	4.8
智障与精神疾病服务机构	**183**	**144**	**27.1**	**209**	**211**	**-0.9**
社会福利医院	106	80	32.5	103	100	3.0
复退军人精神病院	77	64	20.3	106	111	-4.5
儿童收养救助服务机构	**382**	**275**	**38.9**	**338**	**291**	**16.2**
儿童福利机构	332	236	40.7	294	250	17.6
未成年人救助保护中心	50	39	28.2	44	41	7.3
其他提供住宿的服务机构	**441**	**375**	**17.6**	**472**	**396**	**19.2**
生活无着人员救助管理站	372	320	16.3	381	313	21.7
安置农场				11	1	1000.0
军供站	42	33	27.3	53	45	17.8
其他提供住宿的机构	27	22	22.7	27	37	-27.0

A-1-8续表

单位:人

指　标	社会工作师			助理社会工作师		
	2013年	2012年	比上年增减(%)	2013年	2012年	比上年增减(%)
不提供住宿的社会服务机构	**4758**	**3604**	**32.0**	**11961**	**8765**	**36.5**
老龄机构	113	99	14.1	84	90	-6.7
为残疾人提供服务的机构	749	710	5.5	1900	2180	-12.8
救助低保服务机构	114	77	48.1	96	76	26.3
救灾储备单位	22	20	10.0	17	15	13.3
福利彩票发行机构	100	115	-13.0	137	114	20.2
军队离退休人员管理中心	48	39	23.1	32	23	39.1
军队离退休人员活动中心	6	5	20.0	5	5	
烈士纪念建筑物管理机构	150	141	6.4	103	112	-8.0
社区服务机构	3456	2398	44.1	9587	6150	55.9
二、成员组织和其他社会服务机构	**13554**	**10499**	**29.1**	**27565**	**24158**	**14.1**
成员组织	**12994**	**10056**	**29.2**	**26871**	**23513**	**14.3**
社会组织	**8561**	**6788**	**26.1**	**13399**	**13000**	**3.1**
社会团体	3556	1850	92.2	5437	5944	-8.5
基金会	78	232	-66.4	151	140	7.9
民办非企业	4927	4706	4.7	7811	6916	12.9
自治组织	**4433**	**3268**	**35.6**	**13472**	**10513**	**28.1**
居委会	3964	2741	44.6	11852	9090	30.4
村委会	469	527	-11.0	1620	1423	13.8
其他社会服务	**560**	**443**	**26.4**	**694**	**645**	**7.6**
婚姻服务机构	**162**	**100**	**62.0**	**135**	**106**	**27.4**
殡葬服务机构	**398**	**343**	**16.0**	**559**	**539**	**3.7**
殡仪馆	204	184	10.9	308	313	-1.6
公墓	97	93	4.3	150	130	15.4
骨灰堂				1		
殡葬管理单位	97	66	47.0	100	96	4.2
三、其他事业单位	**349**	**326**	**7.1**	**265**	**280**	**-5.4**
行政机关	**1280**	**1114**	**14.9**	**1264**	**1163**	**8.7**

A-1-9 性别统计情况

指　标	人员总数 （人）	#女性	占总人数的比重 （%）	比上年增减 （百分点）
社会服务	**11976467**	**3688093**	**30.8**	**0.4**
一、社会工作	**2692329**	**1008579**	**37.5**	**-0.6**
提供住宿的社会服务机构	**422870**	**224650**	**53.1**	**0.1**
老年人与残疾人服务机构	**356071**	**190908**	**53.6**	**0.2**
城市养老服务机构	109752	70387	64.1	-0.5
农村养老服务机构	164144	75976	46.3	0.2
社会福利院	44645	26899	60.3	-1.5
光荣院	11949	5569	46.6	-2.5
荣誉军人康复医院	5319	2881	54.2	1.4
复员军人疗养院	2995	1682	56.2	1.9
军休所	17267	7514	43.5	0.3
智障与精神疾病服务机构	**25114**	**14118**	**56.2**	
社会福利医院	13835	7660	55.4	0.3
复退军人精神病院	11279	6458	57.3	-0.4
儿童收养救助服务机构	**13641**	**8623**	**63.2**	**-1.6**
儿童福利机构	11598	7862	67.8	-2.1
未成年人救助保护中心	2043	761	37.2	-0.1
其他提供住宿的服务机构	**28044**	**11001**	**39.2**	**-2.6**
生活无着人员救助管理站	17587	5924	33.7	-0.4
安置农场	1227	483	39.4	16.9
军供站	5587	2266	40.6	-1.5
其他提供住宿的机构	3643	2328	63.9	1.7

A-1-9续表

指　标	人员总数（人）	#女性	占总人数的比重（%）	比上年增减（百分点）
不提供住宿的社会服务机构	**2269459**	**783929**	**34.5**	**-0.5**
老龄机构	10134	4417	43.6	-0.4
为残疾人提供服务的机构	1373351	439224	32.0	-0.3
救助低保服务机构	7187	3237	45.0	-2.2
救灾储备单位	2157	650	30.1	-1.1
福利彩票发行机构	10636	4315	40.6	-0.2
军队离退休人员管理中心	1904	866	45.5	1.2
军队离退休人员活动中心	647	282	43.6	0.0
烈士纪念建筑物管理机构	10221	4077	39.9	-1.0
社区服务机构	853222	326861	38.3	-5.1
二、成员组织和其他社会服务机构	**9263658**	**2670323**	**28.8**	**0.6**
成员组织	**9172941**	**2641665**	**28.8**	**0.6**
社会组织	**6365813**	**1880817**	**29.5**	**0.6**
社会团体	3531635	795902	22.5	0.3
基金会	18646	5202	27.9	-2.8
民办非企业	2815532	1079713	38.3	0.6
自治组织	**2807128**	**760848**	**27.1**	**0.5**
居委会	484015	234413	48.4	-0.4
村委会	2323113	526435	22.7	0.6
其他社会服务	**90717**	**28658**	**31.6**	**-0.8**
婚姻服务机构	**9949**	**6650**	**66.8**	**0.1**
殡葬服务机构	**80768**	**22008**	**27.2**	**-1.1**
殡仪馆	46178	11524	25.0	-1.0
公墓	25397	8142	32.1	-1.6
骨灰堂	173	30		
殡葬管理单位	9020	2312	25.6	-0.6
三、其他事业单位	**20480**	**9191**	**44.9**	**-0.8**
行政机关	**93911**	**30161**	**32.1**	

A-1-10 社会服务机构固定资产与上年比较

单位：亿元

指　标	2013年	2012年	比上年增减(%)
社会服务	**6810.2**	**6675.4**	**2.0**
一、社会工作	**3030.7**	**2898.9**	**4.5**
提供住宿的社会服务机构	**843.7**	**783.2**	**7.7**
老年人与残疾人服务机构	**724.1**	**661.0**	**9.5**
城市养老服务机构	200.8	160.0	25.5
农村养老服务机构	313.0	333.1	-6.0
社会福利院	119.9	92.3	29.9
光荣院	24.7	22.2	11.3
荣誉军人康复医院	19.8	10.8	83.3
复员军人疗养院	10.1	6.2	62.9
军休所	35.8	36.4	-1.6
智障与精神疾病服务机构	**40.1**	**35.4**	**13.3**
社会福利医院	20.5	15.6	31.4
复退军人精神病院	19.6	19.8	-1.0
儿童收养救助服务机构	**33.0**	**31.5**	**4.8**
儿童福利机构	30.3	28.8	5.2
未成年人救助保护中心	2.7	2.7	
其他提供住宿的服务机构	**46.5**	**55.3**	**-15.9**
生活无着人员救助管理站	27.6	25.3	9.1
安置农场	0.5	0.5	
军供站	13.0	16.7	-22.2
其他提供住宿的机构	5.4	12.8	-57.8

A-1-10续表

单位：亿元

指 标	2013年	2012年	比上年增减(%)
不提供住宿的社会服务机构	**2187.0**	**2115.7**	**3.4**
老龄机构	8.4	9.0	-6.7
为残疾人提供服务的机构	1760.1	1814.7	-3.0
救助低保服务机构	1.3	1.1	18.2
救灾储备单位	11.5	9.7	18.6
福利彩票发行机构	68.5	62.4	9.8
军队离退休人员管理中心	12.9	12.4	4.0
军队离退休人员活动中心	6.7	6.7	
烈士纪念建筑物管理机构	49.1	42.3	16.1
社区服务机构	268.5	157.4	70.6
二、成员组织和其他社会服务机构	**3732.7**	**3729.5**	**0.1**
成员组织	**3465.7**	**3477.7**	**-0.3**
社会组织	**1496.6**	**1425.4**	**5.0**
社会团体	325.8	310.0	5.1
基金会	14.3	17.9	-20.1
民办非企业	1156.5	1097.5	5.4
自治组织	**1969.1**	**2052.3**	**-4.1**
居委会	349.8	440.8	-20.6
村委会	1619.3	1611.5	0.5
其他社会服务	**267.0**	**251.8**	**6.0**
婚姻服务机构	**9.4**	**8.5**	**10.6**
殡葬服务机构	**257.6**	**243.3**	**5.9**
殡仪馆	165.0	142.2	16.0
公墓	72.1	81.0	-11.0
骨灰堂	0.4		
殡葬管理单位	20.1	20.1	
三、其他事业单位	**46.8**	**47.0**	**-0.4**
行政机关	**185.4**	**344.1**	**-46.1**

A-1-11 社会服务机构增加值（按国民经济行业分类）

单位：亿元

指　标	2013年	2012年	比上年增减(%)
社会服务	**2251.9**	**2128.9**	**5.8**
一、社会工作	**1167.1**	**1125.2**	**3.7**
提供住宿的社会服务机构	**332.7**	**301.1**	**10.5**
老年人与残疾人服务机构	**273.3**	**247.1**	**10.6**
城市养老服务机构	26.5	22.8	16.2
农村养老服务机构	36.8	34.3	7.3
社会福利院	30.7	27.1	13.3
光荣院	5.1	4.7	8.5
荣誉军人康复医院	7.1	6.1	16.4
复员军人疗养院	3.1	2.4	29.2
军休所	164.0	149.7	9.6
智障与精神疾病服务机构	**26.2**	**22.5**	**16.4**
社会福利医院	15.0	13.0	15.4
复退军人精神病院	11.2	9.5	17.9
儿童收养救助服务机构	**11.8**	**10.7**	**10.3**
儿童福利机构	10.6	9.4	12.8
未成年人救助保护中心	1.2	1.3	-7.7
其他提供住宿的服务机构	**21.4**	**20.8**	**2.9**
生活无着人员救助管理站	15.0	14.1	6.4
安置农场	0.8	0.8	
军供站	4.7	1.2	291.7
其他提供住宿的机构	0.9	4.7	-80.9

A-1-11续表

单位：亿元

指　标	2013年	2012年	比上年增减(%)
不提供住宿的社会服务机构	**834.4**	**824.1**	**1.2**
老龄机构	6.6	6.2	6.5
为残疾人提供服务的机构	693.2	702.9	-1.4
救助低保服务机构	2.7	3.4	-20.6
救灾储备单位	1.3	1.1	18.2
福利彩票发行机构	17.6	19.3	-8.8
军队离退休人员管理中心	24.1	28.4	-15.1
军队离退休人员活动中心	0.9	1.3	-30.8
烈士纪念建筑物管理机构	8.0	7.6	5.3
社区服务机构	80.0	53.9	48.4
二、成员组织和其他社会服务机构	**1064.7**	**984.9**	**8.1**
成员组织	**972.9**	**900.7**	**8.0**
社会组织	**571.1**	**525.6**	**8.7**
社会团体	155.5	142.1	9.4
基金会	16.2	14.0	15.7
民办非企业	399.4	369.5	8.1
自治组织	**401.8**	**375.1**	**7.1**
居委会	107.0	103.4	3.5
村委会	294.8	271.7	8.5
其他社会服务	**91.8**	**84.2**	**9.0**
婚姻服务机构	**3.3**	**2.9**	**13.8**
殡葬服务机构	**88.5**	**81.3**	**8.9**
殡仪馆	48.2	46.1	4.6
公墓	33.5	29.5	13.6
骨灰堂	0.1		
殡葬管理单位	6.7	5.7	17.5
三、其他事业单位	**20.1**	**18.8**	**6.9**
行政机关	**211.7**	**192.7**	**9.9**

A－1－12 社会服务机构增加值（按登记类型分类）

单位：亿元

指　标	2013年	2012年	比上年增减(%)
民政管理单位增加值合计	**2251.9**	**2128.9**	**5.8**
一、事业单位	**585.8**	**525.3**	**11.5**
收养类	147.8	134.8	9.6
城市老年福利机构	26.5	22.8	16.2
农村老年福利机构	36.8	34.3	7.3
社会福利院	30.7	27.1	13.3
光荣院	5.1	4.7	8.5
荣誉军人康复医院	7.1	6.1	16.4
复员军人疗养院	3.1	2.4	29.2
复退军人精神病院	11.2	9.5	17.9
社会福利医院	15.0	13.0	15.4
儿童福利机构	10.6	9.4	12.8
安置农场	0.8	0.8	
其他提供住宿的机构	0.9	4.7	-80.9
救助类	16.2	15.4	5.2
生活无着人员救助管理站	15.0	14.1	6.4
未成年人救助保护中心	1.2	1.3	-7.7
救灾储备类	1.3	1.1	18.2
救灾储备单位	1.3	1.1	18.2
筹集资金类	17.6	19.3	-8.8
福利彩票发行单位	17.6	19.3	-8.8

A-1-12续表

单位：亿元

指　标	2013年	2012年	比上年增减(%)
优抚安置类	201.7	188.2	7.2
军休所	164.0	149.7	9.6
军供站	4.7	1.2	291.7
军队离退休人员管理中心	24.1	28.4	-15.1
军队离退休人员活动中心	0.9	1.3	-30.8
烈士纪念建筑物管理单位	8.0	7.6	5.3
社区服务类	80.0	53.9	48.4
社区服务指导中心	3.1	2.2	40.9
社区服务中心	17.5	16.6	5.4
社区服务站	40.1	35.1	14.2
养老等其他社区服务机构	19.3		
婚姻登记服务类	3.3	2.9	13.8
殡葬服务类	88.5	81.3	8.9
殡仪馆	48.2	46.1	4.6
公墓	33.5	29.5	13.6
骨灰堂	0.1		
殡葬管理机构	6.7	5.7	17.5
其他	29.4	28.4	3.5
老龄行政机构	6.6	6.2	6.5
救助低保服务机构	2.7	3.4	-20.6
其他事业单位	20.1	18.8	6.9
二、成员组织			
社会组织	571.1	525.6	8.7
社会团体	155.5	142.1	9.4
基金会	16.2	14.0	15.7
民办非企业	399.4	369.5	8.1
自治组织	401.8	375.1	7.1
居委会	107.0	103.4	3.5
村委会	294.8	271.7	8.5
三、企业	**693.2**	**702.9**	**-1.4**
为残疾人提供服务的机构	693.2	702.9	-1.4
四、行政机关	**211.7**	**192.7**	**9.9**

A-1-13 基本建设投资与上年比较

单位：亿元、个

项　目	2013年	2012年	比上年增减(%)
计划总投资	**1036.1**	**727.9**	**42.3**
本年计划投资	**311.9**	**222.3**	**40.3**
提供住宿的社会工作机构	**195.3**		
老年人与残疾人服务机构	173.0		
智障与精神疾病服务机构	6.6		
儿童收养救助服务机构	11.1		
其他提供住宿的服务机构	4.6		
不提供住宿的社会工作机构	**55.4**		
其他	**61.2**		
自开始建设至本年底累计完成投资	**549.2**	**359.3**	**52.9**
本年完成投资	**292.8**		
提供住宿的社会工作机构	**188.8**		
老年人与残疾人服务机构	167.3		
智障与精神疾病服务机构	6.4		
儿童收养救助服务机构	10.5		
其他提供住宿的服务机构	4.6		
不提供住宿的社会工作机构	**49.2**		
其他	**54.8**		
国家投资	120.1	104.2	15.3
国内贷款	1.4	3.8	-63.2
利用外资	1.7	1.1	54.5
福利彩票公益金	64.7	51.1	26.6
其他	104.8	74.6	40.5
本年完工项目个数	**15328**	**6095**	**151.5**

A-1-14 社会服务经费与上年比较

单位：亿元

指　标	2013年	2012年	比上年增减(%)
社会服务经费合计	**4276.6**	**3683.8**	**16.1**
占国家财政支出比重（%）	3.1	3.0	0.1(百分点)
# 中央转移支付的事业费	2149.7	1794.6	19.8
占社会服务经费的比重（%）	50.3	48.7	1.6
# 国家基本建设投资	120.1	104.2	15.3
# 公益金支出	195.5	159.0	23.0
按支出性质分			
抚恤	618.4	517.0	19.6
退役安置	435.3	372.1	17.0
社会福利	397.6	319.5	24.4
社会救助	2172.4	1866.1	16.4
# 城市居民最低生活保障	756.7	674.3	12.2
农村最低生活保障	866.9	718.0	20.7
其他社会救助	291.4	243.2	19.8
医疗救助	257.4	230.6	11.6
自然灾害生活救助	178.7	163.4	9.4
离退休人员经费	43.6	39.0	11.8
其他	430.6	406.7	5.9

A-1-15 中央级社会服务费和转移支付的社会服务费与上年比较

单位：万元

指　标	2013年	2012年	比上年增减(%)
合计	**21634580.4**	**18046116.8**	**19.9**
中央级民政事业费	**137419.9**	**100110.8**	**37.3**
民政管理事务	46609.8	52806.5	-11.7
# 行政运行	6043.8	5745.8	5.2
一般行政管理政务	3431.9	10194.1	-66.3
机关服务	244.4	249.4	-2.0
拥军优属	298.7	300.9	-0.7
老龄事务	1030.6	837.6	23.0
民间组织管理	19691.7	20970.0	-6.1
行政区划和地名管理	807.2	2499.5	-67.7
基层政权和社区建设	443.8	417.7	6.2
其他民政管理政务支出	14617.7	11591.5	26.1
自然灾害生活救助	43506.0	16170.0	169.1
其他款项用于民政支出	47304.1	31134.3	51.9
中央财政转移支付的民政经费	**21497160.48**	**17946006**	**19.8**
# 抚恤	3697979	3333318	10.9
退役安置	2774042	2654268	4.5
社会福利	543649.48	419812	29.5
最低生活保障	11687897	8704961	34.3
医疗救助	1566688	1499582	4.5
自然灾害生活救助	1019248	1127379	-9.6
其他	207657	206686	0.5

A-1-16 按支出形式分类的社会服务经费支出情况

单位：万元

项 目	2013年	2012年	占全部(%)	比上年增减额	比上年增长(%)
总计	**42765370.8**	**36837379.4**	**100.0**	**5927991.4**	**16.09**
直接发放	**33690680.3**	**29216223.3**	**78.8**	**4474457.0**	**15.31**
按标准发放和报销	25426105.1	22582978.1	59.5	2843127.0	12.59
发放数	24938318.7	22146150.8	58.3	2792167.9	12.61
定期发放	24705123.8	21958524.9	57.8	2746598.9	12.51
军队干部离休金	287951.3	283732.7	0.7	4218.6	1.49
军队干部退休金	1662363.8	1549064.4	3.9	113299.4	7.31
军队无军籍退休金	316383.0	300927.6	0.7	15455.4	5.14
地方干部、人员退休金、退职金	128819.7	124670.9	0.3	4148.8	3.33
离休、退休、退职金小计	2395517.8	2258395.6	5.6	137122.2	6.07
烈属和牺牲病故定期抚恤金	353112.6	348174.9	0.8	4937.7	1.42
伤残抚恤金	1010354.1	896464.8	2.4	113889.3	12.7
在乡退伍红军老战士生活费	2474.0	2541.6		-67.6	-2.66
红军失散人员补助费	27460.8	32536.8	0.1	-5076.0	-15.6
复员退伍军人定期定量补助费	1593219.6	1456103.0	3.7	137116.6	9.42
“参战”退伍军人补助费	547642.4	476959.6	1.3	70682.8	14.82
“涉核”退伍军人补助费	84506.7	74194.5	0.2	10312.2	13.9
抚恤、补助费小计	3618770.2	3286975.2	8.5	331795.0	10.09
军队离休干部遗属、退休人员遗属定期定量补助费	13433.6	12417.7		1015.9	8.18
农村五保供养救济费	1723213.1	1449614.7	4.0	273598.4	18.87
农村最低生活保障金	7440641.9	6581923.3	17.4	858718.6	13.05
城市居民最低生活保障金	7567087.0	6743253.7	17.7	823833.3	12.22
传统救济	303280.7	257322.1	0.7	45958.6	17.86
定期定量救济费小计	17047656.3	15044531.5	39.9	2003124.8	13.31
分散安置伤残军人护理费	24257.9	20487.8	0.1	3770.1	18.4
军队离休、退休人员护理费	31162.3	31313.2	0.1	-150.9	-0.48
儿童福利支出	512724.7	504974.7	1.2	7750.0	1.53
老年人福利	1075034.6	811846.9	2.5	263187.7	32.42
非定期发放	233194.9	187625.9	0.6	45569.0	24.29
烈士和牺牲病故人员一次性抚恤金	203231.1	161812.7	0.5	41418.4	25.6
企事业退休人员一次性抚恤金	7600.7	5942.6		1658.1	27.9
离休、退休干部死亡丧葬补助费	22363.1	19870.6	0.1	2492.5	12.54
城市居民最低生活保障对象临时补助	921889.5	517398.0	2.2	404491.5	78.18
农村最低生活保障对象临时补助	1228397.2	597619.2	2.9	630778.0	105.55
报销数	487786.4	436827.3	1.1	50959.1	11.67
伤残补助费	61431.8	61300.8	0.1	131.0	0.21
离休、退休干部其他费用	426354.6	375526.5	1.0	50828.1	13.54

A-1-16续表

单位：万元

项　目	2013年	2012年	占全部(%)	比上年增减额	比上年增长(%)
临时性发放	8264575.2	6633245.2	19.3	1631330.0	24.59
烈军属复员退伍军人临时补助费	2260265.7	1637004.1	5.3	623261.6	38.07
退伍军人建房补助费	20198.2	19067.9	0.1	1130.3	5.93
义务兵优待金	964378.5	680039.7	2.3	284338.8	41.81
退役士兵自谋职业金	830837.0	628126.4	1.9	202710.6	32.27
城镇退役士兵生活补助	132257.2	88192.0	0.3	44065.2	49.97
优抚对象临时补助费小计	4207936.6	3052430.1	9.8	1155506.5	37.86
灾民生活救济费	1009445.7	931776.4	2.4	77669.3	8.34
医疗救助	2574119.1	2306113.1	6.0	268006.0	11.62
其他对象临时救助	473073.8	342925.6	1.1	130148.2	37.95
单位拨款	**2812021.9**	**2296220.1**	**6.6**	**515801.8**	**22.46**
民政部门举办事业单位经费	2293641.8	1873416.8	5.4	420225.0	22.43
优抚事业单位	435144.3	351154.2	1.0	83990.1	23.92
荣誉军人康复医院	68539.2	48518.6	0.2	20020.6	41.26
复员军人慢性病疗养院	32160.6	33020.6	0.1	-860.0	-2.6
复员退伍军人精神病院	93801.9	81101.9	0.2	12700.0	15.66
光荣院	80831.4	68462.1	0.2	12369.3	18.07
烈士纪念建筑物管理机构	91133.4	72968.9	0.2	18164.5	24.89
其他优抚事业单位	68677.8	47082.1	0.2	21595.7	45.87
社会福利事业单位	928043.8	852153.5	2.2	75890.3	8.91
社会福利院	495319.7	442989.2	1.2	52330.5	11.81
儿童福利院	133016.6	116834.7	0.3	16181.9	13.85
精神病人福利院	132519.6	128586.0	0.3	3933.6	3.06
流浪乞讨人员救助站	167187.9	163743.6	0.4	3444.3	2.1
军队离退休干部管理机构	375917.5	248751.8	0.9	127165.7	51.12
殡葬事业单位	554536.2	421357.3	1.3	133178.9	31.61
火葬场	243437.4	178204.5	0.6	65232.9	36.61
其他殡葬事业单位	311098.8	243152.8	0.7	67946.0	27.94
集体办事业单位补贴	285014.9	225593.4	0.7	59421.5	26.34
优抚事业单位	2117.0	1325.5		791.5	59.71
社会福利事业单位	282897.9	224267.9	0.7	58630.0	26.14
生产单位拨款	18563.6	19487.3		-923.7	-4.74
假肢厂、站	8118.9	7169.1		949.8	13.25
安置农场	10444.7	12318.2		-1873.5	-15.21
灾民紧急抢救、转移、安置费	110119.6	109752.3	0.3	367.3	0.33
救灾储备	104682.0	67970.3	0.2	36711.7	54.01
其他支出	**6262668.6**	**5324936.0**	**14.6**	**937732.6**	**17.61**

A-1-17 按支出性质分类的社会服务经费支出情况

单位：万元

项　目	2013年	2012年	占全部(%)	比上年增减额	比上年增长(%)
总计	**42765370.8**	**36837379.4**	**100.0**	**5927991.4**	**16.1**
优待抚恤支出合计	**6184310.6**	**5169949.0**	**14.5**	**1014361.6**	**19.6**
死亡抚恤	596955.5	532843.8	1.4	64111.7	12.0
伤残抚恤	1071785.9	957765.6	2.5	114020.3	11.9
在乡复员、退伍军人生活补助	2255303.5	2042335.5	5.3	212968.0	10.4
优抚事业单位	699863.5	497901.0	1.6	201962.5	40.6
义务兵优待金	964378.5	680039.7	2.3	284338.8	41.8
其他优抚支出	596023.7	459063.4	1.4	136960.3	29.8
退役安置	**4352600.2**	**3720969.5**	**10.2**	**631630.7**	**17.0**
退伍军人安置	1098342.4	811471.4	2.6	286871.0	35.4
军队移交政府的离退休人员安置	2693052.7	2509251.2	6.3	183801.5	7.3
军队移交政府离退休干部管理机构	375917.5	248751.8	0.9	127165.7	51.1
其他退役安置支出	185287.6	151495.1	0.4	33792.5	22.3
社会福利	**3975669.6**	**3194500.1**	**9.3**	**781169.5**	**24.5**
儿童福利	512724.7	504974.7	1.2	7750.0	1.5
老年人福利	1075034.6	811846.9	2.5	263187.7	32.4
假肢矫形	14227.7	10532.9		3694.8	35.1
殡葬	554536.2	421357.3	1.3	133178.9	31.6
社会福利事业单位	1054198.5	924996.0	2.5	129202.5	14.0
其他社会福利支出	764947.9	520792.3	1.8	244155.6	46.9
社会救助	**21724118.2**	**18661169.5**	**50.8**	**3062948.7**	**16.4**
最低生活保障	16236126.1	13922796.2	38.0	2313329.9	16.6
城市居民最低生活保障	7567087.0	6743253.7	17.7	823833.3	12.2
农村最低生活保障	8669039.1	7179542.5	20.3	1489496.6	20.8

A-1-17续表

单位：万元

项　目	2013年	2012年	占全部(%)	比上年增减额	比上年增长(%)
其他社会救助	2913873.0	2432260.2	6.8	481612.8	19.8
医疗救助	2574119.1	2306113.1	6.0	268006.0	11.6
民政部门资助参合	300427.0	258295.7	0.7	42131.3	16.3
民政部门资助参保	144061.2	116470.7	0.3	27590.5	23.7
直接医疗救助	1804596.5	1663140.0	4.2	141456.5	8.5
优抚对象医疗补助	325034.4	268206.7	0.8	56827.7	21.2
自然灾害生活救助	**1786987.6**	**1633832.7**	**4.2**	**153154.9**	**9.4**
生活救济费	1009445.7	931776.4	2.4	77669.3	8.3
紧急抢救、安置、转移灾民支出	110119.6	109752.3	0.3	367.3	0.3
救灾储备	104682.0	67970.3	0.2	36711.7	54.0
自然灾害灾后重建补助	436158.1	429372.0	1.0	6786.1	1.6
其他救助	126582.2	94961.7	0.3	31620.5	33.3
民政管理事务	**2967378.9**	**2484897.7**	**6.9**	**482481.2**	**19.4**
行政运行	703821.7	642355.5	1.7	61466.2	9.6
一般行政管理事务	140587.2	138963.2	0.3	1624.0	1.2
机关服务	21345.4	21035.1	0.1	310.3	1.5
拥军优属	204454.4	197229.7	0.5	7224.7	3.7
老龄事务	263798.2	200114.9	0.6	63683.3	31.8
民间组织管理	57838.9	44892.4	0.1	12946.5	28.8
行政区划和地名管理	54308.6	63817.9	0.1	-9509.3	-14.9
基层政权和社区建设	758420.3	553175.9	1.8	205244.4	37.1
部队供应	40981.0	39433.3	0.1	1547.7	3.9
其他民政管理事务支出	721823.2	583879.8	1.7	137943.4	23.6
行政事业单位离退休	**435817.7**	**390037.5**	**1.0**	**45780.2**	**11.7**
地方离退休人员经费	143243.2	140402.5	0.3	2840.7	2.0
行政单位离退休	159588.6	136930.9	0.4	22657.7	16.6
事业单位离退休	111312.1	94878.8	0.3	16433.3	17.3
离退休人员管理机构	2522.8	1583.6		939.2	59.3
其他行政事业单位离退休支出	19151.0	16241.7		2909.3	17.9
其他	**1338488.0**	**1582023.4**	**3.1**	**-243535.4**	**-15.4**

A-2-1 社会服务类机构财务状况

单位：万元

指　标	2013年	2012年	比上年增减(%)
执行企业会计制度单位情况			
固定资产原价	17819100.0	18364881.6	-2.97
本年折旧	1770212.0	1757971.0	0.70
营业收入	52462724.8	51911562.3	1.06
营业成本	20749655.3	20130883.0	3.07
营业税金及附加	1082070.2	1007793.8	7.37
销售费用	2554860.8	2897368.7	-11.82
管理费用	2236730.0	2468470.9	-9.39
# 税金	269064.9	269901.2	-0.31
差旅费	89652.4	109617.4	-18.21
财务费用	1014560.9	1116746.2	-9.15
# 利息支出	706436.7	754607.3	-6.38
公允价值变动收益	15392.8	3513.0	338.17
投资收益	24948.6	16108.3	54.88
营业利润	1596719.6	1424365.7	12.10
营业外收入	165738.3		
# 政府补助	20078.2		
应付职工薪酬	2275714.5	2505244.2	-9.16

A-2-1续表

单位：万元

指　标	2013年	2012年	比上年增减(%)
执行行政事业单位会计制度情况			
固定资产原价	9487436.7	7757606.5	22.30
上年结转和结余	940370.5	669600.4	40.44
本年收入合计	8240070.7	8143597.3	1.18
#事业收入	3687462.0	3269349.4	12.79
经营收入	173418.9	229205.6	-24.34
本年支出合计	8066596.6	7721130.8	4.47
#工资福利支出	1447814.4	1300998.5	11.28
商品和服务支出	1585510.2	1515216.6	4.64
#取暖费	50429.3	46224.4	9.10
差旅费	24857.0	23814.9	4.38
因公出国（境）费用	680.3	1568.7	-56.63
劳务费	106408.1	98968.1	7.52
工会经费	6830.4	13011.6	-47.51
福利费	29917.2	31764.9	-5.82
对个人和家庭的补助	2327616.2	2162854.5	7.62
#抚恤金	24940.0	23177.0	7.61
生活补助	342933.4	164697.0	108.22
救济费	102462.2	58994.8	73.68
助学金	2852.6	2983.4	-4.38
奖励金	5823.3	2375.4	145.15
生产补贴	398.8	207.0	92.66
经营支出	45952.7	25567.5	79.73
收支结余	437944.9		
销售税金	4669.1	5450.0	-14.33
执行民间非营利组织单位会计制度情况			
固定资产原价	3000559.9	2867358.7	4.65
上年结余	53953.7	36977.0	45.91
本年收入合计	1187693.9	818731.5	45.07
# 捐赠收入	94629.9	76248.8	24.11
会费收入	90566.1	84187.6	7.58
本年费用合计	1117084.4	874290.8	27.77
# 业务活动成本	557800.1	376337.9	48.22
# 人员费用	263059.8	180840.8	45.46
日常费用	119702.1	85585.5	39.86
固定资产折旧	76876.5	47721.4	61.09
税费	2045.2	1309.5	56.18
管理费用	297372.7	268245.6	10.86
# 人员费用	134034.0	135633.6	-1.18
日常费用	73135.5	65892.4	10.99
固定资产折旧	34124.9	31018.6	10.01
税费	1450.9	1169.1	24.10
净资产变动额	43329.3	27879.2	55.42

A-2-2 社会服务床位数和收养人员与上年比较

指 标	床位数（万张、%）			收养救助人数（万人、%）			年末床位利用率（%）
	2013年	2012年	比上年增减（%）	2013年	2012年	比上年增减（%）	
合计	**526.6**	**449.3**	**17.2**	**322.6**	**309.5**	**4.2**	**44.7**
老年人与残疾人服务机构	**493.7**	**416.5**	**18.5**	**307.5**	**293.6**	**4.7**	**44.9**
城市养老服务机构	97.1	78.2	24.2	53.5	44.9	19.2	38.4
农村养老服务机构	272.9	261.0	4.6	201.2	200.0	0.6	52.8
社会福利院	34.6	30.9	12.0	21.1	20.3	3.9	45.7
光荣院	8.8	8.4	4.8	5.5	5.3	3.8	43.3
荣誉军人康复医院	0.9	0.8	12.5	0.5	0.6	-16.7	47.5
复员军人疗养院	0.7	0.7		0.5	0.4	25.0	55.3
军休所（万户）	14.6	16.7	-12.6	15.9	18.5	-14.1	109.2
社区服务机构	64.1	19.8	223.7	9.3	3.6	158.3	5.6
智障与精神疾病服务机构	**7.4**	**6.7**	**10.4**	**6.0**	**5.8**	**3.4**	**65.0**
社会福利医院	4.5	4.1	9.8	3.7	3.6	2.8	65.0
复退军人精神病院	2.9	2.6	11.5	2.3	2.2	4.5	65.1
儿童收养救助服务机构	**9.8**	**8.7**	**12.6**	**5.6**	**5.4**	**3.7**	**44.5**
儿童福利院	8.7	7.7	13.0	5.4	5.2	3.8	49.2
流浪儿童救助保护中心	1.1	1.0	10.0	0.2	0.2		9.1
其他提供住宿的服务机构	**15.7**	**17.4**	**-9.8**	**3.5**	**4.7**	**-25.5**	**29.0**
生活无着人员救助管理站	9.7	9.0	7.8	2.2	2.1	4.8	21.3
军供站	3.7	3.8	-2.6				44.4
其他	2.3	4.6	-50.0	1.3	2.6	-50.0	36.5

A-2-3 儿童收养与上年比较

单位：人、%

指　标	2013年	2012年	比上年增减(%)
孤儿数	**548845**	**570075**	**-3.72**
集中供养孤儿	93899	95251	-1.42
社会散居孤儿	454946	474824	-4.19
儿童收养服务			
收养登记合计(人)	24460	27278	-10.33
中国公民收养登记	21230	23157	-8.32
# 香港居民	139	149	-6.71
澳门居民	6	17	-64.71
台湾居民	28	26	7.69
华侨	24	27	-11.11
外国人收养登记	3230	4121	-21.62
被收养人合计（人）	24491	27310	-10.32
# 女性	17164	19658	-12.69
残疾儿童	2632	3016	-12.73
社会福利机构抚养的儿童	9657	1760	448.69
# 被外国人收养	2695	308	775.00
社会福利机构抚养的弃婴	7814	12202	-35.96
# 被外国人收养	524	3771	-86.10
社会弃婴	2466	10398	-76.28
父母无力抚养的儿童	640	677	-5.47
# 被外国人收养	11	42	-73.81
其他	3914	2273	72.20

A-2-4 社会救助与上年比较

指　标	2013年	2012年	比上年增减(%)
救助总人数	**17602.9**	**17090.7**	**3.00**
城市			
城市居民最低生活保障人数（万人）	2064.2	2143.5	-3.7
# 女性	867.0	889.9	-2.6
残疾人	169.2	174.5	-3.0
三无对象	58.0	64.9	-10.6
# 老年人	330.3	339.3	-2.7
在职人员	45.1	49.6	-9.1
灵活就业	462.1	459.3	0.6
登记失业	365.5	400.4	-8.7
未登记失业	416.8	422.1	-1.3
在校生	303.2	318.3	-4.7
其他未成年人	141.3	154.5	-8.5
城市居民最低生活保障家庭数（万户）	1097.2	1114.9	-1.6
城市居民最低生活保障费（亿元）	756.7	674.3	12.2
城市居民最低生活保障平均标准（元/人、月）	373.3	330.1	13.1
城市居民最低生活保障平均支出水平（元/人、月）	264.2	239.1	10.5
城市“三无”救助人数（万人）	**8.6**	**9.9**	**-13.1**
城市临时救助户次数（万户次）	**323.0**	**256.6**	**25.9**
农村			
农村最低生活保障人数（万人）	5388.0	5344.5	0.81
农村最低生活保障家庭数（万户）	2931.1	2814.9	4.13
农村最低生活保障费（亿元）	866.9	718.0	20.74
农村最低生活保障平均标准（元/人、年）	2433.9	2067.8	17.70
农村最低生活保障平均支出水平（元/人、年）	1393.5	1247.9	11.67

A−2−4续表

指 标	2013年	2012年	比上年增减(%)
五保供养			
农村五保集中供养人数（万人）	183.5	185.3	-0.97
农村五保集中供养救济费（亿元）	74.7	63.6	17.45
农村五保集中供养平均标准(元/人、年)	4685.0	4060.9	15.37
农村五保集中供养平均支出水平(元/人、年)	4078.3	3496.6	16.64
农村五保分散供养人数（万人）	353.8	360.3	-1.80
农村五保分散供养救济费（亿元）	97.6	81.3	20.05
农村五保分散供养平均标准(元/人、年)	3498.5	3008.0	16.31
农村五保分散供养平均支出水平(元/人、年)	2724.3	2237.3	21.77
传统救济人数（万人）	**73.0**	**79.6**	**-8.29**
农村临时救助户次数（万户次）	**375.1**	**383.2**	**-2.11**
医疗救助			
民政部门直接救助人次数	2126.4	2173.7	-2.18
民政部门直接救助平均支出水平（元/人、次）	848.7	765.2	10.91
民政部门资助参加医疗保险人数（万人）	1490.1	1387.1	7.43
民政部门资助加医疗保险平均支出水平（元/人）	96.7	84.0	15.12
民政部门资助参加合作医疗人数（万人）	4868.7	4490.4	8.42
民政部门资助参加合作医疗平均支出水平（元/人）	61.7	57.5	7.30
生活无着人员救助（万人次）	**348.5**	**276.6**	**25.99**

A-2-5 各省城市居民最低生活保障平均标准与上年比较

单位：元/人、月

地　区	2013年	2012年	比上年增减(%)
全　国	**373.3**	**330.1**	**13.1**
北　京	580.0	520.0	11.5
天　津	600.0	520.0	15.4
河　北	378.5	335.0	13.0
山　西	351.1	308.5	13.8
内蒙古	460.3	407.7	12.9
辽　宁	411.5	366.6	12.2
吉　林	322.5	291.1	10.8
黑龙江	387.7	323.7	19.8
上　海	640.0	570.0	12.3
江　苏	485.1	434.3	11.7
浙　江	515.5	462.7	11.4
安　徽	380.5	339.4	12.1
福　建	363.3	324.1	12.1
江　西	395.7	345.9	14.4
山　东	417.7	364.1	14.7
河　南	309.2	271.8	13.8
湖　北	375.1	334.5	12.1
湖　南	356.1	304.5	17.0
广　东	380.4	314.0	21.2
广　西	334.7	270.5	23.8
海　南	353.3	316.2	11.7
重　庆	346.8	326.0	6.4
四　川	306.4	276.7	10.7
贵　州	347.6	308.0	12.8
云　南	323.9	284.4	13.9
西　藏	432.4	399.7	8.2
陕　西	374.7	363.1	3.2
甘　肃	279.0	251.3	11.0
青　海	330.8	310.8	6.4
宁　夏	287.6	252.5	13.9
新　疆	300.4	261.0	15.1

A-2-6 各省城市居民最低生活保障支出水平与上年比较

单位：元/人、月

地　区	2013年	2012年	比上年增减(%)
全　国	**264.2**	**239.1**	**10.5**
北　京	510.9	463.0	10.4
天　津	433.4	435.0	-0.4
河　北	231.9	217.0	6.9
山　西	240.7	221.9	8.5
内蒙古	367.5	329.3	11.6
辽　宁	312.7	296.3	5.5
吉　林	321.7	254.4	26.4
黑龙江	290.3	261.7	10.9
上　海	500.9	404.4	23.9
江　苏	296.5	251.7	17.8
浙　江	400.4	378.9	5.7
安　徽	271.5	257.3	5.5
福　建	240.4	199.6	20.5
江　西	226.5	202.0	12.1
山　东	286.4	250.2	14.5
河　南	207.2	189.3	9.4
湖　北	246.6	218.7	12.8
湖　南	244.4	236.8	3.2
广　东	253.6	196.6	29.0
广　西	228.3	212.3	7.6
海　南	237.1	233.3	1.6
重　庆	257.9	234.7	9.9
四　川	206.9	192.0	7.7
贵　州	245.9	222.2	10.7
云　南	224.2	205.1	9.3
西　藏	384.4	357.1	7.7
陕　西	308.3	261.0	18.1
甘　肃	268.9	223.8	20.2
青　海	267.9	248.5	7.8
宁　夏	202.5	203.5	-0.5
新　疆	266.7	244.1	9.3

A-2-7 社会捐赠与上年比较

指　标	2013年	2012年	比上年增减(%)
社会捐赠合计（万元）	**5750775.5**	**5787842.5**	**-0.6**
民政部门直接接收的捐赠（万元）	**1163269.0**	**1079883.1**	**7.7**
直接接收捐赠情况			
捐赠款数额（万元）	1076179.2	1016640.2	5.9
捐赠衣被合计（万件）	10405.0	12538.2	-17.0
捐赠其他物资价值（万元）	87089.8	63242.9	37.7
间接接收捐赠情况			
捐赠款数额（万元）	50195.9	50328.8	-0.3
捐赠衣被合计（万件）	739.1	485.6	52.2
捐赠其他物资价值（万元）	35081.4	54836.0	-36.0
受益人次数（万人次）	1246.0	1325.0	-6.0
社会捐赠接收工作站、点数（个）	30703	30920	-0.7
# 社会捐赠接收工作站数（个）	15149	15355	-1.3
慈善超市数（个）	9492	9053	4.8
各类社会组织接收捐赠（万元）	**4587506.5**	**4707959.4**	**-2.6**

注：由于社会组织年检工作滞后于年报汇总工作，社会组织捐赠数据为2012年。

A-2-8 自然灾害与上年比较

指　标	2013年	2012年	比上年增减(%)
农作物受灾情况总计(千公顷)			
受灾	31349.8	24962.0	25.6
绝收	3844.4	1826.3	110.5
旱灾			
受灾	14100.4	9339.8	51.0
绝收	1416.1	374.0	278.6
洪涝(含山体滑坡和泥石流)			
受灾	8765.8	7729.6	13.4
绝收	1539.4	889.0	73.2
风雹			
受灾	3387.3	2780.8	21.8
绝收	412.4	213.4	93.3
台风			
受灾	2670.1	3490.8	-23.5
绝收	289.5	206.3	40.3
地震			
受灾	115.1	3.2	3496.9
绝收	6.3	0.7	800.0
雪灾、低温冷冻			
受灾	2320.1	1617.8	43.4
绝收	180.7	142.9	26.5
人口受灾情况			
受灾（万人次）	38818.7	29421.7	31.9
死亡人口（含失踪）（人）	2284	1530	49.3
紧急转移人口（万人次）	1215	1109.6	9.5
损失情况			
倒塌房屋（万间）	87.5	90.6	-3.4
损坏房屋（万间）	770.3	427.9	80.0
直接经济损失（亿元）	5808.4	4185.5	38.8

A-2-9 国家优抚、安置对象与上年比较

单位：人

指 标	2013年	2012年	比上年增减(%)
重点优抚对象人数	**9504555**	**9444470**	**0.6**
抚恤	1178219	1260777	-6.5
烈士家属抚恤	240375	277712	-13.4
因公牺牲抚恤	55734	59478	-6.3
病故军人家属抚恤	70291	74521	-5.7
伤残人员抚恤	811819	849066	-4.4
补助	8326336	8183693	1.7
在乡红军老战士	647	757	-14.5
在乡西路军红军老战士	117	164	-28.7
红军失散人员	18976	25961	-26.9
在乡复员军人	1260945	1474790	-14.5
带病回乡退伍军人	1306479	1324325	-1.3
60岁以上农村籍退伍军人	3566766	3210986	
参战退役人员	1523763	1538805	-1.0
参试退役人员	199215	194987	2.2
部分60周岁以上烈士(含错杀被平反)人员子女	222838	173174	
其他补助人数	226590	239744	-5.5
本年接收离退休人员和安置复原干部数	**39343**	**19124**	**105.7**
军队干部（含地方）	11427	14341	-20.3
军队退休士官	570	1047	-45.6
军队无军籍职工	26709	2847	838.1
复员干部	637	889	-28.3
当年批准的烈士	**200**	**172**	**16.3**
零散烈士纪念建筑物	**13601**	**13151**	**3.4**
优待			
优待优抚对象（万户）	340.3	347.2	-2.0
# 军属（万户）	95.8	100.8	-5.0
优待金（亿元）	135.1	112.1	20.5
# 军属（亿元）	64.6	52.1	24.0

A-2-10 社区服务与上年比较

单位：万个、个、人、张

指　标	2013年	2012年	比上年增减(%)
社区服务			
社区服务机构总数	**25.2**	**20.0**	**26.0**
社区服务指导中心	890	809	10.0
社区服务中心	19014	15497	22.7
社区服务站	108377	87931	23.3
养老等其他社区服务机构	123658	95925	28.9
社区服务机构覆盖率	**36.9**	**29.5**	**25.1**
便民利民网点数	**35.9**	**39.7**	**-9.6**
日间照料床位	**417686**	**163390**	**155.6**
留宿照料床位	**223757**	**34557**	**547.5**
社区服务志愿者组织数	**12.8**	**9.3**	**37.6**

A-3-1 社会组织财务状况

单位：万元

指　标	2013年	2012年	比上年增减(%)
执行行政事业单位会计制度情况			
固定资产原价	230469.3	225515.6	2.2
上年结转和结余	21577.4	19823.3	8.8
本年收入合计	360143.7	335934.3	7.2
# 事业收入	25508.0	228323.0	-88.8
经营收入	22245.2	15970.2	39.3
本年支出合计	76056.5	382537.5	-80.1
# 工资福利支出	25773.6	60449.0	-57.4
商品和服务支出	14702.8	229712.0	-93.6
# 取暖费	390.0	1698.7	-77.0
差旅费	967.2	831.7	16.3
因公出国（境）费用		3340.0	-100.0
劳务费	660.6	702.3	-5.9
工会经费	351.3	3.0	11610.0
福利费	962.1	941.4	2.2
对个人和家庭的补助	6087.2	69289.2	-91.2
# 抚恤金	12.0	8.0	50.0
生活补助	142.1	328.6	-56.8
救济费	16.6	69289.2	-100.0
助学金	127.5	156.8	-18.7
奖励金	235.0	220.0	6.8
生产补贴	232.0	220.0	5.5
经营支出	197.6	35.0	464.6
收支结余	1053.5		
销售税金	1373.80	397.2	245.9

A-3-1续表

单位：万元

指　标	2013年	2012年	比上年增减(%)
执行民间非营利组织单位会计制度情况			
固定资产原价	14735831.8	14028087.9	5.0
上年结余	5849439.7	15701044.9	-62.7
本年收入合计	18488799.5	19842972.2	-6.8
# 捐赠收入	4587506.5	4707959.4	-2.6
会费收入	2290481.7	1689306.1	35.6
本年费用合计	16676894.8	14844816.1	12.3
# 业务活动成本	10519432.3	8929283.7	17.8
# 人员费用	3065213.8	2930113.9	4.6
日常费用	1915178.4	1534635.1	24.8
固定资产折旧	589198.6	519164.1	13.5
税费	153772.2	113066.7	36.0
管理费用	3894350.8	3583647.9	8.7
# 人员费用	1458542.1	1317960.5	10.7
日常费用	577864.5	552648.5	4.6
固定资产折旧	278985.0	238241.1	17.1
税费	99149.8	44940.3	120.6
净资产变动额	4398132.3	4579482.9	-4.0

A-3-2 社会组织与上年比较

单位：个

指　标	2013年	2012年	比上年增减(%)
社会组织合计	**547245**	**499268**	**9.6**
社会团体	**289026**	**271131**	**6.6**
按活动区域分			
中央级	1908	1873	1.9
省级	26569	25713	3.3
地级	72075	70064	2.9
县级	188474	173481	8.6
基金会	**3549**	**3029**	**17.2**
按性质分类			
公募性	1378	1316	4.7
非公募性	2137	1694	26.2
涉外基金会	8		
境外代表机构	26	19	36.8
民办非企业	**254670**	**225108**	**13.1**
按性质分类			
法人	194827	167028	16.6
合伙	6951	7105	-2.2
个体	52892	50975	3.8

A-3-3 自治组织财务状况

单位：万元

指　标	2013年	2012年	比上年增减(%)
执行企业会计制度单位情况			
固定资产原价	2710492.8	2562622.7	5.8
本年折旧	97026.5	65368.5	48.4
营业收入	1170136.8	597027.1	96.0
营业成本	597710.7	299646.4	99.5
营业税金及附加	17664.6	15250.6	15.8
销售费用	34488.4	47304.5	-27.1
管理费用	298542.1	300728.7	-0.7
# 税金	3606.1	6829.4	-47.2
差旅费	1130.1	1386.6	-18.5
财务费用	-26013.1	-588.2	43.2
# 利息支出	-44993.2	-13342.6	2.4
公允价值变动收益	33.1	41.4	-20.0
投资收益	34940.6	25360.3	37.8
营业利润	15205.5	18789.9	-19.1
营业外收入	64087.7		
#政府补助	40936.3		
应付职工薪酬	100144.0	91363.2	9.6

A-3-3续表

单位：万元

指　标	2013年	2012年	比上年增减(%)
执行行政事业单位会计制度情况			
固定资产原价	14761875.6	15476814.2	-4.6
上年结转和结余	782291.3	649574.2	20.4
本年收入合计	7356717.6	6984200.8	5.3
#事业收入	2054096.4	734756.1	179.6
经营收入	495967.9	290589.6	70.7
本年支出合计	6948677.2	6462119.2	7.5
#工资福利支出	1862284.5	1794886.1	3.8
商品和服务支出	1742872.7	1751296.8	-0.5
#取暖费	44509.3	47894.7	-7.1
差旅费	63052.8	70228.0	-10.2
因公出国（境）费用	1087.9	782.4	39.0
劳务费	167196.7	152258.2	9.8
工会经费	14104.7	23406.0	-39.7
福利费	129752.6	158130.9	-17.9
对个人和家庭的补助	284576.1	333285.2	-14.6
#抚恤金	3249.3	23327.4	-86.1
生活补助	66111.3	78707.8	-16.0
救济费	1745.6	1144.2	52.6
助学金	9155.5	10131.7	-9.6
奖励金	6210.2	662.1	838.0
生产补贴	2604.9	19881.8	-86.9
经营支出	28273.5	50717.9	-44.3
收支结余	12307.2		
销售税金	18291.0	14581.8	25.4
执行民间非营利组织单位会计制度情况			
固定资产原价	2218317.5	2483705.1	-10.7
上年结余	78777.9	52059.3	51.3
本年收入合计	2277945.9	2010688.2	13.3
# 捐赠收入	27077.5	32054.3	-15.5
会费收入	97933.6	78755.7	24.4
本年费用合计	840258.8	701893.2	19.7
# 业务活动成本	468877.2	376442.4	24.6
# 人员费用	146171.0	159826.6	-8.5
日常费用	76432.4	68175.6	12.1
固定资产折旧	88263.4	69550.7	26.9
税费	8037.7	2990.6	168.8
管理费用	219837.9	185177.9	18.7
# 人员费用	88616.2	74013.3	19.7
日常费用	45350.9	41447.5	9.4
固定资产折旧	19105.3	24691.1	-22.6
税费	5913.3	2198.9	168.9
净资产变动额	107540.8	60617.5	77.4

A-3-4 自治组织与上年比较

单位：个、人

指　标	2013年	2012年	比上年增减(%)
城市			
社区居委会	94620	91153	3.8
居民小组	1356954	1334923	1.7
居民委员会成员人数	484015	468786	3.2
# 中共党员	258341	253447	1.9
# 女性	234413	228933	2.4
居委会选举情况			
当年进行选举的居委会数	19674	27898	-29.5
当年参选人口数	47359318	66888743	-29.2
# 登记选民数	41752811	56201179	-25.7
# 参选人数	33317825	41714870	-20.1
农村			
村民委员会	588547	588475	0.0
村民小组	4664307	4693825	-0.6
村民委员会成员人数	2323113	2322731	0.0
# 中共党员	1344643	1340391	0.3
# 女性	526435	512780	2.7
村委会选举情况			
当年进行选举的村委会数	130763	81469	60.5
当年参选村人口数	169057485	88279294	91.5
# 登记选民数	157432303	76688850	105.3
# 参选人数	139419135	70099796	98.9

A-3-5 其他社会服务机构财务状况

单位：万元

指　标	2013年	2012年	比上年增减(%)
执行企业会计制度单位情况			
固定资产原价	767595.3	761162.0	0.8
本年折旧	71829.7	63738.4	12.7
营业收入	650281.3	649298.6	0.2
营业成本	211523.7	164215.7	28.8
营业税金及附加	5339.6	6370.6	-16.2
销售费用	79569.2	91198.9	-12.8
管理费用	128439.2	141112.3	-9.0
# 税金	5116.3	7352.8	-30.4
差旅费	1478.3	2224.8	-33.6
财务费用	7413.6	8156.8	-9.1
# 利息支出	3069.0	2049.4	49.8
公允价值变动收益		32.3	-100.0
投资收益	396.2	779.3	-49.2
营业利润	159947.2	101271.1	57.9
营业外收入	6575.1		
#政府补助	4195.2		
应付职工薪酬	54139.4	59815.6	-9.5

A-3-5续表

单位：万元

指　标	2013年	2012年	比上年增减(%)
执行行政事业单位会计制度情况			
固定资产原价	1875873.8	1734053.9	8.2
上年结转和结余	87091.2	80579.1	8.1
本年收入合计	1410394.2	1452829.6	-2.9
#事业收入	688144.0	661406.2	4.0
经营收入	248893.1	239258.2	4.0
本年支出合计	1363074.6	1372530.6	-0.7
#工资福利支出	310350.7	283359.1	9.5
商品和服务支出	513727.7	484926.5	5.9
#取暖费	7598.5	7448.6	2.0
差旅费	4824.8	6355.4	-24.1
因公出国（境）费用	78.3	168.7	-53.6
劳务费	32503.7	23873.7	36.1
工会经费	2061.8	1706.3	20.8
福利费	10034.0	12861.0	-22.0
对个人和家庭的补助	61841.9	55321.3	11.8
#抚恤金	1407.2	1012.0	39.1
生活补助	3113.0	2846.0	9.4
救济费	285.1	129.0	121.0
助学金	136.9	145.5	-5.9
奖励金	1143.3	567.7	101.4
生产补贴	1760.3	1032.6	70.5
经营支出	122128.3	89088.3	37.1
收支结余	38633.2		
销售税金	3254.3	3585.3	-9.2
执行民间非营利组织单位会计制度情况			
固定资产原价	26728.9	22842.7	17.0
上年结余	2144.3	2295.4	-6.6
本年收入合计	8069.1	11549.6	-30.1
# 捐赠收入	424.9	374.8	13.4
会费收入	209.0	158.5	31.9
本年费用合计	6377.1	9526.1	-33.1
# 业务活动成本	3582.0	6214.2	-42.4
# 人员费用	995.7	1407.8	-29.3
日常费用	917.4	856.7	7.1
固定资产折旧	355.4	222.1	60.0
税费	37.4	256.2	-85.4
管理费用	1615.9	2190.7	-26.2
# 人员费用	556.8	629.4	-11.5
日常费用	430.7	330.3	30.4
固定资产折旧	184.1	264.3	-30.3
税费	3.9	229.0	-98.3
净资产变动额	620.0	858.7	-27.8

A-3-6 其他社会服务与上年比较

指　标	2013年	2012年	比上年增减(%)
婚姻服务			
结婚登记	13469267	13235949	1.8
内地居民登记结婚对数（对）	13414255	13182663	1.8
初婚人数（人）	23859646	23611741	1.0
再婚人数（人）	3078888	2860157	7.6
其中：女性	1565397	1457935	7.4
恢复结婚（对）	298766	229607	30.1
涉外及华侨、港澳台居民登记结婚（对数）	6538	53286	-87.7
每千居民之结婚宗数（‰）	9.9	9.8	0.1(千分点)
办理离婚登记（对）	3500111	3103837	12.8
民政部门办理离婚对数（对）	2815369	2423393	16.2
内地居民办理离婚	2808831	2417232	16.2
华侨、港澳台居民登记离婚	6538	6161	6.1
各级法院办理离婚件数（件）	684742	680444	0.6
每千居民之离婚宗数（‰）	2.6	2.3	0.3 (千分点)
办理婚姻登记业务的处数（处）	6780		
殡葬服务			
火化炉数(台)	5743	5539	3.7
全年处理遗体数（具）	4688910	4777014	-1.8
火化率(%)	48.2	49.5	-1.3 (百分点)
穴位数（个）	13039598	12172893	7.1
安葬数（具）	8932865	8195456	9.0

社会服务
历年统计资料

04

B-1-1 县及以上行政区划

单位：个

年份	省级	地级（不含地级市）	县级（不含县级市、市辖区）	市			市辖区	县级合计
					地级	县级		
1978	30	212	2153	193	98	92	408	2653
1979	30	211	2153	216	104	109	428	2690
1980	30	211	2151	223	107	113	511	2775
1981	30	208	2144	233	108	122	514	2780
1982	30	210	2140	245	112	130	527	2797
1983	30	178	2091	289	144	142	552	2785
1984	30	175	2069	300	147	150	595	2814
1985	30	165	2046	324	162	159	621	2826
1986	30	159	2017	353	166	184	629	2830
1987	30	156	1986	381	170	208	632	2826
1988	31	151	1936	434	183	248	647	2831
1989	31	151	1919	450	185	262	648	2829
1990	31	151	1903	467	185	279	651	2833
1991	31	151	1894	479	187	289	650	2833
1992	31	148	1848	517	191	323	662	2833
1993	31	139	1795	570	196	371	669	2835
1994	31	127	1735	622	206	413	697	2845
1995	31	124	1716	640	210	427	706	2849
1996	31	117	1696	666	218	445	717	2858
1997	33	110	1693	668	222	442	727	2862
1998	33	104	1689	668	227	437	737	2863
1999	34	95	1682	667	236	427	749	2858
2000	34	74	1674	663	259	400	787	2861
2001	34	67	1660	662	265	393	808	2861
2002	34	57	1649	660	275	381	830	2860
2003	34	51	1642	660	282	374	845	2861
2004	34	50	1636	661	283	374	852	2862
2005	34	50	1636	661	283	374	852	2862
2006	34	50	1635	656	283	369	856	2860
2007	34	50	1635	655	283	368	856	2859
2008	34	50	1635	655	283	368	856	2859
2009	34	50	1636	654	283	367	855	2858
2010	34	50	1633	657	283	370	853	2856
2011	34	48	1627	657	284	369	857	2853
2012	34	48	1624	657	285	368	860	2852
2013	34	47	1613	658	286	368	872	2853

B-1-2 乡镇级行政区划

单位：个

年 份	乡镇级区划数	镇数	乡数	#民族乡	街道办事处	区公所
1978	6195	2173				4022
1979	10424	2361			4444	3619
1980						
1981	11434	2678			4965	3791
1982						
1983	49695	2968	35514		5304	5909
1984	106439	7186	85290		5844	8119
1985	104900	9140	82450	3144	5402	7908
1986	83954	10718	61353	2936	5718	6165
1987	81025	11103	58739	3020	5680	5503
1988	65345	11481	45195	1571	5099	3570
1989	65419	11873	44624	1755	5420	3502
1990	65188	12084	44397	1980	5269	3438
1991	63391	12455	42654	1403	5186	3096
1992	54830	14539	33827	1348	5233	1231
1993	54863	15805	32445	1351	5470	1143
1994	54605	16702	31463	1322	5372	1068
1995	53360	17532	29502	1330	5596	730
1996	51336	18171	27056	1383	5565	544
1997	50967	18925	25966	1545	5678	398
1998	50999	19216	25712	1517	5732	339
1999	50750	19756	24745	1222	5904	345
2000	51024	20312	24555	1356	5902	255
2001	46369	20358	20012	1165	5972	27
2002	44822	20600	18640	1162	5516	66
2003	44067	20226	18064	1149	5751	26
2004	43275	19892	17534	1127	5829	20
2005	41636	19522	15951	1093	6152	11
2006	41040	19369	15306	1089	6355	10
2007	40813	19249	15120	1094	6434	10
2008	40828	19234	15067	1097	6524	3
2009	40858	19322	14848	1098	6686	2
2010	40906	19410	14571	1096	6923	2
2011	40466	19683	13587	1086	7194	2
2012	40446	19881	13281	1064	7282	2
2013	40497	20117	12812	1035	7566	2

B-1-3 全国人口情况

单位：万人、%

年 份	总人口			农村贫困人口	65岁及以上老年人口	65岁及以上人口比重	60岁及以上老年人口	60岁及以上人口比重	出生人口	死亡人口	当年净增人口
		城 镇	乡 村								
1978	96259	17245	79014	25000							
1979	97542	18495	79047								1283
1980	98705	19140	79565								1163
1981	100072	20171	79901								1367
1982	101654	21480	80174		4991	4.9					1469
1983	103008	22274	80734								954
1984	104357	24017	80340	12800							
1985	105851	25094	80757	12500							1164
1986	107507	26366	81141	13100							1476
1987	109300	27674	81626	12200	5968	5.4					1500
1988	111026	28661	82365	9600							1541
1989	112704	29540	83164	10200							1577
1990	114333	30195	84138	8500	6368	5.6			2391	762	1629
1991	115823	31203	84260						2258	768	1490
1992	117171	32175	84996	8000					2119	771	1348
1993	118517	33173	85344						2126	780	1346
1994	119850	34169	85681	7000					2104	771	1333
1995	121121	35174	85947	6540	7510	6.2			2063	792	1271
1996	122389	37304	85085		7833	6.4			2067	799	1268
1997	123626	39449	84177	4962	8085	6.5			2038	801	1237
1998	124761	41608	83153	4210	8359	6.7			1942	807	1135
1999	125786	43748	82038	3412	8679	6.9			1834	809	1025
2000	126743	45906	80837	3209	8821	7.0			1771	814	957
2001	127627	48064	79563	2927	9062	7.1			1702	818	884
2002	128453	50212	78241	2820	9377	7.3			1647	821	826
2003	129227	52376	76851	2900	9692	7.5			1599	825	774
2004	129988	54283	75705	2610	9857	7.6			1593	832	761
2005	130756	56212	74544	2365	10055	7.7	14408	11.03	1617	849	768
2006	131448	57706	73742	2148	10419	7.9	14901	11.3	1584	892	692
2007	132129	59379	72750	4320	10636	8.1	15340	11.6	1594	913	681
2008	132802	60667	72135	4007	10956	8.3	15989	12	1608	935	673
2009	133450	62186	71288	3597	11309	8.5	16714	12.5	1615	943	672
2010	134091	66558	67415	2688	11883.2	8.9	17764.9	13.26	1596	953	642
2011	134735	69079	65656	12238	12288	9.1	18499	13.7	1604	960	644
2012	135404	71182	64222	9899	12714	9.4	19390	14.3	1635	966	669
2013	136072	73111	62961	8249	13161	9.7	20243	14.9	1640	972	668

注：本表资料来源于国家统计局。

B-1-4 城乡居民生活水平、职工工资和住房

单位：元、平方米/人

年　份	平均消费水平			职工平均工资	人均住宅建筑面积
	全　国	农　村	城　镇		
1978	184	138	405	615	6.7
1979	208	159	425	668	6.9
1980	238	178	489	762	7.2
1981	264	201	521	772	7.7
1982	288	223	536	798	8.2
1983	316	250	558	826	8.7
1984	361	287	618	974	9.1
1985	446	349	765	1148	10.0
1986	497	378	872	1329	12.4
1987	565	421	998	1459	12.7
1988	714	509	1311	1747	13.0
1989	788	549	1466	1935	13.5
1990	833	560	1596	2140	13.7
1991	932	602	1840	2340	14.2
1992	1116	688	2262	2711	14.8
1993	1393	805	2924	3371	15.2
1994	1833	1038	3852	4538	15.7
1995	2355	1313	4931	5348	16.3
1996	2789	1626	5532	5980	17.0
1997	3002	1722	5823	6444	17.8
1998	3159	1730	6109	7446	18.7
1999	3346	1766	6405	8319	19.4
2000	3632	1860	6850	9333	20.3
2001	3887	1969	7161	10834	20.8
2002	4144	2062	7486	12373	22.8
2003	4475	2103	8060	13969	23.7
2004	5032	2319	8912	15920	25.0
2005	5596	2657	9593	18200	26.1
2006	6299	2950	10618	20856	27.1
2007	7310	3347	12130	24721	31.6
2008	8430	3901	13653	28898	32.4
2009	9283	4163	14904	32244	32.5
2010	10522	4700	16546	36539	32.9
2011	12570	5870	19108	41799	34.5
2012	14110	6632	21035	46769	35.0
2013	15632	7409	22880	51474	

注：本表资料来源于国家统计局。

B-1-5 城乡居民家庭人均收入和消费支出

单位：元、%

年 份	城镇居民可支配收入	城镇居民家庭		农民纯收入	农村居民家庭	
		人均生活消费支出	恩格尔系数		人均生活消费支出	恩格尔系数
1978	343	311	57.5	134	116	67.7
1979				161	135	64.0
1980	478	412	56.9	191	162	61.8
1981	*458*	457	56.7	223	191	59.8
1982	*495*	471	58.6	270	220	60.6
1983	*526*	506	59.2	310	248	59.4
1984	*608*	559	58.0	355	274	59.3
1985	739	673	52.2	398	317	57.8
1986	900	799	52.4	424	357	56.5
1987	1002	884	53.5	463	398	55.8
1988	1181	1104	51.4	545	477	54.0
1989	1376	1211	54.5	602	535	54.8
1990	1510	1279	54.2	686	585	58.8
1991	1701	1454	53.8	709	620	57.6
1992	2027	1672	53.0	784	659	57.6
1993	2577	2111	50.3	922	770	58.1
1994	3496	2851	50.0	1221	1017	58.9
1995	4283	3538	51.0	1578	1310	58.6
1996	4839	3919	48.8	1926	1572	56.3
1997	5160	4186	46.6	2090	1617	55.1
1998	5425	4332	44.7	2162	1590	53.4
1999	5854	4616	42.1	2210	1577	52.6
2000	6280	4998	39.4	2253	1670	49.1
2001	6860	5309	38.2	2366	1741	47.7
2002	7703	6030	37.7	2476	1834	46.2
2003	8472	6511	37.1	2622	1943	45.6
2004	9422	7182	37.7	2936	2185	47.2
2005	10493	7943	36.7	3255	2555	45.5
2006	11759	8697	35.8	3587	2829	43.0
2007	13786	9997	36.3	4140	3224	43.1
2008	15781	11243	37.9	4761	3661	43.7
2009	17175	11265	36.5	5153	3993	41.0
2010	19109	13471	35.7	5919	4382	41.1
2011	21810	15161	36.3	6977	5221	40.4
2012	24565	16674	36.2	7917	5908	39.3
2013	26955	18023	35.0	8896	6626	37.7

注：1.本表资料来源于国家统计局。
2.斜体下划线为生活费支出，与其他年份不可比。

B-1-6 社会服务机构（按登记类型分类）

单位：万个

年 份	合 计	事业单位	福利企业	社会组织	自治组织	行政机关
1978	1.1	1.1	0.1			
1979	1.3	1.2	0.1			
1980	1.4	1.3	0.1			
1981	1.5	1.3	0.2			
1982	1.7	1.6	0.2			
1983	40.2	1.9	0.6		37.7	
1984	103.6	2.6	0.7		100.3	
1985	107.7	3.3	1.5		103.0	
1986	101.2	3.9	2.0		95.3	
1987	100.1	4.2	2.8		93.2	
1988	106.7	4.3	4.0	0.4	97.8	
1989	111.8	4.4	4.2	0.5	102.8	
1990	119.8	4.5	4.2	1.1	110.0	
1991	129.2	4.7	4.4	8.3	111.9	
1992	136.1	4.8	5.0	15.5	110.8	
1993	139.7	5.3	5.7	16.8	112.0	
1994	140.3	5.2	6.0	17.4	111.7	
1995	133.7	5.2	6.0	18.1	104.4	
1996	133.9	5.3	5.9	18.5	104.2	
1997	131.4	5.3	5.6	18.1	102.4	
1998	122.2	5.4	5.1	16.6	95.2	
1999	115.7	5.4	4.5	14.3	91.6	
2000	109.5	6.1	4.1	15.3	84.0	
2001	110.4	5.7	3.8	21.1	79.2	0.6
2002	111.0	5.8	3.6	24.5	76.7	0.5
2003	110.3	5.8	3.4	26.7	74.0	0.4
2004	111.5	6.7	3.2	28.9	72.2	0.4
2005	113.0	6.6	3.1	32.0	70.9	0.4
2006	116.0	6.7	3.0	35.4	70.5	0.4
2007	118.0	7.0	2.5	38.7	69.5	0.3
2008	119.6	6.6	2.4	41.4	68.8	0.4
2009	126.2	12.1	2.3	43.1	68.4	0.3
2010	126.9	11.6	2.2	44.6	68.2	0.3
2011	129.8	13.1	2.2	46.2	67.9	0.3
2012	146.5	26.3	2	49.9	68	0.3
2013	156.5	31.4	1.8	54.7	68.3	0.3

B-1-7 社会服务机构（按行业分类分）

单位：万个

年 份	合 计	社会工作	成员组织			其他社会服务	其他事业单位	民政系统行政机关
				社会组织	自治组织			
1978	1.1	0.8				0.3		
1979	1.3	1.0				0.3		
1980	1.4	1.1				0.3		
1981	1.5	1.2				0.3		
1982	1.7	1.4				0.3		
1983	40.2	2.2	37.7		37.7	0.3		
1984	103.6	3.0	100.3		100.3	0.3		
1985	107.7	4.5	103.0		103.0	0.3		
1986	101.2	5.6	95.3		95.3	0.3		
1987	100.1	6.6	93.2		93.2	0.3		
1988	106.7	8.1	98.3	0.4	97.8	0.3		
1989	111.8	8.3	103.3	0.5	102.8	0.3		
1990	119.8	8.4	111.1	1.1	110.0	0.3		
1991	129.2	8.7	120.2	8.3	111.9	0.3		
1992	136.1	9.5	126.3	15.5	110.8	0.3		
1993	139.7	10.7	128.7	16.8	112.0	0.3		
1994	140.3	10.9	129.1	17.4	111.7	0.3		
1995	133.6	10.9	122.4	18.1	104.4	0.3		
1996	133.9	10.9	122.7	18.5	104.2	0.3		
1997	131.4	10.6	120.5	18.1	102.4	0.3		
1998	122.2	10.2	111.8	16.6	95.2	0.3		
1999	115.7	9.5	105.9	14.3	91.6	0.3		
2000	109.5	9.8	99.3	15.3	84.0	0.3		
2001	110.4	9.2	100.3	21.1	79.2	0.3		0.6
2002	111.0	9.1	101.2	24.5	76.7	0.3		0.5
2003	110.3	8.9	100.7	26.7	74.0	0.3		0.4
2004	111.5	9.6	101.1	28.9	72.2	0.3		0.4
2005	113.0	9.5	102.9	32.0	70.9	0.3		0.4
2006	116.0	9.2	105.9	35.4	70.5	0.5		0.4
2007	118.0	9.0	108.2	38.7	69.5	0.5		0.3
2008	119.6	8.4	110.2	41.4	68.8	0.6		0.4
2009	126.2	13.8	111.5	43.1	68.4	0.6		0.3
2010	126.9	13.2	112.8	44.6	68.2	0.6		0.3
2011	129.8	14.6	114.1	46.2	67.9	0.7		0.3
2012	146.5	27.5	117.9	49.9	68	0.6	0.2	0.3
2013	156.5	32.3	123.0	54.7	68.3	0.6	0.2	0.3

注：2012年开始社会工作中包含其他社区服务机构。

B-1-8 社会服务机构职工

单位：万人

年份	合计	社会工作	成员组织			其他社会服务	其他事业单位	行政机关	乡、镇民政助理员
				社会组织	自治组织				
1978	19.7	19.7							
1979	21.9	21.9							
1980	25.3	25.3							
1981	27.8	27.8							
1982	29.1	29.1							
1983	41.5	41.5							
1984	48.0	48.0							
1985	497.9	83.4	414.5		414.5				
1986	506.2	104.1	402.1		402.1				
1987	529.1	132.2	396.9		396.9				
1988	569.6	166.9	402.7		402.7				
1989	587.5	171.5	416.0		416.0				
1990	631.8	179.3	452.5		452.5				
1991	661.2	192.7	468.5		468.5				
1992	691.3	213.9	477.4		477.4				
1993	733.9	230.0	503.9		503.9				
1994	749.6	243.1	506.5		506.5				
1995	694.2	245.7	448.5		448.5				
1996	676.0	229.2	446.8		446.8				
1997	681.1	238.2	428.6		428.6			14.3	
1998	649.2	225.0	409.4		409.4			14.8	
1999	629.9	213.7	401.4		401.4			14.8	5.9
2000	580.3	203.4	363.4		363.4			13.5	5.7
2001	577.3	202.4	362.8		362.8			12.1	4.6
2002	537.4	192.4	333.8		333.8			11.2	4.1
2003	562.6	193.0	358.8		358.8			10.8	3.7
2004	543.7	197.8	334.6		334.6			11.3	3.9
2005	509.0	189.5	311.1		311.1			8.4	5.5
2006	903.8	183.0	712.5	425.2	287.3			8.3	4.6
2007	938.4	190.4	739.6	456.9	282.7			8.4	4.7
2008	967.4	206.9	751.8	475.8	276.0			8.7	4.5
2009	1038.1	207.5	821.8	544.7	277.1			8.8	4.7
2010	1138.4	234.0	895.5	618.2	277.3			8.9	5.0
2011	1129.8	235.7	876.6	599.3	277.3	8.5		9.0	4.9
2012	1154.0	241.4	892.5	613.3	279.2	8.6	2.2	9.3	5.2
2013	1207.0	269.2	917.3	636.6	280.7	9.1	2.0	9.4	5.2

注：合计数不含乡镇助理员。

B-1-9 社会工作师

单位：人

年　份	报考人数	考试通过人数	社会服务行业现在人数	行政机关	社会工作	成员组织	其他社会服务	其他事业单位
2008	77698	4192	3144	286	1496	1191	171	
2009	46015	4227	7360	758	3809	2544	249	
2010	25547	2664	9901	922	5176	3473	330	
2011	25500	2338	11604	854	5165	5247	338	
2012	34245	6104	18215	1114	6276	10056	443	326
2013	48287	11658	23197	1280	8014	12994	560	349

B-1-10 助理社会工作师

单位：人

年　份	报考人数	考试通过人数	社会服务行业现在人数	行政机关	社会工作	成员组织	其他社会服务	其他事业单位
2008	60139	20648	17574	609	4727	11840	398	
2009	38204	6611	24095	798	5530	17388	379	
2010	46047	5428	24700	969	6724	16517	490	
2011	54515	8068	29626	963	10686	17419	558	
2012	92621	23846	37599	1163	11998	23513	645	280
2013	121937	27300	44565	1264	15471	26871	694	265

B-1-11 社会服务职业技能人员情况

单位：人

年份	合格总人数	养老护理员	假肢类技能人员	孤残儿童护理员	灾害信息员	殡葬类技能人员
2007	114		21			93
2008	1027		139			888
2009	3575	24	302	23	1397	1829
2010	16809	171	252	196	14554	1636
2011	33240	1538	164	1270	27842	2426
2012	34931	4220	219	2590	25608	2294
2013	17612	4072	193	2216	8989	2142

说明：1.以上数据为民政部职业技能鉴定指导中心及分布在全国31个省、自治区、直辖市76个鉴定站鉴定人数和竞赛晋级人数（不含地方自行组织的鉴定人数）。

2.殡葬类职业包括：殡仪服务员（初中高技师4个级别）、遗体接运工（初中高3个级别）、遗体防腐师（初中高技师高级技师5个级别）、遗体整容师（初中高技师高级技师5个级别）、遗体火化师（初中高技师高级技师5个级别）、墓地管理员（初中高技师4个级别）。

3.假肢类职业包括：假肢师（初中高技师高级技师5个级别）、矫形器师（初中高技师高级技师5个级别）。

B-1-12 社会服务增加值

单位：亿元

年份	合计	民政系统行政机关	社会工作	成员组织	社会组织	自治组织	其他社会服务	其他事业单位
2006	1344.8	72.2	833.6	385.3	112.2	273.1	53.7	
2007	1501.2	83.7	776.7	588.6	307.6	281.0	52.2	
2008	1650.1	108.7	780.8	701.0	372.4	328.6	59.6	
2009	1849.4	141.1	777.7	864.1	493.1	371.0	66.5	
2010	2014.5	190.8	912.4	841.1	531.2	309.9	70.2	
2011	2459.8	212.9	1152.2	1023.3	660.0	363.3	71.4	
2012	2321.6	192.7	1125.2	900.7	525.6	375.1	84.2	18.8
2013	2463.6	211.7	1167.1	972.9	571.1	401.8	91.8	20.1

B-1-13 社会服务机构固定资产原值

单位：亿元

年份	合计	社会工作	成员组织	社会组织	自治组织	其他社会服务	其他事业单位	行政机关
1978								
1979								
1980								
1981								
1982								
1983	13.0	13.0						
1984	14.9	14.9						
1985	20.1	20.1						
1986	24.2	24.2						
1987	28.7	28.7						
1988	40.8	40.8						
1989	44.1	44.1						
1990	51.7	51.7						
1991	63.6	63.6						
1992	75.6	75.6						
1993	100.3	100.3						
1994	119.0	119.0						
1995	142.6	142.6						
1996	168.1	168.1						
1997	211.5	211.5						
1998	962.4	962.4						
1999	1017.3	1017.3						
2000	1199.3	1199.3						
2001	1317.0	1317.0						
2002	1394.9	1394.9						
2003	1644.3	1644.3						
2004	1818.4	1755.6						62.8
2005	3097.8	1858.0	1174.9		1174.9			64.9
2006	4066.7	2103.0	1869.4	423.0	1446.4			94.3
2007	3973.0	1934.3	1905.9	682.0	1223.9			132.8
2008	4592.8	2186.8	2273.1	805.8	1467.3			132.9
2009	5198.0	2326.4	2752.4	1030	1722.4			119.2
2010	6589.3	2671.9	3795.6	1864.1	1931.5			121.8
2011	6989.8	2790.4	3684.2	1885.0	1799.2	231		284.2
2012	7019.5	2898.9	3477.7	1425.4	2052.3	251.8	47	344.1
2013	6995.5	3030.7	3465.7	1496.6	1969.1	267	46.8	185.4

B-1-14 历年财政支出和社会服务经费支出情况

单位：亿元

年 份	国家财政支出	民政事业费支出	占财政支出%	年 份	国家财政支出	民政事业费支出	占财政支出%
1950	68.04	1.32	1.94	1981	1138.41	19.23	1.69
1951	122.32	1.37	1.12	1982	1229.98	19.19	1.56
1952	175.78	2.83	1.61	1983	1409.52	21.61	1.53
1953	220.5	3.55	1.61	1984	1701.02	24.24	1.43
1954	280.93	6.04	2.15	1985	2004.25	29.58	1.48
1955	474.29	4.98	1.05	**“七五”时期**	**12865.67**	**208.49**	**1.62**
“一五”时期	**1367.89**	**25.99**	**1.90**	1986	2204.91	34.41	1.56
1956	536.79	5.69	1.06	1987	2262.18	35.93	1.59
1957	303.43	5.31	1.75	1988	2491.21	39.56	1.59
1958	408.75	3.27	0.80	1989	2823.78	46.65	1.65
1959	553.09	4.48	0.81	1990	3083.59	51.94	1.68
1960	652.25	7.24	1.11	**“八五”时期**	**24387.46**	**386.59**	**1.59**
“二五”时期	**3760.99**	**53.03**	**1.41**	1991	3386.62	62.54	1.85
1961	367.66	9.89	2.69	1992	3742.2	63.71	1.70
1962	305.33	7.45	2.44	1993	4642.3	69.87	1.51
1963	339.15	8.75	2.58	1994	5792.62	87.02	1.50
1964	398.77	16.15	4.05	1995	6823.72	103.45	1.52
1965	467.1	10.79	2.31	**“九五”时期**	**57043.46**	**840.90**	**1.47**
“三五”时期	**2523.24**	**35.83**	**1.42**	1996	7937.55	121.15	1.53
1966	540.49	8.81	1.63	1997	9233.56	133.52	1.45
1967	441.4	8.21	1.86	1998	10798.18	161.84	1.50
1968	359.62	5.61	1.56	1999	13187.67	194.70	1.48
1969	525.2	6.67	1.27	2000	15886.5	229.69	1.45
1970	646.53	6.53	1.01	**“十五”时期**	**127800.69**	**2471.74**	**1.93**
“四五”时期	**3924.37**	**46.70**	**1.19**	2001	18902.58	284.75	1.51
1971	734.41	6.83	0.93	2002	22053.15	392.27	1.78
1972	768.87	8.15	1.06	2003	24649.95	498.92	2.02
1973	810.57	9.97	1.23	2004	28486.89	577.39	2.03
1974	792.98	9.04	1.14	2005	33708.12	718.41	2.13
1975	820	12.71	1.55	**“十一五”时期**	**317654.99**	**9156.70**	**2.88**
“五五”时期	**5198.77**	**84.22**	**1.62**	2006	40213.16	915.35	2.28
1976	804.48	16.17	2.01	2007	49565.4	1215.49	2.45
1977	842.27	18.53	2.20	2008	62427.03	2146.45	3.44
1978	1122.09	13.71	1.22	2009	75874	2181.90	2.88
1979	1281.79	18.33	1.43	2010	89575.4	2697.51	3.01
1980	1228.83	17.48	1.42	**“十二五”时期**	**374385.92**	**11189.38**	**2.99**
“六五”时期	**7483.18**	**113.85**	**1.52**	2011	108930	3229.1	2.96
				2012	125712	3683.7	2.93
				2013	139744	4276.5	3.06

B-1-15 按科目分的社会服务经费

单位：亿元

年　份	民政事业费总支出	抚恤费	离休费	社会福利及其他社会救济费	最低生活保障事业费	自然灾害救济费	退休费	其他民政事业费
1978	13.7	2.8		4.4		4.2	2.3	
1979	18.4	3.5		5.2		6.8	2.9	
1980	17.5	4.4		5.2		4.5	3.4	
“六五”时期	**114.2**	**27.3**	**0.9**	**32.1**		**35.2**	**16.8**	**1.7**
1981	19.2	4.4		5.1		6.3	3.4	
1982	19.6	4.8		5.1		6.0	3.5	
1983	21.6	5.3		6.5		6.4	3.4	
1984	24.2	6.1	0.2	8.0		6.9	3.0	
1985	29.6	6.7	0.7	7.4		9.6	3.5	1.7
“七五”时期	**208.4**	**59.2**	**11.4**	**46.7**		**56.4**	**22.0**	**12.8**
1986	34.4	8.4	1.2	8.3		10.7	3.8	1.9
1987	35.9	9.6	1.8	8.6		9.9	4.1	2
1988	39.6	11	2.3	9		10.4	4.3	2.5
1989	46.6	14	2.9	10		12.3	4.6	2.9
1990	51.9	16.2	3.2	10.8		13.1	5.2	3.5
“八五”时期	**386.6**	**107.8**	**23.2**	**75.6**		**94.1**	**45.5**	**40.5**
1991	62.5	16.8	3.6	11.7		20.9	5.4	4.2
1992	63.7	18	4.2	12.4		17.1	6.6	5.4
1993	69.9	20.1	3.6	14.5		14.9	8.3	8.4
1994	87	24.4	5.5	17.3		17.7	12.1	10.1
1995	103.5	28.5	6.3	19.7		23.5	13.1	12.4

年　份	民政事业费总支出	抚恤费	军队离退休、退职费	社会福利及其他社会救济费	最低生活保障事业费	自然灾害救济费	地方离、退休人员费	其他民政事业费
“九五”时期	**840.9**	**220.6**	**76.9**	**201.8**	**48.7**	**171.5**	**58.0**	**112.2**
1996	121.2	31.9	6.2	22.8	3	30.8	13.9	15.5
1997	133.5	36.1	12.4	27.1	2.9	28.7	10.3	19
1998	161.8	39.4	15.2	34	7.1	41.2	10.9	21.3
1999	194.7	49.7	18.4	52.5	13.8	35.6	11.2	27.2
2000	229.7	63.5	24.7	65.4	21.9	35.2	11.7	29.2

年　份	民政事业费总支出	抚恤费	退役安置	社会福利	社会救助	城市低保及其他城市社会救济	农村低保及其他农村社会救济	医疗救助	自然灾害生活救助	离退休人员经费	其他
“十五”时期	**2471.8**	**479.8**	**302.7**	**444.7**		**668**	**127.6**	**11**	**247.6**	**66.9**	**273.7**
2001	284.8	69.5	31.2	90.6		41.6			41	13	39.5
2002	392.3	74.7	49.5	167.5		108.7			40	13.2	47.3
2003	498.9	87.9	59	78.9	153.1	153.1			52.9	13.1	54
2004	577.4	104.1	74.1	52.1	223.6	172.7	47.7	3.2	51.1	13.9	58.5
2005	718.4	143.6	88.9	55.6	279.6	191.9	79.9	7.8	62.6	13.7	74.4
“十一五”时期	**9156.8**	**1316.2**	**956**	**490**	**3673.6**	**1941.7**	**1710.7**	**436.1**	**1205**	**125.7**	**975.4**
2006	915.4	178.8	115.7	65.3	372	224.2	126.6	21.2	79	14	90.6
2007	1215.5	210.8	165	87.6	509.7	277.4	189.8	42.5	79.8	24.8	137.8
2008	2146.5	253.6	180.6	103.1	806.7	393.4	326.8	86.5	609.8	26.5	166.2
2009	2181.9	310.3	225.7	124.1	1098.1	482.1	487.9	128.1	199.2	30	194.5
2010	2697.5	362.7	269	109.9	1302	564.6	579.6	157.8	237.2	30.4	386.3

年　份	民政事业费总支出	抚恤费	退役安置	社会福利	社会救助	城乡低保	其他社会救助	医疗救助	自然灾害生活救助	离退休人员经费	其他
“十二五”时期	**11189.3**	**1563.7**	**1109.7**	**949.3**	**5804.8**	**4343.5**	**757**	**704.3**	**470.8**	**117.9**	**1173.3**
2011	3229.1	428.3	302.3	232.2	1766.3	1327.6	222.4	216.3	128.7	35.3	336.0
2012	3683.7	517	372.1	319.5	1866.1	1392.3	243.2	230.6	163.4	39	406.7
2013	4276.5	618.4	435.3	397.6	2172.4	1623.6	291.4	257.4	178.7	43.6	430.6

B-1-16 中央级事业费及中央转移支付社会服务费

单位：万元

年　份	合　计	中央级民政事业费	中央专项转移支付	抚恤、退休、救济费	救　灾	社会福利救济事业费	其　他
1978	11	11					
1979	44	44					
1980	103	103					
“六五”时期	**335594**	**1108**	**334486**	**63306**	**270745**	**220**	**215**
1981	138	138					
1982	74120	78	74042	14247	59795		
1983	74368	163	74205	14205	60000		
1984	78872	286	78586	18586	60000		

年　份	合　计	中央级民政事业费	中央专项转移支付	抚　恤	安　置	救　灾	社会福利救济事业费	其　他
1985	108096	443	107653	9698	6570	90950	220	215
“七五”时期	**778310**	**9267**	**769043**	**148718**	**105230**	**512500**		
1986	132802	2526	130276	16396	9285	102000		
1987	133877	2742	131135	21726	19409	90000		
1988	158355	1297	157058	24110	21948	111000		
1989	174374	1185	173189	43206	26483	103500		
1990	178902	1517	177385	43280	28105	106000		
“八五”时期	**1488090**	**15897**	**1472193**	**328272**	**315101**	**828820**		
1991	309432	1792	307640	49010	34210	224420		
1992	209360	3217	206143	52156	40587	113400		
1993	238083	3108	234975	60494	53481	121000		
1994	353831	4077	349754	79084	90670	180000		
1995	377384	3703	373681	87528	96153	190000		
“九五”时期	**2943934**	**104302**	**2839632**	**749824**	**773058**	**1122750**	**190000**	**4000**
1996	426354	6371	419983	102394	102589	215000		
1997	455309	5954	449355	110430	114925	220000		4000
1998	568049	50783	517266	120000	149516	247750		

年　份	合　计（亿元）	中央级民政事业费（亿元）	中央专项转移支付（亿元）	抚恤（亿元）	安置（亿元）	救灾（亿元）	低保（亿元）	医疗救助（亿元）	福利（亿元）	其他（亿元）
1999	62.8	1.2	61.6	18.0	17.6	22.0	4.0			
2000	86.6	2.9	83.7	23.7	23.0	22.0	15.0			
“十五”时期	**1004.3**	**11.9**	**992.4**	**212.1**	**217.3**	**170.1**	**373.1**	**12.0**		**7.9**
2001	109.6	1.4	108.2	26.3	28.7	30.2	23.0			
2002	140.2	1.8	138.4	31.6	37.0	24.3	45.5			
2003	213.6	1.8	211.8	37.1	39.2	40.5	92.0	3.0		0.1
2004	227.7	3.9	223.8	40.7	47.4	32.0	100.6	3.0		0.1
2005	313.2	2.9	310.3	76.4	65.0	43.1	112.0	6.0		7.7
“十一五”时期	**4761.3**	**89.3**	**4658.9**	**767.6**	**699.9**	**856.1**	**1941.6**	**319.6**		**74.2**
2006	406.8	2.8	404.0	111.7	73.9	49.4	136.0	14.3		18.7
2007	523.1	5.6	504.4	110.9	117.4	49.9	189.9	36.3		0.1
2008	1207.7	26.6	1181.1	142.1	142.9	478.4	363.1	54.5		0.1
2009	1232.5	5.5	1227.0	187.3	160.2	174.7	620	84.5		0.3
2010	1391.2	48.8	1342.4	215.6	205.5	103.7	632.6	130		55
“十二五”时期	**5785.4**	**33.1**	**5752.3**	**980.5**	**749.2**	**298.6**	**3044.0**	**456.7**	**121.6**	**101.8**
2011	1817.4	9.4	1808.0	277.4	206.4	84	1004.7	150	25.2	60.3
2012	1804.6	10	1794.6	333.3	265.4	112.7	870.5	150	42	20.7
2013	2163.4	13.7	2149.7	369.8	277.4	101.9	1168.8	156.7	54.4	20.8

B-1-17 彩票公益金使用情况

单位：亿元

年 份	合计	抚恤	退役安置	社会福利	低保及其他社会救济	医疗救助	自然灾害生活救助	其他
2001								
2002								
2003								
2004								
2005								
“十一五”时期	**485.3**	**17.6**	**6**	**204.9**	**26.2**	**48.8**		**175.6**
2006	52.6	2.6	1	24.1	3.3			21.6
2007	77.6	3	0.9	35.5	4.3			33.9
2008	119.2	3.7	1.3	44.9	7.2	17.5		38.5
2009	113.4	3.4	1.2	49.3	5.9	15.5		38
2010	122.5	4.9	1.6	51.1	5.5	15.8		43.6
“十二五”时期	**482.4**	**17.7**	**1.5**	**270.7**	**23.4**	**50.6**	**4.7**	**113.7**
2011	127.9	4.8	0.4	61.4	7.4	16.3	0.8	36.6
2012	159.0	5.4	0.5	92.2	7.3	16.8	1.3	35.6
2013	195.5	7.5	0.6	117.1	8.7	17.5	2.6	41.5

B-1-18 中央彩票公益金使用情况

单位：万元

年 份	合 计	中央级	转移支付					
				养老	残疾人	儿童	社会公益	医疗救助
“十五”时期	**14.91**		**14.91**	**0.70**		**2.06**	**0.15**	**12.00**
2001								
2002								
2003	3.00		3.00					3.00
2004	5.91		5.91	0.70		2.06	0.15	3.00
2005	6.00		6.00					6.00
“十一五”时期	**112.29**	**2.47**	**109.82**	**21.64**		**16.37**	**1.81**	**70.00**
2006	14.03	0.10	13.93	1.59		3.24	0.10	9.00
2007	16.98	0.88	16.10	1.53		1.24	0.33	13.00
2008	28.14	0.10	28.04	4.79		6.67	0.58	16.00
2009	26.61	0.09	26.52	7.79		2.05	0.68	16.00
2010	26.53	1.30	25.23	5.94		3.17	0.12	16.00
“十二五”时期	**110.62**	**1.30**	**109.32**	**40.69**	**2.97**	**12.91**	**4.75**	**48.00**
2011	30.03	1.30	28.73	7.86		3.48	1.39	16.00
2012	33.68		33.68	10.67	0.99	4.35	1.67	16.00
2013	46.91		46.91	22.16	1.98	5.08	1.69	16.00

B-1-19 社会服务基本建设投资（按投资来源分）

单位：亿元、个

年份	计划总投资	本年完成投资	国家投资	国内贷款	自筹	福利彩票公益金	其他	本年完工项目个数
1988								
1989	5.8	2.0	0.8	0.1	0.8		0.2	
1990	6.9	2.4	1.0	0.1	1.0		0.3	
“八五”时期	**63.4**	**27.6**	**39.4**	**1.2**	**13.4**		**2.8**	
1991	7.0	3.0	30.4	0.1	1.5		0.3	
1992	7.3	3.2	0.8	0.1	1.9		0.4	
1993	12.8	5.6	1.3	0.2	3.4		0.7	
1994	15.5	6.2	2.3	0.5	2.9		0.6	
1995	20.9	9.6	4.6	0.3	3.8		0.9	
“九五”时期	**237.9**	**89.8**	**21.3**	**5.9**	**54.3**	**6.8**	**8.3**	**2793**
1996	29.8	10.1	2.1	0.4	6.4	0.0	1.1	
1997	35.7	13.8	2.7	0.8	8.6	0.0	1.6	
1998	41.0	16.6	2.8	0.8	11.1	0.0	1.9	
1999	63.2	24.7	6.0	2.3	14.6	3.5	1.8	1456
2000	68.2	24.7	7.7	1.6	13.6	3.3	1.9	1337
“十五”时期	**376.9**	**151.7**	**47.9**	**8.8**	**78.4**	**21.0**	**16.6**	**22117**
2001	77.5	30.8	10.4	2.2	15.1	3.6	3.1	1360
2002	88.7	30.1	9.5	1.4	15.9	3.3	3.3	3659
2003	87.3	30.0	9.9	1.7	15.1	3.5	3.3	3867
2004	89.7	29.2	8.9	2.4	14.4	4.7	3.5	8982
2005	33.8	31.6	9.1	1.0	17.9	5.8	3.5	4249
“十一五”时期	**485.6**	**487.8**	**210.7**	**12.4**	**148.8**	**96.8**	**82.3**	**62453**
2006	34.8	33.5	9.9	0.9	19.9	8.4	2.5	3626
2007	47.6	47.7	14.5	3.0	26.9	13.0	2.9	2446
2008	63.5	66.6	26.6	1.9	34.6	16.5	3.2	3906
2009	166.5	157.0	70.6	3.7	67.4	26.6	15.3	6457

年份	计划总投资	本年完成投资	国家投资	国内贷款	利用外资	福利彩票公益金	其他	本年完工项目个数
2010	173.2	183.0	89.1	2.9	0.2	32.3	58.5	46018
“十二五”时期	**751.5**	**746**	**302.8**	**11.4**	**3.3**	**169.1**	**259.3**	**25956**
2011	217.3	218.5	78.5	6.2	0.5	53.4	79.9	4533
2012	222.3	234.7	104.2	3.8	1.1	51	74.6	6095
2013	311.9	292.8	120.1	1.4	1.7	64.7	104.8	15328

B-1-20 国家对社会服务基本建设投资

单位：亿元

年 份	国家基本建设投资	#优抚安置单位	#社区服务设施	#收养性福利机构	#殡仪	#救助	#其他
1989	0.7						
1990	0.8			0.2	0.1		
“八五”时期	**10.3**	**4.2**		**1.4**	**1.1**	**0.2**	
1991	1.0	0.1		0.2	0.1		
1992	1.0			0.2			
1993	1.4			0.2	0.4		
1994	2.3	1.2		0.3	0.3		
1995	4.6	2.9		0.5	0.3	0.2	
“九五”时期	**21.3**	**2.0**	**1.6**	**6.6**	**6.5**		**2.6**
1996	2.1	0.1		0.5	0.5		
1997	2.7			0.7	1.1		
1998	2.8	0.2		1.8	0.8		
1999	6.0	0.9	0.6	1.5	1.7		1.2
2000	7.7	0.8	1.0	2.1	2.4		1.4
“十五”时期	**47.9**	**5.0**	**9.4**	**14.3**	**9.2**		**9.8**
2001	10.4	0.7	1.5	3.1	2.1		3.0
2002	9.5	0.7	2.1	2.8	1.9		1.9
2003	9.9	1.2	2.4	3.3	1.5		1.5
2004	9.0	1.1	2.3	2.5	1.1		1.9
2005	9.1	1.3	1.1	2.6	2.6		1.5
“十一五”时期	**210.8**	**27.8**	**31.5**	**85.2**	**19.2**	**8.1**	**39.0**
2006	9.9	1.8	0.8	3.9	1.4	0.3	1.6
2007	14.5	2.5	0.9	6.5	2.4	0.4	1.8
2008	26.6	8.2	1.9	8.5	3.7	1.1	3.2
2009	70.6	7.4	14.0	30.1	5.7	2.5	11.0
2010	89.2	7.9	13.9	36.2	6.0	3.8	21.4
“十二五”时期	**475.5**	**209.6**	**196.7**	**82.6**	**23.4**	**59.1**	**88.2**
2011	78.5	9.5	11.1	31.1	5.8	3.8	17.2
2012	104.2	11.3	18.3	45.1	7.1	6.1	16.2

年 份	国家基本建设投资	#提供住宿的社会工作机构	#为老年人与残疾人提供服务的机构	#为智障与精神病提供服务的机构	#为儿童提供收养救助服务的机构	#不提供住宿的社会工作机构	#其他
2013	292.8	188.8	167.3	6.4	10.5	49.2	54.8

B−1−21 中央预算内

年份	项目合计	投资合计	本级情况			
			本级项目数	本级投资	地方项目小计	补助地方投资小计
1989						
1990		0.1		0.1		
“八五”时期		**0.2**		**0.2**		
1991		0.2		0.2		
1992						
1993						
1994						
1995						
“九五”时期						
1996						
1997						
1998						
1999						
2000						
“十五”时期	**24**	**0.8**	**24**	**0.8**		
2001	3	0.3	3	0.3		
2002	10	0.2	10	0.2		
2003	6	0.1	6	0.1		
2004	3	0.1	3	0.1		
2005	2	0.1	2	0.1		
“十一五”时期	**2088**	**35.9**	**18**	**5.5**	**2070**	**30.37**
2006	2	0.2	2	0.2		
2007	218	2.8	5	0.8	213	2.0
2008	575	6.8	3	2.1	572	4.7
2009	774	13.0	4	1.3	770	11.7
2010	519	13.1	4	1.1	515	12.0
“十二五”时期	**1860**	**76.0**	**4**	**0.7**	**1856**	**75.3**
2011	433	26.0	4	0.7	429	25.3
2012	692	33.0			692	33.0
2013	735	17.0			735	17.0

基本建设投资情况

地方情况					
养老		精神卫生		儿童	
项目数	资金额	项目数	资金额	项目数	资金额
189	**5.0**	**26**	**4.4**	**134**	**5.0**
				15	0.5
				32	1.3
63	2.0			33	1.3
126	3	26	4.37	54	1.9
1364	**55.0**	**91.0**	**16.3**		
338	9	91	16.3		
669	31				
357	15				

B-1-21续表

年份	地方情况					
	流浪		社区		烈建	
	项目数	资金额	项目数	资金额	项目数	资金额
1989						
1990						
“八五”时期						
1991						
1992						
1993						
1994						
1995						
“九五”时期						
1996						
1997						
1998						
1999						
2000						
“十五”时期						
2001						
2002						
2003						
2004						
2005						
“十一五”时期	**254**	**5.0**	**1334**	**6.0**	**133**	**5.0**
2006						
2007	28	0.8	170	0.7		
2008	65	1.4	475	2.0		
2009	78	1.4	463	2.0	133	5.0
2010	83	1.4	226	1.3		
“十二五”时期			**401.0**	**4.0**		
2011						
2012			23	2		
2013			378	2		

B-1-22 中央彩票公益金用于基本建设投资情况

年份	投资合计	本级投资	补助地方投资小计	养老	精神卫生	儿童	流浪未成年人	社区	殡葬
1989									
1990									
“八五”时期									
1991									
1992									
1993									
1994									
1995									
“九五”时期									
1996									
1997									
1998									
1999									
2000									
“十五”时期									
2001									
2002									
2003									
2004									
2005									
“十一五”时期	**38.8**	**2.47**	**36.31**	**21.37**		**10.62**	**2.90**	**1.30**	**0.1**
2006	4.3	0.10	4.18	1.58		2.00	0.60		
2007	5.2	0.88	4.28	1.48		2.00	0.50	0.30	
2008	10.8	0.10	10.72	4.80		4.42	1.00	0.50	
2009	9.9	0.09	9.79	7.79		1.00	0.50	0.50	
2010	8.6	1.30	7.34	5.72		1.20	0.30		0.12
“十二五”时期	**41.69**		**41.69**	**29.79**	**3.58**	**4.35**	**1.77**	**1.2**	**1**
2011	8.57		8.57	7.01	0.59		0.57	0.20	0.20
2012	17.41		17.41	10.67	0.99	4.35	0.60	0.50	0.30
2013	15.71		15.71	12.11	2.00		0.60	0.50	0.50

B-2-1 按收养人员分类的可提供住宿的社会服务机构

单位：个

年 份	单位数	老年及残疾人	智障和精神疾病	儿童	其他	#救助管理站	#安置农场	#军供站
1978	8571	8365	139	67				
1979	8988	8801	135	52				
1980	9669	9460	150	59				
1981	10031	9813	155	63				
1982	12275	12046	165	64				
1983	15807	15582	165	60				
1984	22796	22566	167	63				
1985	29100	28852	161	59	28			
1986	35008	34750	166	58	34			
1987	37372	37109	170	60	33			
1988	39030	38767	173	62	28			
1989	39743	39472	180	64	27			
1990	40583	40340	181	62				
1991	42264	42013	188	63				
1992	43319	43063	189	67				
1993	43681	43375	190	67	49			
1994	43240	42911	188	73	68			
1995	43074	42735	190	77	72			
1996	42829	42518	155	84	72			
1997	42385	42027	192	91	75			
1998	42131	41755	195	105	76			
1999	40430	40030	191	110	99			
2000	40491	39321	201	126	843			
2001	38785	38106	200	160	319			
2002	38200	37591	200	178	231			
2003	37294	36224	205	192	1587			
2004	38593	37880	211	208	1320			
2005	42487	40641	226	224	1396			
2006	43187	40964	219	249	1755			
2007	44958	42713	234	269	1742			
2008	41099	38674	244	290	1891			
2009	43944	39671	266	419	3588			
2010	44482	39904	251	480	3847			
2011	45973	42828	251	638	2256	1547		327
2012	48078	44304	257	724	2793	1770	27	328
2013	45977	42475	261	803	2438	1891	26	325

B-2-2 按收养人员分类的可提供住宿的社会服务床位

单位：万张

年　份	床位数合计	老年及残疾人床位	智障和精神疾病床位	儿童床位	其他床位	#救助管理站	#军供站	每千人口拥有社会服务床位数	每千老年人口拥有养老床位数
1978	16.3	15.7	0.6					0.17	
1979	22.6	20.1	2.1	0.4				0.23	
1980	24.2	21.3	2.4	0.5				0.25	
1981	25.3	22.2	2.5	0.6				0.25	
1982	28.2	24.8	2.8	0.6				0.28	
1983	32.4	29.0	2.8	0.6				0.31	
1984	42.5	39.0	2.9	0.6				0.41	
1985	49.1	45.7	2.9	0.5	0.2			0.46	
1986	58.7	55.0	3.1	0.6	0.3			0.55	
1987	64.9	61.0	3.3	0.6	0.3			0.59	
1988	69.5	65.5	3.4	0.6	0.2			0.63	
1989	73.8	69.5	3.6	0.7	0.2			0.65	
1990	78.0	73.5	3.7	0.8				0.68	
1991	82.8	78.3	3.8	0.7				0.71	
1992	89.8	85.2	3.8	0.8				0.77	
1993	92.7	87.8	4.0	0.9	0.4			0.78	
1994	95.5	90.6	4.0	0.9	0.5			0.80	
1995	97.6	92.5	4.0	1.1	0.6			0.81	
1996	100.8	95.6	4.0	1.2	0.6			0.82	
1997	103.1	97.8	4.0	1.3	0.6			0.83	
1998	105.8	100.2	4.1	1.5	0.6			0.85	
1999	108.9	102.4	4.1	1.6	0.8			0.87	
2000	113.0	104.5	4.1	1.8	2.6			0.89	
2001	140.7	114.6	4.2	2.3	19.6			1.10	
2002	141.5	114.9	4.3	2.5	19.8			1.10	
2003	142.9	120.6	4.5	2.7	15.1			1.11	
2004	157.2	139.5	4.5	3.0	10.2			1.21	
2005	180.7	158.1	4.4	3.2	15.0			1.38	10.97
2006	204.5	179.6	4.4	3.2	17.3			1.56	12.05
2007	269.6	242.9	4.7	3.4	18.6			2.04	15.83
2008	300.3	267.4	5.4	4.3	23.2			2.26	16.72
2009	326.5	293.5	5.9	4.8	22.3			2.45	17.56
2010	349.6	316.1	6.1	5.5	21.9			2.61	17.79
2011	396.4	369.2	6.5	6.8	13.9	7.1	3.8	2.94	19.96
2012	449.3	416.5	6.7	8.7	17.4	9.0	3.8	3.32	21.48
2013	526.7	493.7	7.4	9.8	15.7	9.7	3.7	3.87	24.39

注：老年及残疾人床位含社区服务床位（含日间照料床位）。

B-2-3 可提供住宿的社会服务机构收养人员情况

单位：万人

年　份	总人数	老年及残疾人	智障和精神疾病人	儿童	其他
1978	16.3	14.0	1.9	0.4	
1979	18.6	16.3	1.9	0.4	
1980	19.1	16.7	2.0	0.4	
1981	19.7	17.0	2.2	0.5	
1982	22.5	19.7	2.3	0.5	
1983	25.9	23.0	2.4	0.5	
1984	34.1	31.0	2.6	0.5	
1985	40.8	37.5	2.6	0.5	0.2
1986	47.4	43.9	2.8	0.5	0.2
1987	51.8	48.2	2.9	0.5	0.2
1988	54.8	51.1	3.0	0.6	0.1
1989	56.9	53.0	3.1	0.6	0.2
1990	59.9	56.1	3.2	0.6	
1991	64.6	60.8	3.2	0.6	
1992	69.6	65.6	3.3	0.7	
1993	72.4	68.0	3.4	0.7	0.3
1994	73.6	69.2	3.3	0.8	0.3
1995	74.7	70.1	3.2	1.0	0.4
1996	76.9	72.3	3.1	1.1	0.4
1997	78.5	73.7	3.2	1.2	0.4
1998	80.0	74.9	3.2	1.4	0.5
1999	82.7	77.6	3.2	1.4	0.5
2000	85.4	78.6	3.2	1.8	1.8
2001	88.5	82.0	3.3	2.1	1.1
2002	91.6	85.0	3.4	2.2	1.0
2003	96.5	89.1	3.5	2.5	1.4
2004	110.9	103.9	3.6	2.8	0.6
2005	123.6	116.2	3.7	2.9	0.8
2006	147.0	138.5	3.8	3.2	1.5
2007	200.0	191.3	4.1	3.0	1.6
2008	240.0	211.5	4.5	3.4	20.6
2009	256.0	227.5	5.0	3.7	19.8
2010	278.2	247.0	5.3	4.2	21.7
2011	293.4	279.7	5.5	4.6	3.6
2012	309.5	293.6	5.8	5.4	4.7
2013	322.5	307.4	6.0	5.6	3.5

B-2-4 按城乡分类的可提供住宿的社会服务机构情况

年 份	单位数（个）	城市	农村	床位数（万张）	城市	农村	收养人数（万人）	城市	农村
1978	8571	728	7843	16.3	0.1	16.2	16.3	5.7	10.6
1979	8988	1518	7470	22.6	6.4	16.2	18.6	8	10.6
1980	9669	1407	8262	24.2	7.1	17.1	19.1	7.9	11.2
1981	10031	1487	8544	25.3	7.4	17.9	19.7	8.2	11.5
1982	12275	1689	10586	28.2	7.6	20.6	22.5	8.7	13.8
1983	15807	1760	14047	32.4	7.7	24.7	25.9	9	16.9
1984	22796	1925	20871	42.5	8.5	34	34.1	10	24.1
1985	29100	5478	23622	49.1	18.2	30.9	40.8	14.6	26.2
1986	35008	8330	26678	58.7	23.6	35.1	47.4	18.9	28.5
1987	37372	9358	28014	64.9	25.8	39.1	51.8	20.5	31.3
1988	39030	10498	28532	69.5	28.4	41.1	54.8	22.3	32.5
1989	39743	10118	29625	73.8	28.7	45.1	56.9	22.3	34.6
1990	40583	12697	27886	78	34.5	43.5	59.9	26.8	33.1
1991	42264	13197	29067	82.8	36.7	46.1	64.6	28.5	36.1
1992	43319	16847	26472	89.8	44.6	45.2	69.6	34.5	35.1
1993	43681	17400	26281	92.7	47	45.7	72.4	37.2	35.2
1994	43240	18035	25205	95.5	50	45.5	73.6	39.1	34.5

年 份	单位数（个）	国有社会福利院	社会办敬老院	床位数（万张）	国有社会福利院	社会办敬老院	收养人数（万人）	国有社会福利院	社会办敬老院
1995	43074	11184	31890	97.6	18.6	79	74.7	14.4	60.3
1996	42829	11216	31613	100.8	19.2	81.6	76.9	14.8	62.1
1997	42385	10417	31968	103.1	19.9	83.2	78.5	15.4	63.1
1998	42131	9895	32236	105.8	21	84.8	80	16.1	63.9
1999	40430	3086	37344	108.9	23.6	85.3	82.7	17.9	64.8

年 份	单位数（个）	城 市	农 村	床位数（万张）	城 市	农 村	收养人数（万人）	城 市	农 村
2000	40491	14915	25576	113	57.4	55.6	85.4	42.6	42.8
2001	38785	12135	26650	140.7	72.3	68.4	88.5	39.6	48.9
2002	38200	12503	25697	141.5	75.3	66.2	91.6	42.2	49.4
2003	37294	12951	24343	142.9	75.3	67.6	96.5	46.1	50.4
2004	38593	12151	26442	157.2	79.7	77.5	110.9	51.5	59.4
2005	42487	12806	29681	180.7	91.2	89.5	123.6	55.7	67.9
2006	43187	11814	31373	204.5	90.9	113.6	147.0	55.0	92.0
2007	44958	10274	34684	269.6	89.8	179.8	200.0	43.9	149.3
2008	41099	10731	30368	300.3	107.2	193.1	240.0	79.5	160.5
2009	43944	12658	31286	326.5	117.7	208.8	256.0	83.0	173.0
2010	44482	13010	31472	349.6	124.7	224.9	278.2	95.7	182.5
2011	45973	13833	32140	396.4	154.5	241.9	293.4	100.9	192.5
2012	48078	15291	32787	449.3	188.3	261	309.5	109.5	200.0
2013	45977	15730	30247	526.7	253.9	272.8	322.5	121.3	201.2

B-2-5 孤儿和收养

单位：件、人

年 份	孤儿数	收养登记总数	中国公民收养登记	外国公民收养登记	被收养人合计	福利机构抚养的儿童	被中国公民收养	被外国人收养
1996		18896	14804	4092	20389	2201		
1997		21548	17193	4355	21548	975		
1998		26498	20611	5887	26498	677		
1999		38074	31916	6158	38019	1670	31882	6137
2000		55802	49037	6765	56191	1847	49500	6691
2001		44706	36089	8617	45844	1908	37200	8644
2002		45336	35372	9964	47860	2404	37642	10218
2003		54159	44884	9275	54159	3427	44884	9275
2004		52603	40084	12519	55572	3189	44708	10864
2005		49506	35470	14036	50921	3564	38057	12864
2006		48178	38393	9785	49148	2867	39424	9724
2007		45192	36893	8299	46047	1146	37790	8257
2008	67921	42550	37009	5541	44115	1846	38617	5498
2009	127599	44260	39801	4459	44359	1605	39964	4395
2010	252110	34529	29618	4911	34473	1878	29978	4495
2011	509695	31424	27579	3845	31329	1679	28117	3212
2012	570075	27278	23157	4121	27310	1760	23169	4141
2013	548845	24460	21230	3230	24491	9657	21261	3230

注：福利机构抚养的儿童2012年以前是孤儿，2013年以后含弃婴。

B-2-6 社会福利企业

年 份	单位数 （个）	残疾职工人数 （万人）	利润额 （亿元）
1978	920	3.5	0.8
1979	1106	4.8	0.8
1980	1309	5.5	0.9
1981	1574	6.1	0.7
1982	1704	6.4	0.8
1983	5930	9.6	0.9
1984	6710	11.6	1.3
1985	14872	23.2	5.1
1986	19865	31.4	4.2
1987	27793	43.3	8.8
1988	40496	55.9	16.5
1989	41565	60.5	16.1
1990	41827	63.8	17.8
1991	43805	70.1	21.3
1992	49836	77.8	32.6
1993	56881	84.5	44.7
1994	60233	90.9	44.1
1995	60237	93.9	49.1
1996	59397	93.6	45.1
1997	55509	91.0	66.3
1998	50514	85.6	63.9
1999	44628	79.0	76.7
2000	40670	72.5	99.0
2001	37980	69.9	119.5
2002	35758	68.3	148.3
2003	33976	67.9	189.9
2004	32410	66.2	219
2005	31211	63.7	225.2
2006	30199	55.9	237.8
2007	24974	56.3	169.3
2008	23780	61.9	119.2
2009	22783	62.7	125.4
2010	22226	62.5	150.8
2011	21507	62.8	140.1
2012	20205	59.7	118.4
2013	18227	53.9	106.9

B-2-7 城市社会救济和城市居民最低生活保障

单位：万人

年份	城市居民传统救济总人数	城市居民传统定救人数	城市精简退职老职工人数	享受40%人数	定量救济人数
1978					
1979	33.6	23.7	*9.9*		
1980	32.9	22.9	*10*		
1981	31.5	21.5	*10*		
1982	34.7	21.4	*13.3*		
1983	47.1	22.6	*24.5*		
1984	*207.4*	*160.6*	*46.8*	*25.3*	
1985	30.0	18.2	11.8	6.4	5.4
1986	49.0	35.6	13.4	7.1	6.3
1987	29.8	16.2	13.6	7.2	6.4
1988	32.9	17.6	15.3	7.7	7.6
1989	30.5	16.2	14.3	7.1	7.2
1990	41.8	16.4	25.4	16.4	9.0
1991	33.7	16.1	17.6	8.5	9.0
1992	39.5	19.2	20.3	9.7	10.6
1993	24.6	13.8	10.8	5	5.8
1994	23.0	12.4	10.6	4.9	5.7
1995	109.0	55.2	53.8	23.9	29.9
1996	120.1	66.5	53.6	23.6	30.0

年份	城市居民最低生活保障人数	在职人员	下岗人员	退休人员	失业人员	“三无”人员	其他人员
1996	84.9						
1997	87.9						
1998	184.1						
1999	256.9						
2000	402.6						
2001	1170.7						
2002	2064.7	186.8	554.5	90.8	358.3	91.9	783.1
2003	2246.8	179.3	518.4	90.7	409	99.9	949.3
2004	2205	141	468.9	73.1	423.1	95.4	1003.5
2005	2234.2	114.1	430.7	61.3	410.1	95.8	1122.1
2006	2240.1	97.6	350	53.2	420.8	93.1	1225.3

年份	城市居民最低生活保障人数	残疾人	三无人员	老年人	成年人				未成年人	
					在职人员	灵活就业	登记失业	未登记失业	在校生	其他
2007	2272.1	161.0	125.8	298.4	93.9	343.8	627.2	364.3	321.6	223
2008	2334.8	169.1	106.9	316.7	82.2	381.7	564.3	402.2	358.1	229.6
2009	2345.6	181.0	94.1	333.5	79.0	432.2	510.2	410.9	369.1	210.7
2010	2310.5	180.7	89.3	338.6	68.2	432.4	492.8	420.0	357.3	201.2
2011	2276.8	184.1	80.3	346.9	61.5	429.7	472.5	426.7	348.5	191
2012	2143.5	174.5	64.9	339.3	49.6	459.3	400.4	422.1	318.3	154.5
2013	2064.2	169.2	58	330.3	45.1	462.1	365.5	416.8	303.2	141.3

注：1984年的精简退职老职工人数含农村的数据。

B-2-8 农村社会救济和农村最低生活保障

单位：万人、万户

年份	农村社会救济总人数	农村定期定量救济人数	农村精简退职老职工人数	享受40%人数	定量救济人数
1978					
1979	6847.6	*6837.7*	*9.9*		
1980	4651.8	*4641.8*	*10*		
1981	4265.1	*4255.1*	*10*		
1982	4270.7	*4257.4*	*13.3*		
1983	3526.7	*3502.2*	*24.5*		
1984	3842.7	*3795.9*	*46.8*	*25.3*	
1985	116.7	75.1	41.6	18.1	23.5
1986	103	63.1	39.9	18.1	21.7
1987	92.2	53.2	39	17.7	21.3
1988	93	54.1	38.9	17.6	21.4
1989	75.7	35.0	40.7	18.3	22.3
1990	100.2	46.7	53.5	23.6	29.9
1991	97	43.8	53.2	23.5	29.8
1992	97.5	45.6	51.9	23.3	28.6
1993	80.1	36.3	43.8	19.5	24.3
1994	82.1	38.5	43.6	19.2	24.3
1995	98.3	55.2	43.1	19	24.1
1996	109.2	66.5	42.7	18.6	24.1
1997	104.5	51.4	53.1	23.2	29.8
1998	120.5	65.6	54.9	24.9	30
1999	107.1	55.6	51.5	22.5	28.7
2000	112.2	62.5	49.7	22.1	27.6
2001	130.5	80.7	49.8	21.3	27.8
2002	138.7	*90.0*	48.7	20.9	27.8

年份	农村困难群众救助总人数	农村最低生活保障人数	农村特困户救助人数	农村困难群众救助总户数	农村最低生活保障户数	困难户	其他	农村特困户救助户数	困难户	其他	五保户供养户数	农村传统救济人数
2001	385.3	304.6	80.7									
2002	497.8	407.8	*90.0*	156.7	156.7							
2003	1160.5	367.1	793.4	632.8	146.5	114.5	32	282.1	192.7	89.3	204.2	
2004	1402.1	488	914.1	780.8	197.9	165.2	33.6	317.1	260.4	56.6	265.8	
2005	1891.8	825	1066.8	1061	356.5	298.8	57.7	354.8	290.4	64.4	349.7	
2006	2987.8	1593.1	775.8	1606.3	777.2			325.8			503.3	115.6

年份	农村救助总人数	农村最低生活保障人数	农村集中供养五保人数	农村分散供养五保人数	传统救济人数	农村临时救济人数
2007	4818.6	3566.3	138	393.3	75	646
2008	5757.3	4305.5	155.6	393	72.2	831
2009	5922	4760	171.8	381.6	62.2	546.4
2010	6443.5	5214	177.4	378.9	59.5	613.7
2011	6522.2	5305.7	184.5	366.5	68.7	596.8
2012	5969.7	5344.5	185.3	360.3	79.6	
2013	5998.3	5388	183.5	353.8	73	

注：1984年以前含应保未保的农村救济人数。

B-2-9 最低生活保障和社会救济平均标准

年　份	城市居民最低生活保障平均标准（元/人、月）	农村最低生活保障平均标准（元/人、年）	农村五保集中供养平均标准（元/人、年）	农村五保分散供养平均标准（元/人、年）
1999	149.0			
2000	157.0			
2001	147.0			
2002	148.0			
2003	149.0			
2004	152.0			
2005	156.0			
2006	169.6	850.8	1608.2	1224.5
2007	182.4	840.0	1953.0	1432.0
2008	205.3	987.6	2176.1	1624.4
2009	227.8	1210.1	2587.5	1842.7
2010	251.2	1404.0	2951.4	2102.1
2011	287.6	1718.4	3399.7	2470.5
2012	330.1	2067.8	4060.9	3008.0
2013	373.3	2433.9	4685.0	3498.5

B-2-10 最低生活保障和社会救济平均支出水平

年　份	城市居民最低生活保障平均支出水平（元/人、月）	农村最低生活保障平均支出水平（元/人、年）	农村五保集中供养平均支出水平（元/人、年）	农村五保分散供养平均支出水平（元/人、年）
1999	44.8			
2000	45.3			
2001	29.6			
2002	43.9			
2003	58.0			
2004	65.0			
2005	72.3			
2006	83.6	414.0		
2007	102.7	465.6		
2008	143.7	604.8	2055.7	1121.0
2009	172.0	816.0	2316.0	1284.0
2010	189.0	888.0	2460.0	1416.0
2011	240.3	1273.2	3081.9	1774.9
2012	239.1	1247.9	3496.6	2237.3
2013	264.2	1393.5	4078.3	2724.3

B-2-11 医疗救助

单位：万人次、万人

年　份	农村民政部门医疗救助总数	农村民政部门救助	民政部门资助参加合作医疗	城市医疗救助总数	城市民政部门医疗救助
2004		552.6	121.1		
2005		654.9	199.6		
2006		1317.1	201.3		
2007		2517.3	819.1		
2008	642.6	3432.4	1203.1		
2009	1095.9	4059.1	1140.4		
2010	1461.2	4615.4	1479.3		
2011	1549.8	4825.3	2144		
2012	1387.1	4490.4	2173.7	1141.4	1032.3
2013	1490.1	4868.7	2126.4	1074.0	1052.4

B-2-12 城市生活无着人员救助

年份	救助站（个）	未成年人救助保护中心（个）	生活无着人员救助（人次）	# 未成年人救助	救助类单位床位数（张）	# 未成年人救助保护中心床位
1978	783					
1979	845					
1980	665					
1981	598					
1982	610					
1983	615					
1984	628					
1985	636					
1986	647					
1987	639					
1988	644					
1989	669					
1990	666					
1991	691					
1992	692					
1993	719					
1994	712					
1995	722					
1996	720					
1997	728					
1998	742					
1999	800					
2000	857					
2001	838					
2002	861					
2003	864		634528	60257		
2004	977		820254	104455	47086	
2005	1079	40	1196305	120487	45603	1849
2006	1189	50	1295506	129337	45661	1133
2007	1261	90	1544492	159989	46800	3621
2008	1334	88	1573484	155794	50642	3543
2009	1372	116	1680532	167283	51049	3670
2010	1448	145	1719008	146329	55562	5221
2011	1547	241	2409701	178705	71109	8165
2012	1770	261	2765761	152070	99901	10038
2013	1891	274	3484727	183802	108360	11499

B-2-13 社会捐赠

单位：亿元、亿件

年 份	社会捐赠款物合计	社会捐赠款	民政部门	各类社会组织	社会捐赠其他物资折款	接收社会捐赠衣被数量
1997	14.0	4.2			9.9	0.9
1998	113.2	50.2	50.2		63.0	2.9
1999	17.8	6.9	5.0	2.0	10.8	0.6
2000	16.3	9.3	5.4	3.9	7.0	0.8
2001	20.0	11.7	7.6	4.1	8.3	1.3
2002	20.8	19.0	11.1	7.9	1.8	2.3
2003	43.4	41.0	29.2	11.9	2.4	2.0
2004	35.1	34.0	17.1	16.9	1.2	0.9
2005	61.9	60.3	31.3	29.0	1.6	1.0
2006	89.5	83.1	43.0	40.1	6.4	0.7
2007	148.3	132.8	50.9	81.9	15.6	0.9
2008	764.1	744.5	479.3	265.2	19.6	11.6
2009	485.9	483.7	66.5	417.2	2.2	1.2
2010	601.7	596.8	179.8	417.0	4.9	0.3
2011	494.9	490.1	96.6	393.5	4.8	0.3
2012	578.8	572.5	101.7	470.8	6.3	1.3
2013	575.1	566.4	107.6	458.8	8.7	1

B-2-14 中国福利彩票销售

年　份	福利彩票发行单位（个）	福利彩票销售额（亿元）	提取公益金（亿元）	公益金支出（亿元）
1978				
1979				
1980				
“六五”时期				
1981				
1982				
1983				
1984				
1985				
“七五”时期		**14.2**	**4.6**	
1986				
1987		0.2	0.1	
1988		3.8	1.2	
1989		3.8	1.3	
1990		6.5	2.0	
“八五”时期		**115.2**	**34.3**	
1991		7.7	2.5	
1992		13.8	4.1	
1993		18.4	5.5	
1994		18.0	5.3	
1995		57.3	16.9	
“九五”时期		**358.7**	**103.5**	**72.7**
1996		64.8	19.1	
1997		36.4	10.1	
1998		63.2	19.6	14.1
1999	1169	104.4	30.5	19.9
2000	1253	89.9	24.2	38.7
“十五”时期		**1145.2**	**377.1**	**161.9**
2001	1185	139.6	41.9	19.7
2002	1121	168.0	52.3	25.5
2003	1145	200.1	67.2	30.6
2004	1128	226.4	79.4	33.8
2005	1113	411.2	136.3	52.3
“十一五”时期		**3455.3**	**1127.4**	**484.0**
2006	989	495.7	168.8	52.6
2007	985	631.6	211.0	77.6
2008	999	604.0	205.4	119.2
2009	988	756.0	243.4	113.4
2010	993	968.0	298.8	121.2
“十二五”时期		**4553.6**	**1342.1**	**482.4**
2011	974	1278.0	382.0	127.9
2012	955	1510.3	449.4	159
2013	940	1765.3	510.7	195.5

B-2-15 定期抚恤优抚对象

单位：人

年份	抚恤补助总人数（万人）	定期抚恤人数	烈属	牺牲、病故军人家属	伤残人员（万人）
1978	205.9				73.4
1979	173.6				75.6
1980	222.4				78.6
1981	233.6				79.6
1982	240.8	590104	541516	48588	81.6
1983	251.2	577791	526826	50965	83.0
1984	267.3	585403	536523	48880	84.4
1985	283.3	518566	440000	78566	85.3
1986	339.8	533245	446209	87036	86.5
1987	366.3	548063	453480	94583	88.0
1988	378.5	537472	429271	108201	88.7
1989	411.7	525134	422656	102478	89.1
1990	425.7	516638	407276	109362	87.4
1991	434.8	614945	504462	110483	87.5
1992	433.7	602163	492457	109706	87.6
1993	441.2	495994	383924	112070	88.3
1994	442.0	487256	372850	114406	88.5
1995	448.8	486250	370685	115565	88.8
1996	447.0	484270	366216	118054	89.3
1997	448.3	480464	362086	118378	89.5
1998	447.0	473901	357492	116409	89.2
1999	445.1	458079	336587	121492	88.7
2000	442.4	448276	325116	123160	88.1

年份	抚恤补助总人数（万人）	定期抚恤人数	烈属	牺牲军人家属	病故军人家属	伤残人员（万人）
2001	450.7	480852	348521	60081	72250	85.5
2002	459.0	480466	341109	63953	75404	85.8
2003	464.9	488820	345141	65303	78376	86.0
2004	462.0	485733	339817	65695	80221	85.6
2005	460.3	492517	349253	63603	79661	84.5
2006	462.6	491320	346089	64248	80983	86.0
2007	622.4	488675	342101	64478	82096	86.5
2008	633.2	478880	332390	65001	81489	87.2
2009	630.7	458578	317675	62304	78599	87.2
2010	625.0	447824	307587	62338	77899	86.7
2011	852.5	422439	286449	60534	75456	85.9
2012	944.4	411711	277712	59478	74521	84.9
2013	950.5	366400	240375	55734	70291	811819

B-2-16 定期补助优抚对象

单位：人

年 份	定期补助总人数	红军老战士合计	在乡红军老战士	西路军	红军失散人员	在乡复员军人	带病回乡退伍军人	60岁以上农村籍退伍军人	其 他
1978	9251	9251	9251						
1979	7872	7872	7872						
1980	6922	6922	6922						
1981	6567	6567	6567						
1982	1002181	6383	6383			859055	136743		
1983	1104586	6142	6142			952993	145451		
1984	1243633	6159	6159			1081350	156124		
1985	1461180	6329	6329			1185502	183129		86220
1986	1999872	6315	6315			1673990	210445		109122
1987	2230873	7466	7466			1833402	241290		148715
1988	2360462	7415	7415			1950641	247009		155397
1989	2715258	6628	6628			2272639	283075		152916
1990	2866579	7514	7514			2373873	305045		180147
1991	2939074	7015	7015			2419453	346021		166585
1992	2975175	6599	6599			2402869	373989		191718
1993	2947209	113728	5531	2997	105200	2424984	408497		
1994	2963965	112054	5058	2430	104566	2424435	427476		
1995	2987751	108484	4659	2318	101507	2423191	456076		
1996	3018047	115317	4480	2303	108534	2421517	481213		
1997	3037367	122115	4195	2214	115706	2396017	519235		
1998	3033826	118245	3996	2157	112092	2367266	548315		
1999	3056727	111096	3687	2106	105303	2363466	582165		
2000	3057257	105632	3326	1997	100309	2320739	630886		
2001	3170877	98345	3325	1889	93131	2246954	782802		42776
2002	3251971	94848	3136	1691	90021	2274657	882090		376
2003	3300232	90767	2893	1610	86264	2262264	919349		27852
2004	3277914	87521	2701	1454	83366	2214467	950428		25498
2005	3265797	79639	2681	1370	75588	2145421	977424		63313
2006	3274059	71707	2417	1220	68070	2064713	1072684		64955
2007	4870800	66220	2049	966	63205	1988977	1134414		1681189
2008	4981893	49198	1622	440	47136	1920235	1193622		1818838
2009	4976839	42945	1351	322	41272	1809019	1219752		1905123
2010	4935399	38630	1226	273	37131	1703396	1265664		1927709
2011	7243706	30309	911	190	29208	1587006	1321786	2373772	1930833
2012	8183693	26882	757	164	25961	1474790	1324325	3210986	2146710
2013	8326336	19740	647	117	18976	1260945	1306479	3566766	2172406

B-2-17 接收军队离退休、退职人员

单位：人

年份	合计	军队离退休干部	地方(含军队职工)人员
1978			
1979			
1980			
1981			
1982	21993	801	21192
1983	20038	1507	18531

年份	合计	军队离退休干部	#离休	地方人员	军队职工
1984	9916	1873	117	6228	1815
1985	12429	6137	3327	4472	1820
1986	29260	21564	15598	4236	3460
1987	14146	10035	6224	1719	2392
1988	6050	4242	2329	1287	521
1989	4858	3441	1530	994	423
1990	6214	4988	2573	1008	218
1991	6558	5568	2703	806	184
1992	4420	3551	1516	693	176
1993	5578	916	283	543	4318
1994	5773	1016	447	566	4190
1995	3531	1056	323	476	1999
1996	9346	3210	371	282	5854
1997	6311	3246	401	230	2835
1998	8156	5868	785	691	1597

年份	合计	军队离退休干部	地方离退休干部	军队无军籍职工
1999	12380	9464	305	2611
2000	15238	10197	219	4822
2001	13738	6236	373	7129

年份	合计	军队离退休干部(含地方)	#离休	军队退休士官	军队无军籍职工
2002	14428	3640		161	10627
2003	11057	5055	143	140	6312
2004	10794	8884	200	90	1820

年份	合计	军队离退休干部	#离休	地方离退休干部	#离休	军队退休士官	军队无军籍职工
2005	18512	17280	223	136	14	192	904
2006	31968	20794	259	673	85	365	10136
2007	28058	18534	258	303	23	160	9061
2008	21378	15829	78	205	15	297	5047
2009	18904	13836	143	348	5	1308	3412
2010	13451	11775	148	183	4	1112	381
2011	14530	12355	140	141	8	1405	629
2012	18570	14341	416	335	45	1047	2847
2013	38762	10927	108	500	29	570	26709

B-2-18 烈士褒扬和优待

年　份	烈士纪念建筑物管理机构（个）	本年批准烈士人数（人）	零散烈士纪念建筑物（个）	优待优抚对象户数（户）	#优待军属户数	优待总金额（万元）	#固定优待军属总额
1978			5347				
1979			3779			20393	
1980			2825			31459	
1981			2915			47255	
1982	965	8601	3592	4730756		58750	
1983	928	11024	3826	4387292		59588	
1984	786	8478	3953	4102419		62263	
1985	579	5887	3716	3567165	2884906	71655	577018
1986	582	11758	3871	3355694	2710272	75243	62205
1987	587	10644	4121	3223550	2562036	80915	66321
1988	632	9035	4236	3225253	2477699	87160	71735
1989	637	3960	4466	3086285	2423418	92169	77764
1990	632	3067	6065	2941486	2522476	99535	86739
1991	630	1556	6474	2967881	2540714	106354	93069
1992	684	1338	6957	2967002	2535037	116573	102008
1993	696	1467	6956	3009163	2470099	131555	113330
1994	718	1215	7279	3027420	2462671	155627	133070
1995	715	1277	7067	3051322	2476261	194379	166414
1996	740	1187	7020	3040439	2449077	251798	217527
1997	737	888	7048	3334000	2427586	321741	261865
1998	752	749	7322	3250395	2415838	356413	292305
1999	774	616	7252	3818210	2380675	402998	305386
2000	795	468	7427	3855797	2282584	469054	363675
2001	845	460	7802	3973085	2086464	385859	275456
2002	873	403	8051	4130817	1929011	374819	251854
2003	918	461	7781	3962425	1672205	391581	239410
2004	938	316	7425	3632630	1430630	418499	267458
2005	989	314	7483	3393218	1224036	379631	213968
2006	1072	265	7414	3220933	1183674	421010	224354
2007	1056	168	7186	3277318	1145223	454090	233479
2008	1133	297	7569	3301682	1108878	666011	267750
2009	1137	213	7622	3280522	1190816	751065	297448
2010	1195	173	9729	3308766	1169833	671536	340382
2011	1227	233	12378	3330859	1050918	968175	555402
2012	1306	172	13151	3471611	1008477	1121135	520520
2013	1463	200	13601	3402629	958255	1351368	646023

注：2011年由于部分省份指标理解错误，数据有调整。

B-2-19 自然灾害情况

年 份	受灾人口（万人次）	因灾死亡人口（含失踪）（人）	紧急转移人口（万人）	直接经济损失（亿元）	倒塌房屋（万间）	农作物受灾面积（万公顷）
1978		4965			73.1	4844
1979		6962			152.1	3937
1980		6821			137.3	5003
1981	26710.0	7422			261.5	3979
1982	22900.7	7935			320.3	3313
1983	22439.0	10952		260.9	345.4	3471
1984	20894.0	6927			274.7	3189
1985	26446.0	4394	290.5	410.4	224.9	4437
1986	29928.0	5410	345.8		209.7	4714
1987	23512.0	5495	348.0	326.3	180.0	4207
1988	36169.0	7306	582.9		258.0	5087
1989	34569.0	5952	365.3	525.0	194.1	4699
1990	29348.0	7338	579.2	616.0	247.4	3847
1991	41941.0	7315	1308.5	1215.1	581.5	5547
1992	37174.0	5741	303.6	853.9	196.6	5133
1993	37541.0	6125	307.7	933.2	271.6	4867
1994	43799.0	8549	1054.0	1876.0	512.1	5504
1995	24215.0	5561	1064.0	1863.0	439.3	4587
1996	32305.0	7273	1216.0	2882.0	809.0	5975
1997	47886.0	3212	511.3	1975.0	288.0	5343
1998	35216.0	5511	2082.4	3007.4	821.4	2229
1999	35319.0	2966	664.8	1962.4	174.5	4998
2000	45652.3	3014	467.1	2045.3	147.3	5469
2001	37255.9	2583	211.1	1942.0	92.2	5215
2002	37841.8	2840	471.8	1717.4	175.7	4711.9
2003	49745.9	2259	707.3	1884.2	343.0	5438.6
2004	33920.6	2250	563.2	1602.3	155.0	3710.6
2005	40653.7	2475	1570.3	2042.1	226.4	3881.8
2006	43453.3	3186	1384.5	2528.1	193.3	4109.1
2007	39777.9	2325	1499.1	2363.0	146.7	4899.3
2008	47795.0	88928	2682.2	11752.4	1097.7	3999.0
2009	47933.5	1528	709.9	2523.7	83.8	4721.4
2010	42610.2	7844	1858.4	5339.9	273.3	3742.6
2011	43290.0	1126	939.4	3096.4	93.5	3247.1
2012	29421.7	1530	1109.6	4185.5	90.6	2496.2
2013	38818.7	2284	1215.0	5808.4	87.5	3135

B-2-20 社区服务机构

单位：个

年份	城乡各类服务机构合计	社区服务中心	其他社区服务机构	便民利民网点	社区服务机构覆盖率（%）
1987					
1988	69699		69699		7.1
1989	71357		71357		6.9
1990	84757		84757		7.7
1991	89918		89918		8.0
1992	112171		112171		10.1
1993	92946	3711	89235	169503	8.3
1994	98679	4034	94645	204229	8.8
1995	115175	4380	110795	234024	11.0
1996	132309	5055	127254	259201	12.7
1997	138366	5113	133253	307226	13.5
1998	154196	6154	148042	345075	16.2
1999	164962	7623	157339	405740	18.0
2000	187888	6444	181444	451567	22.4
2001	201758	6179	195579	539544	25.5
2002	206743	7898	198845	622986	27.0
2003	203945	7520	196425	668418	27.5
2004	205926	7804	198122	703760	28.5
2005	203275	8479	194796	664764	28.7
2006	160007	8565	151442	457896	22.7

年份	城乡各类服务机构合计	社区指导中心	社区服务中心	社区服务站	其他社区服务机构	便民利民网点	社区服务机构覆盖率（%）
2007	134852		9319	50116	75417	892656	19.4
2008	146322		9873	30021	106428	748684	21.3
2009	146341		10003	53170	83168	692625	21.4
2010	152941		12720	44237	95984	539136	22.4
2011	160352		14391	56156	89805	452868	23.6
2012	200162	809	15497	87931	95925	397222	29.5
2013	251939	890	19014	108377	123658	358518	36.9

注：社区服务机构覆盖率=(社区服务中心+社区服务站+其他社区服务机构)/村居委会。

B-3-1 社会组织

单位：个

年 份	社会组织合计	社会团体	基金会	民办非企业
1978				
1979				
1980				
1981				
1982				
1983				
1984				
1985				
1986				
1987				
1988	4446	4446		
1989	4544	4544		
1990	10855	10855		
1991	82814	82814		
1992	154502	154502		
1993	167506	167506		
1994	174060	174060		
1995	180583	180583		
1996	184821	184821		
1997	181318	181318		
1998	165600	165600		
1999	136764	136764		5901
2000	130668	130668		22654
2001	128805	128805		82134
2002	133297	133297		111212
2003	142121	141167	954	124491
2004	154251	153359	892	135181
2005	172125	171150	975	147637
2006	354393	191946	1144	161303
2007	386916	211661	1340	173915
2008	413660	229681	1597	182382
2009	431069	238747	1843	190479
2010	445631	245256	2200	198175
2011	461971	254969	2614	204388
2012	499268	271131	3029	225108
2013	547245	289026	3549	254670

注：2001年以前的基金会含在社会团体内。

B-3-2 自治组织

年 份	基层群众性自治组织合计（万个）	居民委员会（个）	居民小组（万个）	居民委员会成员（万人）	村民委员会（万个）	村民小组（万个）	村民委员会成员（万人）
1978							
1979		46810					
1980							
1981		57169					
1982							
1983	37.7	65519			31.2		
1984	100.3	75609			92.7		
1985	103.0	80943		34.9	94.9		379.6
1986	95.3	86824		36.2	86.6		365.9
1987	93.2	86799		37.0	84.5		359.9
1988	97.8	95684		36.1	88.3		366.6
1989	102.8	93691		36.6	93.4		379.4
1990	110.0	98814		43.1	100.1		409.4
1991	111.9	100347		44.1	101.9		424.4
1992	110.8	104136		46.5	100.4		430.9
1993	112.0	107173		47.9	101.3		456.0
1994	111.7	110112		48.0	100.7		458.5
1995	104.4	111860		48.0	93.2		400.5
1996	104.2	113690		49.3	92.8		397.5
1997	102.4	117915	108.3	49.8	90.6	535.8	378.8
1998	95.2	119042	117.2	50.8	83.3	537.1	358.6
1999	91.6	114815	124.7	50.1	80.1	555.7	351.3
2000	84.0	108424	127.2	48.4	73.2	553.4	315.0
2001	79.2	91893	125.9	46.4	70.0	541.9	316.4
2002	76.7	86087	124.4	39.6	68.1	528.6	294.2
2003	74.1	77431	122.2	39.7	66.3	519.2	319.1
2004	72.2	77884	129.6	42.5	64.4	507.9	292.1
2005	70.9	79947	123.3	45.4	62.9	490.5	265.7
2006	70.4	80717	123.5	44.3	62.4	453.3	243.0
2007	69.5	82006	122.3	41.6	61.3	466.9	241.1
2008	68.8	83413	128.7	42.2	60.4	480.9	233.9
2009	68.4	84689	129.5	43.1	59.9	480.5	234.0
2010	68.2	87057	130.7	43.9	59.5	479.1	233.4
2011	67.9	89480	134.0	45.4	59.0	476.4	231.9
2012	68.0	91153	133.5	46.9	58.8	469.4	232.3
2013	68.3	94620	135.7	48.4	58.9	466.4	232.3

B-3-3 结婚

年　份	结婚登记总数（万对）	内地居民登记结婚数（万对）	涉外华侨港澳台登记结婚数（万对）	登记结婚人数
1978	597.8	597.8		
1979	637.1	636.3	0.8	
1980	720.9	719.8	1.1	
1981	1041.7	1040.3	1.4	
1982	836.9	835.5	1.4	
1983	765.4	764.2	1.3	
1984	784.8	783.4	1.4	
1985	831.3	829.1	2.2	
1986	884.0	882.3	1.7	
1987	926.7	924.7	2.0	
1988	899.2	897.2	2.0	
1989	937.2	935.2	2.0	
1990	951.1	948.7	2.4	
1991	953.6	951.0	2.6	
1992	957.5	954.5	3.0	
1993	915.4	912.2	3.3	
1994	932.4	929.0	3.4	
1995	934.1	929.7	4.4	
1996	938.7	934.0	4.7	1877.4
1997	914.1	909.1	5.1	1828.3
1998	891.7	886.7	5.0	1783.4
1999	885.3	879.9	5.4	1770.6
2000	848.5	842.0	6.5	1697.0
2001	805.0	797.1	7.9	1610.0
2002	786	778.8	7.3	1572.0
2003	811.4	803.5	7.8	1622.8
2004	867.2	860.8	6.4	1734.4
2005	823.1	816.6	6.4	1646.2
2006	945	938.2	6.8	1890.0
2007	991.4	986.3	5.1	1982.8
2008	1098.3	1093.2	5.1	2196.6
2009	1212.4	1207.5	4.9	2424.8
2010	1241	1236.1	4.9	2482.0
2011	1302.4	1297.5	4.9	2604.8
2012	1323.6	1318.3	5.3	2647.2
2013	1346.9	1341.4	5.5	2693.8

每千居民之结婚宗数（粗结婚率）计算方法：

$$每千居民之结婚宗数=\frac{结婚宗数}{（当年期初人口数+当年期末人口数）/2}\times 1000‰$$

登记

初婚人数	再婚人数	#女	#恢复结婚件数	每千居民之结婚宗数（粗结婚率）（‰）
				6.2
				6.7
				7.3
				10.4
				8.3
				7.5
				7.5
				7.9
				8.2
				8.6
				8.3
				8.4
				8.2
				8.3
				8.3
				7.8
				7.8
				7.7
1781.7	86.2	41.1	48044	7.7
1726.0	92.2	46.3	62752	7.4
1675.4	97.9	49.8	69160	7.2
1659.4	100.5	50.0	57815	7.1
1581.4	102.6	50.8	56324	6.7
1481.7	112.5	58.0	63442	6.3
1440.3	117.2	60.2	68081	6.1
1483.9	123.3	60.7	68204	6.3
1569.6	152.0	77.1	84799	6.7
1483.0	163.1	74.3	115003	6.3
1705.6	184.4	86.7	107113	7.2
1779.7	203.1	97.3	138967	7.5
1972.5	224.1	108.0	162244	8.3
2168.8	256.0	124.7	181162	9.1
2200.9	281.1	138.8	190356	9.3
2309.9	294.9	146.5	209781	9.7
2361.2	286.0	145.8	229607	9.8
2386.0	307.9	156.5	298766	9.9

B-3-4 离婚办理

年　份	离婚总数（万对）	民政部门登记离婚数（万对）			法院部门办理离婚数（万对）	每千居民之离婚宗数（粗离婚率）（‰）
			内地居民登记离婚数（万对）	涉外华侨港澳台登记离婚数（对）		
1978	28.5	17.0	17		11.5	0.18
1979	31.9	19.3	19.3	82	12.6	0.33
1980	34.1	18.0	18	330	16.1	0.35
1981	38.9	18.7	18.7	46	20.2	0.39
1982	42.8	21.1	21.1	116	21.7	0.42
1983	41.8	19.7	19.7	126	22.1	0.42
1984	45.4	19.9	19.9	110	25.5	0.40
1985	45.8	19.6	19.6	108	26.2	0.44
1986	50.6	21.4	21.4	205	29.2	0.47
1987	58.1	23.6	23.6	220	34.5	0.55
1988	65.5	26.4	26.4	310	39.1	0.60
1989	75.3	28.8	28.7	518	46.5	0.68
1990	80.0	30.1	30	602	49.9	0.69
1991	83.1	30.1	30	588	53	0.72
1992	85.0	31.6	31.5	833	53.4	0.74
1993	91.0	33.6	33.5	968	57.4	0.77
1994	98.2	35.5	35.4	737	62.7	0.82
1995	105.6	36.8	36.7	813	68.8	0.88
1996	113.4	39.4	39.3	1175	74	0.93
1997	119.9	44.0	43.9	1385	75.9	0.97
1998	119.2	46.6	46.5	948	72.6	0.96
1999	120.2	47.8	47.7	975	72.4	0.96
2000	121.3	48.9	48.8	1075	72.4	0.96
2001	125.0	52.8	52.5	2856	72.2	0.98
2002	117.7	57.3	56.8	5221	60.4	0.90
2003	133.0	69	68.7	3333	64	1.05
2004	166.5	104.6	104.0	5830	61.9	1.28
2005	178.5	118.4	117.5	8267	60.1	1.37
2006	191.3	129.1	128.3	8414	62.2	1.46
2007	209.8	145.7	144.8	8852	64.1	1.59
2008	226.9	161.0	160.0	9470	65.9	1.71
2009	246.8	180.2	179.6	5608	66.6	1.85
2010	267.8	201.0	200.4	5783	66.8	2.00
2011	287.4	220.7	220.2	5761	66.7	2.13
2012	310.4	242.3	241.7	6161	68.1	2.29
2013	350.0	281.5	280.9	6538	68.5	2.58

每千居民之离婚宗数（粗离婚率）计算方法：

$$每千居民之离婚宗数=\frac{离婚宗数}{（当年期初人口数+当年期末人口数）/2}\times 1000‰$$

B-3-5 殡葬服务

年　份	殡仪馆（个）	公墓（个）	骨灰堂	殡葬管理机构（个）	火化炉数（台）	火化遗体数（万具）	火化率（%）
1978					1712	117.5	
1979					2300	102.1	
1980					2510	98.7	
1981					2586	85.4	
1982					2622	96.2	
1983					2622	108.0	
1984					2686	128.2	
1985	9	24		122	2729	155.2	
1986	5	25		143	2745	155.5	26.2
1987	6	29		195	2752	162.0	27.0
1988	14	37		219	2729	180.9	29.5
1989	17	50		217	2768	182.3	30.1
1990	1260	73		211	2795	201.3	31.5
1991	1283	84		234	2714	215.6	34.0
1992	1288	88		228	2852	242.6	31.2
1993	1264	136		296	2891	247.6	31.6
1994	1272	163		284	2882	257.1	33.4
1995	1281	209		302	2927	262.7	33.2
1996	1283	256		313	3005	282.7	35.2
1997	1289	359		340	2959	295.0	36.8
1998	1310	425		374	3157	319.7	39.6
1999	1318	624		402	*3340*	336.4	41.5
2000	1363	692		466	*3565*	373.7	46.0
2001	1415	757		540	4299	386.7	47.3
2002	1486	854		542	3945	415.2	50.6
2003	1515	855		599	4159	434.9	52.7
2004	1549	937		633	4792	436.9	52.5
2005	1594	1009		681	5037	450.2	53
2006	1635	1109		805	5649	430.2	48.2
2007	1708	1162		799	4838	442.1	48.4
2008	1692	1209		853	4789	453.4	48.5
2009	1729	1266		901	5123	454.2	48.2
2010	1724	1308		919	5229	474.1	49
2011	1745	1406		952	5209	468.1	48.8
2012	1782	1597		978	5539	477.7	49.5
2013	1784	1506	29	1063	5743	468.9	48.2

注：斜体下划线数据经过修正。1989年以前部分数据统计不完全。

社会服务
当年分省统计资料

05

C-1-1 省级行政区划

地 区	面积（万平方千米）	省级合计（个）	直辖市	省	自治区	特别行政区
全 国	**960**	**34**	**4**	**23**	**5**	**2**
北 京	1.68	1	1			
天 津	1.1	1	1			
河 北	19	1		1		
山 西	15	1		1		
内蒙古	110	1			1	
辽 宁	15	1		1		
吉 林	18	1		1		
黑龙江	46	1		1		
上 海	0.58	1	1			
江 苏	10	1		1		
浙 江	10	1		1		
安 徽	13	1		1		
福 建	12	1		1		
江 西	16	1		1		
山 东	15	1		1		
河 南	16	1		1		
湖 北	18	1		1		
湖 南	21	1		1		
广 东	18	1		1		
广 西	23	1			1	
海 南	3.4	1		1		
重 庆	8.23	1	1			
四 川	48	1		1		
贵 州	17	1		1		
云 南	38	1		1		
西 藏	120	1			1	
陕 西	19	1		1		
甘 肃	39	1		1		
青 海	72	1		1		
宁 夏	6.6	1			1	
新 疆	160	1			1	
香 港		1				1
澳 门		1				1
台 湾		1		1		

C−1−2 地级与县级行政区划

单位：个

地区	地级合计	地级市	地区	自治州	盟	县级合计	市辖区	县级市	县	自治县	旗	自治旗	特区	林区
全国	**333**	**286**	**14**	**30**	**3**	**2853**	**872**	**368**	**1442**	**117**	**49**	**3**	**1**	**1**
北京						16	14		2					
天津						16	13		3					
河北	11	11				172	37	22	107	6				
山西	11	11				119	23	11	85					
内蒙古	12	9			3	102	22	11	17		49	3		
辽宁	14	14				100	56	17	19	8				
吉林	9	8		1		60	20	21	16	3				
黑龙江	13	12	1			128	64	18	45	1				
上海						17	16		1					
江苏	13	13				100	55	23	22					
浙江	11	11				90	34	21	34	1				
安徽	16	16				105	43	6	56					
福建	9	9				85	26	14	45					
江西	11	11				100	20	10	70					
山东	17	17				137	48	29	60					
河南	17	17				159	50	21	88					
湖北	13	12		1		103	38	24	38	2				1
湖南	14	13		1		122	35	16	64	7				
广东	21	21				121	58	23	37	3				
广西	14	14				110	36	7	55	12				
海南	3	3				20	4	6	4	6				
重庆						38	19		15	4				
四川	21	18		3		183	48	14	117	4				
贵州	9	6		3		88	13	7	56	11			1	
云南	16	8		8		129	13	12	75	29				
西藏	7	1	6			74	1	1	72					
陕西	10	10				107	24	3	80					
甘肃	14	12		2		86	17	4	58	7				
青海	8	2		6		43	5	3	28	7				
宁夏	5	5				22	9	2	11					
新疆	14	2	7	5		101	11	22	62	6				

C-1-3 乡镇级行政区划

单位:个

地区	乡镇级合计	镇	乡	#民族乡	街道办事处	区公所
全 国	**40497**	**20117**	**12812**	**1035**	**7566**	**2**
北 京	325	144	38	5	143	
天 津	240	121	6	1	113	
河 北	2246	1045	914	50	286	1
山 西	1398	564	632		202	
内蒙古	1010	493	275	18	242	
辽 宁	1521	636	228	60	657	
吉 林	900	434	184	28	282	
黑龙江	1279	495	398	56	386	
上 海	208	108	2		98	
江 苏	1265	797	79	1	389	
浙 江	1324	639	264	14	421	
安 徽	1508	927	330	9	251	
福 建	1104	616	313	19	175	
江 西	1546	807	594	8	145	
山 东	1826	1107	91		628	
河 南	2406	1085	755	12	566	
湖 北	1232	757	175	10	300	
湖 南	2407	1138	925	97	344	
广 东	1585	1128	11	7	446	
广 西	1247	722	405	59	120	
海 南	224	182	21		21	
重 庆	1016	611	213	14	192	
四 川	4657	1853	2502	98	302	
贵 州	1507	782	606	215	119	
云 南	1388	652	574	141	162	
西 藏	694	140	544	9	10	
陕 西	1420	1142	74		204	
甘 肃	1347	478	750	34	119	
青 海	395	137	228	28	30	
宁 夏	237	101	92		44	
新 疆	1035	276	589	42	169	1

C-1-4 民政部门

地 区	单位数	年末职工人数	#女性	受教育程度		职业资
				大学专科人数	大学本科及以上人数	助理社会工作师人数
全 国	**3492**	**93911**	**30161**	**37524**	**38614**	**1264**
中央级	1	356	98	12	343	
北 京	18	1102	427	203	838	66
天 津	18	588	153	155	377	
河 北	196	6251	2296	2324	1910	118
山 西	131	2636	796	1180	935	22
内蒙古	117	3051	1018	1421	1200	1
辽 宁	124	2965	901	1117	1621	41
吉 林	72	1472	389	508	748	21
黑龙江	146	2597	948	1099	1190	58
上 海	19	744	297	148	531	37
江 苏	122	3459	869	1067	1969	149
浙 江	102	2503	660	944	1291	25
安 徽	122	2702	687	1094	1175	38
福 建	97	1783	375	673	685	23
江 西	117	3129	934	1116	1070	27
山 东	182	6648	2102	2597	3124	115
河 南	183	8211	2981	3594	2583	125
湖 北	117	4055	1219	1842	1528	21
湖 南	146	6400	2190	2398	2312	41
广 东	141	3880	1175	1503	1783	74
广 西	128	2356	718	1038	988	13
海 南	23	628	200	277	206	22
重 庆	41	1200	290	479	653	2
四 川	208	5291	1778	2242	2084	69
贵 州	98	2910	928	1337	1100	9
云 南	148	4356	1456	1839	1664	21
西 藏	82	923	379	372	319	2
陕 西	119	3638	1010	1545	1224	18
甘 肃	101	3041	907	1179	1138	45
青 海	55	846	299	331	327	41
宁 夏	28	684	228	273	346	2
新 疆	290	3506	1453	1617	1352	18

行政机构

单位:个、人、人次、时

格水平	年龄结构				志愿服务	
社会工作师人数	35岁及以下人数	36岁至45岁人数	46岁至55岁人数	56岁及以上人数	志愿者服务人次数	志愿服务时间
1280	**23903**	**34702**	**28031**	**7275**	**280443**	**643668.0**
	136	97	77	46		
24	266	370	371	95		
	97	152	259	80	2122	4340.0
83	1858	2408	1630	355	2122	7717.0
13	653	963	863	157	218	435.0
11	770	1115	953	213		
23	616	916	1091	342	35	74.0
20	284	555	523	110	72	180.0
34	630	1005	854	108		
78	168	220	246	110	4978	13644.0
170	558	1173	1278	450	33740	63190.0
36	436	743	972	352	2023	6245.0
89	475	1051	930	246	23597	59269.0
46	311	631	661	180	35343	110651.0
30	595	1245	988	301	516	1667.0
95	2127	2511	1676	334		
139	2893	2956	1839	523	35	120.0
30	760	1441	1362	492	327	807.0
33	2013	2400	1484	503	6504	23432.0
78	949	1335	1218	378	3920	10150.0
25	305	834	978	239	169	489.0
5	104	253	206	65	642	1200.0
11	208	401	450	141	1056	2782.0
44	1206	2095	1621	369	160345	329636.0
3	697	1203	859	151	357	891.0
26	897	1679	1501	279	735	1649.0
4	450	319	134	20		
54	1052	1303	1028	255	1029	3885.0
41	1002	1116	777	146	144	236.0
18	200	401	204	41		
6	161	261	199	63		
11	1026	1550	799	131	414	979.0

C-1-4续表

地　区	职工按行政级别分				乡、镇、街道民政助理员
	中央级	省级	地级	县级	
全　国	**356**	**3746**	**13867**	**75942**	**51772**
中央级	356				
北　京		219		883	714
天　津		130		458	396
河　北		114	666	5471	3109
山　西		93	394	2149	1485
内蒙古		78	462	2511	1594
辽　宁		93	734	2138	1140
吉　林		89	275	1108	334
黑龙江			643	1954	461
上　海		178		566	408
江　苏		167	673	2619	1692
浙　江		107	418	1978	1885
安　徽		106	504	2092	1993
福　建		120	316	1347	1656
江　西		81	415	2633	1131
山　东		140	883	5625	2784
河　南		144	801	7266	2424
湖　北		108	562	3385	1560
湖　南		181	733	5486	5407
广　东		135	940	2805	780
广　西		108	451	1797	2572
海　南		76	101	451	338
重　庆		193		1007	2915
四　川		128	759	4404	3370
贵　州		109	361	2440	3285
云　南		142	694	3520	1930
西　藏		96	251	576	76
陕　西		150	516	2972	3732
甘　肃			619	2422	1470
青　海		105	166	575	354
宁　夏		140	98	446	219
新　疆		216	432	2858	558

单位:个、人、万元

执行行政事业单位会计制度财务指标					
固定资产原价	上年结转和结余	本年收入合计	本年支出合计	收支结余	行政事业单位增加值
1853515.6	**1395302.7**	**6738435.8**	**6735101.8**	**278474.0**	**2116799.6**
84149.2	33413.1	150890.8	153813.0	30490.8	22186.7
32202.2	48587.6	343857.7	344544.2	34620.5	85091.8
12403.7	8051.8	81794.0	81731.7	7638.4	33631.8
49260.8	6504.7	285589.9	304055.6	1725.9	91053.0
53488.6	9826.4	138694.1	136451.5	2247.8	38774.1
32727.4	7217.6	59721.3	61426.6	5512.3	27625.1
332569.8	6909.9	116155.6	119190.3	4718.0	51292.9
26143.5	2203.8	70351.6	55655.2	0.8	30774.0
26027.0	1296.8	107610.5	108765.3		26126.4
17278.3	54977.8	323747.6	327545.4	690.9	119748.7
66396.1	29420.0	342500.6	357110.3	3521.6	150556.3
53921.7	41190.0	573277.0	567110.6	3804.0	188011.6
58660.5	9418.1	228422.0	225152.9	298.3	65110.7
26936.6	17707.7	233993.9	232244.5	10718.5	96992.8
33013.0	15960.4	76374.3	65737.8	33434.8	22236.3
99021.7	10828.9	231055.6	231509.3	893.0	104771.0
37630.4	13396.8	184293.1	183171.5	4.7	77482.5
84450.7	6252.9	118102.5	90778.0	793.0	42156.8
61516.5	3591.3	323537.9	331404.4	27.4	144656.2
105868.0	699207.0	644794.4	629153.0	5074.4	166737.9
60700.0	76207.0	369503.2	437750.3	21912.3	66109.4
13580.4	20768.5	160223.2	118703.8	8661.5	16309.4
35625.2	5512.7	72382.8	73701.5	1804.0	27932.8
74535.5	41024.5	269569.5	264555.0	14151.3	127264.8
43702.3	65210.3	295305.7	307117.0	4316.5	51159.2
92541.6	79181.7	333838.7	314617.3	36873.4	68588.8
27706.4	1751.8	26328.7	21504.4		4052.7
42114.6	6926.2	149266.9	148582.8	5789.5	42884.4
65408.8	37777.9	53271.3	62831.1	28090.6	37002.5
19030.3		151348.1	159499.2		23345.8
21245.2	14439.3	48961.5	48394.8	7849.2	15014.2
63659.6	20540.2	173671.8	171293.5	2810.6	52119.1

C−1−5 社会服务

地区	单位数	按登记类型分		
		工商登记	编制登记	民政登记
全 国	**1562298**	**19141**	**26465**	**589954**
中央级	2221		31	2190
北 京	27294	616	812	8756
天 津	12254	234	156	5102
河 北	97126	762	1001	19166
山 西	47087	469	834	12290
内蒙古	27457	187	595	11038
辽 宁	44927	2007	860	20732
吉 林	22906	448	1211	9528
黑龙江	28419	543	752	14139
上 海	22453	1150	289	12372
江 苏	107643	2833	1421	61000
浙 江	98175	2194	1234	38021
安 徽	47808	380	782	24266
福 建	40992	320	578	19761
江 西	40167	333	1784	16412
山 东	148894	1319	1241	40355
河 南	82755	964	1083	26638
湖 北	67665	652	1522	29010
湖 南	81710	605	1834	23788
广 东	115248	274	1109	42747
广 西	43287	159	595	17624
海 南	9304	26	76	4673
重 庆	31774	765	515	13856
四 川	99246	773	2449	36625
贵 州	46447	132	723	9946
云 南	34333	339	589	17423
西 藏	6391	3	41	831
陕 西	50839	264	696	18876
甘 肃	36998	87	547	15066
青 海	8260	44	47	3137
宁 夏	7821	74	129	4549
新 疆	24397	185	929	10037

总表

单位:个、人

	按行业分类分			
未登记	社会工作	成员组织	其他社会服务	其他事业单位
926738	**323061**	**1230412**	**6441**	**2384**
	2	2190		29
17110	11791	15357	69	77
6762	2417	9777	37	23
76197	27931	68895	249	51
33494	4870	42014	130	73
15637	3183	24092	163	19
21328	9321	35122	362	122
11719	2165	20431	215	95
12985	3696	24440	224	59
8642	5063	17260	93	37
42389	29660	77589	321	73
56726	28704	68994	287	190
22380	8705	38812	269	22
20333	4627	36094	202	69
21638	5892	33626	214	435
105979	28302	120261	282	49
54070	7433	74861	292	169
36481	11880	55438	271	76
55483	12691	68551	322	146
71118	47638	67146	421	43
24909	9579	33518	131	59
4529	1874	7389	20	21
16638	7408	24193	150	23
59399	10462	88165	455	164
35646	18953	27110	294	90
15982	2861	31163	272	37
5516	339	6027	25	
31003	4430	46183	177	49
21298	6162	30585	211	40
5032	556	7669	32	3
3069	1019	6747	47	8
13246	3447	20713	204	33

C-1-5续表1

地　区	年末职工人数		受教育程度		职业资
		#女性	大学专科人数	大学本科及以上人数	助理社会工作师人数
全　国	**11976467**	**3688093**	**1984651**	**1120189**	**43301**
中央级	32528	14132	1102	23725	711
北　京	237464	104090	54218	68795	6596
天　津	99383	43961	23839	22210	938
河　北	548878	141082	64506	37693	969
山　西	316012	83016	55365	26982	310
内蒙古	163498	55298	41903	15594	173
辽　宁	440884	147660	76513	53915	1317
吉　林	177583	43536	31080	8479	996
黑龙江	271762	100832	52231	17688	847
上　海	319586	110500	55417	21038	1644
江　苏	955434	312068	168258	104576	6614
浙　江	782019	254992	138149	73236	3188
安　徽	351059	104250	68809	30338	1488
福　建	366272	83263	35149	25294	1093
江　西	318369	94341	30973	10226	855
山　东	879871	249386	204002	114535	1354
河　南	518837	148341	90429	43314	853
湖　北	480036	171836	98928	34017	945
湖　南	467849	148902	86717	36781	864
广　东	801068	319188	156618	102971	5584
广　西	426358	91773	48606	30200	580
海　南	65162	22784	8405	6420	71
重　庆	280467	103102	49993	39241	1325
四　川	829552	236697	126114	76429	1853
贵　州	329963	78892	45811	16319	361
云　南	510882	164667	48153	25001	614
西　藏	35590	11355	1079	359	2
陕　西	401465	94309	40491	16011	317
甘　肃	283728	63229	31514	13630	273
青　海	41454	9917	3563	1168	151
宁　夏	56463	18626	9439	5169	92
新　疆	186991	62068	37277	18835	323

单位:个、人、人次、时

格水平	年龄结构				志愿服务	
社会工作师人数	35岁及以下人数	36岁至45岁人数	46岁至55岁人数	56岁及以上人数	志愿者服务人次数	志愿服务时间
21917	**3677999**	**4624544**	**2664241**	**1009683**	**13687495**	**35800508.3**
1450	9770	10951	6642	5165		
2745	66861	81153	60652	28798	6139567	16974276.8
256	28720	34245	26311	10107	191960	457700.0
919	163777	229008	123293	32800	83748	239409.0
245	95877	113693	76409	30033	11045	30934.0
136	49640	63473	38130	12255	34834	98840.0
766	118383	160403	100291	61807	160021	458346.0
283	52379	78970	37125	9109	1601	5370.0
380	100903	104044	52531	14284	16072	56582.0
945	83219	125958	78580	31829	64731	173889.0
2310	273711	362607	240619	78497	671164	1698911.0
2053	238311	289591	168981	85136	652855	1513318.3
545	98609	139679	83992	28779	154976	415776.0
609	85718	120583	99752	60219	143959	405152.0
266	98720	143570	59709	16370	8241	25902.7
777	276747	363523	185716	53885	2408027	5156080.6
541	178059	208283	101290	31205	2208	6783.0
353	169204	176427	103649	30756	14696	41583.5
469	141049	199022	99382	28396	173615	558893.0
2847	343132	251137	153842	52957	177817	605820.4
706	107538	160021	112960	45839	8046	24011.0
27	20967	28909	11076	4210	25419	75791.0
488	93595	102663	57950	26259	757627	2164239.0
971	273371	312359	151045	92777	97281	262133.0
86	94105	143188	69151	23519	1588415	4045288.0
205	157817	199893	108047	45125	2372	6505.0
3	8224	14279	9052	4035	218	729.5
171	100326	145457	123417	32265	28425	90373.5
117	61212	144924	60461	17131	21726	63593.0
31	10420	17825	10677	2532	13578	40834.0
33	12781	22625	15730	5327	5454	16288.0
184	64854	76081	37779	8277	27797	87156.0

C-1-5续表2

地 区	增加值合计	执行企业会计制度单位财务指标					执行行政	
		固定资产原价	营业收入	费用合计	营业利润	企业单位增加值	固定资产原价	上年结转和结余
全 国	**22519112.4**	**21348404.5**	**54311279.7**	**6345407.3**	**1769764.3**	**7397369.0**	**26772248.1**	**1915367.5**
中央级	176825.8	40852.2	23416.8	14544.5	-1728.2	7345.3	128251.2	32417.1
北 京	1216566.7	2669567.7	1848324.5	372336.5	27317.0	271264.5	899021.1	520599.6
天 津	306270.0	248305.9	810720.3	428695.7	12767.3	111681.3	344674.2	39871.0
河 北	800794.3	545277.4	1356268.3	136372.0	13695.3	225564.8	1209048.4	44569.8
山 西	397248.1	361074.6	484699.5	41283.5	373.2	73429.8	1070467.0	24252.2
内蒙古	188824.1	69150.6	73195.7	14671.5	2959.8	18618.7	299882.4	20633.6
辽 宁	949143.0	754016.5	2325936.9	257925.9	79143.7	422619.7	561947.5	31721.5
吉 林	254119.0	196013.9	394656.3	44874.6	6399.0	60119.6	315680.3	5771.4
黑龙江	277561.7	153011.3	203497.4	52118.5	11294.1	48058.2	464182.2	44353.2
上 海	1798903.4	1424453.5	3254927.0	339458.7	381283.9	1021683.7	1132512.4	105059.0
江 苏	2966394.5	4049569.8	13008656.4	1432515.6	338393.0	1250374.7	3153101.1	112247.1
浙 江	3209513.2	5659786.5	17539084.6	1714402.4	602662.0	1926353.9	4479303.5	165111.8
安 徽	498678.2	167904.0	956357.3	67416.2	18841.0	62554.0	819104.0	13741.1
福 建	307740.4	222917.7	388598.2	63904.5	6763.4	68554.4	276309.1	37229.8
江 西	336673.1	120790.9	2089815.3	21082.6	2904.0	19142.8	354078.8	14287.0
山 东	2332858.4	1078621.4	1752909.6	331972.1	134115.1	579847.7	1923978.1	9382.3
河 南	455315.1	312620.6	610715.2	112667.4	16726.0	130988.0	653679.6	19572.4
湖 北	658239.6	227631.1	448004.5	114105.1	6108.2	96557.4	1008313.1	12026.3
湖 南	535950.8	298029.5	578382.5	81179.9	12266.4	85747.3	707356.8	6627.3
广 东	1714733.3	328936.0	341632.4	45704.4	11010.3	72699.5	2895361.3	233328.8
广 西	245733.0	75723.4	400149.1	16116.1	-325.7	28334.4	409538.3	31857.6
海 南	57827.5	24053.1	51139.2	6185.9	1418.7	5755.5	73485.1	57365.6
重 庆	551211.4	596745.7	1774008.3	213804.8	34342.8	270056.0	388063.1	23066.9
四 川	854397.2	500510.1	1634195.8	121671.3	18671.1	316527.3	1067016.9	84156.0
贵 州	228853.1	72484.1	55544.8	19844.7	6063.6	17320.4	206479.7	25951.9
云 南	413736.5	679817.9	1177571.9	172155.2	-2924.8	88214.5	664446.6	96462.6
西 藏	5988.8	3395.3	353.8	119.9	104.4	144.0	72682.9	3159.0
陕 西	370958.4	177887.3	402469.8	59802.2	22500.6	65906.3	465568.9	42376.3
甘 肃	134712.0	32249.3	9175.8	3124.9	215.6	2428.4	281236.6	7367.7
青 海	22085.0	7620.3	10641.8	1526.8	100.0	1971.8	41742.6	1466.1
宁 夏	56064.4	63173.3	41795.9	13405.4	-707.5	14128.9	86474.1	11144.1
新 疆	195192.0	186213.6	264434.8	30418.5	7011.0	33376.3	319261.2	38191.4

单位：万元

事业单位会计制度财务指标				执行民间非营利组织单位会计制度财务指标				
本年收入合计	本年支出合计	收支结余	行政事业单位增加值	固定资产原价	上年结余	本年收入合计	本年费用合计	社会组织增加值
17763568.6	**16878718.9**	**538364.2**	**8607050.4**	**19981438.1**	**5984315.6**	**21962508.4**	**18640615.1**	**6514693.0**
275015.7	242718.1		20678.4	675289.8		3630930.1	2959197.2	148802.1
1059564.5	1260502.3	148641.3	642469.4	1148551.2	1319738.3	1473409.9	1278085.3	302832.8
341501.1	345093.7	4080.3	152852.0	100793.0	17631.6	363478.2	284932.9	41736.7
1282249.7	1262051.3	5645.4	322753.7	837504.0	447886.0	335109.3	397557.7	252475.8
319256.5	352461.7	10873.3	205695.3	386152.0	9998.1	184549.0	165466.8	118123.0
233155.2	226627.4	29266.9	129658.4	107036.6	288.0	79655.7	76585.0	40547.0
606639.3	662695.4	5880.5	275697.6	630252.6	13710.4	591301.6	455437.7	250825.7
273126.2	261772.4	2886.9	170593.5	47213.3	766.9	35190.7	37042.3	23405.9
482488.6	212631.8	77.8	130959.7	100181.0	3280.6	72548.0	207039.3	98543.8
850595.0	707863.7	17579.5	328424.6	408247.1	936740.1	2203311.0	1883224.0	448795.1
1565628.2	1646189.6	38091.5	929375.7	2860105.3	1288865.8	2826314.6	2276037.0	786644.1
1884589.4	1587667.6	19716.6	881344.7	2103425.4	870375.3	1703684.8	1489507.1	401814.6
368378.7	354247.7	3461.8	225375.3	863688.7	11370.4	456365.8	454003.2	210748.9
307290.6	302759.4	10967.8	123118.0	453848.4	114699.0	220066.3	231666.8	116068.0
168280.3	161398.6	-479.7	96306.2	343307.9	6787.8	234442.3	924335.6	221224.1
1809333.8	1808137.7		1031570.8	1285642.2	5834.8	1042522.5	1037728.4	721439.9
451613.8	425408.0	85671.5	223819.7	444472.8	45692.1	261511.3	191941.1	100507.4
585894.5	579020.5	531.1	341119.8	587787.1	6018.5	540962.2	470821.1	220562.4
656790.7	642879.3	5229.9	318253.7	338277.5	65205.1	268465.0	279950.6	131949.8
1586368.8	1406665.6	25498.0	695703.2	2311591.3	271196.5	2195906.6	1630346.8	946330.6
286480.2	269894.7	5450.2	155211.2	341659.7	51852.5	208952.9	87995.8	62187.4
76507.8	77050.4	5719.9	34353.6	92904.9	309.9	24977.8	25145.7	17718.4
282949.1	273559.2	31255.8	145682.8	624156.0	190405.7	412627.7	373676.2	135472.6
626004.3	608896.1	11565.5	299315.5	750333.2	20694.2	657516.8	655696.7	238554.4
179172.2	159309.6	3818.0	103291.1	502233.8	12976.9	142866.2	157172.8	108241.6
244986.6	230411.6	5928.2	148652.1	786761.3	216908.3	223620.7	285466.3	176869.9
10740.5	10991.4		4836.1	5154.3	12474.1	2475.0	2114.3	1008.7
355239.5	351489.8	14221.0	226943.4	506295.8	5156.3	54892.3	130233.2	78108.7
184442.3	133287.1	1262.1	85082.5	109389.2	12218.0	1391821.1	65126.6	47201.1
35289.0	27066.3	834.8	11333.5	64982.8	1071.6	31655.1	26444.8	8779.7
122427.1	41402.0	21714.6	23342.4	54781.0	21670.2	35299.7	43350.8	18593.1
251569.4	246568.9	22973.7	123236.0	109418.9	2492.6	56078.2	57286.0	38579.7

C-1-6 社会服务

地 区	社会服务综合指数(%)	每万人口社会服务机构数(个/万人)	每万人口社会服务职工人员(人/万人)	每百万人口社工助工师(人/百万人)	每千人口社会服务业增加值(万元/千人)	每千人口固定资产原值(万元/千人)
全 国	**100.0**	**11.5**	**88.0**	**90.5**	**16.6**	**50.1**
北 京	272.6	12.9	112.3	729.6	57.5	223.1
天 津	113.1	8.3	67.5	163.3	20.8	47.1
河 北	89.6	13.3	74.9	34.1	10.9	35.4
山 西	81.5	13.0	87.1	37.5	10.9	50.1
内蒙古	80.2	11.0	65.5	23.4	7.6	19.1
辽 宁	115.5	10.2	100.4	100.5	21.6	44.3
吉 林	76.9	8.3	64.6	91.6	9.2	20.3
黑龙江	76.7	7.4	70.9	61.6	7.2	18.7
上 海	156.5	9.3	132.3	246.1	74.5	122.8
江 苏	167.4	13.6	120.3	201.0	37.4	126.7
浙 江	181.4	17.9	142.2	184.1	58.4	222.7
安 徽	90.6	7.9	58.2	49.8	8.3	30.7
福 建	99.7	10.9	97.1	94.1	8.2	25.3
江 西	72.5	8.9	70.4	40.1	7.4	18.1
山 东	114.0	15.3	90.4	56.6	24.0	44.1
河 南	71.1	8.8	55.1	32.1	4.8	15.0
湖 北	101.9	11.7	82.8	53.2	11.4	31.5
湖 南	81.0	12.2	69.9	40.9	8.0	20.1
广 东	129.1	10.8	75.3	231.4	16.1	52.0
广 西	74.3	9.2	90.4	38.7	5.2	17.5
海 南	75.9	10.4	72.8	16.1	6.5	21.3
重 庆	104.1	10.7	94.4	61.0	18.6	54.2
四 川	89.1	12.2	102.3	42.6	10.5	28.6
贵 州	83.9	13.3	94.2	14.3	6.5	22.3
云 南	76.3	7.3	109.0	22.5	8.8	45.5
西 藏	34.7	20.5	114.1	2.6	1.9	26.0
陕 西	96.4	13.5	106.7	36.4	9.9	30.6
甘 肃	77.5	14.3	109.9	22.8	5.2	16.4
青 海	45.2	14.3	71.8	41.5	3.8	19.8
宁 夏	72.0	12.0	86.3	39.9	8.6	31.3
新 疆	67.4	10.8	82.6	39.7	8.6	27.2

综合指数

社会服务事业费占财政支出的比重（‰）	每千人口社会服务事业费（万元/千人）	每百万人口乡镇街道数（个/百万人）	万人口社会服务床位（张/万人）	千老年人口养老床位（张/千人）	每十万人口孤儿数（人/十万人）	每百万人口家庭收养数（件/百万人）
30.6	**31.4**	**29.8**	**38.7**	**24.4**	**40.3**	**18.0**
37.3	73.56	15.4	63.5	39.3	11.2	10.3
21.7	37.5	16.3	38.7	24.6	5.7	11.3
37.9	22.81	30.6	56.6	36.8	20.8	6.0
37.3	31.14	38.5	20.9	13.0	44.4	7.0
33.5	49.51	40.4	35.8	22.5	24.5	7.9
32.2	38.11	34.7	45.0	28.4	17.5	4.7
35.9	35.85	32.7	33.7	19.2	21.4	1.3
47.2	41.45	33.4	30.6	18.7	21.2	2.4
18.4	34.46	8.6	50.1	32.1	8.9	13.1
29.9	29.41	15.9	63.6	41.4	24.6	33.2
30.2	25.99	24.1	56.0	36.5	9.5	73.4
36.8	26.55	25.0	49.3	31.7	44.9	17.4
23.8	19.34	29.3	27.1	16.6	17.6	30.5
35.3	27.08	34.2	38.5	24.8	59.9	19.3
37.4	25.71	18.8	50.2	32.6	19.6	21.5
37.6	22.28	25.6	33.7	21.5	49.8	7.3
42.3	31.89	21.3	43.5	27.2	50.8	23.8
42.6	29.84	36.0	28.4	17.4	77.2	12.6
23.6	18.62	14.9	18.5	11.2	40.9	18.7
40.3	27.39	26.4	28.0	17.6	47.7	30.5
25.2	28.42	25.0	17.1	11.1	26.1	19.4
32.6	33.65	34.2	49.8	32.0	45.6	11.8
46.3	35.53	57.4	49.1	30.1	37.2	13.2
43.5	38.3	43.0	24.1	14.2	64.6	11.1
45.1	39.38	29.6	15.9	9.2	54.1	27.3
15.4	50.02	222.4	33.6	17.3	178.7	36.9
50.2	48.84	37.7	28.1	17.3	35.8	9.5
56.3	50.32	52.2	31.0	19.0	86.8	4.0
30.7	65.35	68.4	28.9	16.2	283.0	10.4
28.9	40.7	36.2	18.5	10.2	108.0	5.4
35.9	48.63	45.7	26.3	13.6	118.3	19.0

C-1-6续表

地 区	每万人口流浪救助人次数（人次/万人）	每十万人口福利企业残疾职工人数（人/十万人）	城市低保平均标准（十元/人、月）	农村低保平均标准（十元/人、月）	五保集中供养平均标准（十元/人、月）	五保分散供养平均标准（十元/人、月）	每万人口优抚对象人数（人/万人）
全 国	**25.6**	**39.6**	**37.3**	**20.3**	**39.0**	**29.2**	**69.9**
北 京	343.0	53.0	58.0	52.2	92.3	92.3	20.5
天 津	9.4	47.9	60.0	44.2	69.8	55.8	30.8
河 北	12.8	24.7	37.9	18.9	32.7	22.6	79.6
山 西	22.6	47.4	35.1	18.0	34.5	21.3	50.9
内蒙古	18.1	21.1	46.0	28.5	56.1	36.7	24.7
辽 宁	13.9	101.0	41.2	23.7	46.7	30.3	53.6
吉 林	17.0	38.8	32.2	17.0	32.6	22.0	44.9
黑龙江	8.4	25.0	38.8	18.6	30.4	22.0	36.9
上 海	15.1	123.3	64.0	50.0	66.5	66.5	16.5
江 苏	11.9	119.6	48.5	39.6	59.8	52.0	62.0
浙 江	10.4	133.9	51.5	39.3	68.2	61.2	47.7
安 徽	24.5	12.0	38.0	20.5	32.2	21.1	84.3
福 建	24.0	22.8	36.3	19.8	47.4	41.5	51.9
江 西	23.5	25.9	39.6	20.1	26.8	23.2	75.4
山 东	13.5	37.9	41.8	20.6	40.2	26.6	103.6
河 南	18.1	28.5	30.9	14.1	31.9	19.8	81.3
湖 北	50.7	28.2	37.5	16.9	29.1	21.4	91.0
湖 南	42.5	26.8	35.6	17.2	42.8	23.3	133.5
广 东	15.4	5.6	38.0	26.9	55.3	52.7	40.8
广 西	15.1	6.9	33.5	16.6	32.1	25.3	63.1
海 南	36.3	14.3	35.3	25.2	44.8	37.4	31.4
重 庆	21.4	86.9	34.7	20.1	41.6	36.7	96.2
四 川	31.8	27.8	30.6	15.3	33.7	27.1	110.0
贵 州	25.1	2.9	34.8	15.3	21.2	13.9	74.6
云 南	16.0	35.5	32.4	16.3	29.9	19.5	80.7
西 藏	20.6	3.4	43.2	16.5	26.1	22.4	16.8
陕 西	28.1	13.5	37.5	17.9	45.9	40.0	77.9
甘 肃	14.2	5.5	27.9	16.2	27.5	25.7	45.2
青 海	27.9	17.7	33.1	17.4	39.2	36.3	25.1
宁 夏	29.8	31.0	28.8	17.0	39.5	26.4	16.2
新 疆	15.8	25.2	30.0	15.0	53.0	34.5	15.5

每千人口福利彩票销售（万元/千人）	社区服务设施覆盖率（%）	城市社区服务中心（站）覆盖率（%）	每十万人口社会组织（个/十万人）	每十万人口村居委会个数（个/十万人）	每万人口结婚对数（对/万人）	每万人口离婚对数（对/万人）	火化率（%）
13.0	**36.9**	**75.4**	**40.2**	**50.2**	**99.0**	**25.7**	**48.2**
24.1	154.0	99.7	40.5	32.1	77.4	30.6	88.1
20.4	33.1	79.0	30.7	35.7	69.7	30.7	74.4
9.6	48.0	51.7	22.5	71.4	101.0	24.4	45.0
8.1	10.1	67.7	32.0	83.8	105.8	16.8	10.4
15.8	15.8	70.9	42.8	53.7	88.7	32.3	46.3
21.2	34.6	97.4	44.4	35.6	84.2	34.7	100.0
15.1	5.6	23.7	33.4	40.9	92.4	45.1	77.1
11.5	18.4	61.0	33.0	30.7	98.2	46.5	73.2
15.5	57.4	63.6	48.1	23.3	61.9	28.8	93.2
16.2	110.9	105.7	70.8	26.9	113.8	27.3	86.6
22.6	73.9	80.3	66.3	59.2	76.8	24.1	100.0
9.8	30.1	78.0	34.3	30.0	133.6	25.9	70.9
12.7	17.4	83.9	51.3	44.3	104.9	21.9	82.8
10.8	15.7	40.7	29.6	44.8	87.1	19.0	32.5
13.8	29.5	82.3	40.0	83.5	91.6	23.1	96.6
6.6	5.7	27.9	25.1	54.5	134.1	22.3	41.1
12.7	28.5	100.7	44.5	51.2	111.4	26.0	60.7
9.0	18.6	46.1	32.4	70.1	92.8	25.0	17
17.8	175.1	127.6	38.8	24.3	82.2	16.6	93.1
10.1	47.0	33.6	36.8	34.2	100.0	19.7	23.8
17.9	51.7	57.4	48.5	34.1	101.9	14.7	5.5
14.7	44.4	73.0	44.3	37.2	102.0	45.0	38.5
8.4	10.5	48.5	43.2	65.5	95.8	33.1	35.8
5.8	91.9	116.0	23.7	53.7	122.7	24.5	27.3
10.7	8.9	48.6	36.2	30.3	96.5	19.5	19.8
13.7	0.6	13.1	18.9	174.3	37.1	5.7	3.9
16.8	10.0	102.8	46.1	76.6	105.1	21.4	20.5
12.8	29.8	137.4	51.6	66.8	72.2	14.9	10.7
16.6	3.7	36.3	52.6	80.1	82.2	18.7	18.4
16.4	28.2	109.0	61.2	42.0	97.6	24.3	12
15.0	18.7	70.9	40.9	50.6	115.1	48.2	25

C-1-7 社会工作师、助理

地区	社会工作师和助理社会工作师累计合格人数	社会工作师		
		累计合格人数	当年考试通过人数	当年报考人数
全国	**123084**	**31183**	**11658**	**48287**
北京	15429	3467	1101	3759
天津	2404	506	160	690
河北	2497	933	234	1134
山西	1361	581	157	817
内蒙古	585	193	74	649
辽宁	4413	1245	481	2074
吉林	2519	460	309	1704
黑龙江	2363	575	188	1167
上海	5943	1948	615	2694
江苏	15955	3621	1528	5222
浙江	10119	3166	1129	4065
安徽	3002	679	246	1838
福建	3552	958	421	2000
江西	1812	452	97	403
山东	5509	1843	482	2014
河南	3017	936	278	956
湖北	3085	548	257	1288
湖南	2738	775	253	1302
广东	24627	5277	2503	8294
广西	1825	427	93	460
海南	144	38	19	95
重庆	1813	488	250	1256
四川	3452	796	326	1547
贵州	500	90	33	194
云南	1056	272	92	582
西藏	8	3		5
陕西	1369	289	124	465
甘肃	588	140	48	234
青海	240	51	15	97
宁夏	261	109	41	247
新疆	623	218	90	851
兵团	275	99	14	184

社工师人员情况

单位：人

	助理社会工作师			
当年实考人数	累计合格人数	当年考试通过人数	当年报考人数	当年实考人数
36695	**91901**	**27300**	**121937**	**97527**
3080	11962	2605	11223	9339
589	1898	373	2415	2063
831	1564	362	1269	1017
664	780	77	492	379
416	392	130	654	470
1702	3168	711	4638	3780
1381	2059	635	4772	3819
881	1788	355	2281	1741
1902	3995	1290	5596	4100
4105	12334	3876	15339	12796
2823	6953	1740	7183	5230
1035	2323	723	3575	2485
1522	2594	933	4737	3925
309	1360	231	961	758
1335	3666	704	2526	1978
862	2081	486	1459	1302
1018	2537	851	5261	4368
928	1963	578	3164	2470
6615	19350	7914	29549	23892
354	1398	222	1014	815
86	106	25	139	122
965	1325	556	2759	2178
1227	2656	840	4670	3771
114	410	64	432	257
382	784	131	932	624
2	5	1	5	4
385	1080	548	1457	1270
190	448	87	317	255
72	189	19	134	113
196	152	36	506	411
605	405	156	2167	1541
119	176	41	311	254

C-1-8 社会服务职业

地 区	累计鉴定合格人数	2013年鉴定合格人数	养老护理员		假肢类技能人员	
			累计鉴定合格人数	2013年鉴定合格人数	累计鉴定合格人数	2013年鉴定合格人数
全 国	**107308**	**17612**	**10025**	**4072**	**1290**	**193**
中央级	4120	1590	1484	1147	355	57
北 京	12431	2471	238	1	58	
天 津	577	112	144	3	2	
河 北	630	189	318	46	10	
山 西	2059	395	390	191		
内蒙古	1738	238	80	3	13	
辽 宁	2410	204	284	132	84	
吉 林	2556	460	87		5	
黑龙江	3201	275	446	66	4	
上 海	2641	15	8	2	131	13
江 苏	2840	191	41	4	126	22
浙 江	30502	4823	22	3	44	9
安 徽	2179	81	182	1	24	
福 建	98	35	2	1	4	
江 西	2313	264	54	2	11	
山 东	4546	354	491	4	25	13
河 南	3816	1150	1103	500	63	
湖 北	2507	122	360		13	
湖 南	4617	411	124	2	20	
广 东	4542	1301	1778	1053	116	43
广 西	1535	449	613	256	93	17
海 南	72	37	14			
重 庆	3531	395	7	3	24	
四 川	2633	650	1011	381	1	
贵 州	2241	142	247	3	8	
云 南	2304	255	58	1	23	
西 藏	24					
陕 西	457	154	73			
甘 肃	907	236	201	129	19	19
青 海	199	162	145	137		
宁 夏	2595	361	18	1		
新 疆	487	90	2		14	

说明：1.以上数据为民政部职业技能鉴定指导中心及分布在全国31个省、自治区、直辖市76个鉴定站鉴定人数和竞赛晋级人数（不含地方自行组织的鉴定人数）。

2.殡葬类职业包括：殡仪服务员（初中高技师4个级别）、遗体接运工（初中高3个级别）、遗体防腐师（初中高技师高级技师5个级别）、遗体整容师（初中高技师高级技师5个级别）、遗体火化师（初中高技师高级技师5个级别）、墓地管理员（初中高技师4个级别）。

3.假肢类职业包括：假肢师（初中高技师高级技师5个级别）、矫形器师（初中高技师高级技师5个级别）。

技能人员情况

单位：人

孤残儿童护理员		灾害信息员		殡葬类技能人员	
累计鉴定合格人数	2013年鉴定合格人数	累计鉴定合格人数	2013年鉴定合格人数	累计鉴定合格人数	2013年鉴定合格人数
6295	**2216**	**78390**	**8989**	**11308**	**2142**
521	161	856	151	904	74
154	3	10651	2092	1330	375
70	59	246		115	50
164	81	11		127	62
176	81	1493	123		
278	136	1072		295	99
160	49	1573		309	23
124	36	2340	424		
178	81	2440	128	133	
71		2420		11	
387	101	1869		417	64
305	84	29877	4718	254	9
88	73	1498		387	7
46	34	46			
209	98	1809	49	230	115
302	119	3052		676	218
437	108	2041	542	172	
256	53	1663	42	215	27
260	70	2157		2056	339
474	120	1238		936	85
172	77	177		480	99
49	37	1		8	
143	1	2587	252	770	139
189	77	1245	162	187	30
168	78	1603		215	61
197	101	1517		509	153
8				16	
377	154	7			
67	55	479		141	33
49	25	5			
64	20	2306	306	207	34
152	44	111		208	46

C-1-9 各省、自治区、直辖市

地 区	1952年	1953年	1954年	1955年	1956年	1957年
全 国	**28265**	**35484**	**60390**	**49842**	**56906**	**53119**
中央级	6	443	20619	8736	270	85
北 京	198	237	276	247	584	302
天 津	208	315	131	157	217	240
河 北	2849	4558	4764	4526	9681	6640
山 西	1253	1398	1531	1373	2096	1953
内蒙古	912	370	306	364	625	417
辽 宁	611	1434	1392	1298	1638	1339
吉 林	346	595	880	856	1331	1610
黑龙江	640	831	912	952	1442	1336
上 海	550	306	411	729	1121	1073
江 苏	1980	1993	2051	3003	4052	5051
浙 江	398	426	505	757	1430	988
安 徽	2051	4061	3382	3453	4748	4306
福 建	828	732	789	933	1473	866
江 西	1519	1040	1368	2253	1889	1802
山 东	2624	3993	5082	3975	3664	5261
河 南	1440	2745	2307	2494	4360	5539
湖 北	2719	1058	2765	2664	1306	1505
湖 南	1255	1089	3381	2205	2259	2177
广 东	1762	1454	1270	1407	2725	2729
广 西	516	645	735	700	1414	1589
海 南						
重 庆						
四 川	1583	2035	2052	2646	3570	2606
贵 州	368	686	633	567	618	494
云 南	630	695	875	740	908	599
西 藏			43	207	91	
陕 西	519	1023	984	1135	1794	1250
甘 肃	390	1074	675	1171	1083	871
青 海	52	134	140	154	281	237
宁 夏						
新 疆	58	114	131	140	236	254

社会服务经费历年支出情况

单位：万元

1958年	1959年	1960年	1961年	1962年	1963年
32693	**44786**	**72444**	**98912**	**74475**	**87533**
82	192	262	39		
376	751	824	658	542	638
194					
2494	4148	5070	10807	5780	15681
2279	1656	2659	2896	2556	2640
505	873	525	785	1468	1124
1098	1249	4475	4392	3933	3467
1126	764	1055	1271	1660	2138
948	782	991	1485	2151	2362
464	475	471	422	539	874
2617	2956	4843	4107	4873	7282
672	874	857	1414	1597	1166
1642	3169	3161	4704	3530	5431
823	4141	2823	2798	1493	1687
1717	1691	2179	3224	3168	2273
3795	4494	8141	11332	6963	7201
2990	2672	10271	11417	8107	10099
1210	2466	4428	4569	3767	3468
1344	967	1690	4299	2697	2834
1223	2982	4608	3475	2830	3146
582	903	997	2687	1505	2125
1982	2583	6315	9758	5918	4227
331	613	750	2390	1429	1792
514	675	880	1692	773	1250
2	1	25	48	117	
588	1109	1113	1530	1422	1640
539	681	1778	4522	2464	2988
164	447	576	1028	1005	
92	239	428	303	365	
300	233	249	860	1823	

C-1-9续表1

地 区	1964年	1965年	1966年	1967年	1968年	1969年
全 国	**161510**	**107869**	**88112**	**81887**	**56154**	**66683**
中央级	31	2325	454	534	308	11
北 京	816	1047	914	939	868	820
天 津				473	439	572
河 北	31433	18545	12395	6983	4443	5333
山 西	2361	2899	4447	2692	2478	2579
内蒙古	1360	1440	2182	2401	1194	842
辽 宁	3382	2942	2572	2781	2473	3542
吉 林	2235	1798	1704	1745	1579	1890
黑龙江	2796	2611	2548	2169	1775	2355
上 海	1074	1220	1472	1654	1410	1359
江 苏	11070	5506	7298	5400	3756	3839
浙 江	1152	1351	1142	1366	1486	1481
安 徽	10567	3347	4119	6861	4025	4246
福 建	1394	1463	1673	1738	1727	1922
江 西	3081	1989	2145	2318	1637	1924
山 东	11079	15807	9458	9844	5878	7622
河 南	48554	17841	9303	8611	4105	6983
湖 北	3319	2790	2579	3177	2651	3509
湖 南	4522	2482	2141	2562	1848	2019
广 东	3056	2664	2454	2644	2046	2639
广 西	4006	1983	1997	2541	1641	1607
海 南						
重 庆						
四 川	4495	5179	4774	4067	3374	3439
贵 州	1808	1726	1730	1926	1224	1314
云 南	1494	1596	1772	1412	807	1018
西 藏	133	192	374			96
陕 西	1918	3137	3623	1874	1477	1733
甘 肃	2310	1611	1161	1963	671	989
青 海	465	695	409	185	190	246
宁 夏	378	284	272	287	200	238
新 疆	1212	1399	1000	740	444	516

单位：万元

1970年	1971年	1972年	1973年	1974年	1975年
65349	**68269**	**81549**	**99675**	**90406**	**127082**
		8	10		
895	974	1192	1506	1284	1461
405	407	546	762	937	881
2054	3591	5482	8727	5925	5960
4777	4563	4025	4696	3587	3420
891	649	1020	1914	1575	1559
2867	3922	4574	5590	3902	18731
1837	1968	1753	2174	2500	2448
2247	2317	2768	3701	3884	3701
1442	1554	1676	1885	2088	2263
4191	4969	7368	6988	7258	8001
1496	1517	2399	2103	1973	1984
5547	3365	4639	4625	3981	5828
1463	1481	1721	2142	2150	1991
2047	2357	2357	4039	3220	2964
6442	9034	8801	8110	8601	10417
4947	4699	4799	5474	4190	24152
4197	3116	3462	4747	3487	4471
1668	1602	2272	3321	2580	2942
2734	2410	2800	4041	5051	3836
1555	1827	1713	1597	1669	1653
3678	4518	5615	6780	5936	6061
1646	1535	2116	3574	1955	2352
2460	1454	1746	1509	2245	2242
100	104	173	228	195	206
1778	2099	2415	3435	2986	2579
952	968	2206	3421	4183	2603
207	291	366	311	342	521
242	354	810	1369	1813	600
584	651	727	896	909	1255

C–1–9续表2

地 区	1976年	1977年	1978年	1979年	1980年	1981年
全 国	**161690**	**185288**	**137135**	**183279**	**174769**	**192267**
中央级			11	44	103	138
北 京	1742	3068	1990	2238	2802	3167
天 津	933	13670	1061	1482	1474	1670
河 北	7041	36568	11605	9140	11165	13597
山 西	4111	4813	5437	8154	6749	7893
内蒙古	2502	1873	2040	5922	5714	6218
辽 宁	14705	7427	6103	5607	6671	8073
吉 林	2834	3677	3869	3477	4482	4970
黑龙江	4176	5463	5545	5149	5370	6562
上 海	2469	2581	2777	3290	3375	3381
江 苏	7719	8031	9208	10019	11269	12914
浙 江	2424	2641	2853	3475	3703	3897
安 徽	15690	6300	6756	13263	9385	9550
福 建	2432	2826	2730	3272	3625	4268
江 西	3606	3981	3953	8610	6289	5309
山 东	9746	10599	12292	15169	16327	14126
河 南	40056	21437	14140	19495	12007	10921
湖 北	5463	5160	6149	9597	9265	12458
湖 南	3442	3550	4380	6747	7026	8924
广 东	4884	5546	5435	8146	8337	7767
广 西	1963	2355	2073	4019	3213	3674
海 南						
重 庆						
四 川	9037	12602	8511	12722	12063	15429
贵 州	2748	3296	2740	4767	4123	4718
云 南	3428	3783	2948	3478	4172	4599
西 藏	289	270	379	1366	1704	1208
陕 西	3174	4575	4834	5780	5390	8198
甘 肃	2240	5485	4030	5204	4801	4338
青 海	407	514	696	853	862	915
宁 夏	1150	1780	1090	1040	1385	1118
新 疆	1279	1417	1500	1754	1918	2267

单位：万元

1982年	1983年	1984年	1985年	1986年	1987年
191874	**216116**	**242371**	**295841**	**344064**	**359278**
78	163	286	443	2526	2742
3416	4063	4904	5719	7287	8906
1669	2194	3101	3583	4113	4531
10179	9692	12427	16654	16581	20578
7854	7015	7924	10683	10193	11833
5135	7379	7909	9030	11684	10867
10591	11727	11741	18341	22112	18104
4951	6300	5952	8391	13570	14016
8005	9546	8782	10119	13791	13686
3215	3170	3540	4467	5503	5603
11991	14750	16403	16254	20586	21208
4070	4808	6480	8174	10211	12353
7521	12093	14059	14340	13524	12942
4773	5506	5601	8298	7657	9238
6183	7093	8360	8364	9768	11546
18998	17811	17413	22757	22496	29017
12862	15216	13710	18456	20939	2260
7956	10798	10760	11860	14581	14846
7546	10428	10373	12357	15013	15167
9550	9035	12337	14516	15526	17076
3897	4779	6382	9438	9634	9054
14542	13943	17823	20667	24973	25524
4354	5211	5833	9182	8657	9092
4231	5251	7025	10137	13752	12712
1151	1357	1821	1391	1789	1828
6271	5820	6313	7545	8586	9299
5778	4902	8983	6541	7655	7238
1068	1270	1674	1918	2134	1837
1819	2329	1497	1826	1990	1780
2220	2467	2958	4395	4768	4896

C−1−9续表3

地 区	1988年	1989年	1990年	1991年	1992年	1993年
全 国	**395646**	**466492**	**519383**	**625359**	**637097**	**698708**
中央级	1297	1185	1517	1792	3217	3108
北 京	11355	12805	14738	16249	19073	26105
天 津	5209	5861	6585	7176	8173	9218
河 北	24272	26484	32162	30785	33344	38161
山 西	13977	15845	15976	17378	19264	19515
内蒙古	11254	10975	13510	13449	14250	15314
辽 宁	19595	22233	26318	26380	29561	32903
吉 林	10692	11439	14155	14619	16553	18461
黑龙江	14205	15127	15982	18411	19734	19377
上 海	3965	4741	5364	6270	7742	10368
江 苏	23816	27647	33150	50604	48290	47590
浙 江	16113	18710	21111	22094	22124	26924
安 徽	14854	16444	19755	80611	39002	26982
福 建	10332	11213	13935	15070	18423	20141
江 西	13240	15076	15791	16915	21249	21410
山 东	31890	39382	44965	46744	52525	62616
河 南	21784	26566	24275	27675	31304	34498
湖 北	17804	20704	21092	23318	23677	28918
湖 南	19110	22384	24981	23436	24712	29096
广 东	16675	20206	21863	25022	29602	43983
广 西	9757	11955	11313	12728	14317	16760
海 南	2338	3659	3366	3843	4270	4630
重 庆						
四 川	28123	32186	36228	39004	42563	49037
贵 州	9408	11568	12079	11043	11761	15154
云 南	14934	31640	33901	38725	41026	30502
西 藏	1795	2116	2909	3499	2647	2598
陕 西	10602	12277	13688	13412	16805	20107
甘 肃	8346	7681	8813	9124	11256	12186
青 海	1750	1802	2086	2036	2387	2965
宁 夏	2609	1805	2000	2206	2456	2464
新 疆	4549	4776	5775	5741	5790	7617

单位：万元

1994年	1995年	1996年	1997年	1998年	1999年
870194	**1034502**	**1211500**	**1335202**	**1618445**	**1946843**
4077	3703	6371	5954	50783	11856
36146	44073	54012	61184	74406	97748
11970	15023	17254	19738	20952	20611
48303	58804	74364	71151	79064	88202
22995	31008	37882	37150	39519	45466
18378	20470	26012	26773	35484	35659
44239	60067	59580	65370	74946	85394
24648	30876	31416	33928	52337	53311
26195	28798	30459	33020	55977	60566
15557	19773	23984	30860	37336	54151
59349	69907	80163	93383	108862	121349
40044	43610	50852	60657	65733	88269
26883	37348	43979	50559	56473	72895
25502	31904	34498	46134	49421	50996
23815	30354	33883	35962	47177	45334
71995	76826	88009	101613	112960	131746
44163	52458	59353	64155	68311	80338
39148	40291	50385	58511	85285	75622
35093	42680	53778	48234	54533	73272
53653	64806	75354	88748	96993	112133
30480	28730	36280	28944	30995	31950
6163	7210	8828	8274	9472	10818
			25048	35054	51123
59629	70257	77059	63016	72283	89492
15641	20528	26419	27866	27126	30834
31529	36916	46048	52043	53384	63169
5304	4466	5228	6987	11749	6824
20404	26336	32108	31702	25791	43230
13897	17748	21484	20366	20554	26371
3454	4342	6473	8088	8669	23784
3244	3458	4279	4397	5442	8651
8297	11732	15706	25387	22690	55676

C-1-9续表4

地 区	2000年	2001年	2002年	2003年	2004年	2005年
全 国	**2296954**	**2847548**	**3922695**	**4989171.81**	**5773906.5**	**7184146**
中央级	29338	13965	18467	18027.2	39289.8	37423
北 京	150746	196540	233429	303795.3	327957	370918
天 津	30547	41580	58202	62682.2	71091.4	92462
河 北	113381	125698	153525	185640.8	216769.6	283480
山 西	56815	71776	105897	124002.5	147569.6	192257
内蒙古	44674	55328	70606	99367.7	126236.7	141727
辽 宁	131675	180547	227704	279736.9	304551.2	368476
吉 林	51153	76026	118392	166702.2	182133.4	218688
黑龙江	61753	80658	177852	167487.2	193823.3	222865
上 海	87021	121538	167719	222539.6	228764.3	282196
江 苏	159691	170800	205763	256062.56	309196	419996
浙 江	97755	124023	159432	189645.4	294720.4	354320
安 徽	72568	89476	138918	208605.9	195411.9	250782
福 建	67797	68897	85353	94060.8	139539.3	157015
江 西	49521	57966	92013	149217.2	176371.5	225667
山 东	159315	180470	233918	283989.3	311522.3	408419
河 南	102698	117574	159157	221712.8	251438.9	337872
湖 北	113381	122382	167653	229233.85	270653.4	345556
湖 南	80343	104818	158443	210815.4	252891.5	326694
广 东	144461	198362	278022	341821	386221.4	483430
广 西	35135	49819	82929	109901	113722.5	156841
海 南	13568	15372	18032	24304.1	27949.8	38103
重 庆	55934	70571	117114	125112.4	145713	174682
四 川	105249	139493	194774	244374.4	302566.3	376043
贵 州	36085	51264	67973	82093.5	102696.6	151257
云 南	78944	98782	115945	150814	183854.7	202346
西 藏	9920	14979	15358	17912.7	23199.7	22574
陕 西	54365	72136	103474	147038.8	149120.1	186935
甘 肃	35251	42851	58315	75346	91876.1	111530
青 海	16159	19790	24812	36616	39139.1	47402
宁 夏	13775	21289	28724	30448.1	34071.3	35346
新 疆	56940	52768	104762	130065	133844.4	160847

单位：万元

2006年	2007年	2008年	2009年	2010年	2011年	2012年	2013年
9153527	**12154874**	**21464484**	**21819430.2**	**26975149**	**32291356.0**	**36837379.4**	**42765370.8**
27907	32841	263213	55240.2	488035.9	93505.4	100110.8	137419.9
450229	575756	575302	745435.4	982144.3	1031493.0	1260515.9	1555734.8
121917	149046	196893	244982.6	313824.7	375011.5	444250.9	552118.0
356510	488387	678036	843485.2	969269.1	1244217.3	1438698.1	1672465.7
236469	339210	457567	562518.4	634004.6	876097.5	936468.5	1130400.3
187147	283105	420111	575897.9	768526.2	968084.5	1127395.6	1236610.0
437608	575209	724799	887386.5	1066504.6	1347428.2	1567755.2	1672890.8
284676	341920	470519	642777.6	750632.3	801698.3	765275.0	986245.5
376619	478896	643011	800947.6	854398.8	1050480.9	1152380.1	1589618.1
316864	406118	515828	557187.9	572521.7	662862.5	727872.8	832211.6
502744	632560	811832	996449.2	1265312.3	1711513.8	1970955.5	2335259.9
415110	508925	610800	704117.9	884859.5	1061597.3	1253870.2	1428845.7
312519	490974	659432	804010.6	971558.4	1263090.4	1421837.3	1601142.2
226313	247500	282403	322487.9	422187.8	503195.6	614533.8	729824.6
340990	434664	596019	693704.1	847650.9	986614.7	1075144.7	1224409.1
526836	715079	885720	1122739	1437374.8	1691804.7	2183629.3	2502270.9
425038	598726	785189	1035342.8	1230796.6	1586875.1	1740800.2	2097496.0
440298	514067	748412	897367.7	1082788.8	1408483.1	1531263.7	1849392.5
422998	521304	771404	997685.9	1165255.4	1545645.5	2003252.4	1996276.3
635940	720130	834465	1021108.9	1154286.9	1480652.6	1668953.2	1981669.0
175928	247212	410162	492763.3	731162.4	971372.9	1173997.1	1292515.6
49003	65929	96527	142315.6	190264.1	223849.3	240254.6	254400.4
216847	307697	435014	514479.6	674873.3	783120.4	907587.4	999446.7
500440	734868	4848630	2289514.1	2408738.2	2168767.6	2375722.4	2880631.2
181266	264299	443051	560108.4	728242.8	1116447.6	1248670.9	1341494.8
228950	420914	687354	930167.6	1224026.2	1432131.1	1730472.3	1845730.7
30224	38363	69982	82169.4	85017.8	130279.7	155073.7	156074.8
244342	365358	849627	867024.3	1139380.6	1356364.3	1424205.1	1838401.7
149598	226791	1063855	577204.8	740624.8	1000902.5	1051754.7	1299304.5
51844	81455	123508	189659.7	330701.5	359785.5	341516.9	377594.3
57593	79705	110375	143479.2	161335.6	195226.4	220055.6	266258.2
222762	267867	395446	519670.9	698848.1	862756.8	983105.5	1101217.0

C-1-10 社会服务经费预算

地 区	预算指标		
	2013年	2012年	增长 (%)
合 计	**43268489.6**	**36691484.0**	**17.9**
中央级	132229.8	105133.9	25.8
北 京	1429615.9	1407329.9	1.6
天 津	561715.2	444186.8	26.5
河 北	1658617.9	1448324.0	14.5
山 西	1145199.4	936323.8	22.3
内蒙古	1274677.4	1150333.0	10.8
辽 宁	1667135.5	1531061.0	8.9
吉 林	982109.1	801885.0	22.5
黑龙江	1629434.3	1139099.9	43.0
上 海	952375.6	889126.6	7.1
江 苏	2277104.5	2024023.3	12.5
浙 江	1449943.3	1257886.2	15.3
安 徽	1588794.1	1389497.5	14.3
福 建	732793.1	604535.8	21.2
江 西	1260784.9	1065920.7	18.3
山 东	2542119.4	2106607.2	20.7
河 南	2089771.4	1672408.6	25.0
湖 北	1837118.4	1519447.5	20.9
湖 南	1995947.6	1860581.3	7.3
广 东	1982305.0	1741587.7	13.8
广 西	1350210.3	1086183.4	24.3
海 南	294076.0	242617.3	21.2
重 庆	1007108.9	893915.4	12.7
四 川	2909798.8	2286512.0	27.3
贵 州	1458130.4	1217755.6	19.7
云 南	1854957.0	1706053.3	8.7
西 藏	166015.3	147540.7	12.5
陕 西	1996633.1	1493548.8	33.7
甘 肃	1292279.6	1048622.3	23.2
青 海	351399.8	322080.2	9.1
宁 夏	285516.1	223890.6	27.5
新 疆	1112572.5	927464.7	20.0

指标地方安排情况

单位：万元

地方预算安排预算指标		
2013年	2012年	增长 (%)
21610000.3	**18586288.1**	**16.3**
866453.9	808991.9	7.1
421625.2	302364.8	39.4
716433.9	616136.0	16.3
517245.4	437123.8	18.3
700058.4	695314.0	0.7
764356.5	732562.0	4.3
318734.1	226344.0	40.8
788714.3	463823.9	70.0
834706.6	752098.6	11.0
1753758.5	1560461.3	12.4
1229097.3	1083587.2	13.4
726851.1	681654.5	6.6
484266.1	411216.8	17.8
474373.9	403254.7	17.6
1457377.4	1188918.2	22.6
765640.4	585784.6	30.7
723950.4	588977.5	22.9
755067.6	838105.3	-9.9
1518665.0	1379375.7	10.1
618515.3	514022.4	20.3
159519.0	139635.3	14.2
470061.9	413985.4	13.5
1257946.8	908844.0	38.4
393433.4	388081.6	1.4
751076.0	733138.3	2.4
46825.3	52979.7	-11.6
1055311.1	736995.8	43.2
383462.6	350866.3	9.3
136929.8	157092.2	-12.8
122015.1	93965.6	29.9
397528.0	340586.7	16.7

C-1-11 中央专项

地 区	合计	抚恤合计	财社[2012]147号	财社[2012]148号	财社[2013]3号
全 国	**21497160.48**	**3697979**	**1860960**	**15345**	**348081**
北 京	563162	23930	10845	127	1648
天 津	140090	16911	7917	79	1566
河 北	942184	240015	117585	4637	23517
山 西	627954	113639	52472	1298	7571
内蒙古	574619	41989	22337	186	2528
辽 宁	902779	99802	50667	266	8542
吉 林	663375	69909	40380	152	5178
黑龙江	840720	77393	42669	255	5780
上 海	117669	12352	6469	2	1181
江 苏	523346	169093	84429	1447	18235
浙 江	220846	68297	31391	236	7727
安 徽	861943	175241	87528	159	17704
福 建	248527	65065	29115	19	7020
江 西	786411	166730	77733	10	12371
山 东	1084742	420070	215588	4852	39954
河 南	1324131	273208	139944	1004	28479
湖 北	1113168	227394	111195	57	20242
湖 南	1240880	306149	151582	36	31094
广 东	463640	110697	52366	19	14461
广 西	731695	91731	47888	6	9084
海 南	134557	18165	8266	39	1241
重 庆	537047	109151	59483	19	10745
四 川	1651852	336209	175043	48	31569
贵 州	1064697	100217	52249	9	9464
云 南	1103881	136108	71152	28	13613
西 藏	119190	4751	2248		189
陕 西	949223	139552	71556	288	11159
甘 肃	908817	41715	22133	48	4116
青 海	214470	8722	4439	2	506
宁 夏	163501	6923	3387	4	439
新 疆	678044.48	26851	10904	13	1158

拨款对账单

单位：万元

财社[2013]18号	财社[2013]19号	财社[2013]48号	财社[2013]63号	财社[2013]64号	财社[2013]74号	财社[2013]75号
500	**500**	**2500**	**41855**	**269994**	**1045522**	**5081**
			180	3509	6408	50
		70	960	300	5227	30
		130	3100	20734	63067	1197
		70	1150	17071	30851	264
		110	1145	1389	12956	78
		110	500	8207	28577	87
			1390	11700	9136	98
		50	1350	3560	21507	68
			200		4026	1
		50	1800	9080	48724	608
			900	6104	19735	137
		130	1300	14477	49332	51
		60	780	10220	16189	4
		130	1620	28550	42317	2
		140	3250	24171	118095	1860
		120	1950	23268	71167	340
		110	2350	23534	63980	23
		130	1020	23500	90716	10
		120	1440	6836	31766	7
500		130	1750	3960	26115	2
			300	3320	4441	13
		70	790	1220	33736	10
		130	2490	11050	106320	11
			1710	2249	31612	2
	500	120	1750	3330	42020	11
		70	200		1766	
		70	3050	7990	41251	97
		190	1050	485	12441	17
		70	730		2666	1
			650	180	1955	1
		120	1000		7423	1

C-1-11续表1

地 区	财社[2013]148号	财社[2013]149号	财社[2013]154号	新疆兵团	安置合计
全 国	**90902**	**577**	**10928**	**5234**	**2774042**
北 京	601	5	557		513349
天 津	448	3	311		64242
河 北	5362	162	524		152681
山 西	2675	45	172		48800
内蒙古	1187	7	66		31897
辽 宁	2640	9	197		276298
吉 林	1606	7	262		57941
黑龙江	2079	9	66		47885
上 海	358		115		88234
江 苏	4398	60	262		163336
浙 江	1679	11	377		54200
安 徽	4177	6	377		47286
福 建	1468	1	189		44554
江 西	3628		369		29606
山 东	10889	191	1080		249044
河 南	6267	39	630		89151
湖 北	5459	2	442		103820
湖 南	7282	1	778		61216
广 东	2707	1	974		110489
广 西	2230		66		30682
海 南	413	1	131		10800
重 庆	2888	1	189		45629
四 川	8638	2	908		116764
贵 州	2561		361		18491
云 南	3460	1	123		74828
西 藏	147		131		9821
陕 西	3572	11	508		116172
甘 肃	1044	2	189		43615
青 海	242		66		12056
宁 夏	176		131		8277
新 疆	621		377	5234	52878

单位：万元

财社[2012]149号	财社[2012]150号	财社[2013]71号	财社[2013]72号	财社[2013]73号	财社[2013]129号	财社[2013]132号
1303814	**46881**	**89520**	**65462**	**113572**	**2590**	**1012167**
218491	7756		131	57314	40	195133
30275	1088	470	203	2371		28417
70030	2172	4039	3972	3489	180	65191
25624	934	751	849	806	50	19120
17387	908	662	1219	569	100	10421
132749	4668	5264	3178	5700	210	100867
30602	1231	3875	1393	1033	150	18595
22960	1114	3707	2436	755	80	15968
41193	1540		122	7414	10	31730
72525	2207	8815	4983	3785	70	55288
25005	1097	3571	1924	1886	50	19732
18302	607	8146	3715	748	110	14657
23684	947	850	1436	1659	30	15246
11192	454	3396	2784	397	50	8018
113109	3852	9788	5571	5740	270	87865
41007	1739	8170	5600	2029	260	29051
51814	1722	5580	3772	1722	160	37752
28906	796	5255	2925	614	110	21304
59679	1957		2708	3834	50	39603
12753	628	1221	2273	418	30	8274
6042	255	133	370	364	20	3445
22782	764	742	1359	1708	100	17543
57210	2111	5603	5285	2440	210	40934
8396	417	1567	1572	209	40	5979
42493	1572	1581	1226	789	80	25690
5432	95	2	41	127		4026
58445	2114	3439	1808	2957	60	45673
20086	860	1143	1514	1103	40	18146
5826	194	105	57	262	20	5392
3537	173	351	587	249	10	3209
26278	909	1294	449	1081		19898

C-1-11续表2

地 区	财社[2013]133号	军休住房 财社[2013]252号	新疆兵团	社会福利合计	财社[2012]151号
全 国	**45296**	**92492**	**2248**	**543649.48**	**189162**
北 京	10041	24443		5011	486
天 津	1034	384		2886	219
河 北	3593	15		17779	5233
山 西	666			16346	4646
内蒙古	631			11930	2880
辽 宁	4013	19649		9763	1495
吉 林	936	126		8498	2188
黑龙江	865			9465	2459
上 海	1490	4735		2519	439
江 苏	2912	12751		17041	3826
浙 江	844	91		9835	1711
安 徽	974	27		22449	12205
福 建	702			8802	1379
江 西	328	2987		24529	8356
山 东	3179	19670		20450	3521
河 南	1295			37666	14098
湖 北	1298			22548	8869
湖 南	1248	58		36510	15751
广 东	1273	1385		20019	9747
广 西	421	4664		23623	8710
海 南	171			6479	959
重 庆	631			18569	7586
四 川	1641	1330		33076	12100
贵 州	311			19508	7414
云 南	1220	177		27872	16578
西 藏	98			11700	1953
陕 西	1676			18838	5419
甘 肃	723			23603	8222
青 海	200			14959	6406
宁 夏	161			9320	2776
新 疆	721		2248	32056.48	11531

单位：万元

财社[2013]60号	中央补助地方专项彩票公益金合计	财社[2013]242号	财社[2013]242号	财社[2013]242号	财社[2013]242号	财综[2013]99号
37063	**309138**	**122649**	**19798**	**50791**	**16900**	**99000**
112	4413	2195	163	1252	104	699
0	2667	1135	189	491		852
558	11988	3687	575	1280	419	6027
1013	10687	4212	1413	1220	752	3090
448	8602	4102	375	1699	386	2040
490	7778	2491	432	1154	1178	2523
12	6298	2902	402	1320	276	1398
707	6299	2828	447	617	346	2061
97	1983	1539	193	251		
908	12307	4072	1529	1566	742	4398
-268	8392	2748	430	741	702	3771
-2031	12275	4859	549	1305	888	4674
235	7188	2712	410	1032	190	2844
2588	13585	7399	481	1690	1045	2970
924	16005	5114	667	1433	343	8448
4457	19111	6044	704	5146	641	6576
2221	11458	4952	530	1289	490	4197
3931	16828	7680	1560	1254	820	5514
1071	9201	3759	682	1115	210	3435
1894	13019	4297	1488	2401	954	3879
162	5358	3358	327	359	426	888
1835	9148	3886	1354	1127	234	2547
3420	17556	6359	637	2198	799	7563
3103	8991	3439	459	1211	339	3543
666	10628	4031	467	2288	488	3354
726	9021	3444	355	3692	576	954
1299	12120	3783	1426	1924	1144	3843
2804	12577	5399	437	3076	842	2823
1450	7103	3619	361	1350	774	999
652	5892	3454	356	856	203	1023
1579	10660	3150	400	4454	589	2067

C-1-11续表3

地　区	新疆兵团	城市低保合计	财社[2013]51号	财社[2012]158号	财社[2013]4号
全　国	**8286.48**	**5455709**	**1253672**	**3512769**	**638848**
北　京		3324			3324
天　津		44966	8932	31067	4967
河　北		202395	39972	139030	23393
山　西		212430	46450	139400	26580
内蒙古		241088	71714	145366	24008
辽　宁		337595	68293	237541	31761
吉　林		306301	62186	216301	27814
黑龙江		435124	118965	270754	45405
上　海		6880			6880
江　苏		11335			11335
浙　江		2387			2387
安　徽		231376	46823	159918	24635
福　建		27982	8688	14082	5212
江　西		241829	49629	162790	29410
山　东		93000	32161	44741	16098
河　南		347287	68665	238835	39787
湖　北		363375	73459	251418	38498
湖　南		366411	79522	243401	43488
广　东		11233			11233
广　西		132103	26054	90622	15427
海　南		40008	10014	25294	4700
重　庆		173505	35197	122424	15884
四　川		444513	96510	292310	55693
贵　州		135997	34309	85818	15870
云　南		190173	39071	123278	27824
西　藏		13716	5143	7163	1410
陕　西		218245	61632	133688	22925
甘　肃		226109	67124	132929	26056
青　海		66699	20572	39234	6893
宁　夏		52534	14253	32890	5391
新　疆	8286.48	275789	68334	132475	24560

单位：万元

新疆兵团	农村低保合计	财社[2012]159号	财社[2013]52号	财社[2013]4号	五保补助 财社[2013]4号	医疗救助支出合计
50420	**6122955**	**3451200**	**1611600**	**1060155**	**109233**	**1566688**
	1267			1267	82	4008
	1988			1988	260	6017
	230175	137673	51375	41127	4747	55325
	154027	84492	40971	28564	3355	41106
	162985	91829	47418	23738	1778	43352
	89100	48107	23032	17961	2837	34806
	102654	63301	24032	15321	2544	58528
	146040	84894	37428	23718	2897	72391
	715			715	64	3317
	113529	60790	25310	27429	4097	25546
	51504	29786	10295	11423	815	12293
	265040	152526	69846	42668	9034	70495
	68483	33198	20553	14732	1803	15961
	200245	127134	43055	30056	4571	71297
	216056	99379	67271	49406	4702	54021
	443574	252031	117973	73570	9532	92624
	256767	145940	65070	45757	5590	71377
	293809	157908	80815	55086	10372	103642
	142354	70357	36356	35641	5121	23584
	351811	191717	94725	65369	6169	56851
	32789	18334	9614	4841	668	17648
	106774	68209	22831	15734	2856	43756
	467279	259469	121577	86233	10199	142237
	651628	363172	185741	102715	2631	77811
	509476	296845	125188	87443	4397	88182
	37796	24428	8768	4600	305	16672
	312915	196547	73866	42502	2515	72701
	414721	225992	120171	68558	2486	78440
	64797	36446	20360	7991	457	27218
	48294	25002	16101	7191	298	20555
50420	184363	105694	51858	26811	2051	63752

C-1-11续表4

地 区	城市医疗救助合计	财社[2012]187号	财社[2013]105号	新疆兵团	农村医疗合计
全 国	**468166**	**351374**	**109042**	**7750**	**860103**
北 京	1363	1063	300		717
天 津	2185	1705	480		907
河 北	13076	10409	2667		29615
山 西	14980	10624	4356		19945
内蒙古	18753	13299	5454		21436
辽 宁	14623	11640	2983		13750
吉 林	30061	23929	6132		23128
黑龙江	37572	27863	9709		29252
上 海	1441	1124	317		558
江 苏	4577	3570	1007		9472
浙 江	1420	1108	312		5402
安 徽	17256	12237	5019		41929
福 建	2477	1932	545		8608
江 西	24295	19340	4955		38905
山 东	8054	6283	1771		21263
河 南	19131	15229	3902		57684
湖 北	24178	19247	4931		33866
湖 南	30450	24240	6210		54584
广 东	3858	3010	848		10012
广 西	10496	7444	3052		40571
海 南	7472	5300	2172		8237
重 庆	14195	11300	2895		21323
四 川	37877	29548	8329		85190
贵 州	12435	8807	3628		58467
云 南	16133	12842	3291		62770
西 藏	6093	4850	1243		9627
陕 西	20392	16232	4160		44274
甘 肃	20833	14774	6059		54742
青 海	10864	7704	3160		14746
宁 夏	8024	6387	1637		11274
新 疆	33602	18334	7518	7750	27849

单位：万元

财社[2012]186号	财社[2013]106号	优抚医疗补助合计	财社[2012]153号	财社[2013]88号	新疆兵团
675096	**185007**	**238419**	**179155**	**58089**	**1175**
570	147	1928	1545	383	
720	187	2925	2117	808	
23998	5617	12634	9901	2733	
14399	5546	6181	4644	1537	
15476	5960	3163	2545	618	
10920	2830	6433	5081	1352	
17159	5969	5339	4359	980	
21119	8133	5567	4043	1524	
443	115	1318	1023	295	
7522	1950	11497	8834	2663	
4290	1112	5471	3840	1631	
33977	7952	11310	8492	2818	
6836	1772	4876	3549	1327	
29897	9008	8097	6210	1887	
16886	4377	24704	19814	4890	
46743	10941	15809	12365	3444	
27443	6423	13333	9837	3496	
44231	10353	18608	13964	4644	
7951	2061	9714	7048	2666	
29320	11251	5784	4223	1561	
5946	2291	1939	1337	602	
17279	4044	8238	5910	2328	
67652	17538	19170	14523	4647	
47378	11089	6909	5033	1876	
50865	11905	9279	6899	2380	
6950	2677	952	715	237	
35878	8396	8035	5694	2341	
44359	10383	2865	2140	725	
10645	4101	1608	1099	509	
8139	3135	1257	890	367	
20105	7744	2301	1481	820	1175

C-1-11续表5

地 区	流浪乞讨救助合计	财社[2012]154号	财社[2013]46号	新疆兵团	其他城镇社会救济(新疆兵团)	救灾合计
全 国	**200040**	**159856**	**39906**	**278**	**97**	**1019248**
北 京	11226	8930	2296			965
天 津	2400	1878	522			420
河 北	6667	4744	1923			32400
山 西	4751	3985	766			33500
内蒙古	2800	2240	560			36800
辽 宁	5047	4794	253			47531
吉 林	4000	3960	40			53000
黑龙江	3653	2976	677			45872
上 海	3588	3588				
江 苏	7969	6318	1651			11400
浙 江	6115	4811	1304			15400
安 徽	10390	10390				30632
福 建	4841	3402	1439			11036
江 西	8104	6880	1224			39500
山 东	8299	6035	2264			19100
河 南	10418	8373	2045			20671
湖 北	14349	11682	2667			47948
湖 南	14747	11798	2949			48024
广 东	10043	9168	875			30100
广 西	6131	3822	2309			32594
海 南	2000	1280	720			6000
重 庆	5207	4743	464			31600
四 川	17880	12000	5880			83695
贵 州	6014	5200	814			52400
云 南	4433	4000	433			68412
西 藏	1224	640	584			23205
陕 西	6256	5505	751			62029
甘 肃	4116	2496	1620			74012
青 海	2300	640	1660			17262
宁 夏	1000	413	587			16300
新 疆	4072	3165	629	278	97	27440

单位：万元

财社[2013]2号	财社[2013]5号	财社[2013]17号	财社[2013]20号	财社[2013]22号	财社[2013]23号	财社[2013]24号
5000	**134200**	**5848**	**1000**	**6000**	**10000**	**6000**
	100	65				
	100	320				
	6300					
	4700					
	5600					
	4900	431				
	3900					
	5100	572				
	2200					
	700					
	4100	332				
	1700	136				
	6500					
	4300					
	4000	671				
	7100	348				
	6800	324				
	1700					
	4600	194				
	600					
	5000					
	9800	295				6000
	8900					
5000	7800	212			10000	
	2800	105	1000			
	5700	629				
	8000	412		6000		
	3200	362				
	3100					
	4900	440				

C-1-11续表6

地区	财社[2013]42号	财社[2013]43号	财社[2013]44号	财社[2013]82号	财社[2013]83号
全国	**6000**	**5000**	**6000**	**8000**	**6000**
北京					
天津					
河北					
山西					
内蒙古					
辽宁					
吉林					
黑龙江					
上海					
江苏					
浙江					
安徽				8000	
福建					
江西					
山东					
河南					
湖北					6000
湖南		5000			
广东	6000				
广西					
海南					
重庆					
四川					
贵州					
云南			6000		
西藏					
陕西					
甘肃					
青海					
宁夏					
新疆					

单位：万元

财社[2013]84号	财社[2013]85号	财社[2013]91号	财社[2013]92号	财社[2013]93号	财社[2013]113号	财社[2013]114号
6000	**25000**	**9000**	**10000**	**15000**	**6000**	**6000**
		9000				
					6000	
						6000
6000						
	25000					
			10000			
				15000		

C-1-11续表7

地区	财社[2013]115号	财社[2013]116号	财社[2013]117号	财社[2013]118号	财社[2013]122号
全国	**8000**	**7000**	**15000**	**10000**	**10000**
北京					
天津					
河北					
山西					
内蒙古					
辽宁					
吉林					10000
黑龙江					
上海					
江苏					
浙江					
安徽					
福建					
江西					
山东					
河南					
湖北					
湖南	8000				
广东					
广西					
海南					
重庆					
四川					
贵州		7000			
云南					
西藏					
陕西			15000		
甘肃				10000	
青海					
宁夏					
新疆					

单位：万元

财社[2013]123号	财社[2013]124号	财社[2013]125号	财社[2013]126号	财社[2013]130号	财社[2013]131号	财社[2013]142号
20000	**12000**	**10000**	**6000**	**8000**	**7000**	**5000**
				8000		
20000						
	12000					
		10000				
			6000			
					7000	
						5000

C-1-11续表8

地　区	财社[2013]191号	财社[2013]192号	财社[2013]193号	财社[2013]194号	财社[2013]195号	财社[2013]196号
全　国	**2000**	**7000**	**5000**	**6300**	**3000**	**2500**
北　京						
天　津						
河　北						
山　西						
内蒙古						
辽　宁						
吉　林						
黑龙江						
上　海						
江　苏						
浙　江				6300	3000	
安　徽						
福　建						2500
江　西						
山　东						
河　南						
湖　北						
湖　南						
广　东			5000			
广　西						
海　南						
重　庆						
四　川	2000					
贵　州						
云　南		7000				
西　藏						
陕　西						
甘　肃						
青　海						
宁　夏						
新　疆						

注：中央补助新疆兵团合并到新疆。

单位：万元

财社[2013]218号	财社[2013]221号	财社[2013]223号	财社[2013]225号	财社[2013]249号	新疆兵团	民政管理事务（新疆兵团）
7000	**2000**	**2100**	**576200**	**10000**	**2100**	**7520**
			800			
			26100			
			19800			
			23200			
			22200			
7000			22100	10000		
			28200			
			9200			
			5400			
			18200			
			6700			
			27000			
			14800			
			16000			
			28500			
			27900			
			7400			
	2000		19800			
		2100	3300			
			20600			
			40600			
			36500			
			32400			
			12300			
			25700			
			34600			
			13700			
			13200			
			20000		2100	7520

C-1-12 收入支出情况

单位：万元

地 区	收入合计	上年结余	本年收入合计	本年实际支出	收支结余	用事业基金弥补收支差额	结余分配	年末净结余
全 国	**46495564.6**	**2493899.1**	**44001665.5**	**43911908.6**	**2583656.0**	**34844.0**	**109956.3**	**2508543.7**
中央级	184304.0	33413.2	150890.8	153813.2	30490.8	304.4	2460.6	28334.6
北 京	2034092.1	418910.9	1615181.2	1771536.1	262556.0	10588.2	7062.4	266081.8
天 津	647258.1	49999.4	597258.7	579264.9	67993.2	53.5	1046.9	66999.8
河 北	1734657.5	73055.8	1661601.7	1672830.4	61827.1	210.2	316.4	61720.9
山 西	1240392.3	96787.2	1143605.1	1134195.5	106196.8	12.9	751.6	105458.1
内蒙古	1315037.6	64623.4	1250414.2	1246145.0	68892.6	1478.8	118.2	70253.2
辽 宁	1752067.1	47272.6	1704794.5	1713245.4	38821.7	1.6	7055.8	31767.5
吉 林	1005641.5	1659.0	1003982.5	988430.5	17211.0	259.0	338.2	17131.8
黑龙江	1607958.0	7217.2	1600740.8	1589737.6	18220.4		210.8	18009.6
上 海	1076090.3	154276.2	921814.1	915926.3	160164.0	161.9	-649.5	160975.4
江 苏	2431754.4	38968.7	2392785.7	2386211.2	45543.2	1189.8	12940.7	33792.3
浙 江	1625118.6	76794.7	1548323.9	1517738.6	107380.0	150.0	11772.2	95757.8
安 徽	1656309.3	20661.1	1635648.2	1636133.7	20175.6		1471.1	18704.5
福 建	809662.0	57485.5	752176.5	737052.0	72610.0	879.7	4624.8	68864.9
江 西	1228710.2	2424.8	1226285.4	1226813.4	1896.8		733.5	1163.3
山 东	2583710.3	19745.2	2563965.1	2560118.4	23591.9	129.9	2233.5	21488.3
河 南	2153884.4	49691.3	2104193.1	2100817.3	53067.1	599.0	8258.3	45407.8
湖 北	1878898.7	14195.4	1864703.3	1869934.2	8964.5	47.2	788.8	8222.9
湖 南	2075681.1	26809.6	2048871.5	2055289.3	20391.8	1214.1	1840.9	19765.0
广 东	2187544.4	88848.2	2098696.2	2087071.8	100472.6	148.5	16036.1	84585.0
广 西	1595784.7	209314.6	1386470.1	1358975.7	236809.0	968.7	17548.3	220229.4
海 南	350211.6	81306.0	268905.6	256953.6	93258.0	318.0	319.9	93256.1
重 庆	1039589.5	33156.3	1006433.2	1018453.5	21136.0	215.2	1875.5	19475.7
四 川	3113799.2	139038.8	2974760.4	2939141.0	174658.2	85.8	1236.0	173508.0
贵 州	1652995.4	275080.1	1377915.3	1349508.7	303486.7	4282.7	3465.7	304303.7
云 南	2043620.5	151286.8	1892333.7	1859928.8	183691.7	6.8	3773.5	179925.0
西 藏	276080.8	73186.1	202894.7	194603.2	81477.6	150.0	675.0	80952.6
陕 西	1930084.2	37279.5	1892804.7	1876521.5	53562.7	11372.1	1538.6	63396.2
甘 肃	1349030.1	54707.3	1294322.8	1299349.4	49680.7	16.0	112.5	49584.2
青 海	412195.6	17182.2	395013.4	398349.8	13845.8			13845.8
宁 夏	320810.4	42932.7	277877.7	270485.7	50324.7			50324.7
新 疆	1182590.7	36589.3	1146001.4	1147332.9	35257.8			35257.8

C－1－13 行政事业性收费收入情况

单位：万元

地区	行政事业性收费	婚姻登记收费	收养登记收费	殡葬收费
全　国	**327526.7**	**12698.9**	**1168.3**	**313659.5**
中央级				
北　京	16550.9	228.8	5.1	16317.0
天　津	6890.5	126.4	12.3	6751.8
河　北	13345.8	603.6	288.6	12453.6
山　西	16033.5	696.3	5.8	15331.4
内蒙古	14703.4	503.6	1.8	14198.0
辽　宁	9801.1	190.3	74.2	9536.6
吉　林	3192.8	68.7		3124.1
黑龙江	5750.8	176.9	0.6	5573.3
上　海				
江　苏	37121.8	284.6	46.2	36791.0
浙　江	12354.7	282.4	61.4	12010.9
安　徽	13099.0	949.8	17.8	12131.4
福　建	15752.8	396.7	27.1	15329.0
江　西	525.1	4.0	7.8	513.3
山　东	20835.8	724.2	43.3	20068.3
河　南	3311.2	860.7	19.5	2431.0
湖　北	27352.4	359.9	28.5	26964.0
湖　南	3222.3	580.1	9.1	2633.1
广　东	28912.8	690.3	40.5	28182.0
广　西	15119.5	658.1	24.9	14436.5
海　南	3089.8	39.4	346.7	2703.7
重　庆	3658.0	919.9	19.3	2718.8
四　川	26870.8	1604.4	26.2	25240.2
贵　州	2328.0	186.1	3.1	2138.8
云　南	2314.4	182.9	40.3	2091.2
西　藏				
陕　西	1168.3	130.8	0.3	1037.2
甘　肃	6795.0	334.2	2.6	6458.2
青　海	208.7	69.0	0.3	139.4
宁　夏	94.1	62.3	0.3	31.5
新　疆	17123.4	784.5	14.7	16324.2

C-1-14 财政性资金

地 区	上年结余合计	抚恤	退役安置	社会福利
全 国	**2174326.2**	**209375.7**	**335562.4**	**307760.7**
中央级	9373.3	547.7		
北 京	345188.7	12441.4	184163.1	57610.6
天 津	45303.9	2402.7	3829.4	19033.4
河 北	73132.5	6792.4	14864.6	13026.4
山 西	94281.6	9556.6	5928.5	17844.6
内蒙古	64388.7	3468.3	5274.1	10659.2
辽 宁	48203.0	656.1	778.8	5352.9
吉 林	1659.0			650.0
黑龙江	7217.2	2922.5	263.7	19.2
上 海	86429.5	9066.1	10923.5	12119.2
江 苏	36229.0	1379.7	1836.1	6993.7
浙 江	73063.1	13869.7	5467.5	14823.3
安 徽	18424.7		933.9	871.2
福 建	53556.0	7917.5	10105.5	10528.3
江 西	2424.8	1020.5	300.0	628.3
山 东	14004.5	8016.6	1360.8	559.6
河 南	49673.3	4417.8	1788.2	7097.6
湖 北	13761.7	714.5	6237.9	
湖 南	7081.6	492.2	70.9	
广 东	80361.9	8244.0	11515.2	17173.1
广 西	192415.3	32023.3	7153.9	29425.8
海 南	74740.2	8721.1	5431.4	5587.1
重 庆	17689.9	4404.6	1790.7	1801.3
四 川	115695.0	7439.4	8956.8	8620.4
贵 州	269571.6	31871.5	9980.1	30007.8
云 南	147404.8	20395.6	21265.0	14948.8
西 藏	73186.1	398.4	10.0	30.5
陕 西	13603.3	544.6	1422.3	2079.4
甘 肃	54707.3	1900.2	2980.0	1483.1
青 海	17182.2	1098.5	2474.4	124.4
宁 夏	40675.1	729.2	5709.7	2469.2
新 疆	33697.4	5923.0	2746.4	16192.3

收、支、余情况

单位：万元

社会救助	自然灾害生活救助	民政管理事务	行政事业单位离退休	其他款项用于民政支出
697678.4	**120299.3**	**178048.0**	**5631.9**	**268342.0**
	0.8	6940.2	53.0	1831.6
34917.4	2936.5	25165.7	933.8	27020.2
6656.7	750.3	4569.3	925.0	7080.1
12379.6	2899.4	3856.6	22.3	18417.4
52604.8	3865.3	2793.5	28.4	1659.9
13561.1	6320.5	13079.0	17.8	10661.0
18716.0	457.9	1715.4	295.8	18419.6
685.0	324.0			
2949.5	10.5	1051.8		
30739.2	1113.2	15403.9	102.2	6962.2
1351.7	93.0	4585.4		19989.4
19202.1	3392.7	11989.0	1187.8	3127.6
3441.7	30.9	300.0		54.5
12356.0	2005.2	6938.9	908.4	2420.1
201.8	274.2			
721.2	4.4	3275.3	2.4	64.1
30936.8	544.7	221.1	36.4	3691.8
5214.7	635.7	899.2		59.7
6062.3	121.1	133.0		201.1
14251.3	1003.2	8503.3	350.6	4499.0
88700.0	14070.9	7024.6	302.4	10962.1
26308.4	2425.3	7532.7	2.4	9440.2
4662.4	1248.7	1381.4		2400.8
45266.4	14473.6	3898.7	346.6	25876.7
145230.8	26975.8	12050.1	39.5	13178.4
42206.7	15760.0	12617.8	64.8	17975.4
41018.2	847.0			30857.0
4920.7	450.0	1147.2	10.9	2321.6
8497.6	3656.6	14637.2	0.9	21270.5
2057.2	7560.3	404.3		3433.1
17916.0	3321.2	4000.7	0.5	4245.4
3945.1	2726.4	1932.7		221.5

C-1-14续表1

地 区	本年收入合计	抚恤	退役安置	社会福利
全 国	**42552399.9**	**6217310.0**	**4242641.9**	**3959526.0**
中央级	132229.8	617.0		18200.0
北 京	1361510.0	103461.9	622580.7	188925.3
天 津	568977.5	61591.8	89227.8	51912.2
河 北	1660792.7	374507.8	237947.4	136810.7
山 西	1138286.1	196879.4	72084.8	74922.1
内蒙古	1238664.5	92371.8	42035.8	115651.9
辽 宁	1643709.7	186876.7	312180.4	110967.1
吉 林	942549.6	102808.8	74895.3	33048.8
黑龙江	1572713.8	116432.5	65078.8	64715.8
上 海	834706.6	81712.2	138625.6	120456.5
江 苏	2301952.3	386197.4	315898.8	366431.4
浙 江	1446441.5	223362.4	104298.0	299235.8
安 徽	1600659.4	267356.9	148754.6	141177.5
福 建	739455.8	129476.3	78720.1	104587.9
江 西	1223848.1	235511.3	43303.2	106218.9
山 东	2506488.6	704882.2	363099.4	262806.0
河 南	2100424.3	423227.8	164413.7	144446.4
湖 北	1831825.8	334065.3	157749.2	150998.2
湖 南	1987211.1	403099.1	100541.4	104349.8
广 东	1973662.3	296545.4	207617.1	309476.6
广 西	1298522.4	154166.5	62610.0	134634.0
海 南	256915.3	26771.8	22460.4	32800.0
重 庆	983759.5	160105.0	76701.4	91430.3
四 川	2914621.3	451725.1	250099.6	146697.9
贵 州	1367330.7	139656.1	44118.5	86250.5
云 南	1877638.3	179414.3	109518.6	110403.6
西 藏	151847.1	5161.5	9771.4	9114.1
陕 西	1857586.5	249344.2	153034.0	158839.6
甘 肃	1290714.5	53643.8	69450.8	58337.0
青 海	373365.0	14454.6	17144.0	36656.8
宁 夏	271567.4	11663.2	15585.8	18360.9
新 疆	1102422.4	50219.9	73095.3	170662.4

单位：万元

社会救助	自然灾害生活救助	民政管理事务	行政事业单位离退休	其他款项用于民政支出
21710934.9	**1829033.5**	**2919769.4**	**428880.7**	**1244303.5**
	43506.0	47422.3	3815.8	18668.7
159398.1	6042.0	160660.2	54835.4	65606.4
219678.3	2447.8	114802.5	4271.6	25045.5
745480.7	52756.9	73032.2	19581.9	20675.1
668746.9	40651.5	54384.0	9753.4	20864.0
846135.2	38100.0	65429.7	13356.6	25583.5
732930.5	66636.3	144441.8	22543.5	67133.4
601889.2	48651.9	31940.7	8833.5	40481.4
1105164.9	147955.7	59886.1	7477.7	6002.3
306200.1	2159.0	128200.0	8358.5	48994.7
841462.5	21278.6	193650.2	27839.5	149193.9
462859.2	33491.5	219539.3	22453.2	81202.1
911508.3	38751.0	63213.6	13507.3	16390.2
279962.4	28199.7	64735.0	25348.0	28426.4
759088.7	28155.2	37953.5	9024.1	4593.2
918967.6	30255.8	148357.2	12320.2	65800.2
1198762.1	25640.1	86141.5	17845.9	39946.8
980262.9	63749.2	83329.7	18107.2	43564.1
1168290.7	60485.7	100502.9	8304.6	41636.9
746216.1	68681.1	216786.2	34509.5	93830.3
768676.7	49695.2	89952.1	13150.4	25637.5
120731.3	8542.2	27961.6	3654.9	13993.1
520194.1	42377.7	72496.6	9126.4	11328.0
1505494.2	328797.7	151555.0	20567.9	59683.9
932530.2	73109.2	71849.3	3455.0	16361.9
1142649.7	120843.5	120080.1	12431.7	82296.8
73475.3	29641.8	9214.2	744.3	14724.5
1009614.2	129677.7	136501.5	6460.6	14114.7
946063.4	126046.2	27019.3	4612.2	5541.8
195375.5	16496.1	22131.2	2158.2	68948.6
161818.0	15640.3	22016.9	2979.5	23502.8
681307.9	40570.9	74583.0	7452.2	4530.8

C－1－14续表2

地 区	本年支出合计	抚恤	退役安置	社会福利
全 国	**42765370.8**	**6184310.6**	**4352600.2**	**3975669.6**
中央级	137419.9	601.0		
北 京	1555734.8	102474.8	727394.6	206296.2
天 津	552118.0	60296.8	85838.7	56024.9
河 北	1672465.7	373253.3	238659.4	138617.1
山 西	1130400.3	189680.9	71227.4	78624.4
内蒙古	1236610.0	89256.9	42870.4	111753.9
辽 宁	1672890.8	188295.1	314708.3	127870.6
吉 林	986245.5	108104.3	74541.6	49132.2
黑龙江	1589618.1	118039.8	64894.3	63704.6
上 海	832211.6	77346.4	140151.1	122116.2
江 苏	2335259.9	400631.2	326575.3	379483.8
浙 江	1428845.7	217849.4	102960.8	294282.5
安 徽	1601142.2	266882.0	149166.5	138831.0
福 建	729824.6	125926.1	77841.6	103793.8
江 西	1224409.1	236272.0	43109.7	106325.7
山 东	2502270.9	703554.6	362728.1	261399.5
河 南	2097496.0	424921.2	168540.5	133884.1
湖 北	1849392.5	336354.1	159256.8	154221.9
湖 南	1996276.3	403904.7	104740.1	105298.4
广 东	1981669.0	296100.2	206489.9	308414.8
广 西	1292515.6	144002.7	61205.8	123642.3
海 南	254400.4	23833.8	20738.5	23754.4
重 庆	999446.7	162662.9	77564.4	107429.8
四 川	2880631.2	453439.9	251994.8	141954.3
贵 州	1341494.8	130472.4	41237.0	81684.3
云 南	1845730.7	174052.0	102166.4	105467.2
西 藏	156074.8	5758.9	7067.2	9380.6
陕 西	1838401.7	240077.9	153626.1	157737.5
甘 肃	1299304.5	54407.1	71141.6	56931.5
青 海	377594.3	14095.5	17263.9	36209.4
宁 夏	266258.2	10741.9	13476.5	18908.4
新 疆	1101217.0	51020.8	73422.9	172494.3

单位：万元

社会救助	自然灾害生活救助	民政管理事务	行政事业单位离退休	其他款项用于民政支出
21724118.2	**1786987.6**	**2967378.9**	**435817.7**	**1338488.0**
	43506.0	46609.8	3868.8	42834.3
171551.3	5774.6	165510.3	55321.8	121411.2
216924.1	2099.6	107670.6	4817.0	18446.3
746377.8	51898.9	72964.2	19449.5	31245.5
664821.3	40974.4	54300.0	9755.0	21016.9
846880.9	38708.6	66714.8	13433.4	26991.1
740422.9	66572.4	150443.1	24258.8	60319.6
603658.1	49320.9	45574.2	9669.5	46244.7
1120922.9	147381.2	60223.6	7477.7	6974.0
298578.4	2653.8	133420.1	8356.7	49588.9
842306.0	21365.3	196254.0	29719.8	138924.5
460626.0	33198.7	219812.7	22088.5	78027.1
912522.7	38259.5	63165.3	13489.3	18825.9
280355.3	26787.9	62282.0	25076.7	27761.2
758590.7	28361.3	38114.3	9054.1	4581.3
918114.8	30255.5	148135.9	12320.2	65762.3
1197876.1	25747.0	87636.7	18004.0	40886.4
983083.7	63679.5	87020.6	18743.2	47032.7
1171110.2	60529.1	100592.5	8512.7	41588.6
739798.0	68783.5	220372.7	34475.0	107234.9
786103.2	48792.6	87307.8	13372.1	28089.1
126350.0	5754.1	30803.4	3717.3	19448.9
515469.9	42383.5	73061.2	9147.2	11727.8
1507933.9	288148.4	151594.1	21077.1	64488.7
923409.2	72189.8	69493.1	3492.8	19516.2
1142530.1	117987.0	116343.2	12617.5	74567.3
80346.8	30154.6	8826.3	775.9	13764.5
995196.5	129959.3	135883.6	6505.5	19415.3
938276.7	125688.1	42029.6	4609.1	6220.8
195303.3	22423.4	30158.9	2184.7	59955.2
161223.2	15082.4	20968.4	2957.1	22900.3
677454.2	42566.7	74091.9	7469.7	2696.5

C-1-14续表3

地 区	年末结余合计	抚恤	退役安置	社会福利
全 国	**2223392.3**	**265650.7**	**240083.2**	**310004.9**
中央级	10324.7	563.7		
北 京	200178.0	12809.5	79179.1	38672.4
天 津	61952.9	3718.8	7238.9	17035.1
河 北	61830.1	11012.6	14270.5	11185.0
山 西	102098.5	16755.1	6716.1	14154.1
内蒙古	68848.3	7846.2	4185.4	10823.9
辽 宁	32749.2	99.0	108.1	1312.1
吉 林	17131.8	120.8		
黑龙江	18009.6	1529.0	406.4	101.4
上 海	101806.2	13459.2	10358.5	13027.8
江 苏	29395.6	1699.0	2027.6	5505.8
浙 江	89848.7	19743.5	6833.8	19040.1
安 徽	17977.0	190.2	794.8	1912.3
福 建	64593.1	10937.8	10389.5	8616.8
江 西	1163.3	18.2	248.0	546.5
山 东	16118.6	7609.1	1674.1	1291.1
河 南	45389.8	3758.3	2288.5	3680.4
湖 北	7232.0	98.1	2251.1	158.7
湖 南	5597.2	694.5	193.7	39.6
广 东	67202.8	8561.4	8408.5	19375.4
广 西	206451.7	41990.8	9978.9	37839.9
海 南	86436.5	11173.8	6822.8	11820.6
重 庆	19455.7	2030.8	1364.2	2918.3
四 川	153619.2	8877.3	8149.4	12626.4
贵 州	295407.5	41055.2	12861.6	34574.0
云 南	176472.6	25634.5	27264.7	17624.3
西 藏	80952.6	475.4	178.0	109.8
陕 西	39589.0	4089.4	1469.2	4820.4
甘 肃	49584.2	1298.7	2283.1	1031.6
青 海	13845.8	992.9	2281.8	3069.5
宁 夏	46872.3	1692.0	7304.0	2664.0
新 疆	35257.8	5115.9	2552.9	14427.6

单位：万元

社会救助	自然灾害生活救助	民政管理事务	行政事业单位离退休	其他款项用于民政支出
728673.9	**164522.8**	**194116.0**	**7655.7**	**217749.3**
	0.8	7752.7		2007.5
23238.4	3721.7	20565.6	462.1	19598.1
8647.0	1098.5	15325.3	366.2	8523.1
12358.4	3835.3	4170.7	52.7	4791.6
56530.4	3542.4	2879.1	26.8	1494.5
13466.6	5707.4	6851.8	17.2	19357.9
18390.1	2.2	316.2		1927.6
1734.0	324.0			
14108.3	602.0	1246.7		15.6
34511.8	618.4	24045.2	144.8	5640.5
840.3	298.0	4668.3	5.4	14350.9
21456.8	3663.6	11754.4	1551.6	5610.5
3612.7	37.5			30.6
12614.7	3051.2	9724.9	1073.9	2979.7
348.4	2.2			
950.2	4.7	3554.6		
32052.0	537.6	264.7	20.3	2109.3
2793.6	121.1	792.4		580.0
4010.8	309.0	177.9		170.7
18108.2	1815.9	6525.6	2336.0	1364.8
72077.5	15162.2	11744.9	369.7	6588.6
24794.3	4599.1	9495.6	22.4	13014.4
8477.3	1266.8	1230.2	89.6	2078.5
46605.0	55486.3	4298.8	325.4	17248.1
154351.8	27895.2	14406.3	1.7	10024.1
42167.1	19878.0	18170.8	783.3	23695.5
47490.4	1185.7			21085.0
7077.8	584.7	2243.9		562.4
14930.0	3974.7	2195.4	3.9	23866.8
1413.1	925.0	518.3		4266.9
21787.7	3610.7	6387.0	1.4	2812.9
7729.2	660.9	2808.7	1.3	1953.2

C-1-15 预算指标

地 区	本年预算指标合计	上年结转预算指标	本级财政安排预算指标	本年上级下达预算指标	本年下达所属地方预算指标	本年抚恤预算指标
全 国	**45327641.6**	**2312784.4**	**43608679.9**	**67721212.9**	**68315035.6**	**6433764.7**
中央级	132229.8		21853419.8		21721190.0	617.0
北 京	1728390.3	298774.4	866453.9	1174869.0	611707.0	111364.3
天 津	589393.2	26620.5	421625.2	294126.6	152979.1	62908.4
河 北	1741824.5	81193.3	718448.0	3095526.0	2153342.8	382372.5
山 西	1200579.9	55380.5	517245.4	2228101.7	1600147.7	208642.0
内蒙古	1314103.7	47101.8	700058.4	2228211.8	1661268.3	94630.3
辽 宁	1701130.4	38654.3	809715.6	2668543.6	1815783.1	189564.1
吉 林	976860.7	13128.3	319689.5	1445592.0	801549.1	102896.1
黑龙江	1593176.7	21817.0	789472.4	3738124.7	2956237.4	118029.8
上 海	877218.4	74352.3	834706.6	117669.0	149509.5	81712.2
江 苏	2433198.8	120651.7	1797388.5	2208693.8	1693535.2	394421.3
浙 江	1566851.8	104511.1	1243811.4	651174.6	432645.3	239611.5
安 徽	1636681.6	31395.4	743212.0	1888312.3	1026238.1	274265.1
福 建	810901.2	78108.0	484266.1	921483.2	672956.1	135362.6
江 西	1264450.1	1002.0	477037.1	2579742.5	1793331.5	235511.3
山 东	2582469.9	53877.5	1457377.4	3732823.9	2661608.9	709229.8
河 南	2145336.5	47538.7	773666.8	4337438.3	3013307.3	423661.3
湖 北	1867415.0	31271.6	723950.4	2581563.5	1469370.5	336623.9
湖 南	2005669.8	30863.3	755067.6	4138633.7	2918894.8	406016.6
广 东	2068129.4	116698.4	1489024.0	2148375.5	1685968.5	307784.3
广 西	1510665.8	156964.4	622006.4	2067969.5	1336274.5	178527.8
海 南	305824.7	30393.2	159519.0	297774.1	181861.6	29961.2
重 庆	1070256.5	63188.5	470061.9	1202201.4	665195.3	163519.3
四 川	2974200.5	64243.6	1258104.8	5335061.6	3683209.5	455742.9
贵 州	1627101.6	168971.2	393433.4	3230561.2	2165864.2	146488.3
云 南	1899879.0	32393.8	763604.2	4035009.7	2931128.7	182722.8
西 藏	185823.9	79140.6	68109.2	199615.2	161041.1	5706.0
陕 西	2284873.1	288244.1	1058269.4	3787213.8	2848854.2	324567.3
甘 肃	1323497.1	31217.5	383462.6	2055499.6	1146682.6	53655.8
青 海	395920.0	6943.3	136929.8	732415.3	480368.4	14986.6
宁 夏	298112.2	12595.7	122015.1	364007.6	200506.2	12000.6
新 疆	1215475.5	105548.4	397528.0	2234878.2	1522479.1	50661.7

收入情况

单位：万元

上年结转预算指标	本级财政安排预算指标	本年上级下达预算指标	本年下达所属地方预算指标	本年退役安置预算指标	上年结转预算指标	本级财政安排预算指标
150625.1	**6314063.5**	**11317101.2**	**11348025.1**	**4829877.3**	**465671.3**	**4458745.7**
	3693362.0		3692745.0			2679302.0
4145.0	83289.3	43231.8	19301.8	909253.0	229249.9	191097.1
657.6	44484.8	34083.9	16317.9	99060.5	196.7	34756.0
6239.7	134690.9	729298.0	487856.1	249098.6	11785.3	84648.0
6451.4	88551.6	354208.7	240569.7	75610.2	4659.6	22150.6
2316.9	48993.6	146255.2	102935.4	47455.0	2869.8	18022.4
7841.1	95376.7	304920.4	218574.1	319632.2	5505.1	51853.3
1051.9	35759.4	153371.2	87286.4	74917.3	208.0	14667.9
950.2	39775.8	279734.4	202430.6	66207.0	9791.9	11654.8
	81712.2	12352.0	12352.0	173922.0	38872.4	138625.6
6315.2	220740.8	580193.0	412827.7	330207.5	15482.1	163369.1
12270.7	158610.9	163901.1	95171.2	108496.4	3866.1	50521.3
3479.6	95544.4	363851.3	188610.2	150223.3	1695.0	101269.3
6209.9	64087.7	235977.1	170912.1	97144.7	15551.0	37039.7
2.0	68779.3	556476.8	389746.8	43303.2		16684.2
1301.4	287858.4	1340125.5	920055.5	379200.4	19776.4	130050.0
274.8	142350.1	877544.9	596508.5	167474.3	11355.6	67127.5
2972.4	106257.5	506767.6	279373.6	159783.6	3692.3	52271.3
4351.8	98055.5	970468.0	666858.7	101099.4	793.0	44310.1
14937.4	183175.0	469827.9	360156.0	257014.6	49056.5	99062.0
21175.8	65621.0	262003.0	170272.0	67885.7	3889.3	37978.4
3230.6	11420.9	39714.7	24405.0	26900.7	3200.4	17183.6
1461.9	53442.5	237258.5	128643.6	78722.2	2772.3	30320.9
4570.1	114854.4	1066877.4	730559.0	258503.9	11460.7	131608.4
4539.2	41732.1	315280.8	215063.8	45198.9	1387.2	25320.7
2277.8	44337.0	447291.1	311183.1	110516.9	1588.4	34277.5
642.0	1820.2	8085.1	4841.3	10090.7	264.6	856.8
29961.7	163336.0	595410.5	464140.9	244661.8	13759.8	114170.7
74.2	11866.6	87859.5	46144.5	71337.0	2649.1	25072.9
500.0	5764.5	27271.5	18549.4	17144.0		5088.2
109.1	4968.4	14090.2	7167.1	16717.0	281.3	8158.9
313.7	23444.0	93370.1	66466.1	73095.3	11.5	20226.5

C-1-15续表1

地　区	本年上级下达预算指标	本年下达所属地方预算指标	本年社会福利预算指标	上年结转预算指标	本级财政安排预算指标	本年上级下达预算指标
全　国	**6531442.2**	**6625981.9**	**4526844.4**	**408571.2**	**4530644.2**	**2733802.5**
中央级		2679302.0	18200.0		862701.0	
北　京	958712.8	469806.8	212831.3	24860.4	182959.9	64658.7
天　津	127749.8	63642.0	55958.4	5324.0	47742.3	5892.8
河　北	413082.4	260417.1	159957.7	11306.4	130872.4	126135.4
山　西	120865.4	72065.4	81628.7	5721.6	59561.1	58158.6
内蒙古	72393.3	45830.5	133788.6	15366.0	137152.5	122212.3
辽　宁	582682.8	320409.0	114491.3	1143.6	113670.5	58879.8
吉　林	125365.4	65324.0	37967.7	343.3	51269.7	24227.4
黑龙江	115895.9	71135.6	68804.9	6781.4	56794.1	35769.6
上　海	83499.0	87075.0	122439.5	1485.0	120456.5	2519.0
江　苏	467634.4	316278.1	385593.2	11657.2	367656.1	142705.9
浙　江	114203.1	60094.1	370427.9	57629.3	306985.3	73703.5
安　徽	108043.8	60784.8	151931.1	2031.5	127379.5	80907.1
福　建	108363.1	63809.1	130966.8	22771.9	99392.8	56435.1
江　西	61113.5	34494.5	116833.9	1000.0	91304.9	105188.2
山　东	605692.2	376318.2	285517.6	2976.0	262091.6	234022.0
河　南	241624.4	152633.2	159913.3	6465.9	136853.9	146141.3
湖　北	239564.3	135744.3	159851.8	4745.5	132920.3	69111.9
湖　南	183865.9	127869.6	116002.6	7849.0	86806.7	141204.6
广　东	318533.6	209637.5	320475.8	13367.5	287089.3	133378.7
广　西	76169.6	50151.6	191778.4	36833.2	131277.6	119063.9
海　南	20968.9	14452.2	36742.9	1404.5	33203.1	14697.5
重　庆	99881.0	54252.0	106612.1	8107.2	79935.5	49493.6
四　川	371496.9	256062.1	164809.0	5119.2	138584.7	103984.8
贵　州	57258.3	38767.3	115092.7	28193.0	67391.7	94429.0
云　南	215614.8	140963.8	112938.7	5331.0	79735.7	138273.0
西　藏	18940.3	9971.0	9139.1	291.6	6702.8	14024.6
陕　西	389791.8	273060.5	179823.1	15210.6	144920.9	167689.6
甘　肃	93815.2	50200.2	58395.3	192.1	34600.2	57117.0
青　海	30666.7	18610.9	43759.8	3743.3	26249.7	44391.9
宁　夏	21460.2	13183.4	23335.3	37.2	15001.1	13518.0
新　疆	86493.4	33636.1	280835.9	101282.8	111380.8	235867.7

单位：万元

本年下达所属地方预算指标	本年社会救助预算指标	上年结转预算指标	本级财政安排预算指标	本年上级下达预算指标	本年下达所属地方预算指标
3146173.5	**22667598.5**	**791959.7**	**21958675.9**	**42622161.5**	**42705198.6**
844501.0			13395002.0		13395002.0
59647.7	165422.2	5197.1	140318.1	39124.0	19217.0
3000.7	222540.3	2300.0	164662.7	108511.1	52933.5
108356.5	775032.0	29020.7	247098.3	1706402.7	1207489.7
41812.6	697462.2	26025.7	255767.5	1567203.1	1151534.1
140942.2	854259.6	6228.6	395937.5	1724743.2	1272649.7
59202.6	763924.3	18765.5	299444.0	1462968.1	1017253.3
37872.7	612183.7	10973.2	115102.9	1016549.6	530442.0
30540.2	1117394.4	3705.0	498458.8	2944178.3	2328947.7
2021.0	306697.5	342.9	306200.1	14564.0	14409.5
136426.0	910422.9	36122.4	713259.8	846559.2	685518.5
67890.2	478190.6	18648.4	386831.9	237060.6	164350.3
58387.0	924445.6	17625.8	320424.8	1259610.6	673215.6
47633.0	292953.2	17435.5	156447.7	449494.8	330424.8
80659.2	759088.7		233042.7	1776828.0	1250782.0
213572.0	929263.1	4696.6	548488.9	1422941.3	1046863.7
129547.8	1209116.0	12641.7	286037.8	2962312.4	2051875.9
46925.9	994702.4	6842.6	276975.8	1611476.9	900592.9
119857.7	1170159.2	9497.9	373397.3	2643124.1	1855860.1
113359.7	761997.8	25332.9	544329.9	1066685.6	874350.6
95396.3	857173.4	72957.2	231195.8	1487405.1	934384.7
12562.2	149722.8	12863.3	49481.4	207713.6	120335.5
30924.2	577687.1	41250.3	203844.0	747053.3	414460.5
82879.7	1513919.8	16504.2	416498.2	3461740.2	2380822.8
74921.0	1139573.5	115710.6	149781.9	2566554.4	1692473.4
110401.0	1150293.6	8893.7	344738.9	2810967.0	2014306.0
11879.9	84914.2	43522.7	34679.8	108935.7	102224.0
147998.0	1234315.0	211069.9	412819.4	2275666.8	1665241.1
33514.0	959798.0	11725.6	222200.4	1624197.1	898325.1
30625.1	196595.5	470.0	35553.0	488016.6	327444.1
5221.0	175454.0	2311.2	50552.7	267358.1	144768.0
167695.4	682895.9	3278.5	150101.9	1716216.0	1186700.5

C-1-15续表2

地 区	本年城市最低生活保障预算指标	上年结转预算指标	本级财政安排预算指标	本年上级下达预算指标	本年下达所属地方预算指标	本年农村最低生活保障预算指标	上年结转预算指标
全 国	**7935692.1**	**271768.4**	**7644628.5**	**16420215.7**	**16400920.5**	**9152696.5**	**299818.2**
中央级			5405289.0		5405289.0		
北 京	69698.7	1325.6	65049.1	9133.9	5809.9	27996.2	
天 津	134815.3	1689.2	87836.7	90255.4	44966.0	33900.0	240.1
河 北	254893.3	13195.1	39303.2	634215.7	431820.7	339328.9	8173.5
山 西	300639.6	14301.2	73908.4	742982.8	530552.8	260307.5	3485.1
内蒙古	402626.4	1439.4	156839.6	909272.4	664925.0	305720.2	286.3
辽 宁	443163.6	10919.5	107865.0	982908.5	658529.4	171337.3	2299.3
吉 林	374964.3	5945.5	45273.6	648881.2	325136.0	133439.2	2164.5
黑龙江	625939.1	349.2	229915.9	1722278.4	1326604.4	245053.8	2.0
上 海	146154.4	289.2	145755.6	6880.0	6770.4	13837.3	51.5
江 苏	152811.6	1121.5	140042.5	109532.9	97885.3	411432.6	33664.9
浙 江	45332.7	1425.8	41519.9	14212.2	11825.2	210332.1	8579.6
安 徽	306955.2	11214.2	64365.0	484172.5	252796.5	364535.3	3165.0
福 建	53732.4	2971.4	22779.0	93514.6	65532.6	130758.1	10.9
江 西	288126.4		46297.4	732326.1	490497.1	245903.5	
山 东	202548.4	1581.3	107967.1	335768.6	242768.6	476533.5	61.0
河 南	382426.0	8128.8	27009.9	1067907.5	720620.2	546906.4	1321.8
湖 北	443061.2	3747.0	76453.2	796420.4	433559.4	339205.6	550.0
湖 南	463861.7	2813.3	94017.5	1159659.4	792628.5	409851.5	4204.9
广 东	139696.2	2429.0	126034.2	163312.1	152079.1	355932.0	11496.0
广 西	183624.8	31032.0	20489.8	336377.3	204274.3	440404.8	24262.0
海 南	57796.2	3614.0	16693.3	92711.9	55223.0	53017.2	3526.4
重 庆	213561.8	26891.9	13164.5	345591.4	172086.0	151511.6	6003.9
四 川	508287.6	3588.8	59618.0	1380597.7	935516.9	564371.7	3003.1
贵 州	186281.6	14753.6	35531.0	434234.2	298237.2	809831.5	91107.2
云 南	289192.7	1494.5	80695.9	694494.6	487492.3	672313.3	4550.0
西 藏	21712.4	2128.5	11418.5	22551.7	14386.3	39743.3	128.1
陕 西	443741.7	93153.1	132184.2	740752.2	522347.8	533212.3	86775.5
甘 肃	317293.5	7673.2	83511.3	509731.0	283622.0	483971.7	705.6
青 海	78397.4		11877.4	199001.1	132481.1	75017.2	
宁 夏	67937.1	1736.1	13667.0	101455.0	48921.0	74396.9	
新 疆	336418.8	816.5	62255.8	859083.0	585736.5	232594.0	

单位：万元

本级财政安排预算指标	本年上级下达预算指标	本年下达所属地方预算指标	本年其他社会救济预算指标	上年结转预算指标	本级财政安排预算指标	本年上级下达预算指标	本年下达所属地方预算指标
8910467.5	**19213543.8**	**19271133.0**	**2921538.7**	**55670.7**	**2853413.3**	**2124958.0**	**2112503.3**
6122955.0		6122955.0			308995.0		308995.0
26647.2	3888.2	2539.2	44431.5	2841.7	30363.8	17685.2	6459.2
31411.9	4496.0	2248.0	19258.7	370.7	16444.4	3621.1	1177.5
101003.4	801517.8	571365.8	87949.6	2284.7	74633.9	80385.1	69354.1
102795.4	592472.6	438445.6	62087.1	2396.9	51584.2	75469.5	67363.5
144612.5	609948.3	449126.9	74621.9	2496.7	68197.1	52882.0	48953.9
91206.0	330239.5	252407.5	90277.1	317.4	80315.2	45578.5	35934.0
30535.6	228395.1	127656.0	37195.6	891.5	28766.4	21759.7	14222.0
99900.3	664296.0	519144.5	106554.9	174.3	102717.8	210670.0	207007.2
13742.0	715.0	671.2	119577.2	2.2	119573.9	3652.0	3650.9
263944.3	574325.5	460502.1	223693.1	930.7	209468.9	57745.2	44451.7
150208.5	152650.4	101106.4	129892.3	5324.3	117521.5	21102.6	14056.1
96330.5	576089.0	311049.2	146041.4	717.9	125889.3	45817.8	26383.6
62264.2	238943.9	170460.9	56248.8	2313.5	47291.3	55258.7	48614.7
45658.5	605345.6	405100.6	94264.7		81589.7	162643.3	149968.3
260416.5	826029.4	609973.4	132392.3	788.7	118603.0	70608.7	57608.1
102010.6	1452715.1	1009141.1	164230.3	1385.6	135777.0	158142.1	131074.4
81888.6	578568.0	321801.0	103742.1	2270.5	81592.6	83586.1	63707.1
163964.0	999907.0	758224.4	166917.5	1055.5	89163.7	161650.5	84952.2
196961.0	663226.2	515751.2	172535.9	2699.4	159793.5	120908.7	110865.7
58162.8	921921.0	563941.0	142645.0	3613.0	132901.0	78693.6	72562.6
17599.0	74933.8	43042.0	15214.7	949.3	12037.7	4812.0	2584.3
38733.6	244178.7	137404.6	121755.9	2338.7	111353.9	51150.2	43086.9
93363.8	1478203.9	1010199.1	223585.4	7784.0	187271.2	117564.2	89034.0
67096.3	1852549.3	1200921.3	49771.2	1468.4	39657.8	46039.0	37394.0
144291.0	1760316.8	1236844.5	80516.4	1330.8	98070.9	78291.0	97176.3
19940.8	58882.1	39207.7	3678.7	64.6	821.7	4471.1	1678.7
132211.4	1081706.0	767480.6	129809.6	5368.8	119391.3	191427.8	186378.3
66059.1	894846.1	477639.1	68733.0	168.7	64448.3	63234.0	59118.0
10220.0	194997.7	130200.5	11848.8	470.0	8602.0	9412.1	6635.3
26102.9	118804.0	70510.0	9701.4	444.2	7968.0	6281.2	4992.0
48230.8	628435.8	444072.6	32366.6	2408.0	22607.3	24415.0	17063.7

C-1-15续表3

地 区	本年医疗救助预算指标	上年结转预算指标	本级财政安排预算指标	本年上级下达预算指标	本年下达所属地方预算指标
全 国	**2657671.2**	**164702.4**	**2550166.6**	**4863444.0**	**4920641.8**
中央级			1557763.0		1557763.0
北 京	23295.8	1029.8	18258.0	8416.7	4408.7
天 津	34566.3		28969.7	10138.6	4542.0
河 北	92860.2	5367.4	32157.8	190284.1	134949.1
山 西	74428.0	5842.5	27479.5	156278.2	115172.2
内蒙古	71291.1	2006.2	26288.3	152640.5	109643.9
辽 宁	59146.3	5229.3	20057.8	104241.6	70382.4
吉 林	66584.6	1971.7	10527.3	117513.6	63428.0
黑龙江	139846.6	3179.5	65924.8	346933.9	276191.6
上 海	27128.6		27128.6	3317.0	3317.0
江 苏	122485.6	405.3	99804.1	104955.6	82679.4
浙 江	92633.5	3318.7	77582.0	49095.4	37362.6
安 徽	106913.7	2528.7	33840.0	153531.3	82986.3
福 建	52213.9	12139.7	24113.2	61777.6	45816.6
江 西	130794.1		59497.1	276513.0	205216.0
山 东	117788.9	2265.6	61502.3	190534.6	136513.6
河 南	115553.3	1805.5	21240.3	283547.7	191040.2
湖 北	108693.5	275.1	37041.4	152902.4	81525.4
湖 南	129528.5	1424.2	26252.1	321907.2	220055.0
广 东	93833.7	8708.5	61541.2	119238.6	95654.6
广 西	90498.8	14050.2	19642.2	150413.2	93606.8
海 南	23694.7	4773.6	3151.4	35255.9	19486.2
重 庆	90857.8	6015.8	40592.0	106133.0	61883.0
四 川	217675.1	2128.3	76245.2	485374.4	346072.8
贵 州	93689.2	8381.4	7496.8	233731.9	155920.9
云 南	108271.2	1518.4	21681.1	277864.6	192792.9
西 藏	19779.8	41201.5	2498.8	23030.8	46951.3
陕 西	127551.4	25772.5	29032.5	261780.8	189034.4
甘 肃	89799.8	3178.1	8181.7	156386.0	77946.0
青 海	31332.1		4853.6	84605.7	58127.2
宁 夏	23418.6	130.9	2814.8	40817.9	20345.0
新 疆	81516.5	54.0	17008.0	204282.2	139827.7

单位：万元

本年自然灾害生活救助预算指标	上年结转预算指标	本级财政安排预算指标	本年上级下达预算指标	本年下达所属地方预算指标
2027505.0	**136600.6**	**1896321.4**	**3218008.2**	**3223425.2**
43506.0		1060654.0		1017148.0
6962.0	720.0	5277.0	3365.0	2400.0
2447.8	600.0	1427.8	1120.0	700.0
60624.7	13781.7	14321.7	107564.3	75043.0
49840.5	6608.7	9731.8	111488.5	77988.5
60111.8	7914.3	14095.5	114222.0	76120.0
70302.4	4464.5	17159.0	146242.9	97564.0
67061.3	551.9	15376.4	96273.0	45140.0
148921.9	472.2	108570.0	334615.2	294735.5
2159.0		2159.0		
24488.8	3239.1	9624.8	43597.2	31972.3
40421.2	3884.5	20679.7	46969.0	31112.0
42206.0	4199.8	7374.2	65737.0	35105.0
31774.2	5805.4	14932.8	38387.5	27351.5
55155.2		15655.2	69345.0	29845.0
32937.0	2369.2	11467.8	62778.8	43678.8
26588.0	871.6	5616.4	64232.4	44132.4
66464.1	1976.3	16539.8	106823.3	58875.3
61196.4	3592.0	10335.4	149979.0	102710.0
70786.3	484.3	40202.0	137301.4	107201.4
67714.2	14587.3	20532.9	87894.7	55300.7
10667.7	1488.8	3334.9	12951.0	7107.0
48582.2	7994.9	8987.3	64180.0	32580.0
341599.6	16559.9	241114.8	278259.1	194334.2
85030.6	14466.7	18163.9	163613.3	111213.3
124598.6	8311.3	47875.3	272111.8	203699.8
30172.3	688.1	8123.9	45594.1	24233.8
136275.1	6728.2	67521.9	255543.9	193518.9
127992.2	1119.0	52861.2	191510.8	117498.8
30196.1	2102.0	10832.1	22726.0	5464.0
19301.1	459.7	2541.4	33405.0	17105.0
41420.7	559.2	13231.5	90177.0	62547.0

C-1-15续表4

地　区	本年民政管理事务预算指标	上年结转预算指标	本级财政安排预算指标	本年上级下达预算指标	本年下达所属地方预算指标	本年行政事业单位离退休预算指标	上年结转预算指标
全　国	**2957367.6**	**36973.1**	**2911261.4**	**550617.6**	**541484.5**	**429572.1**	**511.8**
中央级	47422.3		47422.3			3815.8	
北　京	160675.2	202.3	160472.9	2646.5	2646.5	54835.4	
天　津	115470.4	963.5	114506.9			4271.6	
河　北	74410.0	1862.2	72547.8	12826.9	12826.9	19581.9	
山　西	55588.3	101.3	55487.0	14964.0	14964.0	9753.4	
内蒙古	70921.8	4167.5	51090.2	32845.9	17181.8	13356.6	
辽　宁	144464.5		159577.1	57634.2	72746.8	22543.5	
吉　林	32024.7		32459.2	8142.5	8577.0	8833.5	
黑龙江	60338.7	116.3	60826.6	27843.6	28447.8	7477.7	
上　海	128200.0		128200.0			8358.5	
江　苏	194369.8	997.3	193218.9	27794.0	27640.4	27839.5	20.9
浙　江	223839.0	2872.1	219786.9	11432.4	10252.4	22493.5	
安　徽	63617.0	1169.5	62447.5	10135.5	10135.5	13519.3	
福　建	65642.3	750.8	64891.5	10813.7	10813.7	25950.1	519.0
江　西	37953.5		37953.5	7497.6	7497.6	9024.1	
山　东	149841.2		149840.8	29524.0	29523.6	12320.2	
河　南	86226.5	101.0	85599.9	4357.2	3831.6	17845.9	
湖　北	85474.4	1215.9	84258.5	18476.4	18476.4	18107.2	
湖　南	101231.1	247.6	102396.3	30053.0	31465.8	8327.6	
广　东	217724.4	1955.1	215769.3	6846.2	6846.2	34509.8	
广　西	94244.5	3793.3	90451.2	19694.2	19694.2	13163.3	-38.6
海　南	30504.2	2997.4	29631.8	874.7	2999.7	3654.9	
重　庆	72941.2	291.0	72650.2	4335.0	4335.0	9126.4	
四　川	152239.0	2105.6	149342.1	12714.2	11922.9	20568.7	
贵　州	72822.2	2559.3	70262.9	24464.9	24464.9	3455.0	
云　南	122070.0	1633.3	120436.7	66168.9	66168.9	12431.7	
西　藏	9214.2		9106.0	108.2		744.3	
陕　西	141801.2	6812.8	134654.2	83841.0	83506.8	6460.6	10.5
甘　肃	27019.3		27019.3	1000.0	1000.0	4612.2	
青　海	22131.2		19328.0	6432.3	3629.1	2158.2	
宁　夏	22362.5	55.0	21427.9	5552.6	4673.0	2979.5	
新　疆	74583.0	3.0	68198.0	11598.0	5216.0	7452.2	

单位：万元

本级财政安排预算指标	本年上级下达预算指标	本年下达所属地方预算指标	本年其他款项用于民政支出预算指标	上年结转预算指标	本级财政安排预算指标	本年上级下达预算指标	本年下达所属地方预算指标
427484.1	**2442.3**	**866.1**	**1455112.0**	**321871.6**	**1111483.7**	**745637.4**	**723880.7**
3815.8			18668.7		111160.7		92492.0
54835.4			107046.9	34399.7	48204.2	63130.2	38687.2
4271.6			26735.8	16578.7	9773.1	16769.0	16385.0
19581.9			20747.1	7197.3	14687.0	216.3	1353.5
9753.4			22054.6	5812.2	16242.4	1213.4	1213.4
13356.6			39580.0	8238.7	21410.1	15539.9	5608.7
22427.9	412.6	297.0	76208.1	934.5	50207.1	54802.8	29736.3
8501.0	332.5		40976.4		46553.0	21330.4	26907.0
7477.7			6002.3		5914.6	87.7	
8358.5			53729.7	33652.0	48994.7	4735.0	33652.0
26711.8	1326.9	220.1	165855.8	46817.5	102807.2	98883.2	82652.1
22493.5			83371.7	5340.0	77901.9	3904.9	3775.1
13519.3			16474.2	1194.2	15253.0	27.0	
25431.1			31107.3	9064.5	22042.8	22011.9	22011.9
9024.1			7580.2		4593.2	3293.4	306.4
12320.2			84160.6	22757.9	55259.7	37740.1	31597.1
17872.4		26.5	54511.2	15828.1	32208.8	41225.7	34751.4
18107.2			46407.6	9826.6	36620.0	29343.1	29382.1
8469.8	54.7	196.9	41636.9	4532.0	31296.5	19884.4	14076.0
34509.8			97836.4	11564.7	84886.7	15802.1	14417.1
13201.9			40178.5	3766.9	31747.6	15739.0	11075.0
3654.9			17670.3	5208.2	11608.4	853.7	
9126.4			13066.0	1310.9	11755.1		
20568.7			66817.6	7923.9	45533.5	39989.0	26628.8
3455.0			19440.4	2115.2	17325.2	8960.5	8960.5
12431.7	124.6	124.6	84306.7	4358.3	79771.4	84458.5	84281.5
600.9	144.4	1.0	35843.1	33731.6	6218.8	3782.8	7890.1
6403.5	46.6		16969.0	4690.6	14442.8	19223.6	21388.0
4612.2			20687.3	15457.5	5229.8		
2158.2			68948.6	128.0	31956.1	112910.3	76045.8
2979.5			25962.2	9342.2	16385.2	8623.5	8388.7
7452.2			4530.8	99.7	3493.1	1156.0	218.0

C−1−15续表5

地 区	本年预算指标结余	抚恤	退役安置	社会福利
全 国	**2775241.7**	**216454.7**	**587235.4**	**567318.4**
中央级				
北 京	366880.3	7902.4	286672.3	23906.0
天 津	20415.7	1316.6	9832.7	4046.2
河 北	81031.8	7864.7	11151.2	23147.0
山 西	62293.8	11762.6	3525.4	6706.6
内蒙古	75439.2	2258.5	5419.2	18136.7
辽 宁	57420.7	2687.4	7451.8	3524.2
吉 林	34311.1	87.3	22.0	4918.9
黑龙江	20462.9	1597.3	1128.2	4089.1
上 海	42511.8		35296.4	1983.0
江 苏	131246.5	8223.9	14308.7	19161.8
浙 江	120410.3	16249.1	4198.4	71192.1
安 徽	36022.2	6908.2	1468.7	10753.6
福 建	71445.4	5886.3	18424.6	26378.9
江 西	40602.0			10615.0
山 东	75981.3	4347.6	16101.0	22711.6
河 南	44912.2	433.5	3060.6	15466.9
湖 北	35589.2	2558.6	2034.4	8853.6
湖 南	18458.7	2917.5	558.0	11652.8
广 东	94467.1	11238.9	49397.5	10999.2
广 西	212143.4	24361.3	5275.7	57144.4
海 南	48909.4	3189.4	4440.3	3942.9
重 庆	86497.0	3414.3	2020.8	15181.8
四 川	59579.2	4017.8	8404.3	18111.1
贵 州	259770.9	6832.2	1080.4	28842.2
云 南	22240.7	3308.5	998.3	2535.1
西 藏	33976.8	544.5	319.3	25.0
陕 西	427286.6	75223.1	91627.8	20983.5
甘 肃	32782.6	12.0	1886.2	58.3
青 海	22555.0	532.0		7103.0
宁 夏	26544.8	337.4	1131.2	4974.4
新 疆	113053.1	441.8		110173.5

单位：万元

社会救助	自然灾害生活救助	民政管理事务	行政事业单位离退休	其他款项用于民政支出
956663.6	**198471.5**	**37598.2**	**691.4**	**210808.5**
6024.1	920.0	15.0		41440.5
2862.0		667.9		1690.3
29551.3	7867.8	1377.8		72.0
28715.3	9189.0	1204.3		1190.6
8124.4	22011.8	5492.1		13996.5
30993.8	3666.1	22.7		9074.7
10294.5	18409.4	84.0		495.0
12229.5	966.2	452.6		
497.4				4735.0
68960.4	3210.2	719.6		16661.9
15331.4	6929.7	4299.7	40.3	2169.6
12937.3	3455.0	403.4	12.0	84.0
12990.8	3574.5	907.3	602.1	2680.9
	27000.0			2987.0
10295.5	2681.2	1484.0		18360.4
10353.9	947.9	85.0		14564.4
14439.5	2714.9	2144.7		2843.5
1868.5	710.7	728.2	23.0	
15781.7	2105.2	938.2	0.3	4006.1
88496.7	18019.0	4292.4	12.9	14541.0
28991.5	2125.5	2542.6		3677.2
57493.0	6204.5	444.6		1738.0
8425.6	12801.9	684.0	0.8	7133.7
207043.3	11921.4	972.9		3078.5
7643.9	3755.1	1989.9		2009.9
11438.9	530.5			21118.6
224700.8	6597.4	5299.7		2854.3
13734.6	1946.0			15145.5
1220.0	13700.0			
13636.0	3660.8	345.6		2459.4
1588.0	849.8			

C-1-16 当年预算

地 区	全国预算安排合计	中央安排合计	全省安排合计				抚 恤	
				省 级	市 级	县级及以下		中央安排
全 国	**43268489.6**	**21658489.3**	**21610000.3**	**6808989.5**	**3584877.2**	**11216133.6**	**6313643.6**	**3690695.0**
中央级	132229.8	132229.8					617.0	617.0
北 京	1429615.9	563162.0	866453.9	330669.3		535784.6	107219.3	23930.0
天 津	561715.2	140090.0	421625.2	62523.1		359102.1	61395.8	16911.0
河 北	1658617.9	942184.0	716433.9	255237.6	128161.6	333034.7	374067.1	240015.0
山 西	1145199.4	627954.0	517245.4	179549.8	159416.0	178279.6	202190.6	113639.0
内蒙古	1274677.4	574619.0	700058.4	249560.3	169612.8	280885.3	90982.6	41989.0
辽 宁	1667135.5	902779.0	764356.5	159996.4	304778.2	299581.9	190475.5	99802.0
吉 林	982109.1	663375.0	318734.1	160200.1	37514.1	121019.9	105458.4	69909.0
黑龙江	1629434.3	840720.0	788714.3	574273.9	83300.2	131140.2	117162.3	77393.0
上 海	952375.6	117669.0	834706.6	106313.3		728393.3	94064.2	12352.0
江 苏	2277104.5	523346.0	1753758.5	395432.8	258801.3	1099524.4	386529.8	169093.0
浙 江	1449943.3	220846.0	1229097.3	194351.4	150360.2	884385.7	238235.4	68297.0
安 徽	1588794.1	861943.0	726851.1	135506.3	110082.4	481262.4	269894.9	175241.0
福 建	732793.1	248527.0	484266.1	122441.9	86305.2	275519.0	129152.7	65065.0
江 西	1260784.9	786411.0	474373.9	192452.1	38941.2	242980.6	235158.2	166730.0
山 东	2542119.4	1084742.0	1457377.4	316428.0	331283.2	809666.2	707928.4	420070.0
河 南	2089771.4	1324131.0	765640.4	278414.7	108996.5	378229.2	414176.9	273208.0
湖 北	1837118.4	1113168.0	723950.4	217871.7	162534.9	343543.8	333651.5	227394.0
湖 南	1995947.6	1240880.0	755067.6	248328.0	112801.0	393938.6	404204.5	306149.0
广 东	1982305.0	463640.0	1518665.0	370742.3	377985.0	769937.7	298841.3	110697.0
广 西	1350210.3	731695.0	618515.3	266971.5	120415.6	231128.2	156846.8	91731.0
海 南	294076.0	134557.0	159519.0	47518.2	21765.9	90234.9	29585.9	18165.0
重 庆	1007108.9	537047.0	470061.9	176487.8		293574.1	162593.5	109151.0
四 川	2909798.8	1651852.0	1257946.8	216632.1	151546.8	889767.9	451063.4	336209.0
贵 州	1458130.4	1064697.0	393433.4	100238.7	83047.7	210147.0	141949.1	100217.0
云 南	1854957.0	1103881.0	751076.0	367403.3	117043.7	266629.0	178920.3	136108.0
西 藏	166015.3	119190.0	46825.3	15566.0	11468.0	19791.3	6146.7	4751.0
陕 西	1996633.1	941322.0	1055311.1	489110.6	324575.2	241625.3	294877.0	131651.0
甘 肃	1292279.6	908817.0	383462.6	268240.7	47941.7	67280.2	53581.6	41715.0
青 海	351399.8	214470.0	136929.8	57782.6	9625.9	69521.3	14486.5	8722.0
宁 夏	285516.1	163501.0	122015.1	69312.0	15431.2	37271.9	11891.4	6923.0
新 疆	1112572.5	715044.5	397528.0	183433.0	61141.7	152953.3	50295.0	26851.0

安排情况

单位：万元

全省安排	省　级	市　级	县级及以下	退役安置	中央安排	全省安排	省　级
2622948.6	**779435.6**	**252401.4**	**1591111.6**	**4450148.7**	**2681550.0**	**1768598.7**	**534419.1**
83289.3	1060.8		82228.5	680003.1	488906.0	191097.1	127932.6
44484.8	5966.7		38518.1	98614.0	63858.0	34756.0	129.4
134052.1	48756.0	12051.6	73244.5	236936.6	152666.0	84270.6	38386.3
88551.6	15438.4	17341.7	55771.5	70950.6	48800.0	22150.6	6253.3
48993.6	8813.7	5671.2	34508.7	49919.4	31897.0	18022.4	11629.8
90673.5	21808.8	22655.5	46209.2	301588.6	256649.0	44939.6	5178.0
35549.4	17377.4	539.8	17632.2	72482.9	57815.0	14667.9	7509.0
39769.3	25996.7	493.7	13278.9	59536.7	47885.0	11651.7	2044.0
81712.2	6558.6		75153.6	222124.6	83499.0	138625.6	5012.3
217436.8	49689.3	9160.9	158586.6	310629.5	150585.0	160044.5	35473.0
169938.4	23240.0	7792.0	138906.4	106639.4	54109.0	52530.4	2717.0
94653.9	17487.2	5010.8	72155.9	146280.5	47259.0	99021.5	7026.1
64087.7	18876.1	7804.5	37407.1	81593.7	44554.0	37039.7	3961.5
68428.2	31324.7	1102.1	36001.4	43278.2	26619.0	16659.2	1117.4
287858.4	59854.5	53012.0	174991.9	359424.0	229374.0	130050.0	24222.0
140968.9	25918.4	17706.1	97344.4	155723.8	89151.0	66572.8	17101.0
106257.5	32894.0	14694.3	58669.2	156091.3	103820.0	52271.3	15598.0
98055.5	33444.4	12439.8	52171.3	105468.1	61158.0	44310.1	20269.9
188144.3	67033.1	25845.7	95265.5	209254.6	109104.0	100150.6	1134.2
65115.8	36630.1	6837.5	21648.2	63865.7	26018.0	37847.7	15323.8
11420.9	2833.2	1046.7	7541.0	27983.6	10800.0	17183.6	3730.8
53442.5	22045.2		31397.3	75949.9	45629.0	30320.9	9440.8
114854.4	32736.3	5928.0	76190.1	247042.4	115434.0	131608.4	24519.0
41732.1	7407.0	5961.5	28363.6	43811.7	18491.0	25320.7	4337.0
42812.3	20965.0	1718.8	20128.5	108562.8	74651.0	33911.8	3844.9
1395.7	232.0	427.3	736.4	10677.8	9821.0	856.8	468.6
163226.0	124237.0	13662.7	25326.3	230342.7	116172.0	114170.7	104016.7
11866.6	5552.2	1217.1	5097.3	68687.9	43615.0	25072.9	20992.2
5764.5	1513.9	30.5	4220.1	17144.2	12056.0	5088.2	4039.3
4968.4	744.1	1022.2	3202.1	16435.9	8277.0	8158.9	4954.0
23444.0	13000.8	1227.4	9215.8	73104.5	52878.0	20226.5	6057.2

C−1−16续表1

地　区	市级	县级及以下	社会福利	中央安排	全省安排	省级	市级	县级及以下
全　国	**247959.3**	**986220.3**	**4249360.4**	**598849.5**	**3650510.9**	**1217808.6**	**1051756.8**	**1380945.5**
中央级			18200.0	18200.0				
北　京		63164.5	187970.9	5011.0	182959.9	108346.7		74613.2
天　津		34626.6	50628.3	2886.0	47742.3	23997.2		23745.1
河　北	16477.2	29407.1	148563.5	17779.0	130784.5	41987.9	43539.4	45257.2
山　西	6750.5	9146.8	75907.1	16346.0	59561.1	5475.9	42610.0	11475.2
内蒙古	1988.6	4404.0	149082.5	11930.0	137152.5	71942.0	30777.4	34433.1
辽　宁	12082.5	27679.1	122010.6	9763.0	112247.6	29406.5	57073.7	25767.4
吉　林	892.5	6266.4	59767.7	8498.0	51269.7	34274.7	8211.3	8783.7
黑龙江	4931.4	4676.3	66243.3	9465.0	56778.3	25417.9	23483.8	7876.6
上　海		133613.3	122975.5	2519.0	120456.5	33022.5		87434.0
江　苏	29991.3	94580.2	379821.2	17041.0	362780.2	82540.9	106197.6	174041.7
浙　江	6407.3	43406.1	300369.2	9835.0	290534.2	64009.5	61364.3	165160.4
安　徽	17207.0	74788.4	147516.0	22449.0	125067.0	37479.6	43397.3	44190.1
福　建	8751.6	24326.6	108194.8	8802.0	99392.8	26377.0	33196.3	39819.5
江　西	2620.1	12921.7	115830.0	24529.0	91301.0	51920.4	10605.1	28775.5
山　东	29807.4	76020.6	282541.6	20450.0	262091.6	96071.8	78097.5	87922.3
河　南	15572.9	33898.9	174377.0	37666.0	136711.0	82700.2	19033.4	34977.4
湖　北	12971.1	23702.2	155468.3	22548.0	132920.3	30700.0	50795.3	51425.0
湖　南	10283.8	13756.4	123316.7	36510.0	86806.7	33707.1	20677.2	32422.4
广　东	12787.3	86229.1	317308.9	20019.0	297289.9	19461.2	156413.5	121415.2
广　西	13293.0	9230.9	154727.3	23623.0	131104.3	63649.2	44544.1	22911.0
海　南	7345.0	6107.8	39682.1	6479.0	33203.1	11033.0	1701.6	20468.5
重　庆		20880.1	98504.5	18569.0	79935.5	37591.1		42344.4
四　川	9422.9	97666.5	171660.7	33076.0	138584.7	30268.0	40539.1	67777.6
贵　州	3589.0	17394.7	86899.7	19508.0	67391.7	27421.0	21026.7	18944.0
云　南	11405.7	18661.2	106219.3	27872.0	78347.3	24896.4	24209.6	29241.3
西　藏	366.9	21.3	17705.5	11700.0	6005.5	1314.0	3875.5	816.0
陕　西	6360.5	3793.5	163697.9	18838.0	144859.9	42611.8	64531.1	37717.0
甘　肃	1796.9	2283.8	58203.2	23603.0	34600.2	10126.3	17005.7	7468.2
青　海	235.5	813.4	41208.7	14959.0	26249.7	15153.0	3908.8	7187.9
宁　夏	1966.1	1238.8	24321.1	9320.0	15001.1	6226.8	4816.0	3958.3
新　疆	2655.3	11514.0	180437.3	69056.5	111380.8	48679.0	40125.5	22576.3

单位：万元

社会救助	中央安排合计	全省安排合计	省级	市级	县级及以下	城市最低生活保障	中央安排	全省安排
21964189.4	**13454722.0**	**8509467.4**	**3133736.9**	**939695.0**	**4436035.5**	**7677377.5**	**5455709.0**	**2221668.5**
160225.1	19907.0	140318.1	13327.1		126991.0	68373.1	3324.0	65049.1
220293.7	55631.0	164662.7	20472.4		144190.3	132802.7	44966.0	87836.7
745958.7	499309.0	246649.7	97954.0	32206.1	116489.6	241698.2	202395.0	39303.2
671436.5	415669.0	255767.5	134505.1	56769.1	64493.3	286338.4	212430.0	73908.4
847940.5	452003.0	395937.5	141572.8	94725.8	159638.9	397927.6	241088.0	156839.6
752082.9	469385.0	282697.9	66002.0	100682.8	116013.1	437951.6	337595.0	100356.6
588712.5	474027.0	114685.5	56415.0	572.9	57697.6	351266.6	306301.0	44965.6
1157839.6	660105.0	497734.6	383400.5	32476.4	81857.7	664406.2	435124.0	229282.2
320764.1	14564.0	306200.1	12567.5		293632.6	152635.6	6880.0	145755.6
862732.7	162476.0	700256.7	201639.8	37255.5	461361.4	148356.6	11335.0	137021.6
468030.7	73114.0	394916.7	79486.3	17844.8	297585.6	44211.0	2387.0	41824.0
898911.7	586335.0	312576.7	56460.0	19482.2	236634.5	293569.3	231376.0	62193.3
275517.7	119070.0	156447.7	40990.0	13780.5	101677.2	50761.0	27982.0	22779.0
757318.6	526046.0	231272.6	96752.7	13900.5	120619.4	287429.6	241829.0	45600.6
924566.9	376078.0	548488.9	118221.3	90393.2	339874.4	200967.1	93000.0	107967.1
1185405.8	903435.0	281970.8	116611.5	25377.4	139981.9	373990.9	347287.0	26703.9
988433.8	711458.0	276975.8	95562.0	39322.1	142091.7	439828.2	363375.0	76453.2
1162378.3	788981.0	373397.3	135639.9	29191.0	208566.4	460428.5	366411.0	94017.5
743998.0	192335.0	551663.0	234138.6	50897.7	266626.7	138495.9	11233.0	127262.9
781882.5	553065.0	228817.5	109125.5	6379.6	113312.4	152592.8	132103.0	20489.8
142594.4	93113.0	49481.4	19879.6	1195.3	28406.5	56701.3	40008.0	16693.3
535942.0	332098.0	203844.0	86160.3		117683.7	186669.5	173505.0	13164.5
1498448.2	1082108.0	416340.2	95256.7	41923.9	279159.6	504011.0	444513.0	59498.0
1023862.9	874081.0	149781.9	49618.0	26867.8	73296.1	171528.0	135997.0	35531.0
1137373.2	796661.0	340712.2	195230.1	35820.1	109662.0	269735.3	190173.0	79562.3
87283.7	69713.0	17570.7	45.0	2382.3	15143.4	21979.8	13716.0	8263.8
1024523.7	612632.0	411891.7	164040.4	153435.9	94415.4	350279.2	218245.0	132034.2
948072.4	725872.0	222200.4	177545.1	11970.1	32685.2	309620.3	226109.0	83511.3
197024.0	161471.0	35553.0	3616.0	2603.1	29333.9	78576.4	66699.0	11877.4
173233.7	122681.0	50552.7	33251.0	856.8	16444.9	66201.0	52534.0	13667.0
681400.9	531299.0	150101.9	98250.7	1382.1	50469.1	338044.8	275789.0	62255.8

C-1-16续表2

地 区	省级	市级	县级及以下	农村最低生活保障	中央安排	全省安排	省级	市级
全 国	**732706.0**	**353913.6**	**1135048.9**	**8937893.0**	**6170883.0**	**2767010.0**	**1290964.0**	**294962.7**
中央级								
北 京	2577.7		62471.4	27996.2	1349.0	26647.2	1190.2	
天 津	579.8		87256.9	33659.9	2248.0	31411.9		
河 北	10000.0	10066.7	19236.5	331178.4	230175.0	101003.4	51439.0	11875.8
山 西	46859.9	12123.0	14925.5	256822.4	154027.0	102795.4	50806.0	28779.6
内蒙古	71445.4	39629.2	45765.0	307597.5	162985.0	144612.5	41996.6	39130.7
辽 宁	15000.0	49276.2	36080.4	175945.2	89100.0	86845.2	43016.0	20077.2
吉 林	18835.0		26130.6	133096.6	102654.0	30442.6	25002.0	
黑龙江	165736.0	23373.4	40172.8	248746.8	148937.0	99809.8	68774.0	5162.2
上 海	4060.1		141695.5	14457.0	715.0	13742.0		
江 苏	31477.7	9680.9	95863.0	378004.5	117626.0	260378.5	144779.5	1620.6
浙 江	7745.6	3148.1	30930.3	204674.1	51504.0	153170.1	44882.9	485.2
安 徽	5500.0	4622.8	52070.5	360155.5	265040.0	95115.5	38500.0	5598.3
福 建	1286.0	1984.6	19508.4	130747.2	68483.0	62264.2	14868.0	3758.9
江 西	600.0	6715.0	38285.6	245133.2	200245.0	44888.2	1318.0	2708.6
山 东	18665.2	21543.3	67758.6	476472.5	216056.0	260416.5	74296.0	33141.5
河 南	12300.0	6251.0	8152.9	553813.2	453106.0	100707.2	53244.0	10851.1
湖 北	9480.0	17836.1	49137.1	338655.6	256767.0	81888.6	44000.0	12319.4
湖 南	28200.0	9411.1	56406.4	468145.0	304181.0	163964.0	100193.1	9811.3
广 东	61347.4	14427.4	51488.1	346281.9	147475.0	198806.9	103614.8	11054.0
广 西	8226.9	369.5	11893.4	416142.8	357980.0	58162.8	42836.2	567.9
海 南	11354.0		5339.3	50388.0	32789.0	17599.0	7510.0	100.0
重 庆			13164.5	145507.6	106774.0	38733.6	30507.0	
四 川	20000.0	7696.6	31801.4	560627.8	467279.0	93348.8	27000.0	21640.9
贵 州	10000.0	9800.2	15730.8	718724.3	651628.0	67096.3	22500.0	8203.2
云 南	39969.1	13211.6	26381.6	657003.0	513873.0	143130.0	90471.3	17829.4
西 藏	10.0	1906.0	6347.8	45214.6	37796.0	7418.6		
陕 西	22027.2	80708.0	29299.0	447428.4	315430.0	131998.4	47832.3	47338.5
甘 肃	57513.0	8609.7	17388.6	483266.1	417207.0	66059.1	60432.1	1899.3
青 海	291.0	1186.6	10399.8	75017.0	64797.0	10220.0		1009.1
宁 夏	5885.0	336.6	7445.4	74396.9	48294.0	26102.9	22216.0	
新 疆	45734.0		16521.8	232593.8	184363.0	48230.8	37739.0	

单位：万元

县级及以下	其他社会救助	中央安排	全省安排	省级	市级	县级及以下	医疗救助	中央安排
1181083.3	**2787601.2**	**261442.0**	**2526159.2**	**757542.2**	**198766.9**	**1569850.1**	**2561317.7**	**1566688.0**
25457.0	41589.8	11226.0	30363.8	8775.6		21588.2	22266.0	4008.0
31411.9	18844.4	2400.0	16444.4	2288.4		14156.0	34986.7	6017.0
37688.6	85619.3	11414.0	74205.3	24000.0	7911.7	42293.6	87462.8	55325.0
23209.8	59690.2	8106.0	51584.2	23977.2	8085.8	19521.2	68585.5	41106.0
63485.2	72775.1	4578.0	68197.1	18422.8	8850.0	40924.3	69640.3	43352.0
23752.0	84180.0	7884.0	76296.0	2986.0	24195.3	49114.7	54006.1	34806.0
5440.6	35310.4	6544.0	28766.4	7678.0	572.9	20515.5	69038.9	58528.0
25873.6	106370.8	3653.0	102717.8	94156.5	2440.4	6120.9	138315.8	72391.0
13742.0	123225.9	3652.0	119573.9	8200.3		111373.6	30445.6	3317.0
113978.4	212589.4	7969.0	204620.4	7229.6	22599.5	174791.3	123782.2	25546.0
107802.0	123869.8	6930.0	116939.8	6076.0	7974.6	102889.2	95275.8	12293.0
51017.2	141327.7	19424.0	121903.7	3260.0	6367.2	112276.5	103859.2	70495.0
43637.3	53935.3	6644.0	47291.3	17291.0	6432.6	23567.7	40074.2	15961.0
40861.6	94178.1	12675.0	81503.1	64825.7	1416.1	15261.3	130577.7	71297.0
152979.0	131604.0	13001.0	118603.0	12998.1	24457.8	81147.1	115523.3	54021.0
36612.1	143983.6	10418.0	133565.6	47967.5	6927.5	78670.6	113618.1	92624.0
25569.2	101531.6	19939.0	81592.6	37197.0	6290.0	38105.6	108418.4	71377.0
53959.6	103910.7	14747.0	89163.7	450.0	6128.5	82585.2	129894.1	103642.0
84138.1	172349.7	10043.0	162306.7	52120.2	14106.4	96080.1	86870.5	23584.0
14758.7	136653.7	6131.0	130522.7	47445.1	3749.3	79328.3	76493.2	56851.0
9989.0	14705.7	2668.0	12037.7	715.6	1095.3	10226.8	20799.4	17648.0
8226.6	119416.9	8063.0	111353.9	36128.8		75225.1	84348.0	43756.0
44707.9	215337.2	28079.0	187258.2	18456.5	5896.0	162905.7	218472.2	142237.0
36393.1	48302.8	8645.0	39657.8	14518.0	8097.5	17042.3	85307.8	77811.0
34829.3	100896.3	4433.0	96463.3	53666.7	4019.2	38777.4	109738.6	88182.0
7418.6	2253.5	1529.0	724.5	35.0	125.5	564.0	17835.8	16672.0
36827.6	125132.7	6256.0	118876.7	80391.9	17993.0	20491.8	101683.4	72701.0
3727.7	68564.3	4116.0	64448.3	55032.0	1021.7	8394.6	86621.7	78440.0
9210.9	11359.0	2757.0	8602.0	1325.0	407.4	6869.6	32071.6	27218.0
3886.9	9266.0	1298.0	7968.0	5150.0	508.6	2309.4	23369.8	20555.0
10491.8	28827.3	6220.0	22607.3	4777.7	1097.1	16732.5	81935.0	64927.0

C-1-16续表3

地区	全省安排	省级	市级	县级及以下	自然灾害生活救助	中央安排	全省安排	省级
全国	**994629.7**	**352524.7**	**92051.8**	**550053.2**	**1894574.7**	**1062754.0**	**831820.7**	**361216.3**
中央级					43506.0	43506.0		
北京	18258.0	783.6		17474.4	6242.0	965.0	5277.0	3700.0
天津	28969.7	17604.2		11365.5	1847.8	420.0	1427.8	447.0
河北	32137.8	12515.0	2351.9	17270.9	46721.7	32400.0	14321.7	9439.9
山西	27479.5	12862.0	7780.7	6836.8	43231.8	33500.0	9731.8	4840.0
内蒙古	26288.3	9708.0	7115.9	9464.4	50895.5	36800.0	14095.5	6750.0
辽宁	19200.1	5000.0	7134.1	7066.0	63950.8	47531.0	16419.8	1495.0
吉林	10510.9	4900.0		5610.9	68356.4	53000.0	15356.4	9140.0
黑龙江	65924.8	54734.0	1500.4	9690.4	154442.0	45872.0	108570.0	101512.3
上海	27128.6	307.1		26821.5	2159.0		2159.0	1938.0
江苏	98236.2	18153.0	3354.5	76728.7	20981.8	11400.0	9581.8	4000.0
浙江	82982.8	20781.8	6236.9	55964.1	36215.9	15400.0	20815.9	8100.0
安徽	33364.2	9200.0	2893.9	21270.3	37855.2	30632.0	7223.2	3124.0
福建	24113.2	7545.0	1604.4	14963.8	25968.8	11036.0	14932.8	7158.9
江西	59280.7	30009.0	3060.8	26210.9	55135.2	39500.0	15635.2	1830.0
山东	61502.3	12262.0	11250.6	37989.7	30567.8	19100.0	11467.8	2852.0
河南	20994.1	3100.0	1347.8	16546.3	26105.4	20671.0	5434.4	2865.3
湖北	37041.4	4885.0	2876.6	29279.8	64487.8	47948.0	16539.8	11200.0
湖南	26252.1	6796.8	3840.1	15615.2	58359.4	48024.0	10335.4	5540.3
广东	63286.5	17056.2	11309.9	34920.4	70573.3	30100.0	40473.3	23009.8
广西	19642.2	10617.3	1692.9	7332.0	53126.9	32594.0	20532.9	13399.3
海南	3151.4	300.0		2851.4	9334.9	6000.0	3334.9	1000.0
重庆	40592.0	19524.5		21067.5	40587.3	31600.0	8987.3	4990.8
四川	76235.2	29800.2	6690.4	39744.6	324809.8	83695.0	241114.8	18280.9
贵州	7496.8	2600.0	766.9	4129.9	70563.9	52400.0	18163.9	2716.0
云南	21556.6	11123.0	759.9	9673.7	115930.9	68412.0	47518.9	32648.5
西藏	1163.8		350.8	813.0	28691.9	23205.0	5486.9	1993.5
陕西	28982.4	13789.0	7396.4	7797.0	129445.3	62029.0	67416.3	10333.8
甘肃	8181.7	4568.0	439.4	3174.3	126873.2	74012.0	52861.2	45200.6
青海	4853.6	2000.0		2853.6	28094.1	17262.0	10832.1	9450.4
宁夏	2814.8		11.6	2803.2	18841.4	16300.0	2541.4	2000.0
新疆	17008.0	10000.0	285.0	6723.0	40671.5	27440.0	13231.5	10260.0

单位：万元

市级	县级及以下	民政管理事务	中央安排	全省安排	省级	市级	县级及以下
116887.9	**353716.5**	**2892944.7**	**54942.3**	**2838002.4**	**467057.2**	**592830.6**	**1778114.6**
		47422.3	47422.3				
	1577.0	160472.9		160472.9	48303.6		112169.3
	980.8	114506.9		114506.9	11510.4		102996.5
1923.6	2958.2	72090.8		72090.8	10217.7	13968.2	47904.9
2459.0	2432.8	55487.0		55487.0	3342.8	25293.0	26851.2
4050.3	3295.2	51090.2		51090.2	4532.3	16392.1	30165.8
12672.0	2252.8	146404.2		146404.2	23736.7	59539.7	63127.8
270.0	5946.4	32151.2		32151.2	8577.0	4307.7	19266.5
	7057.7	60818.1		60818.1	31326.3	14310.3	15181.5
	221.0	128200.0		128200.0	42240.3		85959.7
435.0	5146.8	189435.9		189435.9	19526.0	38340.4	131569.5
4088.0	8627.9	217340.4		217340.4	14604.3	37814.4	164921.7
862.2	3237.0	60174.0		60174.0	11030.1	15398.3	33745.6
1366.3	6407.6	64891.5		64891.5	17028.9	11481.8	36380.8
1908.4	11896.8	37590.0		37590.0	6365.6	6662.0	24562.4
4836.5	3779.3	149840.8		149840.8	9674.0	56830.5	83336.3
849.5	1719.6	84139.6		84139.6	6551.6	22370.9	55217.1
1033.3	4306.5	84258.5		84258.5	11694.0	26158.5	46406.0
193.8	4601.3	102396.3		102396.3	14818.2	27144.4	60433.7
5502.9	11960.6	219954.1		219954.1	13208.4	59110.0	147635.7
1740.9	5392.7	90242.0		90242.0	17143.6	29445.1	43653.3
144.0	2190.9	29631.8		29631.8	6647.6	5698.9	17285.3
	3996.5	72650.2		72650.2	13420.2		59230.0
3197.3	219636.6	149342.1		149342.1	10993.3	24433.2	113915.6
3765.0	11682.9	70262.9		70262.9	7064.4	19542.7	43655.8
6546.5	8323.9	117067.6		117067.6	38852.6	20646.2	57568.8
2257.3	1236.1	8690.0		8690.0	5975.0	1870.5	844.5
51122.4	5960.1	132900.2		132900.2	34112.9	32143.3	66644.0
5294.2	2366.4	27019.3		27019.3	5694.8	8311.0	13013.5
283.0	1098.7	19328.0		19328.0	3610.6	918.2	14799.2
86.5	454.9	21427.9		21427.9	8321.2	4781.3	8325.4
	2971.5	75718.0	7520.0	68198.0	6932.8	9918.0	51347.2

C−1−16续表4

地　区	行政事业单位离退休	中央安排	全省安排	省级	市级
全　国	**425286.9**	**3815.8**	**421471.1**	**55746.2**	**92443.2**
中央级	3815.8	3815.8			
北　京	54835.4		54835.4	2087.7	
天　津	4271.6		4271.6		
河　北	19577.5		19577.5	3474.2	3941.0
山　西	9753.4		9753.4	1949.9	3514.7
内蒙古	13356.6		13356.6	735.3	4444.9
辽　宁	21723.9		21723.9	2605.7	6999.0
吉　林	8501.0		8501.0		4620.0
黑龙江	7477.7		7477.7	4576.2	1936.5
上　海	8358.5		8358.5	2912.1	
江　苏	25963.3		25963.3	1005.0	3692.2
浙　江	23222.7		23222.7	988.5	6556.5
安　徽	13098.5		13098.5	1826.4	3644.0
福　建	25431.1		25431.1	2049.5	4122.8
江　西	8894.5		8894.5	1682.8	1608.5
山　东	12320.2		12320.2	3756.1	3035.6
河　南	17652.0		17652.0	2777.6	5136.2
湖　北	18107.2		18107.2	3529.8	3882.3
湖　南	8469.8		8469.8	694.0	2360.2
广　东	34509.8		34509.8	5200.0	13523.3
广　西	13107.5		13107.5	724.0	3529.8
海　南	3654.9		3654.9	1871.9	648.2
重　庆	9126.4		9126.4	2399.1	
四　川	20568.7		20568.7	3035.6	4415.2
贵　州	3455.0		3455.0		217.9
云　南	11827.4		11827.4	1664.9	1738.3
西　藏	600.9		600.9	312.7	288.2
陕　西	6403.5		6403.5	1460.4	1070.0
甘　肃	4612.2		4612.2	711.2	1294.0
青　海	2158.2		2158.2	774.3	415.8
宁　夏	2979.5		2979.5	941.3	933.7
新　疆	7452.2		7452.2		4874.4

单位：万元

县级及以下	其他款项用于民政支出	中央安排	全省安排	省级	市级	县级及以下
273281.7	**1078341.2**	**111160.7**	**967180.5**	**259569.6**	**290903.0**	**416707.9**
	18668.7	18668.7				
52747.7	72647.2	24443.0	48204.2	25910.8		22293.4
4271.6	10157.1	384.0	9773.1			9773.1
12162.3	14702.0	15.0	14687.0	5021.6	4054.5	5610.9
4288.8	16242.4		16242.4	7744.4	4678.0	3820.0
8176.4	21410.1		21410.1	3584.4	11562.5	6263.2
12119.2	68899.0	19649.0	49250.0	9763.7	33073.0	6413.3
3881.0	46679.0	126.0	46553.0	26907.0	18099.9	1546.1
965.0	5914.6		5914.6		5668.1	246.5
5446.4	53729.7	4735.0	48994.7	2062.0		46932.7
21266.1	101010.3	12751.0	88259.3	1558.8	33728.4	52972.1
15677.7	59889.6	91.0	59798.6	1205.8	8492.9	50099.9
7628.1	15063.3	27.0	15036.3	1072.9	5080.6	8882.8
19258.8	22042.8		22042.8	6000.0	5801.4	10241.4
5603.2	7580.2	2987.0	4593.2	1458.5	534.5	2600.2
5528.5	74929.7	19670.0	55259.7	1776.3	15270.5	38212.9
9738.2	32190.9		32190.9	23889.1	2950.1	5351.7
10695.1	36620.0		36620.0	16693.9	13678.0	6248.1
5415.6	31354.5	58.0	31296.5	4214.2	10510.8	16571.5
15786.5	87865.0	1385.0	86480.0	7557.0	53904.6	25018.4
8853.7	36411.6	4664.0	31747.6	10976.0	14645.6	6126.0
1134.8	11608.4		11608.4	522.1	3986.2	7100.1
6727.3	11755.1		11755.1	440.3		11314.8
13117.9	46863.5	1330.0	45533.5	1542.3	21687.2	22304.0
3237.1	17325.2		17325.2	1675.3	2077.1	13572.8
8424.2	79055.5	177.0	78878.5	49300.9	14958.5	14619.1
	6218.8		6218.8	5225.2		993.6
3873.1	14442.8		14442.8	8297.6	2249.3	3895.9
2607.0	5229.8		5229.8	2418.3	1052.7	1758.8
968.1	31956.1		31956.1	19625.1	1231.0	11100.0
1104.5	16385.2		16385.2	12873.6	968.6	2543.0
2577.8	3493.1		3493.1	252.5	959.0	2281.6

C-1-17 预算资金

地区	民政预算内经费实际支出	抚恤	死亡抚恤				伤残抚恤
				一次性抚恤金	定期抚恤金	其他	
全 国	**42765370.8**	**6184310.6**	**596955.5**	**203231.1**	**353112.6**	**40611.8**	**1071785.9**
中央级	137419.9	601.0					
北 京	1555734.8	102474.8	34826.4	31309.7	3495.0	21.7	13250.6
天 津	552118.0	60296.8	5115.7	3481.2	1489.1	145.4	10249.6
河 北	1672465.7	373253.3	30079.2	9547.1	19718.6	813.5	64585.7
山 西	1130400.3	189680.9	13237.3	3908.9	8639.5	688.9	31018.0
内蒙古	1236610.0	89256.9	4376.6	1419.8	2485.7	471.1	16654.1
辽 宁	1672890.8	188295.1	23389.4	10263.1	7954.8	5171.5	36072.3
吉 林	986245.5	108104.3	10452.9	2035.6	7931.2	486.1	30138.2
黑龙江	1589618.1	118039.8	9980.4	2289.7	7104.5	586.2	24531.7
上 海	832211.6	77346.4	10466.5	4225.4	4525.2	1715.9	14479.2
江 苏	2335259.9	400631.2	48460.0	13051.2	28217.3	7191.5	79343.5
浙 江	1428845.7	217849.4	16133.4	6058.2	9395.7	679.5	34788.5
安 徽	1601142.2	266882.0	17035.9	3661.4	12168.1	1206.4	41541.4
福 建	729824.6	125926.1	14457.9	2245.1	11526.2	686.6	15139.3
江 西	1224409.1	236272.0	33039.5	4981.1	25491.8	2566.6	33519.3
山 东	2502270.9	703554.6	57379.5	14936.3	37446.5	4996.7	163055.8
河 南	2097496.0	424921.2	28862.2	9851.1	18406.8	604.3	82309.2
湖 北	1849392.5	336354.1	40101.4	6741.1	32871.4	488.9	43842.8
湖 南	1996276.3	403904.7	38357.2	11623.6	23876.1	2857.5	72727.6
广 东	1981669.0	296100.2	24372.1	12313.4	10981.2	1077.5	33820.0
广 西	1292515.6	144002.7	6811.0	2105.7	4610.2	95.1	12542.1
海 南	254400.4	23833.8	4506.5	1085.6	3327.1	93.8	2952.9
重 庆	999446.7	162662.9	12557.3	4645.7	5910.1	2001.5	27680.8
四 川	2880631.2	453439.9	43647.2	11979.9	29128.2	2539.1	80664.5
贵 州	1341494.8	130472.4	10907.6	5337.0	5122.4	448.2	18894.1
云 南	1845730.7	174052.0	14655.5	7075.8	7348.8	230.9	24952.4
西 藏	156074.8	5758.9	2899.4	532.6	2319.2	47.6	2329.6
陕 西	1838401.7	240077.9	21418.1	6356.9	13581.1	1480.1	32393.5
甘 肃	1299304.5	54407.1	7967.0	3086.2	4203.0	677.8	12948.0
青 海	377594.3	14095.5	3070.5	1956.8	990.6	123.1	2781.6
宁 夏	266258.2	10741.9	2010.8	1264.1	676.4	70.3	2807.1
新 疆	1101217.0	51020.8	6381.1	3861.8	2170.8	348.5	9772.5

总体支出情况

单位：万元

伤残抚恤金	在乡伤残抚恤金	在职保健金	伤残补助费	分散安置残疾军人护理费	在乡复员、退伍军人生活补助	在乡复退军人定期定量补助费	在乡红军老战士定期定量补助费	红军失散人员定期定量补助费
1010354.1	**754587.3**	**255766.8**	**61431.8**	**24257.9**	**2255303.5**	**1593219.6**	**2474.0**	**27460.8**
12275.9	6974.1	5301.8	974.7	296.1	11769.4	8746.6	4.3	
9256.9	4255.5	5001.4	992.7	378.1	20293.4	14619.5		
62502.5	61890.5	612.0	2083.2	648.2	109744.7	81763.4	13.6	
29526.0	18559.5	10966.5	1492.0	665.3	44926.7	39038.1	30.1	1.5
16221.1	7571.2	8649.9	433.0	101.2	24550.9	23727.3	12.6	4.5
34040.5	21842.2	12198.3	2031.8	722.6	62682.5	58368.4		1.4
28448.9	20804.7	7644.2	1689.3	903.2	27223.6	24906.5		13.1
24104.8	18151.6	5953.2	426.9	163.9	48161.8	45154.8	45.3	25.9
13550.3		13550.3	928.9	311.6	10383.8	8011.3		
74076.6	56767.9	17308.7	5266.9	2544.6	111923.4	97009.0		1.6
31433.5	21514.0	9919.5	3355.0	703.6	70288.2	56017.2		112.6
39864.9	28100.7	11764.2	1676.5	909.5	116734.1	91064.4	10.0	3819.1
14791.4	12682.0	2109.4	347.9	175.2	44120.3	26091.3	3.4	645.6
31605.8	27628.0	3977.8	1913.5	456.9	96596.8	59312.3	68.5	12661.9
152839.9	109437.9	43402.0	10215.9	6211.6	197509.9	161064.9	9.9	36.3
78451.1	56082.5	22368.6	3858.1	1938.1	148977.5	101692.1	41.8	846.8
42102.9	38375.3	3727.6	1739.9	878.3	131305.9	97460.9	9.8	2063.6
66975.0	56630.6	10344.4	5752.6	1350.4	171932.1	111480.2	10.3	2874.9
30829.7	23185.1	7644.6	2990.3	568.1	137878.9	60009.8		134.7
12021.2	9602.2	2419.0	520.9	132.7	67227.2	32823.6	46.0	627.5
2845.7	2677.7	168.0	107.2	14.5	7811.5	5295.3		44.0
25932.0	18820.7	7111.3	1748.8	1381.0	82185.7	56809.3		
76436.5	61144.1	15292.4	4228.0	1409.0	246071.8	186632.9	255.2	1258.1
18154.3	14615.3	3539.0	739.8	293.2	64987.1	35961.5	3.1	36.5
23669.5	17053.1	6616.4	1282.9	179.1	67823.4	28783.3		4.6
2148.9	927.0	1221.9	180.7		196.1	186.1		
30521.2	22316.3	8204.9	1872.3	494.4	89969.5	53635.4	1711.1	2217.3
11772.0	8523.0	3249.0	1176.0	261.3	21403.5	11627.1	150.3	22.8
2735.8	2042.6	693.2	45.8	9.8	3888.1	2938.1		
1730.7	1508.9	221.8	1076.4	20.6	3296.7	2509.1	9.8	5.0
9488.6	4903.1	4585.5	283.9	135.8	13439.0	10479.9	38.9	1.5

C-1-17续表1

地 区	“参战”退伍军人生活补助	“涉核”退伍军人生活补助	优抚事业单位	烈士纪念建筑物管理维修经费
全 国	**547642.4**	**84506.7**	**699863.5**	**353735.6**
中央级			601.0	601.0
北 京	2457.6	560.9	3726.7	850.3
天 津	5520.3	153.6	10541.6	3334.2
河 北	19431.0	8536.7	77371.5	33790.0
山 西	3545.9	2311.1	36596.5	13039.4
内蒙古	757.4	49.1	12138.4	5932.5
辽 宁	2863.8	1448.9	21548.6	12646.4
吉 林	1573.5	730.5	19365.6	12386.7
黑龙江	2839.3	96.5	17528.5	4800.2
上 海	2040.0	332.5	9826.7	7554.0
江 苏	12576.5	2336.3	43193.5	17799.5
浙 江	12839.8	1318.6	13957.1	9225.6
安 徽	16453.0	5387.6	24996.8	15955.8
福 建	17109.6	270.4	13163.2	7971.8
江 西	23485.1	1069.0	33107.1	24923.9
山 东	29803.3	6595.5	83316.9	34903.9
河 南	36719.8	9677.0	42806.3	26529.3
湖 北	28024.4	3747.2	51988.7	28199.7
湖 南	51755.7	5811.0	47086.3	23374.5
广 东	73252.9	4481.5	22978.4	9916.0
广 西	32268.6	1461.5	21843.2	10119.0
海 南	2297.4	174.8	1902.3	1399.6
重 庆	23117.6	2258.8	8026.9	3803.0
四 川	49282.5	8643.1	23677.9	11853.6
贵 州	28824.5	161.5	7846.0	3252.5
云 南	38964.4	71.1	9451.3	4927.9
西 藏	10.0		137.6	122.6
陕 西	21521.6	10884.1	26237.7	15451.7
甘 肃	6339.2	3264.1	4303.8	2497.5
青 海	478.6	471.4	783.9	76.1
宁 夏	535.8	237.0	364.2	245.3
新 疆	953.3	1965.4	9449.3	6252.1

单位：万元

烈士纪念建筑物管理单位经费	荣誉军人康复医院经费	在院人员生活费	复员军人疗养院经费	在院人员生活费
91133.4	**68539.2**	**7366.6**	**32160.6**	**3507.0**
413.8				
2152.5			1721.4	104.6
5976.4	3201.1	539.0	9519.9	883.2
3745.5	2399.6	175.2	2841.0	200.5
826.4	536.9	198.9	42.7	20.0
3837.9	1472.0	363.0		
1273.2	4938.0			
1116.8	7580.7	530.0		
6816.6	775.2	27.2		
8077.2	4536.2		1375.6	152.7
2516.1	2761.0			
3739.3	1929.1	106.0		
1720.7	136.3	110.1		
3969.5	2381.9	785.4	165.0	52.0
11467.2	10896.3	601.0	10842.6	1343.9
5201.5	5445.8	385.4	1386.2	112.7
2283.9	2502.9	310.0		
5683.9	686.5		280.0	
2557.9	351.0	220.0	1705.2	390.0
3336.4	2069.2			
348.3				
433.4	2869.5	228.5		
2983.2	4364.4	2305.8	189.0	78.4
993.1	1499.9	152.0		
1474.5	672.1			
19.6				
3140.1	2996.8	317.1	2092.0	169.0
1810.7	464.2			
50.0				
119.1				
3048.7	1072.6	12.0		

C-1-17续表2

地区	复退军人精神病院经费	在院人员生活费	光荣院经费	在院人员生活费
全 国	**93801.9**	**12614.1**	**80831.4**	**21981.1**
中央级				
北 京			2817.8	517.5
天 津	1935.6	220.0	2438.5	449.2
河 北	8432.5	1890.0	12367.1	3131.8
山 西	6330.5	519.4	7113.2	1591.1
内蒙古	920.7	220.0	4048.7	1196.5
辽 宁	2232.1	400.1	4584.8	1846.7
吉 林	294.1	278.1	721.4	330.6
黑龙江	2548.5	179.9	1312.5	622.8
上 海	89.4	49.8		
江 苏	9061.6		902.9	291.4
浙 江	676.3		1103.7	245.7
安 徽	2088.5	312.0	3164.9	632.4
福 建	176.0	176.0	2091.9	650.8
江 西	8.0	7.0	4095.7	1581.1
山 东	19480.8	2293.1	3578.6	1497.1
河 南	2640.4	435.0	2988.5	780.2
湖 北	12418.8	1317.1	6984.3	1331.1
湖 南	3598.2	750.0	10403.9	2177.5
广 东	5733.9	1299.7	2257.0	846.0
广 西	6641.1	56.1	1272.2	305.1
海 南			350.0	99.2
重 庆			1087.3	339.2
四 川	3129.2	1005.7	2054.1	804.4
贵 州	1020.0	696.0	493.8	337.9
云 南	680.7		37.3	1.0
西 藏				
陕 西	2698.1	509.1	1315.6	200.5
甘 肃	893.9		100.0	45.0
青 海			10.0	
宁 夏			12.0	12.0
新 疆	73.0		1123.7	117.3

单位：万元

其他优抚事业单位经费	集体办优抚事业单位补助费	义务兵优待金	城市义务兵优待金	农村义务兵优待金	其他优抚支出
68677.8	**2117.0**	**964378.5**	**472957.4**	**491421.1**	**596023.7**
58.6		18886.4	14683.0	4203.4	20015.3
1111.9		7881.8	4926.4	2955.4	6214.7
9873.7	187.2	65203.4	35413.6	29789.8	26268.8
4872.8		49310.1	29014.1	20296.0	14592.3
656.9		24230.7	15444.8	8785.9	7306.2
613.3		21903.1	9767.3	12135.8	22699.2
1025.4		14964.2	8261.6	6702.6	5959.8
1175.0	111.6	8159.9	5490.8	2669.1	9677.5
1408.1		26697.9	23063.9	3634.0	5492.3
9200.5	317.2	69534.6	37266.3	32268.3	48176.2
190.5		60742.6	21493.8	39248.8	21939.6
1858.5		48735.6	18275.1	30460.5	17838.2
2755.6	31.6	27026.9	9726.8	17300.1	12018.5
1235.7	296.9	20000.1	10037.2	9962.9	20009.2
3614.7		108617.8	39166.3	69451.5	93674.7
3716.1	100.0	93965.3	46392.3	47573.0	28000.7
1853.0	30.0	47520.1	25852.7	21667.4	21595.2
7848.2	895.0	48174.2	27701.7	20472.5	25627.3
2965.3	50.0	40834.7	15948.8	24885.9	36216.1
1741.7		13886.3	2605.6	11280.7	21692.9
136.7	16.0	1297.7	957.5	340.2	5362.9
267.1		20745.3	8332.4	12412.9	11466.9
2087.6		40683.0	17993.4	22689.6	18695.5
1573.3	6.5	15490.2	8812.4	6677.8	12347.4
3133.3		8525.4	2516.8	6008.6	48644.0
15.0		109.8	46.4	63.4	86.4
1643.5	40.0	47039.4	25152.1	21887.3	23019.7
313.2	35.0	4325.7	1948.5	2377.2	3459.1
697.8		2162.6	921.1	1241.5	1408.8
106.9		1442.2	915.3	526.9	820.9
927.9		6281.5	4829.4	1452.1	5697.4

C-1-17续表3

地 区	退役安置	退伍军人安置	一次性建房补助费	退役士兵自谋职业金	城镇退役士兵生活补助	军队移交政府的离退休人员安置	军队离休干部离休金	军队退休干部退休金
全 国	**4352600.2**	**1098342.4**	**20198.2**	**830837.0**	**132257.2**	**2693052.7**	**287951.3**	**1662363.8**
中央级								
北 京	727394.6	15733.9	39.7	14153.1	376.4	571659.8	20942.4	341586.6
天 津	85838.7	11870.8	140.2	8412.6	560.8	61819.2	6144.9	42682.4
河 北	238659.4	59469.0	479.3	42631.8	8610.6	156485.8	24746.7	99394.3
山 西	71227.4	11919.0	355.3	6329.6	3849.4	46625.6	6463.4	26859.3
内蒙古	42870.4	6083.9	601.1	3486.1	1305.4	29524.8	2992.3	20349.2
辽 宁	314708.3	39320.5	754.6	28298.8	6718.2	238786.3	22036.3	166638.6
吉 林	74541.6	15499.8	503.6	9284.1	4722.3	52654.2	3806.6	29411.4
黑龙江	64894.3	16714.1	972.2	12762.9	1773.1	41141.5	4272.4	26623.0
上 海	140151.1	24024.6	33.3	18204.5	1068.9	88762.2	5017.8	53644.7
江 苏	326575.3	94744.1	571.3	76654.7	4778.3	184050.8	15955.3	102167.5
浙 江	102960.8	39249.4	540.5	30507.1	4410.9	49733.6	8342.5	28956.6
安 徽	149166.5	99743.8	1844.9	85534.0	8226.7	40262.2	7740.2	21887.0
福 建	77841.6	30245.5	103.5	23136.8	4098.1	39045.0	6133.5	27400.8
江 西	43109.7	19509.3	1080.4	13522.9	3191.0	20067.0	4630.5	9607.3
山 东	362728.1	95989.0	636.8	61353.2	17371.3	223921.6	38740.9	131266.1
河 南	168540.5	72826.0	465.9	51916.5	13713.7	75957.6	10851.8	51139.5
湖 北	159256.8	47972.9	479.2	37075.2	4946.8	97645.7	12401.1	60905.4
湖 南	104740.1	32599.8	1233.4	20204.0	7237.6	56084.2	7867.9	33142.4
广 东	206489.9	68639.9	1353.5	56175.9	4683.5	106481.2	8917.2	78938.7
广 西	61205.8	27121.8	539.5	21648.7	2283.6	26959.9	2134.9	17640.1
海 南	20738.5	8620.9	168.1	6383.0	1118.4	9784.7	707.7	6583.2
重 庆	77564.4	26570.2	269.3	22760.4	1050.7	43152.3	2827.9	27381.8
四 川	251994.8	126691.1	4786.3	105972.3	7690.8	109445.7	9322.7	74785.2
贵 州	41237.0	19118.6	231.7	14924.1	2462.3	17865.0	2415.7	8971.1
云 南	102166.4	22163.4	199.2	17184.2	2262.6	71071.2	18003.1	34785.1
西 藏	7067.2	194.7			19.9	6459.9	21.3	1339.2
陕 西	153626.1	21905.3	1213.9	11828.1	6136.4	114594.9	10652.0	80183.0
甘 肃	71141.6	21806.4	290.1	11501.6	6579.7	41713.3	19032.5	13850.9
青 海	17263.9	2460.4	30.2	1673.1	461.1	13405.1	609.9	7449.9
宁 夏	13476.5	6330.4		5827.4	71.8	6043.8	836.5	4634.8
新 疆	73422.9	13203.9	281.2	11490.3	476.9	51848.6	3383.4	32158.7

单位：万元

军队无军籍职工退休金	军队离退休人员其他费用	死亡丧葬费	护理费	遗属生活困难补助费	定期定量补助费	其他费用	军队移交政府离退休干部管理机构	其他退役安置支出
316383.0	**426354.6**	**22363.1**	**31162.3**	**13433.6**	**5568.5**	**359395.6**	**375917.5**	**185287.6**
62283.8	146847.0	2058.2	3777.6	193.0	59.3	140818.2	138515.1	1485.8
6854.4	6137.5	321.2	700.9	118.7	28.6	4996.7	5240.1	6908.6
15054.9	17289.9	1725.3	1940.3	2655.8	822.7	10968.5	19223.3	3481.3
5974.6	7328.3	694.1	878.1	649.9	269.2	5106.2	4476.9	8205.9
3390.4	2792.9	224.6	371.8	290.6	133.0	1905.9	4065.3	3196.4
22130.9	27980.5	2251.4	2537.2	542.9	258.2	22649.0	20120.5	16481.0
8539.9	10896.3	291.2	44.6	133.3	57.5	10427.2	5284.0	1103.6
5349.3	4896.8	202.9	332.9	178.8	77.2	4182.2	4692.2	2346.5
9767.4	20332.3	584.7	1043.9	89.5	73.3	18614.2	24715.7	2648.6
21190.9	44737.1	2892.4	2131.2	858.4	463.3	38855.1	20630.7	27149.7
7411.3	5023.2	438.5	656.2	192.2	106.2	3736.3	10176.8	3801.0
4011.4	6623.6	756.2	922.7	643.6	260.6	4301.1	6796.2	2364.3
2387.7	3123.0	375.1	265.5	196.0	98.6	2286.4	5223.7	3327.4
3191.9	2637.3	80.3	132.8	115.9	58.2	2308.3	1340.9	2192.5
19368.8	34545.8	2679.4	6675.3	1266.2	737.7	23924.9	14533.2	28284.3
6753.0	7213.3	1132.3	1305.4	750.0	331.9	4025.6	10124.6	9632.3
13054.6	11284.6	344.5	678.9	378.1	197.8	9883.1	11658.7	1979.5
9921.6	5152.3	686.9	1225.2	542.0	169.6	2698.2	10516.2	5539.9
13918.0	4707.3	416.8	345.4	294.4	115.3	3650.7	10539.4	20829.4
4048.4	3136.5	242.0	366.7	136.2	86.9	2391.6	3429.8	3694.3
534.2	1959.6	63.6	44.6	113.7	40.7	1737.7	1466.9	866.0
6689.2	6253.4	274.9	345.4	103.5	73.4	5529.6	7366.4	475.5
12101.2	13236.6	1220.2	953.9	526.6	329.0	10535.9	10224.3	5633.7
3241.4	3236.8	242.2	797.5	88.4	65.3	2108.7	1204.9	3048.5
11560.1	6722.9	405.9	338.4	805.7	153.6	5172.9	5087.0	3844.8
5063.7	35.7			2.5	1.0	33.2	335.6	77.0
10923.7	12836.2	1011.7	1484.4	964.8	207.7	9375.3	9687.5	7438.4
5526.8	3303.1	139.3	694.8	235.1	108.6	2233.9	3526.3	4095.6
5115.6	229.7	45.0		62.4	30.2	122.3	1146.2	252.2
443.1	129.4	12.5	27.0	52.6		37.3	567.2	535.1
10580.8	5725.7	549.8	143.7	252.8	153.9	4779.4	4001.9	4368.5

C-1-17续表4

地 区	社会福利	儿童福利	老年人福利	假肢矫形
全 国	**3975669.6**	**512724.7**	**1075034.6**	**14227.7**
中央级				
北 京	206296.2	12694.3	98820.2	383.0
天 津	56024.9	1464.5	16546.1	1154.7
河 北	138617.1	11997.4	30830.6	333.6
山 西	78624.4	14089.0	12716.4	496.9
内蒙古	111753.9	7284.0	41411.2	40.0
辽 宁	127870.6	12342.4	23733.5	
吉 林	49132.2	4182.4	7522.8	371.9
黑龙江	63704.6	6555.6	7683.4	576.1
上 海	122116.2	3830.7	28219.5	
江 苏	379483.8	24331.5	121533.1	353.3
浙 江	294282.5	7694.7	75734.5	924.9
安 徽	138831.0	22504.4	36373.8	155.5
福 建	103793.8	6050.7	26344.0	250.0
江 西	106325.7	29217.7	31565.7	479.1
山 东	261399.5	17896.1	75689.7	602.0
河 南	133884.1	37725.7	21320.6	1536.8
湖 北	154221.9	25275.7	17059.1	71.4
湖 南	105298.4	40361.6	15824.0	403.5
广 东	308414.8	43346.7	91376.1	1059.7
广 西	123642.3	16502.6	38899.6	314.4
海 南	23754.4	2619.4	11903.0	
重 庆	107429.8	12558.0	23484.1	2365.3
四 川	141954.3	27076.5	16435.3	951.3
贵 州	81684.3	18971.3	7896.9	50.0
云 南	105467.2	29682.0	33956.1	60.0
西 藏	9380.6	6122.9	623.9	
陕 西	157737.5	14897.9	86403.9	
甘 肃	56931.5	16729.8	9445.2	
青 海	36209.4	12445.1	9569.5	311.0
宁 夏	18908.4	4745.1	2804.0	
新 疆	172494.3	21529.0	53308.8	983.3

单位：万元

假肢厂(站)专项拨款	其他经费	殡葬	补贴火化场经费	补贴殡葬类单位经费
8118.9	**6108.8**	**554536.2**	**243437.4**	**311098.8**
383.0		23151.7	13618.9	9532.8
	1154.7	14139.2	578.4	13560.8
259.0	74.6	28017.8	11429.1	16588.7
496.9		18924.7	17619.7	1305.0
40.0		10989.0	2548.1	8440.9
		31560.6	17443.1	14117.5
371.9		15724.9	9914.2	5810.7
576.1		6842.8	3167.7	3675.1
40.0	313.3	51490.8	31282.0	20208.8
	924.9	61144.2	25791.9	35352.3
140.0	15.5	21426.4	12491.2	8935.2
250.0		18664.9	12080.3	6584.6
	479.1	4469.9	2108.0	2361.9
600.0	2.0	12624.9	5209.6	7415.3
1456.8	80.0	20514.1	15943.1	4571.0
71.4		28345.1	4842.5	23502.6
402.5	1.0	9380.7	1621.2	7759.5
990.0	69.7	45156.2	12595.2	32561.0
	314.4	15178.2	2675.7	12502.5
		2514.8	41.0	2473.8
	2365.3	21156.4	15757.5	5398.9
951.3		32135.5	7665.6	24469.9
50.0		7281.0	3649.0	3632.0
60.0		12255.3	6324.7	5930.6
		594.1	46.1	548.0
		6569.6	2316.8	4252.8
		8945.9	1531.8	7414.1
	311.0	198.6	70.9	127.7
		4475.2	58.1	4417.1
980.0	3.3	20663.7	3016.0	17647.7

C-1-17续表5

地区	社会福利事业单位	社会福利院经费	在院人员生活费	儿童福利院经费
全国	**1054198.5**	**495319.7**	**80448.2**	**133016.6**
中央级				
北京	14441.4	4895.1	582.1	1136.5
天津	10699.9	2299.6	429.7	1242.3
河北	41617.4	11492.8	1816.3	301.8
山西	15177.7	8194.0	2091.8	1021.9
内蒙古	27216.3	11500.5	3412.2	4071.9
辽宁	30794.4	19448.6	5664.7	1747.9
吉林	14205.5	6918.2	2491.0	2375.8
黑龙江	34140.4	9173.5	949.6	5179.8
上海	47494.6	28419.3	2639.0	7192.9
江苏	110560.0	51303.8	7900.1	4711.2
浙江	112624.3	54959.4	2967.0	7363.3
安徽	32570.8	7709.7	2012.8	10569.0
福建	25759.3	9718.1	2825.3	2764.2
江西	11229.8	6780.1	1862.0	840.5
山东	61659.4	13766.4	3909.3	12080.4
河南	22136.1	8661.9	2870.1	5110.1
湖北	67705.6	48689.5	3702.2	7665.6
湖南	26339.8	15122.9	1691.2	3018.9
广东	98941.6	69896.0	12713.9	13595.4
广西	32525.1	14380.8	3687.0	3779.5
海南	3308.4	1715.0	16.5	42.8
重庆	33528.8	15807.7	1552.3	5338.6
四川	52122.0	25551.0	3334.7	6000.7
贵州	19781.8	4681.6	1153.1	3756.9
云南	17270.7	6455.4	588.3	3179.7
西藏	1935.1	1057.9	425.7	877.2
陕西	21592.1	12170.6	3996.9	3972.9
甘肃	11747.3	4355.2	843.0	2903.8
青海	1244.7	484.8	98.3	308.0
宁夏	4817.1	2161.7	515.8	2256.2
新疆	49011.1	17548.6	1706.3	8610.9

单位：万元

在院人员生活费	精神病人福利院经费	在院人员生活费	补贴安置农场经费	其他社会福利单位	其他社会福利支出
40240.5	**132519.6**	**16686.9**	**10444.7**	**282897.9**	**764947.9**
516.1	3477.1	230.1		4932.7	56805.6
1107.6	2970.2	467.5		4187.8	12020.5
190.9			97.5	29725.3	25820.3
514.7				5961.8	17219.7
1218.0	4587.0	627.7		7056.9	24813.4
757.3	1334.1			8263.8	29439.7
1076.6	2017.7	555.7		2893.8	7124.7
1387.2	16007.9	2813.7	3107.2	672.0	7906.3
1528.1	9027.2	95.2		2855.2	42571.4
977.4	22095.0	1504.8		32450.0	71215.1
937.7	3832.5	33.6	462.0	46007.1	36159.9
3030.7	162.0	23.8	415.1	13715.0	25800.1
801.6	10817.0	2255.3	296.0	2164.0	26724.9
227.7	1422.0	66.0		2187.2	29363.5
2756.9	4341.6	472.4		31471.0	92927.4
3246.5	1898.8	747.0	72.1	6393.2	30650.8
2110.6	287.2			11063.3	15765.0
912.6	2691.4	280.0	78.1	5428.5	12988.8
2182.8	6575.2	1382.5	89.2	8785.8	28534.5
787.8	4375.5	1737.0	438.0	9551.3	20222.4
35.0				1550.6	3408.8
1668.1	6694.0	921.0	18.6	5669.9	14337.2
2467.1	9278.1	1143.8		11292.2	13233.7
2232.3	2279.7	315.7	4153.1	4910.5	27703.3
166.1	3507.5	20.0	1130.9	2997.2	12243.1
811.8					104.6
1305.7	1420.8	208.5		4027.8	28274.0
1688.6	1607.7	60.1	72.2	2808.4	10063.3
3.0	60.0			391.9	12440.5
376.7	365.5		14.7	19.0	2067.0
3217.3	9386.9	725.5		13464.7	26998.4

C－1－17续表6

地 区	社会救助	最低生活保障	城市最低生活保障	城市最低生活保障金	城市最低生活保障对象临时补助	农村最低生活保障	农村最低生活保障金	农村最低生活保障对象临时补助
全 国	**21724118.2**	**16236126.1**	**7567087.0**	**6645197.5**	**921889.5**	**8669039.1**	**7440641.9**	**1228397.2**
中央级								
北 京	171551.3	100591.7	72189.5	65122.1	7067.4	28402.2	25771.1	2631.1
天 津	216924.1	164531.6	129950.1	84857.3	45092.8	34581.5	29463.4	5118.1
河 北	746377.8	569798.9	237558.8	207600.2	29958.6	332240.1	282056.1	50184.0
山 西	664821.3	539033.1	284863.9	252076.6	32787.3	254169.2	222858.5	31310.7
内蒙古	846880.9	699737.4	389142.0	351793.4	37348.6	310595.4	275305.2	35290.2
辽 宁	740422.9	601036.4	432202.9	375515.2	56687.7	168833.5	141612.0	27221.5
吉 林	603658.1	501885.2	370059.1	329842.1	40217.0	131826.1	113869.1	17957.0
黑龙江	1120922.9	880079.2	635661.5	520290.7	115370.8	244417.7	188361.9	56055.8
上 海	298578.4	158414.9	142031.4	127875.7	14155.7	16383.5	11468.0	4915.5
江 苏	842306.0	491467.1	148901.2	126408.8	22492.4	342565.9	293601.1	48964.8
浙 江	460626.0	243223.2	43793.8	36004.5	7789.3	199429.4	172693.9	26735.5
安 徽	912522.7	654609.1	296775.2	260008.7	36766.5	357833.9	293782.1	64051.8
福 建	280355.3	182959.1	52707.6	46579.8	6127.8	130251.5	112201.9	18049.6
江 西	758590.7	533402.4	287900.6	265628.9	22271.7	245501.8	224545.7	20956.1
山 东	918114.8	670645.3	197648.5	174136.0	23512.5	472996.8	415828.1	57168.7
河 南	1197876.1	913278.9	368509.6	329864.7	38644.9	544769.3	475791.9	68977.4
湖 北	983083.7	769996.9	436815.8	376928.1	59887.7	333181.1	271303.5	61877.6
湖 南	1171110.2	868523.0	461420.8	421843.9	39576.9	407102.2	362996.2	44106.0
广 东	739798.0	470564.6	130450.4	107126.5	23323.9	340114.2	269197.8	70916.4
广 西	786103.2	569829.3	150525.9	136456.5	14069.4	419303.4	357056.9	62246.5
海 南	126350.0	86758.9	44196.5	42566.4	1630.1	42562.4	41196.5	1365.9
重 庆	515469.9	302421.6	173196.6	150699.7	22496.9	129225.0	108464.5	20760.5
四 川	1507933.9	1067374.2	507681.9	456962.3	50719.6	559692.3	479221.9	80470.4
贵 州	923409.2	786453.2	174125.3	153414.7	20710.6	612327.9	519890.7	92437.2
云 南	1142530.1	958876.6	294308.9	268775.0	25533.9	664567.7	584951.4	79616.3
西 藏	80346.8	65445.4	24333.8	22175.8	2158.0	41111.6	37015.3	4096.3
陕 西	995196.5	757120.8	313426.7	264901.5	48525.2	443694.1	365147.9	78546.2
甘 肃	938276.7	781835.2	302268.0	282390.9	19877.1	479567.2	434054.6	45512.6
青 海	195303.3	153216.4	78279.2	73119.0	5160.2	74937.2	70651.1	4286.1
宁 夏	161223.2	129387.2	54719.4	42835.9	11883.5	74667.8	56687.8	17980.0
新 疆	677454.2	563629.3	331442.1	291396.6	40045.5	232187.2	203595.8	28591.4

单位：万元

其他社会救助	五保供养	五保集中供养	五保分散供养	城市“三无”救助	流浪乞讨人员救助	流浪乞讨人员救助单位经费	流浪乞讨人员救助经费	临时救助	传统救济
2913873.0	**1723213.1**	**747401.8**	**975811.3**	**41542.1**	**372763.3**	**167187.9**	**205575.4**	**473073.8**	**303280.7**
50003.8	3250.9	1818.9	1432.0	209.8	25282.4	13383.5	11898.9	17734.0	3526.7
17444.0	8684.0	1027.6	7656.4		4492.8	2756.6	1736.2	3308.7	958.5
86811.4	68890.8	33732.1	35158.7	131.9	9515.9	2830.4	6685.5	6896.3	1376.5
58861.8	45234.4	12416.2	32818.2	206.1	7341.7	2629.7	4712.0	3558.6	2521.0
79077.6	36421.1	15363.4	21057.7	8351.0	6242.1	3186.6	3055.5	10875.8	17187.6
88377.7	51730.0	19537.8	32192.2	378.7	13123.2	5957.0	7166.2	17535.6	5610.2
37227.1	29546.9	9882.2	19664.7	478.9	4771.8	1821.3	2950.5	1944.9	484.6
105001.1	44512.2	25123.5	19388.7	2065.2	7711.6	4009.5	3702.1	38604.2	12107.9
115593.0	1809.6	927.6	882.0		14424.4	11428.6	2995.8	80289.3	19069.7
227981.0	108729.1	69754.1	38975.0	2113.4	21196.1	12694.9	8501.2	39086.7	56855.7
125088.4	25412.5	24975.0	437.5	894.8	18210.6	9224.7	8985.9	30964.2	49606.3
150897.9	113496.5	55264.7	58231.8	614.8	17806.3	4962.8	12843.5	9531.8	9448.5
55632.3	37465.6	4788.7	32676.9	957.3	8293.8	4339.6	3954.2	3326.1	5589.5
95317.7	66120.0	37606.1	28513.9	2221.4	10675.2	2568.9	8106.3	5726.0	10575.1
131816.9	93768.7	76203.1	17565.6	761.8	17941.6	8335.6	9606.0	17652.9	1691.9
167200.2	134389.7	68058.6	66331.1	303.8	18882.4	9578.6	9303.8	4327.6	9296.7
106336.9	67441.5	28339.5	39102.0	1445.3	20486.2	6420.2	14066.0	10739.4	6224.5
171234.3	133926.1	44978.2	88947.9	1293.6	20828.8	6006.4	14822.4	10902.7	4283.1
179529.9	127113.8	22200.6	104913.2	3414.5	31624.6	18718.4	12906.2	13895.1	3481.9
138117.5	82006.8	12380.9	69625.9	483.7	9930.5	3863.0	6067.5	15756.6	29939.9
18386.5	14434.8	1741.6	12693.2	165.5	3115.9	1040.0	2075.9	353.4	316.9
122486.0	73054.4	29939.6	43114.8	9228.0	9762.8	3446.2	6316.6	21678.2	8762.6
221562.2	161343.4	90533.6	70809.8	1199.5	26223.6	8479.9	17743.7	13124.2	19671.5
35929.4	17699.3	5571.8	12127.5	379.6	8119.1	1916.9	6202.2	7102.3	2629.1
77966.2	36340.5	9003.6	27336.9	393.6	6552.7	2019.3	4533.4	22295.9	12383.5
5440.4	4188.8	1290.6	2898.2	50.0	1054.6	366.4	688.2	125.3	21.7
123109.2	71527.0	30144.2	41382.8	2710.5	11491.0	6283.0	5208.0	32822.5	4558.2
69369.1	34729.0	4295.9	30433.1	770.9	5235.3	1968.4	3266.9	27611.6	1022.3
11526.5	7546.9	1507.5	6039.4	15.1	1468.3	379.0	1089.3	1904.8	591.4
8181.8	5781.5	3348.0	2433.5		1251.3	244.3	1007.0	861.2	287.8
32365.2	16617.3	5646.6	10970.7	303.4	9706.7	6328.2	3378.5	2537.9	3199.9

C-1-17续表7

地 区	医疗救助					
		资助参加合作医疗	资助参加医疗保险	医疗救助		
					门诊救助	住院救助
全 国	**2574119.1**	**300427.0**	**144061.2**	**1804596.5**	**232038.5**	**1572558.0**
中央级						
北 京	20955.8	430.3	4293.3	11660.2	5150.7	6509.5
天 津	34948.5	168.2	11723.3	15798.2	604.1	15194.1
河 北	89767.5	12925.1	2365.0	50498.9	6078.4	44420.5
山 西	66926.4	6656.9	4395.5	48259.5	4844.2	43415.3
内蒙古	68065.9	4918.6	3670.1	51939.1	7663.6	44275.5
辽 宁	51008.8	10900.3	4887.5	28103.8	7802.0	20301.8
吉 林	64545.8	8726.9	4107.5	47027.8	11703.6	35324.2
黑龙江	135842.6	9383.4	12411.7	107460.4	17479.5	89980.9
上 海	24570.5	168.8	3147.6	19067.9	1323.8	17744.1
江 苏	122857.9	10798.7	8954.4	85973.9	12353.6	73620.3
浙 江	92314.4	6120.7	880.6	72662.6	17660.0	55002.6
安 徽	107015.7	12223.6	2851.7	80668.6	5719.3	74949.3
福 建	41763.9	5452.2	484.0	29558.5	4625.2	24933.3
江 西	129870.6	10809.4	5991.3	103455.3	14551.5	88903.8
山 东	115652.6	14136.5	2405.8	56418.1	2146.7	54271.4
河 南	117397.0	20619.1	3939.9	75890.9	4446.2	71444.7
湖 北	106749.9	15894.2	4255.8	72276.5	9198.2	63078.3
湖 南	131352.9	15827.9	10123.6	85859.8	18259.7	67600.1
广 东	89703.5	12839.0	7557.4	50988.5	6599.7	44388.8
广 西	78156.4	12540.5	3186.2	57661.3	3647.9	54013.4
海 南	21204.6	1369.9	706.9	17543.5	888.4	16655.1
重 庆	90562.3	7170.4	5265.2	63429.9	10293.7	53136.2
四 川	218997.5	31294.2	12627.2	157273.2	20922.9	136350.3
贵 州	101026.6	16073.7	1728.0	65804.1	5049.7	60754.4
云 南	105687.3	26226.1	7653.3	64074.1	6739.1	57335.0
西 藏	9461.0	64.9	0.7	9220.7	498.0	8722.7
陕 西	114966.5	8795.4	1780.0	92833.7	10674.8	82158.9
甘 肃	87072.4	7623.3	3033.6	73197.5	3254.2	69943.3
青 海	30560.4	2014.8	1827.2	25422.0	4492.7	20929.3
宁 夏	23654.2	1613.7	683.0	20094.1	2433.5	17660.6
新 疆	81459.7	6640.3	7123.9	64473.9	4933.6	59540.3

单位：万元

优抚对象医疗补助	自然灾害生活救助	生活救济费	紧急抢救、安置、转移灾民支出	救灾储备	自然灾害灾后重建补助	其他救助
325034.4	**1786987.6**	**1009445.7**	**110119.6**	**104682.0**	**436158.1**	**126582.2**
	43506.0			30950.0	12556.0	
4572.0	5774.6	2658.9	44.1	540.3		2531.3
7258.8	2099.6	1121.0		478.5	38.3	461.8
23978.5	51898.9	36384.5	2781.1	5897.4	6072.9	763.0
7614.5	40974.4	28603.1	1552.0	3230.1	5274.4	2314.8
7538.1	38708.6	24267.2	1490.8	2953.5	8363.4	1633.7
7117.2	66572.4	29860.2	12271.5	2220.4	15172.8	7047.5
4683.6	49320.9	28148.0	4459.8	1560.7	12673.0	2479.4
6587.1	147381.2	51377.3	12754.3	3142.4	69435.3	10671.9
2186.2	2653.8					2653.8
17130.9	21365.3	14425.8	587.2	451.2	2204.7	3696.4
12650.5	33198.7	20777.1	890.2	6175.9	2407.7	2947.8
11271.8	38259.5	28985.6	1683.4	803.1	4930.8	1856.6
6269.2	26787.9	13473.2	1496.7	543.8	3049.7	8224.5
9614.6	28361.3	19228.1	2143.5	860.0	2584.2	3545.5
42692.2	30255.5	24921.4	166.1	2919.0	265.0	1984.0
16947.1	25747.0	22278.6	58.1	1222.1	1422.5	765.7
14323.4	63679.5	44372.5	3259.5	4018.1	8542.0	3487.4
19541.6	60529.1	43182.4	5238.1	862.8	6613.1	4632.7
18318.6	68783.5	25349.6	6786.7	2734.0	28401.6	5511.6
4768.4	48792.6	26996.8	1587.7	2819.2	14988.8	2400.1
1584.3	5754.1	4525.6	27.6	476.3	426.9	297.7
14696.8	42383.5	26603.7	2707.4	5680.2	6365.2	1027.0
17802.9	288148.4	163492.4	16942.3	5736.1	93174.1	8803.5
17420.8	72189.8	51647.3	4090.7	2069.4	9113.3	5269.1
7733.8	117987.0	64809.2	4298.6	4369.7	33092.6	11416.9
174.7	30154.6	7457.1	2093.5	1162.4	563.1	18878.5
11557.4	129959.3	45783.4	12717.1	1910.2	63510.2	6038.4
3218.0	125688.1	95544.7	6494.7	1351.9	21400.9	895.9
1296.4	22423.4	20959.3	130.0	804.5	83.1	446.5
1263.4	15082.4	14014.8		159.0	469.0	439.6
3221.6	42566.7	28196.9	1366.9	6579.8	2963.5	3459.6

C-1-17续表8

地 区	民政管理事务	行政运行	一般行政管理事务	机关服务	拥军优属
全 国	**2967378.9**	**703821.7**	**140587.2**	**21345.4**	**204454.4**
中央级	46609.8	6043.8	3431.9	244.4	298.7
北 京	165510.3	26869.4	4212.1	1991.7	7040.5
天 津	107670.6	17104.8	1061.7	56.4	2722.0
河 北	72964.2	33036.2	3681.2	684.2	3811.4
山 西	54300.0	14347.7	2911.5	152.2	2652.0
内蒙古	66714.8	22585.1	2630.2	878.4	2627.3
辽 宁	150443.1	20341.1	6022.2	448.9	7822.6
吉 林	45574.2	8758.9	2328.8	228.2	1912.0
黑龙江	60223.6	10445.5	2965.0	188.7	1801.7
上 海	133420.1	16117.3			19226.2
江 苏	196254.0	50602.1	10184.6	805.1	18740.3
浙 江	219812.7	51101.5	10040.2	486.7	13001.1
安 徽	63165.3	17742.2	3584.5	841.5	4953.7
福 建	62282.0	16916.9	2137.7	203.2	7967.5
江 西	38114.3	12124.5	3452.6	712.1	1693.9
山 东	148135.9	36390.0	7190.9	2531.3	13450.1
河 南	87636.7	29829.0	8204.4	1481.5	9210.4
湖 北	87020.6	19447.1	3847.9	1456.2	4015.1
湖 南	100592.5	35073.4	11005.4	1619.6	3028.3
广 东	220372.7	47270.4	8307.3	2366.3	29351.8
广 西	87307.8	18929.1	4176.2	680.3	8572.6
海 南	30803.4	4651.2	2884.1	53.9	4533.1
重 庆	73061.2	15614.5	2448.9	316.9	4762.6
四 川	151594.1	43516.2	9241.9	1196.4	9198.1
贵 州	69493.1	25299.7	1483.3	47.0	3266.1
云 南	116343.2	31282.0	4936.6	494.2	5976.1
西 藏	8826.3	3638.5	216.8		207.0
陕 西	135883.6	20848.6	9549.5	170.7	2027.1
甘 肃	42029.6	12477.0	1778.0	490.2	1158.5
青 海	30158.9	4134.0	628.5	31.7	590.3
宁 夏	20968.4	6876.3	1038.1		693.3
新 疆	74091.9	24407.7	5005.2	487.5	8143.0

单位：万元

老龄事务	民间组织管理	行政区划和地名管理	基层政权和社区建设	部队供应	其他民政管理事务支出
263798.2	**57838.9**	**54308.6**	**758420.3**	**40981.0**	**721823.2**
1030.6	19691.7	807.2	443.8		14617.7
12539.9	3506.5	344.8	62970.5	1001.5	45033.4
1116.7	610.5	163.7	63644.0	971.7	20219.1
3188.0	448.7	4501.3	11471.9	1118.0	11023.3
2142.7	239.4	863.4	19997.1	997.1	9996.9
2543.8	128.7	768.1	7867.8	1202.4	25483.0
4024.7	804.1	2659.1	83442.0	1867.9	23010.5
1172.7	154.0	896.1	14189.1	410.3	15524.1
1195.3	378.0	4312.7	13715.7	1519.4	23701.6
21632.0	5717.9	243.5	5130.7	1069.2	64283.3
17030.0	3019.6	2871.5	51412.1	1474.8	40113.9
24056.9	5114.2	5823.3	50769.4	2465.0	56954.4
5811.9	489.1	858.0	14532.5	987.1	13364.8
3280.4	255.4	1984.8	7306.5	873.3	21356.3
5984.2	265.3	560.9	6559.7	869.1	5892.0
3511.4	1215.7	3760.6	45953.8	2068.8	32063.3
4314.7	677.6	1606.2	12530.8	2647.7	17134.4
4382.4	555.8	617.7	29929.5	1865.0	20903.9
5999.8	850.1	1775.2	23254.3	787.4	17199.0
16238.3	8735.8	4296.6	55541.1	3302.4	44962.7
5251.7	420.8	1873.6	16993.2	2641.1	27769.2
2092.9	280.4	1739.1	3562.4	1280.0	9726.3
2857.5	524.6	1127.8	29894.4	593.7	14920.3
19254.0	1274.8	2593.6	27366.5	1387.4	36565.2
3245.9	83.2	905.1	12770.9	1535.2	20856.7
31369.5	94.8	1646.5	13415.5	2791.1	24336.9
62.6	45.0	1181.3	260.2	610.9	2604.0
40866.0	1016.0	1007.5	45622.7	1008.6	13766.9
2108.3	488.0	466.5	570.7	245.0	22247.4
2127.7	86.0	291.2	11948.2	181.6	10139.7
898.8	317.1	465.2	5027.9	249.0	5402.7
12466.9	350.1	1296.5	10325.4	959.3	10650.3

C-1-17续表9

地 区	行政事业单位离退休	地方离退休人员经费	离休人员离休金	退休人员退休金	退职人员退职金	离退休人员其他费用
全 国	**435817.7**	**143243.2**	**10664.3**	**115762.2**	**2393.2**	**14423.5**
中央级	3868.8					
北 京	55321.8	36369.2	241.2	32285.8	367.3	3474.9
天 津	4817.0	2411.7	54.3	1583.9	14.2	759.3
河 北	19449.5	6402.6	951.4	4909.1	42.6	499.5
山 西	9755.0	1854.6	238.1	1465.6	21.3	129.6
内蒙古	13433.4	1102.8	72.8	852.4		177.6
辽 宁	24258.8	4282.1	747.3	3100.3	213.0	221.5
吉 林	9669.5	5683.0	1846.5	3441.0	324.6	70.9
黑龙江	7477.7	77.5	5.1	66.4	6.0	
上 海	8356.7	1404.7	88.1	962.2	109.0	245.4
江 苏	29719.8	15297.3	2199.4	10975.7	321.0	1801.2
浙 江	22088.5	7978.1	184.2	6632.0	63.1	1098.8
安 徽	13489.3	3068.7	712.6	1880.2	145.2	330.7
福 建	25076.7	14432.5	82.0	13414.4	196.8	739.3
江 西	9054.1	3675.6	265.6	3128.8	45.2	236.0
山 东	12320.2	4632.9	193.2	3100.3	43.8	1295.6
河 南	18004.0	4271.9	676.8	3017.9	12.0	565.2
湖 北	18743.2	6849.0	432.5	5723.3	42.0	651.2
湖 南	8512.7	4249.0	345.2	3594.4	20.6	288.8
广 东	34475.0	3831.9	254.5	3150.0	4.0	423.4
广 西	13372.1	484.1	46.1	423.7	2.9	11.4
海 南	3717.3	282.3	77.0	205.3		
重 庆	9147.2	643.0	32.7	527.8	8.7	73.8
四 川	21077.1	4882.9	239.6	3991.9	166.3	485.1
贵 州	3492.8	2152.1	166.4	1827.5	9.9	148.3
云 南	12617.5	2454.6	112.8	2217.4		124.4
西 藏	775.9	384.7		384.7		
陕 西	6505.5	1329.9	171.1	1080.3	54.1	24.4
甘 肃	4609.1	1501.7	166.3	988.2	19.6	327.6
青 海	2184.7	379.8	41.0	233.4		105.4
宁 夏	2957.1	269.0		119.8	137.2	12.0
新 疆	7469.7	604.0	20.5	478.5	2.8	102.2

单位：万元

一次性抚恤金	行政单位离退休	事业单位离退休	离退休人员管理机构	其他行政事业单位离退休支出	其他
7600.7	**159588.6**	**111312.1**	**2522.8**	**19151.0**	**1338488.0**
	2722.0	740.8	406.0		42834.3
2741.2	10105.5	3878.6	176.0	4792.5	121411.2
193.6	311.3	1176.8		917.2	18446.3
293.7	6099.9	6259.9	262.2	424.9	31245.5
111.2	3116.6	4554.4		229.4	21016.9
63.7	7301.6	4953.8		75.2	26991.1
88.5	9300.9	9053.1	40.0	1582.7	60319.6
35.1	2907.6	961.9	24.5	92.5	46244.7
	6282.5	261.1		856.6	6974.0
89.2	3910.9	3026.1		15.0	49588.9
937.5	8185.4	4155.4	50.0	2031.7	138924.5
131.0	8203.7	4753.3	214.0	939.4	78027.1
190.0	6411.5	3835.3	68.8	105.0	18825.9
489.2	5975.8	3834.2	8.0	826.2	27761.2
139.2	3620.7	1655.3	31.5	71.0	4581.3
317.7	2194.8	5482.5		10.0	65762.3
326.2	7052.7	6513.7	34.0	131.7	40886.4
357.1	4310.3	5380.3	363.4	1840.2	47032.7
119.4	2864.7	1089.2	90.0	219.8	41588.6
217.3	14373.4	15833.7	194.3	241.7	107234.9
11.4	5748.4	7028.4		111.2	28089.1
	1510.6	1527.7	358.5	38.2	19448.9
31.8	4913.0	1618.5	2.3	1970.4	11727.8
197.0	9377.3	6023.6	126.7	666.6	64488.7
32.6	1004.9	335.3		0.5	19516.2
92.7	6840.5	2753.5	16.8	552.1	74567.3
	125.9	121.9		143.4	13764.5
15.9	2685.8	2322.8	10.7	156.3	19415.3
268.0	2233.7	801.0	45.1	27.6	6220.8
85.4	1299.1	500.0		5.8	59955.2
12.0	1989.5	622.4		76.2	22900.3
13.1	6608.1	257.6			2696.5

C-1-18 支出水

地 区	优抚对象整体抚恤水平	定期抚恤水平	伤残抚恤	定期补助水平	在乡复退军人定期定量补助水平
全 国	**5770.34**	**9637.35**	**13202.28**	**2708.64**	**2597.28**
中央级					
北 京	22738.87	19690.14	11857.36	3861.73	3584.38
天 津	10969.93	17685.27	14762.49	5401.35	5289.83
河 北	5072.23	8952.42	11803.37	2166.33	2027.38
山 西	8285.13	8364.31	11701.81	3036.94	3311.82
内蒙古	12490.04	9285.39	11829.04	5457.21	5680.74
辽 宁	7084.80	9659.74	11711.41	3192.84	3751.98
吉 林	7178.17	14785.98	16145.18	2733.51	2698.98
黑龙江	7108.65	9838.67	11234.01	4287.34	4293.79
上 海	16947.72	7760.59	20242.14	3866.47	3342.50
江 苏	7267.00	17821.83	15865.84	2627.17	2893.38
浙 江	7768.81	19285.10	15610.72	2987.26	2818.67
安 徽	4761.55	8656.26	11584.97	2548.32	2349.08
福 建	5754.62	9242.40	12438.83	2575.47	2043.86
江 西	5957.65	8451.35	13124.24	3385.66	3392.61
山 东	6151.30	8472.25	13826.14	2334.16	2282.40
河 南	4994.83	8607.34	12633.80	2195.73	1899.51
湖 北	5387.54	8950.44	12042.74	2887.82	2763.52
湖 南	3994.85	8563.27	14305.47	2110.95	1822.42
广 东	6288.14	11843.40	14000.66	3439.10	2907.18
广 西	4105.53	9358.91	11655.14	2385.11	2713.19
海 南	7800.64	10488.97	13734.42	3427.15	3796.19
重 庆	5411.96	9906.30	13100.24	3177.68	3105.62
四 川	4819.05	8723.89	13223.04	3085.90	3037.21
贵 州	4691.23	10763.61	11809.55	2700.63	2416.15
云 南	4353.68	8879.65	13074.35	1933.88	1783.68
西 藏	10731.77	8896.05	15858.41	1687.61	3592.66
陕 西	7296.56	8679.68	13439.61	3551.61	3411.49
甘 肃	4294.00	13944.92	12120.19	2078.31	1548.32
青 海	9187.38	9275.28	8571.96	3820.85	4370.22
宁 夏	9821.79	12388.28	10751.05	4449.59	4719.90
新 疆	11865.03	11608.56	13290.49	5206.09	5571.45

平情况

单位：元/人、年、元/个、年

在乡红军老战士定期定量补助费水平	红军失散人员定期定量补助水平	“参战”退伍军人生活补贴水平	“涉核”退伍军人生活补助水平	烈士纪念建筑物管理单位补助水平
32382.20	**14471.33**	**3594.01**	**4241.98**	**622921.39**
43000.00		7930.30	7438.99	827600.00
		7141.40	6000.00	2391666.67
68000.00		3694.95	4121.22	609836.73
33444.44	15000.00	3851.31	3472.73	634830.51
31500.00	22500.00	3874.17	4632.08	688666.67
	14000.00	4087.06	4421.42	783244.90
	131000.00	4241.24	5513.21	424400.00
32357.14	15235.29	5814.66	4406.39	413629.63
		8336.74	7574.03	6196909.09
	16000.00	3891.48	4436.57	907550.56
	15013.33	5150.96	4567.37	629025.00
33333.33	14082.23	3824.86	4916.14	733196.08
34000.00	15226.42	5130.62	5656.90	318648.15
31136.36	14109.54	5033.46	5873.63	583750.00
33000.00	13961.54	3698.96	3803.85	1033081.08
32153.85	14304.05	3646.13	3830.65	525404.04
32666.67	16197.80	3721.75	3736.74	415254.55
34333.33	15028.23	2859.07	8230.88	1457410.26
	15134.83	4772.02	4711.91	297430.23
30666.67	15570.72	3667.47	4420.75	1588761.90
	15172.41	2891.63	7344.54	387000.00
		3430.37	3562.21	197000.00
31121.95	14394.74	3505.51	3970.92	194980.39
31000.00	14038.46	3205.36	4498.61	177339.29
	15333.33	2115.40	6405.41	230390.63
		909.09		49000.00
32468.69	14568.33	3681.86	3599.60	805153.85
32673.91	15200.00	3376.94	5512.75	229202.53
		3807.48	2280.60	500000.00
32666.67	50000.00	4704.13	8200.69	132333.33
32416.67	15000.00	4759.36	4651.83	2177642.86

C-1-18续表1

地 区	荣誉军人康复医院补助水平	荣誉军人康复医院在院人员补助水平	复员军人疗养院补助水平	复员军人疗养院在院人员补助水平	复退军人精神病院补助水平
全 国	**16318857.14**	**17182.59**	**8463315.79**	**8837.13**	**8849235.85**
中央级					
北 京					
天 津			17214000.00	44497.67	19356000.00
河 北	32011000.00	46465.52	13599857.14	6643.71	42162500.00
山 西	4799200.00	18237.51	28410000.00	4246.33	9043571.43
内蒙古	5369000.00	76500.00	213500.00	8271.95	4603500.00
辽 宁	14720000.00	22025.60			5580250.00
吉 林	24690000.00				420142.86
黑龙江	75807000.00	908215.96			25485000.00
上 海	7752000.00	18133.33			
江 苏	45362000.00		3439000.00	4083.40	90616000.00
浙 江	27610000.00				6763000.00
安 徽	19291000.00	5300.00			20885000.00
福 建	1363000.00	8469.23			586666.67
江 西	23819000.00	12368.50	825000.00	7730.53	80000.00
山 东	54481500.00	15489.69	15489428.57	18913.35	14985230.77
河 南	18152666.67	15993.16	6931000.00	11159.93	26404000.00
湖 北	25029000.00	15715.28			12418800.00
湖 南	6865000.00		1400000.00		4497750.00
广 东	1755000.00	7179.71	8526000.00	14266.67	5733900.00
广 西	10346000.00				16602750.00
海 南					
重 庆	9565000.00	11141.43			
四 川	10911000.00	185174.26	630000.00	3920.00	3476888.89
贵 州	4999666.67	6125.99			1275000.00
云 南	6721000.00				3403500.00
西 藏					
陕 西	29968000.00	19889.59	6973333.33	6688.90	8993666.67
甘 肃	4642000.00				2979666.67
青 海					
宁 夏					
新 疆	10726000.00	13333.33			182500.00

单位：元/个、年、元/人、年

复退军人精神病院在院人员补助水平	光荣院补助水平	光荣院在院人员补助水平	军队离休干部支出水平	军队退休干部支出水平	军队无军籍职工支出水平	孤儿补助水平
6636.81	**567237.89**	**5743.06**	**121477.94**	**85496.27**	**32081.67**	**9341.89**
	2817800.00	29223.27	105238.19	85054.31	32530.97	53472.20
11764.71	4064166.67	15712.31	112338.21	92969.72	42077.35	17538.92
61293.30	870922.54	5390.30	138870.37	88959.37	28056.09	7852.73
4577.24	808318.18	12970.90	114599.29	111449.38	25402.21	8742.79
4701.38	1396103.45	9383.83	100076.92	86445.20	35801.48	11888.36
3532.47	2084000.00	15363.42	99486.68	80474.53	28464.18	16024.93
2811.58	167767.44	4167.21	70492.59	67924.71	47338.69	7112.93
524468.85	525000.00	7524.58	108162.03	88419.13	30222.03	8072.40
			85921.23	87043.16	28286.71	17892.11
	820818.18	10458.82	110112.49	93218.52	44593.64	12475.77
	479869.57	10332.21	114910.47	83328.35	43905.81	14786.13
6347.61	597150.94	5202.49	116745.10	84473.18	30833.21	8311.57
4633.25	373553.57	7529.23	118179.19	86492.42	32092.74	9109.76
3871.21	199790.24	2828.44	122500.00	80261.49	23180.10	10778.65
11747.39	542212.12	5277.58	112815.67	85099.58	40845.21	9380.98
5188.74	304948.98	3511.45	97852.12	79310.64	24494.02	8053.48
4746.40	751000.00	3820.31	117545.97	91518.26	37055.35	8574.43
5932.30	622988.02	4588.72	116045.72	69861.72	25610.74	7817.02
7061.14	347230.77	9490.51	117023.62	102384.82	33488.93	9958.81
548.07	171918.92	3606.50	124122.09	98055.03	35826.55	7333.84
	388888.89	9430.89	141540.00	96669.60	4236.32	11208.39
	1359125.00	16956.05	155379.12	76613.88	39534.28	9280.22
5063.98	437042.55	6024.58	117266.67	86737.65	27966.72	8984.47
19882.60	189923.08	4476.88	118416.67	79320.07	49867.69	8383.25
	124333.33	492.58	180211.21	65250.61	29118.64	11699.18
			106500.00	76525.71	56200.89	10980.81
9610.63	626476.19	7817.06	102226.49	91158.48	23466.60	11057.60
	250000.00	20518.43	592912.77	52366.35	19123.88	7464.99
	100000.00		871285.71	108126.27	40059.51	7611.22
	60000.00	5601.02	134919.35	81886.93	18935.90	6715.40
	401321.43	1568.02	189016.76	101929.32	42750.71	8034.41

C-1-18续表2

地 区	康复辅具机构(站)专项拨款支出水平	补贴火化场人员水平	补贴殡葬类单位补助水平	社会福利院补助水平	社会福利院在院人员生活费补助水平
全 国	**3007000.00**	**519.18**	**709947.06**	**2714080.55**	**5087.01**
中央级					
北 京	3830000.00	1545.78	1765333.33	6118875.00	2124.45
天 津		86.38	4676137.93	7665333.33	10442.11
河 北	2590000.00	508.39	911467.03	2803121.95	3961.55
山 西	4969000.00	8453.94	213934.43	3901904.76	7363.49
内蒙古	400000.00	393.37	659445.31	2674534.88	6203.80
辽 宁		617.37	538835.88	3889720.00	9870.95
吉 林	1859500.00	919.01	397993.15	1356509.80	6944.66
黑龙江	2880500.00	188.21	241782.89	2959193.55	2255.16
上 海				12356217.39	5068.16
江 苏	400000.00	645.01	835074.38	7773303.03	9472.83
浙 江		843.30	1629138.25	6039494.51	2889.08
安 徽	1400000.00	476.07	467811.52	1306728.81	4936.47
福 建	2500000.00	634.29	430366.01	1331246.58	7977.25
江 西		231.34	165167.83	517564.89	2695.64
山 东	6000000.00	86.96	441386.90	5098666.67	11461.87
河 南	7284000.00	606.52	179960.63	1219985.92	5368.15
湖 北	238000.00	221.65	1366430.23	3926572.58	3213.37
湖 南	4025000.00	202.54	367748.82	1718511.36	1907.13
广 东	4950000.00	270.62	1150565.37	4288098.16	5864.12
广 西		374.04	1667000.00	1467428.57	6992.20
海 南		150.29	1455176.47	2450000.00	350.02
重 庆		2043.99	482044.64	4516485.71	3261.12
四 川	9513000.00	382.24	818391.30	1965461.54	3078.50
贵 州	500000.00	535.35	261294.96	821333.33	5957.40
云 南	600000.00	1065.21	296530.00	1344875.00	2675.07
西 藏		588.76	2740000.00	114989.13	2086.94
陕 西		491.62	401207.55	3380722.22	9424.31
甘 肃		897.15	1074507.25	821735.85	4925.31
青 海		96.24	39906.25	404000.00	1593.81
宁 夏		161.12	1299147.06	1965181.82	5869.31
新 疆	9800000.00	1094.82	1020098.27	2166493.83	3996.42

单位：元/个、年、元/人、年、元/人次

儿童福利院补助水平	儿童福利院在院人员生活费补助水平	精神病人福利院补助水平	精神病人福利院在院人员生活费补助水平	城市居民最低生活保障补助水平（不含春节补助）	农村最低生活保障补助水平（不含春节补助）	农村集中五保供养救助水平
2514491.49	**9415.98**	**8549651.61**	**5670.16**	**3219.27**	**1380.96**	**4073.23**
947083.33	5164.00	17385500.00	4888.88	6280.95	4325.82	8920.55
6211500.00	13707.92	29702000.00	7192.31	5291.35	2742.21	7345.25
301800.00	14120.68			2853.04	1271.11	3800.03
1277375.00	26767.95			2964.57	1488.08	4430.24
5817000.00	16513.14	11467500.00	7758.96	4488.63	2196.90	5511.53
1942111.11	3241.10	13341000.00		3909.36	1601.98	5630.33
1319888.89	17444.92	2882428.57	4285.12	3880.24	1407.25	3345.48
3453200.00	12996.73	32015800.00	30809.95	3618.80	1549.86	3617.91
10275571.43	13376.74	30090666.67	552.33	6242.62	3496.77	7659.79
2944500.00	4812.76	20086363.64	4537.09	3745.45	2256.05	5971.64
5259500.00	6188.04	19162500.00	934.40	5012.39	3132.17	6850.35
2577804.88	10202.29	540000.00	2140.76	3322.10	1359.76	3321.36
2764200.00	9945.41	7726428.57	7873.23	2953.81	1523.36	5016.45
1681000.00	9933.49	4740000.00	3403.74	2715.91	1397.71	3149.30
6711333.33	9571.39	21708000.00	16976.58	3574.40	1600.15	4451.45
3930846.15	13807.33	2373500.00	7049.92	2518.37	1217.11	3448.03
1503058.82	8551.68	957333.33		2994.48	1151.05	3184.93
1437571.43	4155.22	2990444.44	2396.06	2939.22	1254.59	4135.81
3486000.00	10630.32	21917333.33	8331.35	3151.60	1649.26	6808.33
4724375.00	17708.82	10938750.00	16210.94	2760.23	1032.28	5381.83
214000.00	8594.01			2940.83	1678.15	7662.12
7626571.43	13341.93	6085454.55	5123.30	3289.65	1730.97	4811.20
1363795.45	11200.48	5457705.88	2340.99	2489.26	1090.49	3404.88
2087166.67	18156.79	991173.91	2096.08	2988.93	1089.78	2018.18
1222961.54	1564.71	8768750.00	413.03	2583.10	1253.80	2536.94
584800.00	6650.17			4442.27	1125.09	1624.83
3611727.27	6352.70	14208000.00	5060.68	3950.39	1826.74	6417.21
1528315.79	13442.63	5359000.00	2108.77	3227.37	1264.41	3962.28
440000.00	40.37	600000.00		3247.53	1753.72	3444.14
3760333.33	11778.93	3655000.00		2384.12	1484.67	8578.02
1722180.00	9534.19	11733625.00	5432.56	3176.56	1510.09	4078.73

C-1-18续表3

地 区	农村分散五保供养补助水平	流浪乞讨人员救助单位补助水平	救助流浪乞讨人员每次补助水平	临时救助户次补助水平	资助参加合作医疗补助水平	资助参加医疗保险补助水平
全 国	**2758.42**	**772230.48**	**589.93**	**677.62**	**61.71**	**96.68**
中央级						
北 京	7029.95	5818913.04	164.05	1073.68	86.33	917.31
天 津	6809.93	2297166.67	1248.62	470.11		410.77
河 北	2350.15	336952.38	711.75	116.99	66.79	110.31
山 西	2404.05	282763.44	575.43	418.89	49.06	70.74
内蒙古	3520.71	838578.95	677.72	1163.95	43.47	62.04
辽 宁	3096.74	902575.76	1172.29	553.87	184.79	206.64
吉 林	2113.03	350250.00	629.99	16.70	104.63	53.30
黑龙江	2521.88	483072.29	1148.22	1530.66	68.17	85.51
上 海	5351.94	5714300.00	821.33	896.30	123.21	613.56
江 苏	4605.07	1232514.56	903.11	914.53	88.53	280.17
浙 江	4750.27	1182653.85	1568.17	2233.47	113.30	167.48
安 徽	2156.86	841152.54	870.41	1021.67	61.59	80.03
福 建	4186.93	638176.47	436.16	636.39	63.01	91.69
江 西	2614.30	244657.14	763.99	1113.90	77.05	120.03
山 东	3088.62	1366491.80	730.84	1062.10	76.01	146.42
河 南	2372.52	1019000.00	546.09	405.55	58.34	55.53
湖 北	2172.10	422381.58	478.82	336.07	65.70	41.07
湖 南	2195.37	370765.43	520.81	358.81	74.00	112.17
广 东	4986.87	2495786.67	787.41	520.47	76.73	185.05
广 西	2562.93	702363.64	852.66	609.95	51.40	127.14
海 南	4167.58	1300000.00	638.44	223.69	49.51	65.25
重 庆	4343.89	801441.86	992.60	1402.52	54.91	71.86
四 川	2897.61	460864.13	689.00	548.52	66.10	84.55
贵 州	1244.50	266236.11	704.50	1172.65	36.03	38.04
云 南	1516.29	197970.59	604.36	668.14	57.65	73.48
西 藏	4028.08	458000.00	1072.97	380.85	61.57	10.53
陕 西	4932.69	698111.11	492.34	1850.02	96.87	160.08
甘 肃	2695.32	371396.23	890.53	3889.34	23.08	36.12
青 海	3256.79	222941.18	676.25	1057.40	47.05	88.27
宁 夏	2308.82	135722.22	516.65	568.22	47.96	62.64
新 疆	1532.50	727379.31	946.17	335.86	65.82	91.17

单位：元/个、年、元/人、年、元/人次

直接医疗救助补助水平	门诊救助人次补助水平	住院救助人次补助水平	优抚对象医疗补助支出水平	救灾物资储备中心补助水平	老龄机构补助水平	军供站补助水平
848.68	**220.48**	**1464.27**	**715.77**	**1335229.59**	**1026052.90**	**1260953.85**
814.28	630.21	1059.04	2775.62	337687.50	7376411.76	10015000.00
739.16	43.67	2015.29	2527.09	2392500.00	697937.50	9717000.00
917.13	364.48	1157.24	1042.89	4536461.54	430810.81	1242222.22
1760.36	642.97	2183.81	813.58	454943.66	187956.14	1661833.33
1748.34	562.80	2751.60	1818.78	1737352.94	591581.40	2404800.00
775.25	383.37	1276.80	1007.03	854000.00	609803.03	1698090.91
621.51	244.22	1273.24	1159.88	3121400.00	344911.76	373000.00
1559.08	390.10	3730.91	818.19	3928000.00	111710.28	1381272.73
2774.08	620.51	3743.32	1921.09		12017777.78	10692000.00
487.19	94.73	1598.15	752.42	644571.43	2432857.14	867529.41
548.38	180.29	1591.83	1661.09	1260387.76	2672988.89	2240909.09
927.13	459.76	1005.10	490.55	617769.23	543168.22	274194.44
540.85	153.38	1017.80	782.86	181266.67	520698.41	727750.00
1760.09	686.01	2366.55	1098.81	505882.35	549009.17	668538.46
1960.16	368.16	2364.61	741.70	5838000.00	232543.05	1088842.11
725.48	177.02	898.79	465.99	940076.92	440275.51	1103208.33
780.12	413.74	895.79	410.48	854914.89	492404.49	2072222.22
743.69	358.99	1046.66	399.71	663692.31	447746.27	656166.67
921.89	185.36	2252.78	913.03	414242.42	1424412.28	2540307.69
1394.19	308.88	1827.96	430.05	1342476.19	807953.85	2031615.38
1157.16	80.31	4063.41	1018.06	2381500.00	3488166.67	6400000.00
271.05	60.55	830.19	607.16	1535189.19	892968.75	1484250.00
949.10	293.89	1442.64	468.95	651829.55	903943.66	991000.00
837.55	144.30	1394.32	1114.95	1881272.73	341673.68	1705777.78
790.27	288.27	993.66	433.15	1065780.49	2571270.49	1162958.33
2628.78	476.01	3543.80	973.80	894153.85	208666.67	6109000.00
1828.99	484.21	2861.60	1162.01	1005368.42	3967572.82	916909.09
1050.59	153.53	1442.84	799.40	365378.38	208742.57	306250.00
480.77	112.64	1611.15	2969.31	113309.86	386854.55	454000.00
612.32	145.59	1096.80	1694.93	176666.67	332888.89	2490000.00
1092.02	222.12	1616.66	2531.31	3870470.59	530506.38	799416.67

C-1-19 中央专项基本

地 区	项目数	地方配套资金合计	中央对地方投资合计	养老发改投资[2013]1075号				社区发改	
				项目数	小计	中央投资	地方投资	项目数	小计
全 国	**735**	**466605**	**170000**	**347**	**573720**	**143500**	**430220**	**377**	**51729**
北 京	2	25987	1000	2	26987	1000	25987		
天 津	3	18914	1300	3	20214	1300	18914		
河 北	36	22897	8400	7	27716	7200	20516	29	3581
山 西	26	26388	5800	16	30238	5000	25238	10	1950
内蒙古	22	15275	7800	12	20525	7000	13525	10	2550
辽 宁	35	28107	7800	21	33895	7000	26895	14	2012
吉 林	34	20648	8000	15	26083	7200	18883	19	2565
黑龙江	44	18565	9800	17	22670	7000	15670	20	2360
上 海	1	18588	950	1	19538	950	18588		
江 苏	10	29676	2000	10	31676	2000	29676		
浙 江	9	32881	2400	9	35281	2400	32881		
安 徽	71	8970	8200	36	11365	7000	4365	35	5805
福 建	16	17723	2400	16	20123	2400	17723		
江 西	39	17875	7000	20	21980	5800	16180	19	2895
山 东	11	17437	2400	11	19837	2400	17437		
河 南	27	9836	8200	7	16270	7000	9270	20	1766
湖 北	43	10474	8400	15	13876	7200	6676	28	4998
湖 南	37	17479	8600	10	21096	7400	13696	27	4983
广 东	4	21300	2000	4	23300	2000	21300		
广 西	21	2681	5800	9	7218	5000	2218	12	1263
海 南	12	3720	2900	5	5970	2500	3470	7	650
重 庆	27	5276	5800	11	9378	5000	4378	16	1698
四 川	33	8230	8200	13	13977	7000	6977	20	2453
贵 州	19	11878	5800	6	15988	5000	10988	13	1690
云 南	27	8455	5800	11	12950	5000	7950	16	1305
西 藏	7		2150	1	1750	1750		6	400
陕 西	23	27649	5800	7	31454	5000	26454	16	1995
甘 肃	29	3624	5800	17	8109	5000	3109	12	1315
青 海	15	1066	3400	10	3904	3000	904	5	562
宁 夏	16	5290	3400	8	7042	3000	4042	8	1648
新 疆	32	6795	7800	17	13310	7000	6310	15	1285
兵 团	3	2921	4900						

建设投资对账单

单位：个、万元

投资[2013]1052号		养老发改投资 [2013]667号				社区发改投资 [2013]667号			
中央投资	地方投资	项目数	小计	中央投资	地方投资	项目数	小计	中央投资	地方投资
19600	**32129**	**10**	**10551**	**6500**	**4051**	**1**	**605**	**400**	**205**
1200	2381								
800	1150								
800	1750								
800	1212								
800	1765								
800	1560	7	3335	2000	1335				
1200	4605								
1200	1695								
1200	566								
1200	3798								
1200	3783								
800	463								
400	250								
800	898								
1200	1253								
800	890								
800	505								
400									
800	1195								
800	515								
400	162								
400	1248								
800	485								
		3	7216	4500	2716	1	605	400	205

C-1-20 中央彩票公益金投资

地 区	合计	老年福利类 财社[2013]242号	残疾人福利类 财社[2013]242号
全 国	**157144**	**121144**	**20000**
北 京	2442	2175	163
天 津	1324	1135	189
河 北	4631	3637	575
山 西	6177	4012	1413
内蒙古	4815	4054	375
辽 宁	3987	2377	432
吉 林	3486	2808	402
黑龙江	3497	2704	447
上 海	1732	1539	193
江 苏	6323	4052	1529
浙 江	3870	2738	430
安 徽	6198	4761	549
福 建	3312	2712	410
江 西	8317	7291	481
山 东	6104	5094	667
河 南	7154	5809	704
湖 北	5764	4744	530
湖 南	9617	7487	1560
广 东	4651	3759	682
广 西	6510	4068	1488
海 南	4111	3358	327
重 庆	5400	3812	1354
四 川	7545	6109	637
贵 州	4162	3364	459
云 南	4798	3843	467
西 藏	4375	3444	355
陕 西	6136	3566	1426
甘 肃	6305	5276	437
青 海	4637	3502	361
宁 夏	3939	3380	356
新 疆	5825	4534	602

基本建设项目对账单

单位：万元

流浪儿童类 财社[2013]242号	殡葬 财社[2013]242号	社区 财社[2013]242号
6000	**5000**	**5000**
104		
234	185	
162	90	500
246	140	
143	535	500
136	140	
176	170	
192		550
152		550
218	170	500
120	70	
325	220	
273	70	
271	370	
310	180	
360	210	
210		
274	180	500
61	65	300
114	120	
459	340	
219	120	
198	290	
106	70	400
174	470	500
257	335	
124	250	400
133	70	
249	140	300

C-1-21 民政事业基本

地 区	在建项目数	#使用彩票公益金项目数	在建项目总投资	开工累计完成投资	本年计划投资	本年实际完成投资
全 国	**19116**	**8326**	**10361089.8**	**5491696.3**	**3119268.8**	**2927692.6**
中央级	7		47763.0	44661.7	2054.0	2505.0
北 京	68		384519.9	266999.8	64978.7	56936.2
天 津	7	2	40137.7	25744.5	12290.0	12401.4
河 北	2781	1439	169783.4	102226.9	51993.9	57914.6
山 西	42	23	37614.2	23009.5	7888.0	9248.4
内蒙古	116	85	109070.6	82679.7	24467.0	36099.3
辽 宁	791	584	185642.9	137315.5	42263.6	60484.1
吉 林	37	15	56653.2	52988.7	35904.4	38367.7
黑龙江	19	17	74012.1	144127.3	12624.4	14886.3
上 海	5	3	35851.5	15674.2	14315.0	11936.2
江 苏	4102	334	3190888.4	1292924.3	991764.8	770939.5
浙 江	93	55	482521.5	253702.8	113645.6	99544.5
安 徽	922	316	244672.7	172061.6	151176.3	140331.9
福 建	62	43	182528.0	78048.7	41705.1	39539.3
江 西	1307	1034	311356.5	171366.5	119643.1	116836.1
山 东	2076	1171	1270890.4	540648.1	338706.7	336182.4
河 南	297	199	234507.5	153723.5	58040.4	67230.1
湖 北	1433	214	588901.3	327661.2	159974.5	161970.6
湖 南	448	311	297095.7	177084.1	86856.7	89610.9
广 东	240	170	495222.8	190992.8	88914.9	78522.3
广 西	1765	1117	136521.4	93552.7	55974.0	56005.6
海 南	78	27	67826.7	51503.7	21953.3	20951.4
重 庆	497	325	188854.3	114042.1	70904.5	81591.3
四 川	114	47	133385.4	101662.1	58282.2	55893.9
贵 州	362	99	313062.4	181019.7	125532.4	136214.3
云 南	309	220	216136.1	144577.6	60764.9	58275.0
西 藏	67	11	49649.2	30413.2	30891.2	22438.2
陕 西	267	74	184872.9	128566.8	71597.4	72379.6
甘 肃	94	52	125886.6	58729.1	35801.0	31462.4
青 海	256	74	92597.0	89575.4	55893.0	68626.3
宁 夏	52	20	102658.1	70526.3	19011.8	15804.0
新 疆	402	245	310006.4	173886.2	93456.0	106563.8

建设投资情况总表

单位：万元、个、平方米、张

国家预算内投资	国内贷款	利用外资	福利彩票公益金	其他	本年完工项目数	未投入使用项目建设床位数
1201038.8	**14220.9**	**16941.7**	**647008.7**	**1048482.5**	**15328**	**378581**
2505.0					3	
54967.1				1969.1	12	3427
4311.2			2500.0	5590.2	11	200
19206.3	435.0		16659.7	21613.6	1889	23185
2563.3			4056.1	2629.0	28	2155
17017.9			12967.4	6114.0	91	7007
16962.5	5000.0		23477.0	15044.6	269	8679
11135.2			20237.0	6995.5	19	4400
805.0			13556.6	524.7	19	3536
8452.2			2035.0	1449.0		948
338216.3	1050.0		62633.9	369039.3	3837	50187
51774.4			36155.4	11614.7	45	15863
64559.6	46.2		19703.5	56022.6	819	20381
12707.2	87.8		14954.4	11789.9	68	7486
36791.5	100.0	5000.0	45074.0	29870.6	1120	18124
104870.4	800.0		72940.9	157571.1	1339	61767
20840.3		345.0	25654.3	20390.5	262	11853
45560.1	1370.3	2726.7	31076.9	81236.6	1316	18492
32289.7	840.0		17997.5	38483.7	416	12508
36663.2			29520.5	12338.6	163	16885
20663.0	129.0		25616.7	9596.9	1468	8855
9895.8	1279.0		4158.5	5618.1	50	1897
25043.7			27849.7	28697.9	445	7544
25725.3			9205.3	20963.3	96	5456
80049.4		3300.0	12039.7	40825.2	187	26807
25874.2	867.2	5570.0	13560.0	12403.6	204	7815
9247.2			12220.0	971.0	42	1189
28702.0	111.4		16849.0	26717.2	167	8782
20590.0	1585.0		6135.7	3151.7	357	2895
38195.4			8227.0	22203.9	249	4195
8898.0			3667.4	3238.6	36	2444
25956.4	520.0		56279.6	23807.8	301	13619

C-1-22 提供住宿的机构

地 区	在建项目数	#使用彩票公益金项目数	在建项目总投资	开工累计完成投资	本年计划投资	本年实际完成投资
全 国	**6933**	**3738**	**6962003.9**	**3589726.0**	**1953321.1**	**1887702.0**
中央级						
北 京	62		328556.6	236042.7	59618.4	51606.8
天 津	3		12193.7	12982.5	1060.0	3895.6
河 北	421	313	124736.4	76216.8	37863.1	42843.1
山 西	21	16	23447.0	12977.1	4696.0	5463.0
内蒙古	65	53	84677.3	63606.2	18361.0	27774.2
辽 宁	141	115	115355.7	83559.1	24890.5	35802.3
吉 林	17	10	43833.9	43108.5	29028.5	29907.5
黑龙江	10	10	47692.6	142647.4	12006.6	13406.6
上 海	3	2	32169.7	13563.5	14000.0	11572.5
江 苏	1431	115	2114024.6	779321.6	593994.8	500024.6
浙 江	59	42	364114.7	195499.7	81104.2	71951.7
安 徽	488	213	157592.7	126193.2	112108.1	111137.2
福 建	50	39	154587.5	62934.8	32218.7	34006.6
江 西	757	647	249587.5	134343.5	94921.1	93994.1
山 东	731	474	969440.0	369716.5	218211.0	205497.7
河 南	197	163	135068.7	96334.6	39513.4	44738.3
湖 北	299	143	412021.8	207568.4	88787.1	94123.4
湖 南	242	195	204840.8	131431.0	53713.8	64592.0
广 东	126	92	313536.0	96517.2	61762.3	50482.7
广 西	534	447	68401.7	45539.0	23917.6	24824.7
海 南	45	13	55439.6	45889.6	15911.2	16756.8
重 庆	236	160	95149.1	71071.3	40565.0	47564.1
四 川	53	28	75874.8	54601.9	31286.1	26419.6
贵 州	255	78	148678.5	102506.0	61212.7	79008.2
云 南	121	78	85061.1	82431.1	25554.5	29204.4
西 藏	41	8	44278.0	24208.0	27304.0	17975.0
陕 西	122	39	90985.8	46909.5	37075.3	32314.0
甘 肃	56	21	85676.6	41597.2	27226.0	22459.5
青 海	89	43	26116.1	24811.5	13499.6	17102.6
宁 夏	24	8	87555.9	57517.1	12351.6	10422.1
新 疆	234	173	211309.5	108079.5	59558.9	70831.1

基本建设投资情况

单位：万元、个、平方米、张

国家预算内投资	国内贷款	利用外资	福利彩票公益金	其他	本年完工项目数	未投入使用项目建设床位数
761862.9	**5577.2**	**5371.7**	**469028.2**	**645862.0**	**6043**	**336020**
51606.8					9	3427
1805.4				2090.2	4	200
12747.7			11885.2	18210.2	348	13395
2058.5			2704.5	700.0	4	2140
16899.9			7047.3	3827.0	49	6557
13296.5	2000.0		11308.9	9196.9	129	7923
4630.0			19008.0	6269.5	6	4400
500.0			12806.6	100.0	4	3536
8131.0			1992.5	1449.0		948
201314.8	1000.0		39179.8	258530.0	1454	45696
33136.6			29565.3	9249.8	31	15850
45996.6	46.2		17209.4	47885.0	488	19275
11088.3			14476.4	8441.9	32	7486
28839.0	100.0	5000.0	39815.5	20239.6	687	17354
60918.2	800.0		49717.8	94061.7	441	46959
14984.5		345.0	19243.8	10165.0	189	10399
28510.6		26.7	18957.9	46628.2	240	17331
19854.7	540.0		14844.6	29352.7	236	11670
21405.7			21658.7	7418.3	79	16791
10432.5	129.0		11637.2	2626.0	458	7123
9675.8			3201.0	3880.0	29	1673
17080.3			18905.3	11578.5	201	7517
14849.3			5618.3	5952.0	44	5100
56133.5			11249.5	11625.2	123	26556
14114.1	442.0		7151.8	7496.5	90	7398
6363.0			11458.0	154.0	25	1107
12267.0			13766.0	6281.0	52	7782
17429.1			3824.7	1205.7	305	2865
5893.0			5968.0	5241.6	84	3113
7179.7			1422.8	1819.6	12	2332
12720.8	520.0		43403.4	14186.9	190	12117

C-1-23 不提供住宿的机构

地 区	在建项目数	#使用彩票公益金项目数	在建项目总投资	开工累计完成投资	本年计划投资	本年实际完成投资
全 国	**10277**	**3573**	**1085558.5**	**696166.6**	**553592.6**	**491837.8**
中央级						
北 京	4		20101.3	7611.0	3360.3	3360.3
天 津						
河 北	2289	1062	19612.0	13587.3	8520.5	8750.7
山 西	11	3	1365.0	584.8	463.0	460.8
内蒙古	32	23	10445.3	9000.7	3838.0	4650.0
辽 宁	446	281	27584.7	22904.0	7909.7	9090.1
吉 林	5	1	4274.3	4585.2	2230.9	3665.2
黑龙江	2		3120.0	437.9	0.6	437.8
上 海	1	1	179.8	68.7		68.7
江 苏	2401	191	344903.3	213029.0	217866.0	145159.9
浙 江	15	3	18097.7	11085.1	5917.7	6897.2
安 徽	316	67	45226.6	21588.0	22173.3	18540.0
福 建	2		2046.5	1646.1	595.4	669.9
江 西	404	251	27362.0	21596.0	16156.0	14502.0
山 东	1279	680	183339.6	99876.2	85013.9	88357.9
河 南	62	24	37791.1	17973.7	9027.8	8033.9
湖 北	1067	49	49734.8	37726.1	26879.7	25751.5
湖 南	174	97	71123.9	34671.9	23798.9	18772.9
广 东	58	41	18780.0	17114.4	4828.0	6285.0
广 西	984	493	23764.4	18835.9	13846.9	15492.7
海 南	16	13	2697.4	2461.4	1612.4	1341.9
重 庆	180	115	9662.3	9795.3	6353.5	9605.3
四 川	22	4	25389.8	18634.0	14717.3	15396.7
贵 州	67	19	23444.2	13322.6	10021.9	9998.1
云 南	97	71	11529.8	9416.9	6141.4	5474.5
西 藏	21	3	2940.3	3724.3	2590.3	3251.3
陕 西	85	21	15477.5	9584.9	8056.0	7347.4
甘 肃	13	11	4059.0	3624.0	2533.0	2638.9
青 海	117	12	38538.5	36983.5	28249.0	35125.3
宁 夏	26	11	12333.2	10650.2	5260.2	3981.9
新 疆	81	26	30634.2	24047.5	15631.0	18730.0

基本建设投资情况

单位：万元、个、平方米、张

国家预算内投资	国内贷款	利用外资	福利彩票公益金	其他	本年完工项目数	未投入使用项目建设床位数
221892.4	**481.7**	**100.0**	**77154.3**	**192209.4**	**7949**	**42561**
3360.3					3	
4103.8			2463.5	2183.4	1482	9790
204.8			206.0	50.0	19	15
			3260.0	1390.0	30	450
3062.0			4320.8	1707.3	95	756
3525.2			50.0	90.0	9	
0.6			437.2		1	
26.2			42.5			
71637.5			7683.0	65839.4	2108	4491
3133.2			3639.0	125.0	11	13
12471.1			1705.3	4363.6	257	1106
623.9			46.0		30	
6617.5			4652.5	3232.0	303	770
24590.0			11644.1	52123.8	873	14808
2890.1			3826.3	1317.5	43	1454
11069.5	370.3		2878.7	11433.0	1038	1161
10234.0			1590.9	6948.0	154	838
3340.0			558.0	2387.0	45	94
4827.5			8522.9	2142.3	811	1732
220.0			857.5	264.4	9	224
2077.4			3936.2	3591.7	174	27
5163.9			2387.0	7845.8	23	356
6718.1			604.0	2676.0	51	251
1431.6		100.0	2335.5	1607.4	59	417
1937.3			542.0	772.0	14	82
3114.8	111.4		698.0	3423.2	84	1000
2435.9			185.0	18.0	26	30
20961.0			1360.0	12804.3	116	1082
1118.3			1644.6	1219.0	21	112
10996.9			5077.8	2655.3	60	1502

C-1-24 其他社会服务机构

地 区	在建项目数	#使用彩票公益金项目数	在建项目总投资	开工累计完成投资	本年计划投资
全 国	**787**	**482**	**1262610.4**	**713475.8**	**368724.8**
中央级					
北 京	2		35862.0	23346.1	2000.0
天 津	4	2	27944.0	12762.0	11230.0
河 北	15	12	9272.0	7226.0	1886.5
山 西	1		6830.0	6080.0	379.0
内蒙古	7	3	6700.0	5154.8	1000.0
辽 宁	194	187	35488.2	25952.2	6789.2
吉 林	4	3	3009.0	1459.0	2009.0
黑龙江					
上 海					
江 苏	94	10	280411.4	184607.6	105078.9
浙 江	11	5	53211.2	29622.0	19232.6
安 徽	4		26100.0	10660.0	5070.0
福 建	5	2	15784.0	6594.8	4031.0
江 西	133	125	12891.0	4911.0	4405.0
山 东	27	6	67356.6	35905.2	16881.6
河 南	14	5	17955.7	11013.2	3078.2
湖 北	29	10	97286.4	61138.4	37024.4
湖 南	16	5	14016.0	6149.0	6827.0
广 东	26	16	116087.2	48624.1	10431.2
广 西	19	15	25005.0	13782.0	7840.0
海 南	7	1	9009.7	2532.7	3749.7
重 庆	17	9	66321.9	22792.5	13930.0
四 川	9		17659.0	14953.8	8293.0
贵 州	20	2	126299.3	57946.1	47810.0
云 南	29	15	93029.9	27032.4	17971.6
西 藏	2		1267.9	1267.9	167.9
陕 西	11	3	53495.5	53740.5	12902.0
甘 肃	5	2	8280.0	6560.0	3715.0
青 海	23	18	9918.0	9756.0	6595.0
宁 夏	1	1	1300.0	1300.0	1300.0
新 疆	58	25	24819.5	20606.5	7097.0

基本建设投资情况

单位：万元、个、平方米

本年实际完成投资	国家预算内投资	国内贷款	利用外资	福利彩票公益金	其他	本年完工项目数
316152.1	**114450.6**	**7738.3**	**11470.0**	**45780.6**	**136712.6**	**445**
1969.1					1969.1	
8505.8	2505.8			2500.0	3500.0	7
2181.0	542.0	435.0		1184.0	20.0	6
469.0				90.0	379.0	2
1285.0	118.0			790.0	377.0	3
11786.2	284.8	3000.0		7643.0	858.4	36
1459.0	800.0			659.0		2
66862.9	36739.0	50.0		5943.0	24130.9	76
17698.8	15057.1			1305.0	1336.7	2
3070.0	3000.0				70.0	1
1002.8	695.0	87.8		32.0	188.0	5
4424.0	1280.0			547.0	2597.0	118
19176.6	10743.0			4220.0	4213.6	18
5592.9	2585.7			433.2	2574.0	9
31702.4	2400.0	1000.0	2700.0	5581.0	20021.4	13
3748.0	340.0	300.0		925.0	2183.0	9
9861.2	7430.7			1252.5	1178.0	14
7103.0	2268.0			1046.2	3788.8	16
2232.7		1279.0		100.0	853.7	3
14314.9	1330.0			3583.2	9401.7	8
8516.9	1804.9			1200.0	5512.0	6
40720.2	10710.0		3300.0	186.2	26524.0	5
13379.2	3491.0	1.5	5470.0	2025.0	2391.7	21
167.9	167.9					1
18302.0	1930.0			182.0	16190.0	3
3650.0	605.0	1585.0		130.0	1330.0	3
8545.0	5837.0			769.0	1939.0	23
1300.0	500.0			600.0	200.0	1
7125.6	1285.7			2854.3	2985.6	34

C-1-25 其他基本

地 区	在建项目数	#使用彩票公益金项目数	在建项目总投资	开工累计完成投资	本年计划投资
全 国	**1119**	**533**	**1050917.0**	**492327.9**	**243630.3**
中央级	7		47763.0	44661.7	2054.0
北 京					
天 津					
河 北	56	52	16163.0	5196.8	3723.8
山 西	9	4	5972.2	3367.6	2350.0
内蒙古	12	6	7248.0	4918.0	1268.0
辽 宁	10	1	7214.3	4900.2	2674.2
吉 林	11	1	5536.0	3836.0	2636.0
黑龙江	7	7	23199.5	1042.0	617.2
上 海	1		3502.0	2042.0	315.0
江 苏	176	18	451549.1	115966.1	74825.1
浙 江	8	5	47097.9	17496.0	7391.1
安 徽	114	36	15753.4	13620.4	11824.9
福 建	5	2	10110.0	6873.0	4860.0
江 西	13	11	21516.0	10516.0	4161.0
山 东	39	11	50754.2	35150.2	18600.2
河 南	24	7	43692.0	28402.0	6421.0
湖 北	38	12	29858.3	21228.3	7283.3
湖 南	16	14	7115.0	4832.2	2517.0
广 东	30	21	46819.6	28737.1	11893.4
广 西	228	162	19350.3	15395.8	10369.5
海 南	10		680.0	620.0	680.0
重 庆	64	41	17721.0	10383.0	10056.0
四 川	30	15	14461.8	13472.4	3985.8
贵 州	20		14640.4	7245.0	6487.8
云 南	62	56	26515.3	25697.2	11097.4
西 藏	3		1163.0	1213.0	829.0
陕 西	49	11	24914.1	18331.9	13564.1
甘 肃	20	18	27871.0	6947.9	2327.0
青 海	27	1	18024.4	18024.4	7549.4
宁 夏	1		1469.0	1059.0	100.0
新 疆	29	21	43243.2	21152.7	11169.1

建设投资情况

单位：万元、个、平方米

本年实际完成投资						本年完工项目数
	国家预算内投资	国内贷款	利用外资	福利彩票公益金	其他	
232000.7	**102832.9**	**423.7**		**55045.6**	**73698.5**	**891**
2505.0	2505.0					3
4139.8	1812.8			1127.0	1200.0	53
2855.6	300.0			1055.6	1500.0	3
2390.1				1870.1	520.0	9
3805.5	319.2			204.3	3282.0	9
3336.0	2180.0			520.0	636.0	2
1041.9	304.4			312.8	424.7	14
295.0	295.0					
58892.1	28525.0			9828.1	20539.0	199
2996.8	447.5			1646.1	903.2	1
7584.7	3091.9			788.8	3704.0	73
3860.0	300.0			400.0	3160.0	1
3916.0	55.0			59.0	3802.0	12
23150.2	8619.2			7359.0	7172.0	7
8865.0	380.0			2151.0	6334.0	21
10393.3	3580.0			3659.3	3154.0	25
2498.0	1861.0			637.0		17
11893.4	4486.8			6051.3	1355.3	25
8585.2	3135.0			4410.4	1039.8	183
620.0					620.0	9
10107.0	4556.0			1425.0	4126.0	62
5560.7	3907.2				1653.5	23
6487.8	6487.8					8
10216.9	6837.5	423.7		2047.7	908.0	34
1044.0	779.0			220.0	45.0	2
14416.2	11390.2			2203.0	823.0	28
2714.0	120.0			1996.0	598.0	23
7853.4	5504.4			130.0	2219.0	26
100.0	100.0					2
9877.1	953.0			4944.1	3980.0	17

C-2-1 社会

地区	单位数	工商登记	编办登记	民政登记	未登记	年末职工人数	#女性	受教育 大学专科人数
全国	**323061**	**18505**	**20054**	**41791**	**242711**	**2692329**	**1008579**	**380979**
中央级	2		2			277	156	59
北京	11791	612	670	196	10313	81114	38184	14433
天津	2417	232	107	577	1501	34045	14990	4714
河北	27931	758	745	2616	23812	110604	41696	9038
山西	4870	459	677	662	3072	57655	17240	6425
内蒙古	3183	176	453	335	2219	29077	12587	7677
辽宁	9321	1986	505	1163	5667	149867	60346	19475
吉林	2165	417	976	305	467	31449	10757	5080
黑龙江	3696	534	528	1431	1203	39319	15718	8154
上海	5063	1094	215	746	3008	130809	56611	7410
江苏	29660	2783	1131	4725	21021	413429	150888	48517
浙江	28704	2139	845	1583	24137	302166	110012	26673
安徽	8705	359	593	3512	4241	61882	25063	10304
福建	4627	293	388	373	3573	40347	15396	3680
江西	5892	328	1196	2996	1372	54070	19087	4034
山东	28302	1304	943	1374	24681	220193	78965	48697
河南	7433	935	691	3039	2768	99555	37131	14105
湖北	11880	638	1237	3204	6801	91885	37005	15114
湖南	12691	574	1512	2091	8514	80906	29338	14143
广东	47638	236	817	1375	45210	166724	61921	26499
广西	9579	141	433	252	8753	35506	12433	4723
海南	1874	19	46	332	1477	10079	3169	1284
重庆	7408	757	399	668	5584	92168	33023	10779
四川	10462	728	2053	1523	6158	100712	40123	20821
贵州	18953	81	558	1617	16697	90068	24123	23002
云南	2861	313	410	404	1734	59730	17524	4030
西藏	339	3	27	231	78	1268	704	215
陕西	4430	236	523	1504	2167	37164	15056	7749
甘肃	6162	84	451	1614	4013	24561	8078	4424
青海	556	35	38	89	394	4178	1728	667
宁夏	1019	72	100	528	319	8324	3822	899
新疆	3447	179	785	726	1757	33198	15705	8155

工作总表

单位:个、人、人次、时

程度	职业资格水平		年龄结构				志愿服务	
大学本科及以上人数	助理社会工作师人数	社会工作师人数	35岁及以下人数	36岁至45岁人数	46岁至55岁人数	56岁及以上人数	志愿者服务人次数	志愿服务时间
177956	**15471**	**8014**	**878935**	**1046306**	**595299**	**171789**	**10440283**	**26075272.8**
203			188	38	39	12		
11377	2357	874	22315	30555	22784	5460	5631336	15449792.8
2785	352	123	11757	11854	8386	2048	120365	243665.0
3655	236	140	36432	42879	24219	7074	29954	72934.0
2688	94	103	18357	22339	13871	3088	5187	13504.0
3902	155	124	8431	11750	7890	1006	11543	28967.0
13365	361	319	42474	60802	35559	11032	21045	47714.0
1930	417	148	9611	15351	5797	690	792	2292.0
3108	391	198	13249	17645	7192	1233	15431	54867.0
3520	564	451	38006	43528	36309	12966	37999	94289.0
22682	1840	797	120545	162857	102053	27974	350139	756666.0
12200	1508	881	90472	105082	70548	36064	435479	870954.8
3388	304	190	17877	27380	14088	2537	72327	183135.0
1866	379	252	12407	16966	8386	2588	123866	344873.0
1240	152	105	19166	21903	10588	2413	4107	12807.7
23385	560	417	85446	84096	40482	10169	2193456	4531490.6
6012	255	329	41778	38495	15855	3427	2156	6605.0
6638	539	107	29453	36032	22873	3527	10964	30444.5
5755	423	257	21127	38660	17996	3123	36791	112658.0
16903	2822	1011	56926	66724	33061	10013	140432	488022.4
2595	265	193	12095	10958	8899	3554	1561	4556.0
585	41	23	2742	4472	2146	719	25119	74791.0
5082	320	163	31085	36890	19472	4721	362355	972978.0
6179	407	318	37981	39366	18977	4388	52133	126162.0
5821	68	42	32555	36736	15933	4844	713386	1418080.0
2014	79	104	26753	21118	10412	1447	1117	2763.0
115	2	3	663	432	124	49	215	729.5
2582	221	111	13013	13780	8666	1705	19961	63849.5
2142	104	86	8767	8544	4644	2606	5578	15469.0
323	64	21	1650	1802	586	140	80	340.0
604	45	25	2552	4198	1310	264	1526	4510.0
3312	146	99	13062	13074	6154	908	13883	45363.0

C-2-1续表

地区	增加值合计	执行企业会计制度单位财务指标					执行行政	
		固定资产原价	营业收入	费用合计	营业利润	企业单位增加值	固定资产原价	上年结转和结余
全国	**11670945.9**	**17819100.0**	**52462724.8**	**5806151.7**	**1596719.6**	**6939189.0**	**9487436.7**	**940370.5**
中央级	5258.5						32204.0	17092.5
北京	588710.6	329926.7	670334.6	76018.6	-2176.6	118718.3	332466.5	263705.2
天津	201175.4	242310.3	806819.7	426530.4	12658.7	110511.3	119695.0	9035.4
河北	444469.2	534417.7	1353636.3	133723.9	14221.9	225613.6	509607.0	28576.9
山西	149512.3	351931.5	483618.5	37798.7	358.2	70843.1	184253.8	20736.0
内蒙古	99408.6	65368.6	71928.4	14170.3	2939.8	18450.4	167071.7	15560.1
辽宁	619967.7	726459.2	2302276.6	245949.0	76844.1	408190.2	347040.9	11939.8
吉林	115835.4	177446.3	392720.8	44546.9	6261.3	59549.4	184160.8	4525.8
黑龙江	111077.6	131045.3	195567.6	46882.2	9579.7	43564.1	223832.7	10340.4
上海	1012940.8	937039.2	2900094.6	236301.1	267759.5	843595.6	267134.0	14229.0
江苏	1693483.6	4029222.9	12992091.1	1425670.6	334609.5	1242855.5	974476.6	48718.0
浙江	2213205.2	5620728.9	17497212.9	1701999.7	598447.9	1916491.3	952619.4	56475.4
安徽	182952.7	149712.9	944158.1	61350.8	18353.1	57703.3	400022.7	10363.6
福建	137636.5	175031.0	365156.0	54250.5	3476.9	56901.7	109247.9	31025.1
江西	73338.0	105058.6	2087872.6	20323.9	2879.0	18618.3	206328.8	13778.6
山东	1114888.8	1072121.1	1748874.1	330187.0	133905.6	578684.7	484737.6	9320.6
河南	275062.7	288663.6	602878.2	109292.2	16273.4	128161.1	324877.7	15117.0
湖北	297901.9	217842.1	440263.6	111029.0	5197.4	93915.9	489478.7	6968.9
湖南	230159.7	270953.8	571013.8	77446.8	11832.1	83286.0	314522.4	4116.8
广东	345638.8	189439.1	314701.0	34979.8	5813.3	50651.9	648609.0	58231.3
广西	117870.4	63666.5	388343.1	12579.4	-1888.2	24917.3	205667.8	20078.0
海南	19090.4	16658.7	47908.9	4838.0	1103.7	4138.1	36616.6	54468.3
重庆	364302.7	582186.4	1770626.4	211955.8	34337.2	269192.3	191921.0	22556.3
四川	492644.5	453699.3	1611008.1	114215.6	18158.2	311958.5	708714.5	66150.6
贵州	117334.8	8408.6	20562.3	6505.1	1064.0	2905.3	151731.3	21761.8
云南	183744.1	637215.6	1173966.4	170379.7	-3506.9	85515.1	232111.1	24780.7
西藏	3764.9	3395.3	353.8	119.9	104.4	144.0	47273.9	3018.0
陕西	229999.6	163300.1	384998.8	50379.3	21664.4	62802.6	265957.5	33348.5
甘肃	60010.9	30623.7	8642.6	2698.7	134.8	2320.4	122650.2	7137.9
青海	13496.5	6087.3	10428.8	1313.8	100.0	1908.8	37160.7	984.4
宁夏	32292.9	61470.8	41334.8	13007.4	-699.5	14067.1	40999.2	9675.4
新疆	123769.9	177668.9	263332.3	29707.6	6912.7	33014.0	174245.7	26554.2

单位：万元

事业单位会计制度财务指标				执行民间非营利组织单位会计制度财务指标				
本年收入合计	本年支出合计	收支结余	行政事业单位增加值	固定资产原价	上年结余	本年收入合计	本年费用合计	社会组织增加值
8240070.7	**8066596.6**	**437944.9**	**4220165.6**	**3000559.9**	**53953.7**	**1187693.9**	**1117084.4**	**511591.3**
231847.9	194096.6		5258.5					
737711.0	842205.4	126013.3	454721.7	113480.1	262.8	34236.8	39539.3	15270.6
131268.1	129815.7	4015.2	81512.4	25991.4	649.0	195199.1	184514.2	9151.7
667354.3	663390.1	5529.1	210647.9	77935.4	1245.7	12421.0	14582.9	8207.7
129849.0	151216.0	10821.6	75780.9	21085.9	216.5	3660.3	6277.6	2888.3
147082.5	139697.9	25015.6	77705.0	27883.9	12.0	6554.1	7025.1	3253.2
453674.8	513368.9	5378.3	196755.4	70562.7	1153.5	85143.6	28203.0	15022.1
129975.7	122406.0	2195.9	55623.7	7605.2		3425.1	1719.0	662.3
108395.0	99268.3	60.3	65402.5	12016.2	2114.0	42298.1	9859.8	2111.0
321819.7	307616.8	11711.9	124739.0	103290.7	9907.1	104832.3	99873.8	44606.2
583126.3	602820.5	32256.7	397812.5	370400.0	6456.7	139358.6	128895.9	52815.6
604290.7	477527.0	8163.2	273733.6	228730.6	3327.6	61845.7	63269.6	22980.3
194933.5	185249.6	2771.8	111533.2	119836.4	205.3	26691.3	29458.2	13716.2
131079.2	124757.0	5326.1	77201.8	78612.6	1616.6	7321.2	7970.0	3533.0
84589.1	79612.8	-40.0	49600.5	51924.3	4.2	8777.1	10978.5	5119.2
553007.5	551694.4		333625.6	740758.1	434.8	296859.7	295856.9	202578.5
265351.4	246598.6	83570.4	139239.3	82673.1	702.4	9673.4	13310.4	7662.3
317375.3	319088.1	577.8	193434.2	44003.8	52.1	14519.2	16689.2	10551.8
264162.7	257108.1	4136.5	143399.8	18201.0	1121.1	12286.1	12157.5	3473.9
494286.5	461444.0	10485.5	274728.0	127581.0	14242.4	16984.7	34184.5	20258.9
194345.8	179203.3	4362.1	89877.6	34030.2	22.5	1477.4	4606.8	3075.5
37793.2	42768.1	2195.0	14798.0	3500.1	102.3	776.5	855.7	154.3
184332.2	177311.1	29067.6	85112.1	114127.4	81.9	25029.0	24024.5	9998.3
370772.6	347700.1	5184.5	172621.9	51524.6	1397.9	40057.4	16687.4	8064.1
151781.3	131736.8	3815.1	78883.4	171470.7	8434.0	25017.6	48318.7	35546.1
145220.8	140114.9	5322.3	96392.8	227109.6	19.5	689.8	2725.2	1836.2
9624.0	9922.8		3620.9	769.6		10.0		
248989.7	247226.9	9901.1	165400.5	23155.5	45.6	3677.3	3581.1	1796.5
97995.6	92408.6	1232.5	55291.3	26243.0	78.2	1614.6	3411.7	2399.2
33671.3	25753.9	834.8	10564.9	13671.2		1212.9	1360.3	1022.8
37853.6	33190.8	21510.1	17168.8	4172.1		1306.2	2178.9	1057.0
176510.4	170277.5	16530.6	87977.4	8213.5	48.0	4737.8	4968.7	2778.5

C-2-2 提供住宿的社会

地 区	单位数	工商登记	编办登记	民政登记	年末职工人数	#女性
全 国	**45977**	**111**	**12959**	**17289**	**422870**	**224650**
中央级	1		1		150	108
北 京	600	1	376	196	14021	9019
天 津	408	1	55	239	7022	4746
河 北	1802	5	548	567	21358	11588
山 西	1019		343	457	9279	4301
内蒙古	785		309	230	7294	3627
辽 宁	1749	7	359	1007	20549	11405
吉 林	935		797	116	10411	3946
黑龙江	792		287	368	9578	4651
上 海	678	1	69	590	23607	17340
江 苏	2941	10	898	1387	33280	18643
浙 江	2240	18	635	683	20173	12009
安 徽	2649	5	314	1651	19134	8065
福 建	1235	2	262	187	8669	3698
江 西	2061		931	1004	12859	4847
山 东	2715	3	568	1124	33939	18091
河 南	3243		414	1787	24751	11705
湖 北	2477	1	924	1021	22360	12460
湖 南	3033	1	1165	523	18433	8377
广 东	1913	30	429	566	25909	16096
广 西	1601		237	144	9786	5916
海 南	260	7	31	90	1426	695
重 庆	1638	16	305	408	10420	4871
四 川	3655		1412	861	22147	10431
贵 州	1383		221	347	6274	2898
云 南	992	1	245	202	6047	3145
西 藏	278		15	206	764	469
陕 西	1090		299	517	8630	4395
甘 肃	680	1	151	398	5496	2034
青 海	219		28	42	1261	666
宁 夏	104		45	47	1320	744
新 疆	801	1	286	324	6523	3664

服务机构总表

单位：个、人、人次

			受教育程度		职业资格水平	
工商登记	编办登记	民政登记	大学专科人数	大学本科及以上人数	助理社会工作师人数	社会工作师人数
3560	**180321**	**165638**	**77792**	**44340**	**3510**	**3256**
	150		47	88		
42	7850	5859	2293	2309	150	92
15	1839	4512	1372	852	55	61
95	9976	7189	3286	1728	100	71
	4820	3047	1999	1083	21	67
	3703	2547	2268	918	45	71
50	7554	9848	3930	3358	98	155
	9455	743	1540	1011	59	68
	6059	2840	2044	1126	198	143
71	3794	19557	1620	1088	136	223
394	12779	16096	5745	3413	324	319
737	7912	6912	3104	1781	147	166
88	4758	10666	2235	950	117	94
31	3171	2023	1060	786	94	78
	6380	5828	1440	609	84	61
45	10342	14379	8116	5286	252	195
	6760	10316	4237	1867	104	188
150	11644	8468	4288	2097	141	67
22	10921	2215	4429	1947	97	112
1172	11578	9817	4262	2950	474	334
	5663	1966	2297	1352	129	138
390	503	254	194	154	11	20
210	3316	3637	1585	1064	152	67
	11714	4981	5317	2143	164	185
	2919	1271	1864	649	30	23
9	3017	1268	1336	842	37	61
	119	468	104	50	2	1
	4696	2921	1965	907	90	64
13	2124	2925	1167	640	75	50
	699	131	353	171	27	16
	876	388	234	336	36	19
26	3230	2566	2061	785	61	47

C-2-2续表1

地区	年龄结构				志愿
	35岁及以下人数	36岁至45岁人数	46岁至55岁人数	56岁及以上人数	志愿者服务人次数
全国	**114893**	**164868**	**114223**	**28886**	**543180**
中央级	115	20	11	4	
北京	3713	4901	4297	1110	22184
天津	1582	2368	2625	447	17675
河北	7500	8281	4702	875	7851
山西	2848	3899	2163	369	4200
内蒙古	1619	2660	2495	520	375
辽宁	4260	8212	6429	1648	6283
吉林	3214	4563	2314	320	216
黑龙江	2974	3914	2284	406	358
上海	4938	7666	7967	3036	10976
江苏	7829	11644	10652	3155	81048
浙江	4514	7097	6417	2145	76431
安徽	3961	7933	5872	1368	20906
福建	2141	3260	2437	831	18624
江西	2470	5833	3956	600	2807
山东	12240	13399	6978	1322	169591
河南	8085	9224	5894	1548	1502
湖北	5533	9657	5963	1207	6708
湖南	5125	8505	4273	530	20414
广东	6629	11095	6863	1322	15532
广西	3105	3501	2665	515	1083
海南	380	627	336	83	2242
重庆	1917	4031	3394	1078	22989
四川	6087	8465	5722	1873	10883
贵州	1914	2626	1391	343	8727
云南	1864	2522	1361	300	500
西藏	414	244	73	33	215
陕西	2838	3240	2086	466	6058
甘肃	1787	1624	911	1174	2453
青海	565	456	200	40	80
宁夏	479	504	265	72	1526
新疆	2253	2897	1227	146	2743

单位：张、人天、人、人次、时、%

服务						
志愿服务时间	年末床位数	工商登记	编制登记	民政登记	年末在院（站）人天数	年末床位利用率
1420336.3	**5266653**	**28911**	**1527140**	**1877175**	**858661547**	**44.67**
	150		150		47998	87.67
59072.3	134205	400	75533	47489	26416205	53.93
29715.0	57024		10161	36274	7908238	38.00
24564.0	414651	809	80897	81248	44097425	29.14
11046.0	75897		22003	35869	11106381	40.09
1190.0	89434		29982	33044	16169198	49.53
9730.0	197517	1036	65472	92559	36859187	51.13
510.0	92696		77547	9551	11647686	34.43
1081.0	117257		49993	48945	22013495	51.43
35903.0	121040	70	16522	96611	23905459	54.11
214997.0	504647	2320	155426	193261	71127756	38.62
159197.0	307657	6946	86422	95684	41582319	37.03
52656.0	297435	1149	33516	170938	58654233	54.03
53027.0	102120	215	23468	19724	10140318	27.20
9513.0	174098		76512	85874	33926572	53.39
442400.6	488307	388	92418	162247	90178607	50.60
4656.0	316787		40732	170292	59049752	51.07
18796.5	252349	3200	105628	102006	43718549	47.46
68339.0	189765		79593	31371	38636287	55.78
47664.4	196913	5297	56924	63796	27131234	37.75
3020.0	132205		19972	11703	14058576	29.13
6400.0	15324	5014	2438	4507	1363584	24.38
62170.0	147754	1908	31810	44263	28604575	53.04
33384.0	397668		160031	92690	78140707	53.83
21875.0	84522		17659	17689	11111707	36.02
1365.0	74412	99	25196	19574	12945578	47.66
729.5	10494		1600	6154	1836435	47.94
17881.0	105853		36137	48555	18908608	48.94
7340.0	80148		16121	24039	5020486	17.16
340.0	16688		4439	4124	1615250	26.52
4510.0	12115		4956	5520	1981465	44.81
17264.0	59521	60	27882	21574	8757677	40.31

C-2-2续表2

地区	增加值合计	执行企业会计制度单位财务指标					执行行政	
		固定资产原价	营业收入	费用合计	营业利润	企业单位增加值	固定资产原价	上年结转和结余
全国	**3327309.6**	**126358.1**	**23041.7**	**12736.7**	**3081.4**	**14355.7**	**6447693.5**	**396073.4**
中央级	1546.6						1.0	79.5
北京	338138.3	14293.7	4524.4	732.0	266.5	3255.8	164462.6	41842.3
天津	77007.3						63256.2	6939.8
河北	178522.2	5941.0	384.2	342.3		32.8	397886.3	22384.5
山西	68503.3						149092.4	18512.1
内蒙古	56239.3						117457.3	8532.3
辽宁	170644.3	290.0	730.0		135.0	190.0	273638.0	10224.2
吉林	47614.7	300.0					148162.2	799.6
黑龙江	58637.3	297.0	5.0	4.0	2082.0	2083.0	194494.1	5588.0
上海	121361.6	110.0	165.0	1540.0			141249.4	9657.8
江苏	308391.3	24361.2	2940.6	258.4	33.1	1179.5	632589.3	27839.7
浙江	126570.5	30651.5	5832.0	3554.4	433.6	3254.6	418655.7	19178.1
安徽	87510.6	4137.6	530.4	310.7	-23.3	68.9	283344.7	5483.0
福建	69769.3	3861.1	1191.6	1024.2		151.1	82280.4	10069.0
江西	43741.7	18.0	7.0	7.0			177793.6	11283.4
山东	353825.7	3106.0	353.2	182.2	18.0	186.0	362893.2	6261.8
河南	123447.2	43.0					231209.0	10458.4
湖北	154430.5	7252.0	327.0	503.0		265.0	330171.8	2944.7
湖南	118503.8	461.2	162.0	5.6		40.8	251278.2	2727.0
广东	205167.5	8509.5	5165.1	1208.6	201.0	3122.1	482068.5	46047.2
广西	67095.3	1.6					133112.1	19605.7
海南	9014.3	810.0	416.0	90.0		188.0	22585.7	7248.2
重庆	70099.7	9949.8	233.0	183.2		98.8	128001.7	2039.7
四川	136887.6	7086.0		67.0	4.0	118.4	536942.9	26709.0
贵州	44202.4			2560.3			83277.8	11244.0
云南	50230.9	3461.0		10.0		5.4	156807.7	13372.7
西藏	2096.3						33515.3	2188.0
陕西	122846.9	406.1	75.2	153.1	-68.5	102.4	187751.1	18529.4
甘肃	45398.0	111.0		0.7		11.0	87828.6	6898.2
青海	9587.7						14726.9	707.3
宁夏	15286.8						30793.2	6375.8
新疆	44990.8	899.8				2.1	130366.6	14303.0

单位：万元

事业单位会计制度财务指标				执行民间非营利组织单位会计制度财务指标				
本年收入合计	本年支出合计	收支结余	行政事业单位增加值	固定资产原价	上年结余	本年收入合计	本年费用合计	社会组织增加值
4674392.5	**4668540.9**	**219819.1**	**3091738.3**	**1862852.3**	**40179.0**	**700764.3**	**632303.3**	**221215.6**
3847.9	3296.6		1546.6					
454339.9	458078.5	28663.6	319612.9	113460.1	258.8	34236.8	39538.3	15269.6
85239.5	85152.7	3162.0	70282.9	22878.0	486.0	190781.7	180144.0	6724.4
222505.1	221341.7	3339.1	176103.0	43713.2	385.0	6402.5	6404.8	2386.4
102273.4	125980.7	8931.7	67449.5	15901.6	195.5	979.6	1668.8	1053.8
84451.0	83821.1	10714.8	53390.2	24713.9	12.0	5790.3	6148.2	2849.1
301502.2	374151.0	2593.0	159212.8	65315.2	1090.9	77392.2	19650.3	11241.5
84909.7	83721.0	1096.0	47379.0	6803.0		913.3	569.5	235.7
90438.8	81832.4	51.0	54901.8	9384.0	1114.0	727.7	9219.5	1652.5
159640.4	153208.2	9183.4	81721.1	96705.8	9740.2	93887.0	91227.9	39640.5
404355.6	390391.4	9714.5	291244.1	195899.0	6415.3	38215.9	37733.8	15967.7
215390.8	188710.8	5449.8	113906.7	105881.6	3110.3	28898.7	27660.3	9409.2
114461.3	108461.8	1052.9	78312.1	85466.7	25.3	16572.4	19039.3	9129.6
100633.2	98078.7	3102.3	68184.2	67963.6	1588.1	3468.5	2812.6	1434.0
60670.5	57915.8	3.7	41964.0	40678.6	2.2	2837.0	3613.6	1777.7
397816.8	396746.8		293346.2	492955.3	2.3	99532.9	99462.9	60293.5
161402.2	157575.4	79742.2	117594.0	75153.9	307.3	8651.7	10812.4	5853.2
227191.2	226468.0	446.3	147692.2	35034.8	42.0	10967.4	10847.8	6473.3
186880.5	185694.0	2238.5	117380.6	11591.3	420.0	4222.9	3810.5	1082.4
302527.7	287433.4	7377.8	197212.2	58542.4	10014.3	9179.0	11205.7	4833.2
101746.8	100037.6	3326.0	66017.6	13250.5	22.5	952.4	2065.2	1077.7
11908.2	17247.7	1275.0	8731.9	3149.3	102.3	111.5	172.4	94.4
104460.7	102402.9	3533.1	63465.3	85416.0	78.9	17768.3	17233.0	6535.6
208507.6	199941.9	3021.8	131820.0	39510.0	1394.8	34581.7	11020.3	4949.2
72249.0	70919.5	3174.2	39776.9	76965.2	3260.9	2585.7	8179.5	4425.5
73128.2	69725.4	4257.4	49427.6	14896.2	16.5	685.3	1375.7	797.9
3020.9	3034.6		2096.3	710.0		10.0		
154981.3	156445.7	9341.3	120948.0	23155.5	45.6	3677.3	3581.1	1796.5
76039.2	75373.5	1172.4	45089.8	18240.3		357.2	419.2	297.2
13309.5	12684.6	582.7	8626.8	9466.2		1109.9	1190.9	960.9
20564.4	19426.6	5345.5	14959.5	3111.6		628.5	680.3	327.3
73999.0	73240.9	7927.1	42342.6	6939.5	48.0	4639.0	4815.5	2646.1

C-2-3 老年人与残疾人

地区	单位数	工商登记	编办登记	民政登记	年末职工人数	#女性
全国	**42475**	**106**	**10245**	**17098**	**356071**	**190908**
中央级	1		1		150	108
北京	559	1	339	194	12268	7995
天津	390		38	239	6322	4430
河北	1639	5	475	523	19216	10575
山西	903		243	455	7379	3382
内蒙古	728		254	230	5937	3031
辽宁	1632	7	272	986	18179	10346
吉林	834		713	112	7539	2698
黑龙江	676		182	366	6760	3487
上海	647	1	43	585	22041	16386
江苏	2790	10	791	1386	29753	16654
浙江	2129	17	539	682	18864	11351
安徽	2506	5	195	1646	16527	6682
福建	1124	2	179	186	6969	2832
江西	1934		832	1004	11602	4349
山东	2602	3	469	1124	30914	16383
河南	3098		296	1783	21783	10286
湖北	2251	1	736	1019	17740	10008
湖南	2817		1005	521	14473	6393
广东	1762	29	306	549	21384	13823
广西	1513		161	141	7105	4289
海南	248	7	21	89	1271	634
重庆	1573	16	247	408	9233	4253
四川	3336		1204	824	15946	7170
贵州	1247		102	347	4380	2049
云南	824	1	126	198	4363	2335
西藏	254		1	200	601	396
陕西	971		188	517	6868	3663
甘肃	592		84	392	4307	1538
青海	190		12	42	744	357
宁夏	78		26	46	878	446
新疆	627	1	165	304	4575	2579

服务机构总表

单位:个、人、人次、时、张、人天

			受教育程度		职业资格水平	
工商登记	编办登记	民政登记	大学专科人数	大学本科及以上人数	助理社会工作师人数	社会工作师人数
3449	**120258**	**161789**	**56320**	**28633**	**2491**	**2250**
	150		47	88		
42	6150	5815	1867	1697	115	77
	1154	4512	1198	641	46	45
95	8638	6594	2868	1267	93	56
	2980	3036	1452	696	11	51
	2355	2547	1704	524	37	44
50	5382	9771	3084	2639	76	129
	6711	727	1065	649	55	66
	3284	2812	1291	536	180	112
71	2394	19391	1133	707	87	153
394	9405	16088	4647	2375	251	223
720	6673	6897	2701	1370	118	127
88	2321	10626	1505	498	89	66
31	1552	2012	564	410	72	53
	5239	5828	1008	382	48	44
45	7405	14379	7054	3968	209	154
	3950	10286	3282	1173	74	113
150	7445	8262	2842	1048	99	29
	7489	2044	2955	1206	65	73
1128	7637	9329	2780	1986	265	214
	3033	1941	1322	589	87	95
390	367	240	159	118	8	17
210	2176	3637	1128	644	104	45
	7326	3444	3141	1068	75	102
	1098	1271	1094	307	17	17
9	1568	1246	813	386	17	26
	9	440	54	17		
	2965	2921	1394	631	73	45
	1065	2871	786	411	53	37
	229	131	100	73	17	13
	478	378	105	148	16	4
26	1630	2313	1177	381	34	20

C-2-3续表1

地 区	年龄结构				志愿
	35岁及以下人数	36岁至45岁人数	46岁至55岁人数	56岁及以上人数	志愿者服务人次数
全 国	**91780**	**141427**	**98486**	**24378**	**492469**
中央级	115	20	11	4	
北 京	3002	4325	3928	1013	21749
天 津	1337	2209	2411	365	15670
河 北	6854	7520	4116	726	6934
山 西	2190	3168	1724	297	3887
内蒙古	1194	2289	2032	422	100
辽 宁	3656	7339	5671	1513	6268
吉 林	2478	3285	1564	212	86
黑龙江	1972	3042	1620	126	311
上 海	4297	7350	7562	2832	9894
江 苏	6734	10525	9649	2845	73939
浙 江	4072	6625	6108	2059	66052
安 徽	3203	6956	5169	1199	18958
福 建	1501	2721	1999	748	18559
江 西	2116	5317	3645	524	2273
山 东	11005	12419	6294	1196	153388
河 南	6958	8155	5240	1430	1482
湖 北	3951	7987	4962	840	3838
湖 南	3766	6725	3601	381	17844
广 东	4890	9521	5924	1049	15377
广 西	1970	2697	2061	377	1061
海 南	336	573	286	76	2242
重 庆	1441	3672	3100	1020	20901
四 川	4004	6484	4355	1103	10642
贵 州	1362	1965	934	119	8414
云 南	1370	1808	962	223	364
西 藏	345	166	58	32	180
陕 西	2220	2613	1692	343	5744
甘 肃	1392	1160	638	1117	2383
青 海	314	283	128	19	63
宁 夏	289	326	205	58	1418
新 疆	1446	2182	837	110	2448

单位：张、人天、人、人次、时

服务						
志愿服务时间	年末床位数	光荣间床位	工商登记	编制登记	民政登记	年在院总人天数
1280416.3	**4295261**	**141351**	**28911**	**1281052**	**1854491**	**737107676**
	150			150		47998
57188.3	117090	685	400	68163	47259	10417268
25700.0	49516	663		7013	36274	5619483
20566.0	208782	11272	809	81328	74639	37057732
10558.0	67419	4677		18771	35729	9584789
650.0	76193	2237		25047	33044	14494975
9694.0	175482	5499	1036	54784	91879	26205382
290.0	74575	5260		64780	9344	9231977
907.0	104738	3783		39781	48790	19763042
31037.0	111780	78	70	11360	96416	20855402
192077.0	399449	6517	2320	143110	193243	62785113
135840.0	278418	4242	6946	78644	95594	39195637
48135.0	278191	6780	1149	22354	170528	55388269
52832.0	77282	2241	215	16230	19652	7310470
7383.0	164988	19494		70153	85874	32515145
401942.6	392457	11295	388	82669	162247	79826179
4596.0	298631	15065		28837	169532	54584649
9880.0	230007	10378	3200	93294	101516	38994072
57714.0	164064	9645		65823	30421	34565293
47346.4	154317	3416	5297	40582	62511	22277307
2962.0	53548	2061		13216	11619	10023435
6400.0	14715	205	5014	2826	4407	1104373
56705.0	124270	1257	1908	27927	44263	25493470
32676.0	351798	6498		136458	85115	71319241
21186.0	62044	2151		8124	17689	8969969
843.0	61130	405	99	18242	19350	9752680
620.0	7935			75	5406	1390466
16747.0	93165	2291		28472	48555	15890496
7090.0	36646	1223		10748	23547	3277472
260.0	13243	649		2251	4124	1207216
4246.0	8907	254		3231	5240	1566667
16345.0	44331	1130	60	16609	20684	6392009

C−2−3续表2

地 区	年末在院人数	#女性	工商登记	编办登记	民政登记	在院人员按性质分			
						优抚对象	"三无"对象	自费人员	老人
全 国	**2980938**	**657915**	**16772**	**973449**	**1240591**	**128077**	**1987807**	**705956**	**2685694**
中央级	149	78		149				149	57
北 京	68855	14675	63	52697	17818	176	3181	28789	29662
天 津	29017	13096		7489	19736	489	2150	21969	23440
河 北	132581	16817	636	59054	41987	5888	92887	27718	121900
山 西	41376	3209		14847	19629	2557	31578	5271	33506
内蒙古	48605	6762		18390	17358	2936	27807	16887	45098
辽 宁	120998	22606	483	46916	56856	4900	43596	48885	92592
吉 林	47044	8068		42979	3898	8700	30166	5368	39453
黑龙江	87064	13717		34216	38351	4729	67881	11597	79835
上 海	74625	43838	31	11163	63166	482	2887	67232	67875
江 苏	240975	62512	1474	102052	103343	7572	133059	90110	223752
浙 江	140801	48354	4189	41147	45628	1804	39617	96676	134388
安 徽	199687	32116	128	13105	128328	4065	175736	17245	192005
福 建	30243	6044	201	8694	8963	1487	11555	14502	25666
江 西	154991	38514		64859	81587	11219	132583	9410	143169
山 东	267951	67935	65	65078	101904	11545	177967	63201	249416
河 南	247913	41737		21401	143194	18461	206884	16610	231655
湖 北	178634	48126	20	72506	83089	9665	138017	26073	163820
湖 南	139294	29805		55544	26868	10241	117231	7492	125588
广 东	82045	31803	3780	28420	34185	2637	34639	39919	67995
广 西	37763	8444		9709	7829	1329	23733	11793	34342
海 南	8045	2407	4164	1863	1144	1220	3607	2810	6849
重 庆	87856	17103	1471	20675	28316	899	61599	23815	82645
四 川	296923	40516		115379	71517	9683	262881	20187	282609
贵 州	32951	4999		4453	8804	794	28507	2997	29450
云 南	45777	8610	15	13404	14528	561	37549	3171	39606
西 藏	5800	1297		71	3923	48	5742	10	5370
陕 西	68518	10661		23921	36601	1762	53998	8675	58849
甘 肃	20645	4105		7406	12622	1038	14194	3037	15628
青 海	5825	1128		1083	1611	216	4157	1268	4856
宁 夏	6532	1110		2755	3539	139	5074	707	5315
新 疆	31455	7723	52	12024	14269	835	17345	12383	29303

单位：张、人天、人、人次、平方米

在院人员按年龄分		在院人员按类型分			军休所年末在所人数	康复和医疗门诊人次数	家庭寄养儿童数量	机构建筑面积
青壮年	少年儿童	自理（完全自理）	介助（半自理）	介护（不能自理）				
84752	**51394**	**2083887**	**493123**	**244830**	**199439**	**7504575**	**7949**	**84659058**
28	64	32	106	11		4135		
2196	288	13031	7967	11148	39290	219709	16	1934715
1148	20	13181	5449	5978	4518	135650		803598
2635	1958	97338	20031	9124	11300	246682	247	3865983
2751	3149	30225	5829	3352	4158	51550	1838	1688268
1694	838	35416	9188	3026	1882	13779	53	1424724
4129	660	68757	17594	11030	23736	124388	121	2809058
3875	906	29843	9476	4915	2883	82342	89	991970
3900	472	69191	10494	4522	2944	91693		923555
2640	86	22224	19131	29246	4585	105227		2621260
4480	2509	156051	47102	27588	12244	886262	425	7820546
2602	1107	96613	25082	16402	3089	812171	344	4667365
3220	1821	164021	26430	6595	3459	122024	397	6256435
682	1196	17636	6144	3764	3790	104487	323	1487339
4524	5519	121014	27128	5070	1818	41416	947	3644925
2727	570	215061	27716	9936	21060	507159		9512571
6044	4256	193717	35989	12249	6402	266456	254	5590835
7470	2465	125403	34143	14209	8521	581171	135	5205052
3695	5681	102755	25448	6761	5053	251655	568	3780941
2659	6541	35852	18073	23270	7343	1720412	797	3455226
650	1863	24632	6151	6072	1914	152126	539	1328497
470	318	6645	392	600	1252	1030	14	244361
3330	338	73876	8424	4013	3501	166882	99	3117726
8028	2114	232059	48926	11766	4894	569259	107	5388204
915	1933	18666	12588	1044	959	59205	88	1226056
898	777	28609	9571	3101	4858	28168	37	1071606
47	383	5024	518	258		105		212506
4469	1117	46291	14237	3907	8403	69621	132	1433315
722	1919	12635	3859	1775	3316	47888	33	665440
754	31	3389	1877	375	450	3808		206747
532	73	3659	1707	554	612	7644		288155
838	422	21041	6353	3169	1205	30471	346	992082

C-2-3续表3

地区	增加值合计	执行企业会计制度单位财务指标					执行行政	
		固定资产原价	营业收入	费用合计	营业利润	企业单位增加值	固定资产原价	上年结转和结余
全国	**2732849.1**	**124208.7**	**19662.7**	**9016.9**	**1150.1**	**11012.5**	**5276567.7**	**263256.3**
中央级	1546.6						1.0	79.5
北京	315865.5	14293.7	4524.4	732.0	266.5	3255.8	136321.0	35664.7
天津	65591.0						54001.6	4282.5
河北	168847.2	5941.0	384.2	342.3		63.6	354238.3	19906.0
山西	54486.0						124556.4	14208.5
内蒙古	43045.4						96834.1	4669.2
辽宁	151805.5	290.0	730.0		135.0	190.0	235034.1	6359.5
吉林	31639.4	300.0					112637.7	688.4
黑龙江	45461.7	297.0	5.0	4.0		1.0	148622.8	3553.2
上海	99266.1	110.0	165.0	1540.0			87049.3	2461.6
江苏	258244.8	24122.2	862.5	153.0	6.0	785.2	548859.5	12840.4
浙江	101175.4	30332.5	5391.7	3111.7	534.6	3291.0	374482.8	16529.9
安徽	72618.7	3948.5	488.0	245.0		46.0	243933.0	3371.0
福建	53520.1	3861.1	1191.6	1024.2		151.1	59249.3	6736.1
江西	37926.2	18.0	7.0	7.0			161224.8	9878.6
山东	319126.5	3106.0	353.2	182.2	18.0	186.0	294468.1	6066.9
河南	91243.5	43.0					188108.6	5455.7
湖北	121022.1	7252.0	327.0	503.0		265.0	263707.7	1045.9
湖南	88952.4	399.0					212911.1	1763.3
广东	156000.0	7475.5	4579.1	811.6	181.0	2353.8	383347.4	39124.0
广西	45700.9	1.6					96559.3	12801.4
海南	6751.2	810.0	416.0	90.0		188.0	18633.4	6332.7
重庆	55216.8	9949.8	233.0	183.2		98.8	106057.2	1596.6
四川	88647.6	7086.0		67.0	4.0	118.4	441155.4	12389.8
贵州	24476.7						58515.7	1136.9
云南	37295.1	3461.0		10.0		5.4	115479.6	8530.6
西藏	1173.7						23060.4	2132.0
陕西	110813.7	100.0	5.0	10.0	5.0	0.3	163369.9	10011.0
甘肃	38106.7	111.0		0.7		11.0	58765.8	2778.2
青海	7552.2						7418.1	707.3
宁夏	11495.0						19445.1	4291.5
新疆	28235.2	899.8				2.1	88519.2	5863.4

单位：万元

事业单位会计制度财务指标				执行民间非营利组织单位会计制度财务指标				
本年收入合计	本年支出合计	收支结余	行政事业单位增加值	固定资产原价	上年结余	本年收入合计	本年费用合计	社会组织增加值
3557328.7	**3562101.8**	**89569.1**	**2503060.0**	**1840472.5**	**38736.0**	**697586.0**	**625506.0**	**218776.6**
3847.9	3296.6		1546.6					
395772.4	400095.4	23720.4	297340.3	112099.9	258.8	34236.8	39538.1	15269.4
69712.9	66662.5	3118.7	58866.6	22878.0	486.0	190781.7	180144.0	6724.4
204859.5	204154.8	1448.5	166633.4	33857.2	392.0	5337.9	5508.1	2150.2
79403.6	80693.6	6697.4	53432.2	15901.6	195.5	979.6	1668.8	1053.8
60790.9	60851.9	6160.8	40196.3	24713.9	12.0	5790.3	6148.2	2849.1
264094.5	337187.4	2024.3	140394.3	65110.2	1048.9	77362.1	19619.9	11221.2
60353.2	60371.9	2.8	31403.8	6793.0		911.3	569.4	235.6
59572.7	56837.7	51.0	43808.2	9384.0	1114.0	727.7	9219.5	1652.5
118872.5	110200.9	3042.5	59625.6	96705.8	9740.2	93887.0	91227.9	39640.5
315816.8	309074.8	7648.1	241491.9	195899.0	6415.3	38215.9	37733.8	15967.7
168705.6	143243.6	2209.8	88532.2	105321.6	3095.3	28741.7	27513.3	9352.2
84228.7	80207.8	502.5	63443.1	85466.7	25.3	16572.4	19039.3	9129.6
67569.8	66961.2	1734.6	51935.0	67963.6	1588.1	3468.5	2812.6	1434.0
50081.9	47875.0		36148.5	40678.6	2.2	2837.0	3613.6	1777.7
334865.2	333600.3		258647.0	492955.3	2.3	99532.9	99462.9	60293.5
111483.8	108867.9	492.4	85391.0	75053.9	307.3	8591.7	10807.4	5852.5
155567.5	157566.6	99.3	114283.8	35034.8	42.0	10967.4	10847.8	6473.3
133242.2	132915.5	1389.7	87870.0	11591.3	420.0	4222.9	3810.5	1082.4
215221.2	205052.1	3845.4	148983.1	58337.7	10022.1	8727.5	10813.6	4663.1
54896.4	57184.1	1181.8	44642.5	12976.5	18.9	919.1	2025.4	1058.4
8116.3	13281.2	1401.2	6468.8	3149.3	102.3	111.5	172.4	94.4
69460.6	68797.7	1703.0	48582.4	85416.0	78.9	17768.3	17233.0	6535.6
129032.4	121996.6	1860.9	85511.7	29729.1	-2.4	33207.9	5737.7	3017.5
42814.6	40598.8	418.2	20054.2	76955.2	3260.9	2580.7	8176.5	4422.5
47442.2	45269.0	2818.7	36492.2	14877.2	16.5	684.3	1375.3	797.5
574.7	510.2		1173.7	710.0		10.0		
130750.8	131420.8	5337.3	109016.9	23155.5	45.6	3677.3	3581.1	1796.5
62055.5	63145.9	236.9	37798.5	18240.3		357.2	419.2	297.2
7506.2	7440.6	582.7	6591.3	9466.2		1109.9	1190.9	960.9
14593.2	13579.3	4024.5	11167.7	3111.6		628.5	680.3	327.3
36023.0	33160.1	5815.7	25587.0	6939.5	48.0	4639.0	4815.5	2646.1

C-2-4 城市养老

地　区	单位数	年末职工人数		受教育程度		职业资
			#女性	大学专科人数	大学本科及以上人数	助理社会工作师人数
全　国	**7077**	**109752**	**70387**	**16973**	**7344**	**712**
中央级						
北　京	148	4344	3064	403	209	10
天　津	213	4675	3595	736	363	29
河　北	345	5759	3813	919	142	11
山　西	99	1389	741	165	85	1
内蒙古	150	2165	1456	780	66	14
辽　宁	660	7513	4716	1361	1257	21
吉　林	81	508	341	181	92	5
黑龙江	148	1560	835	459	116	115
上　海	413	13985	10834	443	232	30
江　苏	1030	14539	8696	2631	977	96
浙　江	450	6022	3976	945	469	29
安　徽	227	3021	1831	394	122	15
福　建	171	2187	938	150	70	5
江　西	205	1842	621	128	43	1
山　东	749	10991	6642	2786	1197	94
河　南	310	3975	2611	671	311	37
湖　北	252	3470	2358	381	118	4
湖　南	80	973	568	226	105	2
广　东	254	6899	4691	890	381	62
广　西	147	2331	1434	536	232	20
海　南	17	554	222	42	79	3
重　庆	265	3407	1911	421	249	35
四　川	204	1509	762	258	64	6
贵　州	106	876	407	172	56	3
云　南	63	802	453	87	27	2
西　藏	7	26	13	9	5	
陕　西	83	1698	1116	277	118	40
甘　肃	51	787	475	198	50	14
青　海	7	51	31	16	9	3
宁　夏	6	92	64	6		
新　疆	136	1802	1172	302	100	5

服务机构

单位:个、人、人次、时

格水平	年龄结构				志愿服务	
社会工作师人数	35岁及以下人数	36岁至45岁人数	46岁至55岁人数	56岁及以上人数	志愿者服务人次数	志愿服务时间
603	**28053**	**42139**	**31231**	**8329**	**178761**	**421866.2**
5	878	1404	1622	440	9743	22550.3
17	1034	1628	1741	272	8530	15030.0
7	1990	2501	1092	176	2069	5947.0
7	628	598	136	27	2840	8222.0
3	303	889	816	157	70	560.0
71	1203	3334	2451	525	4841	7588.0
1	138	317	51	2	50	200.0
63	552	667	314	27	130	320.0
81	2656	4546	4925	1858		
62	3320	5260	4475	1484	36292	82939.0
23	1162	1802	2295	763	21680	38480.0
5	939	1151	635	296	11193	26893.0
1	613	982	410	182	1535	1705.0
	400	946	465	31	458	1930.0
31	4110	4287	2179	415	62849	153507.5
73	1180	1498	1005	292		
	661	1492	1165	152	1031	1599.0
2	341	411	207	14	1563	5107.0
38	1567	3022	1897	413	5580	18161.4
38	883	727	613	108	105	315.0
11	200	250	93	11		
13	637	1376	1092	302	1693	4020.0
9	492	470	377	170	1051	2461.0
2	291	369	174	42	2351	6053.0
1	308	334	122	38		
	13	9	3	1	8	24.0
28	646	604	392	56	1020	3054.0
9	435	230	104	18	213	600.0
2	23	21	7		10	40.0
	15	31	32	14	6	10.0
	435	983	341	43	1850	14550.0

C-2-4续表1

地区	年末床位数	#光荣间床位	年在院总人天数	年末在院人数	#女性	在院人员按性质分		
						优抚对象	“三无”对象	自费人员
全　国	**970711**	**7816**	**136133234**	**534546**	**200931**	**8565**	**102575**	**423406**
中央级								
北　京	29491	85	4462364	13117	6660	17	324	12776
天　津	32610	37	4391324	19568	11283	137	650	18781
河　北	56326	582	7512439	30168	5887	389	11727	18052
山　西	9996	485	738880	5288	786	190	1237	3861
内蒙古	25801	116	4073333	12939	3149	193	1004	11742
辽　宁	70387	617	11809064	42467	14725	527	3891	38049
吉　林	7248	192	649452	3048	1233	68	691	2289
黑龙江	18278	138	3157360	12515	3554	677	6469	5369
上　海	64143		13033565	44246	28930	41	535	43670
江　苏	154761	729	19426869	75215	24839	880	16363	57972
浙　江	79947	109	9814521	38112	15162	200	4669	33243
安　徽	30739	198	4771349	16496	5229	102	2088	14306
福　建	24466		2493869	9939	1879	188	1082	8669
江　西	8352	428	1468611	6223	1591	357	4128	1738
山　东	113384	1023	17568125	60643	23935	446	7909	52288
河　南	31185	803	4608117	18128	5395	827	5548	11753
湖　北	30516	341	3236901	17147	7958	265	4050	12832
湖　南	6941	256	1430656	4996	1884	192	3021	1783
广　东	38861	153	6057457	21619	11985	770	2953	17896
广　西	12368	98	1837297	8404	2954	104	567	7733
海　南	7929	11	185347	4599	1333	1081	819	2699
重　庆	34666	220	5406988	19686	6602		2303	17383
四　川	24030	349	2929235	17822	4613	215	11133	6474
贵　州	8748	131	777511	2843	972	81	732	2030
云　南	8007	35	942760	4796	621	82	2763	1951
西　藏	275		27270	174	51	7	167	
陕　西	14201	239	764576	8767	3442	253	1517	6997
甘　肃	7998	147	273519	3577	1234	233	1395	1949
青　海	2165		36868	176	84	7	55	114
宁　夏	1536	11	186241	539	169	6	373	160
新　疆	15356	283	2061366	11289	2792	30	2412	8847

单位：张、人天、人、人次、平方米

在院人员按年龄分			在院人员按类型分			康复和医疗门诊人次数	机构建筑面积
老人	青壮年	少年儿童	自理（完全自理）	介助（半自理）	介护（不能自理）		
523372	**8876**	**2298**	**314658**	**117148**	**102740**	**1438399**	**19816509**
12462	634	21	4190	3142	5785	54953	763655
18792	771	5	10376	3716	5476	99629	495782
29564	447	157	20786	5438	3944	18738	1099188
5207	5	76	3771	800	717	856	258829
12750	159	30	9396	2327	1216		401742
42000	458	9	27779	9005	5683	38641	1076211
3012	36		2012	902	134	1345	72948
12085	343	87	10044	1132	1339	22582	216427
43683	563		12926	10792	20528	27880	1427185
74200	855	160	40843	18669	15703	151145	3403492
37684	386	42	22920	8789	6403	107283	1443126
16355	57	84	9896	4470	2130	11914	478207
9758	135	46	4969	2770	2200	4871	546414
6014	50	159	4301	1619	303	2331	211174
60378	212	53	45806	9644	5193	190006	2894155
17697	353	78	10412	4968	2748	65427	730946
16326	755	66	9275	4754	3118	10370	580192
4354	578	64	3502	1194	300	14199	190288
20496	688	435	6458	4788	10373	425325	718039
8277	90	37	2818	2323	3263	797	181448
4224	375		4408	25	166		74330
19483	202	1	15742	2629	1315	35052	1176725
17415	161	246	12050	4465	1307	127098	506750
2701	75	67	1701	851	291	7539	105142
4739	26	31	3169	1080	547	1286	126339
174			134	35	5		7800
8596	158	13	5966	1519	1282	10077	213781
3189	78	310	1797	1161	619	1150	136859
175	1		154	16	6	240	37711
421	118		355	152	32	362	46873
11161	107	21	6702	3973	614	7303	194752

C–2–4续表2

地　区	增加值合计	执行企业会计制度单位财务指标					执行行政	
		固定资产原价	营业收入	费用合计	营业利润	企业单位增加值	固定资产原价	上年结转和结余
全　国	**264792.9**	**90756.2**	**16187.6**	**7962.2**	**1072.3**	**9238.1**	**903084.8**	**15790.3**
中央级								
北　京	18280.3	3779.9	1934.3	589.0	192.7	1739.0	16602.2	431.3
天　津	15015.0						26190.9	2306.9
河　北	10363.8	1358.0	384.2	342.3		52.6	114872.8	0.5
山　西	2098.8						19892.4	3270.5
内蒙古	5337.9						14124.6	241.4
辽　宁	17658.8	250.0	730.0		135.0	190.0	48538.8	498.3
吉　林	1727.4						18693.0	
黑龙江	3374.8	100.0	5.0	4.0		1.0	38466.3	40.2
上　海	26070.7	110.0	165.0	1540.0			24613.4	-83.5
江　苏	37623.3	17512.2	862.5	153.0	6.0	725.2	189577.3	894.3
浙　江	19245.1	30032.5	5391.7	3111.7	534.6	3291.0	52252.7	1746.3
安　徽	5782.0	3860.5	488.0	245.0		46.0	16404.3	-175.0
福　建	2520.1	1510.1	306.6	189.2		100.4	10885.8	13.2
江　西	2846.1	18.0	7.0	7.0			16923.8	
山　东	33390.3	3106.0	353.2	182.2	18.0	186.0	46612.5	
河　南	6580.1						23127.2	10.1
湖　北	5954.2	7242.0	327.0	503.0		265.0	8492.2	
湖　南	4457.7	50.0					22059.5	102.0
广　东	23339.1	6228.2	4579.1	811.6	181.0	2353.8	61606.3	4254.0
广　西	1021.8						4434.0	-42.8
海　南	239.0	810.0	416.0	90.0		188.0		
重　庆	6072.4	9949.8	233.0	183.2		98.8	16155.6	5.0
四　川	3273.1	1318.0					34449.8	1614.9
贵　州	1672.4						8250.0	
云　南	1437.1	3421.0		1.0		1.0	7137.8	133.0
西　藏	202.5						2620.0	
陕　西	2444.0	100.0	5.0	10.0	5.0	0.3	13525.6	29.8
甘　肃	881.9						12143.4	-10.3
青　海	288.0						2439.2	188.8
宁　夏	90.0						678.5	
新　疆	5505.5						31314.9	321.4

单位：万元

事业单位会计制度财务指标				执行民间非营利组织单位会计制度财务指标				
本年收入合计	本年支出合计	收支结余	行政事业单位增加值	固定资产原价	上年结余	本年收入合计	本年费用合计	社会组织增加值
185850.0	**182773.9**	**4092.7**	**132376.9**	**1014595.8**	**24239.7**	**260025.3**	**263454.1**	**123177.9**
9568.0	8987.9	74.1	6288.6	59276.5	-1319.6	21957.1	24434.2	10252.7
14282.1	13171.8	1339.4	9159.1	15097.9	486.0	25173.8	14631.8	5855.9
6570.8	6381.0		8987.6	17327.5	380.0	4090.7	3961.1	1323.6
5137.4	7691.9	548.4	1934.3	3573.6	27.0	225.0	249.5	164.5
4439.9	4156.3	520.0	2656.4	21570.9	12.0	4313.2	4669.1	2681.5
18162.3	18479.4	187.0	8058.9	47417.1	907.9	10572.4	14794.1	9409.9
1322.0	1322.0		1491.8	6793.0		911.3	569.4	235.6
3582.3	2708.4		3219.3	5334.0	1262.0	398.0	334.4	154.5
6629.4	3804.1	75.0	2531.8	39885.2	3214.1	55982.1	56518.4	23538.9
27666.2	26361.0	368.9	24102.7	138669.6	6377.8	29221.0	29542.1	12795.4
19522.5	17917.9	465.7	11616.6	50124.3	2198.5	14177.1	13392.2	4337.5
2515.2	2618.9	5.0	2448.3	27847.8	22.0	5285.1	6060.4	3287.7
1720.6	1857.5		1866.1	44151.0	1468.4	2031.6	1427.5	553.6
2058.4	2055.5		2342.5	24355.0		1161.6	1572.4	503.6
7198.2	7198.2		5495.3	292470.1	2.3	46875.0	46835.0	27709.0
4243.5	3985.3	84.8	3078.7	39930.5	187.3	4331.8	6699.9	3501.4
2518.3	2111.1		2027.5	18711.5	19.0	5842.3	5808.7	3661.7
5919.4	7105.8		4342.5	967.7		581.7	566.1	115.2
28591.7	31514.6	165.2	18116.9	37861.1	8741.0	4820.4	7122.8	2868.4
348.1	232.2	-3.4	453.3	8223.2	13.9	719.8	1438.0	568.5
350.0				1180.5	100.0	69.0	120.0	51.0
3155.0	3025.0	135.0	1966.8	56028.5	47.6	12324.0	12243.3	4006.8
3156.6	3432.4		2947.7	3358.5	19.0	854.4	1162.9	325.4
95.0	109.6		410.1	9185.1	33.5	619.8	1656.1	1262.3
974.5	777.7		1241.9	5580.2		196.6	385.9	194.2
1.5	103.0		202.5					
1830.4	1452.2		1367.4	15185.7	40.0	2454.7	2161.5	1076.3
854.8	779.3		794.6	16085.3		171.8	171.9	87.3
459.4	520.6	127.6	287.0	340.0		15.0	15.0	1.0
148.0	148.0		62.1	2080.0		102.0	134.9	27.9
2828.5	2765.3		2878.9	5984.5		4547.0	4775.5	2626.6

C-2-5 农村养老

地　区	单位数	年末职工人数		受教育程度		职业资
			#女性	大学专科人数	大学本科及以上人数	助理社会工作师人数
全　国	**30247**	**164144**	**75976**	**17673**	**4294**	**429**
中央级						
北　京	259	4770	3039	450	210	8
天　津	151	1168	597	304	117	5
河　北	966	8488	4247	647	160	14
山　西	616	3623	1466	487	54	
内蒙古	483	2139	828	325	63	2
辽　宁	841	7186	3882	683	313	3
吉　林	624	3484	1496	391	155	21
黑龙江	411	3104	1597	418	91	45
上　海	196	5891	3993	295	141	19
江　苏	1544	11209	5627	922	233	17
浙　江	1503	9590	5261	1051	202	43
安　徽	2113	11449	3750	638	85	46
福　建	767	3118	1036	40	21	13
江　西	1371	6283	2318	327	12	10
山　东	1589	15281	7436	2747	963	34
河　南	2499	14406	5896	1624	301	5
湖　北	1677	8956	4663	861	103	37
湖　南	2370	8566	3501	1084	192	11
广　东	1197	5147	2612	310	60	5
广　西	1156	1974	912	71	16	6
海　南	206	382	256	13	8	
重　庆	1225	4397	1587	217	77	9
四　川	2831	10947	4408	1728	347	18
贵　州	1041	2318	1073	490	61	2
云　南	656	2387	1279	394	80	1
西　藏	155	240	151	29	3	
陕　西	757	3011	1523	383	106	14
甘　肃	459	2479	536	302	38	11
青　海	167	431	209	41	12	8
宁　夏	52	325	197	21	2	3
新　疆	365	1395	600	380	68	19

服务机构

单位:个、人、人次、时

格水平	年龄结构				志愿服务	
社会工作师人数	35岁及以下人数	36岁至45岁人数	46岁至55岁人数	56岁及以上人数	志愿者服务人次数	志愿服务时间
383	**37912**	**67660**	**46953**	**11619**	**192635**	**521836.5**
9	1050	1801	1494	425	4212	11305.0
2	162	451	492	63	4100	6550.0
6	3053	3260	1877	298	3559	10791.0
3	844	1646	984	149	110	294.0
	432	834	705	168	30	90.0
4	1395	2780	2299	712	28	84.0
41	1143	1417	874	50		
23	874	1499	689	42	44	147.0
15	1162	2007	2028	694	6140	19775.0
22	2172	4004	3994	1039	22696	64930.0
49	1941	3818	2826	1005	28071	55598.0
21	1663	4987	3991	808	4185	11592.0
23	437	1083	1126	472		
2	809	2891	2217	366	652	1890.0
12	5434	6527	2873	447	73703	203972.0
16	4454	5471	3496	985	473	1520.0
	1760	4270	2550	376	505	1345.0
23	1662	4273	2434	197	10567	37378.0
21	819	2040	1943	345	320	940.0
3	145	894	825	110	709	1742.0
	46	189	101	46	132	400.0
10	401	1839	1566	591	16583	45153.0
36	2254	4758	3145	790	5719	17265.0
4	712	1105	453	48	4141	11160.0
9	728	1066	487	106	175	346.0
	106	67	36	31	77	267.5
3	897	1201	753	160	2346	7279.0
8	511	572	336	1060	1662	4956.0
8	170	179	78	4		
	86	137	77	25	1358	4074.0
10	590	594	204	7	338	993.0

C-2-5续表1

地区	年末床位数	#光荣间床位	年在院总人天数	年末在院人数	#女性	在院人员按性质分		
						优抚对象	“三无”对象	自费人员
全国	**2728290**	**80302**	**526109236**	**2012116**	**370337**	**73400**	**1749840**	**188876**
中央级								
北京	48259	50	4853459	16135	6578	25	2284	13826
天津	12698	5	960620	3975	1605	73	1110	2792
河北	124279	3538	25217509	83059	9190	630	74085	8344
山西	47087	2140	7151916	28381	1673	329	26984	1068
内蒙古	38325	908	7929388	27830	2731	1049	24124	2657
辽宁	72893	3187	11779165	46143	5593	2964	36053	7126
吉林	50573	4781	6980918	34245	4984	7355	25738	1152
黑龙江	72572	2694	14761653	62422	8092	3103	56908	2411
上海	37954	28	5911775	20784	11634	405	1621	18758
江苏	206771	4629	40014853	142926	32485	5832	110426	26668
浙江	168674	3024	25351547	85985	26722	1294	32288	52403
安徽	232934	3332	48609342	174790	25075	2722	170528	1540
福建	36789	809	3158239	12674	2429	521	7686	4467
江西	124559	13292	26226849	121517	30405	4923	113662	2932
山东	246176	10272	59561535	183754	41970	6940	167338	9476
河南	245049	11544	47083289	212744	33936	15061	193849	3834
湖北	157747	4039	30200281	131667	31892	5620	120325	5722
湖南	128739	3547	28088508	112957	21807	4372	106467	2118
广东	66431	762	7764515	29037	7522	944	22975	5118
广西	28274	371	5871396	20901	2541	200	19902	799
海南	5328	60	708164	2401	818	69	2317	15
重庆	78400	456	18199657	60525	7580	547	57286	2692
四川	293018	3045	63826278	256482	30001	6181	241893	8408
贵州	45030	1089	7119265	25964	2916	489	25255	220
云南	40061	230	7978517	30862	6730	355	29939	568
西藏	3562		618660	2515	615	11	2494	10
陕西	66778	600	13329821	49641	5846	352	47987	1302
甘肃	19262	884	2361185	11641	2183	607	10290	744
青海	8786	617	944681	4455	909	154	3384	917
宁夏	4614	134	1051229	3554	578	97	3311	146
新疆	16668	235	2495022	12150	3297	176	11331	643

单位：张、人天、人、人次、平方米

在院人员按年龄分			在院人员按类型分			康复和医疗门诊人次数	机构建筑面积
老人	青壮年	少年儿童	自理（完全自理）	介助（半自理）	介护（不能自理）		
1947456	**49654**	**15006**	**1613017**	**316005**	**83094**	**2480670**	**51765938**
15017	915	203	7890	3845	4400	107401	947006
3910	53	12	2226	1449	300	30756	259461
81240	1446	373	67505	12610	2944	103785	2060336
25541	2345	495	23750	4152	479	14684	1056395
26502	1127	201	21492	5338	1000		706974
43584	2400	159	35910	7107	3126	38977	1179353
31048	2691	506	22733	7481	4031	34497	720906
59254	2880	288	51969	8296	2157	20514	544046
19469	1229	86	8416	7104	5264	74837	1019967
140472	2014	440	110453	25704	6769	427148	3485546
85136	742	107	66817	13308	5860	478710	2566804
171363	2515	912	150787	20705	3298	72163	5259214
12455	141	78	10252	2062	360	2460	646936
117192	2517	1808	98153	20188	3176	16569	2533428
181988	1448	318	163260	16517	3977	183967	6014767
206442	4714	1588	176674	28811	7259	101052	4439013
125394	4844	1429	100241	23621	7805	321602	3557390
110191	1403	1363	90143	19977	2837	83831	2988802
28377	250	410	19788	6553	2696	48017	1447222
20820	51	30	18987	1791	123	4927	768998
2378	8	15	2104	232	65		122783
58087	2236	202	55025	4651	849	42827	1596295
248743	6550	1189	209102	39842	7538	145776	4098182
24688	422	854	14716	10848	400	47689	931879
29920	662	280	22366	6966	1530	24253	713539
2451	43	21	2172	202	141	105	100514
46600	2524	517	37120	10737	1784	12040	896094
10385	436	820	9221	1804	616	38938	415339
3988	467		2697	1407	351	286	145278
3334	175	45	2108	1212	234	776	137372
11487	406	257	8940	1485	1725	2083	406097

C-2-5续表2

地区	增加值合计	执行企业会计制度单位财务指标					执行行政	
		固定资产原价	营业收入	费用合计	营业利润	企业单位增加值	固定资产原价	上年结转和结余
全　国	**368338.1**	**33452.5**	**3475.1**	**1054.7**	**77.8**	**1774.4**	**2310690.3**	**14553.9**
中央级								
北　京	14828.0	10513.8	2590.1	143.0	73.8	1516.8	41202.1	1119.7
天　津	1779.7						7025.9	4.3
河　北	18685.1	4583.0				11.0	128940.1	134.0
山　西	5583.9						47969.9	167.0
内蒙古	5932.7						46982.8	19.5
辽　宁	11370.9	40.0					79285.3	819.5
吉　林	7043.9	300.0					62684.2	343.6
黑龙江	7310.9	197.0					57525.2	360.8
上　海	17107.8						2236.9	42.5
江　苏	39263.2	6610.0				60.0	201965.3	285.0
浙　江	20281.2	300.0					106651.2	3214.6
安　徽	24302.2	88.0					190340.1	468.4
福　建	4498.2	2351.0	885.0	835.0		50.7	20151.0	29.0
江　西	12016.6						85955.7	1753.5
山　东	43864.1						73298.5	9.0
河　南	20034.8	43.0					126665.9	79.6
湖　北	19982.1	10.0					123808.0	534.8
湖　南	16633.7	349.0					103960.5	18.2
广　东	10983.0	1247.3					148418.1	2111.9
广　西	3917.2	1.6					42176.5	513.6
海　南	984.5						9406.7	34.9
重　庆	8998.4						49077.2	4.5
四　川	28548.8	5768.0		67.0	4.0	118.4	293504.9	1773.9
贵　州	5014.3						26376.1	177.5
云　南	5242.2	40.0		9.0		4.4	65468.9	228.7
西　藏	256.1						6238.4	
陕　西	8260.1						105938.9	104.8
甘　肃	1869.9	111.0		0.7		11.0	23998.1	42.2
青　海	1055.9						2376.0	
宁　夏	979.7						11497.7	
新　疆	1708.7	899.8				2.1	19564.2	158.9

单位：万元

事业单位会计制度财务指标				执行民间非营利组织单位会计制度财务指标				
本年收入合计	本年支出合计	收支结余	行政事业单位增加值	固定资产原价	上年结余	本年收入合计	本年费用合计	社会组织增加值
419792.5	**496162.7**	**996.8**	**272648.6**	**785779.6**	**14017.2**	**434349.4**	**359065.8**	**93915.1**
9034.1	7948.3	110.1	8294.5	52823.4	1578.4	12279.7	15103.9	5016.7
802.0	828.7	1.3	911.2	7780.1		165607.9	165512.2	868.5
28897.7	28746.1		17856.5	16526.7		1237.2	1534.0	817.6
6590.1	6814.5		5200.2	9328.0	68.5	754.6	902.9	383.7
12514.0	12514.4	19.1	5765.1	3143.0		1477.1	1479.1	167.6
21814.7	96627.5	14.0	9559.6	17693.1	141.0	66789.7	4825.8	1811.3
10036.8	9921.8		7043.9					
8692.6	8664.3	51.0	5834.9	3900.0	-148.0	279.7	8857.1	1476.0
2389.2	2101.5	0.9	1006.2	56820.6	6526.1	37904.9	34709.5	16101.6
51331.1	58197.0	9.3	36086.1	54029.4	27.5	8864.9	8078.5	3117.1
28384.4	27785.3	528.2	15389.4	53370.3	861.8	14245.3	13836.8	4891.8
25756.3	26337.7		18460.3	57618.9	3.3	11287.3	12978.9	5841.9
4622.4	4594.0		3619.2	22714.1	118.2	1027.1	1284.1	828.3
15738.2	14404.6		10770.3	15723.6	2.2	1635.9	2004.7	1246.3
13402.8	13402.8		11279.6	200485.2		52657.9	52627.9	32584.5
24761.7	24665.8		17831.7	32824.0	50.0	4162.7	3955.1	2203.1
25746.6	24093.0	18.0	17172.5	14293.3		4800.1	4766.1	2809.6
25986.5	25511.1	150.0	15666.5	10623.6	420.0	3461.2	3244.4	967.2
12069.8	12356.7	20.3	9738.3	11572.2	1132.1	2506.5	2542.5	1244.7
2632.8	2767.0		3457.3	4603.3	5.0	199.3	557.4	459.9
942.2	749.9		947.1	1968.8	2.3	32.5	42.4	37.4
7969.0	7974.2	-3.7	6495.0	26650.5	31.3	5364.9	4920.3	2503.4
30544.0	30517.1	95.2	25828.4	23372.6		32253.5	4416.4	2602.0
16959.4	16745.1		1859.2	58678.3	3127.4	1940.4	6510.4	3155.1
3245.9	3501.6	8.2	4640.9	8917.0	16.5	487.7	977.2	596.9
1.5	11.0		256.1	572.0				
7063.7	6907.8	-25.1	7539.9	7969.8	5.6	1222.6	1419.6	720.2
19567.7	19248.4		1649.0	2155.0		185.4	247.3	209.9
14.0	14.0		122.0	7636.2		1064.9	1145.9	933.9
646.9	354.8		680.3	1031.6		526.5	545.4	299.4
1634.4	1856.7		1687.1	955.0	48.0	92.0	40.0	19.5

C-2-6 社会

地　区	单位数	年末职工人数	#女性	受教育程度		职业资
				大学专科人数	大学本科及以上人数	助理社会工作师人数
全　国	**1825**	**44645**	**26899**	**9975**	**6893**	**864**
中央级	1	150	108	47	88	
北　京	8	1159	817	343	328	18
天　津	3	125	66	40	37	5
河　北	41	968	516	290	159	17
山　西	21	542	323	167	86	1
内蒙古	43	904	460	326	206	17
辽　宁	50	1845	1003	445	494	33
吉　林	51	1739	327	125	202	8
黑龙江	31	1305	745	215	161	13
上　海	23	1902	1430	298	209	26
江　苏	66	2494	1589	592	646	111
浙　江	91	2356	1609	438	305	43
安　徽	59	1160	735	233	107	16
福　建	73	847	465	171	105	34
江　西	131	1858	787	307	160	12
山　东	27	779	483	284	240	49
河　南	71	1245	732	321	157	19
湖　北	124	3068	1888	813	321	42
湖　南	88	2523	1208	843	433	35
广　东	163	7785	5695	1108	1101	159
广　西	98	2195	1620	510	227	53
海　南	7	128	74	41	9	4
重　庆	35	935	531	239	155	52
四　川	130	1884	1104	485	252	31
贵　州	57	738	355	239	103	8
云　南	48	621	371	142	130	7
西　藏	92	335	232	16	9	
陕　西	36	909	452	287	118	11
甘　肃	53	598	323	174	101	13
青　海	12	200	91	23	21	6
宁　夏	11	392	156	68	103	12
新　疆	81	956	604	345	120	9

福利院

单位：个、人、人次、时

格水平	年龄结构				志愿服务	
社会工作师人数	35岁及以下人数	36岁至45岁人数	46岁至55岁人数	56岁及以上人数	志愿者服务人次数	志愿服务时间
694	**13776**	**17812**	**10886**	**2171**	**86563**	**258813.5**
	115	20	11	4		
10	467	363	274	55	7761	23283.0
2	55	33	30	7		
18	322	329	258	59	800	2300.0
11	154	241	130	17	239	717.0
34	312	295	253	44		
34	516	734	493	102	240	720.0
8	539	841	325	34	36	90.0
12	299	592	383	31	130	390.0
38	379	731	524	268	3754	11262.0
81	820	756	749	169	14092	41946.0
50	512	787	802	255	10621	31863.0
24	411	447	266	36	2630	7872.0
17	217	348	243	39	17019	51057.0
5	528	817	493	20	382	1146.0
31	241	264	217	57	5095	15379.0
18	538	371	263	73	886	2658.0
19	919	1298	669	182	1860	5580.0
31	928	1043	470	82	1291	3352.0
108	2038	3795	1725	227	9332	27993.0
45	791	824	458	122	141	513.0
	24	54	45	5	2000	6000.0
19	241	283	324	87	1803	5267.0
36	607	723	485	69	3320	9946.0
7	232	313	181	12	642	1926.0
7	203	227	164	27	149	447.0
	226	90	19		95	328.5
7	315	343	223	28	1455	4365.0
11	239	237	108	14	488	1434.0
2	99	66	27	8	38	155.0
4	172	126	82	12	54	162.0
5	317	421	192	26	210	662.0

C−2−6续表1

地区	年末床位数	#光荣间床位	年在院总人天数	年末在院人数	#女性	在院人员按性质分		
						优抚对象	“三无”对象	自费人员
全　国	**346054**	**13944**	**57722689**	**211014**	**75079**	**7194**	**118586**	**85234**
中央级	150		47998	149	78			149
北　京	3388		1000100	2733	1412	1	564	2168
天　津	700		150200	522	100		350	172
河　北	8303	1910	1673460	5329	866	39	4949	341
山　西	4376		1036882	3273	695	11	3093	169
内蒙古	8548	329	2007565	5398	807	334	2668	2396
辽　宁	10878	245	2094647	7290	2091	246	3570	3474
吉　林	11217	88	1309229	5326	1396	410	3270	1646
黑龙江	9358	279	1536936	7922	1921	335	4064	3523
上　海	7028		1900563	5556	3274	21	731	4804
江　苏	26724	468	3044008	11892	5062	293	6174	5425
浙　江	25748	596	3748443	13218	6185	92	2607	10519
安　徽	7310	379	1488253	4244	1666	128	2764	1352
福　建	11600	431	1292720	3846	1542	132	2581	1133
江　西	16657	1159	2521224	12927	3135	373	8865	3689
山　东	8426		1244906	3969	1477	102	2695	1172
河　南	9662	155	1951484	6687	2028	374	5497	816
湖　北	28253	1793	4205253	19041	6966	537	11936	6568
湖　南	14601	654	3236732	10867	4888	1188	6656	3023
广　东	41941	1390	7913497	24974	11852	296	8391	16287
广　西	9136	547	1924651	6317	2837	89	3225	3003
海　南	768		172061	525	229		447	78
重　庆	8579	204	1737407	5564	2798	33	1963	3568
四　川	25631	1753	3953759	15137	5099	1051	9122	4964
贵　州	5888	497	706485	2520	916	41	2044	435
云　南	8767	30	802705	5543	1259	64	4827	652
西　藏	4098		744536	3111	631	30	3081	
陕　西	7062	546	1547985	5070	1295	443	4361	266
甘　肃	6698	53	624722	2993	686	153	2496	344
青　海	2212	31	225118	1009	135	54	718	237
宁　夏	2451	94	320765	1805	362	21	1386	398
新　疆	9896	313	1558395	6257	1391	303	3491	2463

单位：张、人天、人、人次、平方米

在院人员按年龄分			在院人员按类型分			康复和医疗门诊人次数	家庭寄养儿童数量	机构建筑面积
老人	青壮年	少年儿童	自理（完全自理）	介助（半自理）	介护（不能自理）			
155006	**22949**	**33059**	**108193**	**48934**	**53887**	**2200547**	**7949**	**8981052**
57	28	64	32	106	11	4135		
2024	645	64	872	919	942	42214	16	182004
241	278	3	175	176	171	2178		15384
3661	340	1328	3406	636	1287	9988	247	267389
381	322	2570	690	501	2082	1675	1838	104832
4401	397	600	3408	1259	731	13360	53	224939
5634	1191	465	4108	1180	2002	18755	121	392171
3863	1063	400	3949	875	502	36254	89	98570
7189	636	97	6014	965	943	25318		128234
4709	847		882	1235	3439	2510		170552
8407	1587	1898	4218	2657	5017	118532	425	842252
10984	1276	958	6397	2699	4122	86510	344	603755
2909	511	824	2286	841	1117	9075	397	385213
2377	400	1069	1669	1077	1100	93153	323	193709
8439	1297	3191	8489	3133	1305	2220	947	501419
2838	932	199	2194	1137	638	50610		275820
3318	811	2558	3009	1722	1956	33912	254	209598
16504	1650	887	11483	4667	2891	90040	135	671510
5144	1638	4085	4492	3108	3267	88385	568	280008
17771	1511	5692	8900	6460	9614	1183369	797	929304
4018	503	1796	1991	1811	2515	103874	539	289330
150	87	288	83	98	344	95	14	32092
4651	781	132	2773	1062	1729	65199	99	303013
13454	1058	625	8684	3997	2456	75902	107	678561
1324	234	962	1552	653	315	678	88	137341
4867	210	466	3062	1487	994	2555	37	207461
2745	4	362	2718	281	112			104192
2843	1725	502	2616	1718	736	7462	132	223380
2028	189	776	1600	893	500	7768	33	108792
692	286	31	537	454	18	3282		23258
1538	239	28	1196	326	283	6506		100740
5845	273	139	4708	801	748	15033	346	296231

C-2-6续表2

地　区	增加值合计	执行行政事业单位会计制度财务指标				
		固定资产原价	上年结转和结余	本年收入合计	本年支出合计	收支结余
全　国	**307091.0**	**1158699.9**	**65863.5**	**557372.8**	**538055.2**	**22880.5**
中央级	1546.6	1.0	79.5	3847.9	3296.6	
北　京	17571.5	57976.4	3189.9	28072.9	29319.6	6003.2
天　津	1686.3	3402.2	83.7	2379.4	2259.3	
河　北	5708.9	27476.3	1020.2	9282.5	9498.4	184.4
山　西	3853.5	15285.7	2025.9	9969.0	10340.8	
内蒙古	8075.2	19476.5	656.9	15628.2	15689.7	2178.2
辽　宁	13694.3	48467.9	1224.5	22859.2	22440.7	120.0
吉　林	6948.9	15196.5		11767.5	11147.2	2.0
黑龙江	8136.8	30733.3	937.0	11114.6	11555.8	
上　海	19986.7	55229.3	2425.4	31146.9	29655.5	2108.8
江　苏	38664.0	116817.9	8446.5	57747.2	54190.7	2153.2
浙　江	28116.7	201357.4	2149.0	48108.6	46150.9	454.4
安　徽	5466.6	16865.3	147.2	9016.6	8762.6	115.9
福　建	7083.9	14397.4	4036.6	12491.1	12963.4	95.2
江　西	5225.6	33390.3	1186.6	9697.0	8449.8	
山　东	8388.6	19537.0		18077.3	18077.3	
河　南	4164.2	11573.3	903.7	9827.7	8696.1	18.1
湖　北	15303.9	70699.5	150.1	32710.5	32377.8	-11.4
湖　南	15345.6	36173.1	138.2	31684.9	31444.2	410.9
广　东	34236.9	106486.0	17531.6	66709.1	60699.9	1840.3
广　西	10258.1	32373.2	5748.6	18951.8	19706.1	894.3
海　南	1261.7	4623.9	628.4	702.1	3360.9	
重　庆	6679.9	31760.3	416.8	14501.7	13780.5	997.6
四　川	12991.7	74341.2	4891.9	27949.3	24632.9	603.5
贵　州	4338.5	14966.8	380.9	7967.4	6660.0	160.2
云　南	4032.6	20709.5	1671.2	7281.6	7057.6	601.6
西　藏	715.1	14202.0	2132.0	571.7	396.2	
陕　西	6459.1	15641.0	1358.6	14106.0	13503.5	1669.2
甘　肃	2558.6	17074.6	525.0	6169.3	6264.9	
青　海	445.0	1916.4	3.6	618.8	618.8	
宁　夏	3354.8	6403.9	1167.1	4934.2	5433.9	
新　疆	4790.9	24144.8	606.9	11480.8	9623.6	2280.9

单位：万元

行政事业单位增加值	执行民间非营利组织单位会计制度财务指标				
	固定资产原价	上年结余	本年收入合计	本年费用合计	社会组织增加值
305407.4	**40097.1**	**479.1**	**3211.3**	**2986.1**	**1683.6**
1546.6					
17571.5					
1686.3					
5699.9	3.0	12.0	10.0	13.0	9.0
3347.9	3000.0	100.0		516.4	505.6
8075.2					
13694.3					
6948.9					
8114.8	150.0		50.0	28.0	22.0
19986.7					
38608.8	3200.0	10.0	130.0	113.2	55.2
27993.8	1827.0	35.0	319.3	284.3	122.9
5466.6					
7031.8	1098.5	1.5	409.8	101.0	52.1
5197.8	600.0		39.5	36.5	27.8
8388.6					
4016.2	2299.4	70.0	97.2	152.4	148.0
15301.9	2030.0	23.0	325.0	273.0	2.0
15345.6			180.0		
33686.9	8904.4	149.0	1400.6	1148.3	550.0
10228.1	150.0			30.0	30.0
1255.7			10.0	10.0	6.0
6654.5	2737.0		79.4	69.4	25.4
12901.6	2998.0	-21.4	100.0	158.4	90.1
4333.4	9091.8	100.0	20.5	10.0	5.1
4026.2	380.0			12.2	6.4
715.1	138.0		10.0		
6459.1					
2558.6					
419.0	1490.0		30.0	30.0	26.0
3354.8					
4790.9					

C-2-7 光荣

地区	单位数	年末职工人数	#女性	受教育程度		职业资格水平		年龄	
				大学专科人数	大学本科及以上人数	助理社会工作师人数	社会工作师人数	35岁及以下人数	36岁至45岁人数
全国	**1425**	**11949**	**5569**	**2802**	**1048**	**120**	**115**	**3578**	**5291**
中央级									
北京	10	197	99	42	46	3		31	76
天津	6	124	72	51	31	3	12	32	46
河北	142	1661	884	299	85	25	6	639	730
山西	88	778	335	290	94	4	8	241	340
内蒙古	29	378	154	132	75			73	167
辽宁	22	425	211	146	104	8	6	171	148
吉林	43	805	126	77	26	2	14	300	348
黑龙江	25	283	150	31	26	4	8	94	110
上海									
江苏	11	105	63	23	18	1		24	45
浙江	23	107	54	38	12	2	1	24	58
安徽	53	394	186	76	28	5	2	71	210
福建	56	353	196	77	47	3	3	72	165
江西	205	1147	380	91	22	23	26	234	504
山东	66	562	283	191	72	2	3	171	242
河南	98	659	320	141	21	5	1	273	266
湖北	93	1047	532	341	87	12	5	296	497
湖南	167	1197	574	290	89	4	3	332	552
广东	65	447	256	81	29	9	7	147	183
广西	74	298	189	76	20	3	2	64	151
海南	9	78	31	18	1			15	31
重庆	8	45	20	19	18			13	16
四川	47	282	144	91	47	2	7	87	133
贵州	26	185	100	71	15		1	61	91
云南	3	17	13	6	5			7	2
西藏									
陕西	21	152	83	52	1			59	59
甘肃	4	24	6	7	4			2	10
青海	1	1	1						
宁夏	2	2	2					1	1
新疆	28	196	105	45	25			44	110

院

单位：个、人、人次、时、张、人天

结构		志愿服务		年末				
46岁至55岁人数	56岁及以上人数	志愿者服务人次数	志愿服务时间	年末床位数	光荣间床位	年在院总人天数	年末在院人数	女性
2689	**391**	**21486**	**47762.0**	**88306**	**36320**	**13970077**	**54784**	**9430**
74	16	16	16.0	656	550	64636	161	25
42	4	1000	2000.0	693	471	104350	413	95
267	25	476	1485.0	12550	4682	2120673	6265	617
166	31	656	1227.0	3182	1988	447734	1722	55
134	4			2199	832	465399	1407	74
87	19	1159	1302.0	2512	1378	438734	1333	162
155	2			2778	199	289568	1615	455
77	2			1784	672	302106	1294	150
20	16	46	175.0	713	458	101695	352	113
24	1	3900	6360.0	800	493	86797	257	15
100	13	390	744.0	4572	2871	443684	1325	94
104	12	5	70.0	1673	901	315493	958	159
318	91	200	600.0	12811	4595	2040355	11775	3223
118	31	7002	17649.0	5777		1035402	3281	392
110	10	60	240.0	5391	2118	810984	4041	261
222	32	320	1012.0	8405	4147	1271758	5664	1180
293	20	3884	9786.0	8524	5176	1732047	5872	1066
101	16	120	192.0	2669	976	325367	1124	259
77	6	106	392.0	2494	1025	308780	1012	110
27	5	110		284	134	38393	112	27
12	4	463	1429.0	431	147	73017	244	33
54	8	198	666.0	3233	1171	487347	2352	475
30	3	1220	1847.0	1540	424	275490	746	127
2	6			152	52	7410	34	
33	1	105	430.0	833	456	93619	507	17
12				205	139	8005	37	2
1				50	1	365	1	
				25	15	7820	22	1
29	13	50	140.0	1370	249	273049	858	243

C-2-7续表

地　区	在院人员按性质分			在院人员按年龄分			在院人员按类型分		
	优抚对象	“三无”对象	自费人员	老人	青壮年	少年儿童	自理(完全自理)	介助(半自理)	介护(不能自理)
全　国	**33554**	**16115**	**5115**	**52977**	**960**	**847**	**42699**	**8931**	**3154**
中央级									
北　京	133	9	19	159	2		79	61	21
天　津	149	40	224	367	46		274	108	31
河　北	3771	2126	368	6102	90	73	4826	1188	251
山　西	1401	249	72	1705	9	8	1356	321	45
内蒙古	1314	11	82	1398	2	7	1104	241	62
辽　宁	1091	82	160	1286	20	27	960	256	117
吉　林	867	467	281	1530	85		1149	218	248
黑龙江	560	440	294	1253	41		1110	101	83
上　海									
江　苏	348	2	2	350	2		293	52	7
浙　江	156		101	257			174	66	17
安　徽	1053	225	47	1318	6	1	1052	223	50
福　建	627	206	125	949	6	3	736	187	35
江　西	5081	5843	851	11125	302	348	9704	1862	209
山　东	3281			3269	12		2958	237	86
河　南	1942	1985	114	3972	42	27	3381	429	231
湖　北	3178	1686	800	5496	95	73	4204	1076	384
湖　南	4455	1047	370	5699	40	133	4503	1035	334
广　东	562	298	264	1066	55	3	677	229	218
广　西	776	39	197	1008	4		672	224	116
海　南	70	24	18	97		15	50	37	25
重　庆	190	30	24	240	4		197	32	15
四　川	1663	571	118	2321	27	4	1628	332	392
贵　州	149	462	135	678	20	48	586	147	13
云　南	14	20		34			7	4	23
西　藏									
陕　西	366	125	16	444	4	59	310	160	37
甘　肃	24	13		24		13	17	1	19
青　海	1			1			1		
宁　夏	15	4	3	22				17	5
新　疆	317	111	430	807	46	5	691	87	80

单位：人、人次、平方米、万元

康复和医疗门诊人次数	机构建筑面积	增加值合计	执行行政事业单位会计制度财务指标					
			固定资产原价	上年结转和结余	本年收入合计	本年支出合计	收支结余	行政事业单位增加值
220815	**3239078**	**50787.3**	**247217.8**	**7913.7**	**84680.8**	**84573.5**	**1829.5**	**50787.3**
15141	42050	2462.0	7303.2	371.0	3168.4	3279.2	142.1	2462.0
2074	26328	1689.7	3475.6	9.0	2144.4	2164.4		1689.7
17506	415111	7104.8	34170.3	291.8	12017.6	12288.0	59.8	7104.8
5446	193181	2944.9	9521.3	1724.6	7311.0	7526.1		2944.9
40	73920	2468.7	7083.8	830.5	4887.7	4675.8	1042.4	2468.7
15045	91998	3616.2	12446.4	612.5	6880.7	6769.3	250.5	3616.2
10246	39545	1373.9	6610.3		2373.2	3412.6		1373.9
23279	32247	673.7	6314.6	307.1	1243.1	1296.7		673.7
1376	23130	668.1	4069.1		969.0	945.1		668.1
30	27125	1000.7	956.4	72.8	1555.8	1603.7		1000.7
4083	123801	1729.7	9288.7	161.5	3053.4	2768.0	210.8	1729.7
1178	87782	1459.2	4887.7	142.0	2908.1	2976.7	59.7	1459.2
2730	354761	2269.7	19700.0	841.1	3466.3	3457.9		2269.7
8117	164513	3209.2	14492.2		5112.9	5112.9		3209.2
19117	204777	1167.5	8648.8	2.2	2230.2	2244.9		1167.5
38243	357760	4601.0	30919.5	86.6	6378.9	6234.0		4601.0
9562	282493	4955.4	24440.0	129.0	7624.3	7321.5	29.5	4955.4
4638	311998	1533.9	7788.8	425.1	2227.1	2282.1	16.9	1533.9
22116	87520	896.3	7637.1	242.5	936.9	1011.8	7.6	896.3
935	15156	161.9	1492.0	143.9	369.8	382.1		161.9
9004	16125	463.6	1537.0		798.3	798.3		463.6
10089	91601	1855.2	11099.8	68.4	2646.4	2534.7	10.2	1855.2
94	44395	412.1	3807.0	273.8	655.1	450.3		412.1
74	2314	150.8	222.0		204.2	204.2		150.8
585	33880	725.9	2413.9		1207.6	1264.2		725.9
32	3950	77.3	732.2		131.0	131.0		77.3
	500	0.2	5.0		10.0	10.0		0.2
	3170	8.1	50.0		6.1	6.1		8.1
35	87947	1107.4	6105.1	1178.3	2163.3	1421.9		1107.4

C-2-8 荣誉军人

地区	单位数	年末职工人数	#女性	受教育程度		职业资格水平		年龄	
				大学专科人数	大学本科及以上人数	助理社会工作师人数	社会工作师人数	35岁及以下人数	36岁至45岁人数
全国	**42**	**5319**	**2881**	**1573**	**1756**	**44**	**62**	**2075**	**1521**
中央级									
北京									
天津									
河北	1	212	111	70	90	5		87	47
山西	5	230	102	43	55	2	5	58	76
内蒙古	1	73	39	18	46	1	2	16	25
辽宁	1	162	82	33	30		4	45	55
吉林	2	414	207					174	80
黑龙江	1	126	28					43	47
上海	1	44	24	17	18		4	20	14
江苏	1	181	125	49	62		3	89	35
浙江	1	397	279	118	207		1	301	54
安徽	1	140	52	48	36			27	38
福建	1	57	27	18	19	2	1	22	14
江西	1	300	187	97	122	2	8	97	74
山东	2	560	281	127	321	5	15	218	179
河南	3	453	258	151	127			98	191
湖北	1	349	187	85	152	2	2	114	113
湖南	1	248	166	115	93			165	55
广东	2	237	107	64	75	10	10	84	84
广西	2	61	29	23	24	3	1	17	19
海南									
重庆	3	155	81	92	18	7	3	71	31
四川	4	398	280	181	144	2	1	208	90
贵州	3	151	59	71	39	2	2	32	55
云南	1	101	48	35	24	1		34	32
西藏									
陕西	1	185	78	92	20			31	87
甘肃	1	50	23	9	23			19	13
青海									
宁夏									
新疆	1	35	21	17	11			5	13

康复医院

单位:个、人、人次、时、张、人天

结构		志愿服务		年末床位数		年在院总人天数	年末在院人数	
46岁至55岁人数	56岁及以上人数	志愿者服务人次数	志愿服务时间		光荣间床位			女性
1385	**338**	**429**	**1119.0**	**9036**	**1478**	**1564845**	**4771**	**1309**
63	15			580		42340	116	1
73	23			535	64	35064	313	
20	12			100	26	9490	26	
50	12			322	72	60155	148	35
80	80			620				
36				56		2130	54	
10				50	50	5475	15	
43	14			220	40	50961	100	
34	8	220	660.0	443		158775	435	230
68	7			200		73000	191	52
16	5			250	100	47450	127	35
121	8	204	447.0	750	20	231775	635	75
134	29			700		141620	209	71
139	25			558	345	87957	254	84
94	28			451	28	72000	226	130
23	5			175		57600	167	121
64	5			325	35	111843	292	135
19	6			305	20	80403	221	2
40	13	5	12.0	608	230	74858	294	90
86	14			960	130	45450	501	127
58	6			298	10	90565	225	68
33	2			100	58	16792	46	
53	14			300	200	58192	146	53
17	1			50		7665	21	
11	6			80	50	3285	9	

C-2-8续表

地区	在院人员按性质分			在院人员按年龄分			在院人员按类型分		
	优抚对象	“三无”对象	自费人员	老人	青壮年	少年儿童	自理(完全自理)	介助(半自理)	介护(不能自理)
全国	**2332**	**381**	**2058**	**3063**	**1611**	**97**	**2332**	**1425**	**1014**
中央级									
北京									
天津									
河北	116			67	49		100	4	12
山西	282	15	16	277	36		246	38	29
内蒙古	26			17	9			9	17
辽宁	72		76	88	60			46	102
吉林									
黑龙江	54			54			54		
上海	15			14	1				15
江苏	27	73		89	11			11	89
浙江	22	3	410	267	168		215	220	
安徽	60	131		60	131			191	
福建	19		108	127			10	48	69
江西	435		200	274	358	3	317	251	67
山东	108		101	136	73		160	23	26
河南	156	5	93	145	104	5	201	39	14
湖北	55	20	151	90	126	10	200	20	6
湖南	21		146	134	7	26	56	90	21
广东	38	22	232	252	40		29	33	230
广西	160		61	219	2		164	2	55
海南									
重庆	129	17	148	184	107	3	139	50	105
四川	347	81	73	397	82	22	241	195	65
贵州	34	14	177	59	164	2	111	89	25
云南	46			46			5	34	7
西藏									
陕西	80		66	62	58	26	84	25	37
甘肃	21			2	19				21
青海									
宁夏									
新疆	9			3	6			7	2

单位：人、人次、平方米、万元

康复和医疗门诊人次数	机构建筑面积	增加值合计	执行行政事业单位会计制度财务指标					
			固定资产原价	上年结转和结余	本年收入合计	本年支出合计	收支结余	行政事业单位增加值
823190	**615882**	**70672.9**	**197757.8**	**28379.4**	**144929.1**	**134519.8**	**7547.4**	**70672.9**
		1896.8	4345.0	14.0	2827.0	2840.0		1896.8
8237	44997	2139.6	3510.7	2447.8	4556.2	3454.3	3103.2	2139.6
379	12949	958.7	1999.3	1161.0	1034.5	1051.0	1144.5	958.7
12970	69325	1723.0	6542.0	511.2	2863.0	2890.0		1723.0
	60000	101.6	2540.9					101.6
	2600	291.4	560.0		575.0	575.0		291.4
	3556	691.4	856.3	47.9	1001.9	1025.6		691.4
68993	47726	3741.2	9335.9	165.7	10306.6	7258.8	3213.5	3741.2
139638	25355	4022.8	6377.0	6651.0	22824.0	17924.0		4022.8
24789	10000	1244.3	2925.9	523.0	5154.5	2728.5		1244.3
2825	12498	955.9	2188.0		917.0	917.0		955.9
17566	40043	2656.9	2464.5	5879.0	4317.3	5199.9		2656.9
22359	81099	9455.6	83307.7	1139.9	15858.1	15335.2		9455.6
46948	3900	11433.3	6166.6	699.8	7829.5	7285.1		11433.3
120916	35000	4811.4	17048.8	173.3	7923.5	12738.9		4811.4
50946	30000	738.3	4731.0		5652.0	5984.0		738.3
59063	31500	7118.0	9402.9		10414.5	9508.1		7118.0
20412	1200	1584.0	4853.9	4711.6	2489.7	4095.3		1584.0
14800	25567	1531.0	2746.0	17.0	3918.2	3889.7	28.5	1531.0
170970	9760	6323.6	12468.5	1540.6	16614.6	15266.3	57.7	6323.6
3205	7300	2810.0	2360.3		3465.5	3391.4		2810.0
	21953	1183.8	1868.4	2696.6	4565.8	1717.5		1183.8
32157	32000	2091.6	6416.0		7583.4	7608.2		2091.6
	500	525.5	1206.8		1094.5	733.5		525.5
6017	7055	643.3	1535.4		1142.8	1102.5		643.3

C-2-9 复员军人

地 区	单位数	年末职工人数	#女性	受教育程度：大学专科人数	受教育程度：大学本科及以上人数	职业资格水平：助理社会工作师人数	职业资格水平：社会工作师人数	年龄：35岁及以下人数	年龄：36岁至45岁人数
全 国	**38**	**2995**	**1682**	**936**	**1167**	**19**	**28**	**1116**	**931**
中央级									
北 京									
天 津	1	30	15	6	8			13	3
河 北	7	881	481	265	335	5	3	260	270
山 西	1	252	168	89	113			98	86
内蒙古	2	40	12	8	1			4	20
辽 宁									
吉 林									
黑龙江									
上 海									
江 苏	4	95	42	32	17	2	3	15	40
浙 江	1	77	49	25	40			50	22
安 徽									
福 建									
江 西	2	24	4	3	1			5	18
山 东	7	828	510	197	417	4	13	331	210
河 南	2	79	39	23	11			44	9
湖 北	1	9	4	6				4	5
湖 南	2	108	13	69	32			53	42
广 东	2	148	78	61	63	5	7	39	72
广 西									
海 南									
重 庆									
四 川	3	257	164	111	39			148	59
贵 州									
云 南									
西 藏									
陕 西	3	167	103	41	90	3	2	52	75
甘 肃									
青 海									
宁 夏									
新 疆									

疗养院

单位:个、人、人次、时、张、人天

结构		志愿服务		年末床位数	#光荣间床位	年在院总人天数	年末在院人数	#女性
46岁至55岁人数	56岁及以上人数	志愿者服务人次数	志愿服务时间					
770	**178**	**1179**	**3481.0**	**7172**	**1491**	**1448497**	**4609**	**829**
12	2			150	150	8580	130	13
282	69			1767	560	485223	1556	256
65	3			480		172343	429	
16				240	26	8825	30	1
22	18	370	1110.0	464	193	136493	256	13
5				90	20	32850	90	40
1		132	528.0	150		24552	135	85
205	82	642	1622.0	1595		259353	857	90
24	2			710	100	36860	101	33
				154	30	3000	10	
13				138	12	15420	105	39
36	1			321	100	99778	149	50
50		35	221.0	495	50	73000	457	201
39	1			418	250	92220	304	8

C-2-9续表

地区	在院人员按性质分			在院人员按年龄分			在院人员按类型分		
	优抚对象	"三无"对象	自费人员	老人	青壮年	少年儿童	自理(完全自理)	介助(半自理)	介护(不能自理)
全　国	**3032**	**310**	**1267**	**3820**	**702**	**87**	**2988**	**680**	**941**
中央级									
北　京									
天　津	130			130			130		
河　北	943		613	1266	263	27	715	155	686
山　西	344		85	395	34		412	17	
内蒙古	20		10	30			16	14	
辽　宁									
吉　林									
黑龙江									
上　海									
江　苏	192	21	43	234	11	11	244	9	3
浙　江	40	50		60	30		90		
安　徽									
福　建									
江　西	50	85		125		10	50	75	10
山　东	668	25	164	807	50		683	158	16
河　南	101			81	20		40	20	41
湖　北	10			10				5	5
湖　南	13	40	52	66	29	10	59	44	2
广　东	27		122	33	115	1		10	139
广　西									
海　南									
重　庆									
四　川	226	81	150	279	150	28	354	95	8
贵　州									
云　南									
西　藏									
陕　西	268	8	28	304			195	78	31
甘　肃									
青　海									
宁　夏									
新　疆									

单位：人、人次、平方米、万元

康复和医疗门诊人次数	机构建筑面积	增加值合计	执行行政事业单位会计制度财务指标					
			固定资产原价	上年结转和结余	本年收入合计	本年支出合计	收支结余	行政事业单位增加值
340954	**240599**	**31372.5**	**100942.4**	**6701.4**	**62204.7**	**55762.4**	**2079.9**	**31372.5**
1013	6643	364.8	3271.5	567.4	1734.3	1787.4	514.3	364.8
96665	23959	9950.2	20589.7	30.0	17622.3	16967.3	431.0	9950.2
20652	30035	3119.2	15153.4	1068.1	4788.1	4483.7	1068.1	3119.2
	4200	47.3	729.8		43.0	43.0		47.3
119068	18401	1140.9	3505.4		1483.6	1483.6		1140.9
	1200	0.5	13.6		6.0	6.0		0.5
	4100	68.2	341.0	66.0	254.6	142.0		68.2
52100	82217	7996.1	15753.2	4918.0	13202.9	12460.9		7996.1
	2600	492.5	1396.2	41.8	1169.5	1144.8	66.5	492.5
	3200	14.0	289.8	10.1	120.5	127.0		14.0
4732	9350	967.1	1065.0		940.0	940.0		967.1
	17164	3947.9	34946.7		9215.4	6758.2		3947.9
39424	3350	1563.4	1956.9		3388.4	2702.5		1563.4
7300	34180	1700.4	1930.2		8236.1	6716.0		1700.4

C-2-10 军

地　区	单位数	年末职工人数		受教育程度		职业资
			#女性	大学专科人数	大学本科及以上人数	助理社会工作师人数
全　国	**1821**	**17267**	**7514**	**6388**	**6131**	**303**
中央级						
北　京	134	1798	976	629	904	76
天　津	16	200	85	61	85	4
河　北	137	1247	523	378	296	16
山　西	73	565	247	211	209	3
内蒙古	20	238	82	115	67	3
辽　宁	58	1048	452	416	441	11
吉　林	33	589	201	291	174	19
黑龙江	60	382	132	168	142	3
上　海	14	219	105	80	107	12
江　苏	134	1130	512	398	422	24
浙　江	60	315	123	86	135	1
安　徽	53	363	128	116	120	7
福　建	56	407	170	108	148	15
江　西	19	148	52	55	22	
山　东	162	1913	748	722	758	21
河　南	115	966	430	351	245	8
湖　北	103	841	376	355	267	2
湖　南	109	858	363	328	262	13
广　东	79	721	384	266	277	15
广　西	36	246	105	106	70	2
海　南	9	129	51	45	21	1
重　庆	37	294	123	140	127	1
四　川	117	669	308	287	175	16
贵　州	14	112	55	51	33	2
云　南	53	435	171	149	120	6
西　藏						
陕　西	70	746	308	262	178	5
甘　肃	24	369	175	96	195	15
青　海	3	61	25	20	31	
宁　夏	7	67	27	10	43	1
新　疆	16	191	77	88	57	1

休所

单位:个、人、人次、时

格水平	年龄结构				志愿服务	
社会工作师人数	35岁及以下人数	36岁至45岁人数	46岁至55岁人数	56岁及以上人数	志愿者服务人次数	志愿服务时间
365	**5270**	**6073**	**4572**	**1352**	**11416**	**25538.1**
53	576	681	464	77	17	34.0
12	41	48	94	17	2040	2120.0
16	503	383	277	84	30	43.0
17	167	181	170	47	42	98.0
5	54	59	88	37		
10	326	288	291	143		
2	184	282	79	44		
6	110	127	121	24	7	50.0
15	80	52	75	12		
52	294	385	346	105	443	977.0
3	82	84	122	27	1560	2879.0
14	92	123	109	39	560	1034.0
8	140	129	100	38		
3	43	67	30	8	245	842.0
49	500	710	568	135	4097	9813.1
5	371	349	203	43	63	178.0
3	197	312	262	70	122	344.0
14	285	349	161	63	539	2091.0
23	196	325	158	42	25	60.0
6	70	82	69	25		
6	51	49	20	9		
	78	127	66	23	354	824.0
13	208	251	158	52	319	2117.0
1	34	32	38	8	60	200.0
9	90	147	154	44	40	50.0
5	220	244	199	83	818	1619.0
9	186	98	61	24	20	100.0
1	22	17	15	7	15	65.0
	15	31	14	7		
5	55	61	60	15		

C-2-10续表

地区	增加值合计	执行行政事业单位会计制度财务指标				
		固定资产原价	上年结余	收入合计	支出合计	收支结余
全国	**1639794.4**	**358174.7**	**124054.1**	**2102498.8**	**2070254.3**	**50142.3**
中央级						
北京	262723.7	13237.1	30552.8	345929.0	350560.4	17390.9
天津	45055.5	10635.5	1311.2	48370.7	46450.9	1263.7
河北	115137.6	23844.1	18415.5	127641.6	127434.0	773.3
山西	34746.1	13223.0	3504.6	41051.8	40382.3	1977.7
内蒙古	20224.9	6437.3	1759.9	22243.6	22721.7	1256.6
辽宁	103742.3	39753.7	2693.5	191514.6	189980.5	1452.8
吉林	14443.7	6912.8	344.8	34853.7	34568.3	0.8
黑龙江	25674.1	15023.4	1908.1	34365.1	32037.5	
上海	35409.5	4113.4	29.3	77705.1	73614.2	857.8
江苏	137144.1	23588.6	3048.9	166313.1	160638.6	1903.2
浙江	28508.4	6874.5	2696.2	48304.3	31855.8	761.5
安徽	34093.9	8108.7	2245.9	38732.7	36992.1	170.8
福建	37002.8	6739.4	2515.3	44910.6	43652.6	1579.7
江西	12843.1	2449.5	152.4	14550.1	14165.3	
山东	212822.6	41467.0		262013.0	262013.0	
河南	47371.1	10530.6	3718.5	61421.7	60845.9	323.0
湖北	70355.5	12449.9	91.0	80169.2	79884.8	92.7
湖南	45854.6	20482.0	1375.9	55435.1	54608.9	799.3
广东	74841.2	14698.6	14801.4	85993.6	81932.5	1802.7
广西	28023.5	5084.6	1627.9	29537.1	29371.7	283.3
海南	4104.1	3110.8	5525.5	5752.2	8788.3	1401.2
重庆	31471.5	4781.1	1153.3	39118.4	39330.0	545.6
四川	34091.8	13334.3	2500.1	44733.1	42910.7	1094.3
贵州	10229.4	2755.5	304.7	13672.2	13242.4	258.0
云南	25248.6	20073.0	3801.1	31170.2	32010.4	2208.9
西藏						
陕西	89132.6	17504.3	8517.8	90723.6	93968.9	3693.2
甘肃	32193.5	3610.7	2221.3	34238.2	35988.8	236.9
青海	5763.1	681.5	514.9	6404.0	6277.2	455.1
宁夏	7062.4	815.0	3124.4	8858.0	7636.5	4024.5
新疆	14479.4	5854.8	3597.9	16773.2	16390.1	3534.8

单位：万元、户、人

行政事业单位增加值	机构管理军休干部的户数	#分散安置户数	年末机构管理军休干部人数	#分散安置人数	本年发放离退休金
1639794.4	**180292**	**34600**	**199439**	**40341**	**1420195.0**
262723.7	37739	2443	39290	2581	182952.5
45055.5	2774	109	4518	109	8082.8
115137.6	10486	5509	11300	5212	93345.9
34746.1	3712	1949	4158	2188	31089.0
20224.9	1801	821	1882	907	14349.4
103742.3	18640	150	23736	119	103405.7
14443.7	2212	73	2883	73	10451.9
25674.1	2929	239	2944	87	29228.9
35409.5	3134	529	4585	561	48308.7
137144.1	11453	1657	12244	2010	83423.6
28508.4	3057	341	3089	385	39450.3
34093.9	2973	537	3459	818	25655.7
37002.8	3310	806	3790	1091	33444.3
12843.1	1763	54	1818	39	7820.2
212822.6	21537	5138	21060	5822	161868.9
47371.1	6400	324	6402	444	44031.6
70355.5	8058	3577	8521	3642	67229.5
45854.6	5092	146	5053	723	35756.9
74841.2	6066	2297	7343	2493	55474.7
28023.5	1958	987	1914	1006	18679.7
4104.1	1258	852	1252	844	5296.2
31471.5	3418	1832	3501	1958	35824.2
34091.8	5091	660	4894	722	35621.9
10229.4	815	275	959	306	11154.0
25248.6	5082	1039	4858	362	142424.0
89132.6	4478	905	8403	4320	60659.9
32193.5	3243	810	3316	940	12604.2
5763.1	253	223	450	266	5395.9
7062.4	289	8	612		5063.9
14479.4	1271	310	1205	313	12100.6

C-2-11 智障与精神疾病

地区	单位数	年末职工人数	#女性	受教育程度		职业资格水平		年龄	
				大学专科人数	大学本科及以上人数	助理社会工作师人数	社会工作师人数	35岁及以下人数	36岁至45岁人数
全　国	**261**	**25114**	**14118**	**8405**	**6506**	**209**	**183**	**9226**	**8587**
中央级									
北　京	2	361	253	97	77			185	94
天　津	2	364	165	90	96	3		114	72
河　北	2	495	253	69	272	1	4	112	177
山　西	8	1092	621	240	233	3	3	385	440
内蒙古	6	553	276	224	160	2	5	186	129
辽　宁	5	628	334	244	162	4	5	99	277
吉　林	14	1414	728	159	79			296	651
黑龙江	6	990	332	203	252	3	3	322	358
上　海	3	582	339	178	130	9	10	259	112
江　苏	12	1773	1064	599	540	16	18	625	568
浙　江	3	123	75	23	50	1	3	35	67
安　徽	4	510	291	215	114		1	220	168
福　建	17	982	566	305	181	11	4	411	303
江　西	4	162	94	52	55	5	7	44	69
山　东	15	1711	1041	570	829	11	9	699	530
河　南	9	932	520	261	327	5	22	309	365
湖　北	13	2019	1178	622	567	13	7	668	632
湖　南	17	1884	1155	690	428	3	3	621	884
广　东	13	1293	720	405	375	47	26	592	432
广　西	8	1357	931	595	379	9	10	703	336
海　南									
重　庆	11	467	240	164	101	9	7	146	153
四　川	26	2452	1290	1196	477	22	20	1186	767
贵　州	31	949	440	406	130			211	304
云　南	6	339	189	139	118	2	1	129	115
西　藏									
陕　西	4	427	181	139	79	5	3	118	127
甘　肃	6	254	140	93	49	1	3	77	118
青　海	1	213	151	108	48	3	2	123	50
宁　夏	1	85	70	25	60	10	4	44	39
新　疆	12	703	481	294	138	11	3	307	250

服务机构总表

单位:个、人、人次、时、张、人天

结构		志愿服务		年末床位数		年在院总人天数	年末在院人数	
46岁至55岁人数	56岁及以上人数	志愿者服务人次数	志愿服务时间		#光荣间床位			#女性
5823	**1478**	**13158**	**32474.0**	**74492**	**3600**	**17678981**	**59747**	**17073**
69	13			557		171791	423	158
124	54			950		305505	837	226
157	49			915		112549	877	145
233	34			1825	365	468932	1568	185
195	43	235	300.0	1690	58	466086	1344	338
240	12			1515	45	420642	1347	222
439	28			7180	760	834367	3454	789
305	5			3283	425	334586	1724	585
127	84	272	816.0	1783		629115	1734	489
440	140	1468	3290.0	5399	10	1500356	5085	1554
16	5	6000	16100.0	1110		204250	560	225
72	50			765		219985	641	103
222	46			3849	110	1184198	3460	984
46	3	132	528.0	396		77375	372	35
413	69	4156	8750.0	3376		814050	2553	463
207	51			1947	3	692748	1754	622
526	193			4749	310	1113300	3879	1462
316	63			5082	347	887991	3434	1133
222	47	40	40.0	4308	115	1277512	3862	1139
266	52	8	30.0	2889	154	764707	2782	823
144	24	513	1545.0	2067	2	656149	1952	582
407	92			9687	135	2508263	8453	2759
238	196			2737	177	677513	1982	482
76	19			1127		220542	1285	325
113	69	20	75.0	1137	370	343730	936	219
47	12	20	100.0	941	110	152857	408	127
26	14	9	45.0	260	38	59940	222	78
2				305		61000	305	125
135	11	285	855.0	2663	66	518942	2514	696

C-2-11续表

地区	在院人员按性质分			在院人员按年龄分			在院人员按类型分		
	优抚对象	“三无”对象	自费人员	老人	青壮年	少年儿童	自理（完全自理）	介助（半自理）	介护（不能自理）
全　国	**12228**	**17008**	**30511**	**21610**	**36961**	**1176**	**34084**	**18607**	**7056**
中央级									
北　京	4	6	413	102	314	7	287	89	47
天　津	157	265	415	227	610		790	47	
河　北	482	18	377	397	475	5	371	452	54
山　西	760	346	462	733	811	24	1020	479	69
内蒙古	90	419	835	345	988	11	824	375	145
辽　宁	380	275	692	349	972	26	1170	110	67
吉　林	704	1630	1120	1639	1815		2391	751	312
黑龙江	170	1280	274	607	1116	1	829	879	16
上　海	55	120	1559	536	1198		775	959	
江　苏	1439	1739	1907	2242	2697	146	2798	1578	709
浙　江	122	58	380	208	347	5	379	122	59
安　徽	325	62	254	155	474	12	32	560	49
福　建	459	1114	1887	1063	2318	79	2433	739	288
江　西	25	247	100	139	233		275	71	26
山　东	1730	424	399	1003	1550		1843	560	150
河　南	224	494	1036	321	1344	89	1441	263	50
湖　北	665	565	2649	1175	2649	55	2346	1164	369
湖　南	1067	873	1494	1376	1915	143	1278	995	1161
广　东	820	475	2567	1124	2570	168	2442	1127	293
广　西	380	486	1916	859	1829	94	1242	1043	497
海　南									
重　庆	96	776	1080	907	1027	18	1206	504	242
四　川	1106	1909	5438	3747	4593	113	3798	2904	1751
贵　州	120	702	1160	770	1178	34	809	928	245
云　南	226	723	336	347	919	19	489	677	119
西　藏									
陕　西	506	361	69	332	566	38	754	152	30
甘　肃	76	208	124	144	263	1	210	154	44
青　海	2	4	216	56	166		221	1	
宁　夏	10	213	82	70	207	28	40	180	85
新　疆	28	1216	1270	637	1817	60	1591	744	179

单位：人、人次、平方米、万元

康复和医疗门诊人次数	机构建筑面积	增加值合计	执行行政事业单位会计制度财务指标					
			固定资产原价	上年结转和结余	本年收入合计	本年支出合计	收支结余	行政事业单位增加值
2576826	**2731283**	**261798.8**	**400968.6**	**53897.0**	**490249.8**	**487230.3**	**22514.3**	**261798.8**
42493	10818	4008.6	6089.0	1195.2	15527.1	15600.3	798.3	4008.6
68307	23128	6037.4	6153.9	19.8	5694.3	8712.0	2.8	6037.4
51394	143036	1895.3	16889.0	376.0	2585.4	2553.4		1895.3
49150	86534	8978.3	17489.7	2544.5	13389.6	36045.1	1367.2	8978.3
57017	56824	5530.4	3034.8	1802.2	9494.5	9525.1	1771.6	5530.4
	66136	5928.6	9654.3	1077.7	12165.4	11759.3		5928.6
101286	55150	8627.1	18054.2		12795.7	11278.1	1248.0	8627.1
60870	42200	2476.1	11838.0	1303.0	8868.0	9121.0		2476.1
5042	81738	10245.1	16560.6	1955.1	13606.1	14364.4	1106.4	10245.1
79875	201691	28662.0	44630.8	10213.9	51697.8	45788.7	1247.2	28662.0
	56500	4357.3	6939.1	622.9	7285.6	7636.3	272.2	4357.3
58291	28661	3888.9	3244.1	-74.2	8119.4	6177.5		3888.9
454963	101397	9077.7	11436.0	895.4	19275.1	18617.4	212.0	9077.7
	8862	1156.3	670.8		1974.5	1516.4		1156.3
112194	172760	18207.4	27717.5		34237.9	34237.9		18207.4
256575	56177	15937.5	13244.8	858.0	20538.1	19607.5	1686.1	15937.5
162218	263217	18321.0	35102.4	386.0	40708.3	36021.0	55.0	18321.0
271971	176190	16123.7	16615.0	91.5	30178.4	29009.5	626.8	16123.7
91262	63420	17680.9	25832.8	2291.9	32316.3	27308.7	1614.4	17680.9
146755	377702	11961.9	17327.6	4962.3	27106.7	24814.4	1276.5	11961.9
66198	91340	7288.8	7844.3		17939.7	17246.1	693.6	7288.8
197898	198240	28492.1	38867.5	5237.9	47743.8	45356.9		28492.1
50419	94450	8680.2	14941.5	5345.9	11979.0	13554.9	2482.0	8680.2
16815	78762	4121.2	6526.9	2466.7	8651.7	7977.9	1078.4	4121.2
20130	59835	2795.4	5234.4	4783.1	7060.7	4719.8	3101.9	2795.4
93985	17659	2274.8	4561.7	2565.3	5642.9	4784.7	17.5	2274.8
	18000	1354.0	2529.0		4104.5	3219.2		1354.0
6012	14592	510.8	425.4	863.4	1558.2	1150.6	1271.0	510.8
55706	86263	7180.2	11513.5	2113.5	18005.1	19526.2	585.4	7180.2

C-2-12 福利类

地 区	单位数	年末职工人数	#女性	受教育程度		职业资格水平		年龄	
				大学专科人数	大学本科及以上人数	助理社会工作师人数	社会工作师人数	35岁及以下人数	36岁至45岁人数
全 国	**155**	**13835**	**7660**	**5019**	**3255**	**103**	**106**	**5298**	**4567**
中央级									
北 京	2	361	253	97	77			185	94
天 津	1	247	108	65	69	3		75	65
河 北									
山 西	1	97	46	37	29	1	1	27	30
内蒙古	4	343	156	146	71	2	4	111	84
辽 宁	1	75	52	23	29	1	4	21	32
吉 林	7	763	390	127	66			152	326
黑龙江	5	944	311	189	227	3	3	306	344
上 海	3	582	339	178	130	9	10	259	112
江 苏	11	1485	896	538	388	16	15	527	475
浙 江	2	59	30	10	33		1	27	18
安 徽	3	214	156	89	46		1	124	42
福 建	14	833	472	280	176	8	4	336	261
江 西	3	159	93	52	55	5	7	44	69
山 东	2	231	121	122	69		3	75	81
河 南	8	622	344	179	172	3	10	229	239
湖 北	3	336	196	118	51			69	124
湖 南	9	1061	603	389	243			365	534
广 东	3	657	423	220	293	4	3	326	232
广 西	4	689	444	358	218	3	3	339	167
海 南									
重 庆	11	467	240	164	101	9	7	146	153
四 川	17	1567	837	835	313	15	17	834	428
贵 州	23	695	296	262	73			155	198
云 南	4	217	128	84	75	1		67	76
西 藏									
陕 西	1	147	56	46	32	5	3	74	27
甘 肃	3	149	87	50	15	1	1	29	85
青 海	1	213	151	108	48	3	2	123	50
宁 夏	1	85	70	25	60	10	4	44	39
新 疆	8	537	362	228	96	1	3	229	182

精神病院和医院

单位:个、人、人次、时、张、人天

结构		志愿服务		年末床位数	#光荣间床位	年在院总人天数	年末在院人数	#女性
46岁至55岁人数	56岁及以上人数	志愿者服务人次数	志愿服务时间					
3078	**892**	**3801**	**8809.0**	**45280**	**1722**	**10741697**	**37098**	**11313**
69	13			557		171791	423	158
70	37			650		237250	650	216
38	2			215		54750	215	45
123	25	235	300.0	1188	7	295285	900	208
16	6			235		7230	225	67
268	17			4800	450	473337	2625	474
289	5			3083	425	333334	1615	579
127	84	272	816.0	1783		629115	1734	489
360	123	1468	3290.0	4435	10	1210581	4121	1236
10	4			910		131250	360	198
14	34			265		40579	141	56
195	41			3319	110	1045548	2945	819
43	3	132	528.0	371		70775	347	30
70	5	1132	2110.0	350		101567	292	50
118	36			1347	3	386749	1125	486
103	40			591		100445	398	112
134	28			2273	301	426534	1686	562
78	21			1924		605679	1780	682
153	30			1679		391097	1645	502
144	24	513	1545.0	2067	2	656149	1952	582
245	60			6583	16	1783377	5852	2038
151	191			2092	160	549743	1604	397
57	17			817		176742	1006	261
32	14	20	75.0	500	200	150380	425	120
26	9	20	100.0	301		104025	254	95
26	14	9	45.0	260	38	59940	222	78
2				305		61000	305	125
117	9			2380		487445	2251	648

C-2-12续表

地区	在院人员按性质分			在院人员按年龄分			在院人员按类型分		
	优抚对象	“三无”对象	自费人员	老人	青壮年	少年儿童	自理(完全自理)	介助(半自理)	介护(不能自理)
全　国	**3306**	**14030**	**19762**	**13288**	**22919**	**891**	**21250**	**11311**	**4537**
中央级									
北　京	4	6	413	102	314	7	287	89	47
天　津		265	385	171	479		650		
河　北									
山　西	4	147	64	35	178	2	164	43	8
内蒙古	75	393	432	281	619		399	360	141
辽　宁		146	79	31	168	26	158	47	20
吉　林	401	1577	647	1196	1429		1901	581	143
黑龙江	81	1260	274	498	1116	1	720	879	16
上　海	55	120	1559	536	1198		775	959	
江　苏	1140	1686	1295	1906	2071	144	2219	1297	605
浙　江	60	58	242	150	205	5	209	101	50
安　徽		37	104	77	56	8	32	60	49
福　建	368	904	1673	800	2066	79	2313	535	97
江　西		247	100	114	233		250	71	26
山　东	33	180	79	113	179		102	147	43
河　南	11	494	620	254	782	89	812	263	50
湖　北		26	372	314	84		268	31	99
湖　南	309	578	799	667	928	91	994	380	312
广　东	44	102	1634	532	1167	81	1534	140	106
广　西	112	343	1190	510	1051	84	852	425	368
海　南									
重　庆	96	776	1080	907	1027	18	1206	504	242
四　川	219	1532	4101	2371	3386	95	1971	2320	1561
贵　州	51	618	935	672	900	32	591	836	177
云　南	146	622	238	313	679	14	489	398	119
西　藏									
陕　西	72	353		74	325	26	400	25	
甘　肃	13	127	114	32	221	1	171	58	25
青　海	2	4	216	56	166		221	1	
宁　夏	10	213	82	70	207	28	40	180	85
新　疆		1216	1035	506	1685	60	1522	581	148

单位：人、人次、平方米、万元

康复和医疗门诊人次数	机构建筑面积	增加值合计	执行行政事业单位会计制度财务指标					
			固定资产原价	上年结转和结余	本年收入合计	本年支出合计	收支结余	行政事业单位增加值
1540534	**1451769**	**150158.2**	**205337.4**	**30255.4**	**280905.2**	**271594.4**	**15043.9**	**150158.2**
42493	10818	4008.6	6089.0	1195.2	15527.1	15600.3	798.3	4008.6
34923	13451	4397.7	1935.0		3016.0	6363.0		4397.7
298	8262	1192.6	503.8		1386.0	1386.0		1192.6
12272	26400	3191.6	1231.8	1802.2	4946.0	4976.6	1771.6	3191.6
	12338	678.4	1669.2		1408.3	1405.8		678.4
92813	35099	4747.8	9526.2		6812.7	5901.1	624.0	4747.8
60870	39800	2440.6	10951.0	1303.0	8371.0	8624.0		2440.6
5042	81738	10245.1	16560.6	1955.1	13606.1	14364.4	1106.4	10245.1
79875	163950	20867.1	25096.8	8470.8	42300.1	35644.6	1044.8	20867.1
	35000	3004.1	5467.9		5272.2	5272.2		3004.1
20322	15661	1980.5	1065.6	-74.2	3139.9	3104.8		1980.5
444958	84305	8486.9	10998.2	895.4	18346.8	17697.8	212.0	8486.9
	8362	1155.6	654.2		1969.0	1510.9		1155.6
3995	23538	2993.2	2674.0		3778.3	3778.3		2993.2
231555	53177	7585.9	8640.3	858.0	14284.1	12913.5	892.0	7585.9
39372	8740	1505.0	1503.0	41.0	3233.0	3179.0	55.0	1505.0
94332	37390	7087.6	9631.9	91.5	12637.9	12192.7	626.8	7087.6
53370	3059	11810.0	14863.7	35.0	18512.5	16685.0		11810.0
2635	301405	6338.3	9143.2	2751.6	12541.0	12922.8	148.6	6338.3
66198	91340	7288.8	7844.3		17939.7	17246.1	693.6	7288.8
127779	151834	18481.2	26479.1	2347.4	28473.9	27428.5		18481.2
43482	77068	5653.5	11975.3	4027.2	8266.8	9375.7	2095.0	5653.5
11555	22282	3202.2	3877.5		6438.7	6259.3		3202.2
	24759	1278.9	1747.5	1221.7	4303.6	2423.3	3101.9	1278.9
16712	11001	1667.8	1257.0	357.6	1345.3	2061.3	17.5	1667.8
	18000	1354.0	2529.0		4104.5	3219.2		1354.0
6012	14592	510.8	425.4	863.4	1558.2	1150.6	1271.0	510.8
49671	78400	7004.5	10996.9	2113.5	17386.5	18907.6	585.4	7004.5

C-2-13 复退军人

地区	单位数	年末职工人数		受教育程度		职业资格水平		年龄	
			#女性	大学专科人数	大学本科及以上人数	助理社会工作师人数	社会工作师人数	35岁及以下人数	36岁至45岁人数
全　国	**106**	**11279**	**6458**	**3386**	**3251**	**106**	**77**	**3928**	**4020**
中央级									
北　京									
天　津	1	117	57	25	27			39	7
河　北	2	495	253	69	272	1	4	112	177
山　西	7	995	575	203	204	2	2	358	410
内蒙古	2	210	120	78	89		1	75	45
辽　宁	4	553	282	221	133	3	1	78	245
吉　林	7	651	338	32	13			144	325
黑龙江	1	46	21	14	25			16	14
上　海									
江　苏	1	288	168	61	152		3	98	93
浙　江	1	64	45	13	17	1	2	8	49
安　徽	1	296	135	126	68			96	126
福　建	3	149	94	25	5	3		75	42
江　西	1	3	1						
山　东	13	1480	920	448	760	11	6	624	449
河　南	1	310	176	82	155	2	12	80	126
湖　北	10	1683	982	504	516	13	7	599	508
湖　南	8	823	552	301	185	3	3	256	350
广　东	10	636	297	185	82	43	23	266	200
广　西	4	668	487	237	161	6	7	364	169
海　南									
重　庆									
四　川	9	885	453	361	164	7	3	352	339
贵　州	8	254	144	144	57			56	106
云　南	2	122	61	55	43	1	1	62	39
西　藏									
陕　西	3	280	125	93	47			44	100
甘　肃	3	105	53	43	34		2	48	33
青　海									
宁　夏									
新　疆	4	166	119	66	42	10		78	68

精神病院

单位:个、人、人次、时、张、人天

结构		志愿服务		年末床位数		年在院总人天数	年末在院人数	
46岁至55岁人数	56岁及以上人数	志愿者服务人次数	志愿服务时间		#光荣间床位			#女性
2745	**586**	**9357**	**23665.0**	**29212**	**1878**	**6937284**	**22649**	**5760**
54	17			300		68255	187	10
157	49			915		112549	877	145
195	32			1610	365	414182	1353	140
72	18			502	51	170801	444	130
224	6			1280	45	413412	1122	155
171	11			2380	310	361030	829	315
16				200		1252	109	6
80	17			964		289775	964	318
6	1	6000	16100.0	200		73000	200	27
58	16			500		179406	500	47
27	5			530		138650	515	165
3				25		6600	25	5
343	64	3024	6640.0	3026		712483	2261	413
89	15			600		305999	629	136
423	153			4158	310	1012855	3481	1350
182	35			2809	46	461457	1748	571
144	26	40	40.0	2384	115	671833	2082	457
113	22	8	30.0	1210	154	373610	1137	321
162	32			3104	119	724886	2601	721
87	5			645	17	127770	378	85
19	2			310		43800	279	64
81	55			637	170	193350	511	99
21	3			640	110	48832	154	32
18	2	285	855.0	283	66	31497	263	48

C–2–13续表

地　区	在院人员按性质分			在院人员按年龄分			在院人员按类型分		
	优抚对象	“三无”对象	自费人员	老人	青壮年	少年儿童	自理（完全自理）	介助（半自理）	介护（不能自理）
全　国	**8922**	**2978**	**10749**	**8322**	**14042**	**285**	**12834**	**7296**	**2519**
中央级									
北　京									
天　津	157		30	56	131		140	47	
河　北	482	18	377	397	475	5	371	452	54
山　西	756	199	398	698	633	22	856	436	61
内蒙古	15	26	403	64	369	11	425	15	4
辽　宁	380	129	613	318	804		1012	63	47
吉　林	303	53	473	443	386		490	170	169
黑龙江	89	20		109			109		
上　海									
江　苏	299	53	612	336	626	2	579	281	104
浙　江	62		138	58	142		170	21	9
安　徽	325	25	150	78	418	4		500	
福　建	91	210	214	263	252		120	204	191
江　西	25			25			25		
山　东	1697	244	320	890	1371		1741	413	107
河　南	213		416	67	562		629		
湖　北	665	539	2277	861	2565	55	2078	1133	270
湖　南	758	295	695	709	987	52	284	615	849
广　东	776	373	933	592	1403	87	908	987	187
广　西	268	143	726	349	778	10	390	618	129
海　南									
重　庆									
四　川	887	377	1337	1376	1207	18	1827	584	190
贵　州	69	84	225	98	278	2	218	92	68
云　南	80	101	98	34	240	5		279	
西　藏									
陕　西	434	8	69	258	241	12	354	127	30
甘　肃	63	81	10	112	42		39	96	19
青　海									
宁　夏									
新　疆	28		235	131	132		69	163	31

单位：人、人次、平方米、万元

康复和医疗门诊人次数	机构建筑面积	增加值合计	执行行政事业单位会计制度财务指标					
			固定资产原价	上年结转和结余	本年收入合计	本年支出合计	收支结余	行政事业单位增加值
1036292	**1279514**	**111640.6**	**195631.2**	**23641.6**	**209344.6**	**215635.9**	**7470.4**	**111640.6**
33384	9677	1639.7	4218.9	19.8	2678.3	2349.0	2.8	1639.7
51394	143036	1895.3	16889.0	376.0	2585.4	2553.4		1895.3
48852	78272	7785.7	16985.9	2544.5	12003.6	34659.1	1367.2	7785.7
44745	30424	2338.8	1803.0		4548.5	4548.5		2338.8
	53798	5250.2	7985.1	1077.7	10757.1	10353.5		5250.2
8473	20051	3879.3	8528.0		5983.0	5377.0	624.0	3879.3
	2400	35.5	887.0		497.0	497.0		35.5
	37741	7794.9	19534.0	1743.1	9397.7	10144.1	202.4	7794.9
	21500	1353.2	1471.2	622.9	2013.4	2364.1	272.2	1353.2
37969	13000	1908.4	2178.5		4979.5	3072.7		1908.4
10005	17092	590.8	437.8		928.3	919.6		590.8
	500	0.7	16.6		5.5	5.5		0.7
108199	149222	15214.2	25043.5		30459.6	30459.6		15214.2
25020	3000	8351.6	4604.5		6254.0	6694.0	794.1	8351.6
122846	254477	16816.0	33599.4	345.0	37475.3	32842.0		16816.0
177639	138800	9036.1	6983.1		17540.5	16816.8		9036.1
37892	60361	5870.9	10969.1	2256.9	13803.8	10623.7	1614.4	5870.9
144120	76297	5623.6	8184.4	2210.7	14565.7	11891.6	1127.9	5623.6
70119	46406	10010.9	12388.4	2890.5	19269.9	17928.4		10010.9
6937	17382	3026.7	2966.2	1318.7	3712.2	4179.2	387.0	3026.7
5260	56480	919.0	2649.4	2466.7	2213.0	1718.6	1078.4	919.0
20130	35076	1516.5	3486.9	3561.4	2757.1	2296.5		1516.5
77273	6658	607.0	3304.7	2207.7	4297.6	2723.4		607.0
6035	7863	175.7	516.6		618.6	618.6		175.7

C-2-14 为儿童提供住宿的

地区	单位数	年末职工人数		受教育程度		职业资
			#女性	大学专科人数	大学本科及以上人数	助理社会工作师人数
全国	**803**	**13641**	**8623**	**4121**	**3438**	**338**
中央级						
北京	14	544	404	146	264	16
天津	2	124	82	35	62	4
河北	12	108	45	9	13	
山西	11	100	42	21	15	2
内蒙古	7	270	177	112	64	4
辽宁	11	439	264	135	214	6
吉林	18	406	166	55	62	
黑龙江	16	458	292	167	126	2
上海	8	593	505	141	145	26
江苏	46	599	415	175	175	28
浙江	15	373	268	131	131	9
安徽	48	1003	608	260	179	6
福建	10	131	92	47	46	6
江西	18	194	94	71	30	8
山东	24	583	415	207	241	12
河南	17	406	290	67	72	8
湖北	117	1474	865	434	278	17
湖南	64	770	388	254	123	12
广东	40	929	659	174	95	51
广西	15	551	404	146	164	15
海南	2	23	11	4	1	
重庆	12	339	246	131	166	24
四川	84	729	429	282	192	33
贵州	23	283	159	123	79	6
云南	35	343	217	76	110	4
西藏	15	108	59	36	22	2
陕西	11	247	142	81	67	5
甘肃	29	409	184	117	71	12
青海	12	194	122	91	28	4
宁夏	12	272	207	76	89	4
新疆	55	639	372	317	114	12

社会服务机构总表

单位:个、人、人次、时

格水平	年龄结构				志愿服务	
社会工作师人数	35岁及以下人数	36岁至45岁人数	46岁至55岁人数	56岁及以上人数	志愿者服务人次数	志愿服务时间
382	**5665**	**4844**	**2644**	**488**	**17141**	**46362.0**
10	209	228	96	11	32	82.0
11	59	34	25	6		
	34	37	32	5		
5	25	50	22	3		
14	113	87	60	10		
4	153	138	136	12		
	162	143	60	41		
20	216	154	85	3		
36	282	110	159	42		
31	197	180	193	29	2952	6306.0
19	149	115	99	10	616	1356.0
15	332	357	282	32	1295	2580.0
6	48	57	22	4		
1	74	63	49	8	132	528.0
11	303	191	73	16	7783	21509.0
22	200	123	79	4		
21	570	586	239	79	2476	7985.5
21	278	338	132	22	654	2757.0
33	382	355	127	65	80	200.0
10	274	182	86	9		
	8	7	8			
11	223	73	41	2	633	1512.0
23	292	276	132	29		
2	126	103	50	4	30	102.0
18	137	140	63	3	120	480.0
	43	57	7	1	35	109.5
4	106	87	51	3	185	557.0
4	159	165	67	18	10	30.0
	94	80	18	2		
11	122	104	37	9	108	264.0
19	295	224	114	6		4.0

C-2-14续表

地　区	增加值合计	执行行政事业单位			
		固定资产原价	上年结转和结余	本年收入合计	本年支出合计
全　国	**118252.7**	**329511.7**	**35804.1**	**228923.7**	**224286.8**
中央级					
北　京	7683.5	15293.8	1901.7	15109.6	15585.3
天　津	2231.3	1474.9	1237.7	4503.5	4926.8
河　北	388.3	1030.3	341.0	1308.4	1236.4
山　西	555.2	1363.9	220.2	1225.0	828.3
内蒙古	2889.0	8558.0	1024.5	6021.1	5867.1
辽　宁	4481.6	8283.2	2326.1	10252.3	10468.9
吉　林	1695.4	8390.4	40.0	3792.0	4090.2
黑龙江	4374.7	19721.9	318.0	13104.9	6590.7
上　海	5566.1	18075.3	212.0	13427.6	13816.5
江　苏	9695.7	9586.6	3896.6	14030.3	13752.6
浙　江	8109.6	15058.1	1037.9	17646.6	16329.3
安　徽	5381.9	19224.8	662.3	10516.3	10646.0
福　建	2000.5	2236.3	994.5	4073.5	3391.6
江　西	844.3	5246.9		1190.8	1125.6
山　东	7188.2	23058.9		13895.7	13895.7
河　南	4357.5	10143.2	1684.1	8573.2	8566.4
湖　北	7085.4	20355.5	964.1	12407.3	14040.6
湖　南	5437.0	10169.6	11.7	6896.5	7005.2
广　东	4291.4	15065.2	1161.6	9213.1	9292.1
广　西	3315.1	5948.7	486.2	6325.2	5372.6
海　南	451.9	1302.2		569.2	697.9
重　庆	3281.8	7015.3	287.1	8893.9	8082.1
四　川	6539.7	18984.3	5550.3	10552.1	10937.8
贵　州	3262.9	4970.5	3484.9	4719.7	4667.2
云　南	2303.7	15148.9	1180.3	5459.7	5254.4
西　藏	724.6	8613.1	56.0	1510.2	1550.8
陕　西	3350.1	7961.9	2481.2	7450.3	9626.2
甘　肃	2528.5	17341.7	730.9	3706.2	3525.5
青　海	151.7	3792.0		332.2	658.2
宁　夏	2288.9	9199.4	1118.9	2884.6	3199.7
新　疆	5796.8	16896.9	2394.3	9332.7	9259.1

单位：万元、张、人

会计制度财务指标		为儿童提供服务机构床位数	为儿童提供服务机构年末收养人数	#女性
收支结余	行政事业单位增加值			
9879.1	**118252.7**	**98428**	**58514**	**20901**
1197.3	7683.5	1968	984	333
	2231.3	823	684	262
100.0	388.3	713	185	26
	555.2	782	490	104
1178.5	2889.0	1501	798	325
300.0	4481.6	3016	2379	873
-288.2	1695.4	3967	1743	165
	4374.7	2639	1698	745
366.5	5566.1	2599	2261	954
-8.7	9695.7	4055	2136	997
1726.9	8109.6	2645	1557	600
	5381.9	6288	4269	1240
6.7	2000.5	1452	792	347
	844.3	1576	1060	106
	7188.2	7226	3034	1404
601.1	4357.5	2878	2575	1042
98.0	7085.4	7250	4292	1396
	5437.0	5384	3254	1868
969.8	4291.4	4655	2217	805
	3315.1	1918	792	292
4.5	451.9	140	94	45
1098.9	3281.8	3019	1369	623
494.5	6539.7	6488	2950	1141
22.6	3262.9	3191	1332	685
10.5	2303.7	3303	2858	262
	724.6	1695	1543	631
713.6	3350.1	2842	2200	836
	2528.5	3709	2243	754
	151.7	2030	1181	487
11.9	2288.9	1529	593	143
1274.7	5796.8	7147	4951	1410

C-2-15 儿童

地区	单位数	年末职工人数		受教育程度		职业资格水平		年龄	
			#女性	大学专科人数	大学本科及以上人数	助理社会工作师人数	社会工作师人数	35岁及以下人数	36岁至45岁人数
全国	**529**	**11598**	**7862**	**3439**	**2959**	**294**	**332**	**4924**	**4096**
中央级									
北京	12	492	382	136	226	11	8	190	211
天津	2	124	82	35	62	4	11	59	34
河北	10	76	40	9	5			31	32
山西	8	83	37	16	12	2	5	20	47
内蒙古	7	270	177	112	64	4	14	113	87
辽宁	9	416	258	121	207	6	4	148	131
吉林	18	406	166	55	62			162	143
黑龙江	15	453	287	167	121	2	20	213	152
上海	7	532	452	117	139	25	33	248	96
江苏	16	538	387	160	161	25	30	174	154
浙江	14	350	260	123	118	9	19	141	110
安徽	41	949	599	241	169	6	15	323	333
福建	10	131	92	47	46	6	6	48	57
江西	5	82	55	11	9		1	26	24
山东	18	559	404	196	232	12	11	289	182
河南	13	373	280	48	67	8	21	178	113
湖北	51	933	650	314	154	12	17	371	408
湖南	21	327	227	94	55	10	6	114	133
广东	39	838	628	156	82	43	22	363	345
广西	8	483	378	126	134	12	6	257	156
海南	2	23	11	4	1			8	7
重庆	7	315	237	118	158	22	8	214	60
四川	44	585	386	219	148	32	18	235	214
贵州	18	243	144	101	69	5	2	111	87
云南	26	307	200	62	109	4	18	123	127
西藏	15	108	59	36	22	2		43	57
陕西	11	247	142	81	67	5	4	106	87
甘肃	19	326	155	87	57	7	3	136	132
青海	7	177	122	82	28	4		86	71
宁夏	6	237	199	66	64	4	11	113	87
新疆	50	615	366	299	111	12	19	281	219

收养机构

单位:个、人、人次、时、张、人天

结构		志愿服务		年末床位数	#光荣间床位	年在院总人天数	年末在院人数	#女性
46岁至55岁人数	56岁及以上人数	志愿者服务人次数	志愿服务时间					
2263	**315**	**16038**	**42641.0**	**86929**	**1036**	**15598785**	**54447**	**20582**
84	7	32	82.0	1500		364788	984	333
25	6			823		294920	684	262
10	3			603	35	49345	185	26
13	3			678		70183	490	104
60	10			1501		269222	798	325
128	9			2946		852842	2379	873
60	41			3967	4	225257	1743	165
85	3			2539		389581	1698	745
146	42			2499		416960	2261	932
183	27	2884	6102.0	3196	4	741261	2136	995
95	4	616	1356.0	2395		553100	1557	599
263	30	1055	2100.0	5709	5	1084272	3291	1240
22	4			1452		294190	792	347
29	3	132	528.0	965		83667	742	106
72	16	7693	21290.0	6916		1051330	3034	1395
78	4			2643		858220	2550	1017
130	24	2214	7194.5	5691	195	900839	3562	1372
76	4	212	735.0	3831	527	801639	2977	1797
121	9	80	200.0	4355		749481	2217	805
63	7			1355		162375	792	289
8				140		14865	94	45
39	2	632	1507.0	2810		456348	1369	621
114	22			5244	17	803976	2764	1140
43	2	30	102.0	2787	155	448752	1320	685
54	3	120	480.0	2891		387462	1704	259
7	1	35	109.5	1650		445563	1543	631
51	3	185	557.0	2842		750201	2200	836
48	10	10	30.0	3066	19	458496	2243	600
18	2			1780		271232	1181	487
29	8	108	264.0	1223		116730	443	142
109	6		4.0	6932	75	1231688	4714	1409

C-2-15续表

地　区	在院人员按性质分			在院人员按年龄分			在院人员按类型分		
	优抚对象	“三无”对象	自费人员	老人	青壮年	少年儿童	自理(完全自理)	介助(半自理)	介护(不能自理)
全　国	**1839**	**50340**	**2268**	**1176**	**1794**	**51477**	**21825**	**12600**	**20022**
中央级									
北　京		956	28	1	57	926	296	153	535
天　津		666	18		29	655	187	92	405
河　北	17	168				185	149	9	27
山　西		457	33	1		489	353	90	47
内蒙古		798			78	720	328	191	279
辽　宁	1541	787	51		199	2180	1645	652	82
吉　林	10	1665	68	78		1665	1395	72	276
黑龙江	140	1450	108	126	31	1541	1033	428	237
上　海		2013	248			2261	281	359	1621
江　苏	4	2091	41	103	274	1759	491	358	1287
浙　江		1295	262		23	1534	111	395	1051
安　徽	35	3034	222	345	214	2732	748	921	1622
福　建		792			25	767	257	282	253
江　西		742				742	359	12	371
山　东		3034				3034	507	820	1707
河　南	30	2520		6	7	2537	1150	738	662
湖　北		3462	100		48	3514	795	932	1835
湖　南	10	2960	7	16	18	2943	1031	711	1235
广　东	3	1895	319	42	9	2166	596	474	1147
广　西		792			163	629	79	346	367
海　南		94				94	35	14	45
重　庆		1369				1369	382	329	658
四　川	7	2569	188	299	135	2330	676	744	1344
贵　州	3	1268	49	28	43	1249	730	373	217
云　南		1704		20		1684	531	975	198
西　藏	8	1482	53	55	298	1190	1524	19	
陕　西		2194	6		30	2170	616	734	850
甘　肃	2	2114	127	12		2231	813	668	762
青　海	29	952	200			1181	904	256	21
宁　夏		443				443	133	47	263
新　疆		4574	140	44	113	4557	3690	406	618

单位：人、人次、平方米、万元

康复和医疗门诊人次数	家庭寄养儿童数量	机构建筑面积	增加值合计	执行行政事业单位会计制度财务指标					
				固定资产原价	上年结转和结余	本年收入合计	本年支出合计	收支结余	行政事业单位增加值
472769	**20627**	**2179375**	**106471.2**	**302668.2**	**34118.9**	**208479.7**	**204247.4**	**8611.0**	**106471.2**
1259	743	63778	6636.8	14688.9	1815.1	12808.4	13653.7	946.1	6636.8
19427	270	20251	2231.3	1474.9	1237.7	4503.5	4926.8		2231.3
	104	10643	192.1	660.3		427.4	408.4		192.1
730	91	14684	545.1	1110.7	220.2	1069.9	775.7		545.1
13707	15	43905	2889.0	8558.0	1024.5	6021.1	5867.1	1178.5	2889.0
23588	229	107839	4155.6	7999.3	2326.1	9785.1	10019.2	300.0	4155.6
12642	24	19220	1695.4	8390.4	40.0	3792.0	4090.2	-288.2	1695.4
475	132	91210	4191.3	19613.1	318.0	12799.9	6375.1		4191.3
	1325	39141	5147.0	17568.2	0.8	12149.5	12693.7		5147.0
19059	263	97679	9372.9	9121.6	3896.6	13225.3	13088.6	-8.7	9372.9
14220	399	61108	7702.4	14221.0	1037.9	17108.5	15791.2	1726.9	7702.4
14399	403	224531	5216.1	18676.5	662.3	9899.1	10016.3		5216.1
610	722	24179	2000.5	2236.3	994.5	4073.5	3391.6	6.7	2000.5
	2	21310	511.1	1662.7		734.3	658.3		511.1
59750	450	218236	7059.7	21690.0		13486.8	13486.8		7059.7
5011	494	77812	4333.0	9680.2	1684.1	8539.2	8536.4	601.1	4333.0
55434	864	99672	5840.5	15589.5	494.1	9487.7	10673.0	54.0	5840.5
4773	1668	62989	3314.2	6789.8		4265.8	4254.1		3314.2
66141	130	78586	2585.9	11935.4	1161.6	6846.6	7028.0	969.8	2585.9
5218	99	44810	2978.0	5338.2	486.2	5776.6	4824.0		2978.0
84	5	9892	451.9	1302.2		569.2	697.9	4.5	451.9
11845	134	131150	3171.9	6555.5	287.1	8764.8	7953.0	1098.9	3171.9
31075	1616	126340	5913.0	18144.4	5201.7	9523.3	10020.6		5913.0
578	298	38880	2574.1	4686.1	3379.0	4021.5	3902.5	22.6	2574.1
3332	1722	93302	1979.3	14645.6	1175.2	5162.2	4932.4	10.5	1979.3
	25	41014	724.6	8613.1	56.0	1510.2	1550.8		724.6
	405	72869	3350.1	7961.9	2481.2	7450.3	9626.2	713.6	3350.1
18295	78	64270	2155.4	15277.7	625.8	3004.6	2855.7		2155.4
	21	34047	146.8	3670.0		331.0	651.0		146.8
405	107	27075	1835.0	8661.4	1118.9	2310.9	2546.5		1835.0
90712	7789	118953	5570.8	16145.3	2394.3	9031.5	8952.6	1274.7	5570.8

C-2-16 未成年人

地区	单位数	年末职工人数		受教育程度		职业资
			#女性	大学专科人数	大学本科及以上人数	助理社会工作师人数
全　国	**274**	**2043**	**761**	**682**	**479**	**44**
中央级						
北　京	2	52	22	10	38	5
天　津						
河　北	2	32	5		8	
山　西	3	17	5	5	3	
内蒙古						
辽　宁	2	23	6	14	7	
吉　林						
黑龙江	1	5	5		5	
上　海	1	61	53	24	6	1
江　苏	30	61	28	15	14	3
浙　江	1	23	8	8	13	
安　徽	7	54	9	19	10	
福　建						
江　西	13	112	39	60	21	8
山　东	6	24	11	11	9	
河　南	4	33	10	19	5	
湖　北	66	541	215	120	124	5
湖　南	43	443	161	160	68	2
广　东	1	91	31	18	13	8
广　西	7	68	26	20	30	3
海　南						
重　庆	5	24	9	13	8	2
四　川	40	144	43	63	44	1
贵　州	5	40	15	22	10	1
云　南	9	36	17	14	1	
西　藏						
陕　西						
甘　肃	10	83	29	30	14	5
青　海	5	17		9		
宁　夏	6	35	8	10	25	
新　疆	5	24	6	18	3	

救助保护中心

单位:个、人、人次、时

格水平	年龄结构				志愿服务	
社会工作师人数	35岁及以下人数	36岁至45岁人数	46岁至55岁人数	56岁及以上人数	志愿者服务人次数	志愿服务时间
50	**741**	**748**	**381**	**173**	**1103**	**3721.0**
2	19	17	12	4		
	3	5	22	2		
	5	3	9			
	5	7	8	3		
	3	2				
3	34	14	13			
1	23	26	10	2	68	204.0
	8	5	4	6		
	9	24	19	2	240	480.0
	48	39	20	5		
	14	9	1		90	219.0
1	22	10	1			
4	199	178	109	55	262	791.0
15	164	205	56	18	442	2022.0
11	19	10	6	56		
4	17	26	23	2		
3	9	13	2		1	5.0
5	57	62	18	7		
	15	16	7	2		
	14	13	9			
1	23	33	19	8		
	8	9				
	9	17	8	1		
	14	5	5			

C−2−16续表1

地区	本年在站救助人次数	从其他站转入的	女性	未成年人	老年人	肢体残疾人	智障及精神病人
全国	**70873**	**6112**	**9501**	**35461**	**4067**	**5665**	**2209**
中央级							
北京	495		13	495			
天津							
河北	66		4	66			
山西	64			41			
内蒙古							
辽宁	69		3	69			1
吉林							
黑龙江	112						
上海	112		57	112			
江苏	2288	216	262	2033		41	12
浙江	270	57	71	270		2	6
安徽	6078	361	1392	1345	978	741	933
福建							
江西	8256	738	751	1733	318	1423	32
山东	175	13	58	172		39	11
河南	6832		30	6370	25	50	150
湖北	7198	410	557	5017	730	196	117
湖南	16011	1756	2909	7200	277	1812	273
广东	456	456	144	456			
广西	1845	5	190	1113		1	25
海南							
重庆	1327	352	314	1157		50	60
四川	5456	1049	1206	4831	186	368	234
贵州	863	306	135	851	12	66	11
云南	7378	37	486	139	1154	354	94
西藏							
陕西							
甘肃	1550	52	39	1051		4	49
青海	150			120			
宁夏	2841	301	658	690	150	420	171
新疆	981	3	222	130	237	98	30

单位：人次、张

救治的危重病人	自主返乡	跨省接送	床位数	成年人床位数	儿童床位数
218	**5945**	**2998**	**11499**	**2063**	**9436**
		98	468		468
		3	110		110
		1	104		104
			70		70
			100	80	20
			100		100
7	482	114	859	5	854
	6	119	250		250
57	228	131	579	70	509
	204	626	611	166	445
	1	24	310		310
	100		235	130	105
8	591	525	1559	141	1418
2	939	214	1553	418	1135
		151	300		300
3	29	22	563	90	473
	454	143	209	10	199
98	758	305	1244	152	1092
		79	404	242	162
	1145	263	412	129	283
			45	45	
	221	18	643	90	553
			250	50	200
17	681	64	306	150	156
26	106	98	215	95	120

C-2-16续表2

地区	年末在站人数	女性	儿童	本年在站人天数	本年不在站救助人次数	未成年人	在站滞留三个月以上人数	残疾人人数
全　国	**1689**	**319**	**1084**	**380631**	**23578**	**678**	**226**	**25**
中央级								
北　京	46		46	20879			55	
天　津								
河　北								
山　西								
内蒙古					35			
辽　宁				566				
吉　林								
黑龙江	14		14	400				
上　海	57	22	57	19455				
江　苏	42	2	7	12653	540	159	15	2
浙　江	13	1	13	4794			5	3
安　徽	66		64	14198	320		5	4
福　建								
江　西	127			7406	60			
山　东	54	9	21	3375	88			
河　南	28	25	28	1005	2611			
湖　北	178	24	89	72224	3005	12	98	5
湖　南	300	71	186	43947	3471	275	7	6
广　东	134		134	56266				
广　西	25	3	23	5816	106	5	10	
海　南								
重　庆	23	2	23	14527			5	5
四　川	37	1	15	37765	218		13	
贵　州	135		1	50632				
云　南	13	3	3	1857	1569	1	3	
西　藏					191			
陕　西								
甘　肃	382	154	359	5647	1126	226		
青　海					30			
宁　夏	7	1	1	3719	9409		1	
新　疆	8	1		3500	799		9	

单位：万元、人天、人次、人

未成年人人数	增加值合计	执行行政事业单位会计制度财务指标					
		固定资产原价	上年结转和结余	本年收入合计	本年支出合计	收支结余	行政事业单位增加值
108	**11781.5**	**26843.5**	**1685.2**	**20444.0**	**20039.4**	**1268.1**	**11781.5**
55	1046.7	604.9	86.6	2301.2	1931.6	251.2	1046.7
	196.2	370.0	341.0	881.0	828.0	100.0	196.2
	10.1	253.2		155.1	52.6		10.1
	326.0	283.9		467.2	449.7		326.0
	183.4	108.8		305.0	215.6		183.4
	419.1	507.1	211.2	1278.1	1122.8	366.5	419.1
13	322.8	465.0		805.0	664.0		322.8
5	407.2	837.1		538.1	538.1		407.2
5	165.8	548.3		617.2	629.7		165.8
	333.2	3584.2		456.5	467.3		333.2
	128.5	1368.9		408.9	408.9		128.5
	24.5	463.0		34.0	30.0		24.5
12	1244.9	4766.0	470.0	2919.6	3367.6	44.0	1244.9
1	2122.8	3379.8	11.7	2630.7	2751.1		2122.8
	1705.5	3129.8		2366.5	2264.1		1705.5
8	337.1	610.5		548.6	548.6		337.1
5	109.9	459.8		129.1	129.1		109.9
	626.7	839.9	348.6	1028.8	917.2	494.5	626.7
	688.8	284.4	105.9	698.2	764.7		688.8
3	324.4	503.3	5.1	297.5	322.0		324.4
	373.1	2064.0	105.1	701.6	669.8		373.1
	4.9	122.0		1.2	7.2		4.9
1	453.9	538.0		573.7	653.2	11.9	453.9
	226.0	751.6		301.2	306.5		226.0

C-2-17 其他提供住宿的

地区	单位数	年末职工人数	#女性	受教育程度		职业资格水平	
				大学专科人数	大学本科及以上人数	助理社会工作师人数	社会工作师人数
全国	**2438**	**28044**	**11001**	**8946**	**5763**	**472**	**441**
中央级							
北京	25	848	367	183	271	19	5
天津	14	212	69	49	53	2	5
河北	149	1539	715	340	176	6	11
山西	97	708	256	286	139	5	8
内蒙古	44	534	143	228	170	2	8
辽宁	101	1303	461	467	343	12	17
吉林	69	1052	354	261	221	4	2
黑龙江	94	1370	540	383	212	13	8
上海	20	391	110	168	106	14	24
江苏	93	1155	510	324	323	29	47
浙江	93	813	315	249	230	19	17
安徽	91	1094	484	255	159	22	12
福建	84	587	208	144	149	5	15
江西	105	901	310	309	142	23	9
山东	74	731	252	285	248	20	21
河南	119	1630	609	627	295	17	31
湖北	96	1127	409	390	204	12	10
湖南	135	1306	441	530	190	17	15
广东	98	2303	894	903	494	111	61
广西	65	773	292	234	220	18	23
海南	10	132	50	31	35	3	3
重庆	42	381	132	162	153	15	4
四川	209	3020	1542	698	406	34	40
贵州	82	662	250	241	133	7	4
云南	127	1002	404	308	228	14	16
西藏	9	55	14	14	11		1
陕西	104	1088	409	351	130	7	12
甘肃	53	526	172	171	109	9	6
青海	16	110	36	54	22	3	1
宁夏	13	85	21	28	39	6	
新疆	107	606	232	273	152	4	5

社会服务机构总表

单位:个、人、人次、时

年龄结构				志愿服务		年末床位数	年在院(站)总人天数
35岁及以下人数	36岁至45岁人数	46岁至55岁人数	56岁及以上人数	志愿者服务人次数	志愿服务时间		
8222	**10010**	**7270**	**2542**	**20412**	**61084.0**	**157029**	**16883613**
317	254	204	73	403	1802.0	8035	1647726
72	53	65	22	2005	4015.0	1484	83454
500	547	397	95	917	3998.0	11873	1251502
248	241	184	35	313	488.0	2985	224781
126	155	208	45	40	240.0	2667	221450
352	458	382	111	15	36.0	7478	745290
278	484	251	39	130	220.0	3184	331640
464	360	274	272	47	174.0	4770	450273
100	94	119	78	810	4050.0	1504	272433
273	371	370	141	2689	13324.0	6373	709008
258	290	194	71	3763	5901.0	5002	456519
206	452	349	87	653	1941.0	6001	818368
181	179	194	33	65	195.0	3474	353383
236	384	216	65	270	1074.0	4988	557232
233	259	198	41	4264	10199.0	5862	308833
618	581	368	63	20	60.0	10804	744418
344	452	236	95	394	931.0	5986	848963
460	558	224	64	1916	7868.0	5993	655074
765	787	590	161	35	78.0	11365	1005268
158	286	252	77	14	28.0	3533	496378
36	47	42	7			444	95834
107	133	109	32	942	2408.0	1388	134364
605	938	828	649	241	708.0	18634	1947773
215	254	169	24	283	587.0	4597	726880
228	459	260	55	16	42.0	5688	946493
26	21	8				864	406
394	413	230	51	109	502.0	4779	437433
159	181	159	27	40	120.0	2404	105242
34	43	28	5	8	35.0	481	9796
24	35	21	5			367	10581
205	241	141	19	10	60.0	4022	286818

C-2-17续表

地区	增加值合计	执行企业会计制度单位财务指标					执行行政	
		固定资产原价	营业收入	费用合计	营业利润	企业单位增加值	固定资产原价	上年结转和结余
全　国	**214409.0**	**2149.4**	**3379.0**	**3719.8**	**1931.3**	**3343.2**	**440645.5**	**43116.0**
中央级								
北　京	10580.7						6758.8	3080.7
天　津	3147.6						1625.8	1399.8
河　北	7391.4					-30.8	25728.7	1761.5
山　西	4483.8						5682.4	1538.9
内蒙古	4774.5						9030.4	1036.4
辽　宁	8428.6						20666.4	460.9
吉　林	5652.8						9079.9	71.2
黑龙江	6324.8				2082.0	2082.0	14311.4	413.8
上　海	6284.3						19564.2	5029.1
江　苏	11788.8	239.0	2078.1	105.4	27.1	394.3	29512.4	888.8
浙　江	12928.2	319.0	440.3	442.7	-101.0	-36.4	22175.7	987.4
安　徽	5621.1	189.1	42.4	65.7	-23.3	22.9	16942.8	1523.9
福　建	5171.0						9358.8	1443.0
江　西	3814.9						10651.1	1404.8
山　东	9303.6						17648.7	194.9
河　南	11908.7						19712.4	2460.6
湖　北	8002.0						11006.2	548.7
湖　南	7990.7	62.2	162.0	5.6		40.8	11582.5	860.5
广　东	27195.2	1034.0	586.0	397.0	20.0	768.3	57823.1	3469.7
广　西	6117.4						13276.5	1355.8
海　南	1811.2						2650.1	915.5
重　庆	4312.3						7084.9	156.0
四　川	13208.2						37935.7	3531.0
贵　州	7782.6			2560.3			4850.1	1276.3
云　南	6510.9						19652.3	1195.1
西　藏	198.0						1841.8	
陕　西	5887.7	306.1	70.2	143.1	-73.5	102.1	11184.9	1254.1
甘　肃	2488.0						7159.4	823.8
青　海	529.8						987.8	
宁　夏	992.1						1723.3	102.0
新　疆	3778.6						13437.0	3931.8

单位：万元

事业单位会计制度财务指标				执行民间非营利组织单位会计制度财务指标				
本年收入合计	本年支出合计	收支结余	行政事业单位增加值	固定资产原价	上年结余	本年收入合计	本年费用合计	社会组织增加值
397890.3	**394922.0**	**97856.6**	**208626.8**	**22379.8**	**1443.0**	**3178.3**	**6797.3**	**2439.0**
27930.8	26797.5	2947.6	10580.5	1360.2			0.2	0.2
5328.8	4851.4	40.5	3147.6					
13751.8	13397.1	1790.6	7186.0	9856.0	-7.0	1064.6	896.7	236.2
8255.2	8413.7	867.1	4483.8					
8144.5	7577.0	1603.9	4774.5					
14990.0	14735.4	268.7	8408.3	205.0	42.0	30.1	30.4	20.3
7968.8	7980.8	133.4	5652.7	10.0		2.0	0.1	0.1
8893.2	9283.0		4242.8					
13734.2	14826.4	4668.0	6284.3					
22810.7	21775.3	827.9	11394.5					
21753.0	21501.6	1240.9	12907.6	560.0	15.0	157.0	147.0	57.0
11596.9	11430.5	550.4	5598.2					
9714.8	9108.5	1149.0	5171.0					
7423.3	7398.8	3.7	3814.9					
14818.0	15012.9		9303.6					
20807.1	20533.6	76962.6	11908.0	100.0		60.0	5.0	0.7
18508.1	18839.8	194.0	8002.0					
16563.4	16763.8	222.0	7949.9					
45777.1	45780.5	948.2	26256.8	204.7	-7.8	451.5	392.1	170.1
13418.5	12666.5	867.7	6098.1	274.0	3.6	33.3	39.8	19.3
3222.7	3268.6	-130.7	1811.2					
8166.5	8277.0	37.6	4312.3					
21179.3	21650.6	666.4	11276.5	9780.9	1397.2	1373.8	5282.6	1931.7
12735.7	12098.6	251.4	7779.6	10.0		5.0	3.0	3.0
11574.6	11224.1	349.8	6510.5	19.0		1.0	0.4	0.4
936.0	973.6		198.0					
9719.5	10678.9	188.5	5785.6					
4634.6	3917.4	918.0	2488.0					
1366.6	1366.6		529.8					
1528.4	1497.0	38.1	992.1					
10638.2	11295.5	251.3	3778.6					

C-2-18 生活无着人员

地区	单位数	年末职工人数		受教育程度		职业资
			#女性	大学专科人数	大学本科及以上人数	助理社会工作师人数
全国	**1891**	**17587**	**5924**	**6440**	**4364**	**381**
中央级						
北京	21	639	253	154	235	16
天津	12	197	63	47	45	2
河北	82	533	137	133	89	5
山西	90	593	209	241	116	4
内蒙古	38	412	102	176	136	2
辽宁	64	898	280	363	267	9
吉林	52	744	249	173	184	1
黑龙江	82	738	229	305	165	6
上海	19	342	96	154	100	12
江苏	73	704	270	202	262	27
浙江	77	537	179	194	188	16
安徽	52	398	122	127	127	14
福建	68	392	117	109	119	4
江西	92	610	202	211	105	23
山东	55	442	141	168	173	12
河南	90	1041	355	440	180	9
湖北	86	871	322	309	162	11
湖南	119	997	321	426	148	16
广东	74	1733	561	673	380	98
广西	48	406	135	131	124	12
海南	8	94	36	27	29	3
重庆	38	316	110	138	124	14
四川	144	1114	407	430	266	25
贵州	67	389	150	166	102	4
云南	93	506	167	203	150	8
西藏	8	51	14	12	10	
陕西	90	902	339	298	108	7
甘肃	43	384	142	143	88	8
青海	12	71	25	40	11	3
宁夏	12	76	20	22	36	6
新疆	82	457	171	225	135	4

救助管理站

单位:个、人、人次、时

格水平	年龄结构				志愿服务	
社会工作师人数	35岁及以下人数	36岁至45岁人数	46岁至55岁人数	56岁及以上人数	志愿者服务人次数	志愿服务时间
372	**5805**	**6363**	**4338**	**1081**	**18762**	**55222.0**
4	276	179	154	30		
5	62	51	63	21	2005	4015.0
5	152	205	143	33	737	3215.0
7	226	193	145	29	313	488.0
7	92	113	172	35	40	240.0
14	273	283	261	81	15	36.0
1	223	326	174	21	130	220.0
4	198	291	220	29	47	174.0
24	93	88	99	62	810	4050.0
42	236	228	184	56	2485	12548.0
14	185	204	104	44	3577	5265.0
11	115	127	128	28	251	1029.0
15	158	110	105	19	27	81.0
8	180	261	128	41	138	546.0
19	172	153	96	21	4264	10199.0
24	435	352	222	32	20	60.0
8	278	344	176	73	357	795.0
15	383	428	143	43	1916	7868.0
47	509	611	488	125	35	78.0
18	93	143	121	49	14	28.0
3	28	32	28	6		
4	80	115	95	26	942	2408.0
36	385	419	250	60	211	648.0
3	145	148	81	15	273	567.0
9	137	221	126	22	16	42.0
1	24	19	8			
12	344	333	184	41	109	502.0
6	133	128	104	19	20	60.0
1	18	31	19	3		
	23	32	16	5		
5	149	195	101	12	10	60.0

C-2-18续表1

地　区	本年在站救助人次数	从其他站转入的	女性	未成年人	老年人	肢体残疾人	智障及精神病人
全　国	**2891249**	**153301**	**599832**	**144079**	**333172**	**180151**	**183802**
中央级							
北　京	721725	11461	252509	10904	36919	7575	4419
天　津	13530	220	1242	289	938	292	715
河　北	71704	732	10987	2997	9000	3921	7429
山　西	64698	1978	5657	2728	8737	6457	3995
内蒙古	30929	2213	4736	1944	8431	4123	1980
辽　宁	54748	1950	9280	6350	8040	3893	4408
吉　林	38462	4113	11880	1939	7574	3065	3009
黑龙江	31145	3879	5686	2501	5514	3877	2673
上　海	35617	272	7087	2760	3833	1971	1486
江　苏	81424	8149	11919	4316	8747	3351	7697
浙　江	56294	1485	8481	1959	5743	2117	7139
安　徽	90541	7100	13906	4361	13696	7651	7660
福　建	80281	1928	5782	2489	7679	3282	2139
江　西	81549	9583	9041	4368	11396	12376	3522
山　东	78320	5205	13152	3095	8993	8670	3648
河　南	125028	9704	21908	6900	14329	12079	13465
湖　北	257371	7569	55934	24163	36271	10362	20849
湖　南	225730	21037	36452	11751	41370	28592	23076
广　东	140642	9060	17647	6910	16617	7927	7956
广　西	53522	3278	7594	2613	3847	2078	7144
海　南	23937	180	4860	707	6402	815	13825
重　庆	52826	3432	9541	1092	6827	2737	3576
四　川	186135	19678	33490	14225	25321	16325	14115
贵　州	70932	5080	7697	5384	9160	5929	2505
云　南	54469	4236	8493	2914	7094	7538	3023
西　藏	6193	34	545	337	567	858	10
陕　西	90979	5045	11039	6683	10992	5336	2610
甘　肃	28094	3498	5811	1188	5057	1944	1545
青　海	12013	121	1859	3318	754	3641	5387
宁　夏	6184	589	1462	387	400	235	263
新　疆	26227	492	4155	2507	2924	1134	2534

单位：人次、张

救治的危重病人	自主返乡	跨省接送	床位数	成年人床位数	儿童床位数
43016	**970749**	**112296**	**96861**	**76965**	**19896**
519	12850	9145	6803	6621	182
1496	7722	265	1284	1075	209
7131	42121	2410	3114	2380	734
687	35154	1390	2447	1642	805
806	17165	2887	2104	1646	458
352	23950	3119	4698	3533	1165
954	22824	2617	1801	1155	646
17	9693	2068	3511	1970	1541
767	17278	752	1325	1086	239
3120	50527	5226	4277	3478	799
1100	35616	1668	3199	2772	427
3035	47978	4857	3792	2774	1018
516	43906	1897	2247	1657	590
2939	31388	4690	3700	2896	804
143	38221	8846	3557	2720	837
1107	50787	7084	6815	5337	1478
1417	51985	9094	4066	3211	855
2299	84229	10712	4848	4478	370
1053	72046	3384	7820	6178	1642
547	23848	1749	1840	1297	543
461	8196	366	335	244	91
329	35957	1429	1312	1124	188
7215	81541	14280	6865	5753	1112
2854	30439	2225	3406	2120	1286
126	24326	1864	1973	1738	235
218	16	6	864	647	217
718	45014	3677	4234	3803	431
213	15315	2315	1375	1167	208
30	1381	6	325	266	59
101	2319	463	367	270	97
746	6957	1805	2557	1927	630

C-2-18续表2

地区	年末在站人数	女性	儿童	本年在站人天数	本年不在站救助人次数	未成年人	在站滞留三个月以上人数	残疾人人数
全国	**22401**	**5099**	**3130**	**7802190**	**499027**	**3584**	**21857**	**11766**
中央级								
北京	2947	444	559	1523491	3107		2344	646
天津	391	104	89	83454	375	2	317	308
河北	834	267	63	279198	22160	192	776	423
山西	419	148	33	124319	17125	112	704	63
内蒙古	271	52	19	103255	14121	4	247	95
辽宁	869	65	147	150981	6313	120	168	35
吉林	387	92	25	112260	8372		492	274
黑龙江	389	36	128	61915	985		7	2
上海	462	152	68	207098	746		352	352
江苏	1047	408	79	391098	9880	10	1314	718
浙江	601	214	91	322048	738	10	1512	124
安徽	647	209	74	276125	50618	210	642	346
福建	264	64	28	119738	10378	136	526	444
江西	420	6	22	174022	16240	23	655	594
山东	801	296	33	307309	52855	727	1781	1461
河南	1671	727	189	316103	35899	103	430	178
湖北	1719	589	105	625043	26192	13	707	122
湖南	1251	163	125	402198	39390	672	2309	1674
广东	1272	164	184	583628	22810	136	2943	1921
广西	360	65	17	88037	15687	47	230	47
海南	448	97	16	88534	8578		770	655
重庆	196	62	11	117753	9484	32	97	5
四川	990	198	189	471175	65719	58	331	87
贵州	991	99	214	356974	16242	76	727	511
云南	306	88	32	96717	11595	118	407	164
西藏	211		211	406	30			
陕西	955	193	119	260508	14801		669	341
甘肃	315	18	94	58067	5915	159	28	9
青海	45	3		9796	3915		107	95
宁夏	67	12	34	10581	1057		68	63
新疆	855	64	132	80359	7700	624	197	9

单位：万元、人天、人次、人

未成年人人数	增加值合计	执行行政事业单位会计制度财务指标					
		固定资产原价	上年结转和结余	本年收入合计	本年支出合计	收支结余	行政事业单位增加值
3972	**150328.1**	**276475.9**	**38409.5**	**308698.5**	**305533.4**	**21125.2**	**150328.1**
2228	8753.7	3965.6	3040.7	24778.3	23369.2	2947.6	8753.7
31	3147.6	1625.8	1399.8	5328.8	4851.4	40.5	3147.6
49	3101.1	6889.6	1732.6	7953.3	7814.9	1788.7	3101.1
66	3593.0	4204.8	1471.3	7099.0	7341.7	745.9	3593.0
24	3396.9	6521.8	968.9	6458.0	5853.5	1573.4	3396.9
16	6211.9	12117.6	346.7	11359.5	11217.5	268.6	6211.9
36	4089.6	5442.7	71.2	6016.8	5974.9	133.4	4089.6
	2825.1	7018.8	215.3	4562.6	4917.7		2825.1
60	5453.1	17041.6	4945.7	12581.5	13662.9	4596.8	5453.1
55	9276.7	24274.2	987.3	19848.2	18978.4	843.6	9276.7
96	9081.2	9612.5	1749.4	15895.9	15553.3	215.9	9081.2
30	3084.1	8191.4	1483.7	9602.8	9056.8	549.4	3084.1
82	3141.5	4577.7	1238.6	6849.8	6344.2	1055.8	3141.5
84	2687.0	4355.6	967.0	5900.8	5731.9		2687.0
73	6293.7	13226.9	194.9	10579.6	10774.5		6293.7
19	7710.3	7864.6	1930.8	14568.6	14392.5	2176.0	7710.3
18	5509.9	8311.8	509.9	15203.7	15636.2	44.0	5509.9
179	6244.3	8296.1	860.1	13881.8	14107.8	222.0	6244.3
488	22527.2	43849.8	1797.2	38384.2	37698.5	946.4	22527.2
49	3134.4	6404.0	846.9	8760.0	7756.1	765.1	3134.4
8	1774.2	1833.6	806.1	2730.4	2786.5	-130.7	1774.2
5	3586.7	5900.7	156.0	7043.6	7154.1	37.6	3586.7
51	8661.0	29200.6	2819.0	18490.6	18988.7	496.5	8661.0
71	2968.7	3236.5	877.1	6148.4	5561.3	251.4	2968.7
106	3089.5	7749.0	973.8	5535.5	6011.4	249.7	3089.5
	198.0	1841.8		326.0	363.6		198.0
33	4947.0	8983.1	1233.7	8491.6	9516.4	126.4	4947.0
	1736.7	4943.9	822.0	3797.4	3098.5	918.0	1736.7
12	331.8	500.2		886.6	886.6		331.8
2	815.5	1057.3	102.0	1222.2	1176.0	11.9	815.5
1	2957.1	7436.3	3861.8	8413.0	8956.4	251.3	2957.1

C-2-19 安置

地　区	单位数	年末职工人数	#女　性	#残疾职工	#女残疾职工	残疾职工工资总额	残疾职工养老保险总额
全　国	**26**	**1227**	**483**	**131**	**43**	**269.7**	**1.0**
中央级							
北　京							
天　津	1	15	6	1	1	0.1	
河　北	1	29	4	9		27.0	
山　西							
内蒙古							
辽　宁							
吉　林	1	30	20	2		4.0	
黑龙江	1	456	241	20	5	30.0	
上　海							
江　苏	1	139	84	39	27	93.5	
浙　江	2	45	5	3		14.0	
安　徽	3	72	20	2		6.0	
福　建	4	51	13	4		7.3	
江　西							
山　东							
河　南							
湖　北							
湖　南	3	48	9	17	1	22.4	0.8
广　东	3	59	10	17	3	48.1	
广　西	1	41	3	1		2.5	
海　南							
重　庆							
四　川	1	46	11	8	5	4.0	
贵　州	2	149	45	3		3.8	0.2
云　南							
西　藏							
陕　西	1	34	10	1		3.0	
甘　肃	1	13	2	4	1	4.0	
青　海							
宁　夏							
新　疆							

农场

单位:个、人、万元

残疾职工补贴	纳税总额				应减免税金总额	实际减免税金总额	盈利总额
		增值税总额	营业税总额	所得税总额			
	156.1	**131.6**	**16.5**	**6.2**	**141.1**	**141.1**	**129.7**
	131.6	131.6			131.6	131.6	127.9
	9.5		9.5		9.5	9.5	1.8
	15.0		7.0	6.2			

C-2-19续表1

地　区	单位数	年末职工人数	受教育程度		职业资
			大学专科人数	大学本科及以上人数	助理社会工作师人数
全　国	**26**	**1227**	**170**	**72**	**11**
中央级					
北　京					
天　津	1	15	2	8	
河　北	1	29	2		
山　西					
内蒙古					
辽　宁					
吉　林	1	30			
黑龙江	1	456	2		5
上　海					
江　苏	1	139	56	13	
浙　江	2	45	10	5	
安　徽	3	72	2	3	3
福　建	4	51	10	10	
江　西					
山　东					
河　南					
湖　北					
湖　南	3	48	14	1	
广　东	3	59	15	6	
广　西	1	41	6	15	
海　南					
重　庆					
四　川	1	46	4	2	1
贵　州	2	149	47	9	2
云　南					
西　藏					
陕　西	1	34			
甘　肃	1	13			
青　海					
宁　夏					
新　疆					

单位:个、人、人次、时

格水平	年龄结构				志愿服务	
社会工作师人数	35岁及以下人数	36岁至45岁人数	46岁至55岁人数	56岁及以上人数	志愿者服务人次数	志愿服务时间
	326	**297**	**296**	**308**	**38**	**114.0**
	10	2	2	1		
	3	10	13	3		
	10	10	10			
	217	3	2	234		
	7	51	64	17		
		10	22	13		
	7	23	35	7		
	3	13	32	3	38	114.0
	20	20	3	5		
	8	35	11	5		
	9	9	16	7		
	3	18	20	5		
	25	61	55	8		
	2	27	5			
	2	5	6			

C-2-19续表2

地 区	增加值合计	执行企业会计制度单位财务指标				
		固定资产原价	营业收入	费用合计	营业利润	企业单位增加值
全 国	**8414.7**	**2149.4**	**3379.0**	**3719.8**	**1931.3**	**3343.2**
中央级						
北 京						
天 津						
河 北	56.3					-30.8
山 西						
内蒙古						
辽 宁						
吉 林	141.1					
黑龙江	2082.1				2082.0	2082.0
上 海						
江 苏	394.3	239.0	2078.1	105.4	27.1	394.3
浙 江	-36.4	319.0	440.3	442.7	-101.0	-36.4
安 徽	182.8	189.1	42.4	65.7	-23.3	22.9
福 建	668.4					
江 西						
山 东						
河 南						
湖 北						
湖 南	70.4	62.2	162.0	5.6		40.8
广 东	996.1	1034.0	586.0	397.0	20.0	768.3
广 西	167.4					
海 南						
重 庆						
四 川	135.8					
贵 州	3454.3			2560.3		
云 南						
西 藏						
陕 西	102.1	306.1	70.2	143.1	-73.5	102.1
甘 肃						
青 海						
宁 夏						
新 疆						

单位：万元

执行行政事业单位会计制度财务指标					
固定资产原价	上年结转和结余	本年收入合计	本年支出合计	收支结余	行政事业单位增加值
2810.0	**130.7**	**8414.8**	**8634.9**	**43.6**	**5071.5**
80.6		95.6	95.6		87.1
82.9		178.4	178.4		141.1
3.0		2320.0	2320.0		0.1
160.6		60.1	224.6		159.9
1313.1	110.9	1052.2	1010.3	41.8	668.4
19.8		63.1	63.1		29.6
137.4		299.9	298.1	1.8	227.8
110.0	3.8	172.0	170.5		167.4
47.7		31.4	180.1		135.8
854.9	16.0	4142.1	4094.2		3454.3

C-2-20 军

地 区	单位数	年末职工人数		受教育程度		职业资
			#女性	大学专科人数	大学本科及以上人数	助理社会工作师人数
全 国	**325**	**5587**	**2266**	**1772**	**1029**	**53**
中央级						
北 京	1	46	12	5	24	
天 津	1					
河 北	9	94	28	30	27	
山 西	6	108	42	45	23	1
内蒙古	5	106	32	50	26	
辽 宁	11	217	67	82	48	3
吉 林	11	258	74	86	32	3
黑龙江	11	176	70	76	47	2
上 海	1	49	14	14	6	2
江 苏	17	288	136	62	48	2
浙 江	11	136	63	42	35	3
安 徽	36	624	342	126	29	5
福 建	12	144	78	25	20	1
江 西	13	291	108	98	37	
山 东	19	289	111	117	75	8
河 南	24	535	221	179	110	5
湖 北	9	236	75	81	42	1
湖 南	12	258	109	89	40	1
广 东	13	256	114	103	78	6
广 西	13	301	134	96	81	4
海 南	2	38	14	4	6	
重 庆	4	65	22	24	29	1
四 川	14	220	77	83	32	4
贵 州	9	96	38	24	17	
云 南	24	332	156	84	49	
西 藏	1	4		2	1	
陕 西	11	139	56	50	21	
甘 肃	8	123	27	28	15	1
青 海	4	39	11	14	11	
宁 夏	1	9	1	6	3	
新 疆	12	110	34	47	17	

供站

单位:个、人、人次、时

格水平	年龄结构				志愿服务	
社会工作师人数	35岁及以下人数	36岁至45岁人数	46岁至55岁人数	56岁及以上人数	志愿者服务人次数	志愿服务时间
42	**1147**	**2204**	**1732**	**504**	**853**	**2589.0**
	6	20	7	13		
1	21	17	38	18		
1	17	48	37	6		
1	31	37	30	8		
2	37	85	69	26		
1	41	138	63	16		
4	49	66	52	9		
	7	6	20	16		
5	20	83	118	67	204	776.0
3	17	48	57	14	50	142.0
1	84	302	186	52	402	912.0
	20	56	57	11		
1	56	123	88	24	132	528.0
2	61	106	102	20		
7	167	209	128	31		
2	63	96	55	22	37	136.0
	56	108	78	16		
4	65	95	68	28		
5	52	126	102	21		
	8	15	14	1		
	27	18	14	6		
1	38	71	87	24		
1	37	29	29	1		
	46	162	97	27		
	2	2				
	42	49	38	10		
	24	42	49	8	20	60.0
	16	12	9	2	8	35.0
	1	3	5			
	36	32	35	7		

C-2-20续表

地 区	增加值合计	执行行政事业单位会计制度财务指标			
		固定资产原价	上年结转和结余	本年收入合计	本年支出合计
全 国	**46727.5**	**129677.6**	**2964.9**	**70242.0**	**69828.3**
中央级					
北 京	1041.0	1901.0		1612.0	1963.0
天 津					
河 北	1143.5	4108.4	28.9	2559.6	2290.9
山 西	861.2	737.6	67.6	1156.2	1072.0
内蒙古	1234.3	2430.3	57.2	1520.8	1547.5
辽 宁	1066.1	3378.1	7.7	1885.0	1887.3
吉 林	1365.6	3524.3		1703.5	1755.4
黑龙江	1417.6	7289.6	198.5	2010.6	2045.3
上 海	831.2	2522.6	83.4	1152.7	1163.5
江 苏	2013.8	4188.2	-98.5	2861.5	2695.9
浙 江	3618.1	12563.2	-762.0	5547.1	5667.3
安 徽	2354.2	8590.8	40.2	1934.0	2149.1
福 建	1361.1	3468.0	93.5	1812.8	1754.0
江 西	1127.9	6295.5	437.8	1522.5	1666.9
山 东	3009.9	4421.8		4238.4	4238.4
河 南	3871.2	11378.3	529.8	5472.4	5375.0
湖 北	2466.1	2044.4	38.8	3304.4	3203.6
湖 南	1666.8	3186.6	0.4	2553.5	2527.9
广 东	3981.7	13680.1	826.4	6426.0	6270.8
广 西	2796.3	6762.5	505.1	4486.5	4739.9
海 南	37.0	816.5	109.4	492.3	482.1
重 庆	725.6	1184.2		1122.9	1122.9
四 川	2147.5	4852.8	105.0	2277.4	2216.8
贵 州	1200.2	632.1	383.2	2240.6	2233.2
云 南	2675.1	9150.1	220.3	4785.0	4131.4
西 藏				610.0	610.0
陕 西	806.8	1541.8	20.4	1170.9	1105.5
甘 肃	728.2	2137.5	1.8	778.0	778.9
青 海	198.0	487.6		480.0	480.0
宁 夏	176.6	666.0		306.2	321.0
新 疆	805.0	5737.7	70.0	2219.2	2332.8

单位：万元、张、人次、人天

收支结余	行政事业单位增加值	床位数	接待人次数	#接待军队人次数	本年在站人天数
76687.7	**46727.5**	**36994**	**4514838**	**3380293**	**5990286**
	1041.0	349	104000	104000	
		200			
1.9	1143.5	527	99911	97011	130305
121.2	861.2	418	57334	45355	89302
30.5	1234.3	483	62871	62871	107985
	1066.1	1330	39734	26187	443000
	1365.6	986	87088	51126	102565
	1417.6	1259	46640	27816	388358
71.2	831.2	179	73865	35785	65335
-15.7	2013.8	1770	264984	129868	292745
1025.0	3618.1	1401	268918	144651	106845
1.0	2354.2	2209	158670	96020	542243
51.4	1361.1	1227	98427	98032	233645
3.7	1127.9	1288	179915	114980	383210
	3009.9	2305	254088	254088	1524
74786.6	3871.2	3209	419367	268317	207685
150.0	2466.1	1840	111268	104580	219220
	1666.8	1128	253092	205639	252848
	3981.7	3086	239175	202866	335800
102.6	2796.3	1609	103795	100332	388829
	37.0	109	44745	44745	7300
	725.6	76	129732	129732	16611
169.9	2147.5	3508	338295	337795	296200
	1200.2	1090	188274	124381	343226
100.1	2675.1	2655	447438	197112	682915
			20000	20000	
62.1	806.8	445	111292	111292	155125
	728.2	949	75410	75410	47085
	198.0	156	122752	122752	
26.2	176.6				
	805.0	1203	113758	47550	150380

C-2-21 其他提供住宿的

地　区	单位数	年末职工人数		受教育程度		职业资
			#女性	大学专科人数	大学本科及以上人数	助理社会工作师人数
全　国	**196**	**3643**	**2328**	**564**	**298**	**27**
中央级						
北　京	3	163	102	24	12	3
天　津						
河　北	57	883	546	175	60	1
山　西	1	7	5			
内蒙古	1	16	9	2	8	
辽　宁	26	188	114	22	28	
吉　林	5	20	11	2	5	
黑龙江						
上　海						
江　苏	2	24	20	4		
浙　江	3	95	68	3	2	
安　徽						
福　建						
江　西						
山　东						
河　南	5	54	33	8	5	3
湖　北	1	20	12			
湖　南	1	3	2	1	1	
广　东	8	255	209	112	30	7
广　西	3	25	20	1		2
海　南						
重　庆						
四　川	50	1640	1047	181	106	4
贵　州	4	28	17	4	5	1
云　南	10	164	81	21	29	6
西　藏						
陕　西	2	13	4	3	1	
甘　肃	1	6	1		6	
青　海						
宁　夏						
新　疆	13	39	27	1		

社会服务机构

单位:个、人、人次、时

格水平	年龄结构				志愿服务	
社会工作师人数	35岁及以下人数	36岁至45岁人数	46岁至55岁人数	56岁及以上人数	志愿者服务人次数	志愿服务时间
27	**944**	**1146**	**904**	**649**	**759**	**3159.0**
1	35	55	43	30	403	1802.0
5	324	315	203	41	180	783.0
	5		2			
	3	5	6	2		
1	42	90	52	4		
	4	10	4	2		
	10	9	4	1		
	56	28	11		136	494.0
	16	20	18			
	3	12	5			
	1	2				
10	183	46	23	3		
	4	8	13			
3	179	430	471	560	30	60.0
	8	16	4		10	20.0
7	45	76	37	6		
	6	4	3			
		6				
	20	14	5			

C-2-21续表1

地 区	年末床位数	#光荣间床位	年在院总人天数	年末在院人数	#女性	在院人员按性质分		
						优抚对象	"三无"对象	自费人员
全 国	**23174**	**409**	**3091137**	**12686**	**3404**	**276**	**3286**	**9124**
中央级								
北 京	883		124235	340	195		5	335
天 津								
河 北	8232	306	841999	3370	565	28	704	2638
山 西	120		11160	31	16		31	
内蒙古	80		10210	29			19	10
辽 宁	1450		151309	531	51	22	24	485
吉 林	397		116815	347	154		92	255
黑龙江								
上 海								
江 苏	326		25165	138	73		80	58
浙 江	402		27626	209	10	8		201
安 徽								
福 建								
江 西								
山 东								
河 南	780	20	220630	638	52	22	492	124
湖 北	80		4700	47			11	36
湖 南	17	17	28	15			15	
广 东	459		85840	364	54		136	228
广 西	84		19512	65	44		45	20
海 南								
重 庆								
四 川	8261	34	1180398	5325	2020	139	882	4304
贵 州	101	2	26680	73	31	1	13	59
云 南	1060		166861	861	105	5	716	140
西 藏								
陕 西	100	30	21800	70		50	20	
甘 肃	80		90	55		1	1	53
青 海								
宁 夏								
新 疆	262		56079	178	34			178

单位：张、人天、人、人次、平方米

在院人员按年龄分			在院人员按类型分			康复和医疗门诊人次数	机构建筑面积
老人	青壮年	少年儿童	自理（完全自理）	介助（半自理）	介护（不能自理）		
11647	**608**	**431**	**7019**	**3067**	**2600**	**47021**	**471492**
340			168	44	128	4850	35581
3313	55	2	1717	773	880	133	177424
		31	31				5000
	29			29			2100
509	18	4	282	195	54	1037	38491
190	75	82	214	113	20	487	6700
							1000
138			106	29	3	3241	2030
197	12		198	4	7	439	2500
556		82	590	16	32	710	9700
47			40	6	1		850
15			15				600
47	94	223	93	36	235	28000	13902
64	1		18	18	29		1520
5226	92	7	2577	1612	1136	8102	127929
73			73				8100
634	227		728	95	38	22	28165
65	5		70				1500
55			35	6	14		1600
178			64	91	23		6800

C-2-21续表2

地　区	增加值合计	执行行政事业单位会计制度财务指标				
		固定资产原价	上年结转和结余	本年收入合计	本年支出合计	收支结余
全　国	**8938.7**	**31682.0**	**1610.9**	**10535.0**	**10925.4**	**0.1**
中央级						
北　京	786.0	892.2	40.0	1540.5	1465.3	
天　津						
河　北	3090.5	14650.1		3143.3	3195.7	
山　西	29.6	740.0				
内蒙古	143.3	78.3	10.3	165.7	176.0	
辽　宁	1150.6	5170.7	106.5	1745.5	1630.6	0.1
吉　林	56.5	30.0		70.1	72.1	
黑龙江						
上　海						
江　苏	104.0	1050.0		101.0	101.0	
浙　江	265.3			310.0	281.0	
安　徽						
福　建						
江　西						
山　东						
河　南	327.2	469.5		766.1	766.1	
湖　北	26.0	650.0				
湖　南	9.2	80.0		65.0	65.0	
广　东	-309.8	155.8	846.1	667.0	1513.1	
广　西	19.3					
海　南						
重　庆						
四　川	2263.9	3834.6	607.0	379.9	265.0	
贵　州	159.4	126.6		204.6	209.9	
云　南	746.3	2753.2	1.0	1254.1	1081.3	
西　藏						
陕　西	31.8	660.0		57.0	57.0	
甘　肃	23.1	78.0		59.2	40.0	
青　海						
宁　夏						
新　疆	16.5	263.0		6.0	6.3	

单位：万元

行政事业单位增加值	执行民间非营利组织单位会计制度财务指标				
	固定资产原价	上年结余	本年收入合计	本年费用合计	社会组织增加值
6499.7	**22379.8**	**1443.0**	**3178.3**	**6797.3**	**2439.0**
785.8	1360.2			0.2	0.2
2854.3	9856.0	-7.0	1064.6	896.7	236.2
29.6					
143.3					
1130.3	205.0	42.0	30.1	30.4	20.3
56.4	10.0		2.0	0.1	0.1
104.0					
208.3	560.0	15.0	157.0	147.0	57.0
326.5	100.0		60.0	5.0	0.7
26.0					
9.2					
-479.9	204.7	-7.8	451.5	392.1	170.1
	274.0	3.6	33.3	39.8	19.3
332.2	9780.9	1397.2	1373.8	5282.6	1931.7
156.4	10.0		5.0	3.0	3.0
745.9	19.0		1.0	0.4	0.4
31.8					
23.1					
16.5					

C-2-22 不提供住宿的

地 区	单位数	工商登记	编办登记	民政登记
全 国	**277084**	**18394**	**7095**	**24502**
中央级	1		1	
北 京	11191	611	294	
天 津	2009	231	52	338
河 北	26129	753	197	2049
山 西	3851	459	334	205
内蒙古	2398	176	144	105
辽 宁	7572	1979	146	156
吉 林	1230	417	179	189
黑龙江	2904	534	241	1063
上 海	4385	1093	146	156
江 苏	26719	2773	233	3338
浙 江	26464	2121	210	900
安 徽	6056	354	279	1861
福 建	3392	291	126	186
江 西	3831	328	265	1992
山 东	25587	1301	375	250
河 南	4190	935	277	1252
湖 北	9403	637	313	2183
湖 南	9658	573	347	1568
广 东	45725	206	388	809
广 西	7978	141	196	108
海 南	1614	12	15	242
重 庆	5770	741	94	260
四 川	6807	728	641	662
贵 州	17570	81	337	1270
云 南	1869	312	165	202
西 藏	61	3	12	25
陕 西	3340	236	224	987
甘 肃	5482	83	300	1216
青 海	337	35	10	47
宁 夏	915	72	55	481
新 疆	2646	178	499	402

社会服务机构总表

单位:个、人

年末职工人数	#女性	工商登记	编办登记	民政登记
2269459	**783929**	**1370795**	**64066**	**112483**
127	48		127	
67093	29165	28274	4329	
27023	10244	18248	559	1128
89246	30108	43901	2055	6866
48376	12939	37446	2719	944
21783	8960	9970	1746	392
129318	48941	94188	1663	762
21038	6811	15678	1999	1690
29741	11067	17659	1805	5669
107202	39271	85250	2916	5351
380149	132245	273949	1933	20237
281993	98003	223284	1540	1739
42748	16998	18230	2422	7538
31678	11698	18245	859	957
41211	14240	28563	1616	8529
186254	60874	94327	4052	1421
74804	25426	60706	3176	4164
69525	24545	38317	2829	7521
62473	20961	33915	3708	4683
140815	45825	14143	3440	5170
25720	6517	8763	1515	1264
8653	2474	1256	129	896
81748	28152	67649	744	946
78565	29692	54346	3318	2940
83794	21225	2213	4512	7406
53683	14379	45089	1191	1101
504	235	209	62	149
28534	10661	13990	2132	3954
19065	6044	3972	1398	3479
2917	1062	1838	187	297
7004	3078	3741	679	1842
26675	12041	13436	2706	3448

C-2-22续表1

地 区	受教育程度		职业资格水平	
	大学专科人数	大学本科及以上人数	助理社会工作师人数	社会工作师人数
全 国	**303187**	**133616**	**11961**	**4758**
中央级	12	115		
北 京	12140	9068	2207	782
天 津	3342	1933	297	62
河 北	5752	1927	136	69
山 西	4426	1605	73	36
内蒙古	5409	2984	110	53
辽 宁	15545	10007	263	164
吉 林	3540	919	358	80
黑龙江	6110	1982	193	55
上 海	5790	2432	428	228
江 苏	42772	19269	1516	478
浙 江	23569	10419	1361	715
安 徽	8069	2438	187	96
福 建	2620	1080	285	174
江 西	2594	631	68	44
山 东	40581	18099	308	222
河 南	9868	4145	151	141
湖 北	10826	4541	398	40
湖 南	9714	3808	326	145
广 东	22237	13953	2348	677
广 西	2426	1243	136	55
海 南	1090	431	30	3
重 庆	9194	4018	168	96
四 川	15504	4036	243	133
贵 州	21138	5172	38	19
云 南	2694	1172	42	43
西 藏	111	65		2
陕 西	5784	1675	131	47
甘 肃	3257	1502	29	36
青 海	314	152	37	5
宁 夏	665	268	9	6
新 疆	6094	2527	85	52

单位：张、人天、人、人次、时

年龄结构				志愿服务	
35岁及以下人数	36岁至45岁人数	46岁至55岁人数	56岁及以上人数	志愿者服务人次数	志愿服务时间
764042	**881438**	**481076**	**142903**	**9897103**	**24654936.5**
73	18	28	8		
18602	25654	18487	4350	5609152	15390720.5
10175	9486	5761	1601	102690	213950.0
28932	34598	19517	6199	22103	48370.0
15509	18440	11708	2719	987	2458.0
6812	9090	5395	486	11168	27777.0
38214	52590	29130	9384	14762	37984.0
6397	10788	3483	370	576	1782.0
10275	13731	4908	827	15073	53786.0
33068	35862	28342	9930	27023	58386.0
112716	151213	91401	24819	269091	541669.0
85958	97985	64131	33919	359048	711757.8
13916	19447	8216	1169	51421	130479.0
10266	13706	5949	1757	105242	291846.0
16696	16070	6632	1813	1300	3294.7
73206	70697	33504	8847	2023865	4089090.0
33693	29271	9961	1879	654	1949.0
23920	26375	16910	2320	4256	11648.0
16002	30155	13723	2593	16377	44319.0
50297	55629	26198	8691	124900	440358.0
8990	7457	6234	3039	478	1536.0
2362	3845	1810	636	22877	68391.0
29168	32859	16078	3643	339366	910808.0
31894	30901	13255	2515	41250	92778.0
30641	34110	14542	4501	704659	1396205.0
24889	18596	9051	1147	617	1398.0
249	188	51	16		
10175	10540	6580	1239	13903	45968.5
6980	6920	3733	1432	3125	8129.0
1085	1346	386	100		
2073	3694	1045	192		
10809	10177	4927	762	11140	28099.0

C-2-22续表2

地区	增加值合计	执行企业会计制度单位财务指标					执行行政	
		固定资产原价	营业收入	费用合计	营业利润	企业单位增加值	固定资产原价	上年结转和结余
全　国	**8343636.3**	**17692741.9**	**52439683.1**	**5793415.0**	**1593638.2**	**6924833.3**	**3039743.2**	**544297.1**
中央级	3711.9						32203.0	17013.0
北　京	250572.3	315633.0	665810.2	75286.6	-2443.1	115462.5	168003.9	221862.9
天　津	124168.1	242310.3	806819.7	426530.4	12658.7	110511.3	56438.8	2095.6
河　北	265947.0	528476.7	1353252.1	133381.6	14221.9	225580.8	111720.7	6192.4
山　西	81009.0	351931.5	483618.5	37798.7	358.2	70843.1	35161.4	2223.9
内蒙古	43169.3	65368.6	71928.4	14170.3	2939.8	18450.4	49614.4	7027.8
辽　宁	449323.4	726169.2	2301546.6	245949.0	76709.1	408000.2	73402.9	1715.6
吉　林	68220.7	177146.3	392720.8	44546.9	6261.3	59549.4	35998.6	3726.2
黑龙江	52440.3	130748.3	195562.6	46878.2	7497.7	41481.1	29338.6	4752.4
上　海	891579.2	936929.2	2899929.6	234761.1	267759.5	843595.6	125884.6	4571.2
江　苏	1385092.3	4004861.7	12989150.5	1425412.2	334576.4	1241676.0	341887.3	20878.3
浙　江	2086634.7	5590077.4	17491380.9	1698445.3	598014.3	1913236.7	533963.7	37297.3
安　徽	95442.1	145575.3	943627.7	61040.1	18376.4	57634.4	116678.0	4880.6
福　建	67867.2	171169.9	363964.4	53226.3	3476.9	56750.6	26967.5	20956.1
江　西	29596.3	105040.6	2087865.6	20316.9	2879.0	18618.3	28535.2	2495.2
山　东	761063.1	1069015.1	1748520.9	330004.8	133887.6	578498.7	121844.4	3058.8
河　南	151615.5	288620.6	602878.2	109292.2	16273.4	128161.1	93668.7	4658.6
湖　北	143471.4	210590.1	439936.6	110526.0	5197.4	93650.9	159306.9	4024.2
湖　南	111655.9	270492.6	570851.8	77441.2	11832.1	83245.2	63244.2	1389.8
广　东	140471.3	180929.6	309535.9	33771.2	5612.3	47529.8	166540.5	12184.1
广　西	50775.1	63664.9	388343.1	12579.4	-1888.2	24917.3	72555.7	472.3
海　南	10076.1	15848.7	47492.9	4748.0	1103.7	3950.1	14030.9	47220.1
重　庆	294203.0	572236.6	1770393.4	211772.6	34337.2	269093.5	63919.3	20516.6
四　川	355756.9	446613.3	1611008.1	114148.6	18154.2	311840.1	171771.6	39441.6
贵　州	73132.4	8408.6	20562.3	3944.8	1064.0	2905.3	68453.5	10517.8
云　南	133513.2	633754.6	1173966.4	170369.7	-3506.9	85509.7	75303.4	11408.0
西　藏	1668.6	3395.3	353.8	119.9	104.4	144.0	13758.6	830.0
陕　西	107152.7	162894.0	384923.6	50226.2	21732.9	62700.2	78206.4	14819.1
甘　肃	14612.9	30512.7	8642.6	2698.0	134.8	2309.4	34821.6	239.7
青　海	3908.8	6087.3	10428.8	1313.8	100.0	1908.8	22433.8	277.1
宁　夏	17006.1	61470.8	41334.8	13007.4	-699.5	14067.1	10206.0	3299.6
新　疆	78779.1	176769.1	263332.3	29707.6	6912.7	33011.9	43879.1	12251.2

单位：万元

事业单位会计制度财务指标				执行民间非营利组织单位会计制度财务指标				
本年收入合计	本年支出合计	收支结余	行政事业单位增加值	固定资产原价	上年结余	本年收入合计	本年费用合计	社会组织增加值
3565678.2	**3398055.7**	**218125.8**	**1128427.3**	**1137707.6**	**13774.7**	**486929.6**	**484781.1**	**290375.7**
228000.0	190800.0		3711.9					
283371.1	384126.9	97349.7	135108.8	20.0	4.0		1.0	1.0
46028.6	44663.0	853.2	11229.5	3113.4	163.0	4417.4	4370.2	2427.3
444849.2	442048.4	2190.0	34544.9	34222.2	860.7	6018.5	8178.1	5821.3
27575.6	25235.3	1889.9	8331.4	5184.3	21.0	2680.7	4608.8	1834.5
62631.5	55876.8	14300.8	24314.8	3170.0		763.8	876.9	404.1
152172.6	139217.9	2785.3	37542.6	5247.5	62.6	7751.4	8552.7	3780.6
45066.0	38685.0	1099.9	8244.7	802.2		2511.8	1149.5	426.6
17956.2	17435.9	9.3	10500.7	2632.2	1000.0	41570.4	640.3	458.5
162179.3	154408.6	2528.5	43017.9	6584.9	166.9	10945.3	8645.9	4965.7
178770.7	212429.1	22542.2	106568.4	174501.0	41.4	101142.7	91162.1	36847.9
388899.9	288816.2	2713.4	159826.9	122849.0	217.3	32947.0	35609.3	13571.1
80472.2	76787.8	1718.9	33221.1	34369.7	180.0	10118.9	10418.9	4586.6
30446.0	26678.3	2223.8	9017.6	10649.0	28.5	3852.7	5157.4	2099.0
23918.6	21697.0	-43.7	7636.5	11245.7	2.0	5940.1	7364.9	3341.5
155190.7	154947.6		40279.4	247802.8	432.5	197326.8	196394.0	142285.0
103949.2	89023.2	3828.2	21645.3	7519.2	395.1	1021.7	2498.0	1809.1
90184.1	92620.1	131.5	45742.0	8969.0	10.1	3551.8	5841.4	4078.5
77282.2	71414.1	1898.0	26019.2	6609.7	701.1	8063.2	8347.0	2391.5
191758.8	174010.6	3107.7	77515.8	69038.6	4228.1	7805.7	22978.8	15425.7
92599.0	79165.7	1036.1	23860.0	20779.7		525.0	2541.6	1997.8
25885.0	25520.4	920.0	6066.1	350.8		665.0	683.3	59.9
79871.5	74908.2	25534.5	21646.8	28711.4	3.0	7260.7	6791.5	3462.7
162265.0	147758.2	2162.7	40801.9	12014.6	3.1	5475.7	5667.1	3114.9
79532.3	60817.3	640.9	39106.5	94505.5	5173.1	22431.9	40139.2	31120.6
72092.6	70389.5	1064.9	46965.2	212213.4	3.0	4.5	1349.5	1038.3
6603.1	6888.2		1524.6	59.6				
94008.4	90781.2	559.8	44452.5					
21956.4	17035.1	60.1	10201.5	8002.7	78.2	1257.4	2992.5	2102.0
20361.8	13069.3	252.1	1938.1	4205.0		103.0	169.4	61.9
17289.2	13764.2	16164.6	2209.3	1060.5		677.7	1498.6	729.7
102511.4	97036.6	8603.5	45634.8	1274.0		98.8	153.2	132.4

C-2-23 老龄事业

地区	单位数	编制登记	民政登记	未登记	年末职工人数	#女性	受教育 大学专科人数
全　国	**2571**	**1933**	**138**	**500**	**10134**	**4417**	**3794**
中央级							
北　京	17	17			165	69	32
天　津	16	13		3	66	37	22
河　北	74	50	4	20	224	103	65
山　西	114	105		9	520	220	225
内蒙古	43	31	3	9	150	79	53
辽　宁	66	46	8	12	248	118	93
吉　林	34	27	4	3	135	74	45
黑龙江	107	75	20	12	359	176	132
上　海	18	18			146	84	38
江　苏	70	52	4	14	260	114	71
浙　江	90	65	2	23	328	148	109
安　徽	107	84	4	19	265	99	95
福　建	63	52	1	10	173	64	63
江　西	109	94	2	13	404	160	187
山　东	151	141		10	1031	319	399
河　南	98	58	13	27	357	165	129
湖　北	89	78	1	10	388	143	161
湖　南	134	53	11	70	482	224	167
广　东	114	75	3	36	359	150	122
广　西	65	44	3	18	194	90	83
海　南	6	3	2	1	22	14	10
重　庆	32	24		8	118	51	49
四　川	213	193	1	19	689	313	290
贵　州	95	76	4	15	344	159	156
云　南	122	71	16	35	528	220	228
西　藏	3	1	2		3		
陕　西	103	98	3	2	666	298	227
甘　肃	101	84	6	11	484	200	120
青　海	55			55	106	59	12
宁　夏	27	24	1	2	103	41	51
新　疆	235	181	20	34	817	426	360

机构情况

单位：个、人、人次、时

程度	职业资格水平		年龄结构				志愿服务	
大学本科及以上人数	助理社会工作师人数	社会工作师人数	35岁及以下人数	36岁至45岁人数	46岁至55岁人数	56岁及以上人数	志愿者服务人次数	志愿服务时间
3330	**84**	**113**	**2505**	**3993**	**2993**	**643**	**224751**	**649583.0**
128	1	6	40	52	60	13	32817	98451.0
42		2	20	21	21	4	1090	3270.0
83	3	3	84	94	41	5	1445	4320.0
81	4	2	148	217	129	26	38	90.0
68		5	27	68	43	12		
120	2	1	81	81	66	20	9799	28497.0
33	2		43	54	32	6	230	690.0
103	10		72	134	115	38	8111	26006.0
86	2	9	41	53	47	5	40	120.0
98	3	4	57	88	89	26	689	1995.0
124	5	2	82	115	106	25	4328	12984.0
116		6	56	104	82	23	26179	78537.0
55	1	1	27	67	66	13	105242	291846.0
59		6	118	162	104	20	360	1080.0
441	2	14	256	387	312	76	1705	5115.0
79	6	5	166	142	48	1	400	1200.0
104	1	1	66	147	121	54	2580	7452.0
70	3	3	119	221	126	16	1997	5991.0
142	6	7	104	126	103	26	4652	13156.0
57	3		33	77	69	15	420	1260.0
9		1	5	12	5			
52	2	1	20	33	52	13	3827	11481.0
244	8	9	149	284	210	46	4113	11139.0
123	4	1	53	127	143	21	1596	4788.0
183	1	4	104	193	196	35	5	15.0
1			2	1				
176		1	213	258	165	30	8549	25647.0
78	4	1	107	197	152	28	94	270.0
5			5	86	14	1		
46		1	14	36	46	7		
324	11	17	193	356	230	38	4445	14183.0

C-2-23续表

地区	增加值合计	执行	
		固定资产原价	上年结转和结余
全国	**65544.3**	**83690.9**	**10996.3**
中央级			
北京	2444.6	881.7	4434.7
天津	1424.4	269.6	751.5
河北	749.0	306.6	5.0
山西	1262.9	804.3	166.6
内蒙古	1296.0	897.9	682.9
辽宁	2000.9	504.4	21.3
吉林	740.3	664.0	20.0
黑龙江	1255.5	3043.6	57.6
上海	2344.9	4745.6	660.4
江苏	2765.0	13233.7	16.4
浙江	3498.9	3394.0	653.5
安徽	779.9	753.5	35.9
福建	1434.7	645.0	186.3
江西	691.4	712.7	8.7
山东	5954.8	4395.3	
河南	1056.9	2468.3	2.0
湖北	1658.3	1989.2	
湖南	2327.2	7819.9	2.6
广东	4398.4	8354.7	721.1
广西	1183.8	604.5	23.5
海南	160.9	8.1	25.3
重庆	906.7	1556.9	1.4
四川	3100.0	4305.8	416.6
贵州	2071.5	1341.1	693.0
云南	2031.2	11005.8	647.5
西藏	8.5	213.0	
陕西	12898.8	2627.2	472.6
甘肃	1348.9	1640.1	100.1
青海	119.8	546.9	84.6
宁夏	518.9	516.1	28.2
新疆	3111.1	3441.4	77.0

单位：万元

行政事业单位会计制度财务指标			
本年收入合计	本年支出合计	收支结余	行政事业单位增加值
186264.0	**179008.4**	**6116.1**	**65544.3**
22738.8	22242.2	4024.9	2444.6
3930.3	3620.5	306.6	1424.4
1542.3	1533.0	16.0	749.0
2404.4	2476.7	10.3	1262.9
2708.1	3346.7	12.4	1296.0
3401.5	3429.9	1.7	2000.9
965.3	966.4	77.1	740.3
4065.9	3193.7	9.3	1255.5
14039.3	14433.0	457.5	2344.9
4964.7	4950.5	25.1	2765.0
11693.0	11922.1	38.1	3498.9
1919.5	1931.1		779.9
4950.0	4902.4	212.6	1434.7
1507.9	1438.8		691.4
9925.4	9925.4		5954.8
1715.0	1651.4		1056.9
4184.1	4120.0	4.0	1658.3
3140.3	3009.0		2327.2
16597.6	11967.2	34.6	4398.4
2218.8	2136.3	7.6	1183.8
568.8	513.2	240.8	160.9
2377.8	2375.7	2.1	906.7
8511.5	7435.7	263.4	3100.0
4831.1	4163.9	62.0	2071.5
7851.8	8007.0	278.5	2031.2
15.9			8.5
34898.0	34316.8		12898.8
2171.4	2212.6		1348.9
378.4	363.6	15.0	119.8
1484.9	1375.1	11.5	518.9
4562.2	5048.5	5.0	3111.1

C-2-24 为老年人提

地区	老龄人口情况							
							老年维权	
	60岁以上老年人口数	65岁以上老年人口数	80岁以上老年人口数	100岁以上老年人口数	纯老年人家庭人口数	老龄系统接待来信来访次数	老年法律援助中心	涉老案件数
全　国	**201124413**	**125163633**	**26854212**	**60648**	**30828374**	**428077**	**21093**	**55613**
中央级								
北　京	2802110	1918733	466322	613	487691	57497	339	1068
天　津	2008802	1187766	267019	324	395198	1896	101	4137
河　北	11072241	6247938	1107311	2082	921473	6223	370	600
山　西	4591697	2499005	455166	1358	613819	4982	685	852
内蒙古	3336807	1825092	343255	314	516181	1380	178	262
辽　宁	7217160	4227033	898688	1342	1935606	14867	1997	2946
吉　林	4410302	345544	67101	116	101099	1228	39	150
黑龙江	5698810	2540230	575751	555	1106470	4645	614	971
上　海	3762570	2550132	693599	1867	864294	44213	56	3746
江　苏	14553085	9953604	2162730	4451	3326251	30956	1543	4530
浙　江	7730188	5715230	1325787	1756	2134467	40811	382	4427
安　徽	9424577	6614831	1419463	3174	1861624	10842	680	1145
福　建	4796754	3346830	851698	1793	879715	17736	1350	2656
江　西	6172735	3337342	749495	1080	313277	3765	576	635
山　东	16994499	10056012	2142749	5439	4360882	7936	2055	2820
河　南	13300569	8594558	1916268	5071	1019061	6724	1020	1015
湖　北	8797083	5431004	1005988	2072	796154	12975	675	1004
湖　南	10751794	6344959	1526936	2355	1367377	26177	927	2486
广　东	11623248	7555352	1926142	6125	724569	20040	789	1086
广　西	6413121	4823061	1154879	5024	467054	13906	260	1109
海　南	1058221	814073	246465	1730	71544	1892	48	204
重　庆	5901390	3999963	922234	1266	1670085	14900	628	3785
四　川	15516013	10267700	2035983	4740	1932973	22954	1452	4107
贵　州	4727997	3423384	628653	1102	502452	5984	1020	949
云　南	5591114	3273837	704965	1332	766956	12331	1293	4840
西　藏	249320	61746	16987	31	384			
陕　西	5732115	3286144	563441	710	547751	11202	602	1026
甘　肃	3377491	2336894	302573	457	411099	7782	794	710
青　海	622280	428287	68929	180	138484		3	20
宁　夏	739235	374838	55199	82	94117	11065	134	427
新　疆	2151085	1782511	252436	2107	500267	11168	483	1900

供的服务情况

单位：个、人次、件、张、人

老龄事业发展情况：维权协调组织数	老年活动设施：老年活动站/中心/室数	老年活动设施：老年人参与人数	老年活动设施：年末活动人次数	老年福利：享受高龄补贴的老年人数	老年福利：享受护理补贴的老年人数	老年福利：享受养老服务补贴的老年人数	老年医疗护理机构：老年医院数	老年医疗护理机构：床位数
78383	**359896**	**45571722**	**269904433**	**15578750**	**117153**	**1018962**	**3288**	**136900**
4138	7175	970531	4353073	389385	435	115413	20	4619
1964	2180	544407	679337	22306	1231	6685	32	1746
2028	9547	947837	38286832	423215	3637	7258	167	2837
4983	16404	1411693	3274763	274525		7010	81	2012
293	1208	312985	12871786	279272	65	6746	2	150
3167	7597	1163226	3198738	78318	318	1728	43	3379
813	1072	71055	130588	12282	1385	1286	86	1287
1109	3563	636726	2682610	102585	3014	4146	297	3386
2050	6267	341579	3774787	135446	26629	100077	13	2826
6741	18998	4594809	82117929	2179545	14877	68560	406	23075
3675	32673	7512439	50216831	1136256	9816	121953	28	3357
2378	7317	1327410	5116621	647088	9728	7620	235	13422
2208	17471	1424654	2644921	273021	779	18471	61	3752
1958	11191	1498905	1731829	327517	541	42303	55	2860
5046	55327	2712584	3863533	1168297	9555	170278	104	10844
3086	37010	1278153	1732869	249533	1191	11920	238	4865
3130	9170	1710062	6089667	510049	3474	10236	117	5229
5282	19122	2312438	2913477	220208	16213	61785	169	8650
2550	15482	2375932	4043543	2177441	411	99571	106	9740
1409	6743	1091160	2068721	163937	183	997	38	4694
95	1011	176605	210105	74531		1045		
2461	8749	1736408	2403505	256125	556	15280		
7585	22410	3821904	21454946	796332	2239	63095	601	13567
2145	4452	832726	2629961	146097	1095	28976	97	1196
2615	14957	2615388	7791523	880309	675	17877	68	4135
	9	2755	3943	16827				
2454	5846	725188	948031	2002124	7634	25625	146	3129
1698	4366	595090	1016193	80818	1472	2870	60	445
	673	89221	125901	296601				
796	915	133122	348567	31105		151	8	496
526	10991	604730	1179303	227655			10	1202

C-2-24续表

地区	老龄事业							
	老年医疗护理机构			老年人协会个数	参加人数	村、居老年人协会	参加人数	乡、街道老年人协会
	老年临终关怀医院数	床位数	年底在院人数					
全　国	**713**	**34343**	**14947**	**419202**	**44485278**	**342390**	**32600686**	**38924**
中央级								
北　京	5	419	268	7014	433452	5994	425923	103
天　津	1	30	28	3440	414822	3227	326237	190
河　北	21	374	75	21997	852667	16465	538899	3098
山　西	74	5509	824	16409	962944	14367	726492	881
内蒙古				1546	230236	1203	103569	212
辽　宁	8	750	264	10678	1068727	8100	575035	1402
吉　林	1	50	43	1434	92199	1035	48227	251
黑龙江	50	1192	539	6124	547742	4494	393691	1097
上　海	6	114	43	1908	200140	1708	148174	182
江　苏	67	6328	3671	19511	3818641	17587	3257605	1340
浙　江	5	654	634	30867	5975682	29280	5998873	737
安　徽	16	421	136	11518	1273141	10135	879872	1017
福　建	43	2168	902	16144	2027647	14141	1525548	931
江　西	9	322	224	12172	1588068	9985	784247	1062
山　东	40	1756	918	68510	2137408	56843	1476840	7398
河　南	24	458	242	20313	1157606	15542	828639	1256
湖　北	24	518	219	10903	1910031	8882	890881	1259
湖　南	91	2618	1019	30488	2700235	20627	1793076	2227
广　东	33	4231	2390	17472	2686699	15032	2309535	1421
广　西	3	200	144	10480	1865898	8701	1381669	892
海　南				839	122269	689	78661	111
重　庆				8561	2038652	4837	1348838	3361
四　川	127	3357	803	24376	4344825	20277	2664220	3159
贵　州	20	133	53	17795	1526097	15079	871564	1781
云　南	13	910	702	16902	2432497	10457	1708108	1250
西　藏				7	477			
陕　西	12	971	214	15356	1075895	13462	783588	920
甘　肃	16	650	460	8870	606233	7856	526926	593
青　海				734	30323	685	13491	35
宁　夏	2	40		1743	86622	1563	59970	136
新　疆	2	170	132	5091	277403	4137	132288	622

单位：个、人、万元

发展情况								
参加人数	县、市老年人协会	参加人数	老年基金会	事业投入经费	其他老年社团组织	参加人数	老年学校 老年学校个数	在校人数
7150061	**7226**	**2652585**	**11173**	**38195**	**40501**	**4624543**	**53821**	**6920219**
47985	8	10700	5	80	7246	631735	2514	259215
61321	7	1977	2	971	1203	149857	422	209994
110321	885	133457	503	27	174	134057	331	43162
134406	707	61996	13	21	597	55697	2794	291177
63531	127	68703			23	5321	61	9646
240235	255	44379			1466	64975	662	130834
32324	28	8833	1	6	150	21967	305	26639
161553	55	22613	3	1	98	12318	354	27936
46951	8	3912	13	3867	53	31615	1338	503312
383679	218	85520	12	7903	10538	959594	3737	809813
416081	56	222273	294	1725	1057	130509	7954	767350
203126	171	62117	6	12	867	84422	2568	214420
201898	124	34542	328	6139	2581	410984	11808	943389
266178	289	157747	7163	101	1743	93237	974	203927
334446	513	232006	8	307	2992	101471	3047	406735
130125	346	40456	13	29	334	32215	2706	153695
446393	303	234833	702	186	591	181547	1000	187996
476645	801	187132	45	395	793	214206	1015	173355
350076	152	59981	714	14158	2043	150514	643	134996
294544	130	86909	396	111	670	145230	741	75157
21433	34	17471	187		17	7646	9	2594
535012	280	253217	5	331	1226	237727	1465	276289
1422267	408	335631	5	201	1045	456533	2429	477951
195209	363	49951	19	386	1091	57019	1572	151211
235132	468	120525	50	988	850	123358	2043	309640
	4	245						
144169	93	35874	25	228	506	89890	358	51227
101786	64	16860	660	11	169	27997	123	13076
13381	6	1969					7	4953
21954	27	6096			81	3821	29	2852
57900	296	54660	1	13	297	9081	812	57678

C−2−25 为残疾人提供

地　区	单位数	年末职工人数	#女　性	#残疾职工	#女残疾职工	残疾职工工资总额	残疾职工养老保险总额
全　国	**14225**	**1085968**	**352245**	**420082**	**132843**	**2037315.7**	**206630.4**
中央级							
北　京	583	26801	9261	10708	3479	24598.1	6066.8
天　津	229	18241	4776	7045	1986	11437.3	4237.8
河　北	501	31192	9022	12864	3381	1261697.2	5090.7
山　西	253	26998	6259	11905	3432	9936.5	2464.9
内蒙古	77	4622	1656	1944	710	2689.1	609.7
辽　宁	1680	76612	23424	37477	10102	52656.9	17242.8
吉　林	267	10435	2795	8428	1186	5589.4	513.5
黑龙江	470	14773	4242	7838	2624	37123.2	1707.3
上　海	1081	84430	26904	29553	9258	58627.4	42317.1
江　苏	2708	270346	93458	93683	33684	169082.4	37326.7
浙　江	1809	198371	68129	64159	24068	157101.2	46863.0
安　徽	249	13984	4948	5460	1705	9568.4	2184.0
福　建	160	9579	3199	4526	619	4750.9	334.6
江　西	255	19837	6003	8295	2689	9688.2	372.6
山　东	1128	84080	23750	33023	9060	60936.1	20918.3
河　南	759	45910	14952	20563	6100	19000.6	1112.7
湖　北	256	15983	4816	7697	2684	9135.1	841.2
湖　南	359	22942	6221	11171	2972	14412.8	2758.3
广　东	118	10627	3866	4779	1498	5537.9	636.7
广　西	52	2655	576	1036	275	42788.9	69.7
海　南	3	90	34	62	11	12.5	7.3
重　庆	396	31022	9353	11838	3225	22615.1	6069.9
四　川	322	26628	11090	10305	3227	23184.4	3003.6
贵　州	13	363	141	193	59	441.3	48.7
云　南	109	12586	2663	5309	1136	7717.7	1552.2
西　藏							
陕　西	193	11653	3711	4126	1443	7133.5	1169.1
甘　肃	56	3101	1133	1124	348	772.9	28.0
青　海	5	96	55	10		12.0	
宁　夏	18	1000	323	507	230	1776.0	11.0
新　疆	116	11011	5485	4454	1652	7292.7	1072.2

工作岗位的企业

单位:个、人、万元

残疾职工补贴	纳税总额				应减免税金总额	实际减免税金总额	盈利总额
		增值税总额	营业税总额	所得税总额			
19218.1	**1399320.3**	**1042847.5**	**97648.7**	**192715.8**	**820947.1**	**726397.3**	**944740.4**
1967.1	22848.0	19066.3	729.1	1092.7	26375.5	20328.1	7969.4
172.3	16472.6	13625.1	186.4	1320.7	14089.4	12890.7	29072.6
530.9	38565.9	26147.0	1470.4	5013.0	21232.1	14788.7	7999.6
448.1	18256.6	13813.2	3053.6	604.0	9300.2	6009.0	2368.6
72.9	8356.4	6925.0	818.8	603.5	7379.5	6988.0	2666.4
301.8	54207.7	53996.3	7958.0	9530.8	41578.2	43517.7	28928.0
98.7	847.7	954.1	19.0	38.7	779.0	752.7	10.4
520.9							
847.1	153766.6	97239.2	24801.8	54527.5	98365.3	95559.0	160158.6
4144.1	418341.0	323454.9	11443.3	50319.4	245164.8	192304.9	253410.6
1731.6	383100.6	320586.3	35881.9	39930.2	179489.3	186054.0	307604.2
209.5	13495.3	11569.1	175.1	1153.5	7847.6	6753.4	8055.6
175.6	4955.3	3020.8	1.0	79.8	2874.6	3557.8	842.2
63.0	49052.3	3035.8	491.5	1738.0	15391.9	15415.4	6177.8
5895.1	115678.0	65823.4	7308.0	21237.3	68414.1	62253.3	85836.2
185.8	14927.6	10004.5	395.7	971.4	10206.8	8487.1	3043.0
168.6	7576.0	4612.1	71.2	1402.6	4068.0	3959.1	2150.1
646.7	5733.2	2856.0	746.8	162.5	4119.4	3331.3	1047.1
68.2	11335.7	1438.6	174.9	18.0	4741.1	3757.1	5898.3
3.7	489.2	371.9	19.0	15.1	165.7	165.3	151.9
			0.2	0.2			
285.2	47121.5	41726.8	213.0	2369.7	48447.8	29275.2	29420.5
416.3	1550.8	941.1	150.0	42.7	1459.1	847.0	4054.8
19.7	45.9	42.0			42.0	42.0	1.7
110.4	6403.7	5508.2	52.1	53.5	3568.4	4641.5	-17064.7
102.0	2403.7	14037.0	834.9	478.0	1766.8	992.5	13751.7
6.0							
6.5	610.0		610.0		1525.0	1525.0	355.0
20.3	3179.0	2052.8	43.0	13.0	2555.5	2201.5	830.8

C-2-25续表1

地区	单位数	年末职工人数	受教育程度		职业资
			大学专科人数	大学本科及以上人数	助理社会工作师人数
全国	**14225**	**1085968**	**71925**	**29711**	**1327**
中央级					
北京	583	26801	1930	794	35
天津	229	18241	1025	344	56
河北	501	31192	1206	567	6
山西	253	26998	1564	517	4
内蒙古	77	4622	434	125	4
辽宁	1680	76612	3910	2973	80
吉林	267	10435	791	230	264
黑龙江	470	14773	1599	150	32
上海	1081	84430	2499	475	102
江苏	2708	270346	20636	9234	245
浙江	1809	198371	10177	4429	165
安徽	249	13984	932	193	20
福建	160	9579	145	48	2
江西	255	19837	747	198	5
山东	1128	84080	9213	4158	59
河南	759	45910	2766	866	18
湖北	256	15983	421	499	12
湖南	359	22942	1301	285	7
广东	118	10627	643	427	70
广西	52	2655	217	43	1
海南	3	90	1		
重庆	396	31022	2170	1141	31
四川	322	26628	4091	895	20
贵州	13	363	49	9	
云南	109	12586	422	76	5
西藏					
陕西	193	11653	1426	590	75
甘肃	56	3101	94	28	1
青海	5	96	2	9	5
宁夏	18	1000	31	8	2
新疆	116	11011	1483	400	1

单位:个、人、人次、时

格水平	年龄结构				志愿服务	
社会工作师人数	35岁及以下人数	36岁至45岁人数	46岁至55岁人数	56岁及以上人数	志愿者服务人次数	志愿服务时间
580	**361495**	**418606**	**230799**	**75068**	**27916**	**55412.0**
11	6890	11497	6820	1594	1100	1100.0
18	7279	6317	3629	1016	1150	2450.0
2	12665	12596	5158	773	1265	5330.0
	9037	9712	6895	1354		
3	1225	2086	1147	164		
24	20903	32222	19153	4334		200.0
6	3428	4604	2170	233		
4	4970	6513	2800	490		
56	29273	26607	20899	7651	280	900.0
84	79218	107694	65771	17663	10616	17090.0
217	59323	67395	42550	29103	11015	21817.0
5	4478	6634	2600	272	128	382.0
2	3261	4379	1552	387		
3	8611	8329	2555	342		
17	34662	31439	14719	3260	1455	3579.0
20	21894	16588	6492	936	107	321.0
3	8101	4648	2641	593		
5	4460	14139	3511	832	557	1081.0
24	4670	4370	1253	334		
	1386	757	407	105		
	3	58	19	10		
41	9096	13052	7353	1521	94	732.0
16	10726	11128	3840	934		
	101	148	84	30		
1	3810	5464	3038	274		
12	5193	4202	1940	318	89	250.0
1	850	1501	437	313	60	180.0
	12	42	19	23		
	310	604	78	8		
5	5660	3881	1269	201		

C-2-25续表2

地区	增加值合计	执行企业会计制度单位财务指标				
		固定资产原价	营业收入	费用合计	营业利润	企业单位增加值
全国	**5996694.6**	**14957540.3**	**44778306.0**	**4891883.3**	**1394922.0**	**5995405.5**
中央级						
北京	106758.4	279360.2	631324.8	66709.7	-3036.4	106758.4
天津	110503.0	242030.2	806786.5	426541.0	12663.2	110503.0
河北	179102.7	372006.6	900506.1	80771.2	16786.2	179102.7
山西	55976.7	266895.9	397054.5	30766.5	-1943.0	55976.7
内蒙古	10977.4	33113.1	53644.9	10213.8	1222.9	10977.4
辽宁	353474.7	612088.3	1946312.2	211749.9	65353.9	353474.7
吉林	22332.6	84815.5	254043.8	11191.8	2228.3	22332.6
黑龙江	33662.0	116463.5	159541.6	36051.7	6572.3	33662.0
上海	840836.9	930725.1	2877537.3	230291.0	267080.7	840836.9
江苏	1230265.1	3976065.3	12901774.6	1416773.2	332658.6	1230265.1
浙江	1713656.3	5212194.7	15361140.9	1547784.2	531566.3	1713656.3
安徽	39424.2	103970.0	736881.5	42851.2	8809.9	39404.2
福建	42676.4	95207.6	224470.5	19472.9	1289.0	42590.8
江西	15863.7	91573.2	2029730.4	20092.9	2879.0	15863.7
山东	528462.9	956873.2	1547554.4	297808.5	123814.5	528462.9
河南	104433.7	238375.9	437844.8	86725.7	8002.4	104428.2
湖北	43359.9	64234.4	181823.6	50059.4	3869.3	43359.9
湖南	30700.3	98082.6	383839.6	37471.3	-1129.1	30627.6
广东	37076.6	120564.6	260128.4	26151.5	5416.9	37076.6
广西	12538.5	27060.5	137543.1	7921.9	-224.2	12538.5
海南	107.7	1089.0	20.0	8.0		107.7
重庆	120172.7	257135.0	657929.2	72314.0	8706.7	120172.7
四川	250415.8	233530.2	948936.6	61590.6	6476.6	250415.8
贵州	1686.4	1689.1	6005.7	776.0	414.6	1000.2
云南	27281.8	244634.6	425988.0	25146.7	-29450.7	27043.6
西藏						
陕西	48057.1	104932.3	238578.6	38728.5	18046.6	48031.4
甘肃	1141.0	8624.3	3386.1	442.1	-34.2	1141.0
青海	155.2	500.0				
宁夏	6594.9	20058.5	19077.0	10351.5	478.8	6594.9
新疆	29000.0	163646.9	248901.3	25126.6	6402.9	29000.0

单位：万元

执行行政事业单位会计制度财务指标					
固定资产原价	上年结转和结余	本年收入合计	本年支出合计	收支结余	行政事业单位增加值
1884.7	**210.6**	**2183.9**	**2002.6**	**192.5**	**1289.1**
200.0			12.0		20.0
427.0		114.0	91.4		85.6
14.9		42.6	42.6		5.5
154.0		56.5	56.5		72.7
534.6	18.1	1163.9	1095.2		686.2
278.4		294.6	330.8		238.2
42.1		44.0	24.0		25.7
233.7	192.5	468.3	350.1	192.5	155.2

C-2-26 为残疾人提供服务的

地区	单位数	年末职工人数	#女性	#残疾职工	#女残疾职工	残疾职工工资总额	残疾职工养老保险总额
全国	**27**	**1545**	**526**	**153**	**64**	**2657.5**	**43.1**
中央级							
北京	1	110	27	6	1	51.0	10.0
天津	1	5		2		2.0	
河北	1	18	3	1	1	4.5	
山西	1	79	28	2		5.4	
内蒙古	1	41	13	25	16	61.2	12.6
辽宁							
吉林	2	99	41	3		2204.0	
黑龙江	2	28	8	9	2	10.0	5.1
上海	1	91	30	1		8.0	3.0
江苏	1	65	30	2		18.0	
浙江							
安徽	1	10	10	2	1	5.0	
福建	1	27	5	3		12.3	
江西							
山东	1	116	30	4		13.9	
河南	2	128	34	12	2	7.0	
湖北	3	167	63	5	2	15.3	0.2
湖南	1	105	38	3	1	15.2	4.2
广东	2	94	24	11	4	35.6	
广西							
海南							
重庆							
四川	1	106	50	43	29	108.4	
贵州	1	52	17	1		9.2	
云南	1	74	33	5	1	29.9	
西藏							
陕西	1	97	25	12	4	36.0	8.0
甘肃							
青海							
宁夏							
新疆	1	33	17	1		5.6	

康复辅具机构

单位：个、人、万元

残疾职工补贴	纳税总额	增值税总额	营业税总额	所得税总额	应减免税金总额	实际减免税金总额	盈利总额
18.6	**154.3**	**257.9**	**28.2**	**2.2**	**1213.8**	**1413.8**	**82.8**
12.0	47.0	4.0	12.0		298.0	298.0	82.0
3.9	15.0	10.0	2.6	1.8	14.0	14.0	-25.0
2.6							
							-75.7
	48.4	40.7	2.4	0.4			1.5
					425.0	425.0	-10.0
0.1	35.0		3.7				
	7.7	3.2	4.5		355.4	355.4	
	1.2		3.0		121.4	121.4	110.0
		200.0				200.0	

C-2-26续表1

地 区	单位数	年末职工人数	受教育程度		职业资
			大学专科人数	大学本科及以上人数	助理社会工作师人数
全 国	**27**	**1545**	**385**	**294**	**25**
中央级					
北 京	1	110	23	20	
天 津	1	5	1		
河 北	1	18	4	4	
山 西	1	79	17	25	
内蒙古	1	41	9	1	
辽 宁					
吉 林	2	99			
黑龙江	2	28	10		
上 海	1	91	13	7	
江 苏	1	65	40	15	2
浙 江					
安 徽	1	10	2		
福 建	1	27	5	4	
江 西					
山 东	1	116	27	22	
河 南	2	128	30	30	6
湖 北	3	167	40	21	
湖 南	1	105	23	21	
广 东	2	94	20	40	14
广 西					
海 南					
重 庆					
四 川	1	106	42	35	
贵 州	1	52	12	18	
云 南	1	74	33	9	1
西 藏					
陕 西	1	97	27	18	2
甘 肃					
青 海					
宁 夏					
新 疆	1	33	7	4	

单位:个、人、人次、时

格水平	年龄结构				志愿服务	
社会工作师人数	35岁及以下人数	36岁至45岁人数	46岁至55岁人数	56岁及以上人数	志愿者服务人次数	志愿服务时间
19	**405**	**461**	**504**	**175**	**10**	**40.0**
	42	22	29	17		
		1	4			
	4	4	4	6		
2	18	36	23	2		
		2	12	27		
	42	40	15	2		
	14	5	8	1		
	5	35	35	16		
1	19	15	14	17		
1	2	4	4			
	4		20	3		
	10	31	65	10		
7	53	30	28	17		
2	41	35	72	19	10	40.0
	28	31	37	9		
5	26	37	27	4		
	44	26	26	10		
	9	28	12	3		
1	29	9	34	2		
	8	53	30	6		
	7	17	5	4		

C-2-26续表2

地区	增加值合计	执行企业会计制度单位财务指标				
		固定资产原价	营业收入	费用合计	营业利润	企业单位增加值
全国	**14816.6**	**24184.0**	**20241.3**	**9566.9**	**-109.9**	**5232.5**
中央级						
北京	380.3	1992.0	2412.0	672.0	-212.0	380.3
天津	8.3	86.0	33.2	-10.6	-4.5	8.3
河北	182.3					
山西	870.0	5135.0	916.0	157.0	-63.0	870.0
内蒙古	81.0	205.0	125.0	142.0	-24.0	81.0
辽宁						
吉林	644.2					
黑龙江	111.1	188.3	164.3	39.5	9.5	111.1
上海	579.5	2475.5	2241.7	1176.6	-76.7	579.5
江苏	2853.5					
浙江						
安徽	-3.7	474.0	979.0	394.0	-166.0	-3.7
福建	857.3	1152.0	2931.0	843.5	290.0	857.3
江西						
山东	608.1	3261.0	2596.0	1383.0	-10.0	608.1
河南	-419.7	4502.0	1983.0	775.0	-179.0	-419.7
湖北	937.2	29.4	40.2	19.4	-5.0	19.8
湖南	202.4	1193.5	1141.0	1190.2	132.0	202.4
广东	1118.9	1538.3	3276.9	2264.3	96.8	1118.9
广西						
海南						
重庆						
四川	1521.3					
贵州	1232.7					
云南	1881.7					
西藏						
陕西	819.3	1952.0	1402.0	521.0	102.0	819.3
甘肃						
青海						
宁夏						
新疆	351.0					

单位：万元

执行行政事业单位会计制度财务指标					
固定资产原价	上年结转和结余	本年收入合计	本年支出合计	收支结余	行政事业单位增加值
13375.4	**-2.4**	**18807.1**	**18612.6**	**30.4**	**9584.1**
58.0		252.0	258.0		182.3
1138.0		938.0	964.8		644.2
3502.9		6784.7	6783.2	1.5	2853.5
2086.6	-36.4	3303.6	3264.6		917.4
3199.9	15.9	2471.1	2442.2	28.9	1521.3
1373.0		1984.0	1930.0		1232.7
1135.0	18.1	1853.7	1761.8		1881.7
882.0		1220.0	1208.0		351.0

C-2-27 其他为残疾人

地 区	单位数	年末职工人数	#女 性	#残疾职工	#女残疾职工	残疾职工工资总额	残疾职工养老保险总额
全 国	**3975**	**285838**	**86453**	**118890**	**33494**	**323637.8**	**35444.5**
中央级							
北 京	28	1473	696	486	125	1023.9	353.8
天 津	1	2	1	10		30.0	
河 北	251	12857	4160	5235	1446	8575.0	3126.7
山 西	170	10544	2283	5280	1132	6590.0	863.2
内蒙古	85	4967	977	3291	988	3256.4	889.8
辽 宁	298	17571	5958	6848	2388	9242.3	3094.4
吉 林	150	5265	1449	2249	832	2883.0	8.2
黑龙江	62	2858	963	1737	494	37158.5	178.2
上 海	9	713	260	223	68	435.5	231.6
江 苏	62	3586	1420	1285	543	2005.0	154.8
浙 江	312	24913	7596	9474	3555	23362.9	7150.5
安 徽	107	4394	1545	1780	410	2383.8	762.3
福 建	130	8684	2710	4066	523	5359.6	560.9
江 西	76	8923	2498	3408	120	6838.2	6.8
山 东	169	10215	2647	3863	1223	7326.5	1881.6
河 南	176	14773	4110	6203	2208	10270.4	214.1
湖 北	366	22159	6045	8675	3176	14118.4	1324.8
湖 南	190	11520	3019	6757	1536	9996.2	1198.1
广 东	31	3327	1219	1180	397	1959.6	332.3
广 西	90	6119	1041	2221	744	57052.4	443.9
海 南	9	1166	294	1216	309	949.8	45.0
重 庆	345	36627	13025	13963	4605	35351.3	7868.6
四 川	395	28145	9522	12218	3159	22395.5	2286.9
贵 州	32	1860	490	803	345	1385.1	232.7
云 南	210	32632	9152	11312	1928	34942.8	1306.5
西 藏	3	209	73	105	34	10192.7	18.1
陕 西	45	2284	725	926	402	2135.6	457.5
甘 肃	21	843	185	302	40	697.8	27.0
青 海	31	1753	532	1013	202	1702.5	37.6
宁 夏	60	3039	966	1520	244	2802.0	334.0
新 疆	61	2417	892	1241	318	1215.1	54.6

服务的福利机构

单位：个、人、万元

残疾职工补贴	纳税总额	增值税总额	营业税总额	所得税总额	应减免税金总额	实际减免税金总额	盈利总额
3880.9	**162789.0**	**129982.1**	**18082.4**	**16765.0**	**120341.5**	**108127.9**	**124556.2**
98.7	1375.2	132.5	829.5	191.0	1333.5	1321.6	328.5
125.3	10726.5	4066.0	115.0	898.2	7131.1	4704.1	3560.2
46.1	10583.0	7921.7	23.0	5.5	8821.7	5464.1	1934.2
80.0	4248.6	3977.3	150.0	75.1	2060.8	2028.8	1378.6
20.9	12303.3	11728.6	159.8	1181.3	10369.5	8435.6	5513.6
82.7							
31.2	517.7	473.7	31.2	14.0	476.7	466.2	1077.8
	1705.0	1670.5	48.0	57.3	902.8	391.2	734.4
	13412.1	32729.0	12540.0	3176.2	21062.3	27801.2	55823.1
71.6	1907.2	834.1	21.4	90.7	603.9	662.2	838.5
146.6	3615.5	611.8	20.0	16.7	195.2	194.2	3349.0
2.0							
286.2	12289.1	7724.9	438.4	1332.7	9277.3	5204.0	5212.3
8.2	1809.5	1446.9	11.2	134.4	555.1	343.5	569.6
234.3	9017.1	9701.0	550.0	792.1	8920.6	8279.6	1931.5
835.9	4156.0	189.0	760.0	95.0	2925.3	2889.9	183.8
74.0	2046.3	1047.3	134.0	822.9	1787.9	1675.3	30.7
22.8	1961.9	1856.0	90.6		973.0	859.5	-139.5
	1030.0	915.0		40.0	580.0	553.0	70.0
974.8	50771.6	25450.0	876.4	7024.5	33017.7	27157.2	37497.0
500.4	3592.0	3573.9	680.8	252.6	5151.5	5414.1	2771.3
37.7	47.8	47.8			62.8	58.0	19.0
117.4	11602.0	9588.0	592.4	240.5	1943.0	2934.4	-2414.2
24.6	4011.5	3649.4	3.5	220.0	1412.0	1019.5	4227.8
32.0							
20.9					251.4	251.4	
	20.0				18.0		20.0
6.6	40.1	647.7	7.2	104.3	508.4	19.3	39.0

C-2-27续表1

地 区	单位数	年末职工人数	受教育程度		职业资
			大学专科人数	大学本科及以上人数	助理社会工作师人数
全 国	**3975**	**285838**	**19374**	**7637**	**548**
中央级					
北 京	28	1473	83	51	2
天 津	1	2			
河 北	251	12857	463	213	24
山 西	170	10544	133	36	12
内蒙古	85	4967	961	246	3
辽 宁	298	17571	1206	606	32
吉 林	150	5265	325	228	70
黑龙江	62	2858	68	8	4
上 海	9	713	5	1	
江 苏	62	3586	190	61	6
浙 江	312	24913	1129	480	3
安 徽	107	4394	304	105	14
福 建	130	8684	80	101	
江 西	76	8923	6	10	3
山 东	169	10215	574	315	4
河 南	176	14773	2500	1857	
湖 北	366	22159	1405	654	225
湖 南	190	11520	595	65	40
广 东	31	3327	147	43	5
广 西	90	6119	467	50	2
海 南	9	1166	118	49	21
重 庆	345	36627	2660	1011	31
四 川	395	28145	4735	1091	14
贵 州	32	1860	196		
云 南	210	32632	426	216	15
西 藏	3	209	1		
陕 西	45	2284	247	37	8
甘 肃	21	843	45	10	
青 海	31	1753	9	1	10
宁 夏	60	3039	107	27	
新 疆	61	2417	189	65	

单位：个、人、人次、时

格水平	年龄结构				志愿服务	
社会工作师人数	35岁及以下人数	36岁至45岁人数	46岁至55岁人数	56岁及以上人数	志愿者服务人次数	志愿服务时间
150	**109508**	**108423**	**58056**	**9851**	**17429**	**42135.0**
5	576	408	444	45	76	76.0
		1	1			
6	4143	6126	2137	451	40	117.0
5	3524	3641	2667	712		
	822	1812	2273	60		
16	4676	7150	4031	1714	492	1214.0
59	1609	2842	757	57		
	865	1465	494	34		
	170	345	139	59		
7	1363	1352	606	265	780	1010.0
	6987	8978	7829	1119		
1	1531	1697	1000	166	214	430.0
	2797	3814	1690	383		
	4186	2894	1723	120		
3	3118	4339	2387	371		
	6458	6564	1371	380		
	5540	7655	8617	347	57	171.0
4	3362	5539	2185	434	4741	14806.0
3	1441	1126	581	179	470	1365.0
1	3323	1827	794	175		
2	689	398	65	14		
17	15563	13872	5959	1233	10383	22646.0
5	13577	10042	3986	540		
	753	659	334	114	176	300.0
7	18727	9343	4023	539		
	45	106	45	13		
6	784	726	679	95		
	352	399	85	7		
3	766	734	191	62		
	842	1545	517	135		
	919	1024	446	28		

C-2-27续表2

地 区	增加值合计	执行企业	
		固定资产原价	营业收入
全 国	**920004.0**	**2604245.4**	**7634739.6**
中央级			
北 京	8147.2	34111.2	32048.4
天 津		0.1	
河 北	46475.7	156385.1	452689.3
山 西	13996.4	79900.6	85648.0
内蒙古	7091.2	31236.0	17263.7
辽 宁	54500.3	113564.8	355183.4
吉 林	37210.8	92330.8	138668.0
黑龙江	7425.3	13812.0	35854.7
上 海	2179.2	3727.6	20150.6
江 苏	11353.6	28425.2	87297.1
浙 江	199417.3	363048.6	2129371.9
安 徽	18115.2	40855.7	205065.7
福 建	13181.2	73820.3	136011.3
江 西	2744.1	9444.0	57945.2
山 东	49361.6	108694.9	198309.5
河 南	23498.3	44604.7	162120.5
湖 北	50076.2	145035.3	257644.0
湖 南	52172.0	171118.5	185681.2
广 东	8101.3	11315.9	45078.0
广 西	12378.8	36524.4	250800.0
海 南	3718.2	13133.9	47467.9
重 庆	148920.8	289040.4	1112453.2
四 川	61330.9	211771.1	661926.3
贵 州	1884.1	5430.0	14443.6
云 南	58464.1	388774.8	747975.4
西 藏	144.0	3395.3	353.8
陕 西	13849.5	56006.7	144943.0
甘 肃	1156.9	21269.7	5256.5
青 海	1908.8	5064.3	10428.8
宁 夏	7469.7	40557.3	22257.8
新 疆	3731.3	11846.2	14402.8

单位：万元

会计制度单位财务指标		
费用合计	营业利润	企业单位增加值
888914.0	**198626.7**	**920004.0**
7646.9	834.6	8147.2
52551.6	-2564.3	46475.7
6875.2	2364.2	13996.4
3689.3	1740.9	7091.2
34120.1	11355.2	54500.3
33346.1	4033.0	37210.8
10784.9	915.9	7425.3
3293.5	755.5	2179.2
8611.6	1904.6	11353.6
150352.9	66447.3	199417.3
17225.3	9732.5	18115.2
32517.3	1889.6	13181.2
169.0		2744.1
30791.3	10062.1	49361.6
21408.2	8450.0	23498.3
60149.3	1323.4	50076.2
38696.7	12759.2	52172.0
5229.0	-5.4	8101.3
4657.5	-1664.0	12378.8
4740.0	1103.7	3718.2
139447.6	25630.5	148920.8
52458.3	11676.8	61330.9
3156.5	649.4	1884.1
145223.0	25942.8	58464.1
119.9	104.4	144.0
10976.7	3584.3	13849.5
2251.4	169.0	1156.9
1313.8	100.0	1908.8
2655.9	-1178.3	7469.7
4455.2	509.8	3731.3

C-2-28 残疾人教育

地 区	职业培训基地数（个）	本年度城镇职业培训人数（人次）	残疾人就业服务机构（个）
合 计	**5357**	**378247**	**2760**
北 京	62	10471	17
天 津	30	2837	20
河 北	386	20775	187
山 西	512	8422	122
内蒙古	66	12213	83
辽 宁	158	14869	117
吉 林	180	13823	71
黑龙江	94	12399	127
上 海	16	11666	16
江 苏	216	23208	113
浙 江	291	14397	99
安 徽	86	12114	77
福 建	201	8799	91
江 西	227	3802	85
山 东	683	22642	135
河 南	230	51062	157
湖 北	269	10749	105
湖 南	185	6368	135
广 东	130	13117	133
广 西	65	6327	119
海 南	12	2322	18
重 庆	32	4762	38
四 川	517	31184	132
贵 州	40	4423	62
云 南	111	8451	118
西 藏	5	193	2
陕 西	80	12337	121
甘 肃	42	19494	91
青 海	28	2131	31
宁 夏	31	2861	19
新 疆	370	9257	94
兵团	2	772	24
黑龙江农垦			1

指标解释：
职业培训基地数：指承担着残疾人就业前培训，在职培训、下岗失业人员转岗转业培训、农村务工人员培训等项职能的实体的个数。
本年度城镇职业培训人数：指本年度城镇残疾人中在各类职业培训机构（基地）接受培训（含统计时正在接受培训）的实际人次数。
残疾人就业服务机构：指截止到本年度12月31日，省（自治区、直辖市）、地（州、盟）、市（地市级市、县级市）、县（旗）、市辖区各级残联所建的残疾人就业服务机构数。
残疾人就业人数：包括城镇就业残疾人和农村在业残疾人，其中城镇就业残疾人指截止到本年度12月31日城镇（非农业户口）残疾人集中就业、分散按比例就业（包括实施按比例就业前已在社会各单位就业的残疾人）、辅助性就业、公益性岗位就业、个体及其他形式就业的人数，农村在业残疾人指截止到本年度12月31日农村残疾人（农业户口）从事各种生产劳动，包括种植业、养殖业、家庭手工业及在各种类型企事业、服务业、商业及个体从业的实际人数。
未入学适龄残疾儿童少年总人数：指截止到本年度12月31日，在省级人民政府依照《义务教育法》规定的入学年龄段内的，因各种原因未能入学的各类参加儿童少年人数。

就业情况

残疾人就业人数（万人）	未入学残疾儿童、少年（人）	省市县乡残联实有人员（人）
2202.7	**83532**	**110870**
13.6	243	1202
10.6	445	962
109.3	1135	5529
52.1	2481	4750
39.5	1576	3015
71.4	2094	4171
46.4	2896	2857
36.7	1037	2864
9.2	9	1108
99.0	1435	4978
53.0	526	4319
100.7	5034	3453
44.8	1474	2404
71.2	5234	4268
164.2	3752	6006
222.4	7948	8048
113.3	2461	3507
120.9	5839	5519
81.6	4303	6850
71.7	4804	3028
7.9	443	632
63.8	943	1966
207.4	4436	8811
87.2	4427	3098
104.9	4878	3532
2.1	178	202
81.1	4017	4640
64.5	3137	3993
5.3	928	1196
13.4	1021	689
30.2	4183	2779
1.8	49	284
1.6	166	210

C-2-29 孤儿和

地　区	孤儿数	集中供养孤儿	社会散居孤儿	收养登记合计	中国公民收养登记
全　国	**548845**	**93899**	**454946**	**24460**	**21230**
中央级					
北　京	2374	1952	422	218	149
天　津	835	526	309	166	123
河　北	15278	2119	13159	439	391
山　西	16115	3800	12315	255	97
内蒙古	6127	1274	4853	198	155
辽　宁	7702	2933	4769	208	193
吉　林	5880	1691	4189	37	18
黑龙江	8121	1721	6400	93	66
上　海	2141	2013	128	316	250
江　苏	19503	3518	15985	2636	2423
浙　江	5204	2667	2537	4037	3956
安　徽	27076	3721	23355	1046	882
福　建	6642	2196	4446	1150	1104
江　西	27107	6084	21023	872	619
山　东	19077	3276	15801	2092	2005
河　南	46844	5384	41460	690	260
湖　北	29478	5227	24251	1381	1302
湖　南	51633	7410	44223	844	751
广　东	43526	9823	33703	1989	1433
广　西	22502	2404	20098	1438	1269
海　南	2337	323	2014	174	167
重　庆	13532	1459	12073	350	280
四　川	30137	3687	26450	1068	1029
贵　州	22630	2703	19927	387	311
云　南	25371	2241	23130	1278	1175
西　藏	5576	988	4588	115	115
陕　西	13473	2917	10556	357	168
甘　肃	22411	3313	19098	102	52
青　海	16351	1212	15139	60	50
宁　夏	7066	273	6793	35	22
新　疆	26796	5044	21752	429	415

儿童收养

单位：人、件

香港居民	澳门居民	台湾居民	华　侨	外国人收养登记	协议解除收养关系登记	#中国公民
139	**6**	**28**	**24**	**3230**	**609**	**601**
		1	1	69	5	5
1				43	1	
				48	2	2
1		1		158	1	1
				43		
				15	2	1
				19	1	1
1		1	2	27	26	26
1			1	66	9	7
				213	5	5
			8	81	42	42
1				164	2	2
13		7	3	46	57	57
				253	31	31
1		2	1	87	244	244
3				430		
6		2	3	79	14	13
5		2		93	17	16
93	5	5	3	556	16	15
8	1	1		169	18	18
3		2		7	1	1
1		1	2	70	11	10
1		2		39	84	84
				76	10	10
				103	1	1
				189		
		1		50	1	1
				10		
				13		
				14	8	8

C-2-30 被收养的

地区	被收				
	合计	#女性	残疾儿童	社会福利机构抚养的孤儿	
					#被外国人收养
全　国	**24491**	**17164**	**2632**	**9657**	**2695**
中央级					
北　京	218	126	54	142	69
天　津	166	122	41	29	18
河　北	434	252	79	134	48
山　西	255	137	161	63	
内蒙古	198	94	20	23	16
辽　宁	208	109	12	81	15
吉　林	38	12		20	19
黑龙江	93	46	10	44	27
上　海	316	248	66	91	66
江　苏	2638	2032	181	717	213
浙　江	4037	3372	9	1930	81
安　徽	1089	793	135	361	164
福　建	1149	879	59	358	46
江　西	871	815	135	482	253
山　东	2092	1325	140	911	87
河　南	690	340	419	528	423
湖　北	1381	491	11	512	79
湖　南	841	607	92	323	92
广　东	1984	1432	412	1372	556
广　西	1432	1183	114	379	10
海　南	178	117	15	55	5
重　庆	354	221	64	187	70
四　川	1064	630	16	299	39
贵　州	387	314	53	135	76
云　南	1278	887	79	90	6
西　藏	115	56	5	82	
陕　西	356	183	155	219	189
甘　肃	102	68	47	12	
青　海	60	26	20	1	1
宁　夏	35	21	13	16	13
新　疆	432	226	15	61	14

儿童情况

单位：人

养人					
社会孤儿数	#被外国人收养	近亲属抚养人数	生父母有特殊困难无力抚养人数	#被外国人收养	其他
7814	**524**	**2466**	**640**	**11**	**3914**
34		1			41
81	25	27	8		21
135		36	22		107
175	158	4	3		10
60	27	40	30		45
51		21	6		49
2		1	3		12
4		2	28		15
117		56	1		51
983		450	19		469
1553		181	3		370
369		88	15		256
444		104	2		241
291		55	7		36
533		305	5		338
21		4	23	7	114
368		153	77		271
247		121	34	1	116
351		51	28		182
530	159	211	60		252
19		31	13	2	60
68		15	24		60
316		83	85		281
129		43	4		76
676	97	245	35		232
7		3	22		1
48		13	20		56
70	49	8	1	1	11
25	9	3	3		28
3		8	2		6
104		103	57		107

C-2-31 救助、低保

地区	单位数	年末职工人数	#女性	受教育程度		职业资
				大学专科人数	大学本科及以上人数	助理社会工作师人数
全国	**987**	**7187**	**3237**	**2552**	**2518**	**96**
中央级						
北京	17	110	63	27	77	5
天津	1	5	2	2	3	
河北	4	28	14	5	13	
山西	101	748	368	303	225	17
内蒙古	24	256	144	85	145	6
辽宁	16	98	38	20	31	
吉林	58	700	182	156	134	2
黑龙江	39	359	170	134	117	1
上海	7	75	46	6	57	10
江苏	8	30	15	10	17	
浙江	22	111	66	18	73	1
安徽	32	125	46	50	51	2
福建	20	65	38	33	19	3
江西	64	379	176	123	69	8
山东	10	53	24	19	27	1
河南	42	279	129	88	48	4
湖北	62	565	250	221	198	6
湖南	92	771	346	313	212	5
广东	3	24	13	6	14	8
广西	98	435	239	160	211	1
海南	2	14	9	5	8	
重庆	35	231	126	83	142	1
四川	54	254	118	103	65	7
贵州	55	806	332	328	333	3
云南	28	93	32	30	27	1
西藏	1	2	1	1	1	
陕西	26	249	123	109	64	2
甘肃	24	153	60	41	67	
青海	3	7	3	1	4	
宁夏	12	88	46	28	50	1
新疆	27	74	18	44	16	1

服务机构

单位:个、人、人次、时

格水平	年龄结构				志愿服务	
社会工作师人数	35岁及以下人数	36岁至45岁人数	46岁至55岁人数	56岁及以上人数	志愿者服务人次数	志愿服务时间
114	**3391**	**3002**	**694**	**100**	**1372**	**4128.0**
6	41	43	23	3	26	78.0
		2	2	1		
	25	3				
6	363	287	93	5	6	18.0
6	109	125	21	1		
2	37	34	11	16		
5	353	304	40	3	15	45.0
3	132	177	45	5		
7	49	20	4	2		
1	12	11	7		13	39.0
9	53	47	9	2		
2	41	62	18	4	110	342.0
	28	34	3			
9	147	198	29	5		
5	28	20	5			
1	152	92	30	5		
7	220	282	54	9	72	216.0
15	355	327	69	20	670	2010.0
1	6	15	2	1		
5	174	205	52	4	18	54.0
	3	7	4			
1	111	86	30	4	252	756.0
7	122	108	19	5		
3	503	253	50		161	483.0
	29	50	14			
		2				
1	140	80	25	4	9	27.0
9	99	43	11		20	60.0
	3	1	3			
3	15	56	17			
	41	28	4	1		

C-2-31续表

地　区	增加值合计	执行	
		固定资产原价	上年结转和结余
全　国	**26926.9**	**12923.6**	**844.3**
中央级			
北　京	888.3	265.2	8.7
天　津	36.0		
河　北	19.3	33.5	
山　西	1167.0	1491.4	36.8
内蒙古	938.5	361.7	
辽　宁	233.6	78.0	8.7
吉　林	1328.0	669.7	198.6
黑龙江	850.1	711.3	
上　海	1991.3	281.2	65.5
江　苏	204.1	56.6	
浙　江	1065.6	568.5	60.1
安　徽	352.0	394.5	
福　建	266.4	49.9	48.3
江　西	770.8	878.5	6.0
山　东	209.6	70.8	
河　南	597.9	813.1	
湖　北	2252.2	1058.2	5.3
湖　南	2683.4	1714.5	157.4
广　东	28.6	61.7	
广　西	5949.8	810.6	237.8
海　南	17.2	5.0	
重　庆	1190.6	670.3	1.1
四　川	935.9	239.0	
贵　州	1646.6	942.4	10.0
云　南	274.0	24.0	
西　藏	17.9	50.0	
陕　西	726.6	267.7	
甘　肃	150.8	149.5	
青　海	0.4	10.0	
宁　夏	129.6	74.0	
新　疆	4.9	122.8	

单位：万元

行政事业单位会计制度财务指标			
本年收入合计	本年支出合计	收支结余	行政事业单位增加值
76190.1	**68168.5**	**808.7**	**26926.9**
2049.1	2039.2	19.6	888.3
37.0	37.0		36.0
77.0	77.0		19.3
2445.2	2473.1	6.7	1167.0
1423.7	1423.7		938.5
988.6	946.8		233.6
9360.6	9517.2	269.6	1328.0
1597.6	1476.3		850.1
11181.2	10347.0	146.8	1991.3
229.1	229.1		204.1
4884.5	4638.3		1065.6
575.4	586.4		352.0
624.6	657.8	3.0	266.4
1350.0	1370.8		770.8
256.4	256.4		209.6
848.8	812.7		597.9
4039.4	4082.4	15.8	2252.2
5377.1	4430.7	240.4	2683.4
132.0	362.5		28.6
11926.6	11653.2	106.8	5949.8
1752.1	1752.1		17.2
2684.4	2684.4		1190.6
2223.4	2263.8		935.9
8311.9	2017.3		1646.6
145.5	276.5		274.0
331.0	331.0		17.9
1005.8	1000.1		726.6
211.5	221.0		150.8
4.6	4.6		0.4
89.0	173.1		129.6
27.0	27.0		4.9

C-2-32 城市居民最低生活

地 区	城市居民最低生活保障人数	按人员性质分类			老年人	成	
		#女 性	#残疾人	#三无人员		在职人员	灵活就业
全 国	**20641935**	**8669831**	**1691870**	**580490**	**3302718**	**450840**	**4621362**
中央级							
北 京	103682	46425	20124	2289	13661	6677	14007
天 津	160370	78574	22703	845	17953	5011	15302
河 北	727646	297880	45967	17438	118703	16833	188372
山 西	850298	364613	52374	14328	92072	26705	259062
内蒙古	783744	387721	63726		106864	4526	190755
辽 宁	960553	419024	129277	13631	129975	9702	147126
吉 林	850056	423562	81044	9401	126518	729	582076
黑龙江	1437744	585156	128429	30643	156574	14241	266790
上 海	204843	75635	28840	586	4443	17340	2132
江 苏	337500	144579	40107	5791	82070	7844	47134
浙 江	71831	26693	14088	4113	16376	1867	9995
安 徽	782663	323693	77390	38679	218325	9090	148589
福 建	157694	57541	22311	6867	34193	2482	29084
江 西	978048	412525	159167	59464	188204	26542	225850
山 东	487176	197161	34365	13072	72985	22234	87293
河 南	1309834	522270	87832	44544	231515	19545	233964
湖 北	1258743	588684	76348	38179	219288	89498	386521
湖 南	1435222	551573	88725	55576	293238	22485	195690
广 东	339911	136650	40749	15528	68474	9044	69467
广 西	494366	172795	36843	35271	127390	13524	115000
海 南	144743	58760	9827	5512	30603	4254	31630
重 庆	458103	209176	63399	1925	93240	1023	94055
四 川	1835734	718173	108033	49810	314598	17825	397617
贵 州	513277	210907	30106	14569	75926	8037	109759
云 南	1040515	387912	55785	30514	160336	26780	210741
西 藏	49920	23588	3659	9228	10681	5414	10196
陕 西	670571	318392	27341	6911	48910	8644	140665
甘 肃	874989	315069	39151	15490	88670	19717	172993
青 海	225153	112955	9320	3479	20933	7580	37045
宁 夏	179672	77113	15917	6191	22731	3469	47152
新 疆	917334	425032	78923	30616	117269	22178	155300

保障及其他社会救济

单位：人、户、万元、人次

年人		未成年人		城市居民最低生活保障户数	城市低保资金全年计划支出	城市“三无”救助人数
登记失业	未登记失业	在校生	其 他			
3654505	**4167892**	**3031873**	**1412745**	**10971634**	**4805316.0**	**86438**
26943	17410	16236	8748	58457	65394.3	59
46258	33438	26144	16264	86929	84797.2	1
125629	123971	113589	40549	389970	183449.6	479
96220	138515	178211	59513	420570	158833.9	415
127807	243471	66201	44120	445872	336954.1	13022
239243	208080	170932	55495	515099	264188.4	1569
24300	19991	92777	3665	521793	67086.8	7702
335629	413053	181910	69547	751815	213783.7	2083
68577	65112	44732	2507	136088	130405.4	
52045	89654	41199	17554	178011	123564.0	2305
9149	14702	14133	5609	46420	16105.4	950
103122	159142	97783	46612	461104	245183.9	2480
29736	37755	16597	7847	83057	37717.9	968
180306	131960	131125	94061	452893	181606.3	16859
147691	77649	59821	19503	243483	173239.4	1664
271095	262758	171246	119711	719127	210317.3	156
207530	205607	99643	50656	667091	373804.9	8783
361060	262781	176850	123118	789383	353452.3	2421
40457	70845	62843	18781	161431	69920.4	3923
64573	77465	63126	33288	252800	116985.9	1516
17779	30843	20507	9127	62376	35068.6	317
67541	101923	77827	22494	266832	172012.4	9785
274125	461299	239191	131079	1027660	255459.6	
60207	132965	95198	31185	267684	163647.8	1211
196662	219231	158747	68018	633165	152796.8	52
4474	7249	6639	5267	27085	16125.4	883
119292	78383	172235	102442	321125	197213.3	2499
188322	182775	159736	62776	374176	135228.9	1699
22189	54012	53210	30184	104838	25181.2	57
25847	33247	33116	14110	90622	18934.4	152
120697	212606	190369	98915	414678	226856.5	2428

C-2-33 农村最低

地区	农村最低生活保障人数	女性	老年人	未成年人	残疾人	农村最低生活保障户数
全国	**53880178**	**18665358**	**20780811**	**6146317**	**4728926**	**29311123**
中央级						
北京	59575	24920	23358	7946	18243	34816
天津	107444	43556	26718	18224	18748	47710
河北	2218981	679050	1301604	121957	177713	1606259
山西	1497629	529593	852921	73814	169001	1182460
内蒙古	1253151	564945	660925	39495	66071	964849
辽宁	883982	310284	388681	69000	112982	533416
吉林	809162	372663	433962	28593	144144	591109
黑龙江	1215350	439948	516798	79892	87014	648789
上海	32796	16413	11222	1968	10403	25222
江苏	1301395	475996	495363	136093	141807	703140
浙江	551355	192449	202517	72283	108411	346522
安徽	2160542	764581	816941	203060	269940	1175239
福建	736542	244181	207123	83482	103213	358562
江西	1606531	630174	472461	287160	341261	699239
山东	2598685	879595	1491896	170701	220041	1743032
河南	3909196	1172211	1994214	311774	372629	2893314
湖北	2357011	1011395	944274	146587	244625	1485054
湖南	2893347	799410	1101923	323114	213319	1489541
广东	1632234	525581	461340	307717	161566	721482
广西	3458922	982488	1211587	542429	200801	1334863
海南	245488	98297	62704	37904	15429	95276
重庆	626612	279667	193381	101064	86355	348587
四川	4394553	1286831	1878508	479749	366885	2501780
贵州	4770600	1738581	1588398	757371	307670	2236280
云南	4665411	1729219	1338711	563475	265582	2456760
西藏	329000	126621	157966	60369	16330	90163
陕西	1998903	817394	639932	204651	139702	858286
甘肃	3432860	1139217	722927	557302	170979	1131886
青海	402865	122262	72695	74406	25943	137781
宁夏	381821	118789	127948	23921	59370	287628
新疆	1348235	549047	381813	260816	92749	582078

生活保障

单位：人、户、万元

农村低保资金全年计划支出	农村五保集中供养人数	女性	老年人	未成年人	残疾人	农村五保集中供养资金全年计划支出
5695881.2	**1834910**	**340635**	**1636854**	**57551**	**295537**	**573478.8**
26641.2	2039	218	1524	18	1059	1793.8
29655.0	1399	158	1274	6	289	1013.0
247315.5	88768	10198	78140	1816	17164	20995.2
154393.5	28026	2094	22334	600	6730	8643.2
268882.2	27875	2338	23626	303	6290	14784.2
109800.7	34701	3819	30210	638	7877	14384.5
17103.8	29539	7155	26383	1378	8281	1096.1
79012.3	69442	13589	56072	2110	17268	8396.4
10642.6	1211	244	1107	4	217	815.2
270909.6	116809	20855	109102	1777	16727	67470.1
75773.8	36458	6199	34322	447	5423	11419.3
265368.3	166392	24365	154433	2882	21131	39537.7
116069.0	9546	1409	8246	342	1647	2009.6
111977.7	119411	43702	100382	11607	16340	25255.3
444854.2	171187	34792	163533	2106	16401	74052.1
295999.1	197384	39355	180689	6068	26582	38296.4
274446.8	88980	20713	81027	1557	14953	24961.3
275562.1	108753	23076	95850	4973	16522	36486.7
173227.0	32608	6859	31108	599	2669	13077.5
311799.6	23005	4385	21495	589	3689	6457.7
36476.3	2273	784	2211	26	146	988.0
127676.2	62229	6922	54463	735	12016	29591.5
280393.7	265894	32256	233981	7468	43423	58102.5
573364.7	27608	5219	21925	3535	4344	8210.1
370628.8	35490	8640	30244	1766	7983	5897.7
51683.4	7943	4217	7941	2	57	32500.5
265971.7	46974	7729	39227	745	12807	18436.2
231070.9	10842	1882	8856	921	2114	1861.1
29175.8	4377	1525	2842	1057	713	299.7
25317.5	3903	894	3245	193	1150	825.8
144688.2	13844	5044	11062	1283	3525	5820.4

C-2-34 农村五保

地区	农村五保分散供养人数	女性	老年人
全国	**3537579**	**679377**	**3007781**
中央级			
北京	2037	179	1582
天津	11243	1095	9713
河北	149602	15140	131313
山西	136512	15631	98816
内蒙古	59811	4794	50595
辽宁	103955	13430	88363
吉林	93064	20055	81676
黑龙江	76882	15883	56850
上海	1648	245	1322
江苏	84635	15453	78625
浙江	921	119	874
安徽	269984	49928	249109
福建	78045	12388	61152
江西	109069	37640	89446
山东	56872	12045	54260
河南	279581	53520	249082
湖北	180019	39506	163329
湖南	405162	80068	343322
广东	210379	41068	197107
广西	271665	48039	242550
海南	30457	10112	28556
重庆	99254	10915	83588
四川	244373	36829	210160
贵州	97449	21627	69554
云南	180288	44945	126299
西藏	7195	3737	7142
陕西	83895	14349	65198
甘肃	112911	23314	92272
青海	18544	5782	14148
宁夏	10540	2720	7905
新疆	71587	28821	53873

供养情况

单位：人、户、万元

未成年人	残疾人	农村五保分散供养资金全年计划支出
177239	**632898**	**737316.7**
10	1048	1638.9
68	2547	7184.1
3885	26370	27264.4
7139	41557	22553.1
1110	13827	20075.3
2664	23005	24061.6
4064	28557	1776.4
2586	24191	9283.4
16	496	842.7
1756	11553	35387.5
11	141	200.1
5729	32526	39590.4
3928	19240	20009.0
11882	16701	16677.1
766	5440	16975.4
9910	38268	35364.9
3785	25062	33845.5
22533	65604	73043.6
7531	19357	64195.7
14930	37480	59703.0
740	2801	11684.9
2363	18070	44725.8
8649	43452	40642.8
18771	15374	18431.9
19635	48755	16952.5
53	316	30779.0
3896	22569	28714.0
6949	23860	17221.1
2754	3344	2251.4
654	3563	828.0
8472	17824	15413.2

C-2-35 医疗救助及

地 区	传统救济	临时救助户次	临时救助按户籍性质分类		临时救助按属地分类	
			城市家庭户次	农村家庭户次	当地常住人口户次	非当地常住人口户次
全 国	**729532**	**6981385**	**3229955**	**3751430**	**6809669**	**171716**
中央级						
北 京		165171	72373	92798	165171	
天 津	150	70382	62219	8163	70288	94
河 北	5671	589467	270024	319443	587832	1635
山 西	7506	84954	20617	64337	81505	3449
内蒙古	27742	93439	35830	57609	81642	11797
辽 宁	7238	316600	145258	171342	300107	16493
吉 林	25047	1164417	656005	508412	1161555	2862
黑龙江	13730	252207	117826	134381	249413	2794
上 海	13	895791	818302	77489	879608	16183
江 苏	77733	427397	147461	279936	418921	8476
浙 江	5299	138637	30524	108113	135671	2966
安 徽	49361	93296	40485	52811	87452	5844
福 建	3821	52265	16072	36193	50964	1301
江 西	30629	51405	16160	35245	48003	3402
山 东	2188	166208	43634	122574	165731	477
河 南	23663	106709	35683	71026	97335	9374
湖 北	23358	319555	136128	183427	310325	9230
湖 南	112575	303854	103941	199913	289929	13925
广 东	4357	266971	96267	170704	254610	12361
广 西	111153	258327	7164	251163	257390	937
海 南	24737	15799	3022	12777	14508	1291
重 庆	13514	154566	82748	71818	151391	3175
四 川	65403	239267	77488	161779	228376	10891
贵 州	18283	60566	12461	48105	53831	6735
云 南	44802	333701	49443	284258	329652	4049
西 藏		3290	454	2836	3258	32
陕 西	5400	177417	46651	130766	172867	4550
甘 肃	21881	70993	21511	49482	62611	8382
青 海	31	18014	6453	11561	17347	667
宁 夏	74	15156	4110	11046	14585	571
新 疆	4173	75564	53641	21923	67791	7773

其他农村救济

单位：人、户、万元、人次

临时救助按救助类型分类		民政部门资助参保人数	民政部门资助参合人数	民政部门直接医疗救助人次数		
支出型临时救助户次	应急型临时救助户次				住院救助	门诊救助
6205447	**775938**	**14900867**	**48687404**	**21263657**	**10739549**	**10524108**
162148	3023	46803	49843	143196	61466	81730
68779	1603	285401		213733	75394	138339
575357	14110	214401	1935194	550618	383848	166770
71549	13405	621343	1356756	274146	198805	75341
73479	19960	591546	1131517	297077	160908	136169
256402	60198	236518	589880	362514	159005	203509
1139115	25302	770616	834034	756665	277435	479230
225080	27127	1451521	1376458	689257	241177	448080
845469	50322	51301	13700	68736	47402	21334
367699	59698	319601	1219723	1764700	460659	1304041
119089	19548	52579	540198	1325051	345530	979521
73386	19910	356343	1984524	870089	745692	124397
40413	11852	52786	865358	546518	244973	301545
36171	15234	499133	1402937	587785	375668	212117
149428	16780	164309	1859876	287824	229515	58309
70061	36648	709483	3534105	1046075	794902	251173
287109	32446	1036339	2419075	926482	704164	222318
229818	74036	902513	2138891	1154505	645868	508637
230424	36547	408401	1673262	553086	197040	356046
250730	7597	250598	2439585	413584	295485	118099
14542	1257	108333	276681	151608	40988	110620
131674	22892	732678	1305887	2340153	640047	1700106
194604	44663	1493457	4734504	1657081	945146	711935
43249	17317	454224	4461035	785677	435729	349948
287942	45759	1041581	4549282	810783	577007	233776
2945	345	665	10541	35076	24614	10462
122276	55141	111191	907916	507567	287108	220459
53646	17347	839808	3303193	696725	484760	211965
14997	3017	207000	428195	528773	129903	398870
12382	2774	109033	336438	328163	161020	167143
55484	20080	781362	1008816	590410	368291	222119

C-2-36 救灾储

地区	单位数	年末职工人数		受教育程度		职业资
			#女性	大学专科人数	大学本科及以上人数	助理社会工作师人数
全　国	**784**	**2157**	**650**	**711**	**577**	**17**
中央级						
北　京	16	57	13	14	20	
天　津	2	27	10	7	17	3
河　北	13	64	17	15	13	
山　西	71	182	50	80	37	
内蒙古	17	45	6	24	7	
辽　宁	26	121	43	48	49	
吉　林	5	34	9	3	1	
黑龙江	8	30	7	9	11	
上　海						
江　苏	7	16	5	7	7	
浙　江	49	101	33	16	12	2
安　徽	13	35	12	12	6	1
福　建	30	58	25	6	21	
江　西	17	37	13	7	3	
山　东	5	24	7	9	12	
河　南	13	77	17	18	38	1
湖　北	47	131	49	55	37	
湖　南	13	35	11	16	10	
广　东	66	188	74	56	57	3
广　西	21	52	11	18	15	
海　南	2	7	1	3	4	
重　庆	37	61	19	14	25	1
四　川	88	250	85	110	64	2
贵　州	11	21	5	11	6	
云　南	41	130	42	54	49	4
西　藏	13	21	3	1	1	
陕　西	19	77	23	23	12	
甘　肃	37	97	28	27	10	
青　海	71	95	15	17	14	
宁　夏	9	33	8	12	2	
新　疆	17	51	9	19	17	

备机构

单位:个、人、人次、时

格水平	年龄结构				志愿服务	
社会工作师人数	35岁及以下人数	36岁至45岁人数	46岁至55岁人数	56岁及以上人数	志愿者服务人次数	志愿服务时间
22	**732**	**854**	**453**	**118**	**817**	**2163.0**
	15	25	13	4		
	18	5	2	2		
	18	20	20	6		
1	60	82	33	7		
	14	15	15	1		
1	42	43	26	10		
	14	14	6		1	
	11	12	7		6	40.0
2	8	2	5	1		
1	39	40	16	6	10	10.0
2	8	13	12	2		
2	21	24	11	2		
	12	10	14	1		
	1	13	8	2	146	411.0
	24	30	17	6		
1	40	70	16	5	135	405.0
	17	15	2	1	27	70.0
3	82	69	31	6		
	14	18	16	4		
	3	2	2			
	18	25	10	8	395	1061.0
2	87	102	56	5	1	3.0
	8	7	4	2	78	109.0
3	55	46	27	2	1	3.0
	14	7				
1	18	22	24	13	5	15.0
	21	41	23	12	10	30.0
	18	57	16	4		
	16	10	5	2		
3	16	15	16	4	2	6.0

C-2-36续表

地区	增加值合计	执行行政事业单位会计制度财务指标				
		固定资产原价	上年结转和结余	本年收入合计	本年支出合计	收支结余
全　国	**13253.9**	**114831.0**	**16474.9**	**75810.8**	**42699.0**	**125343.0**
中央级						
北　京	480.0	1710.4	1875.6	27950.8	5331.8	47090.0
天　津	425.2	2156.5	360.7	636.1	492.0	
河　北	201.0	535.6	7.7	334.6	327.6	748.0
山　西	552.5	1360.7	561.5	2347.0	2250.8	13375.0
内蒙古	345.4	2186.6	280.5	1242.0	1149.1	
辽　宁	751.2	3996.8	1009.2	2056.2	2022.8	3320.0
吉　林	177.0	1001.8		296.3	263.5	
黑龙江	268.7	590.4	59.4	693.9	425.9	5450.0
上　海						
江　苏	112.0	1067.2	4457.9	132.5	3113.7	750.0
浙　江	310.0	2952.3		866.8	837.6	500.0
安　徽	126.4	840.7	315.2	292.4	256.1	1000.0
福　建	256.4	873.3	39.7	667.0	438.3	1260.0
江　西	89.1	908.0		404.5	411.3	
山　东	270.4	2531.1	19.2	492.3	524.3	
河　南	590.7	2604.4	339.5	1356.0	1191.0	
湖　北	462.0	2866.0	20.1	1183.2	1083.7	12247.0
湖　南	67.5	419.6		402.0	412.0	19700.0
广　东	1579.8	7756.5	321.8	5609.7	5565.8	8588.0
广　西	417.0	3871.7	100.1	2145.4	2127.6	700.0
海　南	85.0	869.4	21.3	155.1	133.8	1436.0
重　庆	223.2	2526.6		1501.2	1506.2	2595.0
四　川	1966.0	19460.1	82.5	6009.1	3039.1	3310.0
贵　州	96.1	1957.5		31.2	22.5	
云　南	928.6	6376.3	2160.3	1122.4	3000.2	314.0
西　藏	311.3	7683.4	150.0	5.0	85.0	1210.0
陕　西	367.4	3106.6	6.0	1144.1	1011.1	920.0
甘　肃	402.8	8794.2	1.0	394.8	320.3	
青　海	889.1	17470.1		7553.7	2840.7	
宁　夏	215.8	2862.7	2303.6	2125.5	232.2	
新　疆	286.2	3494.5	1982.1	6660.0	2283.0	830.0

单位：万元、平方米、顶

行政事业单位增加值	库房建筑面积	仓储面积	#租用仓储面积	#空余仓储面积	仓储物资种类			
					单帐篷	#中央储备	棉帐篷	#中央储备
13253.9	**956220.3**	**819663.4**	**125343**	**62185**	**522508**	**159848**	**199354**	**96421**
480.0	60456.0	55320.0	47090	1880	35521	1126	12695	
425.2	10466.0	9420.0		60	5010	5010	3916	3916
201.0	28157.8	9687.0	748	935	1558		920	
552.5	25675.5	30601.0	13375	1414	14999		8977	
345.4	29792.2	26019.8		500	875		1684	
751.2	37439.0	34234.0	3320	1537	13626	5260	10013	9402
177.0								
268.7	11300.0	8130.0	5450	85	7252	6952	17802	17802
112.0	9797.0	8237.0	750		2121		2000	
310.0	13053.3	11010.0	500	1000	385		50	
126.4	11512.0	9980.0	1000	1200	28211	25500	1972	1000
256.4	24963.0	19863.0	1260	290	18463	4697	200	
89.1	9999.0	8011.0		420	2850		690	
270.4	8565.0	7800.0			6670		3460	
590.7	19517.0	16063.0		750	31420	13078	2037	1900
462.0	52521.0	38767.0	12247	3970	21198	16415	6408	5785
67.5	19810.0	33855.0	19700	1815	16061	14499	2600	1000
1579.8	55317.7	49651.0	8588	5332	14503		99	
417.0	17804.0	15074.0	700	1360	10965	6648	1219	82
85.0	4154.0	4156.0	1436	500	6019			
223.2	15431.0	13476.0	2595	650	12271			
1966.0	182020.4	137538.5	3310	26904	136113	23115	20592	3768
96.1	12173.0	9739.0		315	1260		400	
928.6	58880.4	43750.6	314	4018	32128	8902	2176	20
311.3	39647.0	35087.3	1210	1007	8330	3030	15668	562
367.4	53901.0	53910.0	920	460	65813	17950	18681	16522
402.8	34501.7	31802.1		4472	8339	150	9982	5606
889.1	74691.2	68236.0		411	560	200	32173	14140
215.8	14200.1	14065.1			11471		6900	
286.2	20475.0	16180.0	830	900	8516	7316	16040	14916

C-2-37 民政部门

地区	直接接收捐赠情况			间接接收
	捐赠款数额	捐赠衣被合计	捐赠其他物资价值	捐赠款数额
全 国	**1076179.2**	**10405.0**	**87089.8**	**50195.9**
中央级	13477.3			
北 京	89292.2	43.0	11456.9	
天 津	13413.9	0.4	701.8	413.7
河 北	3484.7	5.6	6.2	24.8
山 西	5391.3	27.5	19.3	967.8
内蒙古	2114.0	41.5	6755.1	720.0
辽 宁	75854.7	2.2	52.2	261.8
吉 林	28467.3	6886.8	694.0	
黑龙江	5116.9	0.3	900.0	79.0
上 海	17763.6	46.0	237.0	
江 苏	181040.1	27.8	28346.1	5854.2
浙 江	117014.6	32.8	820.9	1945.4
安 徽	4016.3		140.0	410.0
福 建	32747.0	0.1	6147.2	1631.2
江 西	8370.9	155.5	55.0	580.0
山 东	110899.0			
河 南	3841.6	762.8	10.5	48.8
湖 北	8745.4	2.3	1216.0	2182.4
湖 南	38311.1	1.7	1405.2	2008.5
广 东	175933.0	1717.8	1806.7	11726.1
广 西	3192.7	20.2	303.2	2025.7
海 南	88.4	0.2	0.2	13.0
重 庆	42448.3	0.8	3506.5	4406.1
四 川	56503.4	557.0	21703.4	14017.7
贵 州	9264.7	50.7	94.1	41.3
云 南	5392.8	10.8	2.8	298.0
西 藏	2418.3		7.0	189.7
陕 西	13291.1		543.3	144.4
甘 肃	1685.4	7.2	1.3	
青 海	556.3			60.0
宁 夏	3573.4		151.0	
新 疆	2469.5	4.0	6.9	146.3

接收的社会捐赠

单位：万元、万件、人次、个

捐赠情况					
捐赠衣被合计	捐赠其他物资价值	受益人次数	社会捐赠接收工作站、点数	社会捐赠接收工作站数	慈善超市数
739.1	**35081.4**	**12460163**	**30703**	**15149**	**9492**
		1314145	1822	20	222
4.8		48836	1331	208	72
0.2	5.2	27919	653	538	45
		62352	1197	533	159
		13735	465	11	157
1.0	11303.6	1086196	1673	979	300
		186408	527	416	117
2.1		26362	1412	978	429
		288274	851	641	207
0.1	23.2	1390378	3731	1081	2377
	9.2	1466217	1002	557	337
		131450	361	265	91
	19519.3	190948	805	317	465
0.4		404141	542	214	58
		1005231	1999	1058	727
19.0		180831	719	438	40
2.1		336077	708	503	281
102.3	428.4	415192	1472	678	717
500.6	1369.6	1687105	1085	769	108
	55.3	171012	1139	716	212
		2965	40	19	8
	232.3	760157	1776	978	540
5.0	2130.6	841919	2658	1309	1394
	0.7	240161	1097	724	179
		82240	173	163	7
	4.0		46	31	1
		16771	401	178	37
		42421	248	214	40
			30	23	
		9156	114	63	62
101.5		31564	626	527	103

C-2-38 福利彩票发

地　区	单位数				年末职工人数		受教育
		编办登记	民政登记	未登记		#女性	大学专科人数
全　国	**940**	**747**	**48**	**145**	**10636**	**4315**	**3606**
中央级	1	1			127	48	12
北　京	18	18			153	62	53
天　津	9	8	1		91	36	22
河　北	16	15		1	281	114	79
山　西	12	12			222	99	77
内蒙古	16	16			236	90	115
辽　宁	21	20		1	513	212	194
吉　林	53	45		8	571	115	82
黑龙江	22	19		3	170	68	50
上　海	17	6	10	1	181	72	39
江　苏	81	75	3	3	717	296	219
浙　江	73	48	3	22	607	319	190
安　徽	37	25	5	7	525	263	230
福　建	14	11		3	352	140	118
江　西	52	35	5	12	170	61	45
山　东	19	18		1	872	374	317
河　南	73	51	8	14	580	245	197
湖　北	54	43	1	10	536	249	236
湖　南	113	85	4	24	644	271	244
广　东	68	57	3	8	722	315	213
广　西	33	27		6	589	230	246
海　南	3	3			47	19	22
重　庆	1	1			139	34	46
四　川	12	12			128	54	71
贵　州	12	12			188	82	72
云　南	17	12	2	3	91	38	38
西　藏	1	1			34	16	12
陕　西	42	31	1	10	520	116	119
甘　肃	16	13	1	2	188	87	72
青　海	2	2			41	20	4
宁　夏	6	4	1	1	148	74	60
新　疆	26	21		5	253	96	112

行机构情况

单位:个、人、人次、时

程度	职业资格水平		年龄结构				志愿服务	
大学本科及以上人数	助理社会工作师人数	社会工作师人数	35岁及以下人数	36岁至45岁人数	46岁至55岁人数	56岁及以上人数	志愿者服务人次数	志愿服务时间
3231	**137**	**100**	**5346**	**3506**	**1450**	**334**	**2263**	**6395.7**
115			73	18	28	8		
80	3	4	64	47	30	12	28	105.0
52		1	52	18	20	1		
71	3		174	72	27	8		
76	1		111	70	31	10		
57		2	119	66	35	16		
193			307	121	70	15		
82	3	1	265	246	50	10	180	560.0
59	2	8	70	74	23	3		
49		1	80	50	39	12	40	96.0
253	28	17	305	277	113	22	865	2298.0
162		3	271	218	89	29	450	1100.0
165	5	5	324	133	56	12	315	759.0
85			107	165	68	12		
17	5	1	58	77	28	7	111	422.7
354	13	18	488	259	110	15		
157	19	1	290	217	69	4		
138	2	1	301	167	62	6	97	293.0
169	4	13	365	211	61	7	50	185.0
241	22	12	376	221	97	28		
121	9	4	319	191	70	9		
12	4		17	15	15			
77	1		75	49	13	2		
38	2		69	33	18	8		
86		3	116	49	18	5		
30	5		38	31	20	2		
5			14	15	2	3		
106	2	3	194	166	100	60	107	517.0
42	3	2	88	73	25	2	20	60.0
22			23	13	4	1		
49			94	41	13			
68	1		99	103	46	5		

C-2-38续表

地　区	增加值合计	执行	
		固定资产原价	上年结转和结余
全　国	**176245.0**	**685015.8**	**145877.5**
中央级	3711.9	32203.0	17013.0
北　京	3146.2	14348.3	308.1
天　津	2100.3	15865.1	155.1
河　北	2989.7	31980.7	383.4
山　西	1768.4	7851.6	386.4
内蒙古	4871.6	25834.7	5361.4
辽　宁	6639.7	26771.2	70.4
吉　林	3798.7	25197.5	1367.0
黑龙江	1693.2	11256.4	4006.1
上　海	2307.9	34711.0	77.8
江　苏	12280.3	63412.2	16009.5
浙　江	7053.1	39798.9	7075.9
安　徽	4922.5	20898.6	1793.4
福　建	3003.3	4140.2	20457.5
江　西	3406.6	12179.0	2311.3
山　东	16640.6	49009.0	3039.6
河　南	6985.0	32135.2	879.5
湖　北	3388.8	23859.4	4319.2
湖　南	4878.5	22774.2	-158.6
广　东	12669.3	40960.2	4639.9
广　西	6263.5	12777.1	-20.0
海　南	1456.1	377.0	558.8
重　庆	6990.0	11177.4	20385.9
四　川	3121.8	65933.3	29007.3
贵　州	2078.0	12091.3	4235.6
云　南	34562.1	8473.7	42.5
西　藏	318.5	391.8	
陕　西	2681.8	14591.8	343.4
甘　肃	2375.3	10505.9	99.8
青　海	684.4	1944.1	
宁　夏	1009.3	3524.6	967.8
新　疆	6448.1	8041.4	760.5

单位：万元

行政事业单位会计制度财务指标

本年收入合计	本年支出合计	收支结余	行政事业单位增加值
1554945.0	**1384842.4**	**86078.2**	**176245.0**
228000.0	190800.0		3711.9
71671.7	75063.9	-3612.4	3146.2
33952.3	32062.4	23.6	2100.3
56235.6	51652.3	141.2	2989.7
13762.0	11583.1	766.2	1768.4
36497.0	29756.0	12102.4	4871.6
113118.7	95830.3	2583.9	6639.7
29818.5	22364.2	-114.0	3798.7
4641.3	4216.6		1693.2
56842.4	58762.6	257.7	2307.9
68585.9	59739.4	20542.7	12280.3
46764.3	35209.6	1921.3	7053.1
41223.4	36761.0	1572.1	4922.5
14274.3	12077.0	1630.4	3003.3
15489.5	13720.6		3406.6
103635.1	103359.0		16640.6
73622.3	62333.8	1493.7	6985.0
27851.9	32395.9	221.9	3388.8
40692.2	37447.0	1657.1	4878.5
69997.0	61350.1	1389.4	12669.3
66095.6	53743.0	575.5	6263.5
18004.7	17584.0	400.7	1456.1
56990.6	51977.1	25399.4	6990.0
81936.5	74830.3	-14.1	3121.8
29559.9	21621.9	394.0	2078.0
52745.2	49062.9	220.9	34562.1
5351.2	5605.8		318.5
17013.0	13661.0	369.4	2681.8
11739.9	7179.3		2375.3
11682.8	9236.3		684.4
13147.0	11486.4	16136.3	1009.3
44003.2	42369.6	18.9	6448.1

C-2-39 优抚对象享受

地区	抚恤、补助优抚对象总人数	在院集中供养人数	定期抚恤人数合计	烈属	城市
全国	**9504555**	**103592**	**366400**	**240375**	**48149**
中央级					
北京	43427	203	1775	533	236
天津	45356	196	842	362	138
河北	583337	4664	22026	14168	1831
山西	184770	2314	10329	7472	445
内蒙古	61744	2116	2677	1590	706
辽宁	235358	2672	8235	3466	886
吉林	123623	1081	5364	3257	1788
黑龙江	141393	3861	7221	5040	2053
上海	39840	468	5831	4542	3976
江苏	491864	6740	15833	9958	1142
浙江	262450	1698	4872	2498	387
安徽	507997	3467	14057	8328	1910
福建	195952	890	12471	9873	758
江西	341015	11025	30163	27061	4199
山东	1008304	12947	44199	29015	4734
河南	765021	14815	21385	11493	1875
湖北	527820	6012	36726	27440	3816
湖南	893197	10824	27882	18346	4385
广东	434344	1633	9272	6530	2501
广西	297549	699	4926	3269	423
海南	28115	62	3172	2882	496
重庆	285730	983	5966	3213	792
四川	891799	8841	33389	19056	4278
贵州	261395	457	4759	2734	589
云南	378073	629	8276	4988	886
西藏	5238	22	2607	1658	492
陕西	293070	2192	15647	8692	1205
甘肃	116682	1144	3014	1065	274
青海	14489	97	1068	552	221
宁夏	10566	222	546	278	132
新疆	35037	618	1870	1016	595

定期抚恤、补助情况

单位：人

	因公牺牲军人遗属			病故军人遗属		
农　村		城　市	农　村		城　市	农　村
192226	**55734**	**14200**	**41534**	**70291**	**21287**	**49004**
297	145	65	80	1097	694	403
224	131	50	81	349	232	117
12337	3336	675	2661	4522	1054	3468
7027	1029	224	805	1828	393	1435
884	512	222	290	575	270	305
2580	1822	614	1208	2947	923	2024
1469	755	428	327	1352	823	529
2987	960	516	444	1221	631	590
566	157	130	27	1132	941	191
8816	2136	528	1608	3739	940	2799
2111	876	219	657	1498	440	1058
6418	2582	652	1930	3147	955	2192
9115	1416	206	1210	1182	327	855
22862	1394	421	973	1708	559	1149
24281	7652	1716	5936	7532	1998	5534
9618	4806	1050	3756	5086	1342	3744
23624	5259	938	4321	4027	1125	2902
13961	4058	1384	2674	5478	1829	3649
4029	924	480	444	1818	847	971
2846	597	121	476	1060	247	813
2386	125	47	78	165	62	103
2421	1121	320	801	1632	496	1136
14778	7050	1507	5543	7283	1848	5435
2145	772	191	581	1253	294	959
4102	1131	243	888	2157	547	1610
1166	434	85	349	515	78	437
7487	2925	575	2350	4030	752	3278
791	788	183	605	1161	281	880
331	201	70	131	315	66	249
146	149	49	100	119	55	64
421	491	291	200	363	238	125

C-2-39续表

地　区	定期补助人数合计	在乡退伍红军老战士	在乡西路红军老战士	红军失散人员	在乡复员军人
全　国	**8326336**	**647**	**117**	**18976**	**1260945**
中央级					
北　京	30477	1			4214
天　津	37571				2683
河　北	506593	2			63166
山　西	147934	9		1	31065
内蒙古	44988	4		2	18426
辽　宁	196322			1	32102
吉　林	99592			1	22391
黑龙江	112335	13	1	17	47008
上　海	26856				2598
江　苏	426022			1	57358
浙　江	235293			75	23048
安　徽	458082	3		2712	56614
福　建	171310	1		424	23114
江　西	285312	22		8974	37892
山　东	846172	3		26	138484
河　南	678486	13		592	78029
湖　北	454688	2	1	1274	62123
湖　南	814476	3		1913	134826
广　东	400916			89	27243
广　西	281862	15		403	36032
海　南	22793			29	5924
重　庆	258634				33657
四　川	797407	11	71	874	142355
贵　州	240637	1		26	49395
云　南	350712			3	43350
西　藏	1162				247
陕　西	253320	527		1522	57588
甘　肃	102985	11	35	15	15358
青　海	10176				2552
宁　夏	7409	1	2	1	2345
新　疆	25814	5	7	1	9758

单位：人

抗　日	带病回乡退伍军人	60岁以上农村籍退伍军人	参战退役人员	参试退役人员	部分60周岁以上烈士子女(含错杀被平反人员子女)	其　他
54872	**1306479**	**3566766**	**1523763**	**199215**	**222838**	**226590**
348	1536	18652	3099	754	1998	223
152	11356	13598	7730	256	1194	754
10140	49316	290814	52588	20714	28312	1681
3335	27021	59789	9207	6655	9542	4645
374	10543	12799	1955	106	763	390
401	15291	108174	7007	3277	1972	28498
495	11675	58215	3710	1325	1819	456
1231	12429	45726	4883	219	1506	533
30	561	20809	2447	439		2
6244	52569	225352	32318	5266	14565	38593
165	23536	152152	24927	2887	1163	7505
2136	150867	180179	43016	10959	5562	8170
48	12668	91875	33348	478	7733	1669
139	51984	84952	46658	1820	48699	4311
14936	99972	467225	80572	17339	42551	
4403	95005	362326	100709	25262	13577	2973
3904	117639	172907	75299	10028	14487	928
832	164707	312183	181023	7060	8905	3856
498	30910	148266	153505	9511	2901	28491
110	3954	80992	87986	3306	3236	65938
790	764	7261	7945	238	137	495
59	71397	77870	67391	6341	1103	875
435	197742	274390	140586	21766	7727	11885
265	20379	79064	89926	359	202	1285
115	27184	90836	184194	111	1156	3878
	238	33	110			534
1661	30943	68689	58453	30237	1431	3930
436	5750	53987	18772	5921	518	2618
2	1317	2854	1257	2067	45	84
33	1042	1929	1139	289	32	629
1155	6184	2868	2003	4225	2	761

C-2-40 伤残人员

地区	伤残人员合计	按伤残				
		一级				二级
			因战	因公	因病	
全国	**811819**	**3507**	**885**	**2362**	**260**	**2014**
中央级						
北京	11175	48	1	44	3	37
天津	6943	31		29	2	12
河北	54718	233	27	188	18	81
山西	26507	75	29	45	1	47
内蒙古	14079	71	25	41	5	15
辽宁	30801	101	32	67	2	75
吉林	18667	134	24	102	8	70
黑龙江	21837	74	15	45	14	29
上海	7153	31	3	25	3	16
江苏	50009	190	51	127	12	133
浙江	22285	77	13	59	5	94
安徽	35858	142	33	103	6	33
福建	12171	48	6	41	1	23
江西	25540	178	40	60	78	192
山东	117933	320	94	219	7	281
河南	65150	298	64	207	27	288
湖北	36406	185	50	121	14	55
湖南	50839	304	128	165	11	114
广东	24156	97	20	70	7	42
广西	10761	39	17	21	1	22
海南	2150	7		6	1	3
重庆	21130	135	46	76	13	36
四川	61003	196	55	135	6	119
贵州	15999	110	41	69		30
云南	19085	119	27	84	8	65
西藏	1469	19		19		9
陕西	24103	92	21	69	2	36
甘肃	10683	64	8	54	2	18
青海	3245	26	10	15	1	4
宁夏	2611	25		25		9
新疆	7353	38	5	31	2	26

享受抚恤情况

单位：人

等级分类

因战	因公	因病	三级	因战	因公	因病
268	**1249**	**497**	**19480**	**5880**	**11026**	**2574**
3	26	8	203	42	127	34
	9	3	120	29	73	18
6	53	22	987	333	504	150
10	29	8	547	235	235	77
2	7	6	199	52	125	22
16	49	10	689	221	414	54
22	34	14	665	220	341	104
2	19	8	443	124	200	119
1	15		163	39	100	24
29	87	17	1484	632	724	128
1	52	41	451	48	253	150
12	12	9	853	305	476	72
4	14	5	172	18	129	25
9	19	164	665	136	251	278
15	235	31	3923	1305	2353	265
28	223	37	1281	414	609	258
14	28	13	848	208	507	133
25	80	9	1289	386	755	148
4	17	21	452	118	270	64
7	11	4	216	77	112	27
1	2		65	25	34	6
4	22	10	457	113	286	58
14	90	15	1229	291	809	129
13	15	2	293	101	172	20
9	23	33	795	167	491	137
	9		65	1	64	
13	21	2	458	141	285	32
2	14	2	220	52	139	29
	4		64	20	41	3
	7	2	50	13	33	4
2	23	1	134	14	114	6

C-2-40续表1

地区	按伤残					
	四级	因战	因公	因病	五级	因战
全国	**10685**	**1286**	**5704**	**3695**	**61572**	**22361**
中央级						
北京	122	27	65	30	485	114
天津	70	10	48	12	503	80
河北	502	62	221	219	4132	1678
山西	234	50	84	100	1901	930
内蒙古	100	14	50	36	845	254
辽宁	237	81	100	56	2067	801
吉林	572	144	259	169	2352	710
黑龙江	278	10	54	214	1733	960
上海	79	12	40	27	403	111
江苏	876	123	526	227	3760	1389
浙江	373	23	118	232	1265	238
安徽	230	43	146	41	2431	911
福建	122	11	57	54	1216	148
江西	733	28	119	586	2138	617
山东	1982	121	1683	178	10265	5348
河南	1687	156	644	887	5360	1536
湖北	369	34	236	99	2806	812
湖南	390	67	241	82	4172	1385
广东	250	61	118	71	1502	418
广西	56	14	34	8	742	297
海南	19	4	11	4	147	53
重庆	270	45	164	61	1291	444
四川	561	76	377	108	4328	1326
贵州	83	9	64	10	911	389
云南	183	25	59	99	1158	508
西藏	23		22	1	91	1
陕西	97	12	35	50	1862	560
甘肃	70	6	39	25	704	159
青海	8	1	6	1	247	50
宁夏	27	6	21		142	30
新疆	82	11	63	8	613	104

单位：人

等级分类					
因公	因病	六级	因战	因公	因病
27488	**11723**	**186214**	**55660**	**93947**	**36607**
312	59	1898	401	1250	247
210	213	1469	275	888	306
1397	1057	13209	4548	5447	3214
665	306	5683	2438	2365	880
510	81	3717	738	2557	422
1050	216	6764	2397	3667	700
1456	186	5743	1560	3692	491
619	154	4422	2279	1575	568
230	62	1211	294	676	241
1394	977	12910	3983	6344	2583
516	511	4387	615	2011	1761
1131	389	8623	2515	4189	1919
425	643	3572	402	1406	1764
903	618	5127	1751	2260	1116
4156	761	30876	11441	15469	3966
2076	1748	15882	4495	7724	3663
1496	498	8277	2036	4251	1990
2114	673	11309	3134	5945	2230
625	459	4714	1200	2472	1042
373	72	2015	682	947	386
78	16	438	190	173	75
659	188	3977	1018	2167	792
2096	906	13172	3005	7178	2989
429	93	2787	870	1447	470
493	157	3289	1069	1619	601
90		215		215	
796	506	5559	1415	2656	1488
447	98	2095	377	1269	449
189	8	570	154	373	43
86	26	651	110	473	68
467	42	1653	268	1242	143

C-2-40续表2

地区	按伤残							
	七级	因战	因公	八级	因战	因公	九级	因战
全国	**248692**	**76394**	**172298**	**240949**	**81535**	**159414**	**24393**	**1215**
中央级								
北京	3637	788	2849	3906	812	3094	634	14
天津	2069	375	1694	2281	446	1835	278	4
河北	17267	6804	10463	16394	6151	10243	1339	43
山西	8841	3833	5008	7743	3249	4494	551	13
内蒙古	4523	1119	3404	4039	1293	2746	421	17
辽宁	9514	3349	6165	10051	4006	6045	899	76
吉林	4072	916	3156	3326	842	2484	955	22
黑龙江	7267	4274	2993	7336	4736	2600	206	17
上海	2098	474	1624	2677	632	2045	296	11
江苏	14003	4410	9593	14454	4830	9624	1416	104
浙江	5784	874	4910	8599	1167	7432	780	16
安徽	10868	2967	7901	10760	3338	7422	1292	50
福建	2975	578	2397	3398	759	2639	511	11
江西	6556	2018	4538	8233	3229	5004	323	18
山东	37507	14596	22911	28859	12587	16272	2752	75
河南	19269	5403	13866	16621	4946	11675	2321	84
湖北	11615	2785	8830	10823	2751	8072	1036	63
湖南	14971	4124	10847	15813	5186	10627	1759	208
广东	6893	1774	5119	8746	2754	5992	1098	65
广西	3335	1113	2222	3679	1446	2233	484	27
海南	654	257	397	664	268	396	133	8
重庆	7387	1756	5631	6547	2039	4508	711	69
四川	19844	4635	15209	18714	5339	13375	1730	80
贵州	5382	1584	3798	5699	2152	3547	462	14
云南	6025	2022	4003	6714	2708	4006	500	33
西藏	409		409	391		391	140	8
陕西	7906	2073	5833	7528	2231	5297	399	30
甘肃	3697	563	3134	3415	657	2758	275	7
青海	1320	296	1024	870	280	590	96	3
宁夏	755	148	607	786	147	639	120	6
新疆	2249	486	1763	1883	554	1329	476	19

单位：人

等级分类				按人员种类分类				优抚对象享受医疗保障人数
	十级			残疾军人	伤残国家机关工作人员	伤残人民警察	伤残民兵民工	
因公		因战	因公					
23178	**14313**	**1676**	**12637**	**755817**	**32651**	**17646**	**5705**	**4541027**
620	205	6	199	10139	426	568	42	16472
274	110	4	106	6390	128	394	31	28724
1296	574	16	558	52384	1454	637	243	229924
538	885	39	846	25144	1042	196	125	93593
404	149	3	146	10932	2169	810	168	41446
823	404	7	397	27219	1440	1754	388	70675
933	778	14	764	14152	2377	1995	143	40380
189	49	5	44	20944	441	355	97	80508
285	179	15	164	6682	122	333	16	11380
1312	783	59	724	48343	905	619	142	227678
764	475	12	463	20941	764	151	429	76158
1242	626	22	604	32845	2136	638	239	229781
500	134	3	131	11606	306	192	67	80081
305	1395	970	425	23405	1367	501	267	87500
2677	1168	21	1147	114658	1790	940	545	575599
2237	2143	143	2000	61930	2002	976	242	363676
973	392	17	375	34561	1094	620	131	348940
1551	718	74	644	46463	2884	1409	83	488889
1033	362	55	307	23598	230	283	45	200636
457	173	21	152	9668	327	162	604	110879
125	20	3	17	2051	57	25	17	15562
642	319	50	269	20048	608	389	85	242058
1650	1110	48	1062	56926	2425	1222	430	379635
448	242	11	231	14653	868	408	70	156248
467	237	27	210	17058	865	577	585	178549
132	107		107	627	651	110	81	1794
369	166	10	156	22675	1092	217	119	99460
268	125	8	117	9982	408	203	90	40255
93	40	1	39	2536	507	144	58	4366
114	46	1	45	2133	280	149	49	7454
457	199	11	188	5124	1486	669	74	12727

C-2-41 优待、烈士褒扬和

地区	优待		
	优待优抚对象户数	优待军属户数	优待总金额
全国	**3402629**	**958255**	**1351367.8**
中央级			
北京	30301	6668	29300.2
天津	9072	4994	9982.8
河北	170932	54574	63217.0
山西	63321	23576	41497.1
内蒙古	29679	14537	22982.4
辽宁	96904	24762	37704.4
吉林	26276	13645	8779.7
黑龙江	53646	10677	10082.8
上海	22533	8130	28690.6
江苏	275441	50127	125635.1
浙江	124408	40806	79708.8
安徽	136489	46058	60631.1
福建	122647	18688	34507.5
江西	85309	34129	26580.6
山东	612496	96523	180298.7
河南	274696	94403	95328.6
湖北	206419	59733	74449.6
湖南	233789	62801	44173.5
广东	89631	42939	45810.5
广西	145325	35634	25331.9
海南	12728	5568	4463.9
重庆	161123	25003	37658.8
四川	193270	77502	65746.2
贵州	53050	27667	20548.2
云南	63211	23037	13128.1
西藏	2165	650	397.9
陕西	45551	26462	145369.2
甘肃	23786	13917	5996.2
青海	1191	971	772.0
宁夏	5522	2550	1715.1
新疆	31718	11524	10879.3

义务兵、士官安置

单位：户、万元、人、处

固定优待军属总额	烈士褒扬		复员干部
	本年批准烈士人数	零散烈士纪念建筑物数	
646022.7	**200**	**13601**	**637**
16498.6	2	188	43
6259.9	3	5	7
41900.4	5	1522	16
23764.8	2	1427	12
8164.4	2	170	6
15714.7	4	291	46
4843.2	4	527	24
3373.8	1	102	7
16307.0	2	5	11
45325.9	8	892	40
46926.1	2	359	10
27822.4	2	451	17
13718.4	8	229	9
10892.2	1	531	31
108617.8	20	548	31
67818.3	11	500	4
36116.6	11	662	28
22814.4	5	300	19
22990.7	5	832	26
9839.8	2	904	24
1515.3	1	214	20
16429.8	3	426	20
26682.4	22	259	26
15762.5	5	1371	6
5077.6	17	181	31
171.7	2	3	2
21798.7	7	168	26
3371.5	2	362	58
614.1	1	37	1
739.3		6	5
4150.4	40	129	31

C-2-42 离退休、

地　区	本年接收人员合计	军队离退休干部	离　休	地方离退休干部	离　休	军队退休士官	军队无军籍职工
全　国	**38706**	**10927**	**108**	**500**	**29**	**570**	**26709**
中央级							
北　京	8474	3643	9	5		14	4812
天　津	234	234					
河　北	1986	788	12	31	1	76	1091
山　西	959	121	4			41	797
内蒙古	330	150		26		5	149
辽　宁	4094	879	22	23	4	29	3163
吉　林	1045	166				8	871
黑龙江	599	93	1	14	1	4	488
上　海	1690	407	1	2		4	1277
江　苏	1267	444	2	8	7	18	797
浙　江	835	215	3	25	3	5	590
安　徽	409	103		12	4	16	278
福　建	616	173	19	40		5	398
江　西	406	78	3	1		3	324
山　东	2237	720				62	1455
河　南	1498	286				51	1161
湖　北	2075	243	1	7		37	1788
湖　南	1063	91		13	1	25	934
广　东	767	133	3	26		14	594
广　西	342	90	2	105		8	139
海　南	639	52				5	582
重　庆	517	194	1	14		11	298
四　川	1414	368	5	72	1	35	939
贵　州	96	61		31	1	1	3
云　南	185	170	3			9	6
西　藏	34	30					4
陕　西	2291	513	5	17	5	31	1730
甘　肃	1188	152	6	15	1	6	1015
青　海	370	71				7	292
宁　夏	83	44				28	11
新　疆	963	215	6	13		12	723

退职人员

单位：人

本年实有人数合计	军队离退休干部	离休	地方离退休干部	离休	军队退休士官	军队无军籍职工	军队离退休干部服务站
349617	**210868**	**23704**	**32858**	**1449**	**7273**	**98618**	**147**
68327	41574	1990	7030	10	577	19146	
7864	5061	547	1097	23	77	1629	
20216	11935	1782	1895	101	1020	5366	12
5671	2728	564	345	27	246	2352	7
3911	2584	299	311	20	69	947	5
32252	22405	2215	1555	197	517	7775	22
7207	4622	540	533	45	248	1804	5
5212	3334	395	36	3	72	1770	6
10369	6740	584	169	6	7	3453	
20001	12183	1449	2840	230	226	4752	13
7481	4146	726	1592	26	55	1688	5
5171	3077	663	616	121	177	1301	8
7982	3621	519	3551	15	66	744	8
4476	995	378	1524	71	580	1377	1
24457	17726	3434	856	38	1133	4742	9
11639	7081	1109	1325	150	476	2757	8
13192	7511	1055	1959	114	199	3523	
11533	5241	678	2237	94	181	3874	6
13134	8410	762	506	20	62	4156	2
3238	1953	172	137		18	1130	2
1995	722	50	3		9	1261	
5590	3626	182	142	3	130	1692	8
14880	8981	795	1136	24	436	4327	8
2306	1323	204	321	16	12	650	1
10562	6253	999	262	10	77	3970	2
1080	177	2	2			901	
14893	9633	1042	400	55	205	4655	6
6170	2739	321	314	24	227	2890	2
1987	658	7	14	2	38	1277	
908	575	62	46		53	234	
5913	3254	179	104	4	80	2475	1

C-2-43 军队离退休

地区	单位数	年末职工人数		受教育程度		职业资
			#女性	大学专科人数	大学本科及以上人数	助理社会工作师人数
全国	**145**	**1904**	**866**	**594**	**944**	**32**
中央级						
北京	27	340	168	105	202	9
天津	1	41	26	10	31	1
河北	22	293	146	102	77	4
山西	1	7	3			
内蒙古	1	12	6	2	8	
辽宁	7	352	120	61	231	1
吉林						
黑龙江						
上海	7	99	49	48	35	2
江苏	1	2	1	1	1	
浙江	7	58	26	8	41	
安徽	7	25	7	10	11	1
福建	3	8	4	1		
江西						
山东	2	44	23	12	27	
河南	4	73	30	39	25	
湖北	4	33	10	10	19	
湖南	6	25	17	9	11	
广东	4	78	34	19	54	9
广西	3	16	6	5	11	2
海南	1	5	2	2		
重庆	4	35	13	20	14	1
四川	12	138	71	57	35	
贵州	2	3	2	2	1	
云南	8	90	46	27	43	
西藏	2	5	3	3	2	
陕西	4	50	23	11	33	
甘肃	1	2	1		2	
青海						
宁夏	1	1	1	1		
新疆	3	69	28	29	30	2

人员管理中心

单位：个、人、人次、时

格水平	年龄结构				志愿服务	
社会工作师人数	35岁及以下人数	36岁至45岁人数	46岁至55岁人数	56岁及以上人数	志愿者服务人次数	志愿服务时间
48	**724**	**580**	**479**	**121**	**972**	**3878.0**
16	97	121	113	9		
1	25	10	4	2		
2	154	89	44	6	960	3854.0
	4	2	1			
	4	1	7			
2	116	90	98	48		
	38	21	28	12		
		1	1			
2	22	16	13	7		
1	7	10	6	2	12	24.0
	1	3	3	1		
3	15	14	12	3		
4	14	39	14	6		
	6	11	12	4		
1	10	14	1			
15	36	31	10	1		
	6	4	5	1		
	1	2	2			
	14	6	14	1		
	38	39	49	12		
	1	2				
	37	32	19	2		
	1	4				
1	42	3	5			
	1	1				
		1				
	34	13	18	4		

C-2-43续表

地　区	增加值合计	执行行政事业单位会计制度财务指标		
		固定资产原价	上年结余	收入合计
全　国	**241079.0**	**128826.0**	**245440.9**	**333699.9**
中央级				
北　京	89917.0	68996.3	210713.2	110426.6
天　津	398.0	500.0		426.0
河　北	14264.3	3763.5	3626.0	26773.1
山　西	1.2	30.0		74.5
内蒙古	5763.3	115.5	306.1	6815.5
辽　宁	20734.8	15945.3		19639.4
吉　林				
黑龙江				
上　海	14767.1	4231.6	652.4	28040.8
江　苏	31.8	500.0		30.0
浙　江	10845.7	1740.9		14301.3
安　徽	2406.5	409.7	23.3	2655.8
福　建	13.7	30.0		245.4
江　西				
山　东	449.7	433.5		822.9
河　南	1424.3	2413.7	2361.2	5512.5
湖　北	4244.3	10513.5		5105.8
湖　南	533.2	540.0		786.0
广　东	13154.1	5345.5	279.8	13855.7
广　西	1135.6	519.3		2181.8
海　南	0.1	3.1		
重　庆	882.2	524.5		1720.2
四　川	16340.5	3372.1	4740.2	38789.3
贵　州	15.3	1.8	5.0	17.2
云　南	1204.4	1994.0	1344.0	1624.8
西　藏	19.6	43.9		20.0
陕　西	17720.7	347.9	13819.0	26891.9
甘　肃	4.5			
青　海				
宁　夏	9.0	5.0		8.8
新　疆	24798.0	6505.4	7570.7	26934.6

单位：人、万元

支出合计	收支结余	行政事业单位增加值	年末机构管理军休干部人数	分散安置人数	本年发放离退休金
456854.1	**101177.9**	**241079.0**	**18642**	**9860**	**183104**
229094.0	94876.4	89917.0	54		26878
426.0		398.0	404	404	3966
27870.1	1473.4	14264.3	2256	1163	11650
38.0		1.2			
5922.8	1198.8	5763.3	581	497	5013
24340.4		20734.8	2990	1199	17995
27414.0	853.1	14767.1	1839	997	14909
26.0		31.8			
14265.4		10845.7	1105	68	10093
2519.8	55.8	2406.5	79	36	584
245.7		13.7	54	46	294
822.9		449.7			
5824.9	2048.8	1424.3	224	163	2350
5150.2		4244.3	4		
823.4		533.2	81	72	328
13849.5	36.0	13154.1	896	853	10497
2336.4		1135.6	78	78	715
		0.1			
1720.2		882.2	75	41	471
38185.0	24.5	16340.5	4126	703	39116
16.2		15.3			
2061.7		1204.4	87	35	706
20.0		19.6	152		172
27540.1		17720.7	1741	1704	16180
10.0		4.5			
8.8		9.0	8	7	
26322.6	611.1	24798.0	1808	1794	21187

C-2-44 军队离退休

地 区	单位数	年末职工人数	#女性	受教育程度		职业资
				大学专科人数	大学本科及以上人数	助理社会工作师人数
全 国	**28**	**647**	**282**	**182**	**154**	**5**
中央级						
北 京	12	508	215	126	111	3
天 津	1	11	3			
河 北	1	3	2	1	1	
山 西						
内蒙古						
辽 宁	1	4		1	2	
吉 林						
黑龙江						
上 海	2	50	24	21	19	2
江 苏	3	15	7	4	8	
浙 江						
安 徽						
福 建						
江 西	1	23	14	10	3	
山 东						
河 南						
湖 北	1	5	3	2	3	
湖 南						
广 东						
广 西						
海 南	1	12	5	9	2	
重 庆						
四 川	5	16	9	8	5	
贵 州						
云 南						
西 藏						
陕 西						
甘 肃						
青 海						
宁 夏						
新 疆						

人员活动中心

单位:个、人、人次、时

格水平	年龄结构				志愿服务	
社会工作师人数	35岁及以下人数	36岁至45岁人数	46岁至55岁人数	56岁及以上人数	志愿者服务人次数	志愿服务时间
6	**275**	**179**	**144**	**49**	**34**	**170.0**
3	240	135	101	32		
	4	1	4	2		
	1	2				
	1	2	1			
1	16	18	14	2	34	170.0
1	2	4	8	1		
	1	4	10	8		
	1	3	1			
	7	1	2	2		
1	2	9	3	2		

C-2-44续表

地区	增加值合计	执行	
		固定资产原价	上年结转和结余
全国	**9219.1**	**67381.6**	**3651.5**
中央级			
北京	3621.6	29662.9	2460.5
天津	920.1	18853.0	
河北	238.0	654.0	
山西			
内蒙古			
辽宁	477.9	6767.4	
吉林			
黑龙江			
上海	724.2	5408.2	173.0
江苏	392.8	2162.9	0.3
浙江			
安徽			
福建			
江西	167.5	260.3	-69.5
山东			
河南			
湖北	244.1	3180.8	
湖南			
广东			
广西			
海南	2346.3	213.7	1087.2
重庆			
四川	86.5	218.4	
贵州			
云南			
西藏			
陕西			
甘肃			
青海			
宁夏			
新疆			

单位：万元

行政事业单位会计制度财务指标			
本年收入合计	本年支出合计	收支结余	行政事业单位增加值
16234.4	**15303.9**	**2292.5**	**9219.1**
4251.3	4764.9	1897.4	3621.6
1935.0	1871.0		920.1
351.0	351.0		238.0
1058.7	1058.7		477.9
4138.6	3010.7	175.7	724.2
435.4	416.9	11.5	392.8
309.3	286.5	-43.7	167.5
772.0	814.0		244.1
2889.5	2637.8	251.6	2346.3
93.6	92.4		86.5

C-2-45 烈士纪念

地区	单位数	年末职工人数	#女性	受教育程度		职业资
				大学专科人数	大学本科及以上人数	助理社会工作师人数
全国	**1463**	**10221**	**4077**	**3092**	**1851**	**103**
中央级						
北京	5	49	25	11	14	2
天津	9	146	59	38	51	1
河北	98	898	349	190	201	8
山西	59	404	165	113	37	3
内蒙古	12	115	36	51	25	3
辽宁	49	339	138	108	111	1
吉林	30	383	95	113	58	8
黑龙江	27	194	74	93	52	1
上海	11	247	92	103	55	
江苏	89	711	278	182	184	15
浙江	40	186	80	35	75	2
安徽	51	405	170	126	52	7
福建	54	177	64	37	22	2
江西	68	308	136	67	35	
山东	111	926	354	356	291	10
河南	99	1380	655	457	147	12
湖北	55	695	293	248	80	1
湖南	39	385	160	87	32	3
广东	86	330	140	70	61	5
广西	21	243	102	78	42	9
海南	9	34	7	4	4	
重庆	22	76	24	36	26	
四川	153	423	167	153	44	6
贵州	56	140	38	44	23	
云南	64	164	27	53	15	
西藏	4	13	5	4	4	
陕西	39	358	191	117	38	
甘肃	79	369	109	83	43	3
青海	1	9	3	7	2	
宁夏	9	29	10	7	4	
新疆	14	85	31	21	23	1

建筑物管理机构

单位:个、人、人次、时

格水平	年龄结构				志愿服务	
社会工作师人数	35岁及以下人数	36岁至45岁人数	46岁至55岁人数	56岁及以上人数	志愿者服务人次数	志愿服务时间
150	**3127**	**4044**	**2480**	**570**	**29571**	**78021.0**
2	22	16	9	2	126	378.0
	39	48	47	12	1080	2240.0
14	281	334	237	46	762	3284.0
6	108	158	113	25	1	
3	28	43	34	10		
3	104	111	94	30	35	132.0
4	127	169	81	6	150	487.0
	44	77	64	9		
2	41	59	100	47		
28	157	291	211	52	1650	4464.0
5	55	65	53	13	802	2481.0
10	92	183	118	12	1114	2171.0
1	25	73	60	19		
	78	133	88	9	132	528.0
19	342	352	188	44	13143	32135.0
33	593	515	238	34	6	18.0
2	196	285	143	71	304	796.0
	124	171	83	7	408	520.0
2	76	136	102	16	60	210.0
2	78	98	52	15		
	12	14	6	2		
	24	40	10	2	70	203.0
5	102	200	87	34	8015	24025.0
1	29	56	44	11	1363	2869.0
	38	76	44	6	200	600.0
	8	5				
2	147	157	46	8	120	390.0
5	122	132	93	22	30	90.0
	1	1	6	1		
	7	16	4	2		
1	27	30	25	3		

C-2-45续表

地区	增加值合计	执行行政事业单位会计制度财务指标				
		固定资产原价	上年结转和结余	本年收入合计	本年支出合计	收支结余
全　国	**80212.9**	**491017.7**	**59163.0**	**144568.8**	**141956.6**	**7317.4**
中央级						
北　京	562.8	5328.0	3.7	428.2	437.0	1.2
天　津	2095.8	11293.7	1.4	1563.0	2505.8	18.4
河　北	6279.5	27432.5	1728.7	17023.9	17166.3	542.7
山　西	2252.0	10317.7	986.6	5199.5	5065.7	1101.1
内蒙古	1448.0	8045.8	161.7	2117.2	2206.6	422.3
辽　宁	2001.5	7244.6	579.0	4980.6	3619.1	199.7
吉　林	995.2	6235.6	1901.6	2701.1	3492.4	867.2
黑龙江	987.7	5803.7	627.0	1228.0	1314.1	
上　海	5854.6	64482.1	1102.7	6885.6	6954.8	102.9
江　苏	8516.7	36144.2	195.8	12868.9	12589.0	252.3
浙　江	2413.3	11102.4	919.2	4012.4	4066.0	240.9
安　徽	3604.4	24383.0	23.7	4858.6	4401.4	91.0
福　建	1066.9	3965.9	206.8	2206.3	1940.0	196.7
江　西	1309.9	9259.2	232.6	2407.0	2237.4	
山　东	9008.8	56163.0		28699.7	28699.7	
河　南	5060.1	40039.5	758.9	9365.4	9274.6	184.8
湖　北	2977.4	19958.2	-462.0	5599.0	5421.4	-314.2
湖　南	2961.8	18223.3	66.3	3984.8	3830.6	0.5
广　东	4152.9	20280.8	417.6	7984.5	6835.9	1536.3
广　西	4686.1	13165.4	0.4	5182.4	4019.9	211.8
海　南	206.9	2421.0	45521.9	217.0	224.1	5.6
重　庆	467.0	3755.3	35.3	882.4	917.0	
四　川	3055.8	44027.7	2197.5	2844.7	3255.6	
贵　州	809.0	8890.7	2.3	555.8	548.9	
云　南	598.3	8795.9	148.0	344.1	394.4	6.5
西　藏	46.2	1111.4			2.0	
陕　西	2196.7	14393.8	145.1	2984.7	3001.0	57.4
甘　肃	3783.2	4597.1	6.8	4391.8	4364.5	
青　海	17.5	437.0		273.0	273.0	
宁　夏	104.2	1041.0		88.9	115.3	16.8
新　疆	692.5	2678.2	1654.4	2690.3	2783.1	1575.5

单位：万元、平方米、个、人次

行政事业单位增加值	管理单位占地面积	烈士纪念建筑物面积	烈士纪念建筑物数	纪念馆(陈列馆)个数	藏品数	参观人次数	本机构管理的其他烈士纪念园地数
80212.9	**45848852.4**	**5152041.2**	**13602**	**1282**	**227764**	**70627378**	**977**
562.8	63559.0	22895.0	39	6	1022	233800	6
2095.8	339913.3	43191.3	35	14	1563	357000	
6279.5	3132969.4	240304.9	1232	95	39017	4183234	81
2252.0	1517862.0	317264.8	152	54	3905	1563682	4
1448.0	602523.0	38690.0	31	15	311	288390	
2001.5	1042700.4	261805.0	200	28	14565	1866667	
995.2	3369351.0	132368.0	72	24	5437	755423	2
987.7	426888.7	98644.7	391	16	8675	2662072	
5854.6	357466.0	42189.7	62	16	3145	1777641	2
8516.7	3000274.7	521749.0	1053	108	19725	7228783	3
2413.3	631145.7	65463.4	139	38	6982	1798886	
3604.4	4863769.8	275537.0	687	198	7564	3985821	5
1066.9	769709.6	59311.3	174	23	1578	3293099	18
1309.9	667024.8	180221.0	231	19	7928	918926	388
9008.8	5492198.2	502822.1	667	156	29442	13866500	3
5060.1	2527706.9	232586.2	896	99	10441	3458286	85
2977.4	2006234.7	168646.5	481	69	18103	2980270	19
2961.8	1080985.0	170192.0	96	19	3674	1425853	1
4152.9	1611558.4	235811.7	2198	20	1861	3204041	288
4686.1	2025606.2	124379.1	59	9	1204	922841	2
206.9	691997.0	170808.0	2499	25	1021	1182081	29
467.0	235790.0	87165.8	142	19	3046	2328205	19
3055.8	5291640.8	578376.8	866	93	9433	3272107	9
809.0	755061.0	81195.0	283	12	250	1135692	1
598.3	993622.1	183625.1	208	21	2827	670490	9
46.2	68100.0	14734.0	10	3	5702	13992	
2196.7	493303.0	89332.0	413	37	4572	1550518	2
3783.2	588720.6	104575.0	232	28	7864	2699446	
17.5	59236.8	9990.0	12	3	5400	45000	
104.2	293044.0	42479.6	9	5	859	131192	
692.5	848890.3	55687.2	33	10	648	827440	1

C-2-46 社区服务

地　区	单位数	农村社区服务机构	可以为居民提供便民办事服务的机构	可以为居民提供活动场所的机构	可以为居民提供养老等服务的机构
全　国	**251939**	**108214**	**142422**	**73229**	**45677**
中央级					
北　京	10467	4908	8317	4462	846
天　津	1739	308	1286	341	23
河　北	25148	19800	1565	5877	17714
山　西	3069	1344	1548	1323	82
内蒙古	2122	54	1277	476	285
辽　宁	5408	591	3749	492	1630
吉　林	631	157	561	31	28
黑龙江	2167	96	1527	438	29
上　海	3232	361	1832	924	40
江　苏	23689	11400	11863	5716	7412
浙　江	24062	12013	15945	5755	736
安　徽	5452	1525	4195	724	36
福　建	2917	411	1514	584	1030
江　西	3189	195	1611	1122	170
山　东	23991	10852	21485	12053	2872
河　南	2924	418	1701	790	62
湖　北	8466	1729	5385	2019	178
湖　南	8711	819	6148	3676	630
广　东	45233	13795	21976	20244	1584
广　西	7595	6434	444	500	6309
海　南	1578	1302	1055	366	3
重　庆	4898	1490	2663	1287	1230
四　川	5552	1610	4195	345	99
贵　州	17293	12572	14094	994	422
云　南	1269	253	1073	113	8
西　藏	34	10	22	12	
陕　西	2868	472	1851	798	38
甘　肃	5147	3051	1712	1129	2055
青　海	169	2	115	43	
宁　夏	773	222	403	214	117
新　疆	2146	20	1310	381	9

机构总表

单位:个、人、人次

		年末职工人数		受教育程度	
农村	可以为居民提供便民信息服务的机构		#女性	大学专科人数	大学本科及以上人数
33147	**40749**	**853222**	**326861**	**196972**	**83369**
219	3531	37327	18566	9736	7571
	305	8388	5294	2215	1393
16051	202	43388	16178	3622	684
34	122	8672	3464	1914	571
	149	11339	5953	3675	2302
238	458	33460	18890	9904	5691
	11	3416	2051	2025	153
	173	10970	5359	4015	1482
3	436	21170	11710	3018	1648
4818	3191	104401	36621	21412	9391
329	2637	57318	21606	11887	5023
	688	22980	9898	6308	1739
87	288	12555	5449	2132	725
1	334	11130	5179	1402	237
1889	12545	88893	33346	29655	12452
1	450	11247	5089	3644	898
57	951	28863	12624	8027	2788
180	3761	25564	10654	6959	2933
411	5812	125066	39990	20941	12874
5853	344	15417	4222	1152	693
2	183	7256	2089	916	343
995	402	13439	5507	4116	1530
13	913	21788	8213	5844	1520
280	1811	80017	19959	20268	4573
2	85	7295	2126	1383	524
		217	134	89	51
	211	12580	5426	3478	601
1677	252	13828	4241	2775	1222
	13	810	375	262	95
2	43	2563	1609	368	82
5	448	11865	5039	3830	1580

C-2-46续表1

地区	职业资格水平		年龄结构			
	助理社会工作师人数	社会工作师人数	35岁及以下人数	36岁至45岁人数	46岁至55岁人数	56岁及以上人数
全国	**9587**	**3456**	**276534**	**337790**	**183024**	**55874**
中央级						
北京	2147	729	10575	13288	10845	2619
天津	236	40	2738	3062	2027	561
河北	88	42	11383	15258	11849	4898
山西	32	14	2136	4235	1723	578
内蒙古	94	34	4464	4872	1808	195
辽宁	147	115	11947	12736	5580	3197
吉林	9	5	516	2515	332	53
黑龙江	143	40	4097	5274	1352	247
上海	310	152	3355	8654	7037	2124
江苏	1217	333	31575	41478	24576	6772
浙江	1183	476	19126	21111	13466	3615
安徽	137	63	7377	10607	4320	676
福建	277	168	3995	5147	2476	937
江西	47	25	3485	4263	2081	1301
山东	219	143	34286	33843	15698	5066
河南	85	70	4049	5054	1654	490
湖北	151	23	9408	13072	5171	1212
湖南	264	104	7162	9487	7648	1267
广东	2206	605	43480	49498	23992	8096
广西	109	43	3657	4280	4769	2711
海南	5		1622	3336	1690	608
重庆	100	36	4247	5696	2637	859
四川	184	88	6978	8930	4961	919
贵州	31	11	29068	32781	13853	4315
云南	10	27	2022	3352	1636	285
西藏		2	165	48	4	
陕西	42	20	3436	4873	3566	705
甘肃	18	18	5340	4533	2907	1048
青海	22	2	257	412	133	8
宁夏	6	2	775	1385	365	38
新疆	68	26	3813	4710	2868	474

单位：个、人次、张、人 、时

志愿服务						
志愿者服务人次数	志愿服务时间	床位数合计	日间照料床位数	农村	住宿收养床位数	农村
9591968	**23813010.8**	**641443**	**417686**	**228437**	**223757**	**161183**
5574979	15290532.5	6555	5356	1998	1199	66
99370	205990.0	4251	3981	1172	270	
17631	31465.0	192368	123583	101538	68785	60218
942	2350.0	2886	2834	1510	52	
11168	27777.0	7383	6310	28	1073	
4436	7941.0	10026	8051	1021	1975	319
		3790	3190	300	600	66
6956	27740.0	1827	1592	10	235	
26629	57100.0	3374	2927	214	447	193
254478	514773.0	89371	79294	32093	10077	4675
342443	673365.8	20482	18520	8732	1962	993
23349	47834.0	6190	5074	194	1116	26
		16063	7839	794	8224	566
697	1264.0	2150	2051	29	99	12
2007416	4047850.0	79386	58436	37831	20950	15494
141	410.0	2527	1428	182	1099	57
1001	2275.0	4357	2981	400	1376	235
7927	19656.0	9242	6345	733	2897	957
119718	425627.0	22268	6941	1440	15327	4430
40	222.0	70317	10788	10285	59529	56236
22877	68391.0	25	13		12	
324345	873929.0	17010	6053	1715	10957	9028
29121	57611.0	11061	6853	768	4208	627
701285	1387656.0	11953	9330	5284	2623	1097
411	780.0	3164	2287	242	877	247
5024	19122.5	3930	2609	515	1321	244
2891	7439.0	36448	30531	19372	5917	5374
		674	674			
		1007	988	14	19	
6693	13910.0	1358	827	23	531	23

C-2-46续表2

地区	年末收养人数合计	日间照料人数	农村	住宿收养人数	农村
全国	**93443**	**60036**	**26799**	**33407**	**37361**
中央级					
北京	2522	1819	204	703	41
天津	1473	1231		242	
河北	19037	10687	8076	8350	6052
山西	521	521	472		
内蒙古	2153	2110	236	43	
辽宁	849	761	125	88	45
吉林	120	120			
黑龙江	110	110			
上海	1322	1321	30	1	
江苏	18039	17279	7735	760	417
浙江	2252	1615	225	637	282
安徽	1601	1601	2930		
福建	266	266			
江西	429	429			
山东	16114	12066	4143	4048	6146
河南	296	109		187	600
湖北	135	51	19	84	4
湖南	1346	881	221	465	397
广东	2925	1533	2	1392	2
广西	12205	1250	1181	10955	18231
海南					
重庆	7390	2113	399	5277	5128
四川	302	282	71	20	
贵州	53	53			
云南	129	125		4	
西藏					
陕西	488	351	45	137	16
甘肃	864	854	685	10	
青海	36	36			
宁夏	255	255			
新疆	211	207		4	

单位:人、人次、个、平方米

本年收养照料人天数	老年人活动人次数	社区服务志愿者组织数	注册社区志愿者人数	城镇便民、利民服务网点数	机构建筑面积
13100189	**8396087**	**127987**	**2286450**	**358518**	**50054452**
431677	1873107	11090	1371885	11004	1877952
		2407		10501	349684
3410265	368069	537	3642	3397	4710379
40616	63790	947	920	6263	392498
362565	278240	708	8333	8552	587417
37877	279	1699	38791	11033	851097
1605	32820			332	115928
35665	6650	7435	200	8816	478716
247358	12278	3589	123264	16843	765440
1654189	2689509	15270	131027	56314	6747889
183763	454180	10568	42115	84291	4603038
167817	107050	969	9908	7940	1045305
15641		802	10	4853	526175
38191	19735	1433	1970	3701	532268
2628208	1179697	9841	22201	35978	7730429
	3054	174		1852	844189
13195	31798	2634	462	3190	1668746
106223	22512	1436	745	16615	1298540
	17777	1249	239338	7013	5903717
2275353	822569	145		1387	1247910
		1	10	19	203614
1288065	260539	33225	115649	11438	1217372
5081	75000	5841	90827	8466	990406
269	347	14427	1160	14577	3066784
		235	82702	27	357017
				2	11190
536	30899	458	747	2654	637615
155908	36284	50	8	8845	658737
90	4	8		1	55975
	1200	117		8896	147055
32	8700	692	536	3718	431370

C-2-46续表3

地区	增加值合计	执行企业会计制度单位财务指标					执行行政	
		固定资产原价	营业收入	费用合计	营业利润	企业单位增加值	固定资产原价	上年结转和结余
全　国	**799640.0**	**106772.2**	**6396.2**	**3050.8**	**199.4**	**4191.3**	**1440796.5**	**61640.5**
中央级								
北　京	34225.9	169.6	25.0	258.0	-29.3	176.6	46811.1	2058.4
天　津	6257.0	194.0					7500.9	826.9
河　北	15445.5	85.0	56.7	58.8		2.4	46956.3	441.6
山　西	3161.9						13305.7	86.0
内蒙古	10356.9	814.5	894.8	125.2		300.8	12172.2	235.2
辽　宁	8508.8	516.1	51.0	79.0		25.2	12095.2	27.0
吉　林	993.9		9.0	9.0		6.0	1092.0	239.0
黑龙江	6186.7	284.5	2.0	2.1		282.7	7933.2	2.3
上　海	19993.6	1.0					12024.9	1839.4
江　苏	116317.4	371.2	78.8	27.4	13.2	57.3	221807.6	198.4
浙　江	148374.5	14834.1	868.1	308.2	0.7	163.1	474406.7	28588.6
安　徽	25714.7	275.6	701.5	569.6		118.7	68798.0	2689.1
福　建	5110.9	990.0	551.6	392.6	8.3	121.3	16836.2	17.5
江　西	4553.2	4023.4	190.0	55.0		10.5	4337.5	6.1
山　东	150096.6	186.0	61.0	22.0	21.0	66.1	9241.7	
河　南	8388.3	1138.0	929.9	383.3		654.3	13179.6	317.5
湖　北	33871.0	1291.0	428.8	297.9	9.7	195.0	93795.0	178.0
湖　南	15129.6	98.0	190.0	83.0	70.0	243.2	11598.7	1322.1
广　东	58191.4	47510.8	1052.6	126.4	104.0	1233.0	83781.1	5803.9
广　西	6222.0	80.0					40807.1	130.5
海　南	1977.7	1625.8	5.0			124.2	10133.6	5.6
重　庆	14449.8	26061.2	11.0	11.0			43708.3	92.9
四　川	13882.4	1312.0	145.2	99.7	0.8	93.4	31015.3	2981.6
贵　州	61612.7	1289.5	113.0	12.3		21.0	41321.1	5553.8
云　南	6287.0	345.2	3.0		1.0	2.0	37220.3	7047.6
西　藏	802.6						4265.1	680.0
陕　西	7834.8	3.0					42829.3	33.0
甘　肃	4249.5	618.7		4.5		11.5	9134.8	32.0
青　海	133.6	523.0					1792.0	
宁　夏	954.7	855.0				2.5	2182.6	
新　疆	10356.0	1276.0	28.2	125.8		280.6	18713.4	206.5

单位：万元

事业单位会计制度财务指标				执行民间非营利组织单位会计制度财务指标				
本年收入合计	本年支出合计	收支结余	行政事业单位增加值	固定资产原价	上年结余	本年收入合计	本年费用合计	社会组织增加值
1156974.2	**1088607.6**	**2727.6**	**505073.0**	**1137707.6**	**13774.7**	**486929.6**	**484781.1**	**290375.7**
43854.6	45153.9	142.6	34048.3	20.0	4.0		1.0	1.0
3548.9	3648.3		3829.7	3113.4	163.0	4417.4	4370.2	2427.3
342259.7	342813.1		9621.8	34222.2	860.7	6018.5	8178.1	5821.3
1343.0	1347.9		1327.4	5184.3	21.0	2680.7	4608.8	1834.5
11828.0	12071.9	191.5	9652.0	3170.0		763.8	876.9	404.1
6928.9	7969.9		4703.0	5247.5	62.6	7751.4	8552.7	3780.6
986.2	1116.5		561.3	802.2		2511.8	1149.5	426.6
5729.5	6809.3		5445.5	2632.2	1000.0	41570.4	640.3	458.5
41051.4	33486.5	534.8	15027.9	6584.9	166.9	10945.3	8645.9	4965.7
84739.5	124581.3	240.5	79412.2	174501.0	41.4	101142.7	91162.1	36847.9
306377.6	217877.2	513.1	134640.3	122849.0	217.3	32947.0	35609.3	13571.1
28947.1	30320.0		21009.4	34369.7	180.0	10118.9	10418.9	4586.6
7364.4	6325.7	4.9	2890.6	10649.0	28.5	3852.7	5157.4	2099.0
2450.4	2231.6		1201.2	11245.7	2.0	5940.1	7364.9	3341.5
11358.9	11359.9		7745.5	247802.8	432.5	197326.8	196394.0	142285.0
11486.6	7892.2	100.9	5924.9	7519.2	395.1	1021.7	2498.0	1809.1
38145.1	36287.9	101.0	29597.5	8969.0	10.1	3551.8	5841.4	4078.5
22843.3	21404.9		12494.9	6609.7	701.1	8063.2	8347.0	2391.5
77582.3	74079.6	6.3	41532.7	69038.6	4228.1	7805.7	22978.8	15425.7
2848.4	3149.3		4224.2	20779.7		525.0	2541.6	1997.8
2297.8	2675.4		1793.6	350.8		665.0	683.3	59.9
13714.9	13727.6	133.0	10987.1	28711.4	3.0	7260.7	6791.5	3462.7
19385.8	16214.1		10674.1	12014.6	3.1	5475.7	5667.1	3114.9
33077.3	29401.4	184.9	30471.1	94505.5	5173.1	22431.9	40139.2	31120.6
6110.5	5494.2	559.0	5246.7	212213.4	3.0	4.5	1349.5	1038.3
880.0	844.4		802.6	59.6				
10026.9	10227.1		7834.8					
3047.0	2727.4	15.1	2136.0	8002.7	78.2	1257.4	2992.5	2102.0
1.0	1.0		71.7	4205.0		103.0	169.4	61.9
345.1	373.3		222.5	1060.5		677.7	1498.6	729.7
16414.1	16994.8		9943.0	1274.0		98.8	153.2	132.4

C-2-47 社区服务

地 区	单位数	农村社区服务机构	可以为居民提供便民办事服务的机构	可以为居民提供活动场所的机构	可以为居民提供养老等服务的机构
全 国	**890**	**32**	**610**	**216**	**78**
中央级					
北 京	18		13	7	3
天 津	11		10	2	
河 北	32	2	20	4	4
山 西	18		10	3	
内蒙古	5		3	2	
辽 宁	26		12	8	2
吉 林	24	3	19	1	
黑龙江	37		21	7	1
上 海	8		6		
江 苏	59	1	41	10	3
浙 江	30	4	13	4	4
安 徽	41	1	32	1	1
福 建	24		16	4	1
江 西	43		29	7	3
山 东	121		113	68	11
河 南	44	3	34	4	4
湖 北	27	1	24	2	
湖 南	67	3	54	29	11
广 东	31	7	23	1	1
广 西	20	3	5	9	5
海 南	1			1	
重 庆	11		4	5	
四 川	64		33	11	7
贵 州	18		15	1	2
云 南	8		8		
西 藏	2		2		
陕 西	49		28	12	2
甘 肃	26	4	8	4	13
青 海					
宁 夏	9		6	2	
新 疆	16		8	7	

指导中心

单位：个、人、人次

		年末职工人数		受教育程度	
农村	可以为居民提供便民信息服务的机构		#女性	大学专科人数	大学本科及以上人数
8	**260**	**8484**	**3812**	**2396**	**1722**
	10	634	371	139	203
	2	63	28	19	31
1	4	273	118	62	14
	5	77	34	12	5
		43	16	16	20
	5	161	95	56	74
	4	101	48	28	20
	8	295	185	113	107
	2	101	54	42	49
	14	657	270	156	131
2	12	1183	189	117	77
	7	331	154	64	38
	3	132	78	19	22
	7	238	144	51	30
	96	1793	886	796	495
	5	331	156	93	28
	1	266	133	62	45
1	38	530	240	171	74
	6	160	85	40	72
2	1	51	24	15	12
		3	2		
	3	32	15	8	14
	13	273	148	94	55
		97	42	23	8
	4	27	16	2	12
		6	2	6	
	7	300	121	126	18
2	1	84	39	18	2
	1	82	37	11	22
	1	160	82	37	44

C-2-47续表1

地　区	职业资格水平		年龄结构			
	助理社会工作师人数	社会工作师人数	35岁及以下人数	36岁至45岁人数	46岁至55岁人数	56岁及以上人数
全　国	**315**	**146**	**3320**	**3750**	**1215**	**199**
中央级						
北　京	76	26	261	234	123	16
天　津	1		26	14	17	6
河　北	1		115	114	37	7
山　西	2	3	40	20	14	3
内蒙古			25	14	4	
辽　宁	3	2	63	75	22	1
吉　林	2	1	30	52	17	2
黑龙江	5	9	127	126	40	2
上　海	4	4	53	25	17	6
江　苏	148	38	344	180	96	37
浙　江	9	3	190	907	82	4
安　徽	4	7	135	157	38	1
福　建	1	13	36	68	21	7
江　西			61	141	26	10
山　东	14	16	913	640	220	20
河　南	2	2	159	114	42	16
湖　北		1	75	131	51	9
湖　南	15	2	208	227	82	13
广　东	11	12	59	72	26	3
广　西	3		12	22	16	1
海　南				2	1	
重　庆	1		9	18	5	
四　川	4	1	99	96	69	9
贵　州			38	39	19	1
云　南			9	17		1
西　藏			4	2		
陕　西	9	5	89	110	80	21
甘　肃			38	32	12	2
青　海						
宁　夏			38	28	16	
新　疆		1	64	73	22	1

单位：个、人次、张、人 、时

志愿服务		床位数合计	日间照料床位数		住宿收养床位数	
志愿者服务人次数	志愿服务时间			农村		农村
485809	**1228560.0**	**14241**	**10195**	**1751**	**4046**	**136**
345511	720593.0	1163	117		1046	
12300	36900.0	110	110			
804	3492.0	1755	1135		620	
5		28	28			
		60	60			
		419	405		14	
		1410	1355	195	55	10
		200	132		68	
348	918.0	479	457		22	
6050	13976.0	1724	1303	1278	421	20
2100	4658.0	191	191	90		
		47	11		36	
		348	323	2	25	
17244	42796.0	2275	1884		391	
		626	204	1	422	
		112	112			4
107	572.0	791	491		300	35
100200	400750.0	95	83	40	12	
40	222.0	191	104	61	87	61
		201	101		100	
167	653.0	809	479		330	
98	246.0	132	106		26	
795	2644.0	555	510		45	
30	90.0	518	492	84	26	6
		2	2			

C-2-47续表2

地　区	年末收养人数合计	日间照料人数	农村	住宿收养人数	农村
全　国	**1706**	**654**	**22**	**1052**	**10**
中央级					
北　京	662			662	
天　津	40	40			
河　北	25	25	10		
山　西	4	4			
内蒙古	52	52			
辽　宁					
吉　林					
黑龙江	10	10			
上　海					
江　苏	107	107	2		
浙　江	185			185	
安　徽	70	70			
福　建					
江　西	87	87			
山　东	212	67		145	
河　南					
湖　北					
湖　南	130	88		42	
广　东					
广　西					
海　南					
重　庆					
四　川					
贵　州					
云　南					
西　藏					
陕　西	114	96	10	18	10
甘　肃	8	8			
青　海					
宁　夏					
新　疆					

单位:人、人次、个、平方米

本年收养照料人天数	老年人活动人次数	社区服务志愿者组织数	注册社区志愿者人数	城镇便民、利民服务网点数	机构建筑面积
294013	**189496**	**5109**	**826743**	**16757**	**958662**
200100	86400	3548	761571	44	131841
		20		20	6705
4500	4920			86	29939
1460	230	3		21	3930
89	1650				6605
					7208
				70	3780
	3650			3	15669
		784	62524	220	6589
9986	2385	294	20	2153	142566
				1816	69453
25550	5350	3	408	80	23754
		66		1637	15526
2052		5		41	15310
49995	71354	292	2106	5811	181449
	1323			235	31060
		2		1252	89304
221	8912	26	21	189	44473
				567	11315
					12826
					120
		29		48	11400
	824	3		803	24403
				1165	6400
					2206
				2	500
60	2418	17	93	38	51754
	80			29	5345
				427	2360
		17			4872

C-2-47续表3

地区	增加值合计	执行企业会计制度单位财务指标					执行行政	
		固定资产原价	营业收入	费用合计	营业利润	企业单位增加值	固定资产原价	上年结转和结余
全　国	**30965.3**	**815.3**	**393.8**	**296.7**	**32.3**	**142.4**	**73118.1**	**945.3**
中央级								
北　京	13319.2						24195.4	529.6
天　津	699.3						1569.4	-26.1
河　北	194.1	13.0	42.0	44.1		2.4	1148.2	
山　西	40.3						33.0	
内蒙古	240.4						522.0	
辽　宁	30.0	4.0	51.0	79.0			123.0	
吉　林	174.1		9.0	9.0		6.0	77.0	1.0
黑龙江	236.8	2.0					314.0	
上　海	1222.5						4974.8	232.6
江　苏	2810.2	3.2	31.1	13.7	13.2	57.3	3624.2	22.2
浙　江	1061.2		52.0	47.8			2916.2	121.1
安　徽	584.7	20.0	21.5	9.6		0.5	3709.4	
福　建	204.2	26.0	31.6	7.6	8.3	33.3	40.0	
江　西	245.9			0.1			383.8	
山　东	4304.8	180.0	30.0	16.0		14.1	4518.2	
河　南	833.6						4351.6	
湖　北	844.3						5927.4	
湖　南	764.3	20.0	20.0	10.0	10.0	10.0	2664.6	
广　东	1386.5	3.1				-8.0	4052.0	44.6
广　西	81.7						578.1	3.0
海　南		3.0						
重　庆	227.7		11.0	11.0			1343.0	
四　川	390.6	90.0	62.6	45.3	0.8	16.7	685.3	6.3
贵　州	86.0	51.0	32.0	3.5		10.1	25.0	10.0
云　南	46.6	107.0					100.0	
西　藏	43.9						120.0	
陕　西	708.6						4488.9	
甘　肃	35.3						73.9	
青　海								
宁　夏	8.4	263.0					175.6	
新　疆	140.1	30.0					384.1	1.0

单位：万元

事业单位会计制度财务指标				执行民间非营利组织单位会计制度财务指标				
本年收入合计	本年支出合计	收支结余	行政事业单位增加值	固定资产原价	上年结余	本年收入合计	本年费用合计	社会组织增加值
40662.1	**38309.5**	**820.3**	**27644.9**	**21618.3**	**1039.7**	**46487.9**	**5565.3**	**3178.0**
17652.5	17096.1	-70.8	13319.2					
382.4	438.5		453.1	102.8	9.0	609.8	646.3	246.2
273.6	311.1		178.6	511.0		21.6	21.0	13.1
41.8	41.8		23.1	40.2		34.3	35.4	17.2
287.6	287.6		240.4					
48.5	38.5		12.9	365.0		42.4	36.6	17.1
287.4	279.4		166.2	6.0		3.5	3.7	1.9
381.6	373.8		228.6	1002.0	1000.0	40801.0	13.2	8.2
3316.0	3003.5	522.7	1184.7	1.0		42.0	43.9	37.8
3234.7	2839.4	240.5	2399.5	1021.4		710.9	811.9	353.4
2245.2	1957.2	21.9	917.7	207.0	5.0	377.0	208.5	143.5
696.6	640.1		541.0	1057.0		96.0	72.2	43.2
267.6	179.1		146.7	32.0	11.0	37.5	36.0	24.2
248.4	242.4		129.8	861.0		151.0	225.8	116.1
3653.0	3653.0		2429.8	13935.3		3106.2	2907.2	1860.9
1574.0	931.0	99.7	803.0	169.1	1.0	29.4	46.7	30.6
1698.4	1595.7		829.6	20.0	10.0	16.0	16.0	14.7
875.4	863.6		662.3	485.5		207.5	190.3	92.0
1747.3	1796.7	6.3	1393.7	6.5		1.0	2.0	0.8
27.5	27.5		43.6	28.4		22.0	52.4	38.1
226.8	221.8		222.2	150.0		5.5	5.5	5.5
457.0	393.9		315.4	300.0	2.6	141.1	116.4	58.5
37.1	37.8		37.7	162.0	1.1	25.1	55.5	38.2
37.8	37.8		41.8	80.0			4.8	4.8
	42.0		43.9					
693.7	730.4		708.6					
71.9	59.4		24.3	3.1		7.1	12.0	11.0
73.4	58.6		8.4					
124.9	131.8		139.1	1072.0			2.0	1.0

C–2–48 社区服务

地　区	单位数	农村社区服务机构	可以为居民提供便民办事服务的机构	可以为居民提供活动场所的机构	可以为居民提供养老等服务的机构
全　国	**19014**	**5909**	**13548**	**4168**	**1288**
中央级					
北　京	192	17	152	76	22
天　津	215	88	135	71	4
河　北	424	70	152	74	132
山　西	435	191	215	210	3
内蒙古	960	28	568	213	172
辽　宁	649	38	429	107	48
吉　林	350	104	302	22	19
黑龙江	480	51	370	61	6
上　海	204	11	176	13	6
江　苏	1492	674	1131	258	235
浙　江	1822	1054	1478	271	38
安　徽	1060	544	866	92	13
福　建	229	25	133	50	46
江　西	352	52	195	111	18
山　东	1039	290	938	403	116
河　南	539	75	425	99	6
湖　北	545	56	437	57	23
湖　南	524	75	460	188	34
广　东	2492	873	1299	979	129
广　西	86	11	22	37	4
海　南	124	54	100		
重　庆	277	21	205	77	9
四　川	977	83	869	30	17
贵　州	1348	704	1162	96	34
云　南	97	2	72	19	4
西　藏	9	2	6	3	
陕　西	432	140	297	139	2
甘　肃	970	567	532	185	144
青　海	13		9	3	
宁　夏	74	6	53	19	2
新　疆	604	3	360	205	2

中心

单位：个、人、人次

农村	可以为居民提供便民信息服务的机构	年末职工人数	#女性	受教育程度	
				大学专科人数	大学本科及以上人数
331	**2642**	**112550**	**48401**	**31567**	**16130**
	103	2291	1306	558	743
	26	1556	977	435	232
49	66	2048	1115	515	123
	7	1823	756	497	166
	49	6465	3318	2119	1281
3	88	4678	2507	1354	927
	7	1708	791	771	109
	43	3850	1693	1724	627
	9	4613	2314	1644	1085
135	184	9303	3809	2397	980
4	136	11042	4335	2453	1285
	179	5830	2367	1408	634
	13	1346	551	225	113
1	28	1627	884	352	79
23	648	6575	2635	2582	1659
1	69	2970	1333	843	275
2	47	3476	1548	1273	503
6	216	3477	1534	1008	361
16	373	9546	3923	1995	1637
1	23	654	321	47	19
	24	872	262	153	82
	16	1760	825	528	234
3	61	4300	1994	1416	473
4	64	9748	3093	2411	1467
	2	737	253	190	92
		77	48	10	8
	9	2166	717	475	126
82	109	3212	1014	658	231
	1	86	36	17	15
1	3	459	302	40	8
	39	4255	1840	1469	556

C-2-48续表1

地区	职业资格水平		年龄结构			
	助理社会工作师人数	社会工作师人数	35岁及以下人数	36岁至45岁人数	46岁至55岁人数	56岁及以上人数
全　国	**1789**	**681**	**40719**	**43976**	**22017**	**5838**
中央级						
北　京	33	30	544	816	770	161
天　津	18	14	433	741	362	20
河　北	6	4	797	821	371	59
山　西	1	5	611	854	279	79
内蒙古	91	33	2448	2878	1009	130
辽　宁	17	17	1776	1754	873	275
吉　林	5	4	419	1026	228	35
黑龙江	45	11	1394	1565	816	75
上　海	220	96	1932	1283	949	449
江　苏	186	74	3344	3433	1915	611
浙　江	373	96	3980	3684	2340	1038
安　徽	52	17	1790	2698	1142	200
福　建	22	8	403	620	283	40
江　西	27	6	529	679	365	54
山　东	10	5	3028	2449	853	245
河　南	24	35	1291	1255	358	66
湖　北	49	6	1266	1504	610	96
湖　南	11	10	1155	1541	689	92
广　东	519	128	3858	3357	1932	399
广　西	1		380	135	98	41
海　南	5		250	362	194	66
重　庆	9	18	496	818	390	56
四　川	26	31	1693	1874	593	140
贵　州	8	6	3484	3519	2092	653
云　南	5	7	179	272	209	77
西　藏		2	62	11	4	
陕　西	4		642	722	548	254
甘　肃	3	5	1136	1068	642	366
青　海	2		15	52	19	
宁　夏	1		157	241	55	6
新　疆	16	13	1227	1944	1029	55

单位：个、人次、张、人 、时

志愿服务		床位数合计	日间照料床位数		住宿收养床位数	
志愿者服务人次数	志愿服务时间			农村		农村
1847159	**5512428.0**	**58768**	**46985**	**9809**	**11783**	**1986**
1440651	4645201.0	626	584	81	42	
41575	58875.0	1868	1598	150	270	
3682	10014.0	4540	3528	1084	1012	550
310	725.0	686	645	32	41	
620	1710.0	4664	3902	28	762	
766	1853.0	1444	959	60	485	32
		1758	1276		482	
		441	335		106	
6503	13853.0	2166	2060		106	
8959	23977.0	9106	7612	2552	1494	601
155711	313715.0	5796	5501	2144	295	19
5239	12504.0	2486	2157	61	329	5
		534	224	19	310	
21	60.0	807	775	8	32	12
43251	111416.0	4048	3514	516	534	14
		896	358	72	538	39
163	456.0	667	453	14	214	
3456	7415.0	1575	1155	178	420	83
2685	8055.0	1540	793	300	747	83
		117	48		69	14
21677	65031.0	7	1		6	
32822	77385.0	1421	921		500	
4567	8378.0	3435	2172	40	1263	8
67386	136245.0	1684	1338	659	346	57
335	552.0	935	511		424	
632	1898.0	742	515	235	227	100
510	1620.0	4171	3579	1572	592	369
		131	131			
		74	66	4	8	
5638	11490.0	403	274		129	

C-2-48续表2

地区	年末收养人数合计	日间照料人数	农村	住宿收养人数	农村
全　国	**10741**	**9789**	**1359**	**952**	**792**
中央级					
北　京	190	190			
天　津	1383	1141		242	
河　北	103	82	19	21	6
山　西	39	39	17		
内蒙古	1366	1364	218	2	
辽　宁	50	45	5	5	5
吉　林	120	120			
黑龙江	15	15			
上　海	1063	1062		1	
江　苏	2223	2083	888	140	126
浙　江	468	308	5	160	
安　徽	1220	1220	10		
福　建					
江　西	169	169			
山　东	869	814	108	55	55
河　南	296	109		187	600
湖　北					
湖　南	133	133	19		
广　东					
广　西					
海　南					
重　庆	181	146		35	
四　川	237	237	48		
贵　州	53	53			
云　南					
西　藏					
陕　西	275	185	22	90	
甘　肃	77	67		10	
青　海					
宁　夏	18	18			
新　疆	193	189		4	

单位:人、人次、个、平方米

本年收养照料人天数	老年人活动人次数	社区服务志愿者组织数	注册社区志愿者人数	城镇便民、利民服务网点数	机构建筑面积
928947	**902914**	**58762**	**573254**	**191094**	**6863278**
5079	147369	4596	401874	4932	254521
		1636		7293	111207
300	2589	308	3284	2774	101529
1136		768	920	4355	76560
300527	217899	521	3711	6700	329981
1028	67	253	327	3384	134047
1605	32820			262	77508
5475	3000	6674	200	4769	119001
236267	2732	2404	35839	16141	121640
133491	193433	1185	3883	10281	1136269
1513	62434	2792	35895	73352	910316
69900	53230	131	1300	3145	302005
		307		604	102161
10006	3010	830	1935	2171	74471
131620	119176	2849	12170	11336	642915
	1599	155		1347	231781
	1439	520		663	154429
	4108	115	95	1681	175726
	360	484		1743	406444
		5		40	36753
					25050
29313	1768	29506	39106	3278	161601
1266	34851	274	31313	2587	229724
269	347	1818	800	10924	433613
				5	42773
					2220
120	126	75	61	465	141688
	11857	12	5	6528	122767
					4409
		1		8106	17886
32	8700	543	536	2228	182283

C-2-48续表3

地区	增加值合计	执行企业会计制度单位财务指标					执行行政	
		固定资产原价	营业收入	费用合计	营业利润	企业单位增加值	固定资产原价	上年结转和结余
全 国	**175361.4**	**7019.3**	**867.1**	**685.7**	**41.4**	**351.4**	**247268.7**	**18936.8**
中央级								
北 京	12082.2						11226.5	1280.5
天 津	1401.2						1007.3	1.0
河 北	1573.8	12.0	14.7	14.7			3893.2	
山 西	717.6						2810.6	
内蒙古	5396.6	296.0	232.0	111.2		4.8	7034.5	17.2
辽 宁	1627.8	238.0				12.2	4133.8	
吉 林	442.2						1003.0	228.0
黑龙江	2161.5	72.5	2.0	2.1		2.0	5787.6	2.0
上 海	7817.8	1.0					5743.6	1530.2
江 苏	20467.1	60.0	43.7	13.7			48324.3	
浙 江	30178.5	1770.0	90.1	86.4	0.7	7.4	24742.0	7845.9
安 徽	10890.3	11.5					30903.3	74.7
福 建	454.1	5.0	80.0	80.0			3798.2	
江 西	1062.8	142.0		4.9		10.5	2465.1	6.0
山 东	16462.1	6.0	31.0	6.0	21.0	52.0	3268.8	
河 南	2197.5	47.3	76.6	29.1		51.7	4834.5	55.5
湖 北	3770.6	600.0	220.0	208.5	9.7	89.3	10594.0	40.0
湖 南	4066.2	40.0	20.0	21.5	10.0	16.6	2705.6	1303.8
广 东	21097.7	868.6				0.6	10864.5	1791.9
广 西	102.1						788.5	123.0
海 南	280.6	5.8					92.1	4.6
重 庆	3048.5	1645.0					10585.8	19.5
四 川	5169.3	252.0	29.4	17.7		16.1	7732.8	550.9
贵 州	15066.5	85.0					10017.4	3804.2
云 南	675.6						2636.1	46.9
西 藏	112.6						962.2	85.0
陕 西	1756.0						13778.2	
甘 肃	945.0	140.6				10.5	2842.9	10.0
青 海	8.0	16.0					192.0	
宁 夏	21.9	375.0					371.0	
新 疆	4308.0	330.0	27.6	89.9		77.7	12129.3	116.0

单位：万元

事业单位会计制度财务指标				执行民间非营利组织单位会计制度财务指标				
本年收入合计	本年支出合计	收支结余	行政事业单位增加值	固定资产原价	上年结余	本年收入合计	本年费用合计	社会组织增加值
348696.0	**335656.2**	**710.2**	**139977.7**	**123703.0**	**780.5**	**55007.5**	**60652.4**	**35032.3**
16208.4	17569.5	213.4	12082.2					
831.3	823.6		931.6	736.0	72.0	867.5	879.1	469.6
145774.2	145701.7		1424.3	2360.2	12.0	195.5	281.2	149.5
570.0	571.0		409.9	1356.4	8.0	1074.0	1154.5	307.7
5928.7	5945.9		5088.0	1686.0		496.6	594.5	303.8
1443.5	1678.5		1174.8	1101.0		1756.2	1235.9	440.8
528.0	618.3		287.8	77.2		348.3	285.1	154.4
2574.5	2618.9		2031.9	470.0		222.0	237.4	127.6
25503.4	18984.4	13.1	7506.5	248.3	38.7	985.3	978.1	311.3
17273.3	16113.3		14495.9	14661.2	1.0	9636.2	9650.2	5971.2
33522.7	31433.4	192.0	27708.9	10916.7	51.0	5145.9	4371.4	2462.2
11453.2	11546.6		9741.6	9165.6		2690.7	2768.3	1148.7
2155.7	2044.3		307.3	424.4	0.2	369.0	495.4	146.8
1041.2	920.0		671.4	3250.0		723.6	1293.4	380.9
4956.9	4956.9		3772.3	38758.4		21316.2	21328.0	12637.8
2690.7	3506.0		1449.6	6329.7		475.6	912.0	696.2
3860.2	3939.3	28.0	3069.1	461.0		910.8	836.5	612.2
7964.7	7402.7		3644.5	569.2		1022.4	828.8	405.1
29085.4	26015.0		16740.6	5931.5	379.0	3134.9	6296.3	4356.5
151.2	109.2		90.6	394.1		4.6	15.4	11.5
700.0	700.0		264.7				18.3	15.9
3164.4	3109.1	63.8	2806.0	6581.5		782.7	612.7	242.5
6101.2	5618.8		3856.3	4726.0	0.5	1267.3	2430.2	1296.9
16153.1	14348.5	184.9	13209.5	11572.0	212.1	1302.8	2492.9	1857.0
748.4	719.1		609.4	324.0			87.2	66.2
110.0	100.3		112.6	9.6				
1781.5	2143.5		1756.0					
1091.9	848.2	15.0	593.2	762.5	6.0	166.6	430.4	341.3
			7.7	458.0		14.0	14.0	0.3
83.0	91.0		21.9	181.5				
5245.3	5479.2		4111.9	191.0		98.8	125.2	118.4

C-2-49 社区

地 区	单位数	农村社区服务机构	可以为居民提供便民办事服务的机构	可以为居民提供活动场所的机构	可以为居民提供养老等服务的机构
全 国	**108377**	**51008**	**74871**	**26850**	**12455**
中央级					
北 京	6315	3657	5154	3491	821
天 津	1282	193	973	206	19
河 北	1564	58	1003	226	449
山 西	2293	1113	1180	974	52
内蒙古	672	26	402	163	52
辽 宁	3685	408	2619	341	1188
吉 林	257	50	240	8	9
黑龙江	1324	45	861	342	14
上 海	2699	339	1387	887	33
江 苏	14972	8645	7344	2845	6214
浙 江	10957	8359	8511	1983	303
安 徽	2587	663	2073	355	17
福 建	1974	289	1147	508	549
江 西	1082	69	446	366	149
山 东	10186	5717	8746	5165	1076
河 南	814	127	628	120	22
湖 北	4442	720	3115	809	131
湖 南	2046	274	1472	813	392
广 东	12381	5645	7689	3708	179
广 西	533	12	274	78	42
海 南	1355	1150	857	365	3
重 庆	2053	335	1536	680	221
四 川	3753	1496	2823	127	19
贵 州	11982	10376	9868	736	205
云 南	1151	247	985	93	
西 藏	23	8	14	9	
陕 西	2062	272	1381	508	15
甘 肃	1742	484	861	571	178
青 海	156	2	106	40	
宁 夏	658	216	342	193	102
新 疆	1377	13	834	140	1

服务站

单位：个、人、人次

				受教育程度	
农村	可以为居民提供便民信息服务的机构	年末职工人数	#女性	大学专科人数	大学本科及以上人数
5576	**18569**	**448884**	**178246**	**105812**	**41200**
219	3360	30197	15053	7896	6090
	260	6152	4123	1703	1111
7	96	6692	3716	2041	412
9	93	5795	2159	1137	332
	78	2957	1628	925	592
119	270	23132	13687	7642	4259
		1607	1212	1226	24
	107	5535	2781	1760	603
3	392	13171	7495	1208	453
4231	1726	67596	24972	13183	4627
101	797	27524	10403	4982	1921
	233	11462	4974	3255	811
12	254	8671	3909	1327	515
	166	3893	1895	455	64
425	4965	45170	18279	14899	6006
	58	3559	1361	831	131
40	435	16892	7160	4733	1638
68	882	9168	3731	2995	1150
2	1033	41725	12830	6568	3182
7	139	4763	1644	634	413
2	159	6099	1731	715	260
40	269	8476	3710	2999	1142
6	784	14162	4815	3798	938
171	1193	53267	12181	10567	1945
	79	6474	1833	1187	415
		134	84	73	43
	173	9195	4316	2814	457
113	132	5733	1950	1478	579
	12	724	339	245	80
1	22	1999	1264	308	52
	402	6960	3011	2228	955

C-2-49续表1

地区	职业资格水平		年龄结构			
	助理社会工作师人数	社会工作师人数	35岁及以下人数	36岁至45岁人数	46岁至55岁人数	56岁及以上人数
全　国	**4929**	**1875**	**143871**	**181220**	**96514**	**27279**
中央级						
北　京	2028	668	8619	10684	8724	2170
天　津	217	24	2153	2066	1443	490
河　北	78	33	2861	2289	1235	307
山　西	5	1	1228	2942	1179	446
内蒙古			1140	1305	467	45
辽　宁	127	96	8362	8489	3434	2847
吉　林	2		67	1437	87	16
黑龙江	91	20	2228	2730	416	161
上　海	64	52	1039	5997	4630	1505
江　苏	757	214	16640	29013	16849	5094
浙　江	403	243	8890	9924	6691	2019
安　徽	64	29	3606	5386	2131	339
福　建	237	147	2799	3627	1738	507
江　西	20	18	1594	1647	618	34
山　东	103	85	17141	17237	7930	2862
河　南	20	7	1296	1339	622	302
湖　北	101	12	4955	7568	3429	940
湖　南	44	65	2809	3583	2428	348
广　东	161	38	14695	17227	8219	1584
广　西	72	28	2382	1512	757	112
海　南			1340	2737	1480	542
重　庆	70	13	3145	3404	1584	343
四　川	154	50	4225	5924	3383	630
贵　州	12	4	20666	20243	10054	2304
云　南	5	8	1812	3048	1417	197
西　藏			99	35		
陕　西	29	7	2510	3745	2515	425
甘　肃	12	5	2417	2063	897	356
青　海	20	2	242	360	114	8
宁　夏	5	2	577	1103	290	29
新　疆	28	4	2334	2556	1753	317

单位：个、人次、张、人 、时

志愿服务		床位数合计	日间照料床位数		住宿收养床位数	
志愿者服务人次数	志愿服务时间			农村		农村
7174692	**16901135.3**	**172304**	**150017**	**56122**	**22287**	**6394**
3788817	9924738.5	4078	3967	1812	111	66
45495	110215.0	2273	2273	1022		
345	1104.0	6077	4203	488	1874	
502	1000.0	1401	1394	777	7	
9968	24087.0	1172	1011		161	
3618	6088.0	5521	4363	610	1158	100
		622	559	105	63	56
4220	16880.0	1021	994	10	27	
14829	36559.0	1078	783	212	295	147
236138	480303.0	64448	60602	27160	3846	1981
180137	344051.8	10520	10126	4270	394	354
15910	30392.0	3287	2580	30	707	21
		5040	4808	403	232	35
636	1117.0	859	817	19	42	
1902170	3785419.5	24322	21189	9187	3133	881
141	410.0	456	389	27	67	18
18	52.0	2960	2026	321	934	223
3954	10643.0	4176	3220	248	956	154
16822	16822.0	3199	940	278	2259	91
		572	362		210	70
1200	3360.0	18	12		6	
291458	796451.0	4183	3230	394	953	
24387	48580.0	4995	3004	559	1991	595
627514	1241398.0	5858	5178	4203	680	507
76	228.0	2086	1747	237	339	158
3594	14556.5	1329	880	120	449	84
1698	4310.0	8432	7423	3597	1009	830
		543	543			
		893	882	10	11	
1045	2370.0	885	512	23	373	23

C-2-49续表2

地 区	年末收养人数合计	日间照料人数		住宿收养人数	
			农村		农村
全 国	**27631**	**26833**	**10568**	**798**	**2889**
中央级					
北 京	1670	1629	204	41	41
天 津	50	50			
河 北	138	91	2	47	
山 西	478	478	455		
内蒙古	368	327		41	
辽 宁	595	520	40	75	40
吉 林					
黑龙江	10	10			
上 海	259	259	30		
江 苏	14399	13992	6117	407	80
浙 江	1307	1307	220		
安 徽	311	311	2920		
福 建	261	261			
江 西	173	173			
山 东	5002	4994	478	8	2720
河 南					
湖 北	63	45	15	18	
湖 南	379	375	23	4	2
广 东					
广 西	21	21			
海 南					
重 庆	1583	1479	28	104	
四 川	53	33	23	20	
贵 州					
云 南	129	125		4	
西 藏					
陕 西	99	70	13	29	6
甘 肃					
青 海	36	36			
宁 夏	229	229			
新 疆	18	18			

单位：人、人次、个、平方米

本年收养照料人天数	老年人活动人次数	社区服务志愿者组织数	注册社区志愿者人数	城镇便民、利民服务网点数	机构建筑面积
2773790	**5712652**	**61215**	**738027**	**134844**	**22507452**
226498	1639338	2946	208440	6028	1138382
		751		3188	178218
14525	160	191		187	236427
38020	63560	176		1887	265114
28976	37156	141	983	1688	119717
4759	212	1446	38464	7202	591936
					34640
3650		743		3790	303953
11091	9546	372	23285	482	594022
1356947	2471425	13687	120098	41767	4377067
104210	376359	7758	6220	9123	2202007
72367	48470	834	8200	3900	507265
15641		429	10	2612	321277
26133	16725	579	35	1448	178343
659137	732559	6072	2520	16538	3153006
	132	19		184	321901
12975	29742	479	462	1093	1008320
18306	8965	1291	514	13612	367932
	781	683	109372	2205	1559448
		124		1330	70503
		1	10	19	168644
179744	184291	3690	76543	7973	660005
365	39325	5299	59213	1291	643074
		12609	360	2423	2168149
		235	82702	22	308888
					8470
356	28355	366	593	2148	403246
	24347	38	3	850	219861
90	4	8		1	51566
	1200	116		363	122085
		132		1490	223986

C-2-49续表3

地区	增加值合计	执行企业会计制度单位财务指标					执行行政	
		固定资产原价	营业收入	费用合计	营业利润	企业单位增加值	固定资产原价	上年结转和结余
全　国	**400785.4**	**83481.5**	**1948.3**	**893.0**	**95.7**	**1808.6**	**544264.2**	**30282.2**
中央级								
北　京	8671.1	167.6	25.0	258.0	-29.3	176.6	8573.9	214.2
天　津	3628.8	194.0					4384.2	852.0
河　北	4737.8						9925.8	58.0
山　西	1980.6						9358.0	86.0
内蒙古	3741.2	516.5	662.8	14.0		296.0	3466.9	218.0
辽　宁	6016.2	250.1				5.0	6177.3	13.0
吉　林	377.6						12.0	10.0
黑龙江	2525.7	210.0					1589.3	0.3
上　海	10607.5						1076.6	44.6
江　苏	80741.0	8.0	4.0				122420.8	176.2
浙　江	52372.2	12991.0	25.0	21.0		57.8	65193.6	13100.6
安　徽	11646.6	165.0	8.0			21.0	31498.6	2614.4
福　建	3660.4	809.0	290.0	290.0			12008.8	17.8
江　西	2285.0	3681.4					840.7	
山　东	89949.8						1454.7	
河　南	1713.4	165.4	162.9	129.1		141.8	1526.3	
湖　北	23097.9	502.0	200.0	75.0		101.0	58047.4	136.0
湖　南	6998.8	30.0	50.0	20.0	20.0	20.0	4729.7	1.8
广　东	19470.6	35462.1	377.8		104.0	788.5	51912.1	926.2
广　西	676.8	15.0					790.9	4.5
海　南	1527.9	1617.0	5.0			124.2	10041.5	1.0
重　庆	8591.0	23342.7					24724.0	66.4
四　川	6845.7		53.2	36.7		26.6	21175.4	2385.5
贵　州	29271.6	1011.4	81.0	8.8		-5.1	22269.4	1637.5
云　南	5508.1	238.2	3.0		1.0	2.0	34300.2	7000.7
西　藏	646.1						3182.9	595.0
陕　西	4791.5	3.0					21847.2	33.0
甘　肃	2101.3	466.1		4.5		1.0	2751.5	
青　海	125.6	507.0					1600.0	
宁　夏	920.4	214.0				2.5	1636.0	
新　疆	5557.5	915.0	0.6	35.9		49.7	5748.5	89.5

单位：万元

事业单位会计制度财务指标				执行民间非营利组织单位会计制度财务指标				
本年收入合计	本年支出合计	收支结余	行政事业单位增加值	固定资产原价	上年结余	本年收入合计	本年费用合计	社会组织增加值
392970.7	**373064.5**	**1145.0**	**228762.5**	**701619.1**	**2525.5**	**258182.6**	**279515.9**	**170214.3**
9429.1	10051.3		8494.5		4.0			
1930.2	1981.2		2018.4	1987.6	82.0	2534.1	2711.7	1610.4
5494.5	5350.9		4638.3	3809.0		285.0	311.4	99.5
481.2	484.1		606.2	3498.7	13.0	1521.9	3170.8	1374.4
4618.4	4644.1	191.5	3420.5	132.0		95.0	109.0	24.7
4728.6	5447.7		3074.7	3371.1	57.9	5670.1	6767.2	2936.5
170.8	218.8		107.3	719.0		2160.0	860.7	270.3
1691.2	2803.5		2241.5	1033.2		519.4	308.2	284.2
10785.8	10179.7		6132.4	4887.8	113.0	6973.7	7407.7	4475.1
58012.4	99867.8		56286.4	115657.4	19.4	64650.8	60913.3	24454.6
148831.5	91983.8	294.7	46285.2	52308.8	132.3	14415.6	13964.3	6029.2
14942.3	16124.3		9755.3	9895.8		4875.8	5036.6	1870.3
4466.2	3639.8	2.5	2162.5	9245.6	10.7	2548.4	3732.6	1497.9
746.6	655.0		349.3	3615.9		2451.6	2747.8	1935.7
2749.0	2750.0		1543.4	135482.3	222.9	116726.7	116520.5	88406.4
2369.4	2351.3		1412.2	31.3		198.7	268.9	159.4
27355.1	26067.1	28.0	20990.1	4870.0		1979.0	3110.2	2006.8
9478.2	8646.9		5633.7	1570.2		4723.4	4640.7	1345.1
27763.6	27301.0		14575.6	33402.4	686.5	291.3	6702.1	4106.5
236.0	328.0		320.0	3717.9		79.2	401.1	356.8
1597.8	1749.8		1359.7	350.8		665.0	665.0	44.0
8171.0	8167.8	69.2	6473.8	16726.0		4727.7	4388.7	2117.2
12019.1	8933.9		5330.9	2977.0		3837.6	2790.7	1488.2
9835.4	8690.1		8857.8	73913.3	1147.8	14700.8	27335.0	20418.9
5274.9	4687.9	559.0	4538.8	211689.4	3.0	4.5	1257.5	967.3
770.0	702.1		646.1	50.0				
6852.6	6662.1		4791.5					
1129.4	1183.2	0.1	956.7	2039.6	33.0	780.6	1740.2	1143.6
1.0	1.0		64.0	3747.0		89.0	155.4	61.6
188.7	219.7		188.2	879.0		677.7	1498.6	729.7
10850.7	11190.6		5507.8	11.0				

C-2-50 其他养老等

地区	单位数	农村社区服务机构	可以为居民提供便民办事服务的机构	可以为居民提供活动场所的机构	可以为居民提供养老等服务的机构
全　国	**123658**	**51265**	**53393**	**41995**	**31856**
中央级					
北　京	3942	1234	2998	888	
天　津	231	27	168	62	
河　北	23128	19670	390	5573	17129
山　西	323	40	143	136	27
内蒙古	485		304	98	61
辽　宁	1048	145	689	36	392
吉　林					
黑龙江	326		275	28	8
上　海	321	11	263	24	1
江　苏	7166	2080	3347	2603	960
浙　江	11253	2596	5943	3497	391
安　徽	1764	317	1224	276	5
福　建	690	97	218	22	434
江　西	1712	74	941	638	
山　东	12645	4845	11688	6417	1669
河　南	1527	213	614	567	30
湖　北	3452	952	1809	1151	24
湖　南	6074	467	4162	2646	193
广　东	30329	7270	12965	15556	1275
广　西	6956	6408	143	376	6258
海　南	98	98	98		
重　庆	2557	1134	918	525	1000
四　川	758	31	470	177	56
贵　州	3945	1492	3049	161	181
云　南	13	4	8	1	4
西　藏					
陕　西	325	60	145	139	19
甘　肃	2409	1996	311	369	1720
青　海					
宁　夏	32		2		13
新　疆	149	4	108	29	6

社区服务机构

单位：个、人、人次

农村	可以为居民提供便民信息服务的机构	年末职工人数	#女性	受教育程度	
				大学专科人数	大学本科及以上人数
27232	**19278**	**283304**	**96402**	**57197**	**24317**
	58	4205	1836	1143	535
	17	617	166	58	19
15994	36	34375	11229	1004	135
25	17	977	515	268	68
	22	1874	991	615	409
116	95	5489	2601	852	431
	15	1290	700	418	145
	33	3285	1847	124	61
452	1267	26845	7570	5676	3653
222	1692	17569	6679	4335	1740
	269	5357	2403	1581	256
75	18	2406	911	561	75
	133	5372	2256	544	64
1441	6836	35355	11546	11378	4292
	318	4387	2239	1877	464
15	468	8229	3783	1959	602
105	2625	12389	5149	2785	1348
393	4400	73635	23152	12338	7983
5843	181	9949	2233	456	249
		282	94	48	1
955	114	3171	957	581	140
4	55	3053	1256	536	54
105	554	16905	4643	7267	1153
2		57	24	4	5
	22	919	272	63	
1480	10	4799	1238	621	410
	17	23	6	9	
5	6	490	106	96	25

C-2-50续表1

地区	职业资格水平		年龄结构			
	助理社会工作师人数	社会工作师人数	35岁及以下人数	36岁至45岁人数	46岁至55岁人数	56岁及以上人数
全　国	**2554**	**754**	**88624**	**108844**	**63278**	**22558**
中央级						
北　京	10	5	1151	1554	1228	272
天　津		2	126	241	205	45
河　北	3	5	7610	12034	10206	4525
山　西	24	5	257	419	251	50
内蒙古	3	1	851	675	328	20
辽　宁			1746	2418	1251	74
吉　林						
黑龙江	2		348	853	80	9
上　海	22		331	1349	1441	164
江　苏	126	7	11247	8852	5716	1030
浙　江	398	134	6066	6596	4353	554
安　徽	17	10	1846	2366	1009	136
福　建	17		757	832	434	383
江　西		1	1301	1796	1072	1203
山　东	92	37	13204	13517	6695	1939
河　南	39	26	1303	2346	632	106
湖　北	1	4	3112	3869	1081	167
湖　南	194	27	2990	4136	4449	814
广　东	1515	427	24868	28842	13815	6110
广　西	33	15	883	2611	3898	2557
海　南			32	235	15	
重　庆	20	5	597	1456	658	460
四　川		6	961	1036	916	140
贵　州	11	1	4880	8980	1688	1357
云　南		12	22	15	10	10
西　藏						
陕　西		8	195	296	423	5
甘　肃	3	8	1749	1370	1356	324
青　海						
宁　夏			3	13	4	3
新　疆	24	8	188	137	64	101

单位：个、人次、张、人 、时

志愿服务		床位数合计	日间照料床位数		住宿收养床位数	
志愿者服务人次数	志愿服务时间			农村		农村
84308	**170887.5**	**396130**	**210489**	**160755**	**185641**	**152667**
		688	688	105		
12800	16855.0	179996	114717	99966	65279	59668
125	625.0	771	767	701	4	
580	1980.0	1487	1337		150	
52		2642	2324	351	318	187
2736	10860.0	165	131		34	
5297	6688.0	130	84	2	46	46
9033	9575.0	15338	10623	2381	4715	2093
545	1623.0	2442	1590	1040	852	600
100	280.0	226	146	13	80	
		10442	2796	372	7646	531
40	87.0	136	136			
44751	108218.5	48741	31849	28128	16892	14599
		549	477	82	72	
820	1767.0	618	390	65	228	8
410	1026.0	2700	1479	307	1221	685
11		17434	5125	822	12309	4256
		69437	10274	10224	59163	56091
65	93.0	11205	1801	1321	9404	9028
		1822	1198	169	624	24
6287	9767.0	4279	2708	422	1571	533
		143	29	5	114	89
3	24.0	1304	704	160	600	60
653	1419.0	23327	19037	14119	4290	4169
		38	38			
		70	41		29	

C-2-50续表2

地区	年末收养人数合计	日间照料人数	农村	住宿收养人数	农村
全国	**53365**	**22760**	**14850**	**30605**	**33670**
中央级					
北京					
天津					
河北	18771	10489	8045	8282	6046
山西					
内蒙古	367	367	18		
辽宁	204	196	80	8	
吉林					
黑龙江	75	75			
上海					
江苏	1310	1097	728	213	211
浙江	292			292	282
安徽					
福建	5	5			
江西					
山东	10031	6191	3557	3840	3371
河南					
湖北	72	6	4	66	4
湖南	704	285	179	419	395
广东	2925	1533	2	1392	2
广西	12184	1229	1181	10955	18231
海南					
重庆	5626	488	371	5138	5128
四川	12	12			
贵州					
云南					
西藏					
陕西					
甘肃	779	779	685		
青海					
宁夏	8	8			
新疆					

单位：人、人次、个、平方米

本年收养照料人天数	老年人活动人次数	社区服务志愿者组织数	注册社区志愿者人数	城镇便民、利民服务网点数	机构建筑面积
9103439	**1591025**	**2901**	**148426**	**15823**	**19725060**
					353208
					53554
3390940	360400	38	358	350	4342484
					46894
32973	21535	46	3639	164	131114
32090				447	117906
26540		18		254	40093
		29	1616		43189
153765	22266	104	7026	2113	1091987
78040	15387	18			1421262
		1		815	212281
					87211
		19		41	264144
1787456	256608	628	5405	2293	3753059
				86	259447
220	617	1633		182	416693
87696	527	4	115	1133	710409
	16636	82	129966	2498	3926510
2275353	822569	16		17	1127828
					9800
1079008	74480			139	384366
3450		265	301	3785	93205
				65	458622
					3150
				3	40927
155908				1438	310764
					4724
					20229

C-2-50续表3

地区	增加值合计	执行企业会计制度单位财务指标					执行行政	
		固定资产原价	营业收入	费用合计	营业利润	企业单位增加值	固定资产原价	上年结转和结余
全国	**192527.9**	**15456.1**	**3187.0**	**1175.4**	**30.0**	**1888.9**	**576145.5**	**11476.2**
中央级								
北京	153.4	2.0					2815.3	34.1
天津	527.7						540.0	
河北	8939.8	60.0					31989.1	383.6
山西	423.4						1104.1	
内蒙古	978.7	2.0					1148.8	
辽宁	834.8	24.0				8.0	1661.1	14.0
吉林								
黑龙江	1262.7					280.7	242.3	
上海	345.8						229.9	32.0
江苏	12299.1	300.0					47438.3	
浙江	64762.6	73.1	701.0	153.0		97.9	381554.9	7521.0
安徽	2593.1	79.1	672.0	560.0		97.2	2686.7	
福建	792.2	150.0	150.0	15.0		88.0	989.2	-0.3
江西	959.5	200.0	190.0	50.0			647.9	0.1
山东	39379.9							
河南	3643.8	925.3	690.4	225.1		460.8	2467.2	262.0
湖北	6158.2	189.0	8.8	14.4		4.7	19226.2	2.0
湖南	3300.3	8.0	100.0	31.5	30.0	196.6	1498.8	16.5
广东	16236.6	11177.0	674.8	126.4		451.9	16952.5	3041.2
广西	5361.4	65.0					38649.6	
海南	169.2							
重庆	2582.6	1073.5					7055.5	7.0
四川	1476.8	970.0				34.0	1421.8	38.9
贵州	17188.6	142.1				16.0	9009.3	102.1
云南	56.7						184.0	
西藏								
陕西	578.7						2715.0	
甘肃	1167.9	12.0					3466.5	22.0
青海								
宁夏	4.0	3.0						
新疆	350.4	1.0				153.2	451.5	

单位：万元

事业单位会计制度财务指标				执行民间非营利组织单位会计制度财务指标				
本年收入合计	本年支出合计	收支结余	行政事业单位增加值	固定资产原价	上年结余	本年收入合计	本年费用合计	社会组织增加值
374645.4	**341577.4**	**52.1**	**108687.9**	**290767.2**	**9429.0**	**127251.6**	**139047.5**	**81951.1**
564.6	437.0		152.4	20.0			1.0	1.0
405.0	405.0		426.6	287.0		406.0	133.1	101.1
190717.4	191449.4		3380.6	27542.0	848.7	5516.4	7564.5	5559.2
250.0	251.0		288.2	289.0		50.5	248.1	135.2
993.3	1194.3		903.1	1352.0		172.2	173.4	75.6
708.3	805.2		440.6	410.4	4.7	282.7	513.0	386.2
1082.2	1013.1		943.5	127.0		28.0	81.5	38.5
1446.2	1318.9	-1.0	204.3	1447.8	15.2	2944.3	216.2	141.5
6219.1	5760.8		6230.4	43161.0	21.0	26144.8	19786.7	6068.7
121778.2	92502.8	4.5	59728.5	59416.5	29.0	13008.5	17065.1	4936.2
1855.0	2009.0		971.5	14251.3	180.0	2456.4	2541.8	1524.4
474.9	462.5	2.4	274.1	947.0	6.6	897.8	893.4	430.1
414.2	414.2		50.7	3518.8	2.0	2613.9	3097.9	908.8
				59626.8	209.6	56177.7	55638.3	39379.9
4852.5	1103.9	1.2	2260.1	989.1	394.1	318.0	1270.4	922.9
5231.4	4685.8	45.0	4708.7	3618.0	0.1	646.0	1878.7	1444.8
4525.0	4491.7		2554.4	3984.8	701.1	2109.9	2687.2	549.3
18986.0	18966.9		8822.8	29698.2	3162.6	4378.5	9978.4	6961.9
2433.7	2684.6		3770.0	16639.3		419.2	2072.7	1591.4
	225.6		169.2					
2152.7	2228.9		1485.1	5253.9	3.0	1744.8	1784.6	1097.5
808.5	1267.5		1171.5	4011.6		229.7	329.8	271.3
7051.7	6325.0		8366.1	8858.2	3812.1	6403.2	10255.8	8806.5
49.4	49.4		56.7	120.0				
699.1	691.1		578.7					
753.8	636.6		561.8	5197.5	39.2	303.1	809.9	606.1
	4.0		4.0					
193.2	193.2		184.2				26.0	13.0

C-2-51 自然灾害损失

地 区	人口受灾情况				
	受灾人口	死亡人口	失踪人口	紧急转移安置人口	其他需紧急生活救助人口
合 计	**38818.7**	**1851**	**433**	**1215.0**	**2643.1**
北 京	21.1	1		0.2	
天 津	8.6				
河 北	1709.6	19		1.7	7.8
山 西	1465.9	49	1	9.6	4.7
内蒙古	565.6	73	2	9.3	34.8
辽 宁	322	81	87	22.4	0.4
吉 林	675.4	22	1	33.7	4.3
黑龙江	666.9	23		32.6	1.8
上 海	12.1	3		1.0	
江 苏	590.7	11		0.9	2.2
浙 江	1702.2	20	3	162.4	75.6
安 徽	2855.9	35	1	30.3	158.7
福 建	404.2	44	1	106.5	5.3
江 西	1160.3	34	1	14.6	199.0
山 东	1157.5	3		2.8	0.2
河 南	2587.8	19	1	1.2	14.3
湖 北	2353.9	46		18.7	279.9
湖 南	3344	44	6	40.9	404.6
广 东	2464	175	14	232.3	50.3
广 西	764.8	90	6	30.5	35.2
海 南	366.3	38	52	46.3	1.4
重 庆	1085.2	26	4	22.4	150.3
四 川	4555.5	372	203	180.4	428.2
贵 州	2278.1	65	1	12.5	201.6
云 南	1984.2	164	15	7.8	284.5
西 藏	151.5	90	24	17.8	3.5
陕 西	1471.9	88	2	90.6	60.1
甘 肃	1540.2	157	8	77.0	147.9
青 海	167.5	36		2.5	7.1
宁 夏	188.7	9		2.1	63.0
新 疆	153.1	12		3.2	11.5
兵 团	44	2		0.8	4.9

注：受灾人口、死亡人口、失踪人口和直接经济损失含森林、海洋等灾害造成受灾人口0.3万人次、死亡人口59人、失踪人口6人、直接经济损失4.7亿元。

情况总表

单位:万人次、人、千公顷、万间、亿元

农作物受灾情况			损失情况			
受灾面积	成灾面积	绝收面积	倒塌房屋	严重损坏房屋	一般损坏房屋	直接经济损失
31349.8	**14303.1**	**3844.4**	**87.5**	**226.9**	**543.4**	**5808.4**
26.9	10.9	3.7				4.8
7.8	1.5	0.8				1.0
1106.5	528.3	94.5	0.5	1.6	2.5	113.3
1592.4	577.9	132.4	3.8	6.7	21.1	146.9
1733.1	858.3	232.6	1.0	5.0	10.8	128.9
450.5	271.3	82.1	1.1	1.4	3.0	125.2
623.2	221.4	67.5	1.8	11.3	24.9	133.3
2734.1	1896.1	828.8	6.6	10.3	11.0	325.2
28.0	8.5	1.6			0.3	3.7
487.1	193.4	25.1	0.1	0.2	0.7	32.7
1326.9	586.6	142.5	0.6	0.5	7.9	695.9
1769.7	509.7	138.2	1.1	2.1	3.6	206.4
276.8	147.7	24.3	0.7	0.9	15.5	120.8
1049.1	606.2	84.8	0.9	0.9	7.3	90.2
1461.7	530.7	145.1	1.3	1.4	4.1	89.7
1179.9	358.8	93.7	0.6	0.7	1.6	109.6
2487.9	954.3	141.3	1.4	1.8	4.4	145.0
3047.2	1550.5	496.5	2.7	4.4	21.0	282.7
1134.5	451.0	119.2	6.7	8.9	10.8	489.8
694.4	178.7	20.1	3.1	3.0	14.5	63.1
164.7	93.1	57.4	0.1	0.2	0.7	37.5
455.3	168.4	38.1	0.9	1.8	8.8	51.1
1602.9	537.9	102.6	15.1	58.6	157.2	1202.6
1522.4	841.5	309.7	2.4	7.9	39.2	129.0
1231.1	558.3	161.7	1.2	11.6	42.5	154.2
22.1	8.9	4.0	0.9	10.1	17.9	42.0
813.4	386.7	90.7	7.5	16.3	27.6	231.7
1282.9	655.4	66.3	22.6	53.5	72.5	542.7
171.2	60.1	8.3	0.1	0.2	1.1	13.6
301.3	160.4	41.9	1.4	1.9	3.0	15.4
355.8	265.2	58.2	0.9	2.8	7.3	44.0
209.0	125.4	30.7	0.4	0.9	0.6	36.4

C−2−52 旱灾

地　区	人口受灾情况		
	受灾人口	需生活救助人口	饮水困难人口
全　国	**16115.8**	**2183.9**	**3046.8**
北　京			
天　津			
河　北	119.8		1.1
山　西	547.1	3.9	14.6
内蒙古	228.3	15.8	25.3
辽　宁	14.9	0.2	
吉　林			
黑龙江			
上　海			
江　苏	283.4	0.5	
浙　江	397.5	72.6	109.9
安　徽	1711.6	152.6	154.4
福　建	26.9		3
江　西	736.7	188.3	184.8
山　东	19		
河　南	1623.2	12.3	34.5
湖　北	1579.5	270.5	367
湖　南	1849.4	373.9	445.7
广　东	0.8		0.8
广　西	47.3	8.2	8.4
海　南			
重　庆	470.1	135.3	166.9
四　川	2014.5	320.1	534.6
贵　州	1623.1	131.2	414.8
云　南	1244.9	269.8	359.6
西　藏	19.3		
陕　西	806.2	39.8	54.5
甘　肃	548.9	130.1	115.4
青　海	65.3	3	0.6
宁　夏	112.4	55.1	47.7
新　疆	24.3	0.4	3.2
兵　团	1.4	0.3	

损失情况

单位:万人次、千公顷、万头、亿元

农作物受灾情况			损失情况	
受灾面积	成灾面积	绝收面积	饮水困难大牲畜	直接经济损失
14100.4	**5851.9**	**1416.1**	**1018**	**905.3**
250.3	138.9	7.4	0.3	2.7
1001.7	257.9	33.9	3.9	24.2
582.6	172.5	24.3	113.7	18.2
23.9	13.5	4.3		1.6
223.1	117.3	11.7		10.9
635.6	247.1	58.4	4.2	78.1
1165.0	234.3	117.7	2.6	83.8
31.9	15.8	0.8	0.1	1.1
576.1	334.2	68.7	25.9	39.2
206.7				1.2
848.1	230.7	72.0	4.9	62.9
1861.9	738.5	110.0	75.1	100.6
2075.9	1134.6	424.7	193.8	170.3
8.4	4.9	0.4		0.1
52.1	36.1	5.6	1.3	2.7
309.1	105.1	26.5	58.1	18.1
800.4	199.4	31.9	200.2	79.3
1175.0	693.3	271.4	59.3	92.9
807.4	369.7	97.7	165.3	66.8
				0.2
400.0	200.0	10.0	3.1	29
694.9	371.5	19.2	48.2	10.1
41.7	24.4		5.8	2.6
194.0	113.2	10.6	52.2	3.4
115.5	91.3	3.7		4.4
19.1	7.7	5.2		0.9

C-2-53 风雹灾害

地　区	人口受灾情况				
	受灾人口	死亡人口	失踪人口	紧急转移安置人口	其他需紧急生活救助人口
合　计	**4336.6**	**246**	**6**	**34.8**	**115.7**
北　京	12.2	1			
天　津	8.6				
河　北	702	8		1.3	3.3
山　西	259.6	1		0.1	
内蒙古	128	26		0.8	6.4
辽　宁	69.7				
吉　林	53.2	3		0.7	0.2
黑龙江	41.8				0.1
上　海		1			
江　苏	179.7	9		0.4	
浙　江	12.6	3		0.4	1
安　徽	238.7	12		1.1	3.2
福　建	24.7	16		1.7	2.8
江　西	44.3	9		3	2.3
山　东	166.9	1		0.9	0.1
河　南	436.4	10		0.4	0.1
湖　北	153.6	12		1.8	2.3
湖　南	254.5	9	3	4.3	12
广　东	18.7	17		0.7	0.8
广　西	81.3	15		3.2	7
海　南	21.1	2		0.7	0.2
重　庆	118.8	10		0.6	2.4
四　川	143.8	17	2	0.7	1.9
贵　州	328.5	5		7.9	45.1
云　南	251.6	28		0.2	3.8
西　藏	17.1	13			0.1
陕　西	214.8	5	1	2.2	1.1
甘　肃	216.9	6		0.1	8.6
青　海	32.3	1		0.9	
宁　夏	16.4				1.1
新　疆	55	6		0.6	6.1
兵　团	33.8			0.1	3.7

损失情况

单位：万人次、人、千公顷、万间、亿元

农作物受灾情况			损失情况			
受灾面积	成灾面积	绝收面积	倒塌房屋	严重损坏房屋	一般损坏房屋	直接经济损失
3387.3	**1682.3**	**412.4**	**5.9**	**17.8**	**113.6**	**456.2**
17.1	7.2	3.4				3
7.8	1.5	0.8				1
386.3	160.2	29.1	0.2	0.5	1	48.1
161.4	129.3	20.5	0.2	0.4	0.9	29.6
469.6	322.1	76.8	0.3	0.6	0.4	31.6
90.5	54.5	19.7			0.2	8.6
196	10.7	5.5	0.1	0.3	0.6	10.7
66.2	44.1	13.1		0.3	0.7	9.4
164.4	50.0	6.3	0.1	0.2	0.7	8.4
3.1	2.2	0.6			0.5	2.7
38.8	10.0	4.3	0.3	0.5	2.1	15.9
20	17.3	3.5			8.4	5.9
24.5	20.1	1.4	0.1	0.5	5.8	5.8
111.6	11.8	1.1	0.1	0.2	2	15.2
198.7	101.2	20.7	0.3	0.4	1	28.5
70	17.7	6.6	0.2	0.4	3	10.2
180.8	101.4	17.1	0.5	1.6	16	21.4
6.1	3.5	1.5		0.1	3.2	9.8
48.7	19.5	6.5	0.1	0.7	10.2	8.3
5.3	3.0	0.4		0.1	0.3	2.7
19.3	4.7	1.5	0.2	0.7	6.2	5.7
62.4	21.2	5.2	0.3	1.1	6.4	9.1
169.2	77.1	23.9	2.1	7.1	35.1	22.3
185.2	70.0	37	0.1	0.7	4.7	25.6
7.8	4.0	2.7				0.8
115.5	39.1	6.6	0.5	0.3	1.7	31.1
200.9	108.3	19.3	0.2	0.7	1.8	35.2
30.8	21.4	5.3			0.1	5
8.3	4.7	1.6			0.4	2.5
174.1	141.8	47.5		0.2	0.1	17
146.9	102.7	22.9		0.2	0.1	25.1

C-2-54 台风灾害

地区	人口受灾情况				
	受灾人口	死亡人口	失踪人口	紧急转移安置人口	其他需紧急生活救助人口
合计	**4922.2**	**179**	**63**	**555.2**	**45.1**
北京					
天津					
河北					
山西					
内蒙古					
辽宁					
吉林					
黑龙江					
上海	12.1	2		1	
江苏	59			0.2	
浙江	1234.7	9	1	160.9	1.9
安徽	5.3			5.1	
福建	313.2	5	1	97	1.4
江西	37.5	2		1.7	0.4
山东					
河南					
湖北					
湖南	321.6	13	1	19.5	1.3
广东	2147.7	90	5	204.4	33
广西	445.9	31	5	19.8	5.9
海南	345.2	27	50	45.6	1.2
重庆					
四川					
贵州					
云南					
西藏					
陕西					
甘肃					
青海					
宁夏					
新疆					
兵团					

损失情况

单位:万人次、人、千公顷、万间、亿元

农作物受灾情况			损失情况			
受灾面积	成灾面积	绝收面积	倒塌房屋	严重损坏房屋	一般损坏房屋	直接经济损失
2670.1	**987.3**	**289.5**	**9.1**	**11.9**	**23.5**	**1260.3**
28	8.5	1.6			0.3	3.7
31.9	6.9					3
612.9	302.9	79.5	0.6	0.5	7.3	609
						0.1
199.7	99.4	17.4	0.5	0.6	6.6	103.6
24.6	10.2	4	0.1		0.1	5.4
176.1	39.9	19.1	0.7	0.7	0.8	38.7
984.1	338.5	104.5	4.6	8.2	4.8	421.8
453.4	90.9	6.4	2.5	1.8	3.2	40.2
159.4	90.1	57	0.1	0.1	0.4	34.8

C-2-55 地震灾害

地 区	人口受灾情况				
	受灾人口	死亡人口	失踪人口	紧急转移安置人口	其他需紧急生活救助人口
合 计	**530.4**	**294**		**154.8**	**54.7**
北 京					
天 津					
河 北					
山 西					
内蒙古	6.2			1.9	
辽 宁					
吉 林	25.9			6.8	
黑龙江					
上 海					
江 苏					
浙 江					
安 徽					
福 建	0.4			0.1	
江 西					
山 东					
河 南					
湖 北					
湖 南					
广 东					
广 西	0.8			0.5	0.4
海 南					
重 庆	2.5				
四 川	233.9	196		86.6	48.5
贵 州					
云 南	42.6	3		6.3	3.2
西 藏	31.5			7.2	
陕 西					
甘 肃	179.1	95		44.1	2.2
青 海	2.5			0.7	
宁 夏					
新 疆	4			0.4	0.1
兵 团	1			0.2	0.3

损失情况

单位：万人次、人、千公顷、万间、亿元

农作物受灾情况			损失情况			
受灾面积	成灾面积	绝收面积	倒塌房屋	严重损坏房屋	一般损坏房屋	直接经济损失
115.1	**37.7**	**6.3**	**22.4**	**107.7**	**226.3**	**1037.7**
			0.1	1.8	4.4	15.6
			0.1	5.8	14.7	20.2
				0.1	0.1	0.4
					0.2	0.7
					0.4	0.3
109.5	34.7	5.9	5	41.7	108.3	683.1
			0.6	10.1	34.1	27.9
			0.6	6.9	11.9	30.2
5.6	3.0	0.4	15.9	40.3	49.4	254.1
				0.1	0.7	
				0.8	1.7	3.1
			0.1	0.1	0.4	2.1

C-2-56 低温冷冻和

地区	人口受灾情况				
	受灾人口	死亡人口	失踪人口	紧急转移安置人口	其他需紧急生活救助人口
合　计	**2324.9**	**20**		**8.4**	**49.5**
北　京					
天　津					
河　北	277.5				1.2
山　西	314.9				0.3
内蒙古	38.9	1			0.1
辽　宁					
吉　林	0.3				
黑龙江	36.2	4			0.1
上　海					
江　苏	57.7	2		0.3	1.7
浙　江	22.5			0.1	
安　徽	319.8			0.1	1
福　建	3.6				
江　西	35.9			0.1	1.6
山　东	167.7				
河　南	43.6				
湖　北	65.8			0.2	2.2
湖　南	154.8			0.9	4.7
广　东					
广　西	29.3				4.9
海　南					
重　庆	55.7				2.2
四　川	49.6	5			6.6
贵　州	57.8			0.3	6.7
云　南	174.7				2.2
西　藏	35.4	8		6.4	3.3
陕　西	130.3				4.8
甘　肃	173.1				0.1
青　海	58.8				4
宁　夏	14.1				1.2
新　疆	4.1				0.5
兵　团	2.8				0.1

雪灾损失情况

单位:万人次、人、千公顷、万间、亿元

农作物受灾情况			损失情况			
受灾面积	成灾面积	绝收面积	倒塌房屋	严重损坏房屋	一般损坏房屋	直接经济损失
2320.1	**885.3**	**180.7**	**0.31**	**0.6**	**1**	**260.4**
158.6	31.5	16.1				30.7
284.2	104.0	59.2				55.3
131.8	69.7	0.4				2.9
0.1	0.1	0.1				0.8
13.9	2.0	0.6		0.1	0.1	2.1
56.0	15.0	5.8				9.8
46.6	20.0	2.0				1.3
248.8	70.6	4.9	0.1	0.1	0.1	41.3
7.7	1.9	0.3				0.4
132.1	79.7	3.1				1.4
242.9	60.0	2.3				13.8
71.8	22.9	0.8				1.1
100.3	40.5	2.2		0.1	0.1	1.9
167.3	114.5	8.3	0.2	0.2	0.3	5.4
66.7	25.1	0.7				1.5
28.3	12.0	1.2				1.2
25.5	9.7	2.4				1.5
54.9	23.4	1.1			0.1	1
112.4	49.3	10.1				3.9
1.7	1.0	0.1	0.01	0.1	0.3	5
98.9	46.9	25.1				41.9
102.9	25.9	5.0				25.6
83.2	13.1	2.6				4.1
44.7	30.0	24.0				4.5
22.5	11.7	1.3				0.6
16.3	4.8	1.0				1.4

C-2-57 洪涝、滑坡和

地区	人口受灾情况				
	受灾人口	死亡人口	失踪人口	紧急转移安置人口	其他需紧急生活救助人口
合计	**10588.5**	**1053**	**358**	**461.8**	**194.2**
北京	8.9			0.2	
天津					
河北	610.3	9		0.4	3.3
山西	344.3	46	1	9.5	0.5
内蒙古	164.2	46	2	6.6	12.5
辽宁	237.4	81	87	22.4	0.2
吉林	596	19	1	26.2	4.1
黑龙江	588.9	19		32.6	1.6
上海					
江苏	10.9				
浙江	34.9	3		1.0	0.1
安徽	580.5	23	1	24.0	1.9
福建	35.4	14		7.7	1.1
江西	305.9	22	1	9.8	6.4
山东	803.9	2		1.9	0.1
河南	484.6	9	1	0.8	1.9
湖北	555	32		16.7	4.9
湖南	763.7	21	2	16.2	12.7
广东	296.8	67	7	27.2	16.5
广西	160.2	42	1	7.0	8.8
海南					
重庆	438.1	14	4	21.8	10.4
四川	2113.7	148	201	93.1	51.1
贵州	268.7	58	1	4.3	18.6
云南	270.1	133	15	1.3	5.5
西藏	48.2	69	24	4.2	0.1
陕西	320.6	68	1	88.4	14.4
甘肃	422.2	56	8	32.8	6.9
青海	8.6	35		0.9	0.1
宁夏	45.8	9		2.1	5.6
新疆	65.7	6		2.2	4.4
兵团	5	2		0.5	0.5

泥石流灾害损失情况

单位:万人次、人、千公顷、万间、亿元

农作物受灾情况			损失情况			
受灾面积	成灾面积	绝收面积	倒塌房屋	严重损坏房屋	一般损坏房屋	直接经济损失
8756.8	**4858.6**	**1539.4**	**49.8**	**88.9**	**179**	**1883.8**
9.8	3.7	0.3				1.8
311.3	197.7	41.9	0.3	1.1	1.5	31.8
145.1	86.7	18.8	3.6	6.3	20.2	37.8
549.1	294.0	131.1	0.6	2.6	6.0	60.6
336.1	203.3	58.1	1.1	1.4	2.8	111.8
427.1	210.6	61.9	1.6	5.2	9.6	101.6
2654.0	1850.0	815.1	6.6	9.9	10.2	313.7
11.7	4.2	1.3				0.5
28.7	14.4	2.0			0.1	4.8
317.1	194.8	11.3	0.7	1.5	1.4	65.3
17.5	13.3	2.3	0.2	0.2	0.4	9.4
291.8	162.0	7.6	0.7	0.4	1.4	38.4
900.5	458.9	141.7	1.2	1.2	2.1	58.1
61.3	4.0	0.2	0.3	0.3	0.6	17.1
455.7	157.6	22.5	1.2	1.3	1.3	32.3
447.1	160.1	27.3	1.3	1.9	3.9	46.9
135.9	104.1	12.8	2.1	0.6	2.8	58.1
73.5	7.1	0.9	0.5	0.5	0.9	9.7
98.6	46.6	8.9	0.7	1.1	2.2	25.8
605.1	272.9	57.2	9.8	15.8	42.5	429.6
123.3	47.7	13.3	0.3	0.8	4.0	12.8
126.1	69.3	16.9	0.5	0.8	3.7	30.0
12.6	3.9	1.2	0.3	3.1	5.7	5.8
199.0	100.7	49.0	7.0	16.0	25.9	129.7
278.6	146.7	22.4	6.5	12.5	21.3	217.7
15.5	1.2	0.4	0.1	0.1	0.3	1.9
54.3	12.5	5.7	1.4	1.9	2.6	5.0
43.7	20.4	5.7	0.9	1.8	5.5	18.9
26.7	10.2	1.6	0.3	0.6	0.1	6.9

C-3-1 成员组

地 区	单位数	民政登记	未登记	年末职工人数	#女性	受教育程度	
						大学专科人数	大学本科及以上人数
全 国	**1230412**	**547245**	**683167**	**9172941**	**2641665**	**1573451**	**925569**
中央级	2190	2190		30769	13241	818	22348
北 京	15357	8560	6797	153535	64840	39268	56430
天 津	9777	4516	5261	64164	28601	18855	19093
河 北	68895	16530	52365	433881	97876	54575	33678
山 西	42014	11611	30403	256623	65112	48441	23946
内蒙古	24092	10685	13407	132113	41986	33539	11385
辽 宁	35122	19494	15628	284660	85136	55098	39293
吉 林	20431	9193	11238	140487	32017	24159	6016
黑龙江	24440	12672	11768	227895	83578	42787	13922
上 海	17260	11626	5634	185022	52546	47374	16988
江 苏	77589	56234	21355	536741	159341	118231	81103
浙 江	68994	36426	32568	475152	143536	110256	60128
安 徽	38812	20705	18107	285647	77960	57602	26659
福 建	36094	19372	16722	322595	66945	30957	23104
江 西	33626	13375	20251	260214	73906	26241	8652
山 东	120261	38976	81285	654972	168880	153679	90312
河 南	74861	23577	51284	410459	108144	73868	36125
湖 北	55438	25778	29660	382971	132777	82035	26741
湖 南	68551	21663	46888	382149	117729	70818	30312
广 东	67146	41317	25829	625638	254684	128298	85132
广 西	33518	17370	16148	388354	78414	43182	27275
海 南	7389	4338	3051	54655	19513	7019	5779
重 庆	24193	13154	11039	186039	69169	38502	33805
四 川	88165	35050	53115	723118	194440	103541	69473
贵 州	27110	8295	18815	235782	53166	21662	9995
云 南	31163	16954	14209	449515	146605	43528	22719
西 藏	6027	589	5438	34245	10615	828	232
陕 西	46183	17360	28823	360860	77918	31825	13050
甘 肃	30585	13335	17250	257746	54632	26691	11289
青 海	7669	3039	4630	37100	8144	2851	833
宁 夏	6747	4002	2745	47828	14695	8449	4496
新 疆	20713	9259	11454	152012	45519	28474	15256

织总表

单位：个、人、人次、时

职业资格水平		年龄结构				志愿服务	
助理社会工作师人数	社会工作师人数	35岁及以下人数	36岁至45岁人数	46岁至55岁人数	56岁及以上人数	志愿者服务人次数	志愿服务时间
26871	**12994**	**2760446**	**3536240**	**2045483**	**830772**	**3213372**	**9632281.0**
703	1439	8855	10543	6294	5077		
4157	1808	43658	49652	37147	23078	506080	1518240.0
583	122	16627	22085	17591	7861	70995	212835.0
698	760	125600	184436	98288	25557	52799	162442.0
211	125	76908	90673	62195	26847	5858	17430.0
7	6	40515	50847	29647	11104	23291	69873.0
914	401	73682	97360	63293	50325	136913	406485.0
563	118	41144	61558	29897	7888	684	2708.0
431	155	86496	84679	44208	12512	466	1405.0
1062	439	43876	81294	41388	18464	25229	75687.0
4699	1447	151498	197754	137319	50170	318550	935387.0
1638	1094	146445	182853	97221	48633	208360	623844.0
1128	314	79634	110814	69137	26062	79826	225616.0
683	314	72257	102209	90683	57446	20087	60261.0
647	125	78093	119828	48468	13825	3052	9176.0
761	306	189584	277619	144314	43455	208612	607975.0
496	150	132032	166841	84118	27468	52	178.0
368	222	138039	138345	79590	26997	3239	9699.0
414	187	117992	158539	80567	25051	135448	440533.0
2684	1789	283244	181001	118935	42458	37350	117696.0
293	484	94710	148157	103555	41932	6485	19455.0
23		18125	24219	8842	3469	300	1000.0
988	311	61765	64851	38019	21404	393150	1184276.0
1387	607	233538	270649	130867	88064	45047	135170.0
279	36	60130	104772	52390	18490	874471	2622936.0
519	86	130424	178084	97389	43618	1217	3645.0
		7513	13830	8916	3986		
82	34	86100	130388	114025	30347	8409	26355.0
153	25	51935	135861	55473	14477	16108	48094.0
84	7	8721	15928	10061	2390	13498	40494.0
47	7	10175	18284	14330	5039	3928	11778.0
169	76	51131	62287	31316	7278	13868	41608.0

C-3-1续表

地　区	增加值合计	执行企业会计制度单位财务指标					执行行政	
		固定资产原价	营业收入	费用合计	营业利润	企业单位增加值	固定资产原价	上年结转和结余
全　国	**9729128.6**	**2710492.8**	**1170139.8**	**34488.4**	**15205.5**	**157810.7**	**14992348.9**	**1142435.0**
中央级	148802.1							
北　京	547827.6	2315877.2	1127813.3	32046.6	15329.4	129289.9	419283.2	224817.4
天　津	67673.7						190944.9	19854.4
河　北	337128.6	6810.3				3.5	627934.9	16867.4
山　西	238377.8	325.0				2444.5	860462.3	3512.7
内蒙古	72649.9	586.0	40.4	8.0		4.0	101112.8	4105.3
辽　宁	271145.9	1204.5				12.5	121777.6	15933.5
吉　林	126647.3	85.7	3.0				53859.7	2316.1
黑龙江	132340.3	4646.0	2.0	0.2		95.3	157694.9	294317.0
上　海	614880.1	244632.1	40610.2	2292.6	-129.9	17383.8	850838.5	86396.8
江　苏	1201513.7		140.0	105.0			1995503.1	73919.1
浙　江	915842.5	271.6				-143.5	3377562.3	102484.6
安　徽	286835.9	20.0				2.0	371881.5	3088.6
福　建	139735.2						117042.4	5332.0
江　西	247317.2	10516.5	993.0	34.0	6.0	397.8	99860.5	562.2
山　东	1172330.3						1343699.7	15.0
河　南	150043.6	6732.0	36.0				252052.1	2849.1
湖　北	320579.4	1767.0					411866.7	3666.1
湖　南	279123.8	212.0					255930.8	7873.1
广　东	1252367.5	106981.6	437.9			8119.6	1883480.1	163827.4
广　西	105010.4	270.5					159474.9	722.8
海　南	28056.9	20.5					27262.0	1083.5
重　庆	167168.8	94.0					147013.2	4933.1
四　川	318414.2	3706.4				99.0	251429.1	18013.1
贵　州	84553.6	7.5					35474.4	4913.0
云　南	217612.9	1279.6		1.0		19.0	397460.0	72213.4
西　藏	1963.8						23567.3	0.2
陕　西	124344.9						167519.5	916.1
甘　肃	67980.8	29.5					142655.2	3183.7
青　海	7878.6	8.0					2325.1	
宁　夏	22060.2	1339.5				27.5	42804.6	660.4
新　疆	60921.2	3069.8	64.0	1.0		56.0	102575.6	4057.9

单位：万元

事业单位会计制度财务指标				执行民间非营利组织单位会计制度财务指标				
本年收入合计	本年支出合计	收支结余	行政事业单位增加值	固定资产原价	上年结余	本年收入合计	本年费用合计	社会组织增加值
7378294.0	**7024732.7**	**13360.7**	**3570349.5**	**16954149.3**	**5928217.6**	**20766745.4**	**17517153.6**	**6000968.4**
				675289.8		3630930.1	2959197.2	148802.1
174006.7	242169.1	697.7	130975.5	1035071.1	1319475.5	1439173.1	1238546.0	287562.2
150831.9	150941.3		35108.8	74764.6	16982.6	168214.3	100356.7	32564.9
567529.9	560484.0		92857.0	759568.6	446640.3	322688.3	382974.8	244268.1
160809.0	176441.4	1.3	120698.6	362763.4	9781.6	180888.7	159189.2	115234.7
55070.9	59172.8		35367.1	79112.7	276.0	73041.6	69499.9	37278.8
59040.4	53496.1		35685.0	558122.2	12556.9	504296.0	425366.7	235448.4
120682.4	119080.2		103903.7	39608.1	766.9	31765.6	35323.3	22743.6
52872.9	57586.4		35828.5	87953.8	1166.6	30240.8	197158.8	96416.5
501291.3	372949.6	1102.8	193307.4	304956.4	926833.0	2098478.7	1783350.2	404188.9
798317.5	897913.3	931.9	467940.8	2487131.5	1282389.1	2685990.7	2146264.4	733572.9
1147695.8	986794.7	8253.8	537250.7	1874329.8	865907.7	1640872.1	1425691.4	378735.3
130093.4	128347.0	60.7	89866.3	742750.2	11165.1	429236.7	424364.5	196967.6
131846.8	133945.6	145.0	27268.7	374663.7	113082.4	212348.7	223596.0	112466.5
54829.0	55954.9		30820.7	291368.6	6783.6	225647.2	913346.8	216098.7
1177250.3	1177259.0		653631.9	543997.4	5400.0	745280.8	741489.5	518698.4
135130.1	131933.7		57198.6	361429.7	44989.7	251687.9	178630.5	92845.0
184609.4	182025.7		110571.5	543758.3	5966.4	526437.0	454125.9	210007.9
254021.5	253110.0	834.3	150647.9	320076.5	64084.0	256172.4	267793.1	128475.9
874549.4	737890.2	609.1	318235.2	2182334.2	256890.3	2178824.4	1596081.1	926012.7
51824.6	52701.2	149.0	45898.5	307626.5	51830.0	207475.5	83389.0	59111.9
19783.6	19047.4	118.0	10492.8	89404.8	207.6	24201.3	24290.0	17564.1
50105.7	54870.5	8.2	41770.5	506528.6	190323.8	387550.7	349532.7	125398.3
167994.7	186917.6	26.7	88405.6	695188.6	18597.8	615328.3	637552.4	229909.6
12425.4	13256.1	2.9	11966.5	327773.6	4542.9	117620.9	108607.1	72587.1
83517.8	77487.6	409.3	42572.2	559584.7	216888.8	222911.2	282721.6	175021.7
495.3	515.2		955.1	4384.7	12474.1	2465.0	2114.3	1008.7
68938.5	65190.8		48033.7	482990.3	5110.7	51205.0	126645.1	76311.2
66871.6	27194.7	10.0	23190.0	83069.0	12139.8	1390193.9	61693.6	44790.8
710.0	442.8		145.8	48601.6	1071.6	30406.6	25046.8	7732.8
79279.8	3220.3		4557.6	49956.9	21448.2	33958.5	41090.9	17475.1
45868.4	46393.5		25197.2	99989.4	2444.6	51213.4	52124.1	35668.0

C-3-2 社会组

地区	单位数	年末职工人数		受教育程度		职业资格水平	
			#女性	大学专科人数	大学本科及以上人数	助理社会工作师人数	社会工作师人数
全国	**547245**	**6365813**	**1880817**	**1225017**	**816422**	**13399**	**8561**
中央级	2190	30769	13241	818	22348	703	1439
北京	8560	119336	47079	28719	48973	1059	859
天津	4516	42573	18833	12877	16908	107	52
河北	16530	248136	65881	43172	31853	574	690
山西	11611	144909	40286	35706	19131	130	73
内蒙古	10685	80051	24944	26075	9431	1	3
辽宁	19494	217509	57810	35842	33415	157	126
吉林	9193	94821	17393	17232	4374	493	97
黑龙江	12672	173745	65848	30989	11570	187	116
上海	11626	158334	37242	41001	14143	406	198
江苏	56234	429104	126770	94840	71844	1925	704
浙江	36426	350782	103275	91518	54444	269	345
安徽	20705	206418	54939	47380	24803	465	123
福建	19372	253138	49584	27906	22457	457	220
江西	13375	183682	53988	22780	8266	531	115
山东	38976	324154	73330	92714	64156	479	237
河南	23577	197277	57666	42981	27895	332	85
湖北	25778	265404	99215	71664	24612	229	172
湖南	21663	215004	69931	54375	26657	292	134
广东	41317	509316	220638	115891	80724	1713	1461
广西	17370	309735	61079	37215	26218	192	453
海南	4338	39414	16159	5079	5642	2	
重庆	13154	132323	52179	28591	31255	644	191
四川	35050	510475	144547	83036	63920	1018	480
贵州	8295	148577	34909	16577	9077	249	24
云南	16954	379387	131954	38698	21605	443	69
西藏	589	9529	3395	585	174		
陕西	17360	252911	51448	29175	12346	70	18
甘肃	13335	190626	42148	22466	9846	118	23
青海	3039	18285	4289	2001	603	60	6
宁夏	4002	36150	11035	7253	4313	6	6
新疆	9259	93939	29782	19861	13419	88	42

织总表

单位:个、人、人次、时

年龄结构				建立党组织的社会组织	社会组织中中共党员人数	志愿服务	
35岁及以下人数	36岁至45岁人数	46岁至55岁人数	56岁及以上人数			志愿者服务人次数	志愿服务时间
2159462	**2306546**	**1266764**	**633041**	**83066**	**826756**	**411467**	**1225910.0**
8855	10543	6294	5077	1143	18293		
36498	38437	24794	19607	1179	29942		
11387	15370	10399	5417	1952	8007	700	1950.0
91163	100501	42100	14372	5074	40464	6506	23563.0
50283	47012	30444	17170	1047	14770	1666	4854.0
27948	27833	16586	7684	1416	9886	160	480.0
58374	70594	43636	44905	2433	25464	6206	14364.0
31534	38986	18085	6216	300	5778		
75958	53682	33009	11096	880	5583	31	100.0
38862	73815	31423	14234	4896	37735	40	120.0
126039	155140	105153	42772	3363	60250	61045	162872.0
119953	128983	61181	40665	5947	50193	46521	138327.0
65499	73653	46808	20458	2964	30231	38264	100930.0
58185	68391	72641	53921	2127	18011		
61693	77822	33375	10792	2180	19177	10	50.0
114225	128981	60838	20110	12356	83966	98551	277792.0
85157	73432	26641	12047	3794	25047	52	178.0
113132	84740	46706	20826	4158	35654	344	1014.0
82634	76943	39204	16223	2617	33770	97633	327088.0
260776	139692	77152	31696	1320	21875	34368	108750.0
81429	119323	74690	34293	953	40983		
15394	17402	4461	2157	318	8070	300	1000.0
49393	41615	23210	18105	928	18136	12142	41252.0
189054	178048	74227	69146	5800	65614	305	944.0
39340	69502	27877	11858	2502	19634	1693	4602.0
111885	147624	79987	39891	2183	26339	8	18.0
3698	3638	1643	550	124	628		
68731	84650	79052	20478	1333	17765	4365	14223.0
37398	101915	40527	10786	4400	25552	243	499.0
4908	7470	4549	1358	1091	4027		
7423	13143	10925	4659	699	5156	62	180.0
32654	37666	19147	4472	1589	20756	252	760.0

C-3-2续表1

地 区	行政执法	行政处罚数	并处没收违法经营额/违法所得	并处罚款
全 国	**3117**	**3071**		**3**
中央级				
北 京	10	6		
天 津				
河 北	659	659		
山 西	75	75		
内蒙古	50	50		
辽 宁	20	20		
吉 林				
黑龙江				
上 海	7	7		
江 苏	115	112		
浙 江	77	77		
安 徽	6	6		
福 建	16	16		
江 西				
山 东	1268	1252		
河 南	1	1		
湖 北	147	124		2
湖 南	12	12		
广 东	177	177		
广 西				
海 南				
重 庆	143	143		
四 川	201	201		
贵 州	42	42		
云 南				
西 藏	2	2		1
陕 西				
甘 肃				
青 海				
宁 夏	2	2		
新 疆	87	87		

单位：起、万元

⑴ 警告	⑵ 限期（责令）停止活动	⑶ 撤销登记	取缔非法社会组织	#并处没收非法财产
652	**86**	**2333**	**46**	**1**
6			4	
		659		
3	1	71		
		50		
15		5		
		7		
31	21	60	3	
8		69		
		6		
		16		
517	44	691	16	1
		1		
3		121	23	
		12		
67	6	104		
	6	137		
		201		
		42		
2				
		2		
	8	79		

C－3－2续表2

地 区	增加值合计	执行行政事业单位会计制度财务指标				
		固定资产原价	上年结转和结余	本年收入合计	本年支出合计	收支结余
全 国	**5710883.6**	**230469.3**	**21577.4**	**360143.7**	**76056.5**	**1053.5**
中央级	148802.1					
北 京	287562.2					
天 津	32546.9					
河 北	239174.1	1799.5	3.0	1567.2	1223.8	
山 西	112846.4	3415.0	66.7	1471.7	1205.9	1.3
内蒙古	35088.6	3698.3	4.6	3952.5	3952.5	
辽 宁	207461.0	1012.2		434.0	394.0	
吉 林	22072.3	476.8	15.0	1601.1	861.9	
黑龙江	92366.0	1146.9	4.0	262598.4	394.3	
上 海	403723.4					
江 苏	713867.8	143359.3	18560.9	46089.7	35979.1	60.0
浙 江	330414.7					
安 徽	181080.9	10.5		670.1	667.1	
福 建	95246.2	6443.0	11.5	4094.4	1962.3	145.0
江 西	206152.2	8917.2		961.0	929.5	
山 东	518698.4					
河 南	76583.0	3463.3		1922.4	1501.2	
湖 北	184390.8	1039.0		742.6	517.9	
湖 南	129462.3	8773.1	1495.4	7157.1	7469.7	834.3
广 东	904692.3	7899.0	251.4	8951.4	5623.5	
广 西	58645.2	2949.8	14.8	586.6	460.6	
海 南	17610.1	699.0		417.0	457.0	
重 庆	115484.3	7698.2	9.0	4828.0	4837.0	
四 川	212085.2	2684.7		2189.8	1130.5	
贵 州	40302.6	2918.0	267.0	2280.3	2271.7	2.9
云 南	164806.2	6366.2	189.5	1940.7	1277.5	
西 藏	1085.5	1920.5		0.2	0.2	
陕 西	76311.2					
甘 肃	45982.9	7875.9	128.8	3145.3	1990.4	10.0
青 海	4693.8					
宁 夏	16965.4	433.3	130.0	621.4	175.4	
新 疆	34679.5	5470.6	425.8	1920.8	773.5	

单位：万元

行政事业单位增加值	执行民间非营利组织单位会计制度财务指标				
	固定资产原价	上年结余	本年收入合计	本年费用合计	社会组织增加值
66022.1	**14735831.8**	**5849439.7**	**18488799.5**	**16676894.8**	**5644861.5**
	675289.8		3630930.1	2959197.2	148802.1
	1035071.1	1319475.5	1439173.1	1238546.0	287562.2
	74740.6	16982.6	168214.3	100320.7	32546.9
558.5	735125.3	446412.3	318846.6	372619.5	238615.6
1108.5	343629.8	9745.6	176707.8	150721.8	111737.9
2216.9	62424.0	246.0	64577.9	62454.3	32871.7
737.4	444999.3	10898.1	460308.4	377149.2	206723.6
418.0	16406.4	765.3	27381.3	31683.6	21654.3
504.4	79815.7	1133.6	23604.0	191452.9	91861.6
	304476.4	926833.0	2098117.7	1782808.4	403723.4
37274.6	1925742.4	1279229.9	2429315.5	1976692.2	676593.2
	1311890.5	852353.9	1387000.0	1231631.2	330414.7
588.7	616896.1	8427.9	401078.6	394717.5	180492.2
257.7	260971.9	90306.0	149637.3	172632.6	94988.5
558.2	275940.4	5670.6	211320.7	897563.1	205594.0
	543997.4	5400.0	745280.8	741489.5	518698.4
570.6	288938.0	44980.7	208884.3	132060.6	76012.4
97.7	500607.2	5244.4	457645.4	398528.7	184293.1
6680.3	316300.7	64084.0	251416.9	260465.2	122782.0
1627.7	2037326.2	242540.2	2154566.6	1554550.6	903064.6
365.8	307006.7	51830.0	206878.5	82514.5	58279.4
46.0	89404.8	207.6	24201.3	24290.0	17564.1
5445.2	441685.4	189611.2	356446.4	319356.4	110039.1
1175.2	632380.6	17187.6	599281.0	605937.6	210910.0
1614.5	235492.0	2909.7	76684.2	60051.1	38688.1
627.7	457987.4	202416.5	205037.2	260321.1	164178.5
76.8	4039.7	12474.1	2465.0	2114.3	1008.7
	482990.3	5110.7	51205.0	126645.1	76311.2
2044.7	73134.4	12139.8	53811.0	60834.2	43938.2
	24248.9	966.1	25244.9	19132.2	4693.8
333.1	46387.2	21412.2	33234.7	39605.8	16632.3
1093.8	90485.2	2444.6	50303.0	48807.7	33585.7

C-3-3 社会

地区	单位数	年末职工人数	#女性	受教育程度		职业资
				大学专科人数	大学本科及以上人数	助理社会工作师人数
全国	**289026**	**3531635**	**795902**	**517856**	**324012**	**5437**
中央级	1908	27578	11872		21637	703
北京	3573	34641	10513	7700	19349	265
天津	2156	8728	2817	2207	3223	11
河北	9536	132639	18252	14809	11374	354
山西	6789	83050	18107	18194	10759	33
内蒙古	6697	50769	13681	17272	5892	
辽宁	8859	117187	15935	15319	10101	76
吉林	5785	74447	10448	11029	2604	378
黑龙江	5683	130183	52168	18677	7967	142
上海	3791	35071	5926	5048	2839	246
江苏	26164	167189	42466	43671	21774	871
浙江	18108	137504	29913	39468	19327	101
安徽	11671	103731	15352	15961	7921	162
福建	12787	186007	22943	16503	7780	157
江西	7783	102116	20342	13700	3999	21
山东	17807	139221	26766	35927	27818	166
河南	10896	74908	18384	11370	5811	120
湖北	11564	134916	48246	27588	7074	11
湖南	11498	117506	28949	23157	11777	88
广东	19000	153018	48766	34321	20168	218
广西	10940	241025	30800	21181	15923	83
海南	2155	15791	4352	1842	1028	
重庆	6693	46713	7977	6971	6518	245
四川	18866	328001	72996	35470	37305	531
贵州	5141	111874	20740	7875	3446	168
云南	11595	322333	103514	28209	11331	91
西藏	560	9389	3358	511	147	
陕西	9623	173947	26696	13124	3990	29
甘肃	10206	163808	36201	13226	6065	69
青海	2022	13916	2919	1315	321	33
宁夏	2958	29880	8006	5507	1758	2
新疆	6212	64549	16497	10704	6986	63

团体

单位:个、人、人次、时

格水平	年龄结构				志愿服务	
社会工作师人数	35岁及以下人数	36岁至45岁人数	46岁至55岁人数	56岁及以上人数	志愿者服务人次数	志愿服务时间
3556	**925218**	**1305050**	**837113**	**464254**	**196107**	**591896.0**
1439	7722	9652	5516	4688		
85	5339	9144	10138	10020		
6	2146	3117	1965	1500	500	1500.0
122	46210	55419	22145	8865	2260	6780.0
22	18278	29533	21916	13323	1603	4809.0
	15229	17901	11793	5846	160	480.0
47	18248	37604	23651	37684	256	768.0
19	24984	29215	15628	4620		
53	61979	37362	22862	7980	31	100.0
75	6565	16875	7107	4524	40	120.0
229	34396	57461	48759	26573	34215	100305.0
257	32540	57447	35366	12151	36314	108942.0
29	22156	37948	29714	13913	9725	29175.0
18	27047	48596	60942	49422		
25	29645	40545	23915	8011	10	50.0
85	42732	53903	29641	12945	40609	121827.0
26	27635	29340	12129	5804		
3	61942	35685	23315	13974	78	231.0
52	34874	42712	27333	12587	50889	152667.0
281	38346	48623	44051	21998	9758	35129.0
405	49506	93952	64921	32646		
	5669	6500	2518	1104	300	1000.0
79	9449	13412	11789	12063	4999	14997.0
105	102830	111982	52303	60886	290	870.0
9	21429	58178	22396	9871	361	1083.0
36	82474	127820	73874	38165		
	3632	3587	1628	542		
15	36343	54783	67523	15298	3424	10484.0
10	28318	92841	33944	8705	213	369.0
1	3082	5787	4000	1047		
3	5073	10686	9917	4204	62	180.0
20	19400	27440	14414	3295	10	30.0

C−3−3续表1

地　区	社会组织负责人	#女性	按活动区域分 中央级社团	省级社团	地级社团
全　国	**610260**	**100266**	**1908**	**26685**	**71922**
中央级	22583		1908		
北　京	24263	4751		1383	
天　津	4334	982		926	
河　北	14331	1949		818	2656
山　西	8558	791		948	2087
内蒙古	12169	2956		726	1888
辽　宁	13044	1996		803	3325
吉　林	7285	985		726	1917
黑龙江	9253	1157		998	2196
上　海	21800	3957		1164	
江　苏	41805	6573		956	5556
浙　江	36913	7697		1030	4349
安　徽	16864	1937		936	3546
福　建	15299	2336		912	2894
江　西	11780	2104		731	2252
山　东	53232	10575		907	5236
河　南	16304	3158		1051	3896
湖　北	31991	5014		901	3249
湖　南	24271	3398		852	3644
广　东	46879	15300		1394	6905
广　西	17247	2141		789	2306
海　南	3547	741		761	324
重　庆	22077	3616		909	
四　川	36017	5728		1107	4023
贵　州	30959	1367		663	1120
云　南	17528	2288		816	2510
西　藏	1040	111		188	146
陕　西	16082	2581		851	1787
甘　肃	13438	2152		569	1616
青　海	2182	256		515	417
宁　夏	4087	199		598	580
新　疆	13098	1470		757	1497

单位：人、个

县级社团	建立党组织的社会组织	社会组织职工中中共党员人数	当年新增单位数	当年年检单位数	行业性社团
188511	**52533**	**513562**	**28658**	**115034**	**38088**
	1017	16350	41	1750	397
2190	674	17053	219	2369	144
1230	1170	4097	172	1431	244
6062	3351	25793	624	3371	1627
3754	545	9447	544	3296	759
4083	905	6421	910	3838	1880
4731	903	14075	420	2815	1503
3142	262	4452	233	370	207
2489	643	3998	267	125	345
2627	1925	13856	155	3165	312
19652	1967	26692	4941	9250	3396
12729	3736	25882	1852	11507	1640
7189	2052	17206	961	6929	1323
8981	1602	15033	1040	3192	2073
4800	1597	8094	531	1753	314
11664	7599	46063	1905	15464	7113
5949	2742	13941	764	1860	901
7414	1862	15803	828	7818	1142
7002	2138	26557	789	4322	1723
10701	713	11588	3252	4626	1593
7845	697	35686	1537	1714	683
1070	167	6642	149	885	425
5784	418	7550	643	4473	876
13736	4048	48469	1298	5448	2333
3358	1780	13958	481	1517	881
8269	1068	21464	976	2964	919
226	123	625	13	271	195
6985	948	11975	562	4119	750
8021	3355	20661	2056	774	380
1090	707	2594	49	687	399
1780	519	3863	151	705	267
3958	1300	17674	295	2226	1344

C-3-3续表2

地区	社会组织					
	科技与研究	生态环境	教育	卫生	社会服务	文化
全　国	**17399**	**6636**	**11753**	**9953**	**41777**	**27115**
中央级	51	3	30	14	18	41
北　京	303	63	152	159	398	336
天　津	125	25	156	138	227	144
河　北	629	135	289	461	1356	884
山　西	457	110	346	188	1130	860
内蒙古	410	163	290	154	879	587
辽　宁	415	128	1062	450	1166	674
吉　林	302	102	221	189	1440	541
黑龙江	291	93	314	262	1029	735
上　海	640	44	156	193	529	288
江　苏	1433	437	921	745	5714	2544
浙　江	1264	316	844	582	1915	1662
安　徽	693	250	328	401	1727	1154
福　建	465	366	664	377	1966	1431
江　西	283	189	410	433	1163	728
山　东	1435	364	502	522	2452	1826
河　南	877	368	551	407	1314	1257
湖　北	911	232	384	471	1474	1072
湖　南	791	406	536	426	2198	1009
广　东	1287	229	664	455	3186	2105
广　西	608	111	231	217	1443	554
海　南	274	21	62	56	123	279
重　庆	454	103	247	174	638	553
四　川	833	678	909	862	2919	1633
贵　州	164	110	115	149	598	533
云　南	370	235	298	461	1304	1130
西　藏	28	25	27	28	107	40
陕　西	532	113	227	220	950	1135
甘　肃	253	897	211	261	1201	686
青　海	76	55	154	177	221	181
宁　夏	174	82	252	84	205	156
新　疆	571	183	200	237	787	357

单位：个

按行业分类

体育	法律	工商业服务	宗教	农业及农村发展	职业及从业组织	国际及涉外组织	其他
17869	**3264**	**31031**	**4801**	**58825**	**19743**	**481**	**38379**
16	4	1531	4	9	2	27	158
218	52	489	42	658	164		539
93	30	207	23	157	177	19	635
559	119	1048	189	1805	624	15	1423
567	110	662	88	740	410	9	1112
371	52	769	68	1543	221	5	1185
497	135	568	139	1435	828	23	1339
283	103	271	74	1082	252	14	911
357	84	435	75	966	591	1	450
340	37	683	70	60	246	12	493
3179	304	2534	370	2971	1562		3450
1342	219	3090	350	1494	2029	55	2946
746	148	1039	178	2964	887	17	1139
761	140	1273	270	1751	952	55	2316
585	126	681	160	1329	612	12	1072
916	172	1905	224	5068	1307	34	1080
570	171	1332	287	1866	690	13	1193
701	161	1409	192	1797	769		1991
519	146	1060	220	1705	1108	40	1334
1430	99	3176	273	1424	1086	31	3555
333	46	646	95	4742	481	14	1419
159	5	355	12	435	99	5	270
358	46	712	94	2135	397	5	777
1133	206	1242	353	4345	1595	14	2144
297	54	517	117	1262	455	1	769
540	165	942	306	3281	610	21	1932
11	9	24	10	112	6		133
336	52	796	170	4089	395	7	601
206	63	395	156	4227	841	5	804
76	71	156	60	407	43	2	343
100	43	141	36	1185	77		423
270	92	943	96	1781	227	25	443

C-3-3续表3

地区	行政执法	行政处罚数	并处没收违法经营额/违法所得	并处罚款
全国	**2173**	**2152**		**3**
中央级				
北京	8	4		
天津				
河北	278	278		
山西	41	41		
内蒙古	50	50		
辽宁	5	5		
吉林				
黑龙江				
上海	2	2		
江苏	45	45		
浙江	25	25		
安徽	5	5		
福建	12	12		
江西				
山东	1253	1237		
河南	1	1		
湖北	55	54		2
湖南	3	3		
广东	86	86		
广西				
海南				
重庆	49	49		
四川	125	125		
贵州	41	41		
云南				
西藏	2	2		1
陕西				
甘肃				
青海				
宁夏	2	2		
新疆	85	85		

单位：起

⑴ 警告	⑵ 限期（责令）停止活动	⑶ 撤销登记	取缔非法社会组织	并处没收非法财产
589	**70**	**1493**	**21**	**1**
4			4	
		278		
3	1	37		
		50		
		5		
		2		
14	7	24		
5		20		
		5		
		12		
516	44	677	16	1
		1		
3		51	1	
		3		
42	6	38		
	4	45		
		125		
		41		
2				
		2		
	8	77		

C-3-3续表4

地区	增加值合计	执行行政事业单位会计制度财务指标				
		固定资产原价	上年结转和结余	本年收入合计	本年支出合计	收支结余
全　国	**1555010.2**	**230469.3**	**360143.7**	**21577.4**	**76056.5**	**1053.5**
中央级	136437.2					
北　京	33356.6					
天　津	7086.4					
河　北	36575.0	1799.5	1567.2	3.0	1223.8	
山　西	42604.3	3415.0	1471.7	66.7	1205.9	1.3
内蒙古	12267.3	3698.3	3952.5	4.6	3952.5	
辽　宁	45811.4	1012.2	434.0		394.0	
吉　林	12301.5	476.8	1601.1	15.0	861.9	
黑龙江	24860.6	1146.9	262598.4	4.0	394.3	
上　海	46569.7					
江　苏	158849.5	143359.3	46089.7	18560.9	35979.1	60.0
浙　江	116942.6					
安　徽	60932.5	10.5	670.1		667.1	
福　建	26907.5	6443.0	4094.4	11.5	1962.3	145.0
江　西	53942.0	8917.2	961.0		929.5	
山　东	150776.8					
河　南	16312.1	3463.3	1922.4		1501.2	
湖　北	46675.6	1039.0	742.6		517.9	
湖　南	36514.4	8773.1	7157.1	1495.4	7469.7	834.3
广　东	281240.2	7899.0	8951.4	251.4	5623.5	
广　西	20662.8	2949.8	586.6	14.8	460.6	
海　南	9662.7	699.0	417.0		457.0	
重　庆	14990.7	7698.2	4828.0	9.0	4837.0	
四　川	42404.7	2684.7	2189.8		1130.5	
贵　州	15754.7	2918.0	2280.3	267.0	2271.7	2.9
云　南	31339.1	6366.2	1940.7	189.5	1277.5	
西　藏	122.8	1920.5	0.2		0.2	
陕　西	30023.0					
甘　肃	26966.8	7875.9	3145.3	128.8	1990.4	10.0
青　海	3439.3					
宁　夏	5420.3	433.3	621.4	130.0	175.4	
新　疆	7260.0	5470.6	1920.8	425.8	773.5	

单位：万元

行政事业单位增加值	执行民间非营利组织单位会计制度财务指标 固定资产原价	上年结余	本年收入合计	本年费用合计	社会组织增加值
66022.1	**3027358.1**	**1824520.3**	**4948958.3**	**5029077.3**	**1488988.1**
	595493.3		1571865.8	1187410.6	136437.2
	191941.6	431069.8	263075.0	263716.0	33356.6
	13622.8	425.8	35200.4	18249.9	7086.4
558.5	65216.0	383382.2	68711.6	65564.8	36016.5
1108.5	73426.8	4637.5	62119.3	57934.7	41495.8
2216.9	18164.8	109.0	24257.3	23614.7	10050.4
737.4	74726.2	1945.6	112611.6	102826.0	45074.0
418.0	9426.6	31.0	14276.9	17676.4	11883.5
504.4	16299.6	747.0	6954.8	38212.2	24356.2
	57790.9	378191.4	431105.6	367298.9	46569.7
37274.6	597180.2	9492.6	367434.8	371564.3	121574.9
	138575.8	368180.3	350666.0	308199.3	116942.6
588.7	118774.7	2555.7	100159.3	94130.4	60343.8
257.7	22285.0	74053.1	62736.1	72495.5	26649.8
558.2	71332.3	829.1	31989.7	683824.3	53383.8
	119081.9	4928.0	225210.5	220979.1	150776.8
570.6	35740.8	5275.9	33705.6	30483.3	15741.5
97.7	61752.6	1105.2	130340.8	131526.5	46577.9
6680.3	50111.0	454.6	54102.1	48159.5	29834.1
1627.7	129935.4	110910.2	588923.7	464677.9	279612.5
365.8	161972.9	7486.4	22465.9	24598.4	20297.0
46.0	10912.4	99.8	10775.6	13441.5	9616.7
5445.2	43503.4	12159.2	71346.5	63249.3	9545.5
1175.2	97960.3	5919.3	140534.8	169737.9	41229.5
1614.5	80455.4	707.3	43442.5	23148.6	14140.2
627.7	56049.8	16097.6	34194.0	48092.8	30711.4
76.8	3322.5	132.0	89.0	76.5	46.0
	43465.6	543.8	16769.9	49297.7	30023.0
2044.7	33684.8	47.5	34129.0	34638.3	24922.1
	10003.5	753.0	21556.6	15597.4	3439.3
333.1	10228.4		6832.8	7741.7	5087.2
1093.8	14920.8	2250.4	11374.8	10912.9	6166.2

C-3-4 基金

地区	单位数	年末职工人数		受教育程度		职业资
			#女性	大学专科人数	大学本科及以上人数	助理社会工作师人数
全国	**3549**	**18646**	**5202**	**4740**	**4217**	**151**
中央级	216	1732	554	450	485	
北京	275	2301	1081	345	1156	
天津	56	345	154	115	212	
河北	49	271	103	85	164	1
山西	55	132	58	85	47	
内蒙古	91	373	125	306	56	
辽宁	63	536	142	245	126	25
吉林	66	103	23			
黑龙江	66	156				
上海	152	1071	159	750	196	
江苏	444	1356	376			
浙江	326	799	319	369		
安徽	71	194	24	23	37	3
福建	141	945	123		11	9
江西	45	233	51	134	74	
山东	86	276	70	158	80	7
河南	98	382	44	228	152	
湖北	73	658	132	230	296	
湖南	174	582	28			
广东	434	2498	755	109	239	
广西	37	355	138	64	19	1
海南	46	163	20	75	88	
重庆	47	456	198	112	86	9
四川	109	875	253	318	95	62
贵州	32	203	5	94	34	17
云南	62	192	75	57	135	12
西藏	10	52	10	41	8	
陕西	79	492	21	16	33	
甘肃	40	409	28	147	94	5
青海	22	45	10	12	8	
宁夏	51	257	117	83	171	
新疆	33	204	6	89	115	

会

单位:个、人、人次、时

格水平	年龄结构				志愿服务	
社会工作师人数	35岁及以下人数	36岁至45岁人数	46岁至55岁人数	56岁及以上人数	志愿者服务人次数	志愿服务时间
78	**5566**	**4844**	**5253**	**2983**	**1419**	**9786.0**
	554	450	485	243		
10	704	538	510	549		
	115	108	75	47		
4	98	73	53	47		
2	18	15	28	71	48	
	135	92	59	87		
6	135	102	238	61		
	89	14				
5			156			
23	302	308	259	202		
	498	226	443	189		
	370	285	102	42		
	10	37	61	86	116	231.0
	105	241	296	303		
	48	169	16			
2	156	120				
	29	16	151	186		
	145	250	184	79		
	16	27	427	112		
	925	389	936	248		
1	67	123	138	27		
	131	21	6	5		
5	102	172	78	104	1255	9555.0
5	374	383	78	40		
	61	62	72	8		
3	42	66	53	31		
	12	31	7	2		
	109	137	134	112		
12	83	126	117	83		
	15	24	6			
	66	130	42	19		
	52	109	43			

C-3-4续表1

地区	社会组织负责人数	#女性	按性质分		
			公募基金会	非公募基金会	涉外基金会
全国	**7331**	**1429**	**1378**	**2137**	**8**
中央级	777	7	90	92	8
北京	699	189	41	234	
天津	201	39	19	37	
河北	72	25	9	40	
山西	55	2	23	32	
内蒙古	96	24	91		
辽宁	70	12	41	22	
吉林	66	12	23	43	
黑龙江	56	19	34	32	
上海	646	175	51	101	
江苏	444	94	149	295	
浙江	317	48	134	192	
安徽	87		23	48	
福建	151	3	31	110	
江西	124	22	17	28	
山东	64	12	36	50	
河南	206	52	37	61	
湖北	532	105	21	52	
湖南	271	21	102	72	
广东	1118	425	112	322	
广西	351	20	18	19	
海南	135		15	31	
重庆	47	18	27	20	
四川	109	20	52	57	
贵州	63	13	29	3	
云南	62	8	34	28	
西藏	25	8	8	2	
陕西	318	35	30	49	
甘肃	47	7	24	16	
青海	22	5	12	10	
宁夏	51	8	25	26	
新疆	49	1	20	13	

单位：人、个

境外基金代表机构	建立党组织的社会组织	社会组织职工中中共党员人数	当年登记单位数	当年年检单位数
26	**604**	**6937**	**491**	**1628**
26	90	1581	16	162
	21	916	62	207
	55	174	2	54
	43	150	12	
	1	16	8	
	10	60		
	46	150		
	7	21	6	
			8	
	35	576	12	127
		865	29	444
	9	348	61	264
	32	126	13	7
	133	410	9	1
	2	15	14	44
	31	132	10	76
	2	228	22	
	6	188	9	60
	3	363	21	
		13	100	
	22	71	6	1
		123	7	27
	8	111	8	39
			21	
		3	3	
	9	43	4	
	18	54	7	71
	16	74	11	
		2	9	41
	5	124	1	3

C-3-4续表2

地　区	社会组织					
	科技与研究	生态环境	教育	卫生	社会服务	文化
全　国	**82**	**46**	**1052**	**130**	**1140**	**213**
中央级			2			
北　京	21	8	55	18	109	46
天　津	2		23	2	16	8
河　北	1		7	1	1	
山　西			21		26	8
内蒙古		2	25	46	1	3
辽　宁			10	4	10	6
吉　林		2	18	1	40	1
黑龙江	2	4	15	2	33	2
上　海	8	6	44	9	57	15
江　苏	3	1	135	6	145	14
浙　江	7		140	5	106	11
安　徽	3	3	21		20	5
福　建		1	76	5	55	2
江　西	2	1	20		17	1
山　东	4	2	29	3	12	5
河　南			16			6
湖　北		3	35	1	20	5
湖　南	3		104		40	7
广　东	16	1	105	17	252	35
广　西			7	1	25	
海　南	1	2	18	2	6	6
重　庆	1		16	2	20	3
四　川	4		50	2	14	4
贵　州			1		29	
云　南		6	16	1	28	3
西　藏		1	2		1	3
陕　西	1		14	2	4	11
甘　肃	2	3	15		13	3
青　海			3			
宁　夏	1		8		37	
新　疆			1		3	

单位：个

按行业分类							
体育	法律	工商业服务	宗教	农业及农村发展	职业及从业组织	国际及涉外组织	其他
33	**39**	**243**	**21**	**43**	**26**	**4**	**477**
1		208				2	3
4	3			2			9
2							3
			3				36
							14
1		20					12
	3	1					
2	1	1	1	1	1		1
1		8			2		2
3	3	1	1	22	4		106
3			2	9			43
1	1	1			7		9
		2					
1	2		1				
1	14			1			15
2							74
1	3		1	2			2
2			5	1	11	1	
4							4
				1			3
	4	1	3	1			2
	1		2				2
1	2			1	1		30
1							1
	1					1	6
2							1
	1		1	1			44
			1	1			2
							19
							5
							29

C-3-4续表3

地　区	行政执法	行政处罚数	(1) 警告	(2) 限期（责令）停止活动	(3) 撤销登记
全　国	**4**	**4**	**3**		**1**
中央级					
北　京	2	2	2		
天　津					
河　北					
山　西					
内蒙古					
辽　宁					
吉　林					
黑龙江					
上　海					
江　苏					
浙　江					
安　徽					
福　建					
江　西					
山　东	2	2	1		1
河　南					
湖　北					
湖　南					
广　东					
广　西					
海　南					
重　庆					
四　川					
贵　州					
云　南					
西　藏					
陕　西					
甘　肃					
青　海					
宁　夏					
新　疆					

单位：起、万元

增加值合计	执行民间非营利组织单位会计制度财务指标				
	固定资产原价	上年结余	本年收入合计	本年费用合计	社会组织增加值
161847.8	**143447.4**	**1592356.2**	**3636553.8**	**2343626.8**	**161847.8**
2.0	52709.6		1974986.9	1686346.1	2.0
30457.1	8976.1	242258.8	177032.4	35876.5	30457.1
243.7	2963.6	10606.5	1688.4	637.5	243.7
339.0	1427.9	14836.5	14654.3	708.6	339.0
375.0	1100.0		14000.0	600.0	375.0
5390.1	381.0		10521.0	8018.0	5390.1
7798.6	1110.0		25074.6	19995.2	7798.6
62.0	328.7			1007.9	62.0
388.5	260.0		250.0	572.0	388.5
48419.9			182397.9	75946.2	48419.9
22075.0		1226854.0	519804.0	28817.0	22075.0
843.1	7188.0	64053.0	285663.4	240043.6	843.1
206.8	1462.0		1373.0	394.0	206.8
21000.0	27370.0		29313.0	25909.0	21000.0
8024.8	715.0		10988.0	8930.4	8024.8
379.7	364.2		2855.1	2509.5	379.7
69.3	126.0	35.0	132.0	150.0	69.3
5650.0	492.0		50484.4	28323.7	5650.0
2819.1	7770.0	1.0	286728.8	141765.8	2819.1
21.3	141.6	4.9	54.8	22.8	21.3
255.0			1890.0	255.0	255.0
3661.1	112.8	50.2	13191.2	6605.0	3661.1
26.4				26.4	26.4
200.7	361.2			365.9	200.7
1100.0			15910.0	13270.0	1100.0
825.6	632.0	11854.6	2100.3	1789.2	825.6
48.5	1340.0		1237.0	928.0	48.5
374.4	100.4	7300.7	1008.3	808.1	374.4
13.3	4250.0		1152.0	865.0	13.3
747.8	12325.3	14501.0	12023.0	12100.4	747.8
30.0	9440.0		40.0	40.0	30.0

C-3-5 民办

地区	单位数	年末职工人数	#女性	受教育程度		职业资
				大学专科人数	大学本科及以上人数	助理社会工作师人数
全　国	**254670**	**2815532**	**1079713**	**702421**	**488193**	**7811**
中央级	66	1459	815	368	226	
北　京	4712	82394	35485	20674	28468	794
天　津	2304	33500	15862	10555	13473	96
河　北	6945	115226	47526	28278	20315	219
山　西	4767	61727	22121	17427	8325	97
内蒙古	3897	28909	11138	8497	3483	1
辽　宁	10572	99786	41733	20278	23188	56
吉　林	3342	20271	6922	6203	1770	115
黑龙江	6923	43406	13680	12312	3603	45
上　海	7683	122192	31157	35203	11108	160
江　苏	29626	260559	83928	51169	50070	1054
浙　江	17992	212479	73043	51681	35117	168
安　徽	8963	102493	39563	31396	16845	300
福　建	6444	66186	26518	11403	14666	291
江　西	5547	81333	33595	8946	4193	510
山　东	21083	184657	46494	56629	36258	306
河　南	12583	121987	39238	31383	21932	212
湖　北	14141	129830	50837	43846	17242	218
湖　南	9991	96916	40954	31218	14880	204
广　东	21883	353800	171117	81461	60317	1495
广　西	6393	68355	30141	15970	10276	108
海　南	2137	23460	11787	3162	4526	2
重　庆	6414	85154	44004	21508	24651	390
四　川	16075	181599	71298	47248	26520	425
贵　州	3122	36500	14164	8608	5597	64
云　南	5297	56862	28365	10432	10139	340
西　藏	19	88	27	33	19	
陕　西	7658	78472	24731	16035	8323	41
甘　肃	3089	26409	5919	9093	3687	44
青　海	995	4324	1360	674	274	27
宁　夏	993	6013	2912	1663	2384	4
新　疆	3014	29186	13279	9068	6318	25

非企业

单位:个、人、人次、时

格水平	年龄结构				志愿服务	
社会工作师人数	35岁及以下人数	36岁至45岁人数	46岁至55岁人数	56岁及以上人数	志愿者服务人次数	志愿服务时间
4927	**1228678**	**996652**	**424398**	**165804**	**213941**	**624228.0**
	579	441	293	146		
764	30455	28755	14146	9038		
46	9126	12145	8359	3870	200	450.0
564	44855	45009	19902	5460	4246	16783.0
49	31987	17464	8500	3776	15	45.0
3	12584	9840	4734	1751		
73	39991	32888	19747	7160	5950	13596.0
78	6461	9757	2457	1596		
58	13979	16320	9991	3116		
100	31995	56632	24057	9508		
475	91145	97453	55951	16010	26830	62567.0
88	87043	71251	25713	28472	10207	29385.0
94	43333	35668	17033	6459	28423	71524.0
202	31033	19554	11403	4196		
90	32000	37108	9444	2781		
150	71337	74958	31197	7165	57942	155965.0
59	57493	44076	14361	6057	52	178.0
169	51045	48805	23207	6773	266	783.0
82	47744	34204	11444	3524	46744	174421.0
1180	221505	90680	32165	9450	24610	73621.0
47	31856	25248	9631	1620		
	9594	10881	1937	1048		
107	39842	28031	11343	5938	5888	16700.0
370	85850	65683	21846	8220	15	74.0
15	17850	11262	5409	1979	1332	3519.0
30	29369	19738	6060	1695	8	18.0
	54	20	8	6		
3	32279	29730	11395	5068	941	3739.0
1	8997	8948	6466	1998	30	130.0
5	1811	1659	543	311		
3	2284	2327	966	436		
22	13202	10117	4690	1177	242	730.0

C-3-5续表1

地　区	民间组织负责人	#女性	按性质分	
			法人	合伙
全　国	**376670**	**125797**	**194827**	**6951**
中央级	196		64	1
北　京	14482	6642	4178	15
天　津	3615	1579	2218	11
河　北	8407	2007	4112	317
山　西	5647	1353	4278	115
内蒙古	5332	1638	2465	171
辽　宁	10184	3628	7721	232
吉　林	3937	1522	1909	15
黑龙江	7837	2581	3620	179
上　海	18947	8535	7614	41
江　苏	37164	10012	24967	794
浙　江	24983	9927	14368	657
安　徽	12081	3463	6155	489
福　建	7335	2387	5317	302
江　西	9787	3320	3504	211
山　东	48898	13919	15696	437
河　南	16124	5650	8948	319
湖　北	21933	5929	11367	456
湖　南	16195	5168	6529	346
广　东	27115	10092	19420	110
广　西	8869	2274	4049	169
海　南	1842	814	1840	30
重　庆	13910	5783	5529	91
四　川	22188	8071	12261	553
贵　州	4146	1365	1537	197
云　南	5779	1973	3552	144
西　藏	21	6	7	3
陕　西	10026	3443	5072	209
甘　肃	4499	1175	2089	198
青　海	981	105	842	23
宁　夏	1039	267	783	82
新　疆	3171	1169	2816	34

单位：人、个

个体	建立党组织的社会组织	社会组织职工中中共党员人数	当年登记单位数	当年年检单位数
52892	**29929**	**306257**	**40605**	**104847**
1	36	362	13	45
519	484	11973	365	3095
75	727	3736	216	763
2516	1680	14521	989	2260
374	501	5307	578	1410
1261	501	3405	839	1826
2619	1484	11239	980	4095
1418	31	1305	278	288
3124	237	1585	433	548
28	2936	23303	910	6096
3865	1396	32693	8984	9044
2967	2202	23963	3420	10172
2319	880	12899	1261	4992
825	392	2568	596	2120
1832	581	11068	904	906
4950	4726	37771	2733	17928
3316	1050	10878	2886	2410
2318	2290	19663	1155	9053
3116	476	6850	2026	5257
2353	607	10274	3235	4555
2175	234	5226	1755	928
267	151	1305	362	546
794	502	10475	937	3921
3261	1752	17145	2126	6645
1388	722	5673	571	1019
1601	1106	4832	735	957
9	1	3	4	6
2377	367	5736	525	2475
802	1029	4817	380	297
130	384	1433	69	183
128	180	1291	80	149
164	284	2958	260	858

C－3－5续表2

地 区	社会组织					
	科技与研究	生态环境	教育	卫生	社会服务	文化
全 国	**13729**	**377**	**145210**	**21234**	**36698**	**11694**
中央级	15		5	2	14	13
北 京	262	4	2988	300	558	217
天 津	33	1	990	166	328	98
河 北	516	1	3662	1403	629	194
山 西	450	7	2786	312	439	257
内蒙古	302	6	2430	235	422	148
辽 宁	321	14	5959	1711	1290	263
吉 林	130		2119	136	661	93
黑龙江	589	2	4612	189	891	156
上 海	324	8	3248	144	2395	355
江 苏	723	14	8066	2206	13743	1433
浙 江	1143	17	11062	755	2364	956
安 徽	444	7	5284	1604	855	263
福 建	375	10	4731	282	243	309
江 西	229	2	3994	484	318	177
山 东	3185	15	8616	2874	2101	1635
河 南	893	77	7462	1208	972	632
湖 北	569	94	5709	1103	2076	1109
湖 南	357	12	7701	684	509	351
广 东	834	29	15355	581	2032	1055
广 西	180	4	5318	176	252	120
海 南	128	3	1368	282	79	121
重 庆	113		4728	81	852	74
四 川	429	6	11616	1738	961	408
贵 州	145	1	2240	304	150	69
云 南	121	3	4094	358	195	128
西 藏	1		9			3
陕 西	389	21	4450	1275	596	474
甘 肃	348	12	1636	297	187	262
青 海	17		611	51	38	97
宁 夏	54	7	518	38	111	76
新 疆	110		1843	255	437	148

单位：个

按行业分类							
体育	法律	工商业服务	宗教	农业及农村发展	职业及从业组织	国际及涉外组织	其他
10353	**511**	**2335**	**94**	**1617**	**1162**	**4**	**9652**
	1	9					7
293	24	13		5	5		43
236	2	7		1	377		65
250	7	44	4	39	22		174
195	20	67	5	22	23		184
105	4	28	21	14	8		174
378	6	52	17	13	195		353
152	3	11	2	6	7		22
285	7	15	3	8	16		150
502	29	208		49	31	4	386
1555	40	392	5	395	62		992
759	55	158	1	21	28		673
286	1	84	5	7	6		117
318	4	57	2	6	17		90
177	3	12		17	7		127
1288	144	304	4	59	49		809
748	14	83	3	3	13		475
297	54	196	3	675	93		2163
153	2	67	6	34	7		108
644	11	173	3	8	45		1113
256	1	20		1	6		59
53		21		1	43		38
253	1	29		78	8		197
310	27	82	3	56	18		421
118	3	11		11	5		65
219	4	26	3	6	8		132
							6
177	31	90	1	13	8		133
93	11	43	3	68	32		97
27		1		1	2		150
77		27			5		80
149	2	5			16		49

C-3-5续表3

地　区	行政执法	行政处罚数	(1) 警告	(2) 限期(责令)停止活动	(3) 撤销登记	取缔非法社会组织
全　国	**940**	**915**	**60**	**16**	**839**	**25**
中央级						
北　京						
天　津						
河　北	381	381			381	
山　西	34	34			34	
内蒙古						
辽　宁	15	15	15			
吉　林						
黑龙江						
上　海	5	5			5	
江　苏	70	67	17	14	36	3
浙　江	52	52	3		49	
安　徽	1	1			1	
福　建	4	4			4	
江　西						
山　东	13	13			13	
河　南						
湖　北	92	70			70	22
湖　南	9	9			9	
广　东	91	91	25		66	
广　西						
海　南						
重　庆	94	94		2	92	
四　川	76	76			76	
贵　州	1	1			1	
云　南						
西　藏						
陕　西						
甘　肃						
青　海						
宁　夏						
新　疆	2	2			2	

单位：起、万元

增加值合计	执行民间非营利组织单位会计制度财务指标				
	固定资产原价	上年结余	本年收入合计	本年费用合计	社会组织增加值
3994025.6	**11565026.3**	**2432563.2**	**9903287.4**	**9304190.7**	**3994025.6**
12362.9	27086.9		84077.4	85440.5	12362.9
223748.5	834153.4	646146.9	999065.7	938953.5	223748.5
25216.8	58154.2	5950.3	131325.5	81433.3	25216.8
202260.1	668481.4	48193.6	235480.7	306346.1	202260.1
69867.1	269103.0	5108.1	100588.5	92187.1	69867.1
17431.2	43878.2	137.0	29799.6	30821.6	17431.2
153851.0	369163.1	8952.5	322622.2	254328.0	153851.0
9708.8	6651.1	734.3	13104.4	12999.3	9708.8
67116.9	63256.1	386.6	16399.2	152668.7	67116.9
308733.8	246685.5	548641.6	1484614.2	1339563.3	308733.8
532943.3	1328562.2	42883.3	1542076.7	1576310.9	532943.3
212629.0	1166126.7	420120.6	750670.6	683388.3	212629.0
119941.6	496659.4	5872.2	299546.3	300193.1	119941.6
47338.7	211316.9	16252.9	57588.2	74228.1	47338.7
144185.4	203893.1	4841.5	168343.0	204808.4	144185.4
367541.9	424551.3	472.0	517215.2	518000.9	367541.9
60201.6	253071.2	39669.8	175046.7	101427.3	60201.6
132065.2	438362.6	4139.2	276820.2	238678.5	132065.2
92947.9	266189.7	63629.4	197314.8	212305.7	92947.9
620633.0	1899620.8	131629.0	1278914.1	948106.9	620633.0
37961.1	144892.2	44338.7	184357.8	57893.3	37961.1
7692.4	78492.4	107.8	11535.7	10593.5	7692.4
96832.5	398069.2	177401.8	271908.7	249502.1	96832.5
169654.1	534420.3	11268.3	458746.2	436173.3	169654.1
24347.2	154675.4	2202.4	33241.7	36536.6	24347.2
132367.1	401937.6	186318.9	154933.2	198958.3	132367.1
137.1	85.2	487.5	275.7	248.6	137.1
46239.7	438184.7	4566.9	33198.1	76419.4	46239.7
18641.7	39349.2	4791.6	18673.7	25387.8	18641.7
1241.2	9995.4	213.1	2536.3	2669.8	1241.2
10797.3	23833.5	6911.2	14378.9	19763.7	10797.3
27389.5	66124.4	194.2	38888.2	37854.8	27389.5

C-3-6 自治组

地 区	单位数	居民1000户以下	居民1000户－3000户	居民3000户以上	社区居委会（村委会）成员	#中共党员
全 国	**683167**	**491077**	**156912**	**35178**	**2807128**	**1602984**
中央级						
北 京	6797	4289	2021	487	34199	19761
天 津	5261	3840	1164	257	21591	10607
河 北	52365	42258	8709	1398	185745	93603
山 西	30403	25019	4517	867	111714	54264
内蒙古	13407	9402	3391	614	52062	26072
辽 宁	15628	7671	6037	1920	67151	36601
吉 林	11238	6700	3400	1138	45666	19690
黑龙江	11768	5887	4749	1132	54150	24425
上 海	5634	2134	3266	234	26688	13810
江 苏	21355	8935	9703	2717	107637	70257
浙 江	32568	24880	6695	993	124370	54765
安 徽	18107	8158	7467	2482	79229	48526
福 建	16722	12371	3862	489	69457	26478
江 西	20251	12619	6814	818	76532	32505
山 东	81285	67485	11465	2335	330818	252578
河 南	51284	34468	14232	2584	213182	116089
湖 北	29660	20818	7228	1614	117567	78096
湖 南	46888	35907	8862	2119	167145	108117
广 东	25829	15713	7817	2299	116322	78303
广 西	16148	11055	4334	759	78619	54811
海 南	3051	2624	289	138	15241	11798
重 庆	11039	6133	3904	1002	53716	32064
四 川	53115	39696	10346	3073	212643	109689
贵 州	18815	15626	2523	666	87205	38916
云 南	14209	9333	4144	732	70128	48394
西 藏	5438	5361	74	3	24716	20432
陕 西	28823	24375	3567	881	107949	50909
甘 肃	17250	13564	3089	597	67120	28083
青 海	4630	4022	331	277	18815	7775
宁 夏	2745	1944	590	211	11678	6818
新 疆	11454	8790	2322	342	58073	28748

织总表

单位：个、人

#女性	社区居委会（村委会）主任	#主任、书记“一肩挑”	#中共党员	#女性	受教育程度 大学专科人数
760848	**680509**	**240700**	**503547**	**108696**	**348434**
17761	6638	3939	5568	2116	10549
9768	5164	1995	3588	1175	5978
31995	52298	11630	32362	5285	11403
24826	30175	16241	21588	3322	12735
17042	13405	3056	8586	3150	7464
27326	15515	6925	11234	4167	19256
14624	11131	3900	7804	2809	6927
17730	11734	2453	6521	3040	11798
15304	5548	1266	3765	2541	6373
32571	21239	5656	17062	4757	23391
40261	31981	2406	18287	2471	18738
23021	18037	3803	14676	2785	10222
17361	16691	892	7938	1994	3051
19918	20188	3300	11274	3441	3461
95550	81285	60821	79695	9652	60965
50478	51181	22154	36246	10978	30887
33562	29545	18654	25512	4408	10371
47798	46838	21978	40813	7455	16443
34046	25748	14618	19800	3539	12407
17335	16134	5184	12993	1590	5967
3354	3047	2126	2625	199	1940
16990	11010	846	9167	1829	9911
49893	52894	4505	36876	10063	20505
18257	18744	1777	11650	3019	5085
14651	14142	6127	10959	1684	4830
7220	5437	1832	4262	1363	243
26470	28775	1943	19206	3863	2650
12484	17223	1841	9930	2503	4225
3855	4627	1382	2916	640	850
3660	2728	1136	1613	330	1196
15737	11407	6314	9031	2528	8613

C-3-6续表1

地　区	受教育程度	职业资格水平		年龄结构			
	大学本科及以上人数	助理社会工作师人数	社会工作师人数	35岁及以下人数	36岁至45岁人数	46岁至55岁人数	56岁及以上人数
全　国	**109147**	**13472**	**4433**	**600984**	**1229694**	**778719**	**197731**
中央级							
北　京	7457	3098	949	7160	11215	12353	3471
天　津	2185	476	70	5240	6715	7192	2444
河　北	1825	124	70	34437	83935	56188	11185
山　西	4815	81	52	26625	43661	31751	9677
内蒙古	1954	6	3	12567	23014	13061	3420
辽　宁	5878	757	275	15308	26766	19657	5420
吉　林	1642	70	21	9610	22572	11812	1672
黑龙江	2352	244	39	10538	30997	11199	1416
上　海	2845	656	241	5014	7479	9965	4230
江　苏	9259	2774	743	25459	42614	32166	7398
浙　江	5684	1369	749	26492	53870	36040	7968
安　徽	1856	663	191	14135	37161	22329	5604
福　建	647	226	94	14072	33818	18042	3525
江　西	386	116	10	16400	42006	15093	3033
山　东	26156	282	69	75359	148638	83476	23345
河　南	8230	164	65	46875	93409	57477	15421
湖　北	2129	139	50	24907	53605	32884	6171
湖　南	3655	122	53	35358	81596	41363	8828
广　东	4408	971	328	22468	41309	41783	10762
广　西	1057	101	31	13281	28834	28865	7639
海　南	137	21		2731	6817	4381	1312
重　庆	2550	344	120	12372	23236	14809	3299
四　川	5553	369	127	44484	92601	56640	18918
贵　州	918	30	12	20790	35270	24513	6632
云　南	1114	76	17	18539	30460	17402	3727
西　藏	58			3815	10192	7273	3436
陕　西	704	12	16	17369	45738	34973	9869
甘　肃	1443	35	2	14537	33946	14946	3691
青　海	230	24	1	3813	8458	5512	1032
宁　夏	183	41	1	2752	5141	3405	380
新　疆	1837	81	34	18477	24621	12169	2806

单位：个、人、人次、时

志愿服务		居民(村民)小组	当年完成选举的居(村)委会数	当年完成选举的居(村)选民登记总数			
志愿者服务人次数	志愿服务时间				本届登记选民数	参加投票人数	委托投票人数
2801905	**8406371.0**	**6021261**	**150437**	**216416803**	**199185114**	**172736960**	**13121553**
506080	1518240.0	87110	3564	2768796	2751006	2382817	347679
70295	210885.0	94634	2593	2180998	2056735	1852256	42548
46293	138879.0	324289	4224	2955898	2419195	1331334	46266
4192	12576.0	121984	3840	2962128	2310926	2168055	95732
23131	69393.0	76219	15	30794	30616	29208	175
130707	392121.0	205110	11070	12756724	12022444	9405930	566583
684	2708.0	81330	4365	6588239	5683974	5041749	87751
435	1305.0	139703	2359	9117049	5161248	4336132	44671
25189	75567.0	207574					
257505	772515.0	344528	15989	41693107	40243332	34648750	3972843
161839	485517.0	322991	28345	32067884	31314801	29451329	2964325
41562	124686.0	271716	1156	2209279	2093241	1530999	42276
20087	60261.0	160032	2631	3720374	3112481	2255864	109527
3042	9126.0	172812					
110061	330183.0	531446					
		388439	1014	1763050	1380857	1291727	42843
2895	8685.0	244764					
37815	113445.0	486843	5432	5244487	4553384	4040775	131878
2982	8946.0	255526	111	327719	327719	315675	35363
6485	19455.0	279696	2419	4160413	3832522	3166585	292610
		28507	2715	4350561	4174960	3343608	144273
381008	1143024.0	93231	4513	9046750	8491777	6967183	563656
44742	134226.0	409178	28256	32851358	30980948	26943236	2280522
872778	2618334.0	184101	9592	15448294	14193055	12390705	569903
1209	3627.0	171228	6888	15540782	14663324	13340156	454467
		17584	3023	990472	965496	895238	7649
4044	12132.0	146033	527	690314	605844	331369	2851
15865	47595.0	92289	3687	4720436	3961807	3835109	222934
13498	40494.0	13912					
3866	11598.0	14064	1047	1248578	1116909	990896	45935
13616	40848.0	54388	1062	982319	736513	450275	6293

C-3-6续表2

地　区	增加值合计	执行企业会计制度单位财务指标					执行行政	
		固定资产原价	营业收入	费用合计	营业利润	企业单位增加值	固定资产原价	上年结转和结余
全　国	**4018245.0**	**2710492.8**	**1170139.8**	**307017.4**	**15205.5**	**157810.7**	**14761879.6**	**782291.3**
中央级								
北　京	260265.4	2315877.2	1127813.3	275877.8	15329.4	129289.9	419283.2	224817.4
天　津	35126.8						190944.9	19854.4
河　北	97954.5	6810.3		99.0		3.5	626135.4	15300.2
山　西	125531.4	325.0		3138.8		2444.5	857047.3	2041.0
内蒙古	37561.3	586.0	40.4	43.2		4.0	97414.5	152.8
辽　宁	63684.9	1204.5		6.0		12.5	120765.4	15499.5
吉　林	104575.0	85.7	3.0				53382.9	715.0
黑龙江	39974.3	4646.0	2.0	151.8		95.3	156548.0	31718.6
上　海	211156.7	244632.1	40610.2	26195.5	-129.9	17383.8	850838.5	86396.8
江　苏	487645.9		140.0	140.0			1852143.8	27829.4
浙　江	585427.8	271.6				-143.5	3377562.3	102484.6
安　徽	105755.0	20.0				2.0	371871.0	2418.5
福　建	44489.0						110599.4	1237.6
江　西	41165.0	10516.5	993.0	436.2	6.0	397.8	90943.3	-398.8
山　东	653631.9						1343699.7	15.0
河　南	73460.6	6732.0	36.0	36.0			248588.8	926.7
湖　北	136188.6	1767.0					410827.7	2923.5
湖　南	149661.5	212.0					247157.7	716.0
广　东	347675.2	106981.6	437.9	744.0		8119.6	1875581.1	154876.0
广　西	46365.2	270.5					156525.1	136.2
海　南	10446.8	20.5					26563.0	666.5
重　庆	51684.5	94.0					139315.0	105.1
四　川	106329.0	3706.4		39.1		99.0	248744.4	15823.3
贵　州	44251.0	7.5					32556.4	2632.7
云　南	52806.7	1279.6		65.0		19.0	391093.8	70272.7
西　藏	878.3						21646.8	
陕　西	48033.7						167519.5	916.1
甘　肃	21997.9	29.5					134779.3	38.4
青　海	3184.8	8.0					2325.1	
宁　夏	5094.8	1339.5		2.0		27.5	42371.3	39.0
新　疆	26241.7	3069.8	64.0	43.0		56.0	97105.0	2137.1

单位：万元

事业单位会计制度财务指标				执行民间非营利组织单位会计制度财务指标				
本年收入合计	本年支出合计	收支结余	行政事业单位增加值	固定资产原价	上年结余	本年收入合计	本年费用合计	社会组织增加值
7356716.6	**6948676.2**	**12307.2**	**3504327.4**	**2218317.5**	**78777.9**	**2277945.9**	**840258.8**	**356106.9**
174006.7	242169.1	697.7	130975.5					
150831.9	150941.3		35108.8	24.0			36.0	18.0
567526.9	559260.2		92298.5	24443.3	228.0	3841.7	10355.3	5652.5
160742.3	175235.5		119590.1	19133.6	36.0	4180.9	8467.4	3496.8
55066.3	55220.3		33150.2	16688.7	30.0	8463.7	7045.6	4407.1
59040.4	53102.1		34947.6	113122.9	1658.8	43987.6	48217.5	28724.8
120667.4	118218.3		103485.7	23201.7	1.6	4384.3	3639.7	1089.3
52868.9	57192.1		35324.1	8138.1	33.0	6636.8	5705.9	4554.9
501291.3	372949.6	1102.8	193307.4	480.0		361.0	541.8	465.5
779756.6	861934.2	871.9	430666.2	561389.1	3159.2	256675.2	169572.2	56979.7
1147695.8	986794.7	8253.8	537250.7	562439.3	13553.8	253872.1	194060.2	48320.6
130093.4	127679.9	60.7	89277.6	125854.1	2737.2	28158.1	29647.0	16475.4
131835.3	131983.3		27011.0	113691.8	22776.4	62711.4	50963.4	17478.0
54829.0	55025.4		30262.5	15428.2	1113.0	14326.5	15783.7	10504.7
1177250.3	1177259.0		653631.9					
135130.1	130432.5		56628.0	72491.7	9.0	42803.6	46569.9	16832.6
184609.4	181507.8		110473.8	43151.1	722.0	68791.6	55597.2	25714.8
252526.1	245640.3		143967.6	3775.8		4755.5	7327.9	5693.9
874298.0	732266.7	609.1	316607.5	145008.0	14350.1	24257.8	41530.5	22948.1
51809.8	52240.6	149.0	45532.7	619.8		597.0	874.5	832.5
19783.6	18590.4	118.0	10446.8					
50096.7	50033.5	8.2	36325.3	64843.2	712.6	31104.3	30176.3	15359.2
167994.7	185787.1	26.7	87230.4	62808.0	1410.2	16047.3	31614.8	18999.6
12158.4	10984.4		10352.0	92281.6	1633.2	40936.7	48556.0	33899.0
83328.3	76210.1	409.3	41944.5	101597.3	14472.3	17874.0	22400.5	10843.2
495.3	515.0		878.3	345.0				
68938.5	65190.8		48033.7					
66742.8	25204.3		21145.3	9934.6		1336382.9	859.4	852.6
710.0	442.8		145.8	24352.7	105.5	5161.7	5914.6	3039.0
79149.8	3044.9		4224.5	3569.7	36.0	723.8	1485.1	842.8
45442.6	45620.0		24103.4	9504.2		910.4	3316.4	2082.3

C-3-7 村民

地 区	单位数	居民1000户以下	居民1000户—3000户	居民3000户以上	社区居委会（村委会）成员
全 国	**588547**	**453615**	**114638**	**20294**	**2323113**
中央级					
北 京	3938	3655	272	11	14460
天 津	3707	3477	218	12	12016
河 北	48703	40758	6963	982	167659
山 西	28273	24417	3259	597	101974
内蒙古	11173	8781	2118	274	40879
辽 宁	11609	7012	3954	643	43340
吉 林	9224	6095	2322	807	34517
黑龙江	8906	5102	3311	493	40090
上 海	1610	1008	562	40	6090
江 苏	14538	6841	6222	1475	71300
浙 江	28339	22966	4956	417	104039
安 徽	14925	7180	5919	1826	62389
福 建	14441	11240	2920	281	57758
江 西	16918	10920	5397	601	64000
山 东	74798	63607	9459	1732	299703
河 南	46997	32451	12531	2015	192454
湖 北	25452	19229	5484	739	97363
湖 南	41922	33372	7019	1531	145875
广 东	19257	13347	4933	977	81572
广 西	14313	10353	3555	405	67204
海 南	2570	2358	169	43	12469
重 庆	8318	5290	2729	299	37886
四 川	46492	36451	8145	1896	183641
贵 州	16859	14486	1876	497	76203
云 南	12137	8581	3288	268	58262
西 藏	5255	5217	36	2	23548
陕 西	26751	23378	2786	587	97884
甘 肃	16022	13069	2510	443	60958
青 海	4170	3757	168	245	16803
宁 夏	2269	1791	414	64	8860
新 疆	8661	7426	1143	92	41917

委员会

单位：个、人

#中共党员	#女性	社区居委会（村委会）主任	#主任、书记“一肩挑”	#中共党员	#女性
1344643	**526435**	**586620**	**202309**	**430329**	**69728**
10714	4155	3848	2345	3153	311
6538	2271	3653	873	2324	137
85386	23065	48644	10360	29776	3779
49319	19770	28051	14999	19909	2313
20836	10165	11171	2085	6847	1675
24749	10941	11532	4219	7886	1337
15322	8395	9165	2804	6232	1753
19704	8297	8874	1392	4662	1100
4553	1971	1592	490	1234	342
48253	16420	14487	3322	11789	2247
42880	29954	27840	1248	15232	805
39319	15366	14865	2899	12101	1703
21913	12333	14417	629	6681	1119
27429	14652	16868	2482	9261	2377
230525	85674	74798	56285	73322	7494
106968	41606	46903	20600	33368	9322
65597	24497	25352	16116	21937	2914
94243	39224	41882	19446	36389	5785
55947	17843	19217	10725	14450	1367
48537	12273	14300	4619	11550	1025
9832	2440	2569	1750	2186	123
22717	9403	8307	341	6811	792
93457	39650	46366	3474	31977	8055
34068	13479	16798	1461	10330	2230
40638	10816	12110	5349	9310	1185
19467	6966	5255	1793	4133	1331
45938	21777	26713	1466	17625	3142
25901	9909	15996	1498	9145	1982
6815	2849	4168	1122	2539	440
5397	1776	2253	850	1225	72
21681	8498	8626	5267	6945	1471

C-3-7续表1

地区	受教育程度		职业资格水平	
	大学专科人数	大学本科及以上人数	助理社会工作师人数	社会工作师人数
全国	**218713**	**57236**	**1620**	**469**
中央级				
北京	3227	1054	157	23
天津	2545	404	2	3
河北	7313	509	19	39
山西	9389	3845	2	3
内蒙古	3815	654		
辽宁	8522	1653	48	22
吉林	3710	582	44	14
黑龙江	6998	1045	160	8
上海	1813	627	75	29
江苏	12771	4271	571	119
浙江	12072	1917	59	20
安徽	6070	949	23	19
福建	1619	232	7	3
江西	1865	148	1	1
山东	51858	21082	51	10
河南	26141	7146	102	30
湖北	5071	689	17	3
湖南	11452	2245	26	25
广东	2885	589	116	38
广西	3419	300	1	6
海南	1152	33		
重庆	4868	699	23	8
四川	14736	3995	61	22
贵州	3343	539	13	6
云南	2665	404	2	1
西藏	205	58		
陕西	836	124	5	15
甘肃	3114	880		
青海	313	88	17	1
宁夏	369	41	1	
新疆	4557	434	17	1

单位：人、人次、时

年龄结构				志愿服务	
35岁及以下人数	36岁至45岁人数	46岁至55岁人数	56岁及以上人数	志愿者服务人次数	志愿服务时间
463479	**1025637**	**663544**	**170453**	**1342354**	**4027718.0**
1021	4854	6668	1917	5668	17004.0
1939	4083	4402	1592	11660	34980.0
28231	76415	52531	10482	38228	114684.0
23615	39325	29818	9216	325	975.0
8781	17967	11075	3056	5396	16188.0
7357	16727	14595	4661	1149	3447.0
6578	17114	9495	1330	684	2708.0
6437	23405	9006	1242	435	1305.0
1373	1914	2273	530	13849	41547.0
15675	28069	22373	5183	128431	385293.0
20376	45434	31320	6909	36803	110409.0
9853	29642	18078	4816	24087	72261.0
11366	28477	14931	2984	20084	60252.0
13060	35263	12974	2703	2	6.0
67579	134764	75941	21419	91551	274653.0
40515	84046	53416	14477		
19465	44639	27779	5480	22	66.0
29439	71820	36751	7865	23257	69771.0
12985	27149	32689	8749	22	66.0
9522	24601	26145	6936	1420	4260.0
2047	5575	3736	1111		
7057	16883	11389	2557	112182	336546.0
37032	79878	49602	17129	11171	33513.0
18007	30771	21622	5803	804799	2414397.0
15717	25374	14383	2788	989	2967.0
3546	9773	6991	3238		
15191	41572	31944	9177	3268	9804.0
12824	30781	13856	3497		
3183	7354	5317	949	6872	20616.0
1642	3771	3075	372		
12066	18197	9369	2285		

C-3-7续表2

地　区	当年完成选举的村委会数	当年完成选举的村选民登记数			
			本届登记选民数	参加投票人数	委托投票人数
全　国	**130763**	**169057485**	**157432303**	**139419135**	**11537922**
中央级					
北　京	3559	2756787	2738997	2381032	347456
天　津	1985	1797697	1765965	1623832	28235
河　北	3917	2273825	1784048	1264159	44761
山　西	3418	2311423	1711403	1759905	79880
内蒙古					
辽　宁	10808	12278266	11608119	9276432	562262
吉　林	3734	5210756	4782600	4345211	85207
黑龙江	1438	4895582	2224159	1913082	8941
上　海					
江　苏	11409	29280589	28814168	25232405	3352241
浙　江	26465	27390639	26726571	25408650	2818193
安　徽	791	1204396	1149288	806226	1928
福　建	2187	2863599	2383159	1874403	106943
江　西					
山　东					
河　南	683	1061676	738474	661925	36808
湖　北					
湖　南	4267	2826030	2462284	2260111	53532
广　东	25	44146	44146	43835	2978
广　西	2229	3640535	3316918	2875770	278831
海　南	2389	3754729	3749867	3091030	131879
重　庆	3403	5730277	5324974	4360083	438240
四　川	25176	27326083	25948882	22532064	1956836
贵　州	8713	13188355	12072287	10733277	531693
云　南	6002	12235285	11989780	11221035	409539
西　藏	2942	934938	915126	844598	6918
陕　西					
甘　肃	3515	4350848	3612642	3520754	203272
青　海					
宁　夏	959	1171079	1113434	989085	45930
新　疆	749	529945	455012	400231	5419

单位：个、人、次

经推举产生的村民代表数	#女性	当年召开村民会议次数	当年召开村民代表会议的次数	自然村	村委会小组数
11602539	**3038904**	**427978**	**734518**	**1948117**	**4664307**
113572	39909	2695	12177	4865	28832
52479	8963	244	2835	3013	36994
84149	14560	2823	10387	66844	282787
119325	17183	7980	11562	44733	104892
		12737	3416	34290	54366
341879	87735	6785	12570	37853	75676
255817	8269	1348	1973	15795	52024
133479	2240	846	886	16915	71732
				1328	25748
3121157	1098640	10946	32673	63197	213304
1127068	408234	38291	67918	93140	253435
24351	4018	953	3571	144621	229033
176513	42382	7	7	66073	134373
				105861	158479
1627351	477703	191123	382610	90786	449401
16645	369	828	30	156902	354051
		1506	3096	103086	200962
686641	274817	3593	259	121887	432161
280	78	778	2156	143978	203151
82258	15597	9399	9664	161926	246052
78118	21097	4115	4760	17272	25123
183719	42614	6591	22701	6159	68936
927489	92036	51579	67611	94625	357308
1019597	173658	31631	45150	91827	160885
1155722	167717	12841	6648	110783	149774
43296	4320	415	349	13888	16746
11272	92	23996	23628	62578	133361
129242	17430	2398	3865	50044	85994
		77	32	5519	13022
59777	15009	1152	1118	7492	11957
31343	4234	301	866	10837	33748

C-3-7续表3

地区	增加值合计	执行企业会计制度单位财务指标					执行行政	
		固定资产原价	营业收入	费用合计	营业利润	企业单位增加值	固定资产原价	上年结转和结余
全　国	**2947947.2**	**2684679.9**	**1169675.5**	**306276.9**	**15199.5**	**154934.9**	**11702273.4**	**616649.9**
中央级								
北　京	158224.6	2315877.2	1127813.3	275877.8	15329.4	129289.9	289016.3	209386.9
天　津	27175.0						172186.6	19658.9
河　北	87248.5	5756.3		68.0		0.6	576754.0	7175.2
山　西	77018.4	210.0		3123.0		2396.0	836761.1	1708.0
内蒙古	26109.7	20.0					73802.2	145.8
辽　宁	40065.4	398.1		6.0		11.0	96599.0	10868.9
吉　林	11927.5	18.0					48362.9	550.0
黑龙江	31704.9	328.0	2.0	2.5			120989.4	31511.9
上　海	164819.5	244629.1	40610.2	26195.5	-129.9	17383.8	742733.4	77469.5
江　苏	310055.4		140.0	140.0			1238861.4	25223.9
浙　江	463265.8	255.0				-143.5	2958168.9	72256.6
安　徽	83135.3	20.0				2.0	286079.6	1627.2
福　建	35281.8						77652.0	1616.8
江　西	31087.5	9393.0	923.0	376.0		282.3	75160.7	-445.3
山　东	563805.5						1092590.4	9.0
河　南	64324.9	5932.0	30.0	30.0			214175.2	779.7
湖　北	103231.2	1040.0					263290.1	654.7
湖　南	111162.1	212.0					187186.7	697.6
广　东	247905.9	95922.8	157.0	398.0		5689.4	1319443.5	79394.3
广　西	38538.8	33.5					130502.6	55.8
海　南	7217.8						21855.0	304.8
重　庆	29704.8	94.0					82430.6	83.7
四　川	84074.0	2935.4		9.1			190982.5	9053.9
贵　州	37690.0	7.5					29437.1	2191.7
云　南	35598.3	460.0		51.0		13.0	261949.3	63681.5
西　藏	415.4						10376.8	
陕　西	43733.2						149801.3	901.1
甘　肃	17497.5	29.5					66054.6	22.8
青　海	2553.8						2020.9	
宁　夏	3814.7	943.0				5.5	32479.0	39.0
新　疆	9560.1	165.5				5.0	54570.3	26.0

单位：万元

事业单位会计制度财务指标				执行民间非营利组织单位会计制度财务指标				
本年收入合计	本年支出合计	收支结余	行政事业单位增加值	固定资产原价	上年结余	本年收入合计	本年费用合计	社会组织增加值
5446189.9	**5108604.9**	**9206.9**	**11421.4**	**1806112.8**	**50543.7**	**2119323.1**	**672441.0**	**277523.3**
54958.6	114116.1							
139610.0	140443.2			0.3				
545605.6	539822.8		55.4	22971.3	226.0	3353.0	9705.3	5335.7
99334.5	98050.1		253.4	16982.0	36.0	3918.2	7932.5	3235.1
40628.4	40767.2		79.3	15032.7		6914.4	5350.5	3278.0
37529.2	31165.7		91.0	105230.0	1653.8	33160.4	34599.2	18783.4
25780.3	23577.3			22897.2		2913.9	2402.1	684.0
39137.7	42626.2			7465.0	33.0	6140.2	5165.4	4228.0
365843.1	242038.0	4935.4	659.4					
538476.0	626425.2	1021.8	6594.3	398195.3	255.0	196460.3	120221.2	38805.6
928545.4	797075.7	2629.0	1434.5	545195.0	13553.8	234905.3	170947.3	40648.8
102518.9	101237.3	60.7	1.6	92594.3	2684.4	21227.5	22918.6	12685.2
100313.5	100261.7		10.0	83584.3	11336.0	49201.6	39275.0	13796.7
43214.4	43568.3			13856.3	1033.0	11257.0	11711.1	7422.0
989920.8	989929.5							
116759.7	113196.4			67632.5	5.0	40520.6	44121.8	15911.0
138996.1	135967.2			37521.9	694.0	60742.4	50471.2	23421.1
185482.0	181441.5			2076.7		3724.9	6419.1	5138.4
475281.6	363783.0		1834.3	112820.2	14012.1	23266.1	29225.2	15740.3
42273.8	42772.8	149.0		507.3		569.0	839.1	797.6
13563.8	12239.3	118.0						
26630.5	26687.3	3.5		47744.4	453.0	22613.6	21697.3	11202.4
139533.0	142066.3	-11.8	211.6	52505.8	1244.2	12606.6	26707.1	16052.2
9989.7	9274.3		15.8	80766.4	1477.1	35394.3	40440.0	29503.9
52590.4	48752.9	301.3	19.0	39655.4	1710.3	8713.4	12629.1	5094.7
491.3	491.0			113.0				
62811.9	59142.9		57.0					
33430.8	22071.9			9579.0		1336370.4	833.1	827.3
639.9	407.5			18788.0	104.0	4084.6	4765.0	2455.5
78004.6	1919.6			3427.5	33.0	673.4	1293.7	739.2
18294.4	17286.7		104.8	8971.0		592.0	2771.1	1737.2

C-3-8 社区

地区	单位数	居民1000户以下	居民1000户–3000户	居民3000户以上	社区居委会（村委会）成员
全　国	**94620**	**37462**	**42274**	**14884**	**484015**
中央级					
北　京	2859	634	1749	476	19739
天　津	1554	363	946	245	9575
河　北	3662	1500	1746	416	18086
山　西	2130	602	1258	270	9740
内蒙古	2234	621	1273	340	11183
辽　宁	4019	659	2083	1277	23811
吉　林	2014	605	1078	331	11149
黑龙江	2862	785	1438	639	14060
上　海	4024	1126	2704	194	20598
江　苏	6817	2094	3481	1242	36337
浙　江	4229	1914	1739	576	20331
安　徽	3182	978	1548	656	16840
福　建	2281	1131	942	208	11699
江　西	3333	1699	1417	217	12532
山　东	6487	3878	2006	603	31115
河　南	4287	2017	1701	569	20728
湖　北	4208	1589	1744	875	20204
湖　南	4966	2535	1843	588	21270
广　东	6572	2366	2884	1322	34750
广　西	1835	702	779	354	11415
海　南	481	266	120	95	2772
重　庆	2721	843	1175	703	15830
四　川	6623	3245	2201	1177	29002
贵　州	1956	1140	647	169	11002
云　南	2072	752	856	464	11866
西　藏	183	144	38	1	1168
陕　西	2072	997	781	294	10065
甘　肃	1228	495	579	154	6162
青　海	460	265	163	32	2012
宁　夏	476	153	176	147	2818
新　疆	2793	1364	1179	250	16156

居委会

单位：个、人

#中共党员	#女性	社区居委会（村委会）主任	#主任、书记“一肩挑”	#中共党员	#女性
258341	**234413**	**93889**	**38391**	**73218**	**38968**
9047	13606	2790	1594	2415	1805
4069	7497	1511	1122	1264	1038
8217	8930	3654	1270	2586	1506
4945	5056	2124	1242	1679	1009
5236	6877	2234	971	1739	1475
11852	16385	3983	2706	3348	2830
4368	6229	1966	1096	1572	1056
4721	9433	2860	1061	1859	1940
9257	13333	3956	776	2531	2199
22004	16151	6752	2334	5273	2510
11885	10307	4141	1158	3055	1666
9207	7655	3172	904	2575	1082
4565	5028	2274	263	1257	875
5076	5266	3320	818	2013	1064
22053	9876	6487	4536	6373	2158
9121	8872	4278	1554	2878	1656
12499	9065	4193	2538	3575	1494
13874	8574	4956	2532	4424	1670
22356	16203	6531	3893	5350	2172
6274	5062	1834	565	1443	565
1966	914	478	376	439	76
9347	7587	2703	505	2356	1037
16232	10243	6528	1031	4899	2008
4848	4778	1946	316	1320	789
7756	3835	2032	778	1649	499
965	254	182	39	129	32
4971	4693	2062	477	1581	721
2182	2575	1227	343	785	521
960	1006	459	260	377	200
1421	1884	475	286	388	258
7067	7239	2781	1047	2086	1057

C-3-8续表1

地 区	受教育程度		职业资格水平	
	大学专科人数	大学本科及以上人数	助理社会工作师人数	社会工作师人数
全 国	**129721**	**51911**	**11852**	**3964**
中央级				
北 京	7322	6403	2941	926
天 津	3433	1781	474	67
河 北	4090	1316	105	31
山 西	3346	970	79	49
内蒙古	3649	1300	6	3
辽 宁	10734	4225	709	253
吉 林	3217	1060	26	7
黑龙江	4800	1307	84	31
上 海	4560	2218	581	212
江 苏	10620	4988	2203	624
浙 江	6666	3767	1310	729
安 徽	4152	907	640	172
福 建	1432	415	219	91
江 西	1596	238	115	9
山 东	9107	5074	231	59
河 南	4746	1084	62	35
湖 北	5300	1440	122	47
湖 南	4991	1410	96	28
广 东	9522	3819	855	290
广 西	2548	757	100	25
海 南	788	104	21	
重 庆	5043	1851	321	112
四 川	5769	1558	308	105
贵 州	1742	379	17	6
云 南	2165	710	74	16
西 藏	38			
陕 西	1814	580	7	1
甘 肃	1111	563	35	2
青 海	537	142	7	
宁 夏	827	142	40	1
新 疆	4056	1403	64	33

单位：人、人次、时

年龄结构				志愿服务	
35岁及以下人数	36岁至45岁人数	46岁至55岁人数	56岁及以上人数	志愿者服务人次数	志愿服务时间
137505	**204057**	**115175**	**27278**	**1459551**	**4378653.0**
6139	6361	5685	1554	500412	1501236.0
3301	2632	2790	852	58635	175905.0
6206	7520	3657	703	8065	24195.0
3010	4336	1933	461	3867	11601.0
3786	5047	1986	364	17735	53205.0
7951	10039	5062	759	129558	388674.0
3032	5458	2317	342		
4101	7592	2193	174		
3641	5565	7692	3700	11340	34020.0
9784	14545	9793	2215	129074	387222.0
6116	8436	4720	1059	125036	375108.0
4282	7519	4251	788	17475	52425.0
2706	5341	3111	541	3	9.0
3340	6743	2119	330	3040	9120.0
7780	13874	7535	1926	18510	55530.0
6360	9363	4061	944		
5442	8966	5105	691	2873	8619.0
5919	9776	4612	963	14558	43674.0
9483	14160	9094	2013	2960	8880.0
3759	4233	2720	703	5065	15195.0
684	1242	645	201		
5315	6353	3420	742	268826	806478.0
7452	12723	7038	1789	33571	100713.0
2783	4499	2891	829	67979	203937.0
2822	5086	3019	939	220	660.0
269	419	282	198		
2178	4166	3029	692	776	2328.0
1713	3165	1090	194	15865	47595.0
630	1104	195	83	6626	19878.0
1110	1370	330	8	3866	11598.0
6411	6424	2800	521	13616	40848.0

C-3-8续表2

地　区	当年完成选举的居委会数	当年完成选举的居选民登记数	本届登记选民数
全　国	**19674**	**47359318**	**41752811**
中央级			
北　京	5	12009	12009
天　津	608	383301	290770
河　北	307	682073	635147
山　西	422	650705	599523
内蒙古	15	30794	30616
辽　宁	262	478458	414325
吉　林	631	1377483	901374
黑龙江	921	4221467	2937089
上　海			
江　苏	4580	12412518	11429164
浙　江	1880	4677245	4588230
安　徽	365	1004883	943953
福　建	444	856775	729322
江　西			
山　东			
河　南	331	701374	642383
湖　北			
湖　南	1165	2418457	2091100
广　东	86	283573	283573
广　西	190	519878	515604
海　南	326	595832	425093
重　庆	1110	3316473	3166803
四　川	3080	5525275	5032066
贵　州	879	2259939	2120768
云　南	886	3305497	2673544
西　藏	81	55534	50370
陕　西	527	690314	605844
甘　肃	172	369588	349165
青　海			
宁　夏	88	77499	3475
新　疆	313	452374	281501

单位：个、人

参加投票人数	委托投票人数	居委会小组数
33317825	**1583631**	**1356954**
1785	223	58278
228424	14313	57640
67175	1505	41502
408150	15852	17092
29208	175	21853
129498	4321	129434
696538	2544	29306
2423050	35730	67971
		181826
9416345	620602	131224
4042679	146132	69556
724773	40348	42683
381461	2584	25659
		14333
		82045
629802	6035	34388
		43802
1780664	78346	54682
271840	32385	52375
290815	13779	33644
252578	12394	3384
2607100	125416	24295
4411172	323686	51870
1657428	38210	23216
2119121	44928	21454
50640	731	838
331369	2851	12672
314355	19662	6295
		890
1811	5	2107
50044	874	20640

C-3-8续表3

地　区	增加值合计	执行企业会计制度单位财务指标					执行行政	
		固定资产原价	营业收入	费用合计	营业利润	企业单位增加值	固定资产原价	上年结转和结余
全　国	**1070297.8**	**25812.9**	**464.3**	**740.5**	**6.0**	**2875.8**	**3059606.2**	**165641.4**
中央级								
北　京	102040.8						130266.9	15430.5
天　津	7951.8						18758.3	195.5
河　北	10706.0	1054.0		31.0		2.9	49381.4	8125.0
山　西	48513.0	115.0		15.8		48.5	20286.2	333.0
内蒙古	11451.6	566.0	40.4	43.2		4.0	23612.3	7.0
辽　宁	23619.5	806.4				1.5	24166.4	4630.6
吉　林	92647.5	67.7	3.0				5020.0	165.0
黑龙江	8269.4	4318.0		149.3		95.3	35558.6	206.7
上　海	46337.2	3.0					108105.1	8927.3
江　苏	177590.5						613282.4	2605.5
浙　江	122162.0	16.6					419393.4	30228.0
安　徽	22619.7						85791.4	791.3
福　建	9207.2						32947.4	-379.2
江　西	10077.5	1123.5	70.0	60.2	6.0	115.5	15782.6	46.5
山　东	89826.4						251109.3	6.0
河　南	9135.7	800.0	6.0	6.0			34413.6	147.0
湖　北	32957.4	727.0					147537.6	2268.8
湖　南	38499.4						59971.0	18.4
广　东	99769.3	11058.8	280.9	346.0		2430.2	556137.6	75481.7
广　西	7826.4	237.0					26022.5	80.4
海　南	3229.0	20.5					4708.0	361.7
重　庆	21979.7						56884.4	21.4
四　川	22255.0	771.0		30.0		99.0	57761.9	6769.4
贵　州	6561.0						3119.3	441.0
云　南	17208.4	819.6		14.0		6.0	129144.5	6591.2
西　藏	462.9						11270.0	
陕　西	4300.5						17718.2	15.0
甘　肃	4500.4						68724.7	15.6
青　海	631.0	8.0					304.2	
宁　夏	1280.1	396.5		2.0		22.0	9892.3	
新　疆	16681.6	2904.3	64.0	43.0		51.0	42534.7	2111.1

单位：万元

事业单位会计制度财务指标				执行民间非营利组织单位会计制度财务指标				
本年收入合计	本年支出合计	收支结余	行政事业单位增加值	固定资产原价	上年结余	本年收入合计	本年费用合计	社会组织增加值
1910526.7	**1840071.3**	**3100.3**	**988838.4**	**412204.7**	**28234.2**	**158622.8**	**167817.8**	**78583.6**
119048.1	128053.0	697.7	102040.8					
11221.9	10498.1		7933.8	23.7			36.0	18.0
21921.3	19437.4		10386.3	1472.0	2.0	488.7	650.0	316.8
61407.8	77185.4		48202.8	2151.6		262.7	534.9	261.7
14437.9	14453.1		10318.5	1656.0	30.0	1549.3	1695.1	1129.1
21511.2	21936.4		13676.6	7892.9	5.0	10827.2	13618.3	9941.4
94887.1	94641.0		92242.2	304.5	1.6	1470.4	1237.6	405.3
13731.2	14565.9		7847.2	673.1		496.6	540.5	326.9
135448.2	130911.6	-3832.6	45871.7	480.0		361.0	541.8	465.5
241280.6	235509.0	-149.9	159416.4	163193.8	2904.2	60214.9	49351.0	18174.1
219150.4	189719.0	5624.8	114490.2	17244.3		18966.8	23112.9	7671.8
27574.5	26442.6		18829.5	33259.8	52.8	6930.6	6728.4	3790.2
31521.8	31721.6		5525.9	30107.5	11440.4	13509.8	11688.4	3681.3
11614.6	11457.1		6879.3	1571.9	80.0	3069.5	4072.6	3082.7
187329.5	187329.5		89826.4					
18370.4	17236.1		8214.1	4859.2	4.0	2283.0	2448.1	921.6
45613.3	45540.6		30663.7	5629.2	28.0	8049.2	5126.0	2293.7
67044.1	64198.8		37943.9	1699.1		1030.6	908.8	555.5
399016.4	368483.7	609.1	90131.3	32187.8	338.0	991.7	12305.3	7207.8
9536.0	9467.8		7791.5	112.5		28.0	35.4	34.9
6219.8	6351.1		3229.0					
23466.2	23346.2	4.7	17822.9	17098.8	259.6	8490.7	8479.0	4156.8
28461.7	43720.8	38.5	19208.6	10302.2	166.0	3440.7	4907.7	2947.4
2168.7	1710.1		2165.9	11515.2	156.1	5542.4	8116.0	4395.1
30737.9	27457.2	108.0	11453.9	61941.9	12762.0	9160.6	9771.4	5748.5
4.0	24.0		462.9	232.0				
6126.6	6047.9		4300.5					
33312.0	3132.4		4475.1	355.6		12.5	26.3	25.3
70.1	35.3		47.5	5564.7	1.5	1077.1	1149.6	583.5
1145.2	1125.3		1154.5	142.2	3.0	50.4	191.4	103.6
27148.2	28333.3		16285.5	533.2		318.4	545.3	345.1

C-3-9 其他社会服务

地区	单位数	工商登记	编办登记	民政登记	未登记	年末职工人数	#女性	受教育大学专科人数
全国	**6441**	**636**	**4138**	**807**	**860**	**90717**	**28658**	**24888**
中央级								
北京	69	4	65			1897	633	362
天津	37	2	26	9		992	279	214
河北	249	4	208	17	20	3806	1141	786
山西	130	10	85	16	19	1243	432	354
内蒙古	163	11	123	18	11	2008	596	616
辽宁	362	21	239	69	33	5455	1794	1721
吉林	215	31	169	1	14	5046	570	1638
黑龙江	224	9	166	35	14	3730	1126	1139
上海	93	56	37			3162	1149	482
江苏	321	50	218	40	13	4606	1516	1246
浙江	287	55	208	3	21	3808	1024	1015
安徽	269	21	170	46	32	3414	1181	870
福建	202	27	124	13	38	3050	784	440
江西	214	5	154	40	15	2282	682	397
山东	282	15	249	5	13	4259	1344	1488
河南	292	29	228	17	18	6145	1927	1773
湖北	271	14	213	24	20	4358	1639	1466
湖南	322	31	185	25	81	3619	1254	1346
广东	421	38	253	51	79	8080	2260	1645
广西	131	18	103	2	8	1643	571	497
海南	20	7	9	3	1	320	56	52
重庆	150	8	93	34	15	2148	867	674
四川	455	45	253	31	126	4692	1693	1426
贵州	294	51	78	31	134	3465	1361	933
云南	272	26	145	62	39	1428	439	514
西藏	25		14	11		77	36	36
陕西	177	28	124	12	13	2874	1058	762
甘肃	211	3	61	112	35	1155	432	338
青海	32	9	6	9	8	164	41	39
宁夏	47	2	21	19	5	259	91	79
新疆	204	6	111	52	35	1532	682	540

机构总表

单位:个、人、人次、时

程度	职业资格水平		年龄结构				志愿服务	
大学本科及以上人数	助理社会工作师人数	社会工作师人数	35岁及以下人数	36岁至45岁人数	46岁至55岁人数	56岁及以上人数	志愿者服务人次数	志愿服务时间
10160	**694**	**560**	**31234**	**34786**	**18984**	**5713**	**24440**	**67535.0**
445	56	34	594	635	494	174	1922	5632.0
231	2	6	286	246	285	175	100	200.0
275	31	17	1429	1501	717	159	273	903.0
223	4	5	507	478	197	61		
230	11	4	591	771	517	129		
945	42	43	1922	1897	1293	343	2047	4103.0
448	7	10	1416	1804	1323	503	110	330.0
451	19	15	898	1433	890	509	175	310.0
283	10	17	1118	939	749	356	1503	3913.0
581	60	43	1382	1803	1096	325	1673	4959.0
539	25	28	1089	1363	975	381	5414	11675.0
264	51	38	1087	1440	713	174	2675	6705.0
195	26	25	945	1314	622	169	6	18.0
107	33	25	812	1010	383	77	354	1075.0
715	31	47	1541	1678	810	230	3885	10374.0
483	52	38	3091	2108	767	179		
409	26	13	1481	1702	973	202	436	1284.0
432	24	9	1508	1405	576	130	1036	4325.0
701	75	36	2731	3209	1701	439	15	42.0
207	15	9	544	680	331	88		
15	1		57	186	59	18		
320	16	13	714	875	428	131	2120	6973.0
464	33	31	1510	1977	960	245	1	1.0
344	8	8	1241	1424	654	146	553	4262.0
206	14	13	562	611	208	47	38	97.0
12			48	17	12		3	
283	12	24	1005	1058	614	197	55	169.0
122	7	4	442	404	274	35		
10			46	91	26	1		
59		1	51	129	68	11		
161	3	4	586	598	269	79	46	185.0

C-3-9续表

地　区	增加值合计	执行企业会计制度单位财务指标					执行行政	
		固定资产原价	营业收入	费用合计	营业利润	企业单位增加值	固定资产原价	上年结转和结余
全　国	**918218.0**	**767595.3**	**650281.3**	**215422.0**	**159947.2**	**291876.9**	**1875873.8**	**87091.2**
中央级								
北　京	39667.0	23677.8	49117.5	20224.3	14264.2	23231.5	99272.8	2016.3
天　津	34811.4	5983.6	3900.6	2154.3	108.6	1170.0	32516.8	5552.4
河　北	17514.1	4049.4	2632.0	2549.1	-526.6	-52.3	66707.2	689.1
山　西	6596.9	8818.1	1081.0	346.0	15.0	142.2	23105.2	1341.4
内蒙古	14924.4	3196.0	1226.9	458.0	20.0	164.3	30208.9	1048.3
辽　宁	52823.2	26292.7	23660.3	11970.9	2299.6	14417.0	83672.6	3978.9
吉　林	9529.1	18481.9	1932.5	327.7	137.7	570.2	76010.2	1.0
黑龙江	30843.3	17320.0	7927.8	5084.5	1714.4	4398.8	69638.8	2235.4
上　海	162942.7	242782.2	314222.2	76962.1	113654.3	160704.3	2157.0	2191.5
江　苏	62717.9	20300.9	15475.8	6276.4	3598.8	7253.7	171370.3	15155.9
浙　江	61322.6	31342.4	39797.4	11043.3	4645.6	9382.4	136921.8	3786.0
安　徽	28514.3	17961.1	12096.2	6027.4	520.9	4868.5	46722.8	958.7
福　建	28109.3	47886.7	23442.2	9654.0	3286.5	11652.7	44371.4	4574.5
江　西	13167.7	5023.0	843.0	233.9	19.0	48.4	38792.7	240.3
山　东	41839.5	6500.3	4035.5	1785.1	209.5	1163.0	93142.1	
河　南	18208.6	17225.0	7801.0	3339.2	452.6	2826.9	52038.3	1057.5
湖　北	33310.1	7780.0	7738.5	3073.7	910.8	2641.5	93877.5	1284.3
湖　南	20306.2	25042.0	7368.7	3733.1	434.3	2461.3	125619.5	289.9
广　东	105818.3	32515.3	26493.5	9980.6	5197.0	13928.0	305805.2	13677.0
广　西	16626.8	11718.4	11806.0	3536.7	1562.5	3397.6	25699.7	7706.0
海　南	2937.7	7373.9	3230.3	1347.9	315.0	1617.4	8185.7	802.3
重　庆	18941.4	14465.3	3381.9	1849.0	5.6	863.7	47008.7	3.9
四　川	38449.5	43104.4	23187.7	7416.6	512.9	4469.8	83611.3	1007.2
贵　州	18536.5	63886.0	34560.5	13211.7	4999.6	14260.1	13867.9	551.0
云　南	11259.2	41322.7	3605.5	1710.5	582.1	2680.4	34278.7	1084.9
西　藏	260.1						1841.7	141.0
陕　西	13850.3	14587.2	17471.0	9422.9	836.2	3103.7	18908.2	7550.0
甘　肃	5669.2	1596.1	533.2	426.2	80.8	108.0	14597.4	50.1
青　海	582.3	1525.0	213.0	213.0		63.0	1772.1	
宁　夏	1330.4	363.0	461.1	396.0	-8.0	34.3	2357.3	1268.7
新　疆	6807.9	5474.9	1038.5	667.9	98.3	306.3	31794.0	6847.7

单位：万元

事业单位会计制度财务指标				执行民间非营利组织单位会计制度财务指标				
本年收入合计	本年支出合计	收支结余	行政事业单位增加值	固定资产原价	上年结余	本年收入合计	本年费用合计	社会组织增加值
1410394.2	**1363074.6**	**38633.2**	**624207.8**	**26728.9**	**2144.3**	**8069.1**	**6377.1**	**2133.3**
108456.1	113476.9	-3822.9	16435.5					
56001.9	55255.2	76.0	33621.3	37.0		64.8	62.0	20.1
42087.3	34777.0	116.3	17566.4					
21497.8	21556.9	50.4	6454.7	2302.7				
23829.3	23895.3	1020.3	14745.1	40.0		60.0	60.0	15.0
83633.1	84891.2	390.2	38051.0	1567.7		1862.0	1868.0	355.2
16208.8	15705.8	88.5	8958.9					
50941.5	48325.3	17.5	26428.2	211.0		9.1	20.7	16.3
7822.5	7579.7	1817.7	2238.4					
120456.1	109375.9	4108.5	55208.6	2573.8	20.0	965.3	876.7	255.6
101708.4	93081.4	3198.3	51841.2	365.0	1140.0	967.0	546.1	99.0
42070.9	39955.1	629.3	23580.7	1102.1		437.8	180.5	65.1
35315.9	32607.8	5021.2	16388.1	572.1		396.4	100.8	68.5
23060.2	20512.2	2.8	13113.1	15.0		18.0	10.3	6.2
74234.6	74234.6		40513.5	886.7		382.0	382.0	163.0
26092.2	25827.1	88.7	15381.6	370.0		150.0	0.2	0.1
72417.8	67515.1	-46.7	30665.9	25.0		6.0	6.0	2.7
118955.9	118967.2	15.2	17844.9			6.5		
164244.9	163460.8	10856.4	91831.3	1676.1	63.8	97.5	81.2	59.0
24335.5	22811.8	752.3	13229.2	3.0				
7072.5	4205.8	2364.7	1320.3					
42152.0	39777.4	2002.4	18001.7	3500.0		48.0	119.0	76.0
58276.9	53667.2	107.3	33399.0	3620.0	698.5	2131.1	1456.9	580.7
4147.2	5347.4		4168.0	2989.5		227.7	247.0	108.4
13089.4	11543.4	196.6	8566.8	67.0		19.7	19.5	12.0
621.0	553.4		260.1					
29561.4	32884.6	4278.2	10745.6	150.0		10.0	7.0	1.0
13995.0	11513.4		5550.1	77.2		12.6	21.3	11.1
762.9	710.9		495.2	2710.0		35.6	37.7	24.1
4477.4	4768.4	204.5	1235.1	652.0	222.0	35.0	81.0	61.0
22867.8	24290.4	5099.5	6368.4	1216.0		127.0	193.2	133.2

C-3-10 婚姻登记

地　区	单位数	编办登记	民政登记	未登记	年末职工人数	#女性	受教育程度 大学专科人数	大学本科及以上人数
全　国	**2059**	**1196**	**358**	**505**	**9949**	**6650**	**4059**	**2619**
中央级								
北　京	15	15			151	109	30	115
天　津	8		8		75	61	22	23
河　北	67	41	8	18	493	384	155	80
山　西	69	46	12	11	313	212	148	79
内蒙古	35	29	1	5	160	99	81	56
辽　宁	100	86	10	4	705	501	280	279
吉　林	69	63		6	501	309	105	91
黑龙江	72	39	25	8	333	230	148	75
上　海	17	17			149	109	43	76
江　苏	79	56	14	9	544	412	219	154
浙　江	70	54	1	15	318	239	116	147
安　徽	78	47	12	19	431	251	160	81
福　建	49	27	7	15	148	103	65	36
江　西	71	41	26	4	282	197	80	24
山　东	114	100	2	12	887	575	392	306
河　南	38	25	4	9	282	183	90	51
湖　北	99	87	6	6	597	434	277	117
湖　南	111	81	9	21	604	385	293	116
广　东	138	66	15	57	636	411	280	160
广　西	56	47	2	7	208	135	105	48
海　南	3	2	1		7	3	3	2
重　庆	38	35	3		196	133	83	101
四　川	156	48	12	96	487	294	242	108
贵　州	155	16	15	124	273	154	145	88
云　南	72	21	40	11	197	120	66	49
西　藏	23	12	11		46	32	28	7
陕　西	71	53	6	12	396	261	150	68
甘　肃	142	26	91	25	363	214	160	48
青　海								
宁　夏	13		9	4	48	31	30	14
新　疆	31	16	8	7	119	69	63	20

服务机构总表

单位:个、人、人次、时、处

职业资格水平		年龄结构				志愿服务		办理婚姻登记事务的处数
助理社会工作师人数	社会工作师人数	35岁及以下人数	36岁至45岁人数	46岁至55岁人数	56岁及以上人数	志愿者服务人次数	志愿服务时间	
135	**162**	**4952**	**3745**	**1150**	**102**	**11601**	**32534.0**	**6780**
5	2	91	45	15		7	7.0	19
		45	19	9	2			20
1	8	265	198	29	1	98	302.0	186
1	3	173	108	31	1			137
		57	80	22	1			118
7	14	362	240	92	11	13	18.0	112
6	5	223	177	91	10			69
4	1	174	137	20	2			200
1	11	66	55	20	8	40	100.0	20
16	12	306	169	60	9	317	1183.0	112
10	8	166	112	36	4	4874	10165.0	113
11	11	181	197	50	3	438	1000.0	113
3	8	64	72	10	2			137
5	4	128	116	37	1	78	234.0	864
10	24	422	349	109	7	3885	10374.0	167
5	10	218	53	9	2			195
13	2	268	240	83	6	66	174.0	132
9	4	329	205	68	2	464	2039.0	153
10	8	290	259	84	3			338
4	2	83	96	28	1			126
		4	1	2				56
4	9	83	83	25	5	1183	4709.0	99
4	7	218	202	57	10			238
		152	91	30		99	2120.0	684
4	5	67	118	12		9	24.0	598
		35	7	4		3		769
2	4	216	135	40	5	27	85.0	119
		195	103	59	6			322
								276
		18	23	7				117
		53	55	11				171

C-3-10续表

地　区	增加值合计	执行企业会计制度单位财务指标					执行行政	
		固定资产原价	营业收入	费用合计	营业利润	企业单位增加值	固定资产原价	上年结转和结余
全　国	**32696.7**	**610.3**	**597.7**	**433.9**	**50.8**	**439.0**	**92373.7**	**1396.9**
中央级								
北　京	1248.4						610.2	32.7
天　津	254.8	66.4	292.7	345.0	28.6	183.6	41.2	52.0
河　北	702.3	20.0	6.0				464.7	3.1
山　西	349.5						206.4	6.4
内蒙古	626.3						324.3	
辽　宁	2617.1	0.8	7.5	1.5		4.5	1907.5	432.1
吉　林	1112.3	4.2				24.0	544.8	1.0
黑龙江	428.2						282.4	
上　海	1560.2						1335.6	41.3
江　苏	2890.1	82.4	198.2	60.8	15.1	130.4	1236.1	6.2
浙　江	1958.7						1503.7	54.4
安　徽	885.2	20.0					1147.5	34.5
福　建	323.0	21.0					416.9	36.5
江　西	290.4	16.0	31.0	2.8		22.8	574.2	0.1
山　东	4762.9						4278.0	
河　南	311.0						160.3	
湖　北	1984.3						1493.2	37.0
湖　南	3677.6						61407.3	18.3
广　东	1285.9	238.0				10.0	2228.4	397.4
广　西	423.0						568.3	33.1
海　南	41.7	1.5					38.8	
重　庆	1014.4						1421.7	
四　川	1373.1						8028.0	8.0
贵　州	568.9	12.0				24.0	295.6	2.0
云　南	416.9	69.0	61.2	23.8	7.1	36.7	356.7	14.0
西　藏	43.8						174.5	141.0
陕　西	1118.7						459.0	45.7
甘　肃	145.5						630.3	0.1
青　海								
宁　夏	86.6	40.0	1.1			3.0	72.2	
新　疆	195.9	19.0					165.9	

单位：万元

事业单位会计制度财务指标				执行民间非营利组织单位会计制度财务指标				
本年收入合计	本年支出合计	收支结余	行政事业单位增加值	固定资产原价	上年结余	本年收入合计	本年费用合计	社会组织增加值
127547.4	**127252.2**	**148.7**	**31881.4**	**591.2**	**20.0**	**574.7**	**697.5**	**376.3**
1995.5	1982.6	24.4	1248.4					
73.2	83.2		51.1	37.0		64.8	62.0	20.1
1103.6	1097.4	6.8	702.3					
423.8	506.6	0.8	349.5	2.7				
893.2	893.2		626.3					
3710.4	3681.6	2.1	2612.3	2.0			3.0	0.3
1315.1	1303.7	1.1	1088.3					
488.4	510.7		422.8	8.0		9.1	9.7	5.4
4148.9	3827.4	17.8	1560.2					
4127.5	3996.1	45.5	2686.9	42.7	20.0	143.0	207.2	72.8
3307.3	3301.8	1.0	1920.1	50.0		25.0	58.0	38.6
1273.7	1300.5		869.3	9.1		26.8	25.5	15.9
675.0	698.1	17.0	318.5	5.0		5.7	4.5	4.5
493.5	492.8	2.8	261.4	15.0		18.0	10.3	6.2
5760.8	5760.8		4762.9					
398.4	412.4		311.0					
2632.7	2560.8		1983.8	20.0		3.0	3.0	0.5
81905.9	81925.4	-8.0	3677.6			6.5		
2155.1	2117.8		1265.5	15.0		11.0	17.8	10.4
514.3	527.1	7.6	423.0	3.0				
88.8	93.8		41.7					
2555.5	2472.3	26.3	1000.4			18.0	19.0	14.0
4792.1	4886.3		1261.4	237.0		203.1	175.5	111.7
339.7	489.2		484.0	72.5		11.0	71.5	60.9
417.7	412.8		368.2	67.0		19.7	19.5	12.0
111.0	43.4		43.8					
1378.2	1391.6		1118.7					
129.7	148.0		142.5	5.2		10.0	11.0	3.0
80.1	84.5		83.6					
258.3	250.3	3.5	195.9					

C-3-11 结婚登

地区	登记结婚件数	登记结婚人数	按居住		
			内地居民登记结婚件数	内地居民登记结婚人数	涉外及华侨、港澳台居民登记结婚件数
全国	**13469267**	**26938534**	**13414255**	**26808974**	**55012**
中央级					
北京	163676	327352	162606	325212	1070
天津	102574	205148	102201	204402	373
河北	740757	1481514	740260	1480520	497
山西	384006	768012	383860	767720	146
内蒙古	221612	443224	221364	442728	248
辽宁	369619	739238	367273	734528	2346
吉林	254091	508182	253018	506036	1073
黑龙江	376612	753224	374511	749022	2101
上海	149535	299070	147481	294962	2054
江苏	903780	1807560	902108	1804216	1672
浙江	422174	844348	416955	832820	5219
安徽	805649	1611298	804284	1608568	1365
福建	395926	791852	386043	772086	9883
江西	393733	787466	390435	780870	3298
山东	891370	1782740	890139	1780278	1231
河南	1262437	2524874	1261382	2522764	1055
湖北	645767	1291534	644163	1272614	1604
湖南	620560	1241120	618499	1236998	2061
广东	874723	1749446	866498	1732996	8225
广西	471895	943790	470148	940296	1747
海南	91214	182428	90370	180740	844
重庆	303084	606168	302313	604626	771
四川	776819	1553638	775297	1550594	1522
贵州	429812	859624	429374	858748	438
云南	452075	904150	448913	897830	3162
西藏	11566	23132	11558	23114	8
陕西	395718	791436	395249	790498	469
甘肃	186461	372922	186335	372670	126
青海	47471	94942	47437	94874	34
宁夏	63838	127676	63787	127574	51
新疆	260713	521426	260394	518070	319

记服务

单位:对、人

地分类

内地居民	#女性	香港居民	澳门居民	台湾居民	华侨	外国人
53685	**31234**	**5083**	**1419**	**10020**	**6919**	**32898**
1002	725	59	8	129	28	914
368	273	12	4	44	19	299
497	277	13	3	64	19	398
138	98	17	1	21	7	108
245	151	8		22	10	211
2331	1649	26	10	200	123	2002
1070	679	26	12	121	40	877
2099	1163	31	13	180	296	1583
1900	1470	108	19	340		1741
1653	1360	55	15	550	33	1038
4351	1650	68	16	288	2834	2881
1364	639	41	7	273	30	1015
9878	4259	832	83	2358	1257	5358
3297	547	49	16	317	25	2892
1200	856	29	8	198	32	995
1009	725	79	25	378	32	587
1604	1575	156	38	597	41	772
2061	1703	178	53	979	50	801
8163	5925	2491	943	947	1781	2125
1747	1193	126	51	520	91	959
844	701	308	14	281	70	171
766	617	62	20	246	21	427
1521	1263	149	36	516	30	792
438	359	59	12	182	18	167
3154	467	22	5	69	13	3061
8	172					8
467	354	20	4	136	16	295
126	112	4		42	1	79
34	10					34
38	30	10	1	10		43
312	232	45	2	12	2	265

C-3-11续表

地 区	按婚姻状况分类			
	初婚人数	再婚人数	#女 性	#恢复结婚件数
全 国	**23859646**	**3078888**	**1565397**	**298766**
中央级				
北 京	251636	75716	35954	11248
天 津	169871	35277	12916	7920
河 北	1266237	215277	114809	2013
山 西	710324	57688	31289	4725
内蒙古	355101	88123	46008	8159
辽 宁	671778	67460	29810	20206
吉 林	468339	39843	20167	17425
黑龙江	651424	101800	51174	17097
上 海	221651	77419	37716	11998
江 苏	1582023	225537	114318	33242
浙 江	712969	131379	62225	11758
安 徽	1401155	210143	108606	19375
福 建	724783	67069	32625	403
江 西	713805	73661	37708	7079
山 东	1516968	265772	140964	4212
河 南	2467531	57343	28972	20617
湖 北	1201344	90190	43515	9594
湖 南	1070438	170682	89061	9841
广 东	1594855	154591	70431	16918
广 西	863772	80018	43654	5348
海 南	169400	13028	5447	823
重 庆	440963	165205	86505	13878
四 川	1242155	311483	166278	24632
贵 州	835350	24274	12462	6021
云 南	804350	99800	49996	2645
西 藏	22776	356	152	14
陕 西	688904	102532	55435	1501
甘 肃	359235	13687	7487	1580
青 海	84835	10107	4787	181
宁 夏	115443	12233	6201	1645
新 疆	480231	41195	18725	6668

单位:对、人

按年龄分类				
20～24岁	25～29岁	30～34岁	35～39岁	40岁及以上
9033542	**9475282**	**2950900**	**1643336**	**3835474**
39911	157786	67745	22419	39491
52311	91463	30629	12429	18316
695549	472955	115522	52262	145226
281863	261031	76051	46468	102599
126534	171289	56811	30495	58095
158880	289056	113446	52313	125543
130369	166200	65487	39453	106673
155574	197260	92692	65795	241903
33979	121823	57455	23629	62184
619341	554907	140465	93591	399256
182687	355455	107521	51451	147234
625653	474462	127364	96820	286999
266505	302218	81267	40882	100980
306584	272596	75608	50209	82469
677035	740819	152810	69305	142771
1039236	819177	240223	140528	285710
407706	463510	135739	78869	205710
442598	461856	143366	67597	125703
558642	716686	244865	88738	140515
283944	374809	141208	62357	81472
50153	61861	29838	13235	27341
189875	196284	64739	45751	109519
495343	495190	164295	126482	272328
244030	247276	110897	84491	172930
291151	279742	114054	77986	141217
13808	7331	1380	494	119
270585	328723	76462	39661	76005
139232	146875	35178	16000	35637
22716	41199	12089	8812	10126
52404	39330	12227	7579	16136
179344	166113	63467	37235	75267

C-3-12 离婚办

地区	总计	民政部门合计	内地居民登记离婚	涉外及华侨、港澳台居民登记离婚	#外国人
全国	**3500111**	**2815369**	**2808831**	**6538**	**2735**
中央级					
北京	64614	54536	54363	173	123
天津	45266	39722	39659	63	47
河北	178798	133622	133562	60	41
山西	61027	41952	41939	13	7
内蒙古	80731	58312	58282	30	21
辽宁	152122	123743	123487	256	187
吉林	124020	107921	107797	124	72
黑龙江	178256	147613	147468	145	65
上海	69573	60885	60467	418	309
江苏	216647	175421	175200	221	107
浙江	132415	108097	107546	551	240
安徽	156218	124815	124723	92	53
福建	82589	65007	63749	1258	449
江西	86117	70247	70094	153	95
山东	225060	172125	171993	132	85
河南	209491	177502	177414	88	34
湖北	150894	127604	127430	174	54
湖南	167305	137627	137301	326	53
广东	176976	150631	149257	1374	292
广西	93190	73592	73406	186	78
海南	13153	9887	9776	111	24
重庆	133718	115691	115575	116	44
四川	268260	222662	222461	201	93
贵州	85739	62337	62270	67	15
云南	91255	70862	70763	99	86
西藏	1764	1167	1167	0	0
陕西	80568	63292	63243	49	25
甘肃	38500	22073	22064	9	4
青海	10805	6013	6008	5	2
宁夏	15902	11536	11523	13	1
新疆	109138	78875	78844	31	29

理服务

单位：件(对)、人

法院部门合计	判决离婚	调解离婚	离婚案件收案	判决不离	调解不离
684742	**170531**	**514211**	**1304841**	**185266**	**91280**
10078	2983	7095	21317	3846	409
5544	1582	3962	13373	2789	765
45176	6985	38191	90253	6625	7070
19075	4246	14829	40158	3697	6632
22419	5010	17409	39448	1683	4844
28379	7693	20686	52212	7691	2022
16099	4403	11696	29260	2721	1185
30643	4409	26234	46169	913	2075
8688	2417	6271	18604	4177	569
41226	8516	32710	91988	16902	9669
24318	6837	17481	49743	12354	2073
31403	8430	22973	62602	12535	1369
17582	6733	10849	34905	6801	962
15870	4573	11297	31218	5204	2055
52935	15280	37655	110594	19790	9337
31989	9254	22735	65864	11414	2851
23290	5547	17743	45266	7545	2716
29678	9240	20438	56062	9631	4846
26345	9014	17331	48465	7992	2799
19598	6119	13479	33767	5212	1757
3266	999	2267	5422	757	673
18027	5376	12651	34826	7022	1344
45598	10611	34987	85374	12158	5786
23402	5050	18352	37144	2783	2137
20393	5555	14838	35355	3516	2749
597	62	535	861	10	134
17276	3400	13876	33666	2610	3784
16427	3778	12649	31010	3505	3317
4792	1094	3698	8398	554	903
4366	1168	3198	9242	1447	608
30263	4167	26096	42275	1382	3840

C-3-13 殡葬服务

地区	单位数				年末职工人数		受教育程度	
		工商登记	编办登记	民政登记		#女性	大学专科人数	大学本科及以上人数
全国	**4382**	**636**	**2942**	**449**	**80768**	**22008**	**20829**	**7541**
中央级								
北京	54	4	50		1746	524	332	330
天津	29	2	26	1	917	218	192	208
河北	182	4	167	9	3313	757	631	195
山西	61	10	39	4	930	220	206	144
内蒙古	128	11	94	17	1848	497	535	174
辽宁	262	21	153	59	4750	1293	1441	666
吉林	146	31	106	1	4545	261	1533	357
黑龙江	152	9	127	10	3397	896	991	376
上海	76	56	20		3013	1040	439	207
江苏	242	50	162	26	4062	1104	1027	427
浙江	217	55	154	2	3490	785	899	392
安徽	191	21	123	34	2983	930	710	183
福建	153	27	97	6	2902	681	375	159
江西	143	5	113	14	2000	485	317	83
山东	168	15	149	3	3372	769	1096	409
河南	254	29	203	13	5863	1744	1683	432
湖北	172	14	126	18	3761	1205	1189	292
湖南	211	31	104	16	3015	869	1053	316
广东	283	38	187	36	7444	1849	1365	541
广西	75	18	56		1435	436	392	159
海南	17	7	7	2	313	53	49	13
重庆	112	8	58	31	1952	734	591	219
四川	299	45	205	19	4205	1399	1184	356
贵州	139	51	62	16	3192	1207	788	256
云南	200	26	124	22	1231	319	448	157
西藏	2		2		31	4	8	5
陕西	106	28	71	6	2478	797	612	215
甘肃	69	3	35	21	792	218	178	74
青海	32	9	6	9	164	41	39	10
宁夏	34	2	21	10	211	60	49	45
新疆	173	6	95	44	1413	613	477	141

机构总表

单位:个、人、人次、时

职业资格水平		年龄结构				志愿服务	
助理社会工作师人数	社会工作师人数	35岁及以下人数	36岁至45岁人数	46岁至55岁人数	56岁及以上人数	志愿者服务人次数	志愿服务时间
559	**398**	**26282**	**31041**	**17834**	**5611**	**12839**	**35001.0**
51	32	503	590	479	174	1915	5625.0
2	6	241	227	276	173	100	200.0
30	9	1164	1303	688	158	175	601.0
3	2	334	370	166	60		
11	4	534	691	495	128		
35	29	1560	1657	1201	332	2034	4085.0
1	5	1193	1627	1232	493	110	330.0
15	14	724	1296	870	507	175	310.0
9	6	1052	884	729	348	1463	3813.0
44	31	1076	1634	1036	316	1356	3776.0
15	20	923	1251	939	377	540	1510.0
40	27	906	1243	663	171	2237	5705.0
23	17	881	1242	612	167	6	18.0
28	21	684	894	346	76	276	841.0
21	23	1119	1329	701	223		
47	28	2873	2055	758	177		
13	11	1213	1462	890	196	370	1110.0
15	5	1179	1200	508	128	572	2286.0
65	28	2441	2950	1617	436	15	42.0
11	7	461	584	303	87		
1		53	185	57	18		
12	4	631	792	403	126	937	2264.0
29	24	1292	1775	903	235	1	1.0
8	8	1089	1333	624	146	454	2142.0
10	8	495	493	196	47	29	73.0
		13	10	8			
10	20	789	923	574	192	28	84.0
7	4	247	301	215	29		
		46	91	26	1		
	1	33	106	61	11		
3	4	533	543	258	79	46	185.0

C-3-13续表1

地　区	火化炉数	全年处理遗体数	国际运尸数	外国人	港澳台	侨民
全　国	**5743**	**4688910**	**471**	**144**	**230**	**34**
中央级						
北　京	90	88104	125	93	2	30
天　津	71	66959				
河　北	361	224811				
山　西	60	20842				
内蒙古	142	64776	7	7		
辽　宁	343	282540				
吉　林	169	107879				
黑龙江	260	168303				
上　海	93	121107	95	33	2	
江　苏	510	484987				
浙　江	343	305846	1	1		
安　徽	238	262383				
福　建	215	190453				
江　西	202	91123				
山　东	477	599057				
河　南	319	262860				
湖　北	310	218474				
湖　南	143	80045				
广　东	403	465419	233	3	226	4
广　西	88	71536	7	7		
海　南	6	2728	3			
重　庆	117	77092				
四　川	267	200546				
贵　州	117	68161				
云　南	163	59375				
西　藏	6	783				
陕　西	85	47126				
甘　肃	48	17074				
青　海	38	7367				
宁　夏	8	3606				
新　疆	51	27548				

单位:具、个、台

穴位数	#本年销售穴位数	安葬数	#本年安葬数	格位数	#格位存放数	#本年格位存放数
13039598	**596575**	**8932865**	**628153**	**653230**	**289627**	**36120**
664634	18134	507723	18873	24730	13168	939
184725	7179	208620	8571	31390	24492	4217
237003	9037	91546	10820	5504	1126	824
88785	4215	48161	3375	17086	7556	847
299051	16525	223692	22457	15450	4852	231
524062	25391	358338	25819	5800	2190	590
41203	2901	33445	6808	4325	3505	124
206855	14907	177352	21721			
1818263	70555	1256029	66730	123790	99421	6716
1383760	92029	1114057	61570	7975	4880	200
995149	32128	743042	30658	33781	9547	443
322497	25621	288989	40168	18954	2840	1811
206518	14153	127035	14186			
95357	16535	60560	18155			
281365	8838	198227	13449			
252913	8845	140036	10817	1166	582	93
833051	26306	575916	38130	16568	2899	37
419093	22820	205427	22866	1662	1134	214
1051541	28709	631444	32329	232686	78706	10530
121945	9948	94365	6291	4500	4002	320
18698	669	10885	465			
471624	16452	297500	17363	43332	12875	994
1090005	50285	632054	56865	30888	11476	3316
345800	18363	144011	16652	1200	500	90
491774	9072	123247	14541			
287411	16158	265582	20338	30331	2235	2170
90890	7738	75068	6711			
5395	1205	1940	358			
30591	4572	20614	3888			
179640	17285	277960	17179	2112	1641	1414

C-3-13续表2

地 区	增加值合计	执行企业会计制度单位财务指标					执行行政	
		固定资产原价	营业收入	费用合计	营业利润	企业单位增加值	固定资产原价	上年结转和结余
全 国	**885521.3**	**766985.0**	**649683.6**	**214988.1**	**159896.4**	**291437.9**	**1783500.1**	**85694.3**
中央级								
北 京	38418.6	23677.8	49117.5	20224.3	14264.2	23231.5	98662.6	1983.6
天 津	34556.6	5917.2	3607.9	1809.3	80.0	986.4	32475.6	5500.4
河 北	16811.8	4029.4	2626.0	2549.1	-526.6	-52.3	66242.5	686.0
山 西	6247.4	8818.1	1081.0	346.0	15.0	142.2	22898.8	1335.0
内蒙古	14298.1	3196.0	1226.9	458.0	20.0	164.3	29884.6	1048.3
辽 宁	50206.1	26291.9	23652.8	11969.4	2299.6	14412.5	81765.1	3546.8
吉 林	8416.8	18477.7	1932.5	327.7	137.7	546.2	75465.4	
黑龙江	30415.1	17320.0	7927.8	5084.5	1714.4	4398.8	69356.4	2235.4
上 海	161382.5	242782.2	314222.2	76962.1	113654.3	160704.3	821.4	2150.2
江 苏	59827.8	20218.5	15277.6	6215.6	3583.7	7123.3	170134.2	15149.7
浙 江	59363.9	31342.4	39797.4	11043.3	4645.6	9382.4	135418.1	3731.6
安 徽	27629.1	17941.1	12096.2	6027.4	520.9	4868.5	45575.3	924.2
福 建	27786.3	47865.7	23442.2	9654.0	3286.5	11652.7	43954.5	4538.0
江 西	12877.3	5007.0	812.0	231.1	19.0	25.6	38218.5	240.2
山 东	37076.6	6500.3	4035.5	1785.1	209.5	1163.0	88864.1	
河 南	17897.6	17225.0	7801.0	3339.2	452.6	2826.9	51878.0	1057.5
湖 北	31325.8	7780.0	7738.5	3073.7	910.8	2641.5	92384.3	1247.3
湖 南	16628.6	25042.0	7368.7	3733.1	434.3	2461.3	64212.2	271.6
广 东	104532.4	32277.3	26493.5	9980.6	5197.0	13918.0	303576.8	13279.6
广 西	16203.8	11718.4	11806.0	3536.7	1562.5	3397.6	25131.4	7672.9
海 南	2896.0	7372.4	3230.3	1347.9	315.0	1617.4	8146.9	802.3
重 庆	17927.0	14465.3	3381.9	1849.0	5.6	863.7	45587.0	3.9
四 川	37076.4	43104.4	23187.7	7416.6	512.9	4469.8	75583.3	999.2
贵 州	17967.6	63874.0	34560.5	13211.7	4999.6	14236.1	13572.3	549.0
云 南	10842.3	41253.7	3544.3	1686.7	575.0	2643.7	33922.0	1070.9
西 藏	216.3						1667.2	
陕 西	12731.6	14587.2	17471.0	9422.9	836.2	3103.7	18449.2	7504.3
甘 肃	5523.7	1596.1	533.2	426.2	80.8	108.0	13967.1	50.0
青 海	582.3	1525.0	213.0	213.0		63.0	1772.1	
宁 夏	1243.8	323.0	460.0	396.0	-8.0	31.3	2285.1	1268.7
新 疆	6612.0	5455.9	1038.5	667.9	98.3	306.3	31628.1	6847.7

单位：万元

事业单位会计制度财务指标				执行民间非营利组织单位会计制度财务指标				
本年收入合计	本年支出合计	收支结余	行政事业单位增加值	固定资产原价	上年结余	本年收入合计	本年费用合计	社会组织增加值
1282846.8	**1235822.4**	**38484.5**	**592326.4**	**26137.7**	**2124.3**	**7494.4**	**5679.6**	**1757.0**
106460.6	111494.3	-3847.3	15187.1					
55928.7	55172.0	76.0	33570.2					
40983.7	33679.6	109.5	16864.1					
21074.0	21050.3	49.6	6105.2	2300.0				
22936.1	23002.1	1020.3	14118.8	40.0		60.0	60.0	15.0
79922.7	81209.6	388.1	35438.7	1565.7		1862.0	1865.0	354.9
14893.7	14402.1	87.4	7870.6					
50453.1	47814.6	17.5	26005.4	203.0			11.0	10.9
3673.6	3752.3	1799.9	678.2					
116328.6	105379.8	4063.0	52521.7	2531.1		822.3	669.5	182.8
98401.1	89779.6	3197.3	49921.1	315.0	1140.0	942.0	488.1	60.4
40797.2	38654.6	629.3	22711.4	1093.0		411.0	155.0	49.2
34640.9	31909.7	5004.2	16069.6	567.1		390.7	96.3	64.0
22566.7	20019.4		12851.7					
68473.8	68473.8		35750.6	886.7		382.0	382.0	163.0
25693.8	25414.7	88.7	15070.6	370.0		150.0	0.2	0.1
69785.1	64954.3	-46.7	28682.1	5.0		3.0	3.0	2.2
37050.0	37041.8	23.2	14167.3					
162089.8	161343.0	10856.4	90565.8	1661.1	63.8	86.5	63.4	48.6
23821.2	22284.7	744.7	12806.2					
6983.7	4112.0	2364.7	1278.6					
39596.5	37305.1	1976.1	17001.3	3500.0		30.0	100.0	62.0
53484.8	48780.9	107.3	32137.6	3383.0	698.5	1928.0	1281.4	469.0
3807.5	4858.2		3684.0	2917.0		216.7	175.5	47.5
12671.7	11130.6	196.6	8198.6					
510.0	510.0		216.3					
28183.2	31493.0	4278.2	9626.9	150.0		10.0	7.0	1.0
13865.3	11365.4		5407.6	72.0		2.6	10.3	8.1
762.9	710.9		495.2	2710.0		35.6	37.7	24.1
4397.3	4683.9	204.5	1151.5	652.0	222.0	35.0	81.0	61.0
22609.5	24040.1	5096.0	6172.5	1216.0		127.0	193.2	133.2

C−3−14 殡仪

地　区	单位数	年末职工人数	#女性	受教育程度		职业资
				大学专科人数	大学本科及以上人数	助理社会工作师人数
全　国	**1784**	**46178**	**11524**	**12826**	**4074**	**308**
中央级						
北　京	12	598	136	150	82	24
天　津	12	555	117	121	105	2
河　北	153	2767	581	501	140	30
山　西	23	378	105	82	76	2
内蒙古	60	1122	286	352	92	1
辽　宁	78	2731	737	831	266	19
吉　林	47	1998	99	1265	238	
黑龙江	101	2756	699	782	279	14
上　海	15	926	219	228	122	3
江　苏	95	2697	646	663	269	33
浙　江	76	2178	446	627	208	10
安　徽	71	1942	602	463	112	24
福　建	63	1804	389	163	54	15
江　西	86	1428	346	199	42	7
山　东	122	2750	548	917	346	18
河　南	115	3620	1016	1052	222	23
湖　北	88	2592	883	870	236	13
湖　南	70	1406	380	508	171	2
广　东	91	4195	904	760	273	36
广　西	29	719	208	198	53	6
海　南	2	66	22	12	6	
重　庆	38	941	316	328	119	7
四　川	77	1813	496	503	139	10
贵　州	44	1450	572	288	100	
云　南	78	709	164	258	83	2
西　藏	2	31	4	8	5	
陕　西	40	1083	303	401	150	3
甘　肃	25	323	100	93	35	4
青　海	19	96	21	37	10	
宁　夏	7	63	21	11	16	
新　疆	45	441	158	155	25	

馆

单位:个、人、人次、时

格水平	年龄结构				志愿服务	
社会工作师人数	35岁及以下人数	36岁至45岁人数	46岁至55岁人数	56岁及以上人数	志愿者服务人次数	志愿服务时间
204	**15073**	**17628**	**10099**	**3378**	**6613**	**18088.0**
14	136	194	195	73	920	2656.0
1	149	94	180	132	50	100.0
7	921	1135	588	123	152	496.0
2	103	136	96	43		
1	327	429	284	82		
14	860	1018	644	209	45	86.0
3	402	668	545	383		
11	569	996	711	480	175	310.0
2	354	240	230	102	1127	3361.0
20	751	1008	724	214	896	2595.0
11	580	857	557	184	186	432.0
20	621	792	429	100	1047	1857.0
14	537	791	372	104		
2	467	643	268	50	276	841.0
19	887	1102	576	185		
7	1873	1200	450	97		
9	867	1014	557	154	225	675.0
	551	551	242	62	535	2150.0
14	1370	1688	905	232	15	42.0
2	260	249	157	53		
	19	38	9			
3	300	372	213	56	814	2015.0
13	591	757	360	105	1	1.0
4	530	674	223	23	146	465.0
2	300	274	107	28		
	13	10	8			
7	397	356	265	65	2	6.0
2	118	108	84	13		
	36	46	14			
	10	29	18	6		
	174	159	88	20	1	

C-3-14续表1

地 区	火化炉数	全年处理遗体数	国际运尸数	外国人
全 国	**5743**	**4688910**	**471**	**144**
中央级				
北 京	90	88104	125	93
天 津	71	66959		
河 北	361	224811		
山 西	60	20842		
内蒙古	142	64776	7	7
辽 宁	343	282540		
吉 林	169	107879		
黑龙江	260	168303		
上 海	93	121107	95	33
江 苏	510	484987		
浙 江	343	305846	1	1
安 徽	238	262383		
福 建	215	190453		
江 西	202	91123		
山 东	477	599057		
河 南	319	262860		
湖 北	310	218474		
湖 南	143	80045		
广 东	403	465419	233	3
广 西	88	71536	7	7
海 南	6	2728	3	
重 庆	117	77092		
四 川	267	200546		
贵 州	117	68161		
云 南	163	59375		
西 藏	6	783		
陕 西	85	47126		
甘 肃	48	17074		
青 海	38	7367		
宁 夏	8	3606		
新 疆	51	27548		

单位:具、个、台

港澳台	侨民	穴位数	#本年销售穴位数	安葬数	#本年安葬数
230	**34**	**1745161**	**83931**	**1180830**	**158543**
2	30	8042	158	7731	164
		26244	2009	20360	1835
		52019	3665	31783	4679
		103174	7016	84901	13533
		13174	784	13447	796
		7979	676	10793	4533
		110017	2068	106734	11189
2		117	35	116	35
		109027	4325	129274	10037
		84647	3685	59637	4198
		48050	1774	60555	20693
		102972	6841	68437	8527
		75330	15417	47275	16679
		65649	1051	63662	5751
		33058	1188	17098	3368
		103205	6236	102667	19063
		152410	4499	107048	6989
226	4	112446	2288	37337	2473
		4612	1382	7537	54
		99456	3288	66609	4131
		18589	1553	12368	1380
		29306	1220	1956	1302
		299676	3998	46210	8968
		50947	1799	46461	774
		6702	2192	12089	1924
		40	40	40	40
		4661	741	1662	748
		23612	4003	17043	4680

C-3-14续表2

地区	增加值合计	执行企业会计制度单位财务指标					执行行政	
		固定资产原价	营业收入	费用合计	营业利润	企业单位增加值	固定资产原价	上年结转和结余
全　国	**482355.1**	**292659.0**	**119507.0**	**43224.1**	**15017.9**	**54475.0**	**1348313.3**	**41119.9**
中央级								
北　京	8238.0						51712.7	421.3
天　津	26209.4						23408.0	1111.0
河　北	14232.4	1943.2	366.0	404.0	-116.0	-109.0	57610.4	598.6
山　西	4599.9						18789.1	1071.8
内蒙古	10817.0	2536.0	468.9	139.0		3.1	27163.7	750.8
辽　宁	30576.8	10889.5	5417.8	3290.3	-68.6	3156.4	64620.2	887.8
吉　林	6008.1	17177.0	92.0	4.0		27.1	66661.2	
黑龙江	23436.0	9835.4	1726.8	1594.1	39.4	864.7	56361.6	1290.0
上　海	25865.2	88363.6	63230.2	17699.0	10447.4	25865.2		
江　苏	40609.6	8210.5	2661.3	498.5	619.2	1076.6	151658.9	11240.1
浙　江	42024.6	4695.4	3516.2	1416.8	388.8	1534.5	125030.9	2153.3
安　徽	16352.4	5168.2	2224.2	1033.9	116.0	1487.9	32665.6	274.0
福　建	16532.1	39539.6	13750.3	7069.0	1810.7	8315.1	34494.7	851.6
江　西	9685.0	4999.0	812.0	231.1	19.0	25.6	22985.3	202.2
山　东	32443.1	630.0	152.0	138.0		75.7	75741.8	
河　南	11577.9	4486.1	943.2	368.1	111.8	378.4	46698.7	902.7
湖　北	20982.0	469.2	250.0	100.0		0.1	61805.2	896.0
湖　南	9245.3	7565.5	1835.0	1014.8	6.2	671.4	32803.9	145.3
广　东	62613.7	1644.9	657.9	259.9		60.4	219694.6	6879.2
广　西	6275.3	3392.5	943.8	535.0	-104.9	23.6	15369.9	1134.5
海　南	950.0	5008.0	1072.0	494.0	1.0	703.0	406.2	38.8
重　庆	10440.3	8502.3	1498.5	811.5	7.0	432.2	32140.1	21.9
四　川	19934.1	21704.7	4977.0	1002.2	116.5	2704.5	45467.6	439.4
贵　州	9470.5	37050.0	12306.4	4767.7	1624.4	7011.5	10537.6	565.1
云　南	7143.7	3947.5	50.0				29243.1	960.3
西　藏	216.3						1667.2	
陕　西	8050.2	30.0	100.0			30.0	15210.7	7502.7
甘　肃	3705.1	150.0					13095.4	42.0
青　海	532.2	1245.0	183.0	183.0		33.0	1725.0	
宁　夏	615.3						669.4	739.5
新　疆	2973.7	3475.9	272.5	170.2		104.0	12874.6	

单位：万元

事业单位会计制度财务指标				执行民间非营利组织单位会计制度财务指标				
本年收入合计	本年支出合计	收支结余	行政事业单位增加值	固定资产原价	上年结余	本年收入合计	本年费用合计	社会组织增加值
844347.0	**822942.9**	**15172.5**	**427720.8**	**8997.0**	**222.0**	**346.2**	**243.7**	**159.3**
31945.3	34222.6	-673.9	8238.0					
29588.7	30058.2		26209.4					
31696.9	25833.7	90.4	14341.4					
13608.6	14132.8	49.6	4599.9					
17467.8	17683.9	572.7	10813.9					
51048.9	50717.4	279.3	27420.4					
7680.3	7273.8	7.4	5981.0					
40706.9	37499.2	17.5	22570.6	3.0			0.8	0.7
86850.5	78382.4	3054.8	39533.0					
78366.3	73306.8	2707.1	40490.1					
26715.8	25273.4	638.4	14864.5					
19804.9	17875.0	207.7	8217.0					
17722.1	15323.6		9659.4					
58121.4	58121.4		32367.4					
19020.0	18794.3	0.1	11199.4	370.0		150.0	0.2	0.1
47799.1	46994.4	51.6	20979.7	5.0		3.0	3.0	2.2
27340.4	27551.4	23.2	8573.9					
110239.1	119028.8	1231.3	62553.3					
12466.7	11593.8	510.0	6251.7					
549.9	565.9		247.0					
28587.1	26746.6	1807.3	9946.1	3500.0		30.0	100.0	62.0
25892.2	24577.2	40.8	17229.6					
2530.9	2881.5		2450.0	1290.0		60.6	17.0	9.0
11068.1	9578.4	198.9	7143.7					
510.0	510.0		216.3					
25683.4	29263.3	4153.8	8019.2	150.0		10.0	7.0	1.0
11248.6	8795.3		3705.1					
743.5	691.5		475.9	2667.0		32.6	34.7	23.3
1492.0	1901.5	204.5	554.3	652.0	222.0	35.0	81.0	61.0
7851.6	7764.8		2869.7	360.0		25.0		

C-3-15 公

地　区	单位数	年末职工人数		受教育程度		职业资
			#女性	大学专科人数	大学本科及以上人数	助理社会工作师人数
全　国	**1506**	**25397**	**8142**	**4979**	**1917**	**150**
中央级						
北　京	34	1046	348	163	175	26
天　津	7	247	75	35	49	
河　北	16	388	144	80	32	
山　西	27	475	89	93	52	1
内蒙古	29	449	140	90	38	4
辽　宁	129	1582	445	429	267	8
吉　林	52	2205	142	209	90	1
黑龙江	36	463	140	138	50	1
上　海	51	2038	803	194	67	5
江　苏	102	1125	368	256	98	4
浙　江	72	931	271	136	62	
安　徽	81	794	254	166	38	13
福　建	22	364	133	45	17	1
江　西	14	211	56	39	21	12
山　东	38	559	203	147	55	2
河　南	52	1079	366	273	78	7
湖　北	62	871	234	207	28	
湖　南	82	1109	393	334	89	10
广　东	84	1934	651	272	102	20
广　西	19	355	128	72	33	
海　南	8	192	20	26	3	1
重　庆	49	870	367	194	56	5
四　川	149	1965	761	507	182	16
贵　州	54	1417	566	356	79	4
云　南	72	326	95	101	23	1
西　藏						
陕　西	37	1159	428	137	28	6
甘　肃	33	390	97	57	22	1
青　海	11	62	16			
宁　夏	11	88	22	16	6	
新　疆	73	703	387	207	77	1

墓

单位:个、人、人次、时

格水平	年龄结构				志愿服务	
社会工作师人数	35岁及以下人数	36岁至45岁人数	46岁至55岁人数	56岁及以上人数	志愿者服务人次数	志愿服务时间
97	**7955**	**9692**	**5953**	**1797**	**2907**	**9047.0**
15	328	366	262	90	693	2079.0
	64	93	60	30		
2	199	105	69	15	23	105.0
	205	203	53	14		
	131	145	140	33		
2	579	464	445	94	20	60.0
2	747	729	632	97		
3	108	237	102	16		
	688	630	482	238	296	352.0
8	269	510	253	93	441	1157.0
1	194	267	297	173	334	958.0
4	225	339	174	56	578	1940.0
	94	160	86	24		
18	87	94	22	8		
2	207	200	116	36		
13	373	465	179	62		
1	251	328	260	32	145	435.0
4	426	424	211	48	32	126.0
1	591	749	434	160		
	79	206	60	10		
	23	123	35	11		
1	294	340	168	68	3	9.0
11	587	807	452	119		
	401	546	366	104	281	1593.0
1	122	135	57	12		
5	288	489	274	108	16	48.0
	98	167	111	14		
	7	43	12			
	11	51	23	3		
3	279	277	118	29	45	185.0

C-3-15续表1

地　区	增加值合计	执行企业会计制度单位财务指标				
		固定资产原价	营业收入	费用合计	营业利润	企业单位增加值
全　国	**334636.6**	**464270.2**	**527264.7**	**169806.5**	**144385.7**	**235874.2**
中央级						
北　京	26426.9	23677.8	49117.5	20224.3	14264.2	23231.5
天　津	5865.1	5917.2	3607.9	1809.3	80.0	986.4
河　北	1457.8	2086.2	2260.0	2145.1	-410.6	56.7
山　西	993.8	8818.1	1081.0	346.0	15.0	142.2
内蒙古	1961.0	660.0	758.0	319.0	20.0	161.2
辽　宁	17113.0	15402.4	18235.0	8679.1	2368.2	11256.1
吉　林	1337.5	1300.7	1840.5	323.7	137.7	519.1
黑龙江	5950.2	6906.6	5451.0	2729.6	1485.0	3322.8
上　海	134839.1	154418.6	250992.0	59263.1	103206.9	134839.1
江　苏	17392.9	12008.0	12616.3	5717.1	2964.5	6046.7
浙　江	12195.9	26542.7	35931.4	9557.2	4233.1	7803.4
安　徽	9189.5	12772.9	9872.0	4993.5	404.9	3380.6
福　建	6430.4	7752.2	8603.4	2178.5	1183.4	2753.3
江　西	2022.9	5.0				
山　东	3785.1	5870.3	3883.5	1647.1	209.5	1087.3
河　南	4499.3	12738.9	6857.8	2971.1	340.8	2448.5
湖　北	8778.6	7287.8	7488.5	2973.7	910.8	2641.4
湖　南	5549.6	10972.5	5176.7	2202.3	428.1	1712.9
广　东	25878.9	30562.4	25733.6	9602.7	5205.0	13784.6
广　西	3837.5	8325.9	10862.2	3001.7	1667.4	3374.0
海　南	1081.8	2354.4	2158.3	853.9	314.0	914.4
重　庆	6421.0	5963.0	1883.4	1037.5	-1.4	431.5
四　川	14734.9	21004.1	18149.1	6356.7	395.0	1730.6
贵　州	7427.6	26584.0	22216.1	8435.5	3375.2	7194.0
云　南	3035.4	37299.2	3494.3	1686.7	575.0	2643.7
西　藏						
陕　西	3416.2	14193.2	17371.0	9422.9	836.2	3073.7
甘　肃	1548.4	1086.1	533.2	426.2	80.8	108.0
青　海	30.8	280.0	30.0	30.0		30.0
宁　夏	323.5	313.0	460.0	396.0	-8.0	31.3
新　疆	1111.8	1167.0	601.0	477.0	105.0	169.0

单位：万元

执行行政事业单位会计制度财务指标					
固定资产原价	上年结转和结余	本年收入合计	本年支出合计	收支结余	行政事业单位增加值
241248.1	**18319.4**	**298220.4**	**271728.5**	**11016.5**	**97200.4**
28512.2	1562.3	57917.7	59117.3	-1607.9	3195.4
7924.2	4159.8	19974.6	19016.8	76.0	4878.7
2617.3	55.0	6151.1	4606.5		1401.1
3830.8	263.2	6693.2	6141.5		851.6
915.6	164.6	3109.4	2934.2	339.8	1784.8
11764.4		17991.1	17282.3	102.8	5502.0
3489.3		5289.7	5204.6	80.0	818.4
8075.4	945.4	7722.1	7835.2		2617.2
15536.8	2325.3	25826.9	23263.2	978.3	11163.4
7215.2	1304.9	10804.6	7499.2	493.9	4332.1
8800.0	650.2	10729.8	10013.5	-9.6	5759.7
835.3	2.0	6581.0	5175.7	1168.5	3637.1
12913.7		3164.0	3165.0		2022.9
11516.4		9365.4	9365.4		2534.8
3813.6	62.1	4062.2	4022.6	78.1	2050.8
25387.1		20332.8	16306.7	-98.3	6137.2
22292.4	126.3	7260.1	7194.9		3836.7
18157.7	5393.6	23675.7	16730.7	9155.3	12057.0
1543.7		2626.5	2313.6		463.5
85.0	256.0	1421.0	681.0		167.4
11603.2	-18.0	9159.5	8676.3	201.1	5989.5
23477.1	553.3	24205.5	20553.4	40.5	12535.3
825.5		91.3	872.4		195.5
4147.1	68.8	324.3	312.8		391.7
944.5		933.2	887.4	18.0	342.5
613.5	8.0	2232.2	2185.6		1432.3
972.0	436.6	2503.0	2418.0		292.2
3439.1		8072.5	7952.7		809.6

C-3-15续表2

地区	执行民间非营利组织单位会计制度财务指标					穴位数
	固定资产原价	上年结余	本年收入合计	本年费用合计	社会组织增加值	
全　国	**16112.7**	**1934.7**	**7088.4**	**5397.7**	**1562.0**	**11294437**
中央级						
北　京						656592
天　津						158481
河　北						184984
山　西	2300.0					88785
内蒙古	40.0		60.0	60.0	15.0	195877
辽　宁	1565.7		1862.0	1865.0	354.9	510888
吉　林						33224
黑龙江	200.0			10.2	10.2	96838
上　海						1818146
江　苏	2531.1		822.3	669.5	182.8	1274733
浙　江	315.0	1140.0	942.0	488.1	60.4	910502
安　徽	1093.0		411.0	155.0	49.2	274447
福　建	417.1		360.7	71.3	40.0	103546
江　西						20027
山　东	886.7		382.0	382.0	163.0	215716
河　南						219855
湖　北						729846
湖　南						266683
广　东	783.1	96.2	56.7	50.6	37.3	939095
广　西						117333
海　南						18698
重　庆						372168
四　川	3383.0	698.5	1928.0	1281.4	469.0	1071416
贵　州	1627.0		156.1	158.1	38.1	316494
云　南						192098
西　藏						
陕　西						236464
甘　肃	72.0		2.6	10.3	8.1	84188
青　海	43.0		3.0	3.0	0.8	5355
宁　夏						25930
新　疆	856.0		102.0	193.2	133.2	156028

单位:万元、个、具

#本年销售穴位数	安葬数	#本年安葬数	格位数	格位存放数	本年格位存放数
512644	**7752035**	**469610**	**628693**	**279505**	**35733**
17976	499992	18709	24730	13168	939
5170	188260	6736	31390	24492	4217
5372	59763	6141	5504	1126	824
4215	48161	3375	17086	7556	847
9509	138791	8924	15450	4852	231
24607	344891	25023	4200	590	590
2225	22652	2275	4325	3505	124
12839	70618	10532			
70520	1255913	66695	123790	99421	6716
87704	984783	51533	7975	4880	200
28443	683405	26460	27303	7908	304
23847	228434	19475	18954	2840	1811
7312	58598	5659			
1118	13285	1476			
7787	134565	7698			
7657	122938	7449	1166	582	93
20070	473249	19067	16568	2899	37
18321	98379	15877	1662	1134	214
26421	594107	29856	217827	72538	10338
8566	86828	6237	4500	4002	320
669	10885	465			
13164	230891	13232	42332	12407	958
48732	619686	55485	30888	11476	3316
17143	142055	15350	1200	500	90
5074	77037	5573			
14359	219121	19564	30331	2235	2170
5546	62979	4787			
1165	1900	318			
3831	18952	3140			
13282	260917	12499	1512	1394	1394

C-3-16 骨灰

地　区	单位数	年末职工人数		受教育程度	
			#女性	大学专科人数	大学本科及以上人数
全　国	**29**	**173**	**30**	**23**	**11**
中央级					
北　京					
天　津					
河　北					
山　西					
内蒙古					
辽　宁	2	16	4	8	7
吉　林					
黑龙江					
上　海					
江　苏					
浙　江	1	3	1		
安　徽					
福　建	1	8	2		
江　西	3	12	3	3	
山　东					
河　南					
湖　北					
湖　南					
广　东	12	76	4		
广　西					
海　南	1	4		1	
重　庆	1	11	6	1	1
四　川					
贵　州					
云　南					
西　藏					
陕　西					
甘　肃					
青　海					
宁　夏					
新　疆	8	43	10	10	3

堂

单位:个、人、人次、时

职业资格水平		年龄结构			
助理社会工作师人数	社会工作师人数	35岁及以下人数	36岁至45岁人数	46岁至55岁人数	56岁及以上人数
1		**78**	**49**	**29**	**17**
1		3	9	3	1
			1	1	1
		5	2	1	
			4	5	3
		55	6	5	10
		1	3		
		3	6	2	
		11	18	12	2

C-3-16续表1

地区	增加值合计	执行企业会计制度单位财务指标				
		固定资产原价	营业收入	费用合计	营业利润	企业单位增加值
全国	**1131.5**	**46.7**	**117.8**	**47.2**	**-20.2**	**-9.4**
中央级						
北京						
天津						
河北						
山西						
内蒙古						
辽宁	61.0					
吉林						
黑龙江						
上海						
江苏						
浙江	-9.4	36.7	117.8	47.2	-20.2	-9.4
安徽						
福建	24.0					
江西	355.7					
山东						
河南						
湖北						
湖南						
广东	427.8					
广西						
海南		10.0				
重庆						
四川						
贵州						
云南						
西藏						
陕西						
甘肃						
青海						
宁夏						
新疆	272.4					

单位：万元

执行行政事业单位会计制度财务指标					
固定资产原价	上年结转和结余	本年收入合计	本年支出合计	收支结余	行政事业单位增加值
2479.6		**1190.7**	**1282.3**		**1106.1**
637.9		86.4	86.7		61.0
379.3		189.5	189.5		355.7
453.8		465.3	465.3		417.0
1008.6		449.5	540.8		272.4

C-3-16续表2

地区	执行民间非营利组织单位会计制度财务指标			
	固定资产原价	上年结余	本年收入合计	本年费用合计
全国	**1028.0**	**-32.4**	**58.8**	**36.3**
中央级				
北京				
天津				
河北				
山西				
内蒙古				
辽宁				
吉林				
黑龙江				
上海				
江苏				
浙江				
安徽				
福建	150.0		30.0	25.0
江西				
山东				
河南				
湖北				
湖南				
广东	878.0	-32.4	28.8	11.3
广西				
海南				
重庆				
四川				
贵州				
云南				
西藏				
陕西				
甘肃				
青海				
宁夏				
新疆				

单位：万元、个

社会组织增加值	格位数	格位存放数	本年格位存放数
34.8	**24537**	**10122**	**387**
	1600	1600	
	6478	1639	139
24.0			
10.8	14859	6168	192
	1000	468	36
	600	247	20

C-3-17 其他殡葬

地 区	单位数	年末职工人数		受教育程度		职业资
			#女性	大学专科人数	大学本科及以上人数	助理社会工作师人数
全 国	**1063**	**9020**	**2312**	**3001**	**1539**	**100**
中央级						
北 京	8	102	40	19	73	1
天 津	10	115	26	36	54	
河 北	13	158	32	50	23	
山 西	11	77	26	31	16	
内蒙古	39	277	71	93	44	6
辽 宁	53	421	107	173	126	7
吉 林	47	342	20	59	29	
黑龙江	15	178	57	71	47	
上 海	10	49	18	17	18	1
江 苏	45	240	90	108	60	7
浙 江	68	378	67	136	122	5
安 徽	39	247	74	81	33	3
福 建	67	726	157	167	88	7
江 西	40	349	80	76	20	9
山 东	8	63	18	32	8	1
河 南	87	1164	362	358	132	17
湖 北	22	298	88	112	28	
湖 南	59	500	96	211	56	3
广 东	96	1239	290	333	166	9
广 西	27	361	100	122	73	5
海 南	6	51	11	10	4	
重 庆	24	130	45	68	43	
四 川	73	427	142	174	35	3
贵 州	41	325	69	144	77	4
云 南	50	196	60	89	51	7
西 藏						
陕 西	29	236	66	74	37	1
甘 肃	11	79	21	28	17	2
青 海	2	6	4	2		
宁 夏	16	60	17	22	23	
新 疆	47	226	58	105	36	2

服务机构

单位:个、人、人次、时

格水平	年龄结构				志愿服务	
社会工作师人数	35岁及以下人数	36岁至45岁人数	46岁至55岁人数	56岁及以上人数	志愿者服务人次数	志愿服务时间
97	**3176**	**3672**	**1753**	**419**	**3319**	**7866.0**
3	39	30	22	11	302	890.0
5	28	40	36	11	50	100.0
	44	63	31	20		
	26	31	17	3		
3	76	117	71	13		
13	118	166	109	28	1969	3939.0
	44	230	55	13	110	330.0
	47	63	57	11		
4	10	14	17	8	40	100.0
3	56	116	59	9	19	24.0
8	149	126	84	19	20	120.0
3	60	112	60	15	612	1908.0
3	245	289	153	39	6	18.0
1	130	153	51	15		
2	25	27	9	2		
8	627	390	129	18		
1	95	120	73	10		
1	202	225	55	18	5	10.0
13	425	507	273	34		
5	122	129	86	24		
	10	21	13	7		
	34	74	20	2	120	240.0
	114	211	91	11		
4	158	113	35	19	27	84.0
5	73	84	32	7	29	73.0
8	104	78	35	19	10	30.0
2	31	26	20	2		
	3	2		1		
1	12	26	20	2		
1	69	89	40	28		

C-3-17续表

地　区	增加值合计	执行企业会计制度单位财务指标					执行行政	
		固定资产原价	营业收入	费用合计	营业利润	企业单位增加值	固定资产原价	上年结转和结余
全　国	**67398.1**	**10009.1**	**2794.1**	**1910.3**	**513.0**	**1098.1**	**191459.1**	**26255.0**
中央级								
北　京	3753.7						18437.7	
天　津	2482.1						1143.4	229.6
河　北	1121.6						6014.8	32.4
山　西	653.7						278.9	
内蒙古	1520.1						1805.3	132.9
辽　宁	2455.3						4742.6	2659.0
吉　林	1071.2						5314.9	
黑龙江	1028.9	578.0	750.0	760.8	190.0	211.3	4919.4	
上　海	678.2						821.4	2150.2
江　苏	1825.3						2938.5	1584.3
浙　江	5152.8	67.6	232.0	22.1	43.9	53.9	3172.0	273.4
安　徽	2087.2						4109.7	
福　建	4799.8	573.9	1088.5	406.5	292.4	584.3	8624.5	3684.4
江　西	813.7	3.0					1940.2	38.0
山　东	848.4						1605.9	
河　南	1820.4						1365.7	92.7
湖　北	1565.2	23.0					5192.0	351.3
湖　南	1833.7	6504.0	357.0	516.0		77.0	9115.9	
广　东	15612.0	70.0	102.0	118.0	-8.0	73.0	65270.7	1006.8
广　西	6091.0						8217.8	6538.4
海　南	864.2						7655.7	507.5
重　庆	1065.7						1843.7	
四　川	2407.4	395.6	61.6	57.7	1.4	34.7	6638.6	6.5
贵　州	1069.5	240.0	38.0	8.5		30.6	2209.2	-16.1
云　南	663.2	7.0					531.8	41.8
西　藏								
陕　西	1265.2	364.0					2294.0	1.6
甘　肃	270.2	360.0					258.2	
青　海	19.3						47.1	
宁　夏	305.0	10.0					643.7	92.6
新　疆	2254.1	813.0	165.0	20.7	-6.7	33.3	14305.8	6847.7

单位：万元、个

事业单位会计制度财务指标				执行民间非营利组织单位会计制度财务指标			殡仪服务站
本年收入合计	本年支出合计	收支结余	行政事业单位增加值	本年收入合计	本年费用合计	社会组织增加值	
139088.7	**139868.7**	**12295.5**	**66299.1**	**1.0**	**1.9**	**0.9**	**21**
16597.6	18154.4	-1565.5	3753.7				2
6365.4	6097.0		2482.1				
3135.7	3239.4	19.1	1121.6				
772.2	776.0		653.7				
2358.9	2384.0	107.8	1520.1				1
10796.3	13123.2	6.0	2455.3				
1923.7	1923.7		1071.2				
2024.1	2480.2		817.6				
3673.6	3752.3	1799.9	678.2				
3651.2	3734.2	29.9	1825.3				
9230.2	8973.6	-3.7	5098.9				
3351.6	3367.7	0.5	2087.2				
8255.0	8859.0	3628.0	4215.5				3
1491.1	1341.3		813.7				
987.0	987.0		848.4				
2611.6	2597.8	10.5	1820.4				
1653.2	1653.2		1565.2				
2449.5	2295.5		1756.7				
27709.7	25118.2	469.8	15538.5	1.0	1.5	0.5	
8728.0	8377.3	234.7	6091.0				
5012.8	2865.1	2364.7	864.2				
1849.9	1882.2	-32.3	1065.7				
3387.1	3650.3	26.0	2372.7				15
1185.3	1104.3		1038.5		0.4	0.4	
1279.3	1239.4	-2.3	663.2				
1566.6	1342.3	106.4	1265.2				
384.5	384.5		270.2				
19.4	19.4		19.3				
402.3	364.4		305.0				
6235.9	7781.8	5096.0	2220.8				

C-4-1 其他

地 区	单位数	编办登记	民政登记	年末职工人数	#女性	受教育程度 大学专科人数	大学本科及以上人数
全 国	**2384**	**2273**	**111**	**20480**	**9191**	**5333**	**6504**
中央级	29	29		1482	735	225	1174
北 京	77	77		918	433	155	543
天 津	23	23		182	91	56	101
河 北	51	48	3	587	369	107	85
山 西	73	72	1	491	232	145	125
内蒙古	19	19		300	129	71	77
辽 宁	122	116	6	902	384	219	312
吉 林	95	66	29	601	192	203	85
黑龙江	59	58	1	818	410	151	207
上 海	37	37		593	194	151	247
江 苏	73	72	1	658	323	264	210
浙 江	190	181	9	893	420	205	369
安 徽	22	19	3	116	46	33	27
福 建	69	66	3	280	138	72	129
江 西	435	434	1	1803	666	301	227
山 东	49	49		447	197	138	123
河 南	169	164	5	2678	1139	683	694
湖 北	76	72	4	822	415	313	229
湖 南	146	137	9	1175	581	410	282
广 东	43	39	4	626	323	176	235
广 西	59	59		855	355	204	123
海 南	21	21		108	46	50	41
重 庆	23	23		112	43	38	34
四 川	164	143	21	1030	441	326	313
贵 州	90	87	3	648	242	214	159
云 南	37	34	3	209	99	81	62
西 藏							
陕 西	49	49		567	277	155	96
甘 肃	40	35	5	266	87	61	77
青 海	3	3		12	4	6	2
宁 夏	8	8		52	18	12	10
新 疆	33	33		249	162	108	106

事业单位

单位:个、人、人次、时

职业资格水平		年龄结构				志愿服务	
助理社会工作师人数	社会工作师人数	35岁及以下人数	36岁至45岁人数	46岁至55岁人数	56岁及以上人数	志愿者服务人次数	志愿服务时间
265	**349**	**7384**	**7212**	**4475**	**1409**	**9400**	**25419.5**
8	11	727	370	309	76		
26	29	294	311	227	86	229	612.0
1	5	50	60	49	23	500	1000.0
4	2	316	192	69	10	722	3130.0
1	12	105	203	146	37		
	2	103	105	76	16		
	3	305	344	146	107	16	44.0
9	7	208	257	108	28	15	40.0
6	12	260	287	241	30		
8	38	219	197	134	43		
15	23	286	193	151	28	802	1899.0
17	50	305	293	237	58	3602	6844.5
5	3	11	45	54	6	148	320.0
5	18	109	94	61	16		
23	11	649	829	270	55	728	2844.0
2	7	176	130	110	31	2074	6241.0
50	24	1158	839	550	131		
12	11	231	348	213	30	57	156.0
3	16	422	418	243	92	340	1377.0
3	11	231	203	145	47	20	60.0
7	20	189	226	175	265		
6	4	43	32	29	4		
1	1	31	47	31	3	2	12.0
26	15	342	367	241	80	100	800.0
6		179	256	174	39	5	10.0
2	2	78	80	38	13		
2	2	208	231	112	16		
9	2	68	115	70	13	40	30.0
3	3	3	4	4	1		
		3	14	22	13		
5	5	75	122	40	12		

C-4-1续表

地　区	增加值合计	执行企业会计制度单位财务指标				
		固定资产原价	营业收入	费用合计	营业利润	企业单位增加值
全　国	**200819.9**	**51216.4**	**28133.8**	**16816.2**	**-2108.0**	**8492.4**
中央级	22765.2	40852.2	23416.8	14544.5	-1728.2	7345.3
北　京	40361.5	86.0	1059.1	215.8	-100.0	24.8
天　津	2609.5	12.0		11.0		
河　北	1682.4					
山　西	2761.1					
内蒙古	1841.2					
辽　宁	5206.2	60.1				
吉　林	2107.2					
黑龙江	3300.5					
上　海	8139.8					
江　苏	8679.3	46.0	949.5	428.6	184.7	265.5
浙　江	19142.9	7443.6	2074.3	1359.4	-431.5	623.7
安　徽	375.3	210.0	103.0	38.0	-33.0	-19.8
福　建	2259.4					
江　西	2850.2	192.8	106.7	88.6		78.3
山　东	3799.8					
河　南	12000.2					
湖　北	6448.2	242.0	2.4	2.4		
湖　南	6361.1	1821.7				
广　东	10908.7					
广　西	6225.4	68.0				19.5
海　南	7742.5					
重　庆	798.5					
四　川	4889.0					
贵　州	8428.2	182.0	422.0	127.9		155.0
云　南	1120.3					
西　藏						
陕　西	2763.6					
甘　肃	1051.1					
青　海	127.6					
宁　夏	380.9					
新　疆	3693.0					

单位：万元

执行行政事业单位会计制度财务指标					
固定资产原价	上年结转和结余	本年收入合计	本年支出合计	收支结余	行政事业单位增加值
416588.7	**84037.1**	**396243.4**	**424315.0**	**48425.4**	**192327.5**
96047.2	15324.6	43167.8	48621.5		15419.9
47998.6	30060.7	39390.7	62650.9	25753.2	40336.7
1517.5	5428.8	3399.2	9081.5	-10.9	2609.5
4799.3	0.6	3714.0	3400.2		1682.4
2645.7	67.1	5695.7	3247.4		2761.1
1489.0	3867.8	3224.6	3861.4	3231.0	1841.2
9456.4	303.3	9857.0	10939.2	112.0	5206.2
1649.6	514.6	4673.2	4580.4	602.5	2107.2
13015.8	54.8	7684.8	7451.8		3300.5
12382.9	2241.7	19661.5	19717.6	2947.1	8139.8
11751.1	1982.9	36199.5	36079.9	794.4	8413.8
12200.0	2365.8	30894.5	30264.5	101.3	18519.2
477.0	0.3	610.8	696.0		395.1
5647.4	381.1	4965.8	11449.0	475.5	2259.4
9096.8	666.9	4841.0	5318.7	-442.5	2771.9
2398.7	46.7	4841.4	4949.7		3799.8
24711.5	2471.2	23117.7	21048.6	2012.4	12000.2
13090.2	849.6	10749.4	10391.6		6448.2
11284.1	9.2	13988.9	13694.0	243.9	6361.1
57467.0	6293.1	44588.0	43870.6	3547.0	10908.7
18695.9	3922.6	15402.5	15178.4	186.8	6205.9
1420.8	1428.5	11441.5	11029.1	1042.2	7742.5
2120.2	392.6	1540.2	1600.2	177.6	798.5
23262.0	1174.9	26770.3	20611.2	6247.0	4889.0
5406.1	739.4	8805.0	8969.3		8273.2
596.8	134.8	1407.4	1265.7		1120.3
13183.7	561.7	7749.9	6187.5	41.7	2763.6
1333.8	12.5	2563.6	2170.4	19.6	1051.1
484.7	481.7	144.8	158.7		127.6
313.0	31.0	324.9	222.5		380.9
10645.9	2226.6	4827.8	5607.5	1343.6	3693.0

附 录

06

《中国民政统计年鉴-2013》勘误

一、93页：社会救助下指标“城市最低生活保障”、“农村最低生活保障”、“其他社会救助”、“医疗救助”应该属于社会救助，而不是与社会救助并列。

二、134页：B-1-16 “十二五”时期数据应该等于2011年和2012年数据的和，数据没有做合计。

三、184页：“说明：1.以上数据为门诊部职业技能指导……”改为“说明：1.以上数据为民政部职业技能指导……”